T0314316

THE

PUBLICATIONS

OF THE

SURTEES SOCIETY

VOL. 208

Hon. General Editors

R. H. BRITNELL and M. M. HARVEY

THE

PUBLICATIONS

OF THE

SURTEES SOCIETY

ESTABLISHED IN THE YEAR
M.DCCC.XXXIV

VOL. CCVIII

THE CARTULARY OF
BYLAND ABBEY

EDITED
BY
JANET BURTON

THE SURTEES SOCIETY

THE BOYDELL PRESS

First published 2004

A Surtees Society Publication
published by The Boydell Press
an imprint of Boydell & Brewer Ltd
PO Box 9, Woodbridge, Suffolk IP12 3DF, UK
and of Boydell & Brewer Inc,
668 Mt Hope Avenue, Rochester, NY 14620, USA
website: www.boydellandbrewer.com

ISBN 0 85444 063 1

ISSN 0307–5362

A catalogue record for this book is available
from the British Library

Details of other Surtees Society volumes are available
from Boydell & Brewer Ltd

This publication is printed on acid-free paper

Printed in Great Britain by
St Edmundsbury Press Ltd, Bury St Edmunds, Suffolk

CONTENTS

TABLES AND MAPS

ACKNOWLEDGEMENTS

The volume has been a long time in the making, and the list of people I would like to thank has grown accordingly. First I would like to mention those associated with the Surtees Society, the Council for agreeing to publish my work on the Byland cartulary, Alan Piper, under whom the project was begun, and the current General Editors, Margaret Harvey and Richard Britnell, and Chairman, Richard Sharpe. Their encouragement, as well as their willingness to read through the text, have been much appreciated. The Vice-Chancellor of University of Wales, Lampeter, Keith Robbins, granted me study leave in 2000 to pursue work on the volume, and I would like to thank him for this and for a grant from the Pantyfedwen Fund towards the production of the maps. These were expertly prepared by Paddie Morrison of York, and to her I am most grateful. My study leave was extended by a research leave award from the Arts and Humanities Research Board and I would like here formally to acknowledge this award.

As will become clear from the pages that follow I have in the course of my research visited many libraries and archive repositories, and I would like to thank those archivists and librarians who patiently answered enquiries, in person and by correspondence, as I sought to track down Byland charters. Particular thanks go to the staff of the British Library, the Bodleian Library, Oxford, the National Archives (Public Record Office), the North Yorkshire County Record Office at Northallerton (and especially Mr Ashcroft), the Cumbria Record Offices at Carlisle and Kendal, the Yorkshire Archaeological Society, and the Historical Manuscripts Commission. The Byland charters in the Bretton collection are quoted by kind permission of Lord Allendale, The Bretton Estate Archive, National Arts Education Service, University of Leeds Bretton Hall Campus, West Bretton, Wakefield, and my thanks are due to Leonard Bartle, custodian, for facilitating access to these charters. I am also grateful to Mr C. H. Bagot of Levens Hall, Cumbria, for permission to quote from the charters in his possession.

Many people have patiently endured my musings on the Byland cartulary, and responded with interest and with perceptive observations. Among these I mention particularly my colleagues in the History Department at Lampeter, who have provided cheerful encouragement, Gill and John in Birmingham, and Veronica Ortenberg in Oxford. Two people, David Smith and Barrie Dobson, rightly appear in the acknowledgements to all my work as they have been a constant source of support, encouragement and sound advice ever since I have known them. David in particular has read much of the text and helped to iron out errors; needless to say for those that remain I am alone responsible.

As always I reserve my biggest thank you for my husband, who has seen me through a project that has seemed to grow over the years. He knows how much he has done to help.

My first sight of Byland Abbey was as a teenager on a cold, wet, Spring day, in the company of my parents, in one of our many expeditions to look at medieval sites. Since I was very young they nurtured my interest in history and historic places. It is to them, with gratitude, wonderful memories, and much love, that I dedicate this volume.

Win Burton (d. 1999)
Eric Burton (d. 2001)

Janet Burton
Lampeter, 2003

ABBREVIATIONS

Add.	Additional
Baildon, *Monastic Notes*	W. P. Baildon, *Notes on the Religious and Secular Houses of Yorkshire*, YASRS, 17, 81 (1895, 1931)
BI	York, Borthwick Institute of Historical Research
BL	British Library
Burton, 'Charters of Byland Abbey'	Janet E. Burton, 'Charters of Byland Abbey relating to the grange of Bleatarn, Westmorland', *TCWAAS*, 79 (1979), 29–50
Burton, 'Settlement of Disputes'	Janet E. Burton, 'The Settlement of disputes between Byland Abbey and Newburgh Priory', *YAJ*, 55 (1983), 67–71
Cal. Ch. R.	*Calendar of the Charter Rolls preserved in the Public Record Office*, 6 vols (London: HMSO, 1903–27)
Cal. Cl. R.	*Calendar of the Close Rolls preserved in the Public Record Office: Henry III to Henry IV* (London: HMSO, 1892– 1938)
Cal. Fine R.	*Calendar of the Fine Rolls preserved in the Public Record Office: Edward I to Henry VI* (London: HMSO, 1911–49)
Cal. Inq. Misc.	*Calendar of Inquisitions Miscellaneous (Chancery) preserved in the Public Record Office: Henry III to Edward III* (London: HMSO, 1916–37)
Cal. Pat. R.	*Calendar of the Patent Rolls preserved in the Public Record Office: Henry III to Henry IV* (London: HMSO, 1891– 1916)
Canivez, *Statuta*	*Statuta Capitulorum Generalium Ordinis Cisterciensis ab anno 1116 usque ad annum 1786*, ed. J. M. Canivez, 8 vols (Louvain: Revue d'Histoire Ecclésiastique, 1933–41)
Cart. Bridlington	*Abstracts of the Charters and Other Documents contained in the Chartulary of the Priory of Bridlington*, ed. W. T. Lancaster (Leeds: privately printed, 1912)
Cart. Fountains	*Abstracts of the Charters and Other Documents contained in the Chartulary of the Cistercian Abbey of Fountains*, ed. W. T. Lancaster, 2 vols (Leeds: privately printed, 1915)
Cart. Guis.	*Cartularium Prioratus de Gyseburne*, ed. W. Brown, 2 vols, SS, 86, 89 (1889–94)
Cart. Monk Bretton	*Abstracts of the Chartularies of the Priory of Monk Bretton*, ed. J. M. Walker, YASRS, 66 (1924)
Cart. Riev.	*Cartularium Abbathiae de Rievalle*, ed. J. C. Atkinson, SS, 83 (1889)

Cart. Whitby	*Cartularium Abbathiae de Whiteby*, ed. J. C. Atkinson, 2 vols, SS, 69, 72 (1879–81)
Chs Vicars Choral	*Charters of the Vicars Choral of York Minster: I: City of York and its Suburbs to 1546*, ed. N. J. Tringham, YASRS, 148 (1993 for 1988 and 1989); *II: County of Yorkshire and Appropriated Churches*, ed. N. J. Tringham, YASRS, 156 (2002)
CP	*The Complete Peerage, or a History of the House of Lords and all its members from the earliest times*, ed. G. E. Cockayne and others, 13 vols in 14 (London: St Catherine's Press, 1910–40)
CPRL	*Calendar of Entries in the Papal Registers Relating to Great Britain and Ireland: papal letters*, ed. W. H. Bliss, C. Johnson, J. A. Twemlow, M. J. Haren (London: HMSO, 1893–in progress)
CPRP	*Calendar of Entries in the Papal Registers Relating to Great Britain and Ireland: petitions to the pope, AD 1342–1419*, ed. W. H. Bliss (London: HMSO, 1896)
Curia Regis Rolls	*Curia Regis Rolls . . . Preserved in the Public Record Office* (London: HMSO, 1922–in progress)
CWAAS	Cumberland and Westmorland Antiquarian and Archaeological Society
d.	died
EEA	*English Episcopal Acta V: York 1070–1154*, ed. J. E. Burton (1988); *XX: York 1154–1181*, ed. Marie Lovatt (2000); *XXIV: Durham 1153–1195*, ed. M. G. Snape (2002); all Oxford: Oxford University Press for the British Academy
EPNS	Publications of the English Place Name Society (*ER*: East Riding of Yorkshire, *NR*: North Riding of Yorkshire, *WR*: West Riding of Yorkshire)
ER	East Riding of Yorkshire
EYC	*Early Yorkshire Charters*, I–III, ed. W. Farrer (Edinburgh, 1914–16), IV–XII and index to I–III, ed. C. T. Clay (YASRS extra series, 1935–65)
EYF	*Early Yorkshire Families*, ed. C. T. Clay and D. E. Greenway, YASRS, 135 (1973)
Farrer, *Kendal*	W. Farrer, *Records Relating to the Barony of Kendal*, I, ed. J. Curwen, CWAAS, Record or Chartulary Series, 4 (1923)
Fasti Monastic Cathedrals	*John le Neve: Fasti Ecclesiae Anglicanae 1066–1300: II Monastic Cathedrals*, ed. D. E. Greenway, (London: University of London and Athlone Press, 1971)
Fasti Parochiales	5 vols, ed. A. Hamilton Thompson and C. T. Clay (I–II), N. A. H. Lawrance (III), N. K. M. Gurney and C. T. Clay (IV), N. A. H. Lawrance (V), YASRS, 85, 107, 129, 133, 143 (1933–82)
Fasti York	*John le Neve: Fasti Ecclesiae Anglicanae 1066–1300: VI York*, ed. D. E. Greenway, (London: University of

	London School of Advanced Study, Institute of Historical Research, 1999)
HMC Rutland	*Historical Manuscripts Commission Twelfth Report, Appendix, Parts IV and V, and Fourteenth Report, Appendix I, The Manuscripts of His Grace the Duke of Rutland Preserved at Belvoir Castle*, 4 vols (London: HMSO, 1888–1905)
HMC Tenth Report	*Tenth Report of the Royal Commission on Historical Manuscripts, appendix IV, The Manuscripts of the Earl of Westmorland, Captain Stewart, Lord Stafford, Lord Muncaster, and others* (London: HMSO, 1885, reissued 1906)
HMC Various Collections	*Historical Manuscripts Commission, Report on Manuscripts in Various Collections*, 8 vols (London: HMSO, 1901–1914)
HRH	*The Heads of Religious Houses: England and Wales, I, 940–1216*, ed. D. Knowles, C. N. L. Brooke and V. C. M. London, 2nd edn (Cambridge: Cambridge University Press, 2001); *II, 1216–1377*, ed. D. M. Smith and V. C. M. London (Cambridge: Cambridge University Press, 2001)
KI	*The Survey of the County of York Taken by John de Kirkeby, commonly called Kirkby's Inquest, and Inquisitions of Knights' Fees, the Nomina Villarum and an Appendix of Illustrative Documents*, ed. R. H. Skaife, SS, 49 (1867 for 1866)
Lord Lieutenants	*The Lord Lieutenants and High Sheriffs of Yorkshire, 1066–2000*, ed. W. M. Ormrod (Barnsley: Wharncliffe Books, 2000)
LP	*Letters and Papers, Foreign and Domestic, of the Reign of Henry VIII, Preserved in the Public Record Office, the British Museum, and elsewhere in England*, 23 vols in 38 (London: HMSO, 1862–1932)
MED	*Middle English Dictionary*, ed. Hans Kurath and others (Ann Arbor: University of Michigan Press, 1952–)
Mon. Ang.	W. Dugdale, *Monasticon Anglicanum*, ed. J. Caley, H. Ellis and B. Bandinel, 6 vols in 8 (London, 1817–30)
Mowbray Charters	*Charters of the Honour of Mowbray 1107–1191*, ed. D. E. Greenway, British Academy Records of Social and Economic History, ns 1 (London: Oxford University Press, 1972)
MRH	*Medieval Religious Houses: England and Wales*, ed. D. Knowles and R. N. Hadcock, 2nd edn (London: Longman, 1971)
MS(S)	manuscript(s)
MS Dodsworth	Oxford, Bodleian Library, MS Dodsworth, with number

MS Top. Yorks.	Oxford, Bodleian Library, MS Top. Yorks., with number
Nicolson and Burn, *Westmorland*	J. Nicolson and R. Burn, *The History and Antiquities of the Counties of Westmorland and Cumberland*, 2 vols (London: W. Strachan and T. Cadell, 1777)
NR	North Riding of Yorkshire
NYCRO	North Yorkshire County Record Office, Northallerton
ns	new series
occ.	occurs, occurred
pa.	parish
pd.	printed
PQW	*Placita de Quo Warranto temporibus Edw. I, II, & III in curia receptae scaccarij West. asservata* (London: Record Commission, 1818)
PRO	London, Public Record Office (now the National Archives)
PUE	*Papsturkunden in England*, ed. W. Holtzmann, 3 vols (Abhandlungen des Gesellschaft der Wissenschaften zu Göttingen, phil.-hist. Klasse, neue Folge, 25, 1930–31; 3 Folge, 14–15, 1935–6; 33, 1952)
Reg. Giffard	*The Register of Walter Giffard, Lord Archbishop of York, 1266–1279*, ed. W. Brown, SS, 109 (1904)
Reg. Gray	*The Register or Rolls of Walter de Gray, Lord Archbishop of York*, ed. J. Raine, SS, 56 (1872)
Reg. Greenfield	*The Register of William Greenfield, Lord Archbishop of York, 1306–1315*, ed. W. Brown and A. Hamilton Thompson, 5 vols, SS, 145, 149, 151–3 (1931–40)
Reg. Melton	*The Register of William Melton, Archbishop of York, 1317–1340*, ed. R. M. T. Hill, D. Robinson, R. Brocklesby and T. C. B. Timmins, 5 vols, Canterbury and York Society, 70–1, 76, 85, 93 (1977–2002)
RRAN	*Regesta Regum Anglo-Normannorum: the acta of William I, 1066–1087*, ed. David Bates (Oxford: Clarendon Press, 1998)
Sandwith, *Exscripta*	NYCRO, MS ZDV 11 (Transcripts of Byland charters made by Henry Sandwith)
SC	F. Madan, H. H. E. Craster and N. Denholm-Young, *A Summary Catalogue of Western Manuscripts in the Bodleian Library at Oxford*, 7 vols (Oxford: Clarendon Press, 1895–1953)
SS	Surtees Society
TCWAAS	*Transactions of the Cumberland and Westmorland Antiquarian and Archaeological Society*
VCH Lancs.	*The Victoria County History of the County of Lancaster*, ed. W. Farrer and W. Brownbill, 8 vols (London: Constable and Co., 1906–14)
VCH NR	*The Victoria History of the Counties of England: A History of Yorkshire, North Riding*, ed. W. Page, 2 vols

	and index (London: Constable and Co., 1914, The St Catherine's Press, 1923–5)
VCH York	*The Victoria History of the Counties of England: A History of Yorkshire, The City of York*, ed. P. M. Tillott (Oxford: Oxford University Press, 1961, repr. Folkestone: Dawson for the Institute of Historical Research, 1982)
VCH Yorks.	*The Victoria History of the Counties England: Yorkshire*, III, ed. William Page (London: Eyre and Spottiswoode, 1913, repr. London and Folkestone: Dawson for the University of London Institute of Historical Research, 1974)
VE	*Valor Ecclesiasticus*, ed. J. Caley and J. Hunter, 6 vols (London: Record Commission, 1802)
Westm.	Westmorland
West Yorks.	Margaret L. Faull and Stephen A. Moorhouse, *West Yorkshire: an archaeological survey to AD 1500*, 4 vols (Wakefield: West Yorkshire Metropolitan County Council, 1981)
WR	West Riding of Yorkshire
YAJ	*Yorkshire Archaeological Journal*
YASRS	Yorkshire Archaeological Society Record Series
YMF	C. T. Clay, ed., *York Minster Fasti*, 2 vols, YASRS, 123–4 (1958–9)
Yorks. Deeds	*Yorkshire Deeds*, ed. W. Brown (I–III), C. T. Clay (IV–VIII), M. J. Hebditch (IX), M. J. Stanley Price (X), YASRS, 39, 50, 63, 65, 69, 76, 83, 102, 111, 120 (1909–55)
Yorks. Fines 1218–1231	*Feet of Fines for the County of York, from 1218 to 1231*, ed. J. Parker, YASRS, 62 (1921)
Yorks. Fines 1232–1246	*Feet of Fines for the County of York, from 1232 to 1246*, ed. J. Parker, YASRS, 67 (1925)
Yorks. Fines 1246–1272	*Feet of Fines for the County of York, from 1246 to 1272*, ed. J. Parker, YASRS, 82 (1932)
Yorks. Fines 1327–1347	*Feet of Fines for the County of York, from 1327 to 1347*, ed. W. Paley Baildon, YASRS, 42 (1910)
Yorks. Fines John	*Pedes finium Ebor. regnante Johanne, A.D. MCXCIX–A.D. MCCXIV*, ed. W. Brown, SS, 94 (1897)

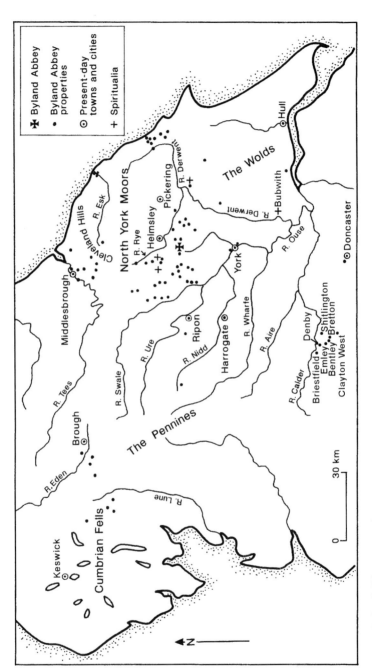

Map 1. Byland Abbey properties

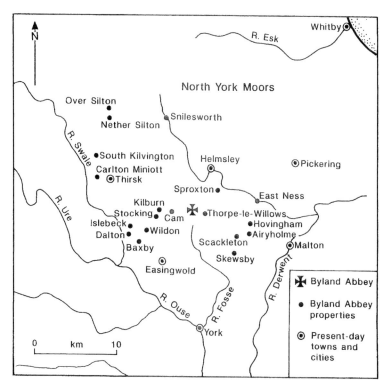

Map 2. Early acquisitions in the vicinity of the abbey

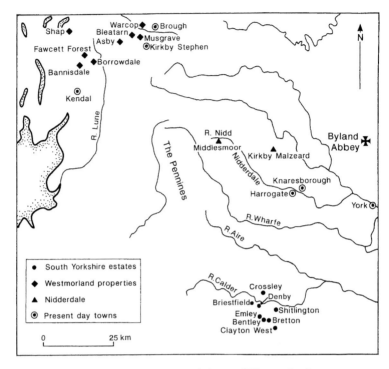

Map 3. Estates in Nidderdale, South Yorkshire and Westmorland

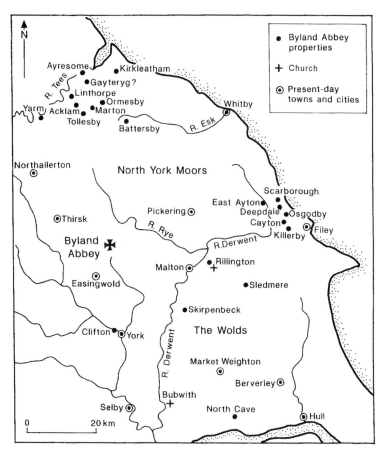

Map 4. Tees valley and East Yorkshire properties

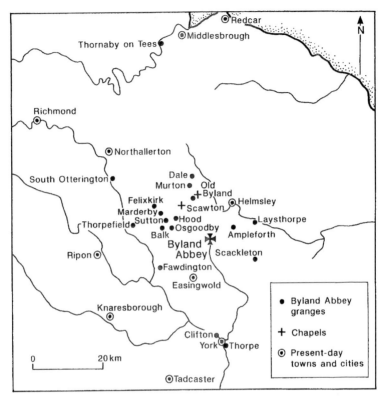

Map 5. The Liberty of Byland

INTRODUCTION

BYLAND ABBEY

Byland Abbey was one of eight Cistercian abbeys in Yorkshire, and its early history was more turbulent than most. The account of the sending of a colony from the Savigniac abbey of Furness (Lancashire) to Calder (Cumberland) in 1134, Calder's destruction by the Scots, the attempt of the monks to return to Furness and their subsequent decision to seek assistance of Archbishop Thurstan of York which led to the offer of the first site of the monastery at Hood (Yorkshire) in 1138, are well documented in the Byland *Historia Fundationis*.[1] Byland was well known to William, author of the *Historia Rerum Anglicarum*, and because the abbey was 'only a mile away from the church of Newburgh which nurtured me in Christ from my boyhood', William was able to include in his history the broad outlines of the foundation of the abbey which he reckoned, alongside the abbeys of Rievaulx and Fountains, as the 'three lights of our province shining out as prime examples of holy religious life'.[2]

---

1   The author of the *Historia* was Abbot Philip of Byland (1196–1197/8). His composition comprised a narrative of the foundation and early history of Byland and its daughter house of Jervaulx in Wensleydale. This sequence, which was copied into a portion of the cartulary that has been lost, survives uniquely in MS Dodsworth 63, fols 9–56. The only printing is in *Mon. Ang.* V, 349–54. I am preparing a new edition, with translation, for the series Borthwick Texts and Calendars. For comment on the sequence see Janet Burton, 'The abbeys of Byland and Jervaulx and the problems of the English Savigniacs', *Monastic Studies* II, ed. J. Loades (Bangor: Headstart History, 1991), 119–31. On the history of Byland see Janet Burton, *The Monastic Order in Yorkshire, 1069–1215*, Cambridge Studies in Medieval Life and Thought, fourth series, 40 (Cambridge: Cambridge University Press, 1999), pp. 109–12; D. Nicholl, *Thurstan, Archbishop of York 1114–1140* (York: Stonegate Press, 1963), pp. 201–4.
2   William of Newburgh, *Historia Rerum Anglicarum*, book I, chapter 15, in *Chronicles of the reigns of Stephen, Henry II, and Richard I*, ed. R. Howlett, 4 vols, Rolls Series (1884–89), I, 49–53; trans. P. G. Walsh and M. J. Kennedy, *The History of English Affairs, Book I* (Warminster: Aris and Phillips, 1988), pp. 77–9.

The site of Hood was provided by a young baron, Roger de Mowbray, later also the founder of Newburgh Priory.[3] However, Hood proved inadequate, and four years later the monks moved to Old Byland, but this in turn was abandoned because of its proximity to Rievaulx Abbey.[4] A major theme of the *Historia* was Byland's trials and tribulations over its affiliation that followed the resettlement of Calder, which saw Byland claimed by both Furness and Savigny as a daughter house, and its disputes with its lay neighbours.[5] William of Newburgh, on the other hand, reduced Byland's first sixty years to a terse summary:

> . . . they first received a tiny plot; but subsequently for various reasons they moved their abode to a second, then a third, then a fourth place while remaining under his [Roger's] patronage, and at last sank roots and settled there. The Lord blessed them, and they have now progressed from poverty to great wealth under their father, Roger, a man of remarkable integrity. He is still alive, enjoying a fruitful old age, having completed about fifty-seven years in authority there.[6]

William's laconic account of the origins of Byland – perhaps so for reasons of economy or politics – certainly reduces to banality one of the most turbulent monastic foundations of the twelfth century, one that provides a fine illustration of the interaction of the nobility and the ecclesiastical hierarchy as well as the monastic order itself in the expansion of monasticism of the period, the uncertainties of foundations, and the ambivalent attitude of lay people. In contrast to the narrative of the foundation history the evidence of the cartulary seems sober indeed, but the two together illustrate William's portrayal of a rise from 'poverty to great wealth'. Although it was forty years before the monks settled on their fourth and final site at New Byland, the period between 1138 and 1177 saw the creation of a sound territorial and economic base for the abbey, and the magnificent church which the community constructed still stands as a monument to early northern Gothic.[7]

---

3   *Mon. Ang.* V, 349.
4   *Ibid.*, 350–51.
5   *Ibid.*, 351–4.
6   William of Newburgh, *Historia*, book 1, chapter 15 (I, 52); Walsh and Kennedy, *History*, pp. 77–9. Roger became abbot in 1142 and ruled for fifty-four years before resigning in 1196.
7   On the church of Byland see, for instance, Peter Fergusson, *Architecture of Solitude: Cistercian Abbeys in Twelfth-Century England* (Princeton: Princeton Univer-

After 1196 narrative sources for the internal history of Byland are exiguous, and the cartulary, London, British Library, MS Egerton 2823, is the single most important record for the development of the abbey, its estate, and its place in the wider community of north Yorkshire. The cartulary demonstrates the importance of the abbey in the economic development of parts of the North Riding, as well as in areas to the south and west of the county, and in Westmorland. Like most religious houses, however, Byland Abbey suffered some periods of economic depression, and the cartulary yields evidence of some of the difficulties. In the 1340s the abbot and convent petitioned to be allowed to appropriate a moiety of Bubwith church and the church of Rillington, and licence was granted because of the damage and poverty caused by the Scottish wars and raids.[8] Some of this disruption may have been caused on the occasion of the 'Battle of Byland Abbey', which was fought nearby in October 1322.

The abbey was surrendered on 30 November 1538 by Abbot John Alanebrigg, *alias* Leeds, the prior, and twenty-three monks.[9] On 22 January 1539 Sir Nicholas Fairfax wrote to Thomas Cromwell to ask that, should Mr Bellasis leave the preferment of Byland he, Fairfax, be granted the demesnes as they were near his house.[10] However, on 22 September 1540 the house, site and abbey of Byland, with appurtenances in Coxwold, Kilburn and elsewhere, were granted to Sir William Pickering of London.[11]

---

sity Press, 1984), pp. 72–90. Fergusson describes Byland as 'the most remarkable of all the Cistercians' buildings in the twelfth century' (p. 106). See also David Robinson, ed., *The Cistercian Abbeys of Britain* (London: B. T. Batsford, 1998), pp. 81–3: 'In all Byland stood as probably the most ambitious twelfth-century Cistercian church and certainly the largest in Britain.'

8   See nos 110, 976.

9   *LP*, vol. XIII, part II, no. 945 (p. 392); see also no. 1064 (p. 454), vol. XIV, part I, no. 185 (p. 67); Claire Cross and Noreen Vickers, eds., *Monks, Friars and Nuns in Sixteenth-Century Yorkshire*, YASRS, 150 (1995 for 1991 and 1992), pp. 98–110. One name, that of Bernard Brodley/Bradley, was entered on the pensions list but crossed out.

10 *LP* XIV, part I, no. 124 (p. 47). Fairfax asked, as second choice, for the demesnes of Newburgh Priory or Whitby Abbey. Mr Bellasis was the ancestor of the viscounts Fauconberg of Newburgh; see below, notes 14–15.

11 *LP* XVI, no. 107/28 (p. 54).

RECORD KEEPING AT BYLAND ABBEY

The cartulary and its arrangement
Provenance, physical description and date
The Byland cartulary, now British Library, MS Egerton 2823, was
acquired by the British Museum in 1899 from the library of Sir
Thomas Phillipps.[12] How it came into Phillipps's ownership is not
recorded. Between 1642 and 1647, when portions were transcribed by
Roger Dodsworth and others, the cartulary's owner was John Rushworth of Lincoln's Inn, and in 1695 Thomas Tanner recorded that it
had also belonged to Brian Fairfax.[13] When Peter le Neve produced
his catalogue/summary of the cartulary in 1702 it was in the hands of
Sir Thomas Frankland, executor of Thomas Bellasis, Viscount
Fauconberg.[14] Pasted at the front, on modern folio 2, is an engraved
view of Byland Abbey by Samuel Buck (1721), which Buck dedicated
to Thomas Bellasis, Viscount Fauconberg.[15]

The cartulary originally comprised 243 folios, but has sustained
physical damage, and now lacks the first 73 and last 25 folios, as well
as several folios in the body of the remaining portion. It has two sets
of foliation, one probably from the seventeenth century and the other
modern. There are roman numerals – in most cases very faint – in the
top right hand corners of a number of folios, but their significance is
unclear. There are numbers written vertically by the bottom margin
of some folios in a post-medieval hand.[16] The cartulary is a large

---

12 *Catalogue of Additions to the Manuscripts in the British Museum in the Years
  1894–1899* (London: British Museum, 1901), p. 565.
13 Thomas Tanner, *Notitia Monastica, or a short history of the religious houses of
  England and Wales* (Oxford: printed at the Theatre, and to be sold at the sign of
  the Black Swan in Pater-Noster-Row London, 1695).
14 MS Top. Yorks. d. 11, fol. 255r; see below, p. xxviii. Thomas Viscount Fauconberg,
  who was created Earl Fauconberg in 1689, died in 1700. His will, dated 1699,
  was proved on 26 May 1701. He was succeeded by his nephew: *CP* V, 264–6.
15 Thomas Bellasis, Viscount Fauconberg, who succeeded in 1701, died in 1718
  and was buried at Coxwold; he was succeeded by his son and heir, Thomas,
  who was born in 1699 and created Earl Fauconberg of Newburgh in 1756. He
  died in 1774: *CP* V, 266.
16 New fols 4r (3), 6r (7), 7r (9), 11r (17), 12r (19), 13r (21), 15r (25), 17r (29), 18r (31),
  19r (33), 20r (35), 21r (27), 22r (39), 23r (41), 24r (43), 25r (45), 26r (47), 27r (49),
  28r (51), 29r (53), 31r (57), 32r (59), 33r (61), 35r (65), 36r (67), 38r (69), 39r (71),
  40r (73), 41r (75), 43r (79), 44r (81), 45r (83), 46r (85), 7r (87), 48r (89), 49r (91), 50r
  (93), 51r (95), 53r (99), 54r (101), 55r (102), 56r (105), 57r (107), 58r (109), 59r (111),

volume; the folios measure between 15.25 inches (385 mm) and 15.55 inches (395 mm), by 10.25 inches (265 mm); the writing area occupies between 7 inches (180 mm) and 7.75 inches (195 mm) in width, by 11.5/11.75 inches (292/300 mm).

The cartulary is carefully written in brown ink in one main hand throughout, the only departures being notes in later hands and an award, dated 1526, inserted at folio 90. There are catchwords, in the cartulary hand, at the bottom of folios 47v, 57v, 69v, 81v, 94v, 106v. There is decoration in the form of red and blue initials. The first initial in each cartulary section, or major division, is a four, five, or six line initial in red and blue.[17] The initial letter of each document within a section is usually a two-line initial, in alternating red and blue. Each document is preceded by a rubric or caption, in whole or in part in red ink and in the same hand as the main text. Red line decorations are used as line fillers. The scribe has extended and embellished the ascenders in words on the top line of folios 60r, 67r, and 108r.

The latest dated document is from 1393 (no. 543) but the reference to Richard II as *rex ultimus* (fol. 92v) dates the cartulary to between 1399 and 1413; moreover, the absence, from the royal charters on folios 163–4, of a copy of Henry IV's confirmation and inspeximus, suggests a date of before 1403.[18]

60r (113), 61r (115), 62r (117), 64r (119), 65r (121), 66r (121), 67r (123), 68r (125), 69r (127), 70r (129), 71r (131), 72r (133), 74r (137), 75r (139), 76r (141), 77r (143), 78r (145), 79r (147), 80r (149), 81r (151), 82r (153), 83r (155), 84r (157), 85r (159), 86r (161), 87r (163), 88r (165), 89r (167), 91r (171), 92r (173), 93r (175), 94r (177), 95r (179), 96r (181), 97r (183), 98r (185), 99r (187), 100r (189), 101r (191), 102r (193), 103r (195), 104r (197), 105r (197), 106r (201), 107r (203), 108r (205), 109r (207), 110r (209), 111r (211), 112r (213), 113r (215), 114r (217), 115r (219), 116r (221), 117r (223), 118r (225).

17 Four-line initials are found on fols 18v, 63v, 70r (blue only); five-line initials are found on fols 6v, 8v, 9v, 10r, 17v, 18r, 19r, 20r (red only), 21r, 22r (blue only), 28r, 29r, 31v, 33r, 60v, 66r, 70v, 111r, 115r, 117v; six-line initials occur on fols 11r, 15v, 17r, 22v, 25r, 31r, 38v, 41v, 43v, 44r, 50r, 51r, 52v, 54v, 68v, 69v, 70r, 73v, 76v, 79r, 84r, 88r, 88v, 89r, 89v, 93r, 93v, 95v, 96r, 97r, 103v, 105r, 109r, 110r, 111v, 114r, 115r, 116r; and seven-line initials occur on fols 36r, 42v, 46r, 47v, 48v, 56v, 65r, 80v, 81r, 92r. There is a single instance of a three-line initial at the beginning of a cartulary section, on fol 64v. Letter 'O' on fol. 117v and letter 'E' on fols 70r, 84r, 109r, contain guides for the insertion of the coloured initial.

18 *Cal. Pat. R. 1401–1405*, p. 194 (dated Westminster, 17 Feb. 1403).

Arrangement

What remains as MS Egerton 2823 represents roughly three fifths of the original cartulary, much having been lost or damaged. Fortunately two compilations, one from the seventeenth and the second from the eighteenth century, enable us to reconstruct the form and organization of the cartulary. Between 1642 and 1649 Roger Dodsworth copied and summarized selected documents from the cartulary, then in the possession of John Rushworth, esquire, of Lincoln's Inn, giving the original folio reference; this manuscript is now MS Dodsworth 63 (SC 5005).[19] However, more important because it is more comprehensive, is the compilation, partly a summary and partly a catalogue of the cartulary, made by Peter le Neve in 1702, and now MS Top. Yorks. d. 11 (SC 55300). Folio 250r is headed *Transcripta cartarum abbatie de Bellalanda*, and this is followed (fols 250r–254r) by copies of various Byland charters. Folio 255r begins: 'An Abstract of the register of Byland Abby (*sic*) in Yorkshire 1702 in the hands of Sir Thomas Fankland (*sic*) executor of the viscount Falconberge'. The table below gives a reconstruction of the shape of the cartulary from these two sources.

Table 1. The structure of the cartulary

Old fol.	New fol.	Subject
1–9	x	? perhaps a table of contents
10–18	x	*Foundation History of Byland and Jervaulx: MS Dodsworth 63, fols 9r–31r and 41r–56r*
19–34	x	*Papal bulls: MS Dodsworth 63, fol. 56: 'Here followe sundry bulls of priveleges graunted unto Bellaland, fol. 19, 20 etc, of which it is consyderable whither any of them are necessarie to be inserted here'; MS Top. Yorks. d. 11, fol. 255r: 'septem magna privilegia', and other papal bulls*
34–52	x	*MS Top. Yorks, d. 11, fol. 258r: 'Postea sequuntur diverse bulle diversorum paparum privilegiorum concessorum omnibus abbatibus ordinis Cisterciensis in omnibus regnis, a fol. 34 ad 52'*
60–62	x	*MS Top. Yorks. d. 11, fol. 258r: 'sequuntur transcripta cartarum particulariter pertinentium abbatie Bellande'; general confirmation by Roger de Mowbray: MS Dodsworth 63, fols 32v–33r*
63	x	*Boundaries of the new abbey: MS Top. Yorks. d. 11, fol. 259r; MS Dodsworth 63, fol. 33r–v*

---

19 At the beginning of MS Dodsworth 63 there is a note: *In registro cartarum monasterii de Bellalanda in com' Ebor' penes Iohannem Ryssheworth armiger' de hospitio Lincolniense 24 Martii 1647.*

237–9	x	*Wilsden (WR): MS Top. Yorks. d. 11, fol. 278v*
240	x	*Whitley (WR): MS Top. Yorks. d. 11, fol. 278v*
241–43	x	*Wind Hill, Woolley, 'Merschaw' (all in Woolley, WR): MS Top. Yorks. d. 11, fol. 278v*

BL MS Egerton 2823, therefore, is a general cartulary compiled at a time of heightened activity of cartulary compilation.[20] There was a significant, though by no means unusual, mixing of historical narrative with legal documents of title, charters and privileges, here achieved by prefacing the legal records with the foundation narrative of Byland and its daughter house of Jervaulx.[21]

Thereafter the compiler followed a conventional organization for the material: papal privileges, first for the abbey and then for the entire Cistercian order; and documents relating to the site of the abbey, *transcripta cartarum particulariter pertinentium abbatie Bellande*, which appear under the title 'Alstede' or Oldstead, and accordingly form the first of the topographical sections, in letter order, which mark the organization of much of the remainder of the cartulary. There are four exceptions to this togographical arrangement. First, there is a separate section for royal privileges (nos 516–43) but this is not placed at the top of the hierarchy of material, merely taking its place under the heading *Libertates* after 'Laysthorpe'. This is followed by a section entitled 'Claims', that brings together documents supporting the abbey's claims to various privileges and liberties (nos 544–77); many appear to be related to *Quo Warranto* proceedings of the reign of Edward I. Third, many of the general charters of confir-

---

20 For a general discussion of cartulary-making see Trevor Foulds, 'Medieval cartularies', *Archives*, 18, no. 77 (April 1987), 3–35 (p. 15).

21 See above, note 1. For examples of cartularies containing foundation narratives and chronicles see Jean-Philippe Genet, 'Cartulaires, registres et histoire: l'exemple anglais', in *Le metier d'historien au moyen âge: Etudes sur l'historiographie médiévale*, ed. Bernard Guenée, Publications de la Sorbonne, série 'Etudes', 13 (Paris, 1977), pp. 95–138 (pp. 121–6). See also the comments by David Dumville, 'What is a Chronicle?', *The Medieval Chronicle* II, ed. Erik Kooper (Amsterdam and New York: Rodopi, 2002), pp. 1–27 (p. 11). What occupied the first nine folios of the cartory is not recorded in either MS Dodsworth 63 or Top. Yorks. d. 11; there are references to two bundles of charters issued by or for the abbot (*baculus abbatum*; see nos 485, 988A), and the extent of these cannot be determined; they may have been placed first or some may have been transcribed under topographical sections. It is more likely that the first folios were used for a *tabula* of contents, followed by the foundation narrative.

mation of Byland's founder, Roger de Mowbray, and his successors
(nos 641–664) are collected together under the title *Mowbray scrinium*,
indicating that the Mowbray muniment was kept in a separate chest.
As with the *Libertates* the charters in the Mowbray chest are not given
priority in the arrangement of the material, but are located between
'Mickley' and the charters of the magnates. The Mowbray section of
the cartulary, however, does not contain copies of all the Mowbray
charters; some formed the basis of the Oldstead section, others are to
be found under other geographical locations. Finally, the section
headed 'Magnates' (nos 665–86) contains charters of confirmation
issued by various members of the nobility and gentry. Their charters
also appear in some of the topographical sections, and, as with the
Mowbray section, the process of selection for inclusion is not always
clear. There was no separate section for episcopal confirmations.

In one respect the Byland compiler had a straightforward way of
classifying and giving hierarchy to the documents at his disposal, but
the deliberate prominence given to the foundation narratives of both
Byland and its daughter house, and to papal confirmations, and to
charters relating to the site of the abbey and its boundaries, suggests
that like many other cartularists the Byland compiler used the
cartulary as a way of affirming the identity of the abbey and its
monks by emphasizing its antiquity, its status and its past, as well as
providing a means to secure its future by enabling the monks to
access their archive.[22] The priority of papal privileges, including
general ones for the entire order, over royal and patronal confirmations, suggests that the identity which the compiler wished to empha-
size was a Cistercian one. The arrangement of the cartulary suggests
that, even in the early years of the fifteenth century, when ties
between English Cistercian houses and their continental counterparts
might have been weakened and superseded by other networks of influence, the monks of Byland retained a strong sense of the meaning
of the 'Cistercian order'.

---

22 Foulds, 'Medieval cartularies', 11 and 35; Genet, 'Cartulaires, registres et
   histoire', 101–2, 128. On the same theme see Georges Declercq, 'Originals and
   Cartularies: the organization of archival memory (ninth–eleventh centuries)',
   in *Charters and the Use of the Written Word in Medieval Society*, ed. Karl Heidecker,
   Utrecht Studies in Medieval Literacy, 5 (Turnhout: Brepols, 2000), pp. 147–70.

The archive from which the cartulary was compiled: Byland's original charters[23]

At the Dissolution some of the original charters of Byland were stored in St Mary's Tower, York, where they were transcribed by Roger Dodsworth and others in the 1630s and 1640s.[24] What happened to them subsequently is not clear. Some at least seem to have passed to the owners of the estates to which they related; certainly some charters appear to have remained together as coherent groups. The largest group of originals comprises seventy-four charters of the twelfth and thirteenth centuries relating to property in the Denby region of south Yorkshire (BL Add. Charters 7409–7482). These were acquired by the British Museum in 1850 from a sale at Colby Hall.[25] The British Library also has Byland charters among the Egerton and Stowe collections, as well as other Add. charters. A further group, relating to Dale, Murton and Thorpe-le-Willows, survives among the archive of the families of Fauconberg/Bellasis/Wombwell of Newburgh Priory into whose hands the properties came, and is now at the North Yorkshire County Record Office in Northallerton. Smaller numbers are in collections at the Cumbria Record Offices (Carlisle and Kendal); these relate to abbey estates in Westmorland. The Yorkshire Archaeological Society (Leeds) has originals of grants and confirmations concerning Islebeck. The Lawrence Batley Centre for the National Arts Education Archive (Trust), Bretton Hall, West Yorkshire (Bretton Estate Archive) has charters relating to the abbey properties in Bretton and Bentley.

This calendar of the cartulary contains 1231 items. Of these 512 are the full text of a document (though in many cases with abbreviated witness lists) prefaced by a rubric. The remaining 719 items are rubrics or headings only, where the compiler has chosen to omit the full document.[26] Original charters survive for forty-six of the documents copied in full into the cartulary, and a further forty-three can be

---

23 A full list of Byland charters appears as Appendix I.
24 See below, pp. xxxix–xli.
25 *Catalogue of Additions to the Manuscripts in the British Museum in the years 1848–1853* (London: British Museum, 1868), p. 278. Additional Charters 74770–74772 also relate to the Denby area, and may have been three of the twelve deeds that were accidentally sold as part of the wrong lot in 1850: *The British Library: Catalogue of Additions to the Manuscripts in the British Museum in the Years 1946–1950, Part I, Description* (London: The British Library, 1979), p. 386. Until 1933 they were at Wroxton Abbey, Oxfordshire.
26 On the significance of this see below, pp. xli–xlv.

matched to rubrics where the compiler has decided, for whatever reason, not to include a text. Approximately one hundred originals are not represented in either way in the surviving portions of the cartulary.

Comparison of originals with cartulary copies suggests that the compiler was a careful copyist. No. 323 is a transcript of a grant of land by William de Wyville which the monks were to hold of William as they had held it of his brother before him. There also exist three thirteenth-century copies or fabricated originals of this same charter. The cartulary has the reading *frater*, whereas the copies have *pater*, and here the cartulary undoubtedly preserves the original reading.[27] The copyist abbreviated witness lists, retaining between three and five witnesses from sometimes upwards of twenty names, ending 'etc' (see, for example, nos 89, 205–6, 211, 224, 233, 236, 242, 253, 257, 259, 260, 429, 451, 593, 728, 1087, 1088, 1157, 1193). Only occasionally does comparison with an original indicate that the copyist mistakenly omitted a witness from the sequence.[28]

In line with common archival practice, many Byland originals have endorsements characterising the document; these are contemporary with the charters, although a number have later medieval and post medieval endorsements as well. A fairly close correspondence can be detected between the rubric in the cartulary and the endorsement of an original, indicating that the copyist used the endorsement when compiling the cartulary text. On occasions the rubric is abbreviated or expanded from the endorsement.[29] Expansions usually occur where a full text has been omitted from the cartulary. The rubric of no. 237 (where the text of the charter has been omitted) has *Carta Mariore quondam uxoris Iohannis de tota predicta cultura et terris etc* where the endorsement of the original has *Carta Mari(ore) de cultura Twich(el)*; the effect of the modification is to make clear that the land in question is the same as in no. 236 and to establish the identity of the donor of no. 237, necessary because of the omission of the text. The endorsement of no. 216 reads: *C. Daniel filii Danielis de remissione iuris in tribus acris*; the text is omitted from the cartulary and so the compiler has added a few words of explanation: *Carta Danielis filii Danielis clerici de toto iure quod habuit in tribus acris terre quas Henricus*

---

27 See note to no. 323.
28 For one example see no. 207.
29 See, for instance, nos 216, 218, 219, 222, 225, 226, 231, 237, 240, 244, 247, 250, 415, 421, 422, 425, 1156.

filius Swani dedit hospitali. In some instances, probably for reasons of economy of effort, the compiler of the cartulary changed and abbreviated an endorsement by adding the word *eiusdem*. *Carta Gilb(ert)i fil(ii) Arnaldi de i acra terre et prato adiacente* of the endorsement of the original of no. 420 becomes *Carta eiusdem Gilberti* . . ., that is, the same Gilbert who granted nos 418 and 419 (see also nos 422, 424, 425). In nos 225–6 the phrase *Carta eiusdem Willelmi* is used for *Carta Willelmi filii Osberti/Osberni* of the endorsements; such an abbreviation was possible within the sequence of documents established in the cartulary, and identified the grantor with that of no. 224. In addition to endorsements some originals have explanatory comments or remarks. The text of no. 221 refers to a *thuriolum*; the scribe of the original has written *estimo quod thuriolum ponitur pro le kylne*, identifying the 'little tower' as a kiln. An abbey archivist noted that no. 246 was a *carta utilis et necessaris*.

In two original charters the name of the scribe occurs. BL Add. Charters 7448 and 7449 are confirmations by Ralph de Neville of lands in Denby. In both cases the last witness is *Romphario capellano meo hanc cartam qui fecit*, indicating that the deeds of grantors of importance might be drafted by their own clerks.[30] On the other hand, there is evidence that charters were drafted at Byland. Greenway pointed to similarities in the writing and style, 'family likenesses', in charters of Byland, Newburgh and Fountains which suggest they were written by the beneficiaries.[31]

Byland's original charters can throw light on the competence of the copyist in transmitting faithful copies into the cartulary. They also have bearing on the storage of records at the abbey. In addition to the endorsements discussed above many of these originals bear a medieval press mark. The press mark is generally a B, followed by an abbreviation for 'us', and one or two numbers. There are similar abbreviations in the margins of the cartulary, with *B^{us}* occasionally written in full as *Baculus* indicating that the compiler has copied from charters kept in a *baculus* or bundle. The purpose of the marginalia was to provide a finding aid, to alert anyone using it as a work of reference to the location of the original charter. The beginning of a

---

30 In one seventeenth-century transcript of an original charter the final witness is named as the scribe: *Serlone de Burgo capellano qui scripsit hoc scriptum* (MS Dodsworth 70, fol. 66r–v; see below no. 75n). The charter may, however, be spurious.

31 *Mowbray Charters*, pp. lxix–lxx.

section of the cartulary is usually marked 'Bundle 1', and the compiler notes when he moves on to 'Bundle 2' and subsequent bundles. The marginalia provide bundle numbers only, but the endorsements of originals indicate a refinement of the system in which charters were given an individual number within the bundle, such as 'Denby bundle 1, 3'. The Denby charters further demonstrate that the numbering was continuous throughout the whole sequence relating to that area, that is, the numbers did not begin afresh with each bundle. Examination of the Denby charters, which have survived in sufficient numbers to make possible comparison with the cartulary section, indicates that with a very few exceptions the arrangement in the cartulary corresponds to the endorsements; in other words, the organization of the material matched the existing archival arrangements, by bundle and by the geographical location which formed the basis of much of the cartulary arrangement.

Other instances, however, suggest that the archival arrangement had been tampered with. BL Stowe charter 499 is a confirmation and quitclaim by Thomas de Aselakeby of homage and rents in Thornaby that his mother, Plesantia, had granted to the monks. The endorsement, *Gaytric iii bac. pur.*, indicates that the charter was originally kept not with a Thornaby bundle but with the 'Gateryg' charters. The same applies to Stowe charter 483, a grant by William de Tamton of a fishery in Stainsby, which is endorsed *ii b^us de Gaiter' pura*. The 'Gateryg' section of the cartulary is complete, yet contains neither of these two charters. It is possible that the compiler deliberately omitted them from the cartulary, but another and more likely explanation is that he chose to create new sections or categories for Thornaby and Stainsby – which we know from MS Top. Yorks. d. 11 did exist – perhaps reflecting changes in administrative arrangements.[32]

Medieval copies

There exist numerous medieval copies of Byland originals, which suggest a layer of archival activity between the drawing up, arrangement and classification of originals and the compilation of the cartulary in the early years of the fifteenth century. Among the Denby charters BL Add. Charters 7414 and 7415 are near identical copies of

---

[32] For similar examples see nos 256, 257, 260, whose endorsements indicate that they were kept in bundles marked 'Murton' but which appear in a section entitled 'Dale'.

no. 205, Add. Charters 7423 and 7447 are copies of no. 217, Add. Charters 7419 and 7468 are copies of no. 254 and Add. Charters 7464, 7470 and 7474 of no. 212. These are not chirographs, but represent a deliberate duplication of material. Some later copies, to be sure, may show signs of interpolation and manipulation, and may be forgeries or fabrications designed to bolster or even falsify claims to lands and privileges. However, unless charters bear signs of anachronistic form or obvious errors, copies may be simply that. In the cartulary rubrics the word *duplicatur* indicates that the charter may exist in more than one copy.[33] A fragment of a charter roll is preserved in MS Dodsworth 76 (SC 5018), a collection of original charters and miscellaneous documents from the twelfth to the fifteenth centuries, which were salvaged in the seventeenth century from St Mary's Tower, York. Folio 146r–v is part of a Byland charter roll relating to Denby, possibly dating from the thirteenth century. The marginalia indicate a correspondence between the numbers of the originals and the number on the roll.

Table 2. MS Dodsworth 76, fol. 146r, a roll of Denby charters (incomplete)

Marginal number		Endorsement of original	No. in present calendar
end of charter		–	211
(a)	xiii	–	220
(b)	x	10	217
(c)			
(d)	xii	12	219
fol. 146 dorso			
end of charter		–	–
no number [?e]		–	238
(f)	xxxv	35	240
(g)		[36]	241
(h)		[37]	242
(i)		[38]	243
(k)		[39]	244
(l)		–	245
no number		–	247
no number		–	249

---

33 It may also, in the case of rubrics for which there is no text, indicate that it was copied elsewhere in the cartulary.

This evidence, fragmentary though it is, may indicate an earlier attempt to group originals into a logical order for reference, either in the abbey archives or for use at outlying granges such as Denby.

The rubrics entered in the cartulary sometimes give the location of the copy which the compiler consulted. These may be, as indicated above, original charters in their bundles; however there is also reference to a book of pleas (*liber placitorum*, nos 447, 448) and a register of pleas (*register placitorum*, no. 625); a register of charters (nos 972–4); records in the treasury (no. 575); a white book (no. 987) and a white or black chest (nos 986). Records were also transcribed from the rolls of the wapentake court of Pickering (nos 879, 880, 882).

The charters in St Mary's Tower, York

At the Dissolution of the religious houses in Yorkshire the muniments of a number of abbeys and priories were stored in St Mary's Tower on the precinct walls of St Mary's Abbey, York. The Tower suffered severe damage during the siege of York in June 1644.[34] Roger Dodsworth had already made some transcripts of charters from the Tower, and in 1644–5 he continued his efforts, copying documents that he and Thomas Fairfax had salvaged. Many of the records were returned after the Restoration, and were subsequently catalogued by James Torre (d. 1699).[35] Some of the charters came into the possession of John Burton (1710–1771), who also copied them, preserving the catalogue marks used by Torre.

Copies of Byland charters from St Mary's Tower survive among the following collections:[36]

---

34 Bernard Barr and Barbara English have done much to elucidate the complex history of those charters from their removal to the Tower and their subsequent fate both before and after the Tower was blown up by Parliamentary forces in June 1644; see B. A. English and C. B. L. Barr, 'The Records formerly in St. Mary's Tower, York', *YAJ*, 42 (1967–70), 198–235, 358–86, 465–518. See also B. A. English and R. Hoyle, 'What was in St Mary's Tower: an inventory of 1610', *YAJ*, 65 (1993), 91–4, in particular the reference to 'Two chestes bound aboute with iron wherin are diverse smale evidences and courte rowles belonginge to the mon[astery] of Byland' (p. 93). See also 'Yorkshire monastic archives' in *The Bodleian Library Quarterly Record*, 8 (1935), 95–100.

35 This catalogue is now fols 214v–61 of MS Top. Yorks. b.14 (SC 55286).

36 See Appendix II for a list of cartulary entries, both full texts and rubrics, which survive as later transcripts.

MSS Dodsworth 7–8 (SC 4149–4150) together form Dodsworth's *Monasticon Boreale*, copied by him and others (1644–5), and begun in October 1644 at the house of Francis Nevill of Chevet. The manuscripts contain some cross references to the cartulary; for instance, in MS Dodsworth 8, fol. 56r, there is a transcript of a confirmation of Roger de Lascy, with a note: *Hic carta etiam legi in cartulario de Bellalanda fol. 86 sub titulo Allerton.*

MS Dodsworth 45 (SC 4187) was written by Roger Dodsworth in 1638.

MS Dodsworth 70 (SC 5012) was compiled by Roger Dodsworth and others *c.* 1646 and is headed simply 'copies of charters', with no note of provenance. However, the notes of endorsements indicate that the Byland charters, which relate to the Westmorland property of Warcop, were transcribed from originals.

MS Dodsworth 71 (SC 5013) is in various hands and written between *c.* 1645 and 1648. These transcripts contain copies of seals and were evidently compiled from originals.

MS Dodsworth 91 (SC 5032) was written in 1636–7 by Roger Dodsworth and others. Folios 1–157 contain transcripts of charters in St Mary's Tower.[37]

MS Dodsworth 94 (SC 5035) contains copies from the originals in St Mary's Tower and was written in and after 1636 by Roger Dodsworth and others. A number of notes throw light on the state of the documents, and their location within the Tower, for instance: fol. 5v: *Incipit carta male scripta et fere deleta de bundis diversarum villarum*; fol. 10r: *Carte abbathie de Bellalanda spectantes in cista cartarum eiusdem domus infra turrim beate Marie iuxta Eboracum reservat'* (27 Sept. 1636); fol. 18r: *In baga 2da de Bellalanda et super filum in Turri Beate Marie Ebor'*; fol. 38r: *In baga cartarum de Bellelanda in turri Beate Marie Ebor'.*

MS Dodsworth 95 (SC 5036) has copies of deeds in St Mary's Tower, written in and after 1645 by Roger Dodsworth and others. There are notes indicating the location of the Byland charters: fol. 40r: *In*

---

37 An indication of the extent of written muniments relating to just one place can be found on fol. 117r, no. 68, a notification by Hugh, eldest son of Lord Geoffrey of Upsall, that he received by the hand of the abbot 64 charters and writings which were found in a chamber at Upsall, and 80 charters and writings found in the chapel of the vill in 1280, in the presence of Brothers Ralph de Stechyll and Henry of Amunderby, monks, and Brother Roger de Wyverthorp *conversus* of the same house, William de Roseles, Simon of Upsall, Geoffrey of Kilvington, William de Bancho.

bundello cartarum monasterio de Bellaland pert(inentium); fol. 74v: *ex quodam rotulo* (possibly the Denby roll now in Dodsworth 76); fol. 75v: *Hec omnia de Bellalanda transcripta sunt ex quodam antiquo rotulo.*

MS Dodsworth 118 (SC 5059) was written between 1618 and 1622 by Roger Dodsworth, and contains copies of monastic deeds in St Mary's Tower.

MS Dodsworth 133 (SC 5074) was written chiefly by Roger Dodsworth in 1629. Folio 139r contains the words: *In certayne transcripts of evidence taken out of St Maries tower in Yorke under the hand of Hen. Sandwithe, clerk.*[38] *Her copyed for Sir Ri. Beaumont*; fol. 139r has: *In tergo rotuli*; and fol. 140r: *This farre out of the transcripts out of St Maryes tower.*

MS Dodsworth 157 (SC 5098) contains rough notes (Part B) made by Roger Dodsworth *c.* 1630. Various notes indicate the location of the Byland documents: *In Byland chest* (fols 30v, 33v); *In baga de Biland* (fol. 31r); *on the file* (fol. 31v).

MSS Top. Yorks. e. 7–e. 12

This sequence of notebooks contains transcripts of a number of Byland charters, some with notes of endorsements and sketches of seals, made by John Burton, whose Yorkshire collections, now MSS Top. Yorks. e. 7–e. 12 (SC 55279–84), were intended to form an appendix to his *Monasticon Eboracense* (York, 1758).

The significance of the transcripts of Dodsworth and Burton will become clear in the following section.

Selection of material for inclusion in the cartulary

The Byland compiler was selective in what he entered in full into the cartulary. Even given the fragmentary nature of the early and final parts of the volume and damage to other sections, it is clear that the compiler did not incorporate all the material at his disposal. Some of

---

38 Henry Sandwith and his father Thomas were deputies to Edward Bee, keeper of the king's evidences at York, 1613–25. Henry was appointed Bee's successor in 1625 and held the office until his death in 1635. Roger Dodsworth, who took notes from records in Thomas Sandwith's custody in 1623, referred to Thomas Sandwith as his cousin. However he was related to the Sandwiths of Oswaldkirk, his mother, Eleanor Sandwith, being the daughter of Ralph Sandwith of Newton Grange, Oswaldkirk. There is no known connection between the Sandwith family of Oswaldkirk and that of York: English and Barr, 'Records formerly in St Mary's Tower, York', pp. 379–81.

the original charters, and transcripts from originals correspond to rubrics for which there is no text. Original charters yield texts that can be matched to forty-three cartulary rubrics, and later transcripts provide texts for a further fifty-six. So, in nearly one hundred cases we are able to identify what the compiler has chosen to refer to without copying. This means that we are in a position to comment on the process of selection.

Trevor Foulds has refined the description accorded to general cartularies by G. R. C. Davies, that they contained 'transcriptions of the entire muniments of a religious house', by demonstrating that compilers might deliberately choose to omit material from a monastery archive.[39] Indeed his examples, many of them from the Thurgarton cartulary, are very telling.[40] In the case of the Byland compiler the strategy is not always clear. Sometimes a complete omission – where neither text nor rubric appear in the cartulary – might be explained by its seeming lack of relevance. BL Egerton charter 2153 is not, at first sight, a Byland charter; rather it is a grant by Stephen de Blaby to the Knights Hospitaller of 1 carucate in Tollesby and 1 bovate in Bagby. Nevertheless, it has a Byland pressmark, *Gaytrik' B. i.*, indicating that at one time it had been in the first 'Gaytrig' bundle. As Byland was a landowner in both Tollesby and Bagby the charter was clearly of sufficient interest for it to be stored at Byland but not, perhaps, central enough to be included in the cartulary.

In other cases a deliberate decision was made not to copy the text of a charter, but to draw attention to its existence by inserting a rubric or heading only. Again the rationale is difficult to discern. However, it may be that when a section, such as that for Laysthorpe, contained a large number of small, and similar grants or quitclaims, the compiler simply did not think it necessary to copy out each text. He is not as engagingly honest as the Thurgarton compiler who wrote: 'Note that there are seven charters that speak of the same matter . . . it is unnecessary to transcribe all on account of their prolixity and tedium, because the tenor of them is similar to the two charters

---

39 Foulds, 'Medieval Cartularies', 7–8. For Davis's catalogue of cartularies see
    G. R. C. Davis, *Medieval Cartularies of Great Britain* (London: Longman, 1958).
    An new edition is in preparation by Professor David Smith of the Borthwick
    Institute, University of York, for publication by the British Library.
40 *The Thurgarton Cartulary*, ed. Trevor Foulds (Stamford: Paul Watkins, 1994).

immediately preceding',[41] but the sentiment may well have been the same.

Undoubtedly the changing status of estates influenced the compiler. The abbey's acquisitions in Skirpenbeck are an interesting case in point. The cartulary section (fol. 115r–v, nos 1154–1172) has the text of three documents and seventeen rubrics. The charter of the original benefactor, Amfrey de Chauncy, which survives as an original (BL Add. Charter 20588) was not copied in full (rubric at no. 1156), nor were a number of confirmations and quitclaims. The only documents copied in full are: an agreement of 1207 between the monks and Walter de Chauncy after a series of disputes (no. 1157), a final concord of 1231 between Roger de Chauncy and the monks (no. 1160), and the lease, by Byland, to John le Romeyn, archdeacon of York, of the manor of 'Staynhow' in Skirpenbeck (no. 1171). Many of these documents do, however, appear in the thirteenth-century cartulary of the Premonstratensian abbey of Easby, BL MS Egerton 2827. On fol. 254v the Easby cartularist copied a grant by Amfrey de Chauncy of one carucate in Skirpenbeck to the Hospital of St Peter, York, and an agreement by which the Hospital granted to Byland that carucate for an annual rent of two marks (no. 1154). This is followed by a note that the two charters were at Easby on one schedule, sealed with the seal of the Hospital and that they had been handed to the canons by John le Romeyn when he enfeoffed them with the land.[42] A further note indicates that the nine *scripta* following were on two schedules, sealed with the seal of the abbot of Byland, that had been handed over to the canons; the main charters remained at Byland.[43] The nine *scripta*, which seem to be copied in full except for the witness lists, correspond to nos 1157, 1162, 1159, 1169, 1167, 1164, 1168, 1165, and a confirmation by Henry II of land granted to Byland by Amfrey de Chauncy (no. 524). This confirmation is followed by a note, *Hic explic' ix carte sigillate sig' abbatis Bellaland*, and by the lease by Abbot Henry to John le Romeyn (no. 1171), a confirmation of the same by

---

41 Foulds, 'Medieval cartularies', 8–9.

42 *Et mem' quod iste ii carte prescripte sunt apud nos in una scedula supscripte et sigillo hospitalis sancti Petri sigillate quas dominus Romanus quando nos feofavit nobis dedit* (BL MS Egerton 2827, fol. 255r).

43 *Item sunt apud nos ix scripta subsequent' in ii scedul(as) sigillata sigillo abbatis de Bell'land que eodem tempore sunt nobis deliberata et carte principales sint apud Bellalandam* (BL MS Egerton 2827, fol. 255r).

Hugh, rector of the Hospital, an earlier version of no. 1171 made when John le Romeyn was subdean,[44] and two charters of Joan Wake relating to the grant to John le Romeyn. The next three charters concerning Skirpenbeck were on a roll sealed with the seal of the prior of Newburgh (fol. 258r–v), and there are two quitclaims to John le Romeyn (fol. 259r–v). Finally, the interest of the canons of Easby becomes clear with the grant, by John le Romeyn, to Easby Abbey, of the manor of 'Staynhow' and common pasture for 400 sheep in Skirpenbeck which he had bought from the monks of Byland, and the undertaking by the abbot of Easby to feed five poor people each day for the salvation of the soul of John le Romeyn and for the souls of all the faithful dead (fols 259v–269r); this was confirmed by Archbishop Walter de Gray (fol. 260r–v). The compiler of the Easby cartulary, leaving nothing to chance, entered the full history of the property from the time of the earliest grant by Amfrey de Chauncy to the hospital of St Peter, and every step of a claim to the manor which his abbey might make could be documented and authenticated – hence his insistence that the cartulary copies were made from rolls and schedules which were appropriately sealed. The Byland compiler, on the other hand, knowing that the section was, in one sense, out of date, since Byland had remitted all right in Skirpenbeck, selected only the three key documents, and contented himself with indicating to anyone interested that the originals still existed at Byland, in the first and apparently the only Skirpenbeck bundle.

The Byland compiler was to a certain extent guided in his selection by what he thought was essential to the interests of the abbey, what might have been useful, and what was not. It is to be expected that perceptions of what was important in the early stages of the development of an estate changed over time. In the Denby section one charter of William son of Michael is copied out in full, and two others are merely given a rubric, despite the fact that one of these survives in an original which is endorsed 'a useful and very necessary charter' (no. 246). What was necessary and useful in the thirteenth century was less so by the fifteenth. A further text, an undertaking by the same that he would undergo a sentence of excommunication if he were to transgress the agreement which he had confirmed by his seal (BL Add. Charter 7433, rubric at no. 250), was probably omitted in its

---

44 This is not in the Byland cartulary but was copied by Dodsworth from the original: MS Dodsworth 91, fol. 96r–v.

entirely as being out of date. Such processes of selection and exclusion reflect the transformations and changes which had taken place in the abbey estate, administration and identity over a period of time.

The cartulary as a work of reference

The cartulary was in some part a statement of the identity of the Byland community and a narrative of its history. It also allowed the monks to access material in their muniments, the great repository of the rights, privileges and liberties which were to be guarded safely. Although the 'intrinsic evidentiary capabilities' of cartulary copies were recognized, for example in the event of the loss of originals, it is unlikely that the cartulary was in any way intended to replace the originals, the *carte autentice* of the community which formed the legal response should those rights be challenged.[45] Rather, the compiler sought to give coherence to the archive and to enable those who might be challenged to find what they wanted. On another level, therefore, the cartulary functioned as a reference tool. This is indicated in a number of ways.

First, there was the *Baculus* system of referencing. This provided a rudimentary, but quick and effective, retrieval method for accessing the archive, with marginal notes directing a user to the location of the original charter.

Second, whereas in the calendar 'rubric only' usually indicates omitted texts, rubrics sometimes function as cross references. A few examples will suffice. In the section relating to Cam, no. 121 has the rubric 'Chirograph agreement between the monks and the prior of Newburgh concerning common pasture in Calvecotedale' etc, and this is followed by the instruction to search for the chirograph in the Newburgh bundle, a cross reference to no. 731. No. 156 under Crossley has marginal note: 'Whitacr', bundle 1'. In the Deepdale section, no. 202 is a rubric noting a confirmation of several manors

---

45 *Thurgarton Cartulary*, p. cxcii; Foulds, 'Medieval cartularies', 31, cites the example of Thomas de Hotot who, in his estate book, stated that he had compiled it to provide evidence of the content of original charters without having to produce them. Foulds notes further (p. 33) that in court evidence of title was provided by the originals (though acceptance of proof of title lay with the court), and that he had been unable to locate an example of a cartulary copy being produced in court in the absence of an original. See also Patrick Geary, *Phantoms of Remembrance: memory and oblivion at the end of the first millennium* (Princeton: University Press, 1994), p. 83.

including Deepdale; it alerts the user to look among the confirmations, and this is a cross reference to no. 960, in the Rillington bundle. Sometimes the instruction is more specific. No. 449 (Cold Kirby) directs the user to look under Sutton in the third bundle, nos 447 and 448 to look in the book of pleas, and no. 485 to search in the bundle of the abbots.

The marginalia, or notes with the rubric, also assisted users to locate the correct document. There is an indication from the marginalia that the royal charters (under the heading *Libertates*) were not stored in bundles but rather in what is referred to in no 531 as the royal chest. They were marked with a letter for further recognition. The first entry (no. 516) is a rubric only: 'Great confirmation of King Henry II of all lands granted to the monks or to be granted in the future. Copied in triplicate and marked with an A'.[46] The second (no. 517) is the full text of a Henry II confirmation. The note reads: 'This charter has not been copied and therefore must be kept carefully. Marked with a B'.[47] The instruction in this case seems to be that, wherever possible, the cartulary copy rather than the original should be used. The charters of Henry II and Richard I (nos 516–26) are marked in sequence from A to K, and lest anyone think he had made an omission the compiler noted, after no. 526, 'we have no general charter of confirmation from King John'.

The compilation of the Byland cartulary was the culmination of record keeping that had included the sorting and arrangement of original charters into bundles for easy retrieval, and the making of copies both in single charter form and on charter rolls. The compilation of a volume was an obvious step to take, and one which many Yorkshire abbeys had taken before Byland.[48] The Byland cartulary,

---

46 The word *duplicatur* often appears at the end of a rubric. As suggested above, it may sometimes mean that the charter has been copied into another portion of the cartulary. It may also mean that the compiler chose not to transcribe it because a copy already existed in the archive, either as a copy charter (as implied here) or on a charter roll such as that preserved in MS Dodsworth 76. A number of charters among the Denby 'originals' are copies rather than originals.

47 For similar comment on the physical state of a document see no. 657, rubric only, which indicates that the original had been placed in a box because its seal was fragile.

48 The Rievaulx cartulary, for instance, was compiled in the late twelfth century (BL Cotton MS Julius D. I); from Fountains Abbey we have one cartulary of the thirteenth century (Oxford, Bodleian Library MS Rawlinson B 449, continued

however, was far from a mechanical transcription of the contents of the abbey archives. The compiler produced a thoughtful, skilled and quite sophisticated volume, which sent out messages about the history, status, antiquity and identity of his monastery, as well as its current concerns, and ensured that the community had access to the repository of its past in order to ensure its future.

THE DOCUMENTS

The documents are here presented in an English calendar, but some comment may be made on a few features of the diplomatic of the Latin charters. This is particularly important since D. E. Greenway, in her edition of *Mowbray Charters,* raised the question of the authenticity of several Byland charters on the grounds of their form.

Addresses

Most charters are addressed generally, with phrases such as *Omnibus sancte matris ecclesie filiis.* However, the following variations occur:

Ebor' archiepiscopo et toti capitulo Sancti Petri (To the archbishop of York and the whole chapter of St Peter): nos 47, 48, 51, 52, 53, 56, 58, 59, 60, 74, 133, 147, 165, 172, 182, 189, 205, 224, 225, 226, 238, 241, 246, 247, 255, 257, 317, 325, 326, 328, 329, 335, 337, 339, 377, 388, 390, 395, 409, 414, 457, 460, 463, 491, 492, 578, 608, 632, 637, 643, 644, 667, 670, 673, 688, 689, 691, 708, 715, 716, 739, 743, 744, 752, 764, 831, 837, 885, 887, 888, 914, 935, 1104, 1107, 1109, 1156, 1161, 1173, 1177

Ebor' archiepiscopo et toti capitulo Sancti Petri et omnibus hominibus suis Francis et Anglis (To the archbishop of York and the whole chapter of St Peter and to all the donor's men, French and English): 310, 655, 995

Ebor' archiepiscopo (To the archbishop of York): nos 55, 154, 158, 159, 296, 327, 341, 343, 387, 456, 458, 524, 855, 1076

Ebor' archiepiscopo et omnibus suis hominibus Francis et Anglis (To the archbishop of York and to all the grantor's men French and English): no. 115.

---

as University College MS 170) and a series from the fifteenth century (BL Cotton MS Tiberius C XII, MSS Add. 40009 and 37770 and Manchester, John Rylands Library Latin MS 224). These were calendared in a sixteenth-century register (London, BL MS Add. 18276).

To a named individual and all the grantor's men French and English: no. 645

To the grantor's bailiffs and other officials and all Christians: no. 690

The address to the archbishop and chapter, and the evidence that nos 47, 56, and 59 were made in the presence of the chapter, and that no. 935 was sealed by the chapter, suggest that the monks were not employing a formulaic address, but made use of the court comprising the archbishop and chapter to have their grants and confirmations strengthened. Greenway noted that the use of the address to the archbishop of York and the whole chapter of St Peter was very common in Byland charters, and that it is found in most Mowbray charters for Byland and more frequently than in charters of other beneficiaries.[49] This would add weight to the likelihood that the charters were drawn up at Byland rather than by a household draughtsman.

Guaranteeing the grant: *laudatio parentum* and warranty

One of the earliest methods of attempting to secure a grant to a religious house was by including a clause indicating the approval of members of the family, especially prospective heirs, for the alienation of land. The *laudatio parentum*, the assent to a grant by the kin of the donor, committed the family to a grant both at the time it was made and for the future. There is evidence that by the late twelfth century the *laudatio* was giving way to a formal 'pledge to warranty' clause.[50] This in itself may have been a result of succession by hereditary right becoming stronger, which demanded a more formal renunciation of rights. Postles suggested that the late twelfth century was a period of transition in the securing of grants, when there was 'fluidity and change in the development of the legal framework and devices available'.[51] In his work on the charters of Oseney Abbey he noted a

---

49 *Mowbray Charters*, pp. lxix–lxx.

50 See David Postles, 'Securing the gift in Oxfordshire charters in the twelfth and thirteenth centuries', *Archives*, 19 (1990), 183–91, and 'Gifts in frankalmoign, warranty of land, and feudal society', *The Cambridge Law Journal*, 50 (1991), 330–46.

51 Postles, 'Securing the gift', 185. See also Marjorie Chibnall, 'Dating the charters of the smaller religious houses of Suffolk in the twelfth and thirteenth centuries', in Michael Gervers, ed., *Dating Undated Medieval Charters* (Woodbridge: Boydell Press, 2000), pp. 51–9. Chibnall noted that express warranties were rare before the latter part of the reign of Henry II (p. 56); before that, warranty was implicit, an expected part of good lordship (p. 57).

preponderance of charters before 1180 using the *laudatio parentum* and/or a pledge of faith. He noted that these devices continued for some time after that watershed, coexisting for a while with the warranty clause which gradually replaced it.

Few Byland charters have the *laudatio* clause. The brother and nephew of William of Cayton agreed his grant of land in Deepdale, and sealed the charter along with the donor (no. 164, of the late twelfth century). William, the brother and heir of Ralph son of Richard of Osgodby attested and agreed Ralph's grant, also in Deepdale (no. 168). William, son and heir of Robert son of Simon of Osgodby, lent his consent and goodwill for his father's grant of land in Deepdale (no. 182). Simon son of Henry of Denby obtained the assent and goodwill of his brother, Jordan, who was also his lord (no. 217), and William son of Osbert obtained the same from his son and heir, another Jordan (no. 226). Adam de Vermenles made a grant with the assent and goodwill of his wife, Albrede (Aubrede), who with her husband sealed the charter (no. 495), an action mirrored by Samson of Laysthorpe (no. 497). Hugh Malebisse made a grant at the request of his wife, Matilda, whose permission was given because the grant was of her dower (no. 632).[52] Gilbert de Meinill's son Walter offered his goodwill and consent for a grant in Osgoodby (no. 743), as did Robert de Buscy's son, William (no. 831). Ralph of Thorpefield secured the assent of his eldest son and his three brothers (no. 914). The examples of *laudatio parentum* are thus very few, and confined to the late twelfth and early thirteenth centuries. Otherwise the consent of heirs seems to have been implicitly conveyed by their witnessing of charters.

Some 120 charters – cartulary copies, originals and post medieval transcripts of documents represented in the cartulary as rubrics only – have evidence of warranty clauses. It is necessary to look at their form, since they have a bearing on the question of the authenticity of certain charters. As mentioned above, scholars have concluded that the warranty clause comes into general use in the late twelfth century, and co-existed with the *laudatio parentum* before replacing it.[53] 'In his

---

52 The consent of a wife was obtained in order to bar dower: Postles, 'Gifts in frankalmoign', 340.

53 Postles, 'Securing the gift' and 'Gifts in frankalmoin'; John Hudson, *Land, Law, and Lordship in Anglo-Norman England* (Oxford: Clarendon Press, 1994), pp. 51–8; P. Hyams, 'Warranty and good lordship in twelfth century England', *Law and History Review*, 5 (1987), 437–503; John Hudson, *The Formation of the English Common Law: law and society in England from the Norman Conquest to Magna Carta*

warranty, the grantor made two different commitments. He made a positive promise, that he (and his family) would maintain the grant against outside challenge . . . If they were unable to do this, the grantee had to be compensated for his loss, as by exchange [*escambium*] of an equivalent holding. Developed warranty also had a negative aspect, . . . once the grant was complete, neither he (nor his family) were to try to resume any part of the property conveyed.'[54]

In charters warranty clauses emerge slowly in the twelfth century, but Hudson suggested that there 'may have been an initial burst during Stephen's reign, perhaps followed by a temporary decrease'.[55] He noted this phenomenon in charters of the earldom of Chester from the 1140s;[56] grants to the church which carried warranty clauses include a confirmation to the nuns of Stixwold (*Et bene sciatis quod ego et heredes mei warantizabimus illis omnes predictas terras in puram et liberam possessionem sancte ecclesie in perpetuum . . .*), dated by Barraclough to between 1140 and 1150; Hartsholme (*Et ego et heredes mei hanc elemosinam ei in perpetuum warantizabimus*), dated to between 1144 and 1146; and the Holy Sepulchre, Lincoln (*. . . ego et heredes mei hec omnia predictis fratribus et pauperibus garantizabimus et adquietabimus et defendemus de omnibus rebus in perpetuum*), dated 1153.[57]

In the Byland charters warranty clauses do indeed become common from the last two decades of the twelfth century. The most common phrase, with minor variants, is: *Affidavi pro me et pro heredibus meis quod nos manutenebimus, warantizabimus et defendemus istam donationem meam dictis monachis contra omnes homines [et feminas] in perpetuum* (e.g., no. 40, dated 1190 x 1220), or *. . . ego et heredes mei fideliter warantizabimus et defendemus omnia predicta dictis abbati et conventui . . . contra omnes homines et feminas in perpetuum* (e.g., no. 41, dated 1180 x 1220). The clause occasionally adds *sine malo ingenio*. The following have the common formula, and are therefore likely to be

(London: Longman, 1996), pp. 121, 207–8; Chibnall, 'Dating the charters of the smaller religious houses of Suffolk', p. 56.

54 Hyams, 'Warranty', 459, quoted in Hudson, *Land, Law and Lordship*, p. 52.

55 Hudson, *Land, Law, and Lordship*, p. 55. See also Postles, 'Gifts in frankalmoign', 335.

56 John Hudson, 'Diplomatic and legal aspects of the charters', in A. T. Thacker, ed., *The Earldom of Chester and its Charters, Journal of the Chester Archaeological Society*, 71 (1991), 153–78 (pp. 173–4).

57 *The Charters of the Anglo-Norman Earls of Chester c. 1071–1237*, ed. Geoffrey Barraclough, Record Society of Lancashire and Cheshire, 126 (1988), nos 20, 76, 107.

nearer the later date within the chronological range suggested for their issue; no. 395 (1177 x 1180); no. 414 (1184 x 1187); no. 457 (1170 x 1186); no. 463 (1179 x 1190); no. 491 (1158 x 1181); no. 578 (*c.* 1170 x 1186); no. 632 (1170 x 1186); no. 648 (1177 x 1189); no. 662 (1186 x 1189); no. 691 (1186 x 1189); no. 708 (1166 x 1175); nos 715, 716 (1175 x 1181); no. 739 (1180 x 1199); nos 885, 888 (1175 x 1181); no. 914 (1181 x 1186); no. 1107 (1186 x 1189); no. 1109 (before 1186). On a handful of occasions grantors named individuals to act as sureties: Archbishop Roger (no. 24), Murdac, rural dean of Appleby (no. 60), Thomas son of Cospatrick (nos 69, 71), William, constable of Appleby (no. 396), Thomas de Coleville (no. 51), the sheriff of York (no. 1101). In a few instances grantors pledged warranty against certain parties: the prior of Guisborough (no. 358), all men except the king (no. 164), the lords of Pickering, Seamer and Topcliffe (no. 493).

In charters of the late twelfth century and later, which account for the vast majority of instances, such formulations arouse no suspicions. However, in apparently early charters they may be indicative of later tampering or interpolation. It is necessary, therefore, to look at the precise wording of charters earlier than the last twenty years of the twelfth century.

Ego quoque coram capitulo sancti Petri hanc donationem confirmavi et affidavi quod hanc terram [quam eis dedi in perpetuam elemosinam liberam de me et heredibus meis] fideliter tenebo et warantizabo contra omnes homines ego et heredes mei (nos 47, 56, 59; 1158 x 1167)

Et ego et heredes mei hec omnia warant(izabimus) prefatis monachis contra omnes homines imperpetuum (no. 153; 1138 x 1147)

Et ego et heredes mei warantizabimus predictis monachis istam donationem contra omnes homines imperpetuum (nos 158, 159; 1160 x 1166)

Et warantizabo eam illis imperpetuum ego et heredes mei contra omnes homines (no. 172; 1145 x 1170)

Istam donationem ego et heredes mei pro salute animarum nostrarum debemus manutenere et warantizare contra omnes homines imperpetuum (no. 323; 1147 x 1157, fabricated)

Et ego et heredes mei manutenebimus et warantizabimus hec omnia predictis monachis contra omnes homines in perpetuum (no. 325; after *c.* 1157, original)

Et ego et heredes mei manutenebimus et warantizabimus predictis monachis istam donationem contra omnes homines imperpetuum (no. 328; 1162 x 1173)

. . . vir meus et ego affidavimus in capitulo quod hec omnia warantizabimus

predictis monachis nos et heredes nostri contra omnes homines inperpetuum (1160 *c.* 1170; no. 343)

Et ego et heredes mei manutenebimus et warantizabimus predictis monachis istam donationem contra omnes homines imperpetuum (no. 643; 1142 x 1147)

Hec omnia ego Rogerus et heredes mei predictis monachis et successoribus suis warantizabimus et manutenebimus contra omnes homines imperpetuum (no. 690; before 1154; fabricated)

Et ego et heredes mei totam hanc donationem eisdem monachis et successoribus suis suis semper debemus manutenere et warantizare contra omnes homines imperpetuum (no. 1104; 1140)

A number of these phrases occur in charters of the Mowbray family. In her discussion of individual charters over a wide range of beneficiaries Greenway notes that the warranty clause, and in particular the style of *contra omnes homines et feminas imperpetuum warantizabimus* and variations, is more common in the thirteenth century than the twelfth. However, she raises no objections to its occurrence in some charters from *c.* 1160.[58] Indeed some charters such as those for Rievaulx Abbey, which she dates to 1154, and Selby, which she dates to 1143 x 1153 are not considered suspicious.[59]

The occurrences of a standard formula in charters of Roger de Mowbray from the 1140s and indeed earlier, that is *Mowbray Charters* nos 35, 42, 49 (below nos 1104, 643, 690), as well as charters surviving from sources other than the cartulary (*Mowbray Charters*, nos 37–8, from the *Historia Fundationis* and MS Dodsworth 94, no. 43 from MSS Dodsworth 7 and 94, no. 55, 1154 x 1175, from MSS Dodsworth 63 and 94), suggest later fabrication or interpolation. They are especially suspicious when they occur either with anachronistic address to the monks of Byland before 1142 (no. 1104) or detailed boundary clauses more likely in a thirteenth-century than a twelfth-century charter. It is also worth noting that Hyams, Hudson, and Postles see no problem in accepting the precocious warranty clauses of Chester charters of

---

58 *Mowbray Charters*, nos 56–7 (1173 x 1180), no. 59 (*c.* 1181), nos 65, 67 (1170 x 1186), no. 70 (1177 x 1190), nos 71, 72, 73, 74 (1186 x 1190), no. 85 (1170 x 1186), no. 86 (1166 x 1190), no. 110 (1174 x 1175), nos 119–21 (1175 x 1176), nos 126–7, 129 (1176), nos 135, 137, 138, 139 (1181/2 and 1181), nos 142, 144–5, 146 (1176 x 1181), no. 148 (1183 x 1186), nos 250, 251, 252 (1163 x 1169), no. 264 (1154 x 1186), no. 291 (1150 x 1169); nos 364, 365 (1170 x 1184), no. 368 (1176 x 1181), no. 382 (1170 x 1186).

59 *Mowbray Charters*, nos 240–241.

the 1140s and 1150s, that is, in a time of tenurial insecurity when 'good lordship was at a premium', and this was a time at which Roger de Mowbray and the earl of Chester (who captured Roger at the Battle of Lincoln in 1141) were in uneasy alliance. Greenway has demonstrated that Roger lost status as a result of having to concede lands to the earl's constable, Eustace Fitz John, as well as to marry Alice de Gant, daughter of the earl's associate, Gilbert de Gant, and as a result of the Stuteville family regaining some estates from him.[60] In such circumstances the appearance of a warranty clause may not be unexpected.

Witnessing

In the vast majority of cases the documents entered into the cartulary are attested. Most witness lists are introduced by the words *Hiis (his) testibus* or, less frequently, *Testibus*, or *Hii sunt testes* (no. 164), in French *Par icelles / iceux testmoignes* (nos 78, 79). Variations are: *coram . . . et ceteris probis hominibus qui tunc fuerunt ibi presentes* (no. 89); *in presentia . . .* (no. 152); *in presentia . . . et aliorum multorum tunc ibi presentium / plurimum* (nos 623, 660); *Huius donationis sed et petitionis et concessionis predicte Mathilde sponse mee testes sunt rogatu eiusdem Mathildis [the donor's wife]* (no. 632); *Presentibus domino . . .* (no. 983). The witness lists are often abbreviated, ending with *etc.*

Sealing

Details of surviving seals appended to original charters are given in the notes to individual documents. Otherwise there is reference to sealing in the text of seventy charters. Agreements and chirographs were normally sealed with the seals of both parties (nos 26, 31, 76, 121, 130, 135, 155, 248, 259, 298, 299, 435, 455, 507, 508, 509, 616, 620, 723, 730, 732, 733, 734, 838, 848, 870, 873, 874, 924, 927A, 959, 970, 1038, 1056, 1059, 1066, 1143, 1151, 1154, 1157, 1171, 1193, 1199). No. 1055, an agreement between the vicar of Felixkirk and the men of the abbot, was sealed by the vicar and by the abbot on behalf of his men.

Some charters were sealed by parties other than the grantor. At Geoffrey de Cottesford's request Robert son of Gilbert of Asby appended his seal because it was well known (no. 25). William of

---

60 *Mowbray Charters*, pp. xxvii–xxviii. For the associations of Roger de Mowbray with the earl of Chester in this period see also Paul Dalton, 'Aiming at the impossible: Ranulf II, earl of Chester and Lincolnshire in the reign of King Stephen', in Thacker, ed., *The Earldom of Chester*, pp. 109–32 (pp. 118–19).

Cayton, son of Durand, added his seal, along with those of his brother and nephew, to his charter (no. 164). Simon de Cliffe sealed his charter with his ring because he did not have a seal (no. 172). Gilbert de Croft secured his undertaking by his own seal and that of Henry of Thurstonland (no. 208). Simon son of Henry of Denby asked his brother Jordan to append his seal as he did not have one (no. 217). The wives of Adam de Vermenles and Samson of Laysthorpe sealed with their husbands (nos 495, 497). Peter of Stonegrave affixed his private seal as he did not have his seal ready, and his charter was also sealed by Sir William de Lascels (no. 718). William of Osgodby's quitclaim was sealed by him, his son and heir, and the chapter of York in whose presence the deed was made (no. 935; *In cuius rei testimonium sigillum capituli Ebor' una cum sigillo meo et sigillo Henrici de Angotby filii et heredis mei qui omnia suprascripta confirmat presenti scripto est appensum*); and the quitclaim by his son, Henry, was sealed by Henry himself, the abbots of Jervaulx and Rievaulx, and the prior and convent of Newburgh (no. 937: *In cuius rei testimonium presenti scripto sigillum meum apposui. Et ad maiorem securitatem sigilla de Rievalle et Ioravalle abbatum necnon et sigillum prioris et conventus de Novoburgo ex assensu meo et voluntate mea presenti scripto in huius rei testimonio sunt appensa*, possibly made at Newburgh Priory). Another Rillington charter is sealed by the chapter of York as well as the grantor (no. 945). A quitclaim by Rievaulx in favour of Byland was sealed by the witnesses, three Cistercian abbots to whom the General Chapter had delegated investigation of the dispute that led to the quitclaim (no. 992); in no. 998 a charter of Thomas Fossard was sealed by the witnesses, who included the abbot of Louth Park, as well as by the donor: *In cuius rei testimonium presenti scripto sigillum meum una cum sigillis testium subscriptorum apposui*). The rubric of no. 816, a multiple quitclaim of land in Osgoodby, notes that the deed was sealed with nine seals.

In cartulary copies where there are no surviving seals, phrases such as the following also indicate sealing:

cum sigillis testium subscriptorum (no. 998)

Et in huius testimonium presenti carte [huic scripto] sigillum meum apposui (nos 41, 91, 128, 151, 152, 201, 375, 376, 412, 429, 430, 452, 453, 584, 592, 626, 627, 656, 658, 660, 671, 672, 673, 675, 684, 685, 686, 699, 701, 703, 796, 799, 906, 909, 960, 1049, 1101, 1148, 1196, 1197)

Et ut hec mea donatio concessio et quieta clamatio perpetue firmitatis robur obtineat presentem cartam eisdem feci et tradidi sigillo meo signatam (nos 70, 869)

Et . . . in testimonium huius rei presentem scriptum sigilli mei appositione roboravi (no. 75)

Et in testimonium huius mee confirmationis sigillum meum feci apposui (no. 189)

In cuius rei testimonium sigillum meum presentibus est appensum (no. 77)

En testmoigne de quel chose [a ceste escrip] ay mis moun seal (nos 78, 79)

In cuius rei testimonium presentem cartam eisdem tradidi [sigilli mei munimine roboratam] [sigillo meo signata] [signatam] (nos 149, 674, 710, 867, 949, 1120, 1146)

Et ut hec mea donatio rata et stabilis permaneat sigillum meum apposui (no. 150)

Et ut hec mea donatio rata et stabilis permaneat huic presenti scripto sigillum meum est appensum (no. 370, spurious)

Ut autem hec mea donatio . . . rata et stabilis permaneat presentem cartam sigilli mei impressione roboravi (no. 445)

Et ut ista donatio (mea) rata sit et inconcussa [stabilis] perpetuo eam scripto presenti [scripti presentis attestatione] firmavi et sigilli mei appositione roboravi (nos 930, 931, 1190)

Et ut hec mea donatio rata in perpetuum perseveret eam presentis scripti serie et sigilli mei appositione confirmavi (no. 264, variant no. 968, Archbishop Geoffrey)

In testimonium huius concessionis et confirmationis sigillum meum feci carte presenti apposui (no. 667)

In huius rei testimonium presenti scripto sigillum communem capituli nostri fecimus apposui (no. 451)

In huius rei testimonium hanc cartam sigilli mei appositione roboravi (no. 464, 466)

In huius rei testimonium sigillum nostrum et sigillum dicti Thome alternatim presenti scripto est appensum (no. 507)

In cuius rei testimonium una pars presentis carte cyrographi quod penes eundem Thome et eandem Feliciam residet sigillo nostro et altera pars quod penes nos est sigillo eiusdem Thome roboratur (no. 508)

In cuius rei testimonium partes alternatim huic indenture sigilla sua apposuerunt (no. 455)

In cuius rei testimonium presentem cartam eisdem tradidi sigillo meo (con)signatam (nos 242, 253, 494)

Et ad maiorem securitatem hanc cartam sigilli mei appositione roboravi (no. 479)

In cuius rei testimonium presentibus sigillum meum apposuimus (no. 484)

Et ut ista conventio rata sit inperpetuum . . . (no. 259)

In cuius rei testimonium dicta Albreda uxor mea presenti carte sigillum suum una cum sigillo meo apposui (no. 495)

In cuius rei testimonium presentem cartam sigillo meo et sigillum Emme uxoris mee roboravi (no. 497)

Such phrases demonstrate the emergence of common formulae associated with sealing.

Place and date
The Mowbray family issued charters from the family property in Epworth and Kirkby Malzeard. Local places of issue include Warcop and Appleby in Westmorland, and in Yorkshire Hawnby, Ampleforth, Laskill, Sutton, Kirkby Moorside, Coxwold, Kilburn, Pickering, Middlemoor, and the Newburgh grange of Brink.

BYLAND AND ITS BENEFACTORS

Cartularies are an important source for identifying those who played a part in the development of the abbey by granting lands and other economic assets to support the monks. They also reveal the reciprocal nature of monastic benefaction and the interaction of the monastery and the wider community of which it was a part. The following sections offer brief notes on those who offered material support to the monks of Byland.

The Mowbrays and their circle
By far the most important lay person in the history of the abbey was its founder, Roger de Mowbray. Roger was born in 1119 or 1120, the son of Nigel d'Aubigny, a landless knight who grew high in royal favour; endowed with lands and an advantageous marriage, Nigel acted from 1107 as a local justice in Yorkshire and Northumberland, and from *c.* 1118 until his death in 1129 was a close adviser of King Henry I. Roger succeeded to a fief that owed a *servitium debitum* of sixty knights.[61] It was around the time that Roger was knighted that he was urged by his mother, Gundreda de Gournay, and Archbishop Thurstan of York to provide for the refugee monks of Calder.[62]

---

61 *Mowbray Charters*, pp. xvii–xxv.
62 The author of the *Historia Fundationis* of Byland was unsure whether the monks

Although both the site that he allocated, Hood, and the food rents that he offered as sustenance, proved to be inadequate, Roger was amenable to persuasion, and at the monks' instance provided alternative sites, first at Old Byland (1142), then at Stocking (1147) and finally New Byland (1177).[63] From 1140 he added landed endowments in Airyholme, Scackleton, Rose Hill, Cam and Hovingham (nos 296, 1104–5).[64] The cartulary bears witness to the continued involvement of successive generations of Mowbrays. Roger's son, Nigel, was associated with some of his father's grants,[65] and issued at least one charter of confirmation in his father's lifetime (no. 689). Some of his confirmations (nos 662, 691, 1107, possibly no. 648) date from the relatively short period between his father's departure on crusade in 1186 or his death in 1188, and Nigel's own journey to the East, undertaken in December 1189. He died at Acre in 1191. Relations between the abbey and Nigel's son and successor, William, who held the honour from 1190 to his death in 1224, were less happy. A dispute over Middlesmoor in Nidderdale, the origin of which was a mortgage of 1172, under which the monks lent Roger de Mowbray 300 marks over ten years,[66] was referred by Pope Innocent III to the dean and chapter of York (no. 695; see also nos 655, 694, 697, 701). The same property was confirmed by chirograph by William's son, Roger, in 1249 (no. 698) in return for a house for his forester and lodgings when he himself came to Nidderdale, and by Roger's son, another Roger (no. 699). Charters in the Mowbray *scrinium* contained general confirmations from every generation from the founder to his great-great-great-great-grandson, John de Mowbray, in 1345 (nos 661, 664), who also gave to the monks a moiety of the church of Bubwith (no. 106).[67]

The names of the Mowbray family dominate the folios of the

---

were settled at Hood in 1138 before or after Roger attained his majority: *Mon. Ang.* V, 349–50.

63 *Ibid.* V, 349–51.

64 See also *Mowbray Charters*, nos 36–7.

65 See *Mowbray Charters*, nos 52–4, not in cartulary. No. 53 bears the hallmarks of interpolation into a genuine deed of the 1160s or 1170s.

66 *Mowbray Charters*, no. 54.

67 In 1385 Thomas de Mowbray, earl of Nottingham and earl marshall, inspected and confirmed the grants of Roger de Mowbray. For this he was received into confraternity at Byland. This does not appear in surviving portions of the cartulary. It was printed from the original in St Mary's Tower in *Mon. Ang.* V, 348–9. The family descended in the male line to the death, without issue, of John de Mowbray in 1476: *EYF*, p. 63.

cartulary, both as grantors and as lords confirming the grants of their tenants. The cartulary reveals that the knightly class of North Yorkshire who held tenancies of Roger de Mowbray and his heirs was also heavily involved in reciprocal relationships with the abbey. Among them were men who in 1147, in that period of insecurity accompanying the resumption of Mowbray estates by the Stutevilles, the visit of Roger de Mowbray to Normandy and then his crusade, chose to try to impede the territorial expansion of the abbey.[68]

The Daiville family held a tenancy of Roger de Mowbray's father, Nigel d'Aubigny, as early as 1114. Robert de Daiville was Roger de Mowbray's constable from c. 1154 until 1186, and in 1166 was holding five knights' fees.[69] In 1147 he was involved with others in harrassing the monks, claiming that they had enclosed a great part of the land which belonged to his vill of Kilburn,[70] and some time later an agreement was made concerning boundaries and rights within the area around Kilburn.[71] These proved to be in constant need of renegotiation (nos 487–90). Hugh Malebisse held the office of steward of the Mowbray household. He granted the monks the vills of Murton and Dale; however, he seems to have regretted his generosity for in 1147, like Daiville, he challenged Byland's rights over land and pasture.[72] Between 1147 and 1157 Mowbray enfeoffed Hugh Malebisse with lands in Carlton Miniott, Over Silton, Kepwick, Scawton, Murton, Dale, Stainton, Arden, Hawnby, and Broughton, for the service of one knight; Greenway suggested that this Hugh was probably the son of Hugh Malebisse I.[73] Hugh II granted – though in effect confirmed – to the monks lands in Murton (nos 578–9), and added Marton in Cleveland (no. 632), and Snilesworth in Hawnby (no. 1076, confirmed by his son, William: nos 1077, 1083).

Hugh I's successor as steward, William de Wyville, held office between 1154 and c. 1157; his son, Richard, held 5 fees in 1166, including Thorpe le Willows.[74] William granted the monks the whole vill of Thorpe le Willows (no. 323), and this was confirmed by his son (nos 324, 325) and by Roger de Mowbray (no. 326). Thomas de

---

68 *Mon. Ang.* V, 351–2. See below, pp. lix–lx.

69 *Mowbray Charters*, pp. xxxiv, lx.

70 *Mon. Ang.* V, 351–2.

71 See no. 486. The detailed boundary clauses are probably interpolations.

72 *Mon. Ang.* V, 352.

73 *Mowbray Charters*, p. lxii and no. 371.

74 *Ibid.*, pp. lxii, 264.

Coleville was enfeoffed by Roger de Mowbray of land in Coxwold, Yearsley and Oulston for the service of one knight in the 1150s.[75] He became a benefactor of Byland, granting land and woodland in Thorpe le Willows (no. 327–8), which were confirmed by Roger de Mowbray (no. 329). Hamo Beler held lands of the honour by 1153[76] and his grant in Hovingham (no. 388) was confirmed by Roger de Mowbray (no. 390). Other Mowbray tenants to develop associations with the abbey were the family of Stonegrave, whose fee was a tenancy created in the twelfth century for the render of scarlet hose (see nos 716–18, relating to Ness and nos 885–88, relating to Thorpefield), the Buscy family, and Philip of Billinghay, successor of his brother Peter, who was enfeoffed of land in Hovingham between 1170 and 1184 and made grants in Kirkby Malzeard (no. 463).[77]

Benefactors from among the nobility
Many of Byland's early problems were created by the Stuteville family,[78] who were both Mowbray tenants and tenants in chief in their own right, half their land being held as a tenancy of the honour and half of the crown. The family had forfeited land after the Battle of Tinchebrai in 1106 and their lands passed to Nigel d'Aubigny and thence to his son, Roger de Mowbray. The family subsequently returned to England, and in 1147 sued for the restoration of land which was then in the hands of the Mowbrays.[79] Between 1154 and 1166 Roger de Mowbray agreed to enfeoff Robert de Stuteville with a fee of nine or ten knights.[80] The family did not become major benefac-

---

75 *Ibid.*, no. 356.
76 *Ibid.*, nos 322, 341, and p. 266.
77 *Ibid.*, no. 349.
78 *Mon. Ang.* V, 352.
79 I. F. Sanders, *English Baronies: a study of their origins and descent 1086–1327* (Oxford: Clarendon Press, 1960), p. 37; *EYF*, pp. 85–6; Paul Dalton, *Conquest, Anarchy and Lordship: Yorkshire 1066–1154*, Cambridge Studies in Medieval Life and Thought, fourth series, 27 (Cambridge: Cambridge University Press, 1994), p. 291.
80 *Mowbray Charters*, p. xxxv and no. 386. According to the *Historia Fundationis* Robert quitclaimed the right he had in the site of the abbey by offering a knife on the altar at Byland: *Mon. Ang.* V, 352. It may have been the tensions between the Stutevilles and the abbey that Walter Map was referring to when he recorded a dispute between the monks of Byland and a knight who held property in Coxwold: Walter Map, *De Nugis Curialium: Courtiers' Trifles*, ed. M. R. James, rev. edn C. N. L. Brooke and R. A. B. Mynors, Oxford Medieval Texts (Oxford, 1983), pp. 104–5 and note 2.

tors of Byland, but confirmed the grants of others (no. 624). The main
line died out in 1233; the elder daughter of Nicholas de Stuteville,
Joan, married Hugh Wake, and their successors conveyed to the
abbey the manor of Middleton (nos 626–9) and confirmed Fossard
grants in Marderby and Sutton (no. 674) suggesting that these were
originally Stuteville lands. More closely involved with the affairs of
Byland Abbey than the Stuteville family were the Fossards. The
Fossards enjoyed a tenurial right in Hood, which they confirmed to
the monks (nos 380–1), and made grants in Marderby (nos 598–601,
603–5, 608–9, 612, 618 (confirmed by Nicholas de Stuteville (no. 624)),
625). A major Fossard donation was the manor of Sutton (no. 998).
This was an important acquisition and the centre of the lordship of
Sutton, carrying with it the vills of Marderby, Laysthorpe and
Felixkirk. A third family of tenants in chief to endow the abbey was
that of Meinill of Whorlton.[81] Stephen de Meinill, who was a minor in
1207 when the boundaries of Snilesworth Moor between the land of
the abbot and convent and Whorlton were perambulated (no. 1080),
granted and quitclaimed Snilesworth moor to the monks in 1230 (no.
1087). Separate branches of the Meinills, those of Thirkleby and
Osgoodby (no. 739), descended from a younger branch of the family,
possibly from Gilbert, younger son of Robert de Meinill of Whorlton
(occurs before 1112) and brother of Stephen (occurs *c.* 1120 and
1143).[82] Their grants are recorded in the Osgoodby section of the
cartulary.

Other tenants in chief and their own tenants became benefactors of
Byland. Agnes de Percy's grant of Moskwith (no. 637) was confirmed
by her son Henry (no. 638), and Percy tenants were important benefactors in Deepdale and Osgodby (nos 667–9). The grants of the
family of Acklam in 'Gayteryg' (nos 335, 337, 338) were confirmed by
Peter and Adam de Brus (nos 336, 336A), and the 'Gayteryg' section
ends with the genealogy of the Acklam family (no. 367). The 'Magnates' section of the cartulary includes confirmations by such families
as Ros, Darel, and Neville. However, with the exception of the
Fossards, Byland does not appear to have attracted high status benefactors outside the orbit of its patrons.

---

81 *CP* VIII, 619–32; *EYF*, p. 60.
82 *EYC* II, 134.

The upper peasantry

In many places the consolidation of lands by the abbey was made possible by the interaction of the monks and the local community, with lesser tenants, subtenants and the more prosperous peasantry, who might make the same kind of demands in return for their grants, confirmations or quitclaims, as more prestigious benefactors. Two examples will illustrate this. The Laysthorpe section contains twenty-two documents (nos 494–515) of which six are full texts and sixteen rubrics only (with texts supplied from later copies for four). The section opens with the grant by John de Cresacre of the homage and service of Adam de Vermenles and his heirs on three bovates (no. 494). Adam and his wife, Aubrede, quitclaimed to the monks the service of Reginald de Helton and his heirs on two bovates (no. 495). Aubrede may well have been the daughter of John de Newton, who gave one bovate when she married Thomas de Anlacby, which Thomas then granted to the monks (no. 496). Samson of Laysthorpe and Emma his wife granted the service of Roger son of Alexander, and this was confirmed by William son of Roger of Carlton (nos 497–8). Further grants and quitclaims of service were made by Emma and her mother, Hugeline Percehay, and a number of other residents of the vill. The Kirkby Malzeard section (nos 456–85) opens with eight grants and confirmations by Mowbrays and their tenants (nos 456–63). The remainder are grants and quitclaims by a host of lesser residents. The Osgoodby section also demonstrates how the monks achieved dominance in a vill through the participation, in land conveyance, of a host of minor players.

Benefactors and benefits

Pro amore dei

The religious or spiritual impulse behind the act of giving to a religious house was only rarely spelt out in the charter which recorded the gift. Of the charters preserved as originals or copied in the Byland cartulary only a few specified that the grant or confirmation was made for the love of God (*pro amore dei*) or through the instincts of charity (*divine pietatis instinctu / caritatis intuitu*) (nos 88, 106, 138, 225, 247, 270, 584, 592, 638, 651, 658, 660, 664, 675, 699, 700, 708, 931, 1142, 1177).

Pro salute anime mee

By far the most common benefit requested by those who granted or confirmed land was that of prayers for the salvation of their soul, and those of their family and kin. Such benefits are requested in 213 charters, usually in the common formula: *pro salute anime mee et omnium antecessorum et heredum meorum.*[83]

Burial rights

Burial within a monastery was a privilege highly prized by many founders, patrons and benefactors.[84] When a family was closely associated with more than one religious house founders and patrons had a choice of burial place, and, over the generations, might favour one establishment over another. Byland did not become or was not chosen by many members of the Mowbray family as their final resting place. The founder and his son both died in the Holy Land, and Roger's wife, Alice de Gant, sought commemoration at Fountains Abbey.[85] According to a document formerly in St Mary's Tower, York, but of unknown provenance, Nigel's grandson, another Nigel, was buried at Newburgh Priory, as was his brother, William.[86] William's son, Roger, is said to have been buried in the church of the Friars Preacher at Pontefract; Roger de Mowbray died at Ghent in 1297 and was buried at Fountains; and John de Mowbray, hanged at

---

83 On the question of lands held for spiritual service, see for instance B. Thompson, 'Free alms tenure in the twelfth century', in *Anglo-Norman Studies XVI, Proceedings of the Battle Conference 1993*, ed. M. Chibnall (Woodbridge, 1994), pp. 221–43.

84 See Janet Burton, *Monastic and Religious Orders in Britain, 1000–1300* (Cambridge: Cambridge University Press, 1994), p. 217, and, in a Yorkshire context, Janet Burton, *The Monastic Order in Yorkshire, 1069–1215*, Cambridge Studies in Medieval Life and Thought, fourth series, 40 (Cambridge: Cambridge University Press, 1999), pp. 209–10. See also Brian Golding, 'Burials and benefactions: an aspect of monastic patronage in thirteenth-century England', *England in the Thirteenth Century, Proceedings of the 1984 Harlaxton Symposium*, ed. W. Ormrod (Harlaxton, 1985), pp. 64–75.

85 *CP* IX, 371, 373; *Mowbray Charters*, no. 131. For a later tradition, emanating from Newburgh Priory, that Roger de Mowbray survived the Third Crusade, returned to England, and lived for a further fifteen years before being buried at Byland, see R. Gilyard-Beer, 'Byland Abbey and the grave of Roger de Mowbray', *YAJ*, 55 (1983), 61–6.

86 *Mon. Ang.* V, 346. There is a parallel here with the Ros family, heirs of Walter Espec, founder of Rievaulx. Members of the Ros family preferred to be buried at Espec's Augustinian foundation at Kirkham rather than Cistercian Rievaulx: see Janet Burton, 'The estates and economy of Rievaulx Abbey in Yorkshire', *Cîteaux: Commentarii Cistercienses*, 49 (1998), 29–94 (pp. 68–9).

York in 1322, was buried at the church of the Friars Preacher there.[87] Only Joan, wife of John de Mowbray, who died in 1349, is known to have been buried before the high altar at Byland (no. 106).

The cartulary reveals nineteen benefactors who requested burial rights, usually expressed in the form of a grant *cum corpore meo*. Of the knightly class Thomas de Coleville requested burial in 1326 (no. 122). Other seeking this privilege were Sir Peter of Stonegrave (no. 718), Gilbert son of Gilbert de Meinill (no. 796) and Robert de Buscy (no. 831). At the end of the twelfth century the prominent York citizen Gerard son of Lewin stated: *sciatis me intuitu salutis anime mee reddidisse me Deo et domui de Bellalanda et ibidem corpori meo elegisse sepulturam et cum corpore meo dedisse et concessisse* . . . (no. 264). However the majority of people who sought burial at Byland were of modest means: John son of Ranulf de Kerby (no. 2); Matthew of Northallerton (no. 19); Guy of Helbeck (no. 35); Gilbert son of Walter and Walter son of Nigel, both of Islebeck (nos 412, 417); William le Pledur of Ormesby (no.851); Robert Belebuche of Thirsk (no. 892); Adam le Norrais (no. 954); Simon son of William of Sproxton (no. 1098); Thomas de Richeburne (no. 1111); Elias de Flamville and Beatrice his wife (nos 1146–7, 1150); Geoffrey of St Peter (no. 1162). Even allowing for the incomplete nature of the evidence, given that the cartulary is missing many folios, it seems that the picture at Byland bears comparison with the Cistercian house of Rievaulx, where few benefactors appear to have asked for burial at the monastery.[88] Rievaulx and Byland present a contrasting picture to Fountains Abbey, where over ninety benefactors were promised burial.[89]

Commemoration, chantries, and confraternity
Pittances, that is small dishes of food or drink allowed to monks on the anniversary of the benefactor who funded them, were a form of commemoration. These were requested by Alan the cook of Ampleforth (no. 5), Michael of Briestwistle, who remitted rent to be used for that purpose (no. 242), Adam de Eyndby (nos 1151–2), John

---

87 *CP* IX, 376–84.
88 Burton, 'Estates and economy of Rievaulx Abbey', 68–9, 92. Among transcripts of charters which survive only in Dodsworth's and Burton's collections I have located only one which furnishes evidence of a request for burial, see MS Dodsworth 91, fol. 126r, no. 89.
89 Joan Wardrop, *Fountains Abbey and its Benefactors 1132–1300*, Cistercian Publications, 91 (Kalamazoo, MI, 1987).

of Stonegrave (no. 1140), William de Richeburne (no. 1125), and
Walter de Skeeftlinge, who requested an annual pittance at Christmas
(no. 720). Also specific as to the time of year when the pittances were
to be made were the requests by Reiner son of William (nos 373–74),
Geoffrey of Upsall (no. 452) and Baldwin Wake, who left money for
eleven pittances annually (no. 626, confirmed at no. 628).[90]

A few charters request the establishment of a chantry. In a final
concord between the monks and Thomas son of William of Emley the
abbot promised that a chaplain would celebrate daily at Byland for
the souls of Thomas and his ancestors and heirs and all the faithful
dead (no. 38). The pittances demanded by Geoffrey of Upsall (no.
452) were later converted into the provision of a chaplain celebrating
for his grandson and all his ancestors and heirs in the chapel of St
Mary Magdalene outside the gates of the abbey (no. 455 and note).
Between 1264 and 1277 the abbot and convent agreed to contribute
towards the maintenance of a chaplain to pray for the soul of Thomas
de Wythen, archdeacon of Nottingham (no. 309). In 1358 the monks
paid towards the chantry for John of Acomb and his family in the
church of St Peter the Little, York (no. 924).[91]

Twenty benefactors acknowledged the benefits (unspecified)
which the monks had bestowed on them (nos 41, 685, 799, 837, 1087,
1120). Most of these were in final concords (nos 258, 487, 489, 722, 927,
947, 948, 999, 1000, 1002, 1003, 1022, 1201, 1204). In a few cases the
word is not *beneficia*, benefits, but (con)fraternity: this is specified for
William of Acklam and his wife and children (no. 335), his son Roger
and Roger's wife (no. 337), Roger Cosin and Emma his wife (no. 343),
Gilbert son of Walter of Islebeck (no. 412), John of Islebeck (no. 429)
and Henry de Percy (no. 669). When William de Surdeval granted a
toft in Ampleforth he asked for benefits of confraternity. His charter
was endorsed: *Sciendum quod monachi Beghlande concesserunt mihi
Willelmo de Surdevalle et Armeste uxori mee et duobus filiis meis Radulfo et
Roberto clerico fraternitatem et beneficia domus sue et quando aliquis de
nobis . . . absolvetur anima eius in capitulo monachorum et orationes pro eo
fiant et in trecennariis recipietur.*[92]

---

90 I have located only one further request for pittances among Dodsworth's and
    Burton's transcripts. See MS Dodsworth 91, fol. 78r–v, no. 16.
91 For the location of the chantry within the church see note to no. 924.
92 This is not in the cartulary; see MS Dodsworth 94, fols 48v–49r.

Entry into the community

In recognition of their material generosity, benefactors might request monasteries to accept them into the community should they ever wish to enter the religious life.[93] The monks of Byland promised Roger Cosin that if he ever wished to take such a course of action they would receive him (no. 343) and a rubric refers to a further grant made by Roger with Richard his son (no. 352). Richard son of Siward of Killerby confirmed land granted by his father and brother when the monks had accepted them into the religious life (no. 491), and Elias son of Alan de Flamville made a grant on his father's entry (no. 1144). Such instances are few and far between.

Grants for particular purposes

In general over the course of the twelfth century benefactors became more confident in specifying how the grant they made was to be used, and whom in particular it should benefit.[94] Among the Byland benefactors only four specified that their benefaction was to help certain groups: the monks and the needy of the house (no. 138); the sick of the house (nos 660, 699); and the sick monks (no. 690). One grant (1240) specified the building of the new church (no. 373).

Peace

In one instance a grant was made in settlement of a quarrel with a third party. Between 1170 and 1184 William of Lancaster granted the monks all his land in Borrowdale (no. 310). This he did for the salvation of his soul and those of his parents and his family, and to end the quarrel which his father, William son of Gilbert, once had with Wimund, bishop of the Isles. William son of Gilbert died in 1170. William II died in 1184 and was buried at Furness Abbey, where Wimund had first entered the religious life and from where he had gone with a founding colony to Rushen in the Isle of Man in 1134. Wimund's subsequent career brought him into conflict with William son of Gilbert, and, having been blinded by his enemies, he became a monk of Byland. William of Lancaster's grant to Byland in restitution was accordingly made to the house to which Wimund had retired.[95]

---

93 Burton, *Monastic and Religious Orders*, pp. 217–18, and *Monastic Order in Yorkshire*, pp. 207–8.

94 See Burton, *Monastic Order in Yorkshire*, p. 210, for examples from Yorkshire monasteries.

95 See no. 310, note.

Material benefits

A handful of charters had an explicit financial dynamic: the remission of a debt to the monks (no. 2), waiving of a loan (nos 655, 673), the fulfilment of an oath (nos 656, 672). The provision of fuel (*estoveria*) is mentioned in just one charter (no. 949). There are also some instances of countergifts and rents. There are forty-eight charters demanding rents (see index); in five cases these were later remitted. The rents were due at different seasons, according to the custom of the district, but chiefly at St Martin and Whitsuntide. In south Yorkshire some rents were due on the feast of St Oswald (nos 208, 209, 213, 215). Countergifts comprised money payments (nos 90, 149, 211, 221, 227, 239, 397, 497, 580, 701, 867, 1053, 1142), and in the last example also a colt.

THE MONASTIC ESTATE

The Byland estate was a long time in the making. In one way this is not surprising, for the first forty years of the existence of the community were unsettled. The initial Yorkshire site was transferred to the Augustinian canons from Bridlington (1142–3), the second was reduced to a grange (1147), and the territorial expansion of the abbey did not go unchallenged by Mowbray rivals and tenants. However, it may be easy to overplay the impediments to Byland's progress. The site at New Byland was evidently cleared and prepared at leisure between 1147 and the final move in 1177;[96] Roger de Mowbray and his knights had ensured that the abbey was on a firm financial footing by the time of the move, and the resources at the command of the abbey are suggested by the scale of the new abbey church.[97] As it was for many religious houses the twelfth century was for Byland an era of territorial expansion when major acquisitions were made. However, the process of consolidation continued throughout the thirteenth century and beyond. The sections that follow offer brief notes on the geographical and chronological formation of the abbey estates, the administration of the estate, and relations with the abbey neighbours.

---

96 *Mon. Ang.* V, 353.
97 On which see, for instance, Peter Fergusson, *Architecture of Solitude*, pp. 72–83.

Temporalia: **The chronology and geography of acquisition**
Early acquisitions in the vicinity of the abbey
When Roger de Mowbray established the monks at Hood in 1138 (no. 377) he granted them a tithe of all the food rents he received. The *Historia Fundationis* records that two years later, in 1140, Roger replaced these with a landed endowment in Cam (no. 115), Wildon, Scackleton and Airyholme. In 1142 the site of Hood was surrendered for the tithes of Wildon and Cam (no. 378).[98] Other early acquisitions were in Hovingham, some seven to eight miles from Byland, and Airyholme (nos 386, 387, 393, 1104) where the endowment was increased by grants of Mowbray tenants (nos 388–392). Roger de Mowbray also made the earliest grant in North Cave, an isolated portion of the Mowbray honour to the north of the River Humber, probably before the move to Stocking in 1147 (no. 153). The fourth and final site of the abbey lay in the parish of Coxwold, the parish church of which was appropriated to Newburgh Priory. The first document in the Coxwold section is the confirmation of 1326 by Thomas de Coleville of all that the monks had by the grants of his ancestors (no. 122). However, there are several folios missing and the monks were acquiring land here at an early date. As with Coxwold the cartulary section for Kilburn lacks a number of charters, and the development of the estate began earlier than the cartulary would suggest. The first document is the agreement by which the monks demised to Robert de Daiville a fishery with millpond, licence to assart at the foot of the valley etc. in return for which the monks had licence to enclose 15 acres and free entry and exit (no. 486). The latest date is 1186 but the charter may contain interpolations.[99]

In the second half of the twelfth century the monks made the important acquisition of Thorpe le Willows, lying about two miles to the south-east of the abbey. This was granted by William de Wyville, a Mowbray tenant (no. 323), and confirmed by his son Richard (no. 324). Richard also confirmed forest which Roger de Mowbray first granted to his uncle, Ralph, and then to his father, William (no. 325). The Wyville grants were supplemented by Thomas de Coleville, another Mowbray tenant, who confirmed land and woodland the monks held (nos 327–8). Thomas reached an agreement with the monks concerning houses they built below their grange (no. 330). Also in the second half of the century came the grant of Snilesworth

---

98   *Mon. Ang.* V, 350–2.
99   For final concords of 1224, 1235 and 1252 see nos 487–9.

(Hawnby), conveyed to the monks by Hugh Malebisse (no. 1076) and confirmed by his son and nephew (nos 1077–8).

Nidderdale

Interests in Kirkby Malzeard (WR), about 6 miles north-west of Ripon, began with the grant by Roger de Mowbray of two bovates with easements in Nidderdale, that is, iron, a tithe of lead mines, and a salt spring (no. 456). Roger made other grants (nos 457–8) which were confirmed by his son Nigel (nos 459–60). These major acquisitions were supplemented by grants and quitclaims by lesser landholders (nos 464–82). The area known as Middlesmoor became a point of contention between the monks and William de Mowbray,[100] and intensive mining activities led to competition with the monks of Fountains who were also developing interests in Nidderdale through grants by Roger de Mowbray.[101]

The Liberty of Byland

By 1284–5 a diverse group of estates both near and at some distance from Byland was known as the Liberty of Byland.[102] The centre of the liberty was Sutton under Whitestonecliffe, where the abbot held his court, and where several charters specify the times and circumstances at which tenants were expected to make suit of court (see, for example, nos 31, 155, 848, 959). The Liberty included Sutton, Marderby, Laysthorpe, Thornaby on Tees, Thorpe near York (Thorpe Maltby, also Middlethorpe),[103] South Otterington, Scackleton, Fawdington, Ampleforth, Osgoodby, Old Byland, Murton (which may have included Dale), and Thorpefield. There was no attempt to group these estates together in the cartulary.

The cartulary section relating to Sutton under Whitestonecliffe is one of the largest in the cartulary (nos 994–1075). Before 1166 Robert de Stuteville enfeoffed Geoffrey Fossard with a knight's fee in Sutton, Marderby and Laysthorpe (no. 995). It was some time later, in 1237, that Thomas Fossard, son of Adam Fossard, granted the monks all his lordship in these places (nos 994, 996, 997), which was confirmed by his son, Thomas (no. 998). This major grant was preceded by Thomas

---

100 See note to no. 695.
101 See note to no. 707.
102 *KI*, pp. 105–6: De Libertate de Belle Lande.
103 The sections of the cartulary relating to Thornaby and Middlethorpe are missing.

son of Adam's confirmation of the grant made by his brother, Robert, whom he succeeded, of pasture in Sutton (no. 1053, dated 1225). Many documents in this section are represented by rubrics only, and appear to be grants and quitclaims by minor players. They are not easy to date, but it seems that Sutton was a fairly late acquisition with little, if any, monastic activity before the thirteenth century. In 1284–5 various tenants held four carucates (making a knight's fee) of the abbot of Byland, who held of the heir of Stuteville, who held of Mowbray, who held of the king by barony.[104]

The Fossard family was also responsible of the acquisition of land in Marderby, Robert Fossard granting twelve bovates which the monks held at farm and other lands for forinsec service before 1219 (nos 598–601) and then all his lordship of the vill (no. 618). Thomas, Robert's brother, confirmed the grants (nos 604–5), as did Nicholas de Stuteville (no. 624). The estate was supplemented by further grants, quitclaims and exchanges. In 1284–5 the abbot held four carucates, where twelve made a knight's fee, of the heirs of Baldwin Wake, who held of the Mowbrays, who held of the king.[105] Acquisitions in Laysthorpe appear to have been made largely in the thirteenth century, and to have comprised the homage and service of tenants. On the whole the estate was acquired from small benefactors among whom there was a close family connection. In 1284–5 the abbot held two carucates under the same tenancy as he did in Marderby.[106]

South Otterington lies about 3 miles south of Northallerton. At the end of the twelfth century Adam de Brus granted to Geoffrey Fossard all his holding in Otterington which he had of his father, to hold of his (Geoffrey's) heirs for the service of half a knight's fee (no. 840). By final concord of 1244 the abbot of Byland remitted to Peter de Brus all right in an annual rent of 1000 haddock, and in return Peter granted him the service of half a knight's fee which Thomas Fossard formerly held of him (no. 841). In 1284–5 the abbot of Byland held two and a half carucates of the heir of Brus, who held of the king.[107] These lands were held of the abbot by Richard Malebisse. In 1316 the abbot and convent took William Malebisse and his lands into their custody following the death of his father (nos 842–3).

---

104 *KI*, p. 105.
105 *Ibid.*, p. 105.
106 *Ibid.*, p. 105.
107 *Ibid.*, p. 105.

The Scackleton section of the cartulary opens with a number of Mowbray grants, the earliest of which may be dated to 1140 (nos 1104–7). The original estate was supplemented by a number of grants and quitclaims by others (nos 1109–40). In 1284–5 the estate had shrunk from the three carucates granted by Mowbray to seven bovates, which the abbot held of Mowbray.[108] For Fawdington, which lies on the river Swale 7–8 miles south west of Byland, the end of the cartulary section only survives. In 1284–5 the abbot held all 15 bovates of Roger de Mowbray.[109] The Ampleforth section of the cartulary is also defective, and all that remains are fourteenth-century quitclaims. It was included in the liberty of Byland in 1284–5. This area shows tenurial complexity, with Walter of London holding half a carucate of Ralph son of William, who held of the abbot of Byland; Geoffrey Attebek holding one carucate of the abbot; the abbot holding one bovate of John de Jarpenville who held of Robert de Ros. Robert held of Roger de Mowbray who held of the king.[110]

Also in the Liberty was Osgoodby (NR), represented in the cartulary by a large section of 100 charters and rubrics (nos 739–839). The earliest grants are associated with Gilbert de Meinill in the last two decades of the twelfth century, and these were confirmed and quitclaimed by other members of the family (nos 739–53). The name of the Meinill family dominates the expansion of the abbey estates here, supplemented by many other local people. In 1284–5 the abbot held four carucates of the heir of Meinill, who held of the Buscy family, who held of Roger de Mowbray, who held of the king.[111] As we have seen, the *Historia Fundationis* links the grant of Murton and Snilesworth to Hugh Malebisse I and they were confirmed by Roger de Mowbray in 1147,[112] but the charters entered in the cartulary are those of his son, Hugh II (nos 578–9). Hugh I or his son subsequently quitclaimed the 40s. required for the vill for 26 marks. However the 40s. rent had been granted to Newbo Abbey, 20s. by Thomas son of Adam of Arncliffe (which he had received from Richard Malebisse) and 20s. which William Malebisse granted Newbo, and was quitclaimed for 26 marks (no. 580); by this time (1242 x 1267) there was a grange. Nos 581–7 all concern the same rent. Dale is related to

---

108 *Ibid.*, p. 105.
109 *Ibid.*, pp. 105–6.
110 *Ibid.*, p. 106.
111 *Ibid.*, p. 106.
112 *Mon. Ang.* V, 352; *Mowbray Charters*, no. 44.

Murton Grange. Although Dale has a separate (short) section in the cartulary (nos 255–60) the endorsements of three surviving originals (nos 256–7, 260) reveal that the charters were kept with those relating to Murton. The earliest benefactor was Ralph del Turp, who granted a spring and a road for their flocks of Murton (255), and quitclaimed all right in the valley of Sproxdale (no. 256). In 1284–5 Murton comprised four carucates, all of which were held by the abbot of Hugh Malebisse of Roger de Mowbray.[113]

Thorpefield lies about two miles SW of Thirsk. The cartulary section begins with the grant of Matilda of Stonegrave of 12 bovates (no. 885), an agreement concerning the same with her son, Simon, and his confirmation (nos 886–7). The family grants, which were confirmed by Roger de Mowbray (no. 888), were supplemented by grants, confirmations and quitclaims by a host of lesser tenants.

In all, therefore, within the liberty of Byland the abbot is recorded as holding three and a half fees and nine bovates of Mowbray, and half a knight's fee, one carucate and five bovates of the Brus family, and it was stated that there was no record of the service for which these lands were held.[114] Some of the estates within the liberty, namely Fawdington, Old Byland, and Murton, represent early acquisitions by the monks. Others, notably the lordship embracing Sutton, Marderby, Laysthorpe and Felixkirk, belong to the first three decades of the thirteenth century and were a welcome boost to the abbey's fortunes on its own doorstep.

The East Riding properties

From the mid twelfth century Byland began to acquire properties in a small area of the East Riding, in Deepdale, Cayton, Osgodby, Scarborough and Rillington. Two families, both Percy tenants, were responsible for the abbey's interest in this area. One was the family of William son of Henry of Cayton, grantors of assets in Cayton (nos 141–2, 144–6), and the other was the family of Durand de Cliffe (of Cayton), with whom the lands in Deepdale originated (nos 158–63). Another family, whose relationship to the family of Durand is not clear, is that of Simon de Cliffe and his son Robert (nos 172–7, 182–3), whose grants were confirmed by Robert's son William (no. 184). The Deepdale section of the cartulary is extensive, with four bundles of original charters, and 46 charters or rubrics (nos 158–204). In 1284–5

---

113 *KI*, p. 106.
114 *Ibid.*, pp. 105–6.

there were in Deepdale four carucates of the barony of the fee of
Henry de Percy subject to geld. Henry of Cayton held two bovates,
William son of Reyner two bovates, the abbot of Byland six bovates,
Thomas de Anlacby thirteen bovates, John Bard four bovates, John de
Percy two bovates, the chapel/chaplain of Osgodby two bovates, and
Henry of Cayton and William son of Reyner one bovate.[115]

The Tees valley
Byland had access to river fisheries along the Swale (nos 305, 488) but
another important area was the Tees valley, where the monks
acquired fisheries at Gayteryg/Florum (probably now part of Middlesbrough). William of Acklam granted a fishery, land and licence to fish
in the Tees, stipulating that the monks were not to construct another
fishery between there and the one William had constructed at
Ayresome (no. 335). This was confirmed by his lord, Peter de Brus
(no. 336), and the estate consolidated by grants in Acklam and
Linthorpe from Roger son of William of Acklam (nos 337–8), Geoffrey
of Ayresome (no. 339), Roger Cosin and Emma his wife (nos 343, 345).
The confirmation by Thomas de Boyton of many of these grants,
which is dated 1392 and is thus one of the latest charters in the
cartulary (no. 366), is followed by a genealogy of the Acklam family
(no. 367).

     The monks also acquired lands in Coatham (Kirkleatham), where
three sons of Ilger, that is, William, Roger, and Ralph, parson of
Kirkleatham, conveyed a toft and croft, houses, saltpan, yard, and
profitable land (nos 133, 134, 136, 137). Their charters precede those of
the Brus family, quitting the monks of toll on fish purchased at
Coatham (nos 138–9) and a general confirmation (no. 140).

The south Yorkshire estates
From the last two decades of the twelfth century the monks of Byland
opened up estates in the Bentley–Bretton–Denby–Emley area of
south Yorkshire. A final concord of 1237 (no. 38) acknowledged that
the abbot of Byland had minerals and pasture for horses, oxen, cows,
a bull, and goats in Emley (which was probably treated as part of the
Bentley estate) of the grant of William son of William, grandfather of
the party to the fine. This indicates that the monks had begun to

---

115 *KI*, p. 139. For Thomas of Anlacby see below, nos 194, 493, 496, 509, 867–8,
     873–4; for John Bard(e), see nos 870, 872.

acquire land in this region in the twelfth century. By 1237 there was a grange at Bentley, for Robert son of William granted the monks the chapel of St Werbergh of Bentley, which was near the grange, with land which the monks were allowed to enclose as they wished. Until 1237 the monks evidently paid rent of 3s. which was then remitted. There was evidently a millpond at Shitlington associated with the Bentley estate, which the monks were allowed to strengthen before 1302 (no. 39).

The Bentley charters are on old fol. 96. Fol. 97 is missing, and may have contained other Bentley charters, as the Bretton section starts on fol. 98, apparently at the beginning. A number of Bretton grants appear to date from the late twelfth century. Peter son of Orm of Bretton granted 10 acres, and pasture for 40 sheep and draught animals (no. 40) and this was quitclaimed by his son William (no. 41). Swane son of Ulkil granted a rood and land from Shitlington to Emley, and common pasture and licence to make a sheepfold, to hold for 6s. yearly (no. 42); this was confirmed by his brother Henry (no. 43) and by his son Hugh (no. 45), as well as Alan son of Adam of Crigglestone (no. 46). Swane then quitclaimed the 6s. rent (no. 44). The endorsements of the Bretton originals suggest that they were designated 'Bentley' charters, probably because the Bretton lands were administered from Bentley grange.

The most extensive cartulary section, even though it is incomplete, is that relating to Denby (three folios, fifty charters and rubrics). It also has a substantial number of surviving originals and, as argued above, the evidence of the endorsements of the originals suggest that the compiler followed the arrangement of the original bundles when he selected and transcribed material.[116] The Byland estate in this area was the product of piecemeal acquisitions from donors such as Henry of Thurstonland and his family (nos 205–9), Henry son of Swane of Denby (no. 211), Simon son of Henry (no. 217), William son of Osbert of Denby (no. 224), William son of William (nos 227–8) and many others. The Denby section illustrates how the monks built up an estate through purchase, rent, exchange and quitclaim to form an important economic asset.

Westmorland

At the time of the foundation of Byland there was little monastic activity in the North West of England. Furness Abbey, from which the

---

116 See above p. xxxvii.

colony was dispatched to Calder in 1134, lay at the northern tip of Lancashire. Calder, abandoned in 1137 and reoccupied in 1142, lay on the Cumbrian coast. St Mary's Abbey, York, had cells at Wetheral and St Bees, and a cathedral served by Augustinian canons had been established at Carlisle in 1133.[117] Nevertheless, this was an area ripe for exploitation, and in the twelfth century Byland made some important acquisitions. The Asby section of the cartulary is damaged, and this makes is difficult to ascertain when the interests of the monks originated. The property was important enough to warrant special confirmation by Henry II (nos 520, 521), and an agreement with Richard de Cottesford was reached before 1181 (nos 24–5). Grants included land to fence and enclose as the monks wished, pasture land for sheep with permission to make a sheepfold (no. 21), arable land (no. 22), and land held rendering rent to the church of Asby (no. 23). The Dodsworth manuscripts also reveal that benefactors in Asby were Gerard de Lascelles and Hugh de Moreville.[118]

Bleatarn was the most important Westmorland property of Byland. Acquisitions seem to have begun in the middle of the twelfth century, and the main donors were members of the family of Torphin son of Robert son of Copsi. Torphin was an early donor (nos 47–52). His son Robert and his uncle Walleve de Bereford were also benefactors (nos 53–59). So was John Tailbois (no. 60), and land acquisitions continued till the fourteenth century. A grange was in existence by 1189 at the latest; this is mentioned in a charter of Henry II (no. 527). There is further reference in 1196 (no. 90). Henry II confirmed the lands in Warcop specifically (no. 522).

The charters relating to Fawcett Forest in Kendal (nos 310–318) show that the origin of the interest of Byland in this area goes back to William II of Lancaster.[119] His daughter and son in law issued confirmations (nos 311–12). Hugh and Ralph, sons of Robert son of Sigge, made a grant (no. 314, see also no. 313), which was confirmed by Henry de Redman, steward of Kendal, Matthew de Redman and Gilbert son of Roger (nos 315–7).

The earliest grant relating to Shap was made by Thomas son of Cospatrick, who conveyed all his part of Shap within specified

---

117 Henry Summerson, *Medieval Carlisle: the city and the borders from the late eleventh to the mid sixteenth century*, 2 vols, CWAAS extra series, XXV (1993), I, 1–54, especially pp. 30–8.

118 MS Dodsworth 63, fol. 59r.

119 For a curious link with Wimund, bishop of the Isles, see no. 310 note.

bounds (nos 395–6), and there were final concords concerning lands
here in 1235 and 1236 (nos 397–8). Thomas's grant was confirmed by
his son Thomas (no. 399) and grandson, Patrick son of Thomas (no.
400). There may have been a grange at Shap (no. 401). This is
mentioned in Henry III's inspeximus of the charter of Henry II (no.
527).

Urban property
The monks acquired several properties in the city of York, but this
cartulary section has sustained much damage. As urban tenements
would have yielded cash rents there was little need for monastic
houses to seek territorial coherence, and the pattern seems to have
been one of casual acquisitions, principally in Coney Street,
Ousegate, Patrickpool, and Cargate (King Street). Just outside the
walls to the north of the city, in the suburbs of Gillygate, other minor
acquisitions were made; three of these are cross referenced under the
York section. In the first half of the thirteenth century the monks
acquired a half toft in Clifton, on the river Ouse to the north-west of
York, from the abbot and convent of St Mary's, York, and they also
held land of Jervaulx Abbey (nos 124–5). The boundaries of the
messuage are described in no. 127. The abbot had a manor house at
Clifton and in 1271 King Henry III ordered that all pleas concerning
the abbot and monks and their men in Yorkshire should be heard at
Clifton rather than Sutton (no. 529, 544, 556).[120]

Spiritualia
Although recent scholarship has argued that Cistercian legislation
concerning 'forbidden revenues' was not a plank of early Cistercian
thought and may have been introduced as late as the mid twelfth
century,[121] by the time of Byland's main territorial expansion it is
certain that churches and tithes, along with ovens and mills, were on
a list of economic assets which the White Monks were expected to

---

120 The monks also held land in Bootham, between the city and Clifton, but the
cartulary section is missing. See MS Top. Yorks. d. 11, fol. 265r.
121 See Constance Brittain Bouchard, *Holy Entrepreneurs: Cistercians, Knights, and
Economic Exchange in Twelfth Century Burgundy* (Ithaca and London: Cornell
University Press, 1991); Constance Hoffman Berman, *Medieval Agriculture, the
South French Countryside, and the Early Cistercians*, Transactions of the American Philosophical Society, 76, no. 5 (Philadelphia, 1986). See also Constance
H. Berman, *The Cistercian Evolution: the invention of a religious order in
twelfth-century Europe* (Philadelphia: University of Pennsylvania Press, 2000).

avoid. The monks came to acquire interests in three churches. The first of these, Old Byland, was in existence when the site of the monastery moved to the vill in 1142, and was retained by the monks after their move to Stocking.[122] Abbot Roger, who accepted the grant of Old Byland church, was less certain about Roger de Mowbray's offer, in 1147, of the patronage of the churches of Thirsk, Hovingham and Kirkby Moorside. Possibly under the influence of the Cistercian Order which Byland joined that year he refused the churches.[123] The monks had licence to appropriate Old Byland before 1181.[124] In 1540 the rectory was valued at £7.[125] The church of Old Byland had a dependent chapel at Scawton, which was built on the initiative of Abbot Roger in 1147 for the convenience of the parishioners (see no. 1089 note), although it was referred to, in an act of Archbishop Geoffrey, as recently constructed (1191 x 1205, no. 968). Although Abbot Roger appointed the first chaplain, Richard,[126] the presentation passed to the Malebisse family, and the monks received 20s. rent from the chapel (no. 1089). In 1247 the pension was in arrears, and was evidently contested again in 1279 and 1333 (nos 1090, 1092, 1095).

The church of Rillington (NR) was acquired in the late twelfth century, although later grants came to specify that the monks were to hold a moiety of the church (nos 930–87). The monks were allowed to appropriate by royal licence in 1317 (nos 534, 971) and a vicarage was ordained in 1344 (no. 981). In 1540 the rectory was valued at £18. 6s. 8d.[127] The third church in which Byland had interests was Bubwith in the East Riding, roughly seven miles to the north east of Selby. The cartulary section opens not with the earliest document relating to Bubwith but with the regrant and confirmation by John de Mowbray of the advowson of a moiety of the church, with licence to appropriate under the Statute of Mortmain (no. 106). This is dated 1349 and was for the salvation of the soul of his wife, Joan, who was buried

---

122 See *Mowbray Charters*, no. 38, a confirmation charter of Roger de Mowbray, printed from the copy of the charter in the *Historia Fundationis*. Old Byland was the dower of Gundreda d'Aubigny: *Mon. Ang.* V, 350.

123 *Mon. Ang.* V, 351: . . . *dictus abbas R. accipere recusabat, homo scrupulosae conscientiae pro cura animarum.*

124 *EEA* XX, no. 8 (*EYC* III, no. 1834); see also *EYC* III, no. 1835, licence and confirmation by the dean and chapter of York. Neither of these charters appear in the cartulary as they were in the (missing) Old Byland section.

125 *Mon. Ang.* V, 355.

126 *Ibid.* V, 351.

127 *Ibid.* V, 355.

before the high altar of Byland. The remainder of the surviving section (nos 107–114) relates to the process of appropriation, which was complete by 1367. There are a number of folios missing, and it is clear from MS Dodsworth 63, fol. 64v, that BL MS Egerton 2823, old fol. 107, contained an inspeximus by John Thoresby, archbishop of York, of a charter of William Tison granting Bubwith to St Peter's, York, holders of the other moiety,[128] and various presentations to the church in 1286, 1310, and 1315. There is no indication that Byland had any other estates in the vill. In 1540 Byland's moiety of the rectory was valued at £12. 13s. 4d.[129]

The cartulary demonstrates that the monks were involved in the provision of pastoral care for the community in another area. On behalf of the men of Sutton and Marderby the abbot sealed an agreement between them and the vicar of Felixkirk concerning the payment of tithes by the men (no. 1055). Abbot Henry and the vicar reached an agreement by which the vicar would celebrate mass three days a week in the chapel of Sutton (no. 1056; see also nos 1057–9).[130]

Administration: the grange economy and the liberty

The *Historia Fundationis* records that during the four years in which the monks were at Hood they created their first grange of Wildon from the grants made by those members of Mowbray's household who entered the religious life at Byland.[131] There is reference to the grangers of Wildon and Stocking in a charter of c. 1147 x 1186 (for example in no. 486), although there appear to be some later interpolations in the charter. Old Byland was reduced to a grange in 1147 following the abandonment of the second conventual site. The *Historia Fundationis* gives a glimpse of the process:

> Cum vero dictus Abbas R. et monachi ejus dictam Bellalandam habuissent decreverunt illam in grangiam unam redigere. Hec illis cogitantibus assignaverunt quandam partem terre eiusdem ville hominibus ibi manentibus scilicet apud Stutekelde, ubi dicti homines de novo inceperunt novam villulam et ibi manserunt per

128 For the grant to St Peter's York by Warin of Bubwith, and confirmations by Roger de Mowbray and William Tison, and the confirmations, by the dean and chapter and by Archbishop Henry Murdac, of the church to William of Winchester, canon of York, see *YMF* I, 51–4.

129 *Mon. Ang.* V, 355.

130 See also no. 610 concerning the provision of a footpath for the parishioners of Sutton living at Marderby.

131 *Mon. Ang.* V, 350: *quibus suffragantibus constructa fuit grangia apud Wildon.*

plures annos, eidem nomen primum imponentes, et sic eadem villa redacta est in grangiam.

(While Abbot Roger and his monks held Byland they decided to reduce it to a grange. With these thoughts in mind they set aside a certain portion of land belonging to the vill for the men who remained there, that is, at 'Stutekelde', where the men began a new village and there they remained for several years and gave it its first name. And so the vill was reduced to a grange).

The grange later contained the abbey tilehouse.[132]

The grange of Thorpe le Willows may have been in existence by the mid 1150s and certainly by *c.* 1180 (no. 728). An agreement reached before 1190 indicates that the monks had constructed houses below their grange, and allowed them to channel water as they thought necessary (no. 330). By 1190 the animals kept on the abbey grange at Murton watered at a spring in Dale around which there was a road (no. 255).[133] There were a number of other granges in the general area of the abbey by the thirteenth century, notably Balk, Cams Head,[134] Fawdington (nos 306, 321, 322), Boscar (nos 321–22; the house is known as Boscar Grange), Thorpefield (no. 899), Scackleton (nos 730, 1111, 1119),[135] Osgoodby (nos 826, 838, 899) and Snilesworth (no. 1081). The group of estates in the East Riding around Scarborough was administered by a grange at Deepdale from at least the late twelfth century (nos 167, 174, 669 etc).[136] On the estates in the south of the county there were granges at Bentley, which lay next to the chapel of St Werbergh (no. 38) and Denby (nos 212, 227). The mention of the monks' houses in a charter dating to before 1189 suggests that the grange may have been in the process of construction at that time (no. 222). The grange was linked by a path to Bentley (nos 210, 214). There is one reference to a monastic official, the granger, at Emley (no. 207), although whether there was a grange at Emley or

---

132 *Mon. Ang.* V, 351. This is now represented as Tylas Farm, on the west bank of the River Rye.

133 See no. 260 for a grant of common pasture in front of the gate of the grange, and no. 258 for a complaint that the monks had been impeded from having access from the grange to the spring in Dale.

134 Colin Platt, *The Monastic Grange in Medieval England* (London: Macmillan, 1969), pp. 188, 196, notes that earthworks of Bagby Grange (for which the cartulary section is lost) lie to the south of the Bagby road, and that Cams Head was a small grange or lodge next to the important abbey fish farm.

135 Platt (*ibid.*, p. 232) notes the outline of a large enclosure to the east of a farmhouse there.

136 For a road running from Seamer past the gate of the grange see no. 185.

whether Denby is intended is not clear. The Westmorland estates were served by three granges, Bleatarn, Asby and Shap, all in existence by 1189 (no. 527).

In the case of some religious houses not all granges were in continuous existence.[137] However, the ministers' accounts of 1540–41 indicate that many of the Byland granges had survived. There were recorded granges at 'Newstede',[138] Snilesworth, Cam (both in 'Estcambe' and 'Westcambe'), 'Lounde iuxta Byland', Deepdale, Scackleton, Marderby, Murton, Thorpe, Wildon, Angram, Osgoodby, Balk, Boscar, The Tilehouse near Old Byland, and Denby. The exceptions were the Westmorland granges. The assets in Wasdale, Hardendale and Shap, Bleatarn with Warcop, and Bretherdale and Asby, were described as lands and tenements. Asby grange had been leased by 1477.[139]

The monks of Byland accordingly seem to have practised what has been described as a 'classic Cistercian economy', a series of granges at the centre of estates which, as the cartulary amply demonstrates, had been built up and consolidated by grant, lease, purchase and exchange over the centuries. The cartulary contains little evidence that the land was leased in preference to being worked in demesne. Small parcels of land were farmed for a money rent (nos 76, 130, 143, 298, 435, 440, 616, 723, 870, 874, 927A, which carried a penalty of half a mark to the fabric of the church in case of default, no. 1171), for rent in kind (no. 75), for homage and service and money rent (nos 507–9, 1199) or for rent and suit of court (nos 31, 155, 848, 959).

Where we see the abbot and convent diverging from the classic Cistercian methods of administration is in the manor and liberty of Sutton under Whitestonecliffe. Details of the estates which formed the liberty are given above. Within the liberty the abbot had his own coroner (no. 549, dated 1241/2, also no. 555, dated 1280) and on more than one occasion the abbot made claim to (unspecified) liberties (nos 550–4, 559) and to have a gallows at Sutton (no. 566) as well as free warren in his lands (nos 566, 572). The royal charters indicate that the abbot enjoyed very wide judicial franchises (see nos 517, 518, 527). He also had a court at Warcop (no. 527, and see nos 573–5).

---

137 For some granges which were short-lived see examples among the granges of Rievaulx: Burton, 'The estates and economy of Rievaulx Abbey', 69–84.
138 Platt (*Monastic Grange*, p. 223) notes Newstead as a grange of Jervaulx.
139 James S. Donnelly, 'Changes in the grange economy of English and Welsh Cistercian Abbeys, 1300–1540', *Traditio*, 10 (1954), 399–458 (p. 438).

A competitive field: relations with other monasteries

Documents entered into the cartulary provide some evidence for the relationship between Byland and other religious houses, especially four that developed territorial interests in the same general geographical areas as Byland. The tensions which could ensue are a feature of the monastic expansion in the twelfth century, and the Cistercian order attempted to anticipate problems by regulating the distance between granges. The first of these houses was the Augustinian priory founded in 1142–3 by Roger de Mowbray on the first site occupied by the monks of Byland, that is, Hood; the canons transferred in 1145 to Newburgh Priory, only 1½ miles from Byland Abbey. The second was Rievaulx Abbey, less than two miles to the south-east of the second abbey site of Old Byland. The small nunnery of Arden was located just a few miles from the abbey. Finally Fountains Abbey had shared interests in Nidderdale. Also near neighbours were the Knights Templar, whose estate at Cold Kirby lay close to Byland's liberty of Sutton under Whitestonecliffe.

Newburgh Priory

The cartulary contains an entire section devoted to agreements between the monks and the canons of Newburgh (nos 725–38) and there are numerous cross references from other portions of the text relating to areas where both houses held lands, in particular Hood (nos 380, 382–4). There was evidently a controversy between the canons of Newburgh and Adam Fossard, which was settled at the instance of the pope by Hugh du Puiset, bishop of Durham in the presence of the Stutevilles (no. 379). Fossard's confirmation is cross referenced to the Newburgh bundle (see nos 380–1). Nos 383–5 are cross referenced to the Sutton bundle, indicating a close connection.

The main sources of contention were Hood, Coxwold and Thirsk (no. 725), Hovingham and Thorpe le Willows (no. 728), and tithes in Scackleton (nos 730, 732) and Coxwold (no. 734). In particular the status of parishioners in the church of Coxwold, appropriated to Newburgh, was called into question, and an agreement reached concerning mortuaries of hired servants of the abbey who lived in the vill or served on granges (no. 733).

Rievaulx Abbey

The overlap of interests with Rievaulx stems from the very close proximity of the second abbey site at Old Byland to Rievaulx (see nos 988–93). The agreement reached between Abbots Ailred of Rievaulx and Roger of Byland, and ratified by Roger and Ailred's successor, Silvanus (no. 988) relates specifically to parcels of land in the immediate vicinity of Old Byland and Rievaulx, to boundaries, bridges, and snares used in the river. It also indicates that by 1167 both abbeys were involved in industrial activities in neighbouring vills in south Yorkshire, in Emley (Byland) and Shitlington and Flockton (Rievaulx).

Arden Priory

The small nunnery of Arden lay about three miles from Old Byland and seven miles from New Byland. There was evidently some disputes concerning boundaries (nos 300–302) which may have arisen as a result of Byland's interests in Dale, Murton and Snilesworth. Dodsworth transcribed a final concord of 1262 between Philip son of Philip and Elizabeth de Carleton and Prioress Agatha of Arden relating to land in Arden. The heading of this copy, *Bene custodiatur istud transcriptum propter varios casus inter nos et moniales*, suggests that this may have been transcribed from a Byland copy.[140]

Fountains Abbey

Roger de Mowbray made extensive grants in Nidderdale to both Byland Abbey and to Fountains Abbey. In 1172 Roger and his sons mortgaged to Byland part of Nidderdale as pasture for eighty mares, in return for which they received 300 marks, to be redeemed at the end of ten years.[141] Within ten years Roger had confirmed west Nidderdale, within specified boundaries (no. 688). At roughly the same time Roger made grants to Fountains in lower Nidderdale, also for financial arrangements.[142] The Mowbray heirs themselves contested Byland's rights in Nidderdale, and by 1225 the two abbeys had come into contention over mineral rights (no. 707), which the Cistercian General Chapter delegated for investigation to the abbots of Furness, Rievaulx and Beaulieu. Their detailed findings indicate that both Byland and Fountains were by that date actively engaged in mining.

---

140 MS Dodsworth 91, fols 99v–100v, no. 48.
141 *Mowbray Charters*, no. 54; not in cartulary.
142 *Ibid.*, nos 110–13.

The Knights Templar

In 1151 x 1153 Abbot Roger reached an agreement with Richard Cruer concerning land in Cold Kirby which Roger quitclaimed to Richard (no. 442). Richard granted 100 acres to the abbey for the term of his life only. The Templars had an interest there, and this accounts for the agreement in 1209 (no. 443). A final concord of the same date was reached by the Templars and Robert Fossard and entered in the cartulary because of obvious overlap of interest (no. 444), as is the grant by Robert to the Templars following the final concord (no. 445; see also no. 446). No 451 is a grant by the Templars to Byland.

EDITORIAL METHOD

The volume contains a full calendar of each document in the cartulary; where the witness list has been inserted by the compiler, this is included in its Latin form. The spelling and orthography of the cartulary have been retained except that i has been treated as the equivalent of i and j, and u is used as a vowel and v as a consonant; the practice of rendering c in some words (e.g. donatio) as t has been followed. Where originals survive these are calendared and variants given from the cartulary copies. In instances where there is damage to the cartulary and readings are supplied from other copies, such readings are enclosed in square brackets [ ]. Conjectured readings are enclosed in < >. Omissions, that is where the text is illegible and cannot be constructed from another source, are marked by . . . Abbreviations have been silently expanded. However, where a name has been abbreviated to an initial letter, the extension is shown in round brackets, for example, H(enry), H(enricus). Where extensions are uncertain, as in the case of place names which could be extended to a noun or an adjective, these are left suspended, for example *Ebor'*. Personal and place names are modernized where possible, and 'of' is used rather than 'de', with a modernized form of the place name where the identification is certain. Where place names cannot be identified they are enclosed in ' ' in the notes and, in the calendar, given in roman instead of italic characters. Less familiar Latin words, or ones whose meaning may be ambiguous, are given in the calendar. In accordance with conventional practice[143] the Latin word *cultura*

---

143 F. M. Stenton, ed., *Documents Illustrative of the Social and Economic History of the*

has not been translated but left in its Latin forms. The *cultura*, as Stenton noted, was an intermediate division between the individual selion or open field strip, and the great arable field; it can 'roughly be defined as a group of parallel strips, recognized as distinct by local usage and generally called by its own name', and was compact, in contrast to the normal tenement.[144] There is no accepted English translation for the *cultura*.

Two dates in square brackets linked by x indicate that the charter was issued within the limits of those dates. Wherever a date is stated to be determined by the dates of a king, bishop, abbot, prior, nobleman, dignitary or canon of a cathedral church, without further reference, it can be assumed that the information derives from one of the standard reference works.

In some instances the copyist has entered a rubric but not copied the document in full. These rubrics have been calendared to allow a view of the full extent of the abbey archives. Where an original charter or a later transcript can be matched to a rubric, a calendar has been included, with the witness list given in its Latin form.

Significant variants between originals and cartulary copies, and between cartulary texts and later copies, are noted.

Each section of the cartulary is preceded by notes giving details of the location of the places concerned and, where appropriate, on the nature of the land and the identity of the principal benefactors. Such notes are also provided for missing sections of the cartulary, using the evidence of original charters, and the collections of Roger Dodsworth and John Burton.

Danelaw from Various Collections (London: British Academy and Oxford University Press, 1920).

144 *Ibid.*, pp. lvi–lvii.

CARTULARY

[old fols 63–6, lost]
OLDSTEAD (SE5380), in the parish of Kilburn and the wapentake of Birdforth (NR). This section, placed first in the topographical arrangement ('Alstede'), contained grants by Roger de Mowbray and quitclaims by the Stuteville family, as well as a declaration of the boundaries of the new abbey (MS Dodsworth 63, fols 34r–v). Oldstead Grange is at SE5379, one mile NW of Byland Abbey.

[old fols 67–73 lost] These contained the beginning of the Ampleforth section.

[fol. 3r, old fol. 74]
AMPLEFORTH (SE5878), township and parish in the wapentake of Ryedale (NR); the parish comprises undulating land from the moors to Thorpe Beck, which marks its southern boundary (*VCH NR* I, 461). Ampleforth was the second topographical section of the cartulary; it began on old fol. 67, and now lacks nine folios (old fols 67–73, 75 and 77). It is possible from MS Dodsworth 63 and Top. Yorks. d. 11 to identify the main donors as members of the Surdeval family. The missing sections contained the main grants to the monks, the surviving portions, which are badly damaged, relating to small parcels of land and rents. In no. 670 below Robert de Ros II confirmed Surdeval grants in the region of Ampleforth, and in no. 671 Robert's grandson, Robert, confirmed all the monks held there. Ampleforth was part of the Liberty of Byland.

1 *Quitclaim in free alms, addressed universally, by Walter de London, to God and St Mary <and the abbot and monks of Byland> and their successors, of 14d. annual rent due from land in Ampleforth. This quitclaim is made for the salvation of the soul of the donor and of his ancestors and heirs. Pledge to warranty. Sealed with the donor's seal.* Byland; Philip and James [1 May] 128[2].
Hiis testibus Willelmo filio Gamelli de Sutton', Roberto . . . Rogero de

Heton', Willelmo filio Thome de Bagby, Willelmo del Bek', et multis aliis.

Note: This folio is much damaged. A later marginal note gives the date as 11 Edward I [1282]. The names of the last two witnesses are legible only under u–v light. In 1202 Walter de London was enfeoffed by Nicholas Basset with half a carucate in Ampleforth. William de London was holding land there in 1250, and Walter, grantor of this charter, was tenant in 1284–5 (*KI*, p. 106; *VCH NR* I, 462–3).

2 *Grant, addressed to all present <and future>, by John son of Ranulf de Kerby, to God and St Mary and the abbot and convent of Byland, of 2 acres with tofts and crofts and other easements in* S[tarthw]ayt *in the region of Ampleforth, and of all its common and easements, and 1 acre of meadow. This land was granted to John by . . . in her widowhood, and granted by John to the monks with his body, for the salvation of his soul and of all his ancestors and heirs. In return the monks have remitted a certain sum of money which John owed them. The monks are to render to Walter de London and his heirs 14d. yearly, 7d. at St Martin in Winter (11 Nov.) and 7d. at Whitsuntide. Sealed with the donor's seal.* [Before 1282; possibly before 1272].

<Hiis testibus> Honorio tunc priore de Bellal', Waltero suppriore, W. <? magistro conver>sorum, . . . Ada de Cundall' socio cellerarii, Ada de [H]usw. . . monacho, Willelmo <de> Car[let]on', . . . Willelmo Maud<uit>, Willelmo Arundell', Henr' de Ca . . . , Waltero . . . Waltero filio eius, Waltero ad portam, et aliis.

Dating: This charter presumably predates no. 1; however, the other occurrences of Prior Honorius (nos 19, 360, 434, 723, 1027) suggest a date considerably earlier than 1282. If Adam of Husthwaite, monk, is the future abbot of Byland then the date is before his first occurrence as abbot, in 1272 (*HRH* II, 270).

[fol. 3r–v]

3 *Quitclaim, addressed <to all present and future> to whom this writing shall come, by Adam de London, kinsman and heir of Walter de London, to John of Myton, abbot of Byland, of the annual rent of 14d. due from 2 acres with tofts and crofts and profitable land and 1 acre in* Staynayt *in Ampleforth given by John son of Ranulf de Kereby to his uncle Walter and his heirs for loyalty and service and for 14d. yearly at <St Martin in Winter> (11 Nov.) and Whitsuntide, and then by Walter to the abbot and convent of Byland. Pledge to warranty. Sealed with the donor's seal.* Ampleforth; Nativity of B. V. M. [8 Sept.] 1332.

Hiis testibus Ricardo de Pykeryng', Roberto de Ever', domino Roberto vicario de Ampilf', Ricardo de Kerby de eadem, Waltero . . . et aliis.

Marginal note (in later hand): 6 Ed. 3
Note: Adam de London was tenant in Ampleforth in 1316, and had died by 1361 (*VCH NR* I, 463). Adam de London (Lond) the elder and the younger appear in a ghost story written at Byland in the late 14th century. Adam the elder and his sister are said to have cheated her husband and children out of a croft in Ampleforth, from which Adam ejected the family after his sister's death. Adam the younger later made restitution. See Andrew Joynes, ed., *Medieval Ghost Stories* (Woodbridge, 2001), p. 125.

[fol. 3v]

4 *Quitclaim in free alms, addressed to all the faithful in Christ to whom the present letters shall come, by Adam de London of Ampleforth, son and heir of William de London, to God and St Mary and the abbot and convent of Byland and their successors, of all claim to 14d. annual rent due from 2 acres with tofts and crofts and 1 acre in* Starthwayt *and in all other customs and services in the vill and region of Ampleforth. Pledge to warranty. Sealed with the donor's seal.* Ampleforth; . . . Jan. 1331 [1332].
<Hiis t>estibus Thoma de Etton', Ade de Thorntona senescallo abbatis de Bellal', Radulfo Iarpenvyle, Roberto . . . ysethorp', Willelmo capellano de Ampilf', Ricardo de Kereby de eadem et <multis> aliis.

5 *Grant and quitclaim, addressed to all the faithful in Christ present and future, by Alan the cook, to God and St Mary and the abbot and convent of Byland, of that half toft in Ampleforth near the toft which belonged to Michael of Fryton, to provide one pittance on the anniversary of his death. Pledge to make no further claim. Sealed with the donor's seal.* [before 1285].
Hiis testibus dominis Iohanne de Scakyncurt', Willelmo de Barton militibus, Willelmo Attebek, Waltero de Lundon, Willelmo filio Gamelli de Sutton', Henrico de Angotby, Willelmo le Pledur, et aliis.
Dating: The second witness, William de Barton, obtained land in Ampleforth with his wife, Emma, one of the daughters of William de Surdeval. William de Barton held 4½ carucates in Ampleforth and Oswaldkirk in 1242–3. He and his wife were still living in 1277. He was succeeded by a son, William, who in turn had been succeeded by his son, Nicholas, by 1284–5 (*EYC* X, 148–50; *VCH NR* I, 462, 549).
Note: The rubric specifies 3s. 4d. annual rent paid to the convent from the half toft.

6 *Grant in free alms, addressed to all the faithful of Christ present and future, by Cecily daughter of Peter of Newton, formerly wife of Walter of (East or West) Harlsey, in her independent widowhood, to God and St Mary and the abbot and convent of Byland, of 2 doles or portions of meadow in St Oswald's marsh, both 2 perches wide, nearest to the dole (portion) of the same meadow near Holbeck, and lying towards the land in Laysthorpe which* *she had from her father in free marriage. The grant is made for the salvation of her soul and those of her ancestors and heirs. Pledge to warranty.* [?early 13th cent.].

Note: The latter part of the charter, including the witness list, is missing. Newton and Laysthorpe are in the parish of Stonegrave, about 3 miles east of Ampleforth and Holbeck is the watercourse that runs to the south and west of Ampleforth and the south of Newton. Peter of Newton witnesses charters of late Henry II (*EYC* IX, no. 148) and *c.* 1160 x 1176 (*ibid.*, no. 161). Walter son of Jocelin of Harlsey and his brother William attest in the time of Agnes, prioress of Marrick, who occurs in the late 12th century and probably *c.* 1211 (*Cart. Riev.*, p. 254, no. 361; see also *EYC* III, no. 1883 and II, 72, 295; *HRH* II, 215). Robert de Ros confirmed to Byland 1 bovate granted by Walter of Harlsey (MS Dodsworth 94, fol. 54r, no. 68), and the witnesses, the first three of whom also attest no. 670 below, suggest a date around 1190 x 1226.

[1 folio lost, evidently old fol. 75]

[fol. 4r, old fol. 76, badly faded]
7   End of text of charter; illegible. Only the names of . . . de Pickering and Adam de London are legible in the witness list.

8   Text of charter illegible.
Rubric: Letter of attorney from John of Holbeck (Ampleforth) to deliver seisin to Robert of Ampleforth and Isabella his wife of lands and tenements in Ampleforth which formerly belonged to Geoffrey del Bek. By the hands of William de Malton and Peter de Pucy. [? early 14th cent.].

Note: A seventeenth-century marginal note gives a genealogy in which Robert of Ampleforth (occ. 14 Edward II [1320–1]), and his sister Isabella are identified as the children of Geoffrey del Bek; Geoffrey was tenant in Ampleforth in 1284–5 (*KI*, p. 106; *VCH NR* I, 463). The genealogy also shows Isabella's husband as John de Councefield, and their son as Thomas son of John, with the note 'infra Oct 1329'. See no. 11.

9   Text of charter illegible.
Rubric: Confirmation by Robert son of Hugh to Dom. John son of Michael de St Andrews, of a capital messuage in Ampleforth with its appurtenant lands and tenements. [Ampleforth; 25 Jan. 1340 x 24 Jan. 1341].

Copies: MS Dodsworth 63, fol. 58v (abbreviated); MS Dodsworth 91, fol. 130v, no. 99. Robert son of Hugh Eure quitclaimed to Dom. John son of Michael de St Andrews of Ampleforth, clerk, all his right in the capital messuage which belonged to Geoffrey del Beck and the assart called 'Geffrey Stockinge'. Teste Marmeduco Darell, Richardo de Esshur seniore, Richardo de Esshuer iuniore.

Marginal note: a later (?17th century) sketch indicates that Robert de Eure was the son of Hugh, and that Robert's daughter was Helen. See no. 13.

Dating: The date is given as 14 Edward III, and the charter is presumably related to no. 10.

Note: The copy in MS Dodsworth 91 has a sketch of a seal with the note 'it may be forged but cannot be discernd'.

[fol. 4r–v]

10 Text illegible on fol. 4r. *Pledge to warranty.* Ampleforth; Tues. after St Scholastica, 14 Edward III [14 Feb. 1340].

Hiis testibus Marmaduco Darell', Ricardo de Eschew seniore, Ricardo de Eschew iuniore, <Ada> de London, Willelmo de Ampilf', Thoma de Pykering et aliis.

Rubric: Quitclaim by Robert de Eur' of a tenement in Ampleforth.

Note: It is possible that this is the Robert de Eure who with Isabel his wife quitclaimed to Geoffrey of Finghall 12 acres in Ampleforth in 1327: *Yorks. Fines 1327–1347*, p. 4. They are likely to be the Robert and Isabella of no. 8. The text of no. 10 is followed by the word 'duplicatur'.

[fol. 4v]

11 *Quitclaim by Thomas son of John [de Cauncefield] to Dom. John of Ampleforth, rector of Thornton in Pickering Lythe* (rest illegible).

Rubric: Quitclaim by Thomas de Cauncefeld' to Dom. John of Ampleforth of a capital messuage in Ampleforth. [c. 1365].

Dating: see no. 12. However, the date of 1329 appears alongside the name of the grantor in the later marginalia by no. 8.

12 Text illegible.

Rubric: Charter of Dom. John of Ampleforth for John de Saylesbery, vicar of Ampleforth, and Richard of Cundall concerning a capital messuage, tofts, crofts and other lands in and around Ampleforth. [c. 1365].

Note: See below, no. 538, a licence for alienation in mortmain by John of Salesbury, vicar of Ampleforth, and Richard of Cundall to the abbot and convent of 1 messuage, 8 tofts, 4 bovates, 20 acres and 1½ acres in Ampleforth (4 Feb. 1365). The grantor seems to have been rector of Thornton in Pickering Lythe: see no. 13.

[fols 4v–5r]

13 Text at bottom of fol. 4v obscure; that on fol. 5r mostly torn away.

Rubric: Quitclaim of Helen de Eure (Ever) to Dom. John of Ampleforth. [Ampleforth; Sat. after the Annunciation [29 Mar.] 1348].

Copies: MS Dodsworth 63, fol. 58v (abbreviated); MS Dodsworth 91, fols 79v–80r, no. 19 (from the original in St Mary's Tower). Quitclaim by Helen de Eure (Ever), daughter of Robert de Eure (Ever), to Dom. John of Ampleforth [MS Dodsworth 63: rector of Thornton in Pickering Lythe; MS Dodsworth 91: chaplain] of all the right she had in the lands which formerly belonged to her father, Robert, of which lands John was enfeoffed by her father. Pledge to warranty. Hiis testibus dominis Richard Malebys, Thoma Ughtred, Alexandro Nevill, Iohanne de Mynyoth, militibus, Iohanne de Upsale, Iohanne de Rillyngton, Roberto Busci et aliis. Place and date.

[1 folio lost, old fol. 77]

[fol. 5r, old fol. 78]
14 mostly torn away.
Rubric: Charter of Edward . . .
Note: Both Edward II and Edward III granted licence for the monks to acquire land in Ampleforth notwithstanding the Statute of Mortmain; for further rubrics relating to Ampleforth, see below, nos 535 and 538 (*Cal. Pat. R. 1317–1321*, p. 322 and *Cal. Pat. R. 1364–1367*, p. 85).

[fol. 5r–v]
15 Text mostly torn away.
Rubric: Writ of King Edward to his escheator.

[fol. 5v]
16 Text mostly torn away.
Rubric: . . . <Ampi>lford'; enrolled in the Chancery.

17 Text torn away.
Rubric: . . . generali de Relig'.
Note: This seems to refer to the statute *De Religiosis*, that is, the Statute of Mortmain, 1279: see note to no. 14 and below nos 535, 538.

[fol. 6r, old fol. 79]
18 Rubric and text mostly torn away; only warranty, sealing clause, and witness list remain. Byland; Mon., Nativity of B. V. M. [8 Sept.] 1365.
Hiis testibus Marmeduco Darell', Thoma Colvyle, Thoma de Etton', Willelmo de Kyrkeby, et aliis.
Note: A later hand adds the date of 39 Edward III.

[fol. 6v]
NORTHALLERTON (SE3794), parish and township in the wapentake of Allerton (NR). These two documents are the only ones in the cartulary to relate to Northallerton.

19 *Grant, addressed to all present and future who will see or hear this charter, by Matthew of Allerton (Northallerton), to God and St Mary and the abbot and convent of Byland, of 3 parts of his toft in (North)allerton,* *nearest to the toft which belonged to Wimark, daughter of Roger Po . . . , being 45 feet long and 25 feet wide. The grant is made, with his body, for the salvation of his soul and those of his father and mother and all his ancestors and heirs, to hold of the chief lord, rendering <1d.> for all service. Pledge to warranty. Sealed with the donor's seal. [c. 1251 x 52].*

Hiis t<estibus> domino Honorio tunc priore, W. cellerario, Willelmo magistro animalium, Ada de Hustw', monachis, ... Willelmo filio Willelmi de Ebor', Willelmo de F. . . Ada, Ricardo, W. . . W. . . . . . Iohanne Long. . . et aliis.

Dating: See also no. 20, dated 1251. The first witness occurs in no. 2, of date *c.* 1282.
Note: The text is damaged. The annual rent of 1d. is conjectured from no. 20.

20 *Final concord reached in the king's court before <Hugh>, abbot of Selby, Gilbert de Preston and Adam de Hilton, between Henry, abbot of Byland, plaintiff, and Matthew of Northallerton, defendant, concerning an annual rent of 1d. [due from 3 parts of] 1 messuage in (North)allerton, about which a claim had been made [for arrears of 3d]. [The 3 parts, which belonged to Wimark, daughter of Roger are acknowledged to be the right of the abbot]. The abbot has conceded to Matthew [the 3 parts] rendering [1d. yearly at St Michael. Pledge to warranty. On Matthew's death these are to revert to the abbey, to hold of the chief lord of the fee by service].* York; [day after St Martin], 36 Henry III; [12 Nov. 1251].

Copy: PRO CP 25/1/265/44, no. 85, from which readings for the damaged portions have been supplied.
Pd: *Yorks. Fines 1246–1272,* p. 39 (from PRO copy).

[3 folios lost, old fols 80–82]

ANGRAM (SE5176), in the parish of Coxwold and wapentake of Birdforth (NR). Angram lies approximately 2 miles to the SW of Byland Abbey and 1 mile south of Wildon Grange. The Angram charters occupied fol. 80: MS Top. Yorks. d. 11, fol. 260v. A charter of Roger de Cundy recorded there mentions a ditch between the meadow of Thomas de Coleville and the land of the abbot and convent.

[fol. 7r, old fol. 83]
ASBY. The townships of Great Asby (NY6813) and Little Asby (NY6909) lie in the parish of Asby (Westm.). Old folios 81–2 and 84–5, which contained charters relating to Asby, have been lost; among the grants were those of the Lasceles and Moreville families. On the Asby

charters (nos 21–5) see F. W. Ragg, 'Charters to St Peter's, York and to Byland Abbey', *TCWAAS*, ns 9 (1909), 236–70, especially 252–70. Ragg cites BL Add. 18388 (which contains eighteenth-century transcripts of some Byland charters) as the Byland cartulary. He states that the Asby charters are the first charters in the manuscript and notes their faded condition. He prints transcripts and translations of five originals evidently not in the cartulary, including one of Richard de Cotesford (see no. 24). The monks had a grange at Asby (NY6810), which lay between Great and Little Asby.

21 *Grant of land (name of donor on missing fol. 82v) within specified bounds, free from all service, to fence and enclose as the monks please. This grant is made for the salvation of the soul of the donor and of all his/her ancestors and heirs. Permission to make a sheepfold above Stannerstones for 300 sheep by the long hundred. Pledge to warranty.* [late 12th or early 13th cent.].

Hiis testibus Ada decano Westm', Iohanne de Hormesheued, Henrico de Suleby, [Willel]mo Anglico, Galfrido del . . . Alano de Warcop, [Roberto] de Cottesford', Galfrido de Cottesford, et multis aliis.

Dating: An Alan of Warcop, donor of no. 85, occurs in the late 12th or early 13th century.

Note: Rubric and opening of charter missing, due to loss of folio; the names in square brackets are conjectured from no. 23, which appears to be of the same period. The first witness appears as dean (nos 23, 25 (as A.)), as dean of Asby (no. 85), and as parson of Asby and dean (no. 87).

22 Original: *Grant, addressed to all the faithful in Christ, by Roger de Montyng, to God and St Mary and the abbot and convent of Byland, for the salvation of his soul and of his ancestors and heirs, of 5 acres of arable land in the* cultura *called Beacham Spring* (Beuchamp) *lying between the land of William le Engleys and that of Thomas de Bueth'. He quitclaims all charges that the monks have been overstocking the pastures.* [before 1272].

Hiis testibus dominis Petro de Brus', Patricio de Curwen', Roberto de Askeby, Thoma de Hellebeck', militibus, Thoma de Musegr', Willelmo de Wardecop', Thoma Bueth', Willelmo le Engleys, Thoma de Slegyll', et aliis.

Location: Kendal, Cumbria Record Office, WD/Kilv/1/1/1.

Copy: MS Dodsworth 63, fol. 65v, from cartulary fol. 83.

Dating: The first witness may be Peter de Brus, son of Peter de Brus and Helewise, sister of William of Lancaster III, who with Walter de Lindsay was William's heir. Peter de Brus died in 1272.

Note: The cartulary text is damaged and faint. The rubric reads 'Charter of Roger

Montyng of Asby concerning 5 acres in the *cultura* called Beacham Spring, and a claim concerning measurement of pasture, which has been relaxed'.

[fol. 7r–v]

23 *Grant, addressed to all the faithful in Christ present and future, by Robert son of William Le Fleming (Fammang), to God and St Mary and <the monks of> Byland, of 1 acre on Great Haber between the land which Robert son of Durand granted to the church of St Peter, Asby, and that of the monks, to hold rendering ½d. yearly to Asby church for incense at Easter. Pledge to warranty. [? late 12th or early 13th cent.].*

Hiis testibus domino [Ada] tunc decano, Roberto filio Gileberti, Roberto de Cottesford, Willelmo Anglico, Galfrido <de> Cottesford', Roberto Scoto, et aliis.

Copy: MS Dodsworth 63, fol. 65v, from which the missing or unclear portions have been restored.

Pd: Ragg, 'Byland Charters', p. 269.

Note: The second witness may be Robert son of Gilbert of Asby who attests no. 25.

[fol. 7v]

24 *Agreement between the monks of St Mary of Byland and Richard de Cottesford, that the monks shall have whatever they possess in Asby, within specified bounds, [that is, as* Masyngile *descends from Skerris etc.], without hindrance or injury from Richard and his heirs. Affidavit in the hands of Archbishop Roger. [1154 x 1181].*

[Hiis testibus Cospatricio filio Hormi, Radulfo de Cundala, Iohanne Taylebois, Humfrido Malocatulo, Roberto de Broi], qui etiam affidaverunt [quod pro toto posse suo sine datione pecunie sue facient (*sic*) Ricardi conventionem prescriptam in omnibus illabatam (*sic*) servatur et per totum (MS totam) episcopatum Carleoleum stabunt cum monachis ad convincendum eum si contra conventionem hanc in aliquo venire temptaverit. Et si necesse fuerit extra episcopatum Carleol' ire unus eorum cum scriptis ceterorum testium ibit ubicunque cause necessitas intra episcopatum Ebor' indixerit. Testes horum omnium sunt Rogerus Bertram et Robertus frater eius, Iohannes etiam seneschallus Rogeri Bertrami.]

Copy: MS Dodsworth 63, fols 65v–66r, from cartulary fol. 83b.

Dating: Roger de Pont l'Evêque, archbishop of York.

Note: The witness list is defective and has been supplied from the copy in MS Dodsworth 63 as has the affidavit, where the Latin seems to be corrupt. The portion of the text giving the boundaries is damaged and faint.

25 Original: *Confirmation in free alms, addressed to all present and future, by Geoffrey de Cottesford for himself and his heirs, of all the agree-*

ments made in the presence of Archbishop Roger of York between the monks of Byland and Richard de Cottesford as contained in their original chirograph. The grantor has requested Robert son of Gilbert of Asby to append his seal, which is well enough known. [1154 x 1181].

Hiis testibus eodem domino Roberto filio Gilberti de Askeby, A(da) tunc decano, Roberto filio Hugonis de Askeby, Willelmo Anglico de Parva Askeby, Willelmo le Flemeng, Ricardo de Camera, Waltero de Meburne, Adam Langstrap, Roberto Schot.

Location: Kendal, Cumbria Record Office, WD/Kilv/1/1/3.
Copy: MS Dodsworth 63, fol. 66r, from cartulary fol. 83b.
Dating: Roger de Pont L'Evêque, archbishop of York.
Note: The cartulary text is damaged and breaks off; the rubric states that the charter has been copied. The second witness is Adam the dean who attests no. 21.

[10 folios lost, old fols 84–93]. These contained further charters relating to Asby (fols 84–5), and the following:

ALLERTON NEAR WILSDEN (SE1134), in the parish of Bradford and wapentake of Morley; the abbot of Byland held land here in 1302/3 but the donor is uncertain (*West Yorks.*, II, 565).

BAGBY (SE4680) and **BALK** (SE4779), in the parish of Kirby Knowle and the wapentake of Birdforth (NR). Bagby and Balk lie about 2 and 3 miles to the east of Thirsk. A number of original charters, then in the possession of Sir Ralph Payne-Gallwey, bart., were printed in *Yorks. Deeds*, II, 10–16, nos 30–42, and the endorsements indicate that these were from the Bagby *baculus*. Among these, Adam Fossard quitclaimed all his right in Bagby as contained in a charter of Roger de Mowbray.

BAGWITH, now Bagwith House (SE1974), in the parish of Kirkby Malzeard, and wapentake of Lower Claro (WR).

[fol. 8r, old fol. 94]
BOSCAR GRANGE (Balschaw) (SE5072), in the parish of Easingwold, and the wapentake of Bulmer (NR). Boscar lies about 2 miles NW of Easingwold and 2 miles SW of Husthwaite. The parish of Easingwold lies in the Vale of York and extends into the forest of Galtres (*VCH NR* II, 128). The beginning of the section (old fol. 93) is missing from the cartulary.

26 *[Agreement between the chapter of St Peter, York, and the monks of Byland concerning a ditch between Boscar Grange and Husthwaite, by* *which the men of Husthwaite and Baxby shall make half the enclosure in the wood of H(usthwaite) and the land of B(axby) by the assent of Meldred, lord of Baxby, that is, from the stream of Easingwold which is the boundary between the monks' land] and the forest, to the higher boundary of* Scalker. *The monks shall make the other half. Sealed with the seals of two chapters.* [Sept. 1177 x 1186].

Hiis testibus Roberto decano Ebor', Radulfo archidiacono, Hamone cantore, Gwydone magistro scolarum, etc.

Copy (abbreviated): MS Top. Yorks. d. 11, fol. 263r (old p. 489), from which the material in square brackets is supplied. Only the end of the cartulary text remains. Dating: Guy became master of the schools in Sept. 1177. Robert Butevilain, dean of York, died in July 1186.

Note: Hamo was precentor of York from *c.* 1170 x 74 and had become treasurer by 1199. The second witness was vice-archdeacon of Richmond. The *Historia Fundationis* notes that land in Boscar was granted to the monks by Bertram de Bulmer: *Mon. Ang.* V, 352. For a prebend of York Minster at Husthwaite, see note to no. 27. Pope Hadrian IV confirmed Byland's possessions there in 1156 (below, no. 595). The stream referred to may be The Kyle, which runs to the south of Boscar and north of Easingwold.

27   *Notification to all present and future of the agreement terminating the controversy between the monks of St Mary of Byland and Hamo, precentor of York, concerning the woodland between Husthwaite and Boscar Grange. They shall make a ditch at the boundaries on the north for the arable land of the monks and on the west for . . . next to the arable land of Boscar. Sealed.* [Sept. 1177 x 1199, probably before 1186].

. . . decano Ebor', . . . Guidone . . .

Dating: Hamo precentor of York and the attestation of Guy. However, the first witness may be Robert Butevilain, and the notification is likely to have been issued on the same occasion as no. 26.

Note: The text is damaged. MS Top. Yorks. d. 11, fol. 263r (old p. 461), follows the copy of no. 26 with: 'alia carta eiusdem ubi mete aliter expresse sunt et Radulfus filius Meldredi dominus de Baxby nominatur. Eisdem testibus'. This agreement is likely to be related to the prebend of York Minster at Husthwaite, which lies approximately 3 miles south-west of Byland and 1½ miles south west of Coxwold. The prebend had been established by 1157, but the church, originally a chapel of Coxwold, which was held by the canons of Newburgh, remained a possession of the priory. A notification by the dean and chapter, which can be dated to *c.* 1177 x 1186, that the prior and convent had placed a resident priest in Husthwaite with the consent of Hamo, canon and precentor, suggests that Hamo held the prebend of Husthwaite (*EYC* I, no. 157; *YMF* I, 2 and II, 41–2). This would explain the agreement made here between Hamo and the monks.

28   *Rubric: Charter of quitclaim.* (rest missing).
This is likely to relate to no. 27.

[fol. 8v]

BAXBY (SE5175), in the township and parish of Husthwaite, and the wapentake of Birdforth (NR). Baxby Manor lies about ½ mile west of Husthwaite.

29   *Grant in free alms, addressed to all the sons of holy church present and future, by Adam of Baxby, to God and the monks of St Mary of Byland, of all the land which he had in* Mirethwayt, *asserted and not asserted, all the assart of Edward, and all the assarts which they hold near the assart of Edward and pasture and easements belonging to 2 bovates. The monks are to have free entry and exit, and to do there as they wish. Pledge to warranty.* [late 12th or early 13th cent.].

[Hiis testibus Thoma de Coleville, Thoma] de Lascell', [Galfrido Fossard], Gilberto de Torn[y, Gilberto de Thirkilby, Stephano filio eius, Willelmo filio Willelmi de Dalton].

Copy (abbreviated): MS Top. Yorks. d. 11, fol. 263r (old p. 461), from which the readings in square brackets are drawn.

Dating: The attestation of Gilbert de Meinill of Thirkleby and his son, Stephen, suggests a date in the late 12th or early 13th cent. For grants by them, and attestation to grants, see nos 761, 762, 786.

Note: The rubric locates the property in Baxby. The land granted by Adam of Baxby is mentioned in a charter of Henry, abbot of Byland (*c.* 1231 x 1268); see below, no. 31.

30   *Confirmation, addressed to all the sons of holy church present and future, by Robert of Bax[by brother of Adam], to God and the monks of St Mary of Byland, of [the same land] . . .* (rest illegible even under ultra violet light). [first half of 13th cent.].

[Test' Ernaldo de Upsala], Galfrido Fossard', [Thoma Lasceles], Gilb(erto) . . .

Copy (much abbreviated): MS Top. Yorks. d. 11, fol. 263r (old p. 461), from which the readings in square brackets are drawn.

Dating: The witnesses suggest that the charter was issued at the same time as no. 29.

Note: The rubric identifies Robert as the brother of Adam (see no. 29) and locates the property in Baxby. It further states that the charter had been copied.

31   *Grant, addressed to all the sons of holy mother church who will see or hear this writing, by Abbot Henry and the convent of Byland to Geoffrey, vicar of Felixkirk, for homage and service [of whatever they have] in the region of Baxby of the grant of Adam of Baxby, as contained in his charter (no. 29), rendering 2s. yearly, 12d. at St Martin in Winter (11 Nov.) and 12d. at Whitsuntide. Geoffrey is to make suit at the abbot's court at Sutton* *three times a year, at the first courts after Michaelmas, Christmas and Easter, and is to be present whenever the king's writ is received or a thief is tried. Pledge to warranty. Sealed in the form of a chirograph with the seal of both parties.* [*c.* 1231 x 1268].

Hiis testibus domino Alano de Leck . . ., fratre Willelmo tunc magistro hospitalis Sancti Iohannis, Roberto capellano, Hugone de Laysethorp, etc.

Copy (abbreviated): MS Top. Yorks. d. 11, fol. 263r (old p. 461).

Dating: Abbot Henry of Battersby occurs between 1231 and 1268; a second Abbot Henry was elected in 1300 and occurs in 1302, but as agreements following disputes were reached between Abbot Henry and Geoffrey in the time of Archbishop Walter de Gray, the earlier period is likely. See below, nos 1055, 1056.

Note: The rubric reads: 'chirograph charter between us and Dom. Geoffrey, vicar of Felixkirk, who holds the said land by inheritance, rendering to us annually 11s. and making three suits at the court of Sutton and at the king's writ or the judging of a thief'. The first witness also attests nos 121, 128, 129, 201, 494, 495, 496, 509, 515, 616, 848, 852, 998, 1146 below. The second witness was probably the master of the preceptory of the Knights Hospitaller at Felixkirk.

32   *Indenture between the abbot and convent of Byland and William Darel of Thornton on the Hill, licensing William to remove and reconstruct his mill of Baxby [16 feet away so that the flow of water can descend in a straight line, saving all matters contained in another agreement].* [1391].

[Testibus Thoma Coleville de Cukewald, Will', Ricardo de Malebysse de Scalton, Thoma Etton de Gilling, Willelmo Darell de Seszay, Willelmo Lasceles de Souclky, Iohanne de Baxeby, Stephano Dayvill de Faldington].

Copy: MS Top. Yorks. d. 11, fol. 263v (old p. 462), from which the text in square brackets is supplied. This is followed by an agreement between the monks and John de Daiville.

Note: The rubric locates the mill on the monks' field. William Darel was a member of the Darel family of Sessay, which descended from Marmaduke Darel, brother of Thomas Darel of Wheldrake and Lund. Marmaduke held a knight's fee of the Percy family. See *EYC* XI, 336–7. At the foot of the folio, in the same hand as the cartulary text, is a note: 1 quaterna de Baxby.

[1 folio lost, old fol. 95]

BORROWBY (SE4289), in the parish of Leake and the wapentake of Allerton. MS Top. Yorks. d. 11, fol. 263v, notes a charter of Ralph son of Uctred relating to lands in Borrowby which were afterwards confirmed by the monks to the brothers of the Hospital of Jerusalem.

[fol. 9r, old fol. 96]

BOLTON ON SWALE (SE2599), township and parish in the wapentake of Gilling East (NR).

33 *Writ of precipe from King Edward [I] to the sheriff of York to order Harsculph de Cleasby to restore without delay to John, abbot of Byland, 1 bovate with its appurtenances in Bolton near Catterick (Bolton on Swale), which he claims to be the right of the church of Byland. Harsculph has no right of entry except through Ralph of Bolton to whom Adam, formerly abbot of Byland, demised it for his lifetime only; after his death the land should have reverted to Abbot John.* St Albans; 14 Apr. 21 Edward [I, 1293].

Teste me ipso apud sanctum Albanum xiiii die Aprilis anno regni nostri xxi.

Dating: Adam, former abbot, is Adam of Husthwaite, who occurs in 1272 and 1283, and again in 1309 x 1310, 1314 and 1315, after Abbots John, Henry and William (*HRH* II, 270). He occurs in nos 157, 309, 435, 870, 959, 989 and 1066. That this belongs to the reign of Edward I rather than Edward III is also indicated by the involvement of Harsculph de Cleasby: see, e.g., *Cal. Pat. R. 1292–1301*, pp. 327, 345, 352, 356 etc., and *VCH NR* I, 155–6. See also no. 34.

34 *Writ of King Edward [I] addressed to Nicholas de Stapleton, Simon le Constable and John Lithergreyns, to hold an assize of novel disseisin to hear the abbot of Byland against Ralph of Bolton near Whitwell (Bolton on Swale). By letters patent.* Westminster; 6 Nov. 16 Edward I [1288].

T(este) Edmundo comiti Cornub', coram nostro.

Dating to Edward I: Edmund earl of Cornwall. Ralph of Bolton also appears in no. 33.

35 *Rubric: Confirmation of Henry Mauvaisur concerning the grant made by Guy of Helbeck.* [before *c.* 1246].

Text: MS Dodsworth 71, fol. 28v, and MS Dodsworth 94, fols 26v–27r, no. 36. Confirmation, addressed to all the sons of holy mother church present and future, by Henry Mauvaisur, to God and St Mary of Byland and the monks serving God there, of a half carucate in Bolton, with its tofts and crofts and houses built on the land, granted by Guy of Helbeck with his body. Of the land Hugh, Gilbert, Arnold, and Norman hold 1 bovate each. Confirmation also of the toft and croft which Robert the chaplain held in the same vill, service on the carucate which Ralph of Bolton held, and rent of 5s. to be taken from Bolton mill at St Michael (29 Sept.). The confirmation is made in free alms, for the salvation of his soul and of all his ancestors and heirs, to do with as they wish. Hiis testibus Ricardo Fitun tunc constabulario

Richemund, Briano filio Alani, Philippo filio Iohannis, Nicholao de Stapilton, Hugone de Magneby, Thoma de Burgo, Roberto de Arundell, Iohanne de Boneville, Radulfo de Smithetun', Thoma de Boleton, Hugone clerico de Richemund.

Dating: The first witness is Richard Fitton of Bollin, Cheshire, justice of Cheshire and constable of Richmond castle, who died *c.* 1246. He probably became constable after the death of Earl Conan in 1217, and held the post after the marriage of Countess Constance to her second husband, Ranulf of Chester. He occurs as constable in 1224 (*EYC* V, nos 338A, 338B, and pp. 277, 283). In 1252 a final concord was levied in the king's court at York (14 Jan. 1252) between Henry, abbot of Byland, plaintiff, and Thomas of Helbeck, defendant, concerning 15s. arrears: *Yorks. Fines 1246–1272*, p. 54.

Note: Guy of Helbeck (Westm.) witnesses a charter of Adam son of Ralph of Bolton quitclaiming to the monks of Rievaulx land in Bolton which they held of the grant of Acaris of Tunstall (*Cart. Riev.*, pp. 101–102, no. 145R). In 1190 x 1192 he attested a charter of Thomas of Helbeck as his son and heir, and a charter of Helen de Hastings granting Startforth church to Egglestone Abbey (*EYC* V, nos 184A, 313). In 1212 he held 7 bovates in North Otterington (*EYC* II, 280). For the grant that Guy made to Byland, copied from the original in St Mary's Tower, see MS Dodsworth 91, fol. 91r–v, no. 34; also in Dodsworth 94, fol. 27r–v, no. 37. See also MS Top. Yorks. e. 7, fol. 151r (old p. 249), continued in Top. Yorks. e. 8, fol. 107r (old p. 178), *ibid.*, fol. 186v (old p. 338), continued in Top. Yorks. e. 9, fol. 24r (old p. 21). By the final concord of 1252 concerning 15s. arrears from an annual rent of 5s. due from Thomas for Bolton mill, Thomas undertook to pay the rent at St Michael (29 Sept.), and also acknowledged the right of the abbot to a half carucate which the abbot had of Guy of Helbeck, Thomas's uncle, whose heir he is, and the homage and service of Thomas of Bolton for 1 carucate which he used to hold of Guy. The abbot quitclaimed the arrears. Guy of Helbeck witnessed a charter of William de Percy to Bridlington Priory, though the Percy connection evident in nos 36–37 is not recorded elsewhere.

36 *Rubric: Confirmation by Cecily de Percy concerning the same.* [before 1252].

Dating: Probably the same time as no. 35, or as the final concord of 1252 (see note to no. 35).
Note: A 17th-century marginal note indicates that Guy of Helbeck married Cecily de Percy.

37 *Rubric: Quitclaim by [Cecily] wife of the said Guy concerning the same.* [before 1252].

Dating: Probably the same time as no. 35, or as the final concord of 1252 (see note to no. 35).

[fol. 9v]

BENTLEY, in the parish of Emley and wapentake of Agbrigg (WR). Bentley Grange (SE266133), along with Denby, was an important iron working site for the monks of Byland, and it has been suggested that monastic timber framed buildings may have been on the site as late as the 19th century (*West Yorks.*, II, 366–7).

38   *Final concord in the king's court before Robert of Lexington, William of York, Adam fitz William and William of Culworth, justices, between Henry, abbot of Byland, plaintiff, through Robert de Hamlby, his monk, and Thomas son of William, defendant, through Bartholomew of Emley, concerning mining rights, and pasture for 2 horses, 4 oxen, 5 cows, 1 bull, 30 she-goats and 3 he-goats in Emley, about which a plea of warranty had been brought. Thomas acknowledges the pasture to be the right of the said abbot and the church of Byland as the gift of William son of William, father of Thomas, whose heir he is, to hold in free alms. Grant by Robert to the abbot of Byland of the chapel of St Werbergh which is located next to the grange of Bentley, with all the land belonging to the chapel, and of all the land which stretches from the gate of Bentley grange along the road which leads to the chapel towards the east, and in width from the western part of the road by the ditches constructed there and the stones which have been set up, and in length as far as the land which belongs to the chapel. The abbot and convent may enclose the land with ditch and hedge as they wish. Quitclaim of 3s. which the abbot used to pay. Pledge to warranty. The abbot remits all claim in the park of Emley and in pastures and minerals, and undertakes to provide a chaplain, monk or secular, in the abbey of Byland or elsewhere to celebrate for the souls of Thomas and his ancestors and successors, and the faithful departed.* Westminster; quindene of St Michael, 21 Henry III [13 Oct. 1237].

Copy: PRO CP 25/1/263/30, no. 15 (damaged).

Pd (calendar): *Yorks. Fines 1232–1246*, pp. 49–50 (from PRO copy).

Note: Robert of Lexington was a long serving justice, who first appears as a justice in eyre in 1218 and retired in 1244; William of York was a clerk then a justice of the King's Bench (1231); Adam fitz William was appointed to the King's Bench in 1232 and died in the middle of May 1238; William of Culworth was a junior justice at Westminster from 1237 to 1238 (Ralph V. Turner, *The English Judiciary in the Age of Glanville and Bracton c. 1176–1239* (Cambridge, 1985), pp. 194, 196, 245).

39   **Original:** *Grant and confirmation in free alms, addressed to all the sons of holy mother church present and future to whom this present charter shall come, by John of Horbury, knight, son of Ralph of Horbury, for himself and his heirs, to the abbot and convent of Byland, of licence to strengthen* *their millpond of Bentley on his land at Shitlington at the head of the assart of* Hutherode *and to repair the same pond in the same place as often as is necessary, without dissent or impairment. The grant is made free from secular service for the salvation of the donor's soul and of his ancestors and heirs. Pledge to warranty. Sealed with the donor's seal.* [before *c.* 1302].

Hiis testibus dominis Willelmo filio Thome, Iohanne de Heton', Ricardo de Thornhill, militibus, Thoma de Horbiri, Henrico de Byri', Ricardo de Bretton', Simone Chyvet, Henrico de Weldon, Willelmo de Hathewaldeley, Henrico filio Rogeri de Emeley, Roberto de Wytheley et multis aliis.

Location: University of Leeds, Bretton Hall, Bretton Estate Archive (Allendale muniments), BEA/C3/B11.98; endorsed: 'C. Iohannis de Horbyri de licentia firmandi stagnum de Benteley'; 'Benteley B.i. vi', that is, Bentley, first bundle, charter 6; seal: oval, brown wax; legend invisible.

Copies: MS Dodsworth 94, fol. 64r–v, no. 9; MS Top. Yorks. e. 8, fol. 139r–v (old pp. 242–3) which has a sketch of the seal.

Pd: (calendared from the original in the possession of Lord Allendale) *Yorks. Deeds,* V, 134, no. 375.

Dating: The donor was still living in 1302; see *EYF,* p. 43.

Note: The cartulary copy has an error in 'Mitelingtona' for Shitlington, the scribe evidently misunderstanding the form of capital 'S' in the original: 'Towards the end of the [thirteenth] century the 'beaver-tailed' capital S (so often since that time misread as M) enjoys its comparatively brief vogue' (L. C. Hector, *The Handwriting of English Documents* (Ilkley, 1958, 2nd edn, 1966), p. 57). The cartulary copy has the first five witnesses only and ends 'etc'.

[1 folio lost, old fol. 97]
It is not clear if missing folio 97 contained the end of the Bentley section or the beginning of Bretton.

[fol. 10r, old fol. 98]
BRETTON (West Bretton (SE2813)), in the parish of Sandal Magna and wapentake of Agbrigg (WR). A number of original charters relating to Bretton survive among the Bretton Estate Archive (Allendale muniments): see Appendix I. Byland's estates in West Bretton, which became an important industrial site, came from the family of Peter son of Orm of Bretton (no. 40), his son William (no. 41), Swane son of Ulkil (nos 42, 44) and his brother Henry (no. 43). Alan of Crigglestone, who attests no. 44, was the grantor of no. 46. The monks reached an agreement with those of Rievaulx to define their respective rights in the south of Yorkshire, including Bretton (no. 988). The lands also provided sheep pastures and arable land.

40 Original: *Grant and confirmation in free alms, addressed to all the sons of holy mother church present and future, by Peter son of Orm of Bretton, to God and the monks of St Mary of Byland, of 10 acres in the region of Bretton, wherever they wish to take them from the lands belonging to him in the same vill, namely, 7 acres in* Rinticlive *or if there are not 7 acres there, in* Trunclive, *until they have the full 7 acres. Afterwards they are to take 3 acres in the northern part below* Trunclive *until they shall have the full 10 acres. The monks are to have 40 sheep throughout the common pasture of Bretton and as many draught animals as are needed to plough the land. The grant is made with all appurtenances, easements and liberties within the vill of Bretton and outside, without anything being held back, free from all secular service or exaction, for the salvation of the soul of the donor and of all his ancestors and heirs, to do with as the monks wish. Pledge to warranty.* [1190 x 1218].

Hiis testibus Willelmo de Sotill', Thoma de Horbiri, Willelmo de Bertona, Ada de Holand, Rogero filio Symonis, Thoraldo de Brectona, Suano de Brectona et multis aliis.

Location: University of Leeds, Bretton Hall, Bretton Estate Archive (Allendale muniments), BEA/C3/B7.14. Endorsed: 'C. Petri filii Orm de x acris terre et de pastura xl ovibus et averiis que terram arari possit. In Brettona'; 'Benteleya i B. vii', that is, Bentley, first bundle, charter 7; seal (detached): round, red-brown wax; SIGILL' . . . TERI DE BETVN.

Pd: (calendared from the original charter, in the possession of Lord Allendale of Bretton Park, Wakefield) *Yorks. Deeds*, VI, 10–11, no. 33; (from the cartulary) *EYC* III, no. 1792.

Dating: The terminal date is provided by the death of the second witness.

Note: The cartulary copy has the first five witnesses only and ends 'etc'. In 1317 the abbot and convent demised to Master John of Dransfield the 10 acres in Bretton which they had of the grant of Peter son of Orm, to hold for 20 years rendering 3s. yearly: *Yorks. Deeds*, VIII, 19, no. 48.

41 Original: *Notification to all present and future by William son of Peter of Bretton, that he remits and quitclaims in free alms, to God and St Mary and the abbot and convent of Byland, all right which he and his heirs ever had or may have in those 10 acres and appurtenances in the region of Bretton, that is, in* Trunclyve *and in* Ruchclive, *which they have of his father, Peter, and in pasture for 40 sheep and draught animals which cultivate the land, also given by his father, as contained in his charter (no. 40). The quitclaim is made for the salvation of the soul of the donor and of his ancestors and heirs, and for the benefits which the monks have bestowed on him. Pledge for himself and his heirs not to bring any claim against the abbot and convent and to warranty the grant. Sealed with the donor's seal.* [c. 1180 x c. 1220].

Hiis testibus domino Willelmo de Bretton', domino Roberto de Holand', Michaele de Breitwisell', Iohanne de Deneby, Hugone filio Swani de Bretton, Roberto, Willelmo, Henrico filiis Swani et aliis.

Location: University of Leeds, Bretton Hall, Bretton Estate Archive (Allendale muniments), BEA/C3/B7.13; endorsed: 'C. Willelmi filii Petri filii Orm de remissione iuris sui de x acris et pastura que habemus de dono patris sui. Breton''; 'Benteleya i B. viii', that is, Bentley, first bundle, charter 8; seal: oval, red-brown wax; SIGILLVM . . . . . . PE . . .

Pd: (calendared from the original charter, in the possession of Lord Allendale of Bretton Park, Wakefield) *Yorks. Deeds*, VI, 11, no. 34.

Dating: see *EYC* I, no. 49, III, nos 1812–3, 1815–6 (occurrences of first 3 witnesses).

Note: The cartulary copy has the first four witnesses only and ends 'etc'.

42 Original: *Grant and confirmation in free alms, addressed to all the sons of holy mother church, present and future, by Swane son of Ulkil of Bretton, to God and the monks of St Mary of Byland, of all that rood in the region of Bretton called Smith Royd and of all the land which he had to the west of Smith Royd from the boundaries of Shitlington as far as the water course of Emley to the north of that road which leads from the water course towards Bretton, with the site (sedes) of Smith Royd and with woodland and other easements contained in the same land. Grant also of common pasture throughout the region for 200 sheep by the long hundred and for the draught animals which plough the land. The monks may construct a sheepfold for the said 200 sheep on whatever side of the watercourse they wish, and may enclose and do with the land whatever they wish. The grant is made in free alms, quit of all service, for the salvation of the soul of the donor and of his ancestors and heirs. Pledge to warranty. The monks are to give to the donor and his heirs 6s. yearly, 3s. at Whitsuntide and 3s. at St Martin (11 Nov.).* [1190 x 1218].

His testibus Roberto Walensi, Iohanne de Birkine, Thoma de Horbiry, Adam Phililli (*sic*), Iordano de Hetona, Adam de Mirefeld, Rogero de Tornet', Thoma de Tornetonia.

Location: University of Leeds, Bretton Hall, Bretton Estate Archive (Allendale muniments), BEA/C3/B7.1; endorsed: 'C. Suani de Bretton' de Smytherod'; 'ix'; 'ix'; 'Benteleya i B. ix', that is, Bentley, first bundle, charter 9; seal: round, brown wax; SIGILL . . . FIL . . . HETE . . . WI . . ., and on reverse SIGILL . . . FIL . . . WIL . . .

Pd: (calendared from the original charter, in the possession of Lord Allendale of Bretton Park, Wakefield) *Yorks. Deeds*, V, 6–7, no. 15; (from the cartulary) *EYC* III, no. 1791.

Dating: as no. 240.

Note: The cartulary copy has the first four witnesses only and ends 'etc'. Clay revised Farrer's date in *EYC*, pointing out that Swane was alive as late as 1243, but the attestation of Robert le Waleys suggests a date earlier in the century. In 1243 Swane of Bretton, son of Ulkil, quitclaimed the rent of ½ mark or a heifer to the same value which the abbot and convent were accustomed to pay at St Peter and St Paul during his lifetime only (*Yorks. Deeds*, V, 8, no. 20, endorsed 'Benteleya i B xi', the same endorsement as no. 44).

[fol. 10r–v]

43   Original: *Confirmation in free alms, addressed to all the sons of holy church present and future, by Henry of Bretton, to God and the monks of St Mary of Byland, of the land and pasture which Swane his brother granted in the region of Bretton, to do there whatever the monks wish, free from all secular service, as Swane's charter (no. 42) attests. Pledge to make no claim or injury to the monks concerning the said land, against his brother's charter.* [c. 1190 x 1210].

His testibus Iordano de Heton', Iordano de Floctona, Adam de Mirefeld', Alano de Brettona, Iordano de Denebi, Willelmo filio Willelmi de Denebi.

Location: University of Leeds, Bretton Hall, Bretton Estate Archive (Allendale muniments), BEA/C3/B7.3; endorsed: 'C. Henrici de Brett' de dono Swani'; 'Benteleya i B'; 'Benteleya i B. x', that is, Bentley, first bundle, charter 10; seal: round, red-brown wax; SIGILL' HENRICI FIL VLKIL.

Pd: (calendared from the original charter, in the possession of Lord Allendale of Bretton Park, Wakefield) *Yorks. Deeds*, V, 7, no. 17.

Dating: The confirmation probably dates from the same period as no. 42. Jordan de Heton (Kirkheaton) occurs possibly as early as 1170 and as late as 1215 (*EYC* III, nos 1696, 1705, 1708); Jordan of Flockton attests between 1190 and 1219 (*ibid.*, no. 1811); Adam of Mirfield witnesses possibly as early as 1190 and as late as 1220 (*ibid.*, nos 1765 and 1816). The appearance of Alan of Bretton, who is recorded in 1154 x 1159, and 1180 x 1190 (*ibid.*, nos 1665, 1757, 1760) suggests a date earlier rather than later in the period.

Note: The cartulary copy has the first four witnesses only and ends 'etc'.

[fol. 10v]

44   Original: *Grant, confirmation and quitclaim in free alms, addressed to all the sons of holy mother church present and future, by Swane son of Ulkil of Bretton, for himself and his heirs, to God and the monks of St Mary of Byland, for the salvation of his soul and of all his ancestors and heirs, of the service of 6s. due yearly to him and his heirs from that rood of land called Smith Royd in the region of Bretton, and for easements and for common pasture throughout the region of Bretton for 200 sheep by the long hundred and for draught animals which plough the land, as contained in his charter (no. 42), which the monks have of him. Pledge to warranty.* [1190 x 1220].

Hiis testibus Thoma filio Willelmi, Willelmo de Bretton', Iohanne de Thorhil, Moriz de Ashe, Petro de Birhewait, Alano de Crigl'ton', Willelmo de Thorhil, Adam de Mirefeld, Alano de Witthelaye, Willelmo de Witthelaye.

Location: University of Leeds, Bretton Hall, Bretton Estate Archive (Allendale muniments), BEA/C3/B7.2; endorsed: 'Quietaclamatio Swani de vi sol.'; 'pura'; 'xii'; Bretton''; 'Benteleya i B. xi', that is, Bentley, first bundle, charter 11; seal: oval, red-brown wax; SIGILL . . . FIL . . . VLK'.

Pd: (calendared from the original charter, in the possession of Lord Allendale of Bretton Park, Wakefield) *Yorks. Deeds*, V, 7, no. 16.

Dating: The charter is evidently contemporary with no. 42. If the first witness is the party to no. 38 then this would suggest a date later rather than earlier in the period.

Note: The cartulary copy has the first four witnesses only and ends 'etc'.

45 Original: *Grant and confirmation in free alms, addressed to all the sons of holy mother church present and future, by Hugh son of Swane of Bretton, to God and St Mary and the abbot and convent of Byland, of all the grants made by his father in the region of Bretton, namely, the rood called Smith Royd and all the land which his father granted to the west of Smith Royd, from the boundaries of Shitlington as far as the water course of Emley to the north of the road which runs from the said water course towards Bretton, with the site* (sedes) *of Smith Royd, and with the wood and all other easements contained in the said land, and common pasture throughout the land of the said vill for 200 sheep by the long hundred and for all other draught animals that plough the land. The monks may construct a sheepfold for 200 sheep on whichever side of the watercourse they wish, and enclose the land and do there as they wish. To hold free from all service for the salvation of the soul of the donor and of his father and of all his ancestors and heirs. Pledge to warranty. Sealed with the donor's seal.* [c. 1190 x 1218].

Hiis t(estibus) domino Willelmo Hayrun, Willelmo de Bretton', Thoma de Horebyri, Ada de Criggeleston', Ada de Holand, Michaele de Breretwisel, Henrico de Byri, Willelmo et Roberto filiis Suani, Willelmo de Foxhol' et aliis.

Location: University of Leeds, Bretton Hall, Bretton Estate Archive (Allendale muniments), BEA/C3/B7.8; endorsed: 'Con' Hugonis filii Suani de omnibus donis patris sui'; 'pur''; 'Bretton''; 'Benteleya i B. xii', that is, Bentley, first bundle, charter 12; seal: oval, red-brown wax; SIGILL HVG FIL SWANI.

Pd: (calendared from the original charter in the possession of Lord Allendale of Bretton Park, Wakefield) *Yorks. Deeds*, V, 8–9, no. 21.

Dating: The witnesses suggest a date roughly contemporary with the charters of Hugh's father Swane (nos 42, 44). The latest date is provided by the death of the third witness.

Note: The cartulary copy has an error in 'Mitelingtona' for Shitlington, the scribe evidently misunderstanding the form of capital 'S' in the original: see note to no. 39 above. It has the first two witnesses only and ends 'etc'.

46 Original: *Confirmation in free alms, addressed to all the sons of holy mother church present and future, by Alan son of Adam of Crigglestone* *(near West Bretton), to God and the monks of St Mary of Byland, of that pasture for 200 sheep throughout the region of Bretton and common pasture of the vill granted by Swane of Bretton. The monks are to have and use the pasture peacefully, without claim or disturbance by the donor or his heirs. The confirmation is made for the salvation of the soul of the donor and of all his ancestors and heirs. [c. 1190 x 1220].*

Hiis testibus Rogero decano de Ledesham, Roberto persona de Sandale, Gileberto de Nottona, Iohanne de Birkinge, Rogero de Birking', Matheo de Scepele, Adam de Holand', Willelmo de Bretton', Willelmo de Sothill, Petro de Birthwait, Thoma de Moald, Swano de Brettona, Willelmo de Denebi, Iohanne de Mora, Thoraldo de Brettona.

Location: University of Leeds, Bretton Hall, Bretton Estate Archive (Allendale muniments), BEA/C3/B7.4; endorsed: 'Confirmatio Alani de Crigl'tona de pastura cc ovibus in Bretton"; 'pur"; 'Benteleya i B. xiii', that is, Bentley, first bundle, charter 13; seal: round, red-brown wax; legend, now faded, recorded in *Yorks. Deeds*, V, as SIGILL ALAIN DE CRIGLESTVN.

Pd: (calendared from the original charter, in the possession of Lord Allendale of Bretton Park, Wakefield) *Yorks. Deeds*, V, 7, no. 18.

Dating: The donor made a grant in 1195 x 1216 (*EYC* I, no. 646). The first witness, rural dean of Pontefract, attests in 1191 x 1203 and without title in 1180 x 1185 (*ibid.* II, no. 1122, III, no. 1739). All the other witnesses attest in the late 12th and early 13th centuries. Robert, parson of Sandal Magna, attests in *c*. 1188 x 1202 and 1202 x 1218 (*ibid.* VIII, no. 136, 143, 167, 172). Matthew of Shepley was steward of the earl of Warenne between *c*. 1215 and *c*. 1225 (*ibid.* VIII, 246–7). It would appear that this is roughly contemporary with the other Bretton charters.

Note: The cartulary copy has the first seven witnesses only.

[fol. 11r, old fol. 99r]

BLEATARN (Westm., NY7313), 2 miles south of Warcop (NY7415), in which township Bleatarn lies. Folios 11r–15r are printed by J. E. Burton in 'Charters of Byland Abbey relating to the grange of Bleatarn, Westmorland', *TCWAAS*, 79 (1979), 29–50. The Bleatarn section of the cartulary is an extensive one, with 59 documents and rubrics. The interests of the monks began with the donations of Torphin son of Robert son of Copsi of Warcop and Waitby, made between 1158 and 1167 (no. 47). Torphin was the grandson of Copsi, whose marriage to Godreda, daughter of Hermer Flauncus, brought the fee of Manfield of the Honour of Richmond. Robert, son of Copsi and Godreda, is last recorded *c*. 1148. The family of Torphin continued to be benefactors of Byland: his daughters Agnes and Matilda (nos 74, 80, 81, 82), who became Torphin's heiresses, his son Robert having predeceased his father, and Torphin's brothers, Robert and

Alan (nos 72, 75, 83–5), as well as later generations (nos 77–8, 93–6). The lands controlled by the monks were extensive, and in addition they received, temporarily at least, the church of Warcop (no. 48) and Torphin's chief house there. By 1189 the monks had established a grange (no. 527). Warcop was the centre of the liberty of the abbot and convent in Westmorland (nos 545, 547, 574); the abbot's court was later removed to Appleby (no. 556).

47   *Grant in free alms, addressed to the archbishop of York and the whole chapter of St Peter (York) and all the sons of holy church, by Torphin son of Robert, to God and the monks of St Mary of Byland, of half the land in Warcop within the following boundaries: from the west of the river Eden as the sike runs down from Fouldberhill and crosses through the middle of* Skermund' *into the river Eden, and as the Eden flows to the ancient ditch which is the boundary between Ormside and Warcop, up along the ditch beyond* Thurgarberth, *down into* Hornegile *and up through* Wlvesdalebech *as far as the boundaries which the donor has shown to the monks; from* Wlvesdalebech *eastwards to Crystal Garth, and thence down the stream which runs from Crystal Garth to where it falls into the river which comes from Bleatarn, across it and up to the nearest valley to the west of Fouldberhill and along the valley bottom as far as the sike of* Skermund. *Torphin grants half the land within these bounds in free alms, quit of all service, for the salvation of his soul and of his father and mother and all his own. Pledge to warranty in the presence of the chapter of St Peter, York.* [1158 x 1167].

Hiis testibus Roberto decano Ebor', Iohanne filio Letholdi, Bartholomeo archidiacono et toto capitulo Sancti Petri, etc.

Marginal note: 'Westmerl'' in an ?18th-century hand by the first line of text.

Pd: J. Nicolson and R. Burn, *The History and Antiquities of the Counties of Westmorland and Cumberland*, 2 vols (London, 1777), I, 614–15 (from the original, now lost, then in the possession of Mr James Richardson of Birks 'within the said manor') with further witnesses: quorum nomina ex altera parte chartae descripta sunt, Murdaco decano Westmerland, Roberto filio Willielmi de Kernebi, Thoma de Colevilla, Gaufrido de Daivilla, Roberto clerico de Manefeld et aliis multis qui ex altera parte descripti sunt; (from cartulary): Burton, 'Charters of Byland Abbey', 36, no. 1.

Dating: The three named officials of York Minster. It is possible that the scribe intended to describe John son of Letold as well as Bartholomew as archdeacon, since the date would accord with his period of office (see no. 56).

Note: For notes on the donor and his family, and on the place names which occur in the Bleatarn charters, see Burton, 'Charters of Byland Abbey', 30–31 and 35–6. It is noteworthy that some of the Bleatarn charters were evidently issued in York, in the presence of the chapter of the cathedral church (nos 47, 56, 58, 59). Murdac the dean occurs without further description in nos 48, 53, 55, 60, 89 and 396, as dean of

Westmorland here and in no. 255, and as dean with the chapter of Appleby in no.
50. Thomas de Coleville who attests here was enfeoffed by Roger de Mowbray of
land in Coxwold, Oulston and Yearsley, and first occurs between 1154 and 1157
(*Mowbray Charters*, no. 356). He was a benefactor of Byland (see nos 327, 328) and
attests many Byland charters. Successive generations of the Coleville family took
the name of Thomas, and individuals who attest are difficult to distinguish.

48   *Grant in free alms, addressed to the archbishop of York and the whole
chapter of St Peter (York) and all the sons of holy church, by Torphin of
Waitby son of Robert, son of Copsi, to God and the monks of St Mary of
Byland and their successors, for the salvation of his soul and of all his ancestors and heirs, of his chief house in Warcop with all its appurtenances, and 5
acres with their appurtenances in the region of the same vill between
Harnishow and the Eden at the head of the Eden towards the west, together
with the advowson of Warcop church, and common pasture for all types of
animals at all times of the year, which his father and he had in Stainmore and
Fallows Hill, that is, along the length of the king's highway which runs from
Rerecross towards Brough but not to the south of it, anywhere to the furthest
boundary of the common pasture belonging to Westmorland to the north and
east. They may pasture pigs wherever they wish. He confirms in free alms all
grants made to the monks by his men and everything within his fee which
the monks may acquire in the future. The monks and their men and tenants
are to be free from the suit of pleas at his court. Pledge to warranty. [before
1194].*
Hiis t(estibus) Roberto filio Thorphini, Iohanne Taylboys, Walthevo
de Bereford, Murdaco decano, Roberto filio Petri, etc.

Pd: Burton, 'Charters of Byland Abbey', 37, no. 2.
Dating: death of the grantor.
Note: The monks of Byland failed to retain the advowson of Warcop church. In the
early 13th century Torphin's daughter, Agnes, granted it to Easby Abbey and this
latter grant proved to be more effective than the first; see Burton, 'Charters of
Byland Abbey', 32. In 1242 Richard, parson of Warcop, claimed that a former
parson, Waldef, was seised of certain common in Warcop of land of the abbot
belonging to the church of Warcop from the time of Henry II, taking profits to the
value of ½ mark: *Curia Regis Rolls*, XVII, 112. In a charter not entered in existing
portions of the cartulary Eva, daughter of Gospatrick son of Waldef and wife of
Robert son of Cospatrick, granted to Byland her dower land in Warcop to the west
of 'Skermund' and Fallows Hill, that is, half the land of the grange of Byland.
Torphin son of Robert was surety. See MS Dodsworth 70, fol. 65v.

49   *Rubric: Charter of the same [Torphin son of Robert] concerning the
same 5 acres. Under the same number.* [before 1194].
Dating: death of the grantor.

50 *Grant in free alms, addressed to all the sons of holy church, present and future, by Torphin son of Robert, to God and the monks of St Mary of Byland, of all his part of* Scheremunde *and half* Harinnes, *to hold quit of all service and to do there whatever they wish, for the salvation of the soul of the donor and those of his ancestors and heirs. Pledge to warranty.* [before 1194].

Hiis testibus Willelmo officiali, Murdaco decano et toto capitulo de Appilby, Thoma de Hellebek', Roberto filio Petri, Conano de Asc, Petro Carrou, Unfrido Malkaell, Willelmo filio Willelmi, Roberto de Cabergh, etc.

Pd: Burton, 'Charters of Byland Abbey', 37, no. 4.

Dating: death of the grantor. The last witness was a brother of Torphin son of Robert: see *EYC* V, 54–6. William son of William may be Torphin's son in law: for his marriage to Agnes, daughter of Torphin, see note to no. 73 below.

[fol. 11v]

51 *Grant in free alms, addressed to the archbishop of York and the whole chapter of St Peter (York) and all the sons of holy church, by Torphin son of Robert, to God and the monks of St Mary of Byland, of the whole of Fouldberhill, free from all service, by the following boundaries: down the valley from the watercourse which comes from Bleatarn and crosses into Bermer* (Brimemire), *along the sike that crosses through the middle of Bermer and down into* Skermund. *Grant also of common pasture of the whole of the land which his stepmother held between Fouldberhill and the Eden, and* Skermund *and the Eden, except for meadow and cornfield. This he gives in exchange for 82 acres, granted by him to Robert son of Peter from the land he first gave to the monks and confirmed by his charter. Pledge to warranty with Thomas de Coleville as surety.* [before 1194].

Hiis testibus predicto Thoma de Colvylla, Radulfo de Beuver', Herberto filio Ricardi, Radulfo de Beverlay, etc.

Pd: Burton, 'Charters of Byland Abbey', 38, no. 5.

Dating: death of the grantor.

52 *Confirmation in free alms, addressed to the archbishop of York and the whole chapter of St Peter (York) and all the sons of holy church present and future, by Torphin son of Robert, to God and the monks of St Mary of Byland, of all the lands the monks have or may acquire in his fee in the region of Warcop, and freedom from suit of pleas belonging to him and his heirs. Promise not to distrain on their animals or chattels for any default or forfeit. The confirmation is made for the salvation of the soul of the donor and of all his ancestors and heirs. Pledge to warranty.* [before 1194].

Hiis testibus Ranulpho filio Walteri, Roberto fratre meo, Thoma de Hellebek, Roberto filio Petri, Humfrido Malkael', etc.

Pd: Burton, 'Charters of Byland Abbey', 38, no. 6.
Dating: death of the grantor.

53 *Grant in free alms, addressed to the archbishop of York and the whole chapter of St Peter (York) and all the sons of holy church, by Robert son of Torphin of Warcop, to God and the monks of St Mary of Byland, of all his part of* Harrun *in the region of Warcop, that is, three parts of a moiety of* Harrun. *The grant is made for the salvation of his soul and that of his wife Juliana, and for the salvation of all his ancestors and heirs. The monks are to do with the land as they wish. Pledge to warranty.* [1158 x c. 1190].

Hiis testibus Murdaco decano, Roberto sacerdote, Roberto de Ormesheved, etc.

Pd: Burton, 'Charters of Byland Abbey', 38–9, no. 7.
Dating: possibly as early as 1158 x 1167 (see no. 56); however Murdac, rural dean, suggests a date later in the century, as does the form of warranty.
Note: The identity of the donor is not certain. Torphin son of Robert, grantor of nos 47–52, and his wife Agnes, had a son named Robert, who may have predeceased his parents (Burton, 'Charters of Byland Abbey', 30). This may be the grantor of the present charter and of nos 54 and 55. In no. 56 Robert son of Torphin is described as holding land of Torphin son of Robert, and as the nephew of Walleve de Berford (see also nos 58, 59). If this is the same Robert son of Torphin, then Walleve his uncle may have been the brother of Agnes, wife of Torphin son of Robert. The close association of Walleve with the charters of Torphin and his family reinforce this suggestion (see nos 48, 58, 59, 64, 72, 73, 74).

54 *Rubric: Charter of the same [Robert son of Torphin] concerning 1½ acres next to the* cultura *on* Lostrum. [2nd half of 12th cent.].

Marginal note: Blaterne B(aculus) i.

[fol. 11v–12r]

55 *Grant in free alms, addressed to the archbishop of York and all the sons of holy mother church, by Robert son of Torphin, to God and the monks of Byland, of all his part of the land of Foulderberhill. To hold of the donor and his heirs quit of all service, for his soul and that of his wife, and those of his father and mother and all his kin* (parentes) *and all his ancestors. Pledge to warranty.* [2nd half of 12th cent.].

Hiis testibus Murdaco decano, Acea sacerdote, Adam (*sic*) sacerdote de Morlunda, Roberto capellano, etc.

Pd: Burton, 'Charters of Byland Abbey', 39, no. 9.
Dating: first witness.

[fol. 12r, old fol. 100]

56 *Grant in free alms, addressed to the archbishop of York and the whole chapter of St Peter (York) and all the sons of holy church, by Robert son of Torphin, to God and the monks of St Mary of Byland, of the land which he had in Warcop within the following boundaries, as specified in (no. 47). This is three parts of that half which the donor and his uncle Walleve held of Torphin son of Robert; Torphin son of Robert has granted the other half contained within the said boundaries (see no. 47). To hold of the donor and his heirs free from all service, for the salvation of the donor's soul and of his father and mother and all his own. Pledge to warranty before the chapter of St Peter's, York.* [1158 x 1167].

Hiis testibus Roberto decano Ebor', Iohanne filio Letholdi et Bartholomeo archidiaconibus (*sic*), Willelmo cantore, Swano magistro hospitalis Sancti Petri, Ernulfo Sotawaina, Symone de Sigillo, Thoma de Ramavilla, etc.

Pd: Burton, 'Charters of Byland Abbey', 39–40, no. 10.

Dating: first three witnesses, who also attest nos 47, 58 and 59; presumably all four charters were issued on the same occasion.

57 *Rubric: Attestation of Robert, archdeacon of Carlisle, of the grant of Robert son of Torphin of land in Warcop (no. 56).* [1158 x 1167].

Dating: As no. 56. Archdeacon Robert of Carlisle first occurs in 1151, perhaps earlier and was probably dead by 1191: *Fasti Monastic Cathedrals*, p. 23.

58 *Confirmation in free alms, addressed to the archbishop of York and the whole chapter of St Peter (York) and all the sons of holy church, by Walleve de Berford, to God and the monks of St Mary of Byland, of the grant of Robert son of Torphin of land in Warcop, as attested in his charter (no. 56). This confirmation is made for the salvation of the soul of the donor and of his father and mother and all his kin.* [1158 x 1167].

Hiis testibus Roberto decano Ebor', Iohanne filio Letholdi et Bartholomeo archidiaconibus (*sic*), et toto capitulo Sancti Petri, Thoma de Colvilla, etc.

Pd: Burton, 'Charters of Byland Abbey', 40, no. 12.

Dating: first three witnesses, who also attest nos 47, 56 and 59.

[fol. 12r–v]

59 *Grant in free alms, addressed to the archbishop of York and the whole chapter of St Peter (York) and all the sons of holy church, by Walleve de Berford, to God and the monks of St Mary of Byland, of all his part of land in Warcop within the following boundaries, as specified in (no. 47) and (no. 56). He gives this as the fourth part of the half which he held of Torphin son of*

*Robert; Torphin son of Robert has granted the other half (no. 47). Pledge as
in (no. 56).* [1158 x 1167].

Hiis testibus Roberto decano Ebor', Iohanne filio Letholdi et
Bartholomeo archdiaconibus (*sic*), Willelmo cantore, Swano magistro
hospitalis, Ernulfo Sotovaina, etc.

Pd: Burton, 'Charters of Byland Abbey', 40, no. 13.

Dating: first three witnesses, who also attest nos 47, 56 and 58. Nos 56 and 59 have
the next three witnesses in common.

[fol. 12v]

60   *Grant in free alms, addressed to the archbishop of York and the whole
chapter of St Peter (York) and all the sons of holy church, by John Tailbois, to
God and the monks of St Mary of Byland, of all the land with all its liberties
which Robert son of Torphin granted him and his heirs in fee and hereditary
right, from the west part of the river Eden, that is, all the lands which Ulf
Burgensis held of the said Robert, and Robert's whole demesne, except for the
part which Henry the cleric had in* Langesite. *He grants all this so that the
monks may assart, build and do whatever they wish with the lands. Pledge to
warranty in front of witnesses with Murdac, dean, as surety.* [before 1191].

Hiis testibus Roberto archidiacono Carleol' et Murdaco decano,
Henrico capellano archidiac(oni), Roberto capellano de Appilby, etc.

Pd: Burton, 'Charters of Byland Abbey', 41, no. 14.

Dating: death of first witness. See no. 57.

Note: Nicolson and Burn, *Westmorland*, I, 614, note the existence of an original
charter, and add witnesses Umfrey Malus-Catulus, Michael de Hardcle (Harcla in
no. 89) etc. The donor attests several of the Bleatarn deeds (nos 48, 69, 71, 74, 82,
89).

61   *Rubric: Charter concerning the same land and demesne. Surrendered.*

Marginal note: B(aculus) i.

Note: No grantor is named and it is not certain if nos 61 and 62 are related to no. 60.

62   *Rubric: Confirmation of the same by Robert son of Torphin.* [before
1194].

Dating: death of the grantor.

63   *Rubric: Confirmation by Torphin son of Robert of all the lands which
the monks have from Robert son of Torphin and John Tailbois.* [before 1194].

Dating: death of the grantor.

64   *Rubric: Confirmation by the same [Torphin son of Robert] of that grant
which his men Walleve de Berford and Robert son of Torphin made (nos 56
and 58).* [before 1194].

Dating: death of the grantor.

65 *Grant in free alms, addressed to all the sons of holy mother church to whom this present writing shall come, by Eva of Warcop daughter of Malreward of Appleby in her widowhood, to God and the monks of St Mary of Byland, of that* cultura *of land in the region of Warcop which lies between the two* culture *which the monks have of John Tailbois east of the road which runs from the Eden to Bleatarn; the* cultura *begins at the land of Warcop church and extends to that road. Further grant of 2 acres and 1 perch in the tofts west of the land which the monks have of Richard Trodherai. The grant is made free from all service to do there whatever the monks wish, for the salvation of the soul of the donor and of her father and mother and all her ancestors and heirs. Pledge to warranty.* [late 12th cent. or later].
Hiis testibus Gervasio capellano de Warcop', Galfrido senescallo de Watheby, etc.
Pd: Burton, 'Charters of Byland Abbey', 41–2, no. 19.
Dating: reference to John Tailbois.

66 *Rubric: Confirmation of the same by Geoffrey son of Eva.* [late 12th cent. or later].
Marginal note: b(aculus) ii.
Dating: The donor was presumably the son of the grantor of no. 65 and the two charters may have been issued at the same time.

67 *Rubric: Charter of Alan son of Wigan concerning a half carucate in Warcop rendering 5s. yearly for all service.*

68 *Rubric: Charter of Girard son of Robert concerning 1 toft and croft in Warcop, etc.*

69 *Rubric: Chirograph charter of Richard son of Ketel concerning a carucate in Warcop called Ploughlands, rendering 20s. and performing forinsec service and service to the lords of the land.*
Original: *Notification to all the faithful in Christ by the abbot and convent of St Mary of Byland that they had received from Richard son of Ketel 1 carucate in Warcop to hold of him and his heirs in fee farm free from all secular service, rendering 20s. yearly for all service, 10s. at Easter and 10s. at St Michael (29 Sept.) and performing forinsec service to the king; Richard and his heirs will render service to their lords; pledge to warranty by Richard, with Thomas son of Gospatrick as his witness and pledge.* [before 1194].

His testibus Thoma de [Hillbek], <Gervasio> de Daencurt, Roberto filio Roberti de Sulebi, Iohanne Tailebois, Ricardo Anglico, Willelmo filio Roberti de Ascabi, Willelmo de Wichintun, Alano de Peningtona, Nivello de Smeredala, Roberto filio Ulfi.

Location: Carlisle, Cumbria Record Office, D/Mus (Musgrave of Edenhall Archives), Box 48; endorsed: Blaterne B iii in fine.
Dating: The grant was confirmed by Torphin son of Robert (MS Dodsworth 70, fol. 65r), for which see no. 71, note.
Note: The name of the second witness is conjectured from no. 71.

[fol. 13r, old fol. 101]

70 *Quitclaim in free alms, addressed to all the faithful of Christ who will see or hear this charter, by Thomas de Newton, son and heir of Richard de Newton, to God and St Mary and the abbot and convent of Byland, for himself and his heirs, for the salvation of his soul and of his father and mother and of all his ancestors and heirs, of that carucate in Warcop called Ploughlands, with all appurtenances, in woodland, plain, roads and paths, meadows, pastures, water, ponds, fishponds, mills, moors, marshes and heathland and other easements, inside and outside the vill, which Richard son of Ketel granted. To hold quit of all service. Pledge to warranty. Sealed with the donor's seal. [mid or late 13th cent.].*

Hiis testibus dominis Ranulpho de Dakerr', Thoma de Musegrave, Ricardo de Crepinges, etc.

Pd: Burton, 'Charters of Byland Abbey', 42, no. 24.
Dating: witnesses.
Note: Ploughlands lies approximately ½ mile south of Warcop.

71 *Rubric: Charter of Richard son of Ketel concerning Ploughlands [to be held] for 20s.* [before 1194].

Text: MS Dodsworth 70, fol. 65r: Demise and confirmation, addressed to all present and future, by Richard son of Ketel, to God and the monks of St Mary of Byland, for the love of God and the salvation of the soul of his lord, Torphin, of that carucate of land which he had in Warcop in fee farm for 20s. yearly to him and his heirs, 10s. at Easter and 10s. at St Michael (29 Sept.), performing forinsec service and saving service to his lord. Pledge to warranty with Thomas son of Gospatrick as his surety. Hiis testibus Gervasio de Daincurt, Thoma de Hellebec, Iohanne Taillebois, Willelmo de Askebi, Roberto filio Roberti de Sulebi, Willelmo [MS Willelmi] de Withington, Ricardo le Engleis, Alano de Peningtun, Nigello de Smeredala, Roberto filio Ulfi.

Dating: The grant was confirmed by Torphin son of Robert (MS Dodsworth 70, fol.

65r, evidently transcribed from the original as there is a note: in dorso: Blaterne confirmatio Thorphini conventionis inter Ric(ardum) fil(ium) Ketelli et nos de carucata terre in Wardecop). There is another copy of Torphin's confirmation in MS Top. Yorks. e. 7, fols 140v–141r (old pp. 228–9), which reads 'Sinerdala' for 'Smeredala'.

Note: For related documents see nos 69 and 70.

72   *Rubric: Confirmation by Torphin son of Robert and his brother Robert of the whole grant of Walleve de Berford (no. 59).* [before 1194].

Dating: first grantor dead by 1194.

Note: Original charter (now lost) noted by Nicolson and Burn, *Westmorland*, I, 615. They state that it also confirmed grants by Robert son of Torphin, John Tailbois and Richard son of Ketel (see nos 53, 54, 55, 56, 60, 69, 71). Witnesses William son of William, Thomas of Helbeck, Robert son of Peter, Conan de Aske, William son of Robert of Asby, Gilbert and Adam his brothers, Richard Anglicus, William his son, Robert of Helton, Richard son of Matilda, Gilbert his son, Robert son of Copsi and John his brother.

73   *Rubric: Confirmation by William son of William and Hugh son of Jernegan, with the assent of their wives Agnes and Matilda, daughters of Torphin (son of Robert of Waitby) of all the lands which the monks have of Torphin son of Robert in Westmorland, and of the grant of Walleve de Berford, etc.* [1194 x 1198].

Dating: Between the death of Torphin and that of the first grantor.

Note: Agnes daughter of Torphin son of Robert married (1) William son of William son of Waldef of Hepple (Northumb.), who was dead by 1198, and (2) in 1200 Adam son of Adam Paynel of Broughton (Lincs.) who was dead by 1224 (*EYC* VI, 264–9); she died without heirs *c.* 1231. Her sister Matilda married (1) Hugh son of Jernegan of the Tanfield fee, Honour of Richmond (died 1201 x 1203), (2) Nicholas de Bueles, (3) Philip de Burgh (died before May 1235), and (4) John de Auno. See *EYC* V, 53–8, 165–6.

74   *Confirmation in free alms, addressed to the archbishop of York and the whole chapter of St Peter (York), by Agnes daughter of Torphin of Waitby, to God and the monks of St Mary of Byland, of all her part of the land which Walleve de Berford had in demesne in Warcop and those 2 bovates which Geoffrey Ruffus and Gille held of Walleve in the vill; also of her share of that land called* Sigeridehuses *with tofts and crofts and all other appurtenances, and her part of Warcop mill. Pledge to warranty. The grant is made in her widowhood, quit of all secular service, to do there as the monks wish, for the salvation of the soul of the donor and of all her ancestors and heirs. Pledge to warranty.* [*c.* 1198 x 1200 or 1224 x 1231].

Hiis testibus Thoma de Hellebek', Willelmo filio Roberti, Iohanne Tayleboys, etc.

Pd: Burton, 'Charters of Byland Abbey', 43, no. 28.

Dating: Either between the death of donor's first husband (by 1198) and her second marriage, or after the death of her second husband. See no. 73.

fol. 13r–v

75 *Notification to all present and future, by Alan son of Robert of Warcop that he received a charter from Robert, abbot of Byland, which he recites. Grant by Abbot Robert of Byland and the convent in fee farm to Alan son of Robert of Warcop, son of Copsi, of all the right they have in Warcop mill, which the monks hold of the gift of Agnes de Moreville, daughter and co-heiress of Torphin son of Robert son of Copsi of Waitby. Alan and his heirs are to hold this rendering 1 basket of flour and 3 bushells of malt yearly at St Martin in Winter (11 Nov.). Witnessed by Gikel prior, Ansketil subprior, Orm of Appleby cellarer, Uspak de Langeton his colleague* (socius) *and the whole convent, and sealed with their seal. Alan seals this charter.* [c. 1219 x 1229, possibly spurious].

Hiis testibus Ada Paynel seniore, Roberto filio Waldevi, Willelmo de Morevill, Willelmo de Morlund, etc.

Copy: MS Dodsworth 70, fol. 66r–v, where recited in a notification by Henry of Warcop, that Alan son of Robert, his grandfather, received and held a charter of Abbot Robert and the convent concerning his right and claim in the mill of Warcop. The witness list omits 'etc' and continues: Ada de Louther, Serlone de Burgo capellano, qui scripsit hoc scriptum. Henry's confirmation is dated at Byland, St Andrew (30 Nov.) 1331, and was evidently issued at the same time as no. 76, whose witnesses it shares. MS Dodsworth 70 has a sketch of the seal and a family tree deriving from Copsi of Warcop.

Pd: Burton, 'Charters of Byland Abbey', 43–4, no. 29.

Dating: Abbot Robert of Byland, but the first witness, father of Adam Paynel the younger who married Agnes daughter of Torphin, died *c.* 1205. It is possible that 'seniore' is a copyist's error for 'iuniore', but the charter may have been forged to support a claim to the rent.

Note: The donor was probably the youngest of the three sons of Robert son of Copsi. For grants by him see nos 83–5 and 103–4 below.

[fol. 13v]

76 *Indenture made between the abbot and convent of Byland and Henry of Warcop son of Richard of Warcop, by which the abbot and convent demise to Henry their land in the region of Warcop called Ploughlands, 7 acres in Thornhow, 2 acres in* Staynbothem, *3 acres in* Greglistedes, *1 acre of meadow in* Thistelsete, *1 acre of woodland and meadow in* Turnemyre, *and a basket of flour and 3 bushells of malt from Warcop mill, with easement of pasture for Henry's animals in the pasture of Bleatarn outside meadow and crops. To hold for 40 years from the day of this agreement. If Henry dies within this term the land and rent shall revert to the abbot and convent with* *no claim by Henry's heirs, assigns or executors. His executors, however, may remove his chattels within the year following his death. Sealed with the seals of both parties.* Byland; St Andrew [30 Nov.] 1331.

Hiis testibus domino Iohanne de Rossegile milite, Willelmo le Engleys de Askeby, Roberto de Sandeford vic(ecomite) Westmer', etc.

Pd: Burton, 'Charters of Byland Abbey', 44, no. 30.

77   *Letters patent with quitclaim in free alms by Henry of Warcop son of Richard of Warcop, to God and St Mary and the abbot and convent of Byland and their successors, of 20s. annual rent which the monks were accustomed to render to him for 1 carucate called Ploughlands in the region of Warcop and which 20s. the donor had of the grant of Thomas de Newton by his charter (no. 78) which Henry has handed over to the abbot and convent along with other muniments which he had relating to the rent (nos 78–9). The quitclaim is made for the salvation of his soul and of his heirs and ancestors. Promise to make no further claim and pledge to warranty. Sealed with his seal.* Warcop; St Martin in Winter [11 Nov.] 1331.

No witnesses.

Pd: Burton, 'Charters of Byland Abbey', 44–5, no. 31.

[fols 13v–14r]

78   *Grant and confirmation, addressed to all who hear and see this writing, by Thomas de Newton, to Henry of Warcop and his heirs and assigns of 20s. annual rent paid by the abbot and convent of Byland for a* cultura *called Ploughlands in the vill of Warcop, to be paid in the same way as they have paid Thomas. Sealed with his seal.* Warcop; Mon. after Decollation of St John the Baptist, 1 Edward I [4 Sept. 1273]. Apparently corrupt. French.

Par icelles testmoignes Ric' de Blenkansop, Thomas de Warcop dounques viscount de Westmerland, William de Helton', et altres.

Pd: Burton, 'Charters of Byland Abbey', 45, no. 32.

Note: For problems with this and no. 79 see Burton, 'Charters of Byland Abbey', 33–4. The date of 1273 is almost certainly too early for Henry of Warcop (if identified with the grantor of no. 77) to have been enfeoffed. The second witness was not sheriff until 1327. A date of 1 Edward III would be more likely than 1 Edward I, 'Edward le fitz Henry' in the text.

[fol. 14r, old fol. 102]

79   *Notification addressed to the abbot and convent of Byland by Thomas, son of Thomas de Newton, of his grant as in no. 78. Sealed with his seal.* Warcop; Monday after the Decollation of St John the Baptist, 1 Edward I [4 Sept. 1273]. Apparently corrupt. French.

Par iceux testmoignes Ric' de Blenkansopp', Thomas de Warcopp' dounq viscount de Westmer', William de Covenale, etc.

Pd: Burton, 'Charters of Byland Abbey', 45, no. 33.

Dating: see note to no. 78.

80 *Rubric: Confirmation by Adam Paynel of the grant of his wife Agnes, daughter of Torphin, of Ploughlands.* [1200 x c. 1224].

Text: This may be the charter copied into MS Dodsworth 94, fol. 14v, no. 14, from the original in St Mary's Tower, York, where the heading locates the land in 'Sigeridhouse'. Confirmation, addressed to all the sons of holy church present and future, by Adam Paynel, to God and the monks of St Mary of Byland, of the grant of his wife, Agnes, daughter of Torphin, in the region of Warcop, as her charter attests, to hold free from service for the salvation of Adam's soul and of his ancestors and heirs, to do there as the monks wish. Pledge to warranty. Hiis testibus Eudone de Bellocampo, vicecomite Westm', Willelmo de Qwichet, Adam de Musgrava, Iohanne de Heltona, Gaufrido de Watebi, Gilberto de Ascabi, Hugone de Cottesford, Thoma de Heltona. Sketch of seal. Headed 'confirmatio Ade Painel iunioris de Sigeridhouse in Wardecop ut in dorso'.

Dating: Marriage of Agnes and Adam Paynel, and death of Adam; see note to no. 73.

81 *Rubric: Charter of Matilda, daughter of Torphin son of Robert, concerning her part of* Sitherildhus *[to hold] for forinsec service to the lords.* [1194 x c. 1235].

Dating: Between the death of Torphin and that of Matilda: see note to no. 73.

82 *Rubric: Quitclaim by Agnes de Moreville and Matilda of the suit of pleas belonging to them and their heirs.* [1194 x c. 1231].

Text: MS Dodsworth 70, fol. 66r. Grant and confirmation, addressed to all the sons of holy mother church present and future, by Agnes de Moreville, daughter of Torphin, to God and St Mary and the monks of Byland, of all pleas in the lands which they hold of her fee, in demesne or at farm. She forbids anyone to molest the monks or their men or their cottars in connection with those pleas. This grant is made for the salvation of her soul and of all her ancestors and heirs. Pledge to warranty. Hiis testibus Roberto filio Petri, Thoma de Hellebec, Iohanne Taillebois, Willelmo de Askebi, Uliano de Mortona, Roberto de Rihle, Nicolao filio suo, Herberto de Tibay, Alano <word deleted>, Br . . .ci (*sic*).

Dating: Between the death of Torphin and that of Agnes; see note to no. 73.

83 *Rubric: Charter of Alan of Warcop concerning land between the meadow of* Chermund (Skermund) *and the* cultura *of Stocking.* [late 12th or early 13th cent.].

Dating: The grantor occurs in the early 13th cent. (above, no. 75), and below no. 85.

84 *Rubric: Charter of the same [Alan of Warcop] concerning 1 acre between the* cultura *of Stocking and his own half carucate.* [late 12th or early 13th cent.].

Dating: as no. 83.

85 *Rubric: Charter of Alan son of Robert of Warcop concerning 1 toft and meadow at the head of the said toft [and stretching] as far as the stream which descends through the centre of the vill.*

Original: *Grant in free alms, addressed to all the sons of holy mother church to whom the present writing shall come, by Alan son of Robert of Warcop, to God and St Mary and the monks of Byland serving God there, of the whole toft in Warcop between the house of William de Trefrman and that of Thomas son of Andrew towards the east, and the meadow at the head of the toft as far as the stream running through the centre of the vill, with appurtenances and common pasture. Pledge to warranty.* [late 12th or early 13th cent.].

Hiis testibus domino Ada decano de Askebia, domino Ada persona de Mileburne, domino Toma persona de Ormeshefed, domino Willelmo filio Simonis, Waltero capellano de Musegraf, Stefano de Sandford, Willelmo filio Goldeburhe, et multis aliis.

Location: Carlisle, Cumbria Record Office, D/Mus (Musgrave of Edenhall Archives), Box 48; endorsed: Blaterne . . . xxxi; C. Alani filii Roberti de Wardecop de uno tofto.

Dating: The grantor occurs in the early 13th cent. (above, no. 75).

86 *Rubric: Charter of Adam son of Geoffrey of Waitby concerning 2 bovates in the region of Warcop [held by] William son of Huck.* [late 12th or early 13th cent.].

Dating: see no. 87.

87 *Rubric: Confirmation by Geoffrey of Waitby father of the said Adam concerning the same 2 bovates.* [late 12th or early 13th cent.]

Text: MS Top. Yorks. e. 9, fol. 25v (old p. 24). Notification, addressed to all the sons of holy mother church, by Geoffrey of Waitby, that he has confirmed to Byland 2 bovates with appurtenances and easements inside and outside the vill, namely, those that Adam his son granted in alms to the monks, free from all service except for forinsec service that the monks will do, as laid down in Adam's charter. Pledge to warranty. H(iis) testibus Ada persona de Askebi tunc decano, Thoma persona de Ormesheved, Thoma capellano de Warthecop, Alano de Warthecop, Iohanne de Heltona, Thomas de Heltona, Willelmo de Santford, Willelmo filio Gaufridi de Wateby.

Dating: A number of the witnesses attest no. 85.

88 *Rubric: Charter of Richard of Hipswell (NR) concerning 1 toft and croft in Warcop between the house of Torky and the lord's* cultura.

Original: *Grant in free alms, addressed to all the faithful in Christ, by Robert of Hipswell, to God and St Mary of Byland and the monks serving God there, of 1 toft and croft in Warcop between the house of Tocki and the* cultura *of Robert de Vipont, with easements and its common pasture. This grant is made by the prompting of love. Pledge to warranty.* [late 12th or early 13th cent.].

Hiis testibus Willelmo de Hareb', Roberto de Helleb', Alano de Warhecop, Willelmo filio Symonis, Simone Brutone, Henrico de Suerdall', Wydone filio suo, Gilberto de Kaberg', Th(oma) de Kaber', et aliis.

Location: Carlisle, Cumbria Record Office, D/Mus (Musgrave of Edenhall Archives), Box 48; endorsed: Blaterne B iii. xxxiiii; C Roberti de Hipleswell de uno tofto et crofto.

Dating: third witness: see no. 85 and note.

Note: The name 'Richard' in the rubric seems to be an error for Robert.

[fol. 14r–v]

89 Original: *Agreement made in the king's court at Appleby between Torphin son of Robert, Robert son of Peter, the monks of Byland, Walleve of Warcop and Robert son of Faith concerning Robert son of Peter's claim to common pasture between Bleatarn and Musgrave. Robert son of Peter is to retain 82 acres from the spur of Huber Hill across the sike below* Maurebergh *as far as the watercourse towards Musgrave. The monks are to retain everything from the spur towards the grange and as far as the watercourse beside the chapel by the boundaries which they have made and perambulated. The animals of neither Robert nor the monks are to enter into the territory of the other. Robert is to have an exit for his animals from Musgrave onto* Maurebergh *between the monks'* cultura *and the valley below Huber Hill by the bounds that they have perambulated beside the meadow, and to have there common pasture as far as the fishpond and from there as far as the road above Crystal Garth which leads towards Appleby, and as far as the* *quarry and then to the head of the fishpond, as perambulated. All this is to be common pasture for the animals of Musgrave and those of the monks but the monks will plough the* cultura *beside the mill ditch as far as the fishpond as perambulated and have their* cultura *on* Maurebergh *and their own meadow as they had before this agreement, and they shall plough nothing more than this. Torphin and Robert have warrantied before their local fellows that they and their heirs will hold faithfully to this agreement. Animals straying to be charged at one penny for twenty, according to the custom of the province.* Appleby; [before 1194].

coram Willelmo filio Hervei ballivo et Murdaco decano et Thoma de Hellebec et Thoma filio Cospatricii et Roberto de Kabergh' et Iohanne Taillebois et Conano de Asc et Willelmo de Aschebi et Ricardo Anglico et Henrico de Cund' et Stephano de Tyrnebi et Rogero Winkenel et Roberto filio Ricardi et Willelmo de Lather et Thoma fratre eius et Herberto clerico, Michaele de Harcla et Waltero filio [eius] et ceteris probis hominibus qui tunc fuerunt ibi presentes.

Location: Carlisle, Cumbria Record Office, D/Mus (Musgrave of Edenhall Archives), Box 48.
Pd: (calendared from original) Nicolson and Burn, *Westmorland*, I, 615–16; (from cartulary) Burton, 'Charters of Byland Abbey', 46–7, no. 43.
Dating: death of the first party.
Note: The cartulary copy includes only first three witnesses, and continues: et ceteris probis hominibus qui tunc fuerunt ibi presentes. The monastic grange at Warcop was stated in a grant of Henry III to have been confirmed by Henry II and Richard I, indicating that it was in existence by 1189 at the latest: see below no. 527 (*Cal. Ch. R. 1226–1257*, I, 314). The charter states that it was issued *in curia domini regis* at Appleby. This refers to the shire court, at which the bailiff was presiding.

[fol. 14v]
90 *Agreement between the monks of St Mary of Byland and Robert son of Robert son of Peter by which Robert demises a spring which rises to the south of their fishpond within their common pasture. He allows them to channel water underground in drains to the offices of their grange as they wish. Repairs to the conduit are to be done by the monks and not to impede Robert's pasture. This grant is made for 1 silver mark which the monks have paid at the making of the agreement.* Appleby; Whitsuntide [9 June] 1196.

Hiis testibus Hugone filio Gernegan, Willelmo filio Roberti de Askeby, Ricardo Anglico, Willelmo filio eius, Waltero filio Durandi, etc.

Marginal note: 7 R I, written in a later hand.
Pd: Burton, 'Charters of Byland Abbey', 47, no. 44.
Note: The donor was probably the son of the main party in no. 89.

91 *Notification to all present and future by Warin son of Ralph of Musgrave of his grant in free alms to God and St Mary and the abbot and convent of Byland serving God and St Mary, of all his land in the* cultura *called Stocking in the region of Warcop. The grant is made for the salvation of his soul and of his ancestors. Pledge to warranty. Sealed with the donor's seal. [c. 1250 x 1282].*

Hiis testibus Thoma de Helleb', Iohanne de Morvyll', Alano de Cabergh' militibus, etc.

Pd: Burton, 'Charters of Byland Abbey', 47–8, no. 45.

Dating: The second witness was still living in 1277 and 1278, and was dead by 1282. His son, Robert, married the widow of the third witness, and died without heirs in 1290. See G. S. H. L. Washington, *Early Westmorland MPs, 1258–1327,* CWAAS Tract Series, 15 (1959), pp. 57–8.

92 *Rubric: Confirmation by Bishop Bernard of Carlisle of all lands and possessions of the monks within his diocese. [May 1203 x July 1214].*

Marginal note: B(aculus) iii.

Dating: Bishop Bernard of Carlisle.

93 *Rubric: Chirograph between the monks and the church of Warcop concerning the annual payment of 1 pound of incense for certain tithes.*

94 *Rubric: Chirograph between the monks and Richard son of Alan of Warcop concerning his closes, buildings and vaccaries, as contained in the beginning of the agreement. Richard is to render 4s. yearly.*

Note: The donor was the grandson or great-grandson of Robert son of Copsi. For Alan see nos 75, 83–5 and 103–4. Richard may have been the father of Henry of Warcop (nos 76, 77, 78). The Latin word 'vaccaria', here translated 'vaccary', can mean cow pasture or grazing farm.

95 *Rubric: Chirograph with the same [Richard son of Alan of Warcop] concerning waste beside Burtergill. Richard is to render 3s. yearly.*

96 *Rubric: Chirograph between the monks and Richard of Warcop concerning the quitclaim of the monks' rights in the* cultura *called Brackenber for the payment of 3s.*

97 *Rubric: Chirograph between the monks and Master William de Coldyngton concerning land which the monks have of the grant of Thomas chaplain of Warcop, rendering to the monks 3½d.*

98 *Rubric: Charter of Thomas chaplain of Warcop concerning a half carucate there. [c. 1240].*

Text: MS Top. Yorks. e. 8, fol. 138r (old p. 240). Notification to all present and future by Thomas, chaplain of Warcop, of his grant and confirmation by this charter which is strengthened by his seal, to God and St Mary and the abbot and convent of Byland, of a half carucate in the vill and region of Warcop, which he had of the grant of Gerard of Hipswell, of which half carucate William de Baywath held 2 bovates of the donor. To hold in free alms, free from all service and demand and suit of court etc. The grant is made for the salvation of his soul and of his ancestors and heirs. Pledge to warranty. Sealed. Hiis testibus Gilberto de Kyrketona vicecomite Westmorlundie, Thoma Cabergh, Adam nepote suo, Willelmo filio meo, Thoma de Musegrava, Thoma de Eltona, Roberto de Cotisford, To(ma) de Wardecoppa, Henrico de Ouleby, et multis aliis.

Dating: Gilbert de Kirketon accounted for Westmorland in 26 Henry III (*Pipe Roll, 26 Henry III*, p. 19).

99 *Rubric: Charter of Girard son of Robert concerning the same. Surrendered.*

100 *Rubric: Chirograph with William son of Thomas the chaplain concerning 2 bovates which have been exchanged, rendering to the monks 6s. yearly.*

Note: The word 'capellanus' has been abbreviated and it is not certain if it relates to William or Thomas.

101 *Rubric: Bond of the same [William son of Thomas] concerning 1 toft and croft which have been exchanged.*

102 *Rubric: Charter of William son of William de Herlyngtona concerning his villein Elias and his family. Copied.*

[fol. 15r, old fol. 103r]
103 *Rubric: Quitclaim by Alan of Warcop of Thomas Causty and his family.*

104 *Rubric: Charter of the same [Alan of Warcop] concerning Thomas Causty and his family.*

105 *Rubric: Quitclaim by Robert of Helbeck (Westm.) of all right against Ralph de Holegile and his family.*

[fol. 15v]
BUBWITH (SE7136), township and parish in the wapentake of Harthill (ER). The cartulary section is incomplete, with three folios (old fols 105–107) lost. However it is clear from MS Top. Yorks. d. 11, that the

section relates to the church of Bubwith, one of three churches appropriated to Byland. This was a late acquisition, granted by John de Mowbray in 1349 (no. 106 and note).

106   *Grant and confirmation in free alms, addressed to all the faithful in Christ to whom the present writing shall come, by John de Mowbray, lord of Axholme (Lincs.), to his beloved in Christ the abbot and convent of Byland in the diocese of York and their successors, of the advowson of a moiety of Bubwith church, with its appurtenances. This grant and confirmation is made from the prompting of love and for the salvation of the soul of his wife Joan, who is buried before the high altar at Byland, and for the souls of their ancestors and heirs. For the same souls and for the health of the conventual church of Byland he grants licence to appropriate the same and hold it for their own use notwithstanding the Statute of Lands in Mortmain. Pledge to warranty. Sealed with the donor's seal.* Epworth (Lincs.); 3 Sept. 1349. No witnesses.

Copies: MS Top. Yorks. e. 7, fols 123v–124r (old pp. 194–5); MS Top. Yorks. e. 9, fol. 56r (old p. 85).

Note: On the donor, see *CP* IX, 380–3. His first wife Joan, sixth and youngest daughter of Henry, earl of Lancaster, died on 7 July (?1349) and was buried at Byland. A moiety of the church of Bubwith was held by the dean and chapter of York. Between *c.* 1138 and 1143 Warin of Bubwith granted to the church of St Peter, York, the church founded in his fee saving the right of William of Winchester, canon of York, with 1 carucate of land, and his grant was confirmed by Roger de Mowbray (*YMF* I, 51–2, nos 1–2; *Mowbray Charters*, no. 321). However, it is clear from a confirmation by Robert, dean, and the chapter of York, to William of Winchester, that the church was already in moieties (*YMF* I, no. 4). Archbishop Henry Murdac confirmed the grant made by Eustace fitz John to William of Winchester of a moiety of the church of Bubwith, and instituted William in the same on the mandate and verbal instruction of Eustace, at the same time as confirming the moiety which William formerly possessed of the grant of Warin (*ibid.*, no. 5; *EEA* V, no. 133). In the late 13th and early 14th centuries the Vescy family were presenting to a moiety, presumably that which had been in the possession of Eustace fitz John (see, for example, *Reg. Greenfield*, III, 163, dated 1309; see also MS Dodsworth 63, fol. 64v). In 1316 Thomas Gynes and his wife, and William Gynes and his wife, brought a plea of *quare impedit* against Clemence de Vescy for preventing them from presenting to a moiety of Bubwith (*Year Books of Edward II*, vol. XX, *10 Edward II, A.D. 1316–1317*, ed. M. D. Legge and W. Holdsworth, Selden Society, 52 (1934), pp. 52–8). There is no indication before no. 106 of any interest of Byland in the church.

107   *Rubric: Letter of the same [John de Mowbray] about delivering seisin.* [*c.* 1349].

Dating: by reference to no. 106.

108 *Rubric: Letter of the convent about receiving seisin, the abbot being dead.* [*c.* 1349].

Dating: by reference to no. 106, and probably predating the election of Abbot John, who was blessed and made profession on 1 Nov. 1349 (*HRH* II, 270).

109 *Rubric: Licence from the king for the appropriation of the said moiety of Bubwith church.* [Westminster; 20 Aug. 1349].

Pd (calendar): *Cal. Pat. R. 1348–50*, p. 367: licence issued by Edward III at the request of Henry, earl of Lancaster, for the alienation in mortmain by John de Mowbray of the advowson of a moiety of Bubwith church and for its appropriation.

110 *Rubric: Bull of Pope Urban [V], sent to the abbot of St Albans, to appropriate Bubwith church.* [Avignon; 18 Oct. 1363].

Pd (calendar): *CPRL IV, 1362–1404*, p. 32.

Note: This is a mandate addressed to the abbot of St Albans to appropriate to the abbot and convent of Byland, who have set forth in their petition to Pope Innocent VI that they have lost possessions and rents during the wars, a moiety of Bubwith church of their patronage, valued at 20 marks. The real value is 40 marks. The report concerning the same by John de Thoresby, archbishop of York (1353–73), had not been sufficient or correct, and Innocent VI had not then appropriated it. Avignon, 18 Oct. 1363. For the mandate of Innocent VI to the archbishop of York to investigate the state of Byland in view of their claims for licence to appropriate, see *ibid. III*, 572, dated 15 Mar. 1355. There was a lapse of 14 years between Mowbray's grant of the advowson and his and the king's licence to appropriate and papal approval of the same. For a letter, also dated 18 Oct. 1363, from Pope Urban to the abbot and convent of Byland, whose rents have been diminished by hostile invasions etc. and on account of the plague, granting them licence to appropriate the church of Bubwith, see M. Hayez, ed., *Urbain V (1362–1370), Lettres communes*, Lettres communes des papes du XIVe siècle, Bibliothèque des Écoles Françaises d'Athènes et de Rome II (1972), no. 5733, pp. 98–9. The abbot of St Albans mentioned here and in no. 111 is Thomas de la Mare, elected in 1349, who died in 1396 (*HRH* II, 64).

111 *Rubric: [Letter of] Proxy for the monk* (procur[atorium] monachi) *coming to the abbot of St Albans for the [documents] written below.* [1364].

[fols 15v–16r, old fols 103v–104r]

112 *Notification to the abbot and convent of the monastery of Byland of the Cistercian order and in the diocese of York, by Thomas, abbot of St Albans, deputed by Pope Urban [V], that he has received letters from the pope with a bull with hemp cords after the manner of the Roman curia (opening line only recited, Urbanus episcopus servus servorum dei dilecto filio abbati monasterii sancti Albani ordinis sancti Benedicti Linc' diocesis salutem et apostolicam benedictionem. Ex iniuncto nobis etc.).*

After receipt of the letters the abbot took care to proceed according to their contents. Acting at the request of the monks of Byland, who have shown him suitable proofs, and considering the state and condition of Byland, and other matters, and accepting that the annexation of the moiety of Bubwith church would be beneficial for the convent and is urgent, he has appropriated to the monastery the moiety and its rights and appurtenances, to possess for its own uses. The abbot and convent are to take corporal possession of the moiety when the rector resigns or dies, and to retain the fruits, revenues and profits but to preserve a suitable portion, agreed by the abbot of St Albans, for a perpetual vicar who is to be appointed by the abbot and convent, and who is to pay all episcopal dues. The archbishop and archdeacons in a time of vacancy are to take from the profits of the church only as much as their predecessors took. An instrument of Hugh de Fletham, clerk of the diocese of York and notary public, is attached as witness. St Martin, Battle; 27 Sept. 1364 [2 Urban V].

Presentibus religioso viro fratre Iohanne de Bukeden monacho dicti monasterii Sancti Albani, magistro Willelmo de Burton' iuris perito dicti domini abbatis <Sancti> Albani clerico speciali, fratre Thoma de Cotun monacho dicti <monasterii> de Bellal' et Adam de Ryd<dy>nges laico Ebor' diocesis testibus ad premissa vocatis specialiter et rogatis.

Notification by Hugh de Fletham, clerk of the diocese of York, notary public by apostolic authority, that he wrote some of the above and checked the rest.

[fol. 16r–v, old fol. 104]

113 *Public instrument with notification, addressed to all the sons of holy mother church to whom this writing shall come, by the abbot and monastery of Byland of the Cistercian order and in the diocese of York, that Pope Urban [V] has allowed the abbot and convent to appropriate a moiety of Bubwith church, except for the portion allowed for the vicarage and vicar, so that when the rector dies or resigns, the convent may take corporal possession of the moiety and keep the fruits, rents and revenues to their own use, as is laid down in the papal letters and other instruments. The abbot and convent have heard that Dom. William de Wyrkesworth, rector of the moiety, has resigned, and have appointed Richard of Yarm, monk and prior, to act on their behalf and take possession of the moiety, and to notify the archbishop and give obedience to him. Sealed with the common seal of the monastery and that of Hugh de Fletham.* Byland, the chapter house; 15 Jan. 1366 [1367].

Presentibus ibidem Iohanne de Baxb', Roberto (*sic*), viris literatis, et Roberto Bisshopp' laico dicte Ebor' diocesis testibus ad premissa vocatis specialiter et rogatis.

Attestation by Hugh de Fletham, clerk of the diocese of York and notary public by apostolic authority, that he was a witness to the above.

[fol. 16v]

114 *Public instrument issued by William de Wirkesworth, rector of the parish church of Bubwith, in the presence of Archbishop John of York, papal legate, and a public notary and witnesses, sitting as a tribunal in the chamber of his manor of Bishopthorpe. . . .* 20 Mar. 1366 [1367], in the fifth year of Pope Urban [V].

Note: Text breaks off at bottom of folio. The rubric adds that this was an instrument of resignation, and admission of the same.

[18 folios lost, old fols 105–119 except for one folio, now fol. 17, which is numbered '105' in a later hand]
The missing folios contained documents at the end of the Bubwith section, and those relating to the following places:

BATTERSBY (NZ5907), in the parish of Ingleby Greenhow and the wapentake of Langbargh West (NR). MS Top. Yorks. d. 11, fol. 264v, notes a charter of Ralph son of Adam. Battersby was part of the Percy fee, and in the 1230s x 1250s William de Percy of Kildale confirmed whatever the monks had of his fee (below, no. 852). Henry of Battersby was abbot of Byland, *c.* 1231–68.

BRETHERDALE (Bretherdale Bank, NY5605, Bretherdale Beck, NY5804, Bretherdale Common, NY5803, Bretherdale Head, NY5705) (Westm.). There are rubrics referring to quitclaims by John le Fraunsays and Adam of Milburn of land in Bretherdale in the Shap section (nos 403, 405). Henry II confirmed the whole of Bretherdale (nos 520, 568), and land there is included in a general confirmation by Henry III (no. 527).

BORROWDALE (NY5603), near Fawcett Forest and Bannisdale (Westm.). Land in Borrowdale was granted by William I of Lancaster and the grant and confirmation entered in the Fawcett Forest section of the cartulary (nos 310, 312); Borrowdale was included in a general confirmation of Henry III (no. 527). Woodland in Borrowdale was the subject of a final concord of 1235 (no. 397).

BOOTHAM, lying outside Bootham Bar, City of York. In 1327 the monks received licence to acquire a messuage in Bootham (no. 532, below); see also MS Top. Yorks. d. 11, fols 264v–265r.

BALK (Balk Grange at SE4779) in the parish of Kirby Knowle and wapentake of Birdforth (NR); charters are noted in MS Top. Yorks. d. 11, fol. 265r.

BRAFFERTON (SE4370), township and parish in the wapentake of Bulmer (NR); charters are noted in MS Top. Yorks. d. 11, fol. 265r.

[fol. 17r]
COLD CAM (Cam), in the township of Oldstead, parish of Kilburn and wapentake of Birdforth (NR). Cams Head lies between Oldstead Grange and Byland Abbey, about ½ mile from each.

115 *Grant in free alms, addressed to the archbishop of York and to all his men, French and English, and all the sons of holy church, by Roger de Mowbray, to God and the monks of St Mary of Byland, of land in Cam and common pasture of the forest of Coxwold, and materials for constructing their houses, by provision of his steward. The grant is made for the salvation of his soul and those of his own.* [1142 x c. 1143 or c. 1147].
Hiis testibus Gundrea matre mea, Sampsone de Albeneio, Rogero de Cundi, Petro de Tresc, Asketil ostiario, etc.
Pd: *Mowbray Charters*, no. 40.
Dating: The grant for building suggests that this is associated with one of the moves made by the convent, either to Old Byland or Stocking, near Coxwold. *Mowbray Charters* prefers the earlier date, which is also suggested by the witnesses.

116 *Remission and quitclaim, addressed to all the sons of holy church present and future, by John de Daiville for himself and his heirs, to the monks of St Mary of Byland, of all the right and claim which he and his ancestors had from the eastern part of these boundaries: as the ditch below* **Midelberga** *runs outside the meadow of the same as far as* **Rutendebeck** *and over* **Rutendebeck** *as far as the highway which comes from the moor, and by the same road from the western part of* **Loftscogha** *as far as* **Flaxepodala**. *Quitclaim in free alms of whatever common pasture he or his ancestors had between these boundaries and their land in Cam, to do there whatever they wish. To hold free from all service, for the salvation of the donor's soul and of his father, mother and wife and all his ancestors and heirs.* [c. 1186 x c. 1210].
Hiis testibus Willelmo de Corneburgo, Willelmo de Buscy, Gikello de Smedtona, etc.
Pd: *EYC* IX, no. 138.
Dating: The donor can be identified as John son of Robert de Daiville to whom Nigel de Mowbray restored lands in Kilburn in 1186 x 1190 (*Mowbray Charters*,

no. 361). John's father Robert held fees of the honour of Mowbray in 1166 (*ibid.*, no. 401) and was still alive in 1180. The present charter probably dates from after the restoration of his father's Yorkshire lands to John. The witnesses occur together between 1184 and 1187: see below, no. 414. The first and third occur together between 1204 and 1209: see below, no. 206.

Note: As noted in *EYC*, the *Historia Fundationis* of Byland Abbey records that Robert de Daiville had been in dispute with the monks in 1147 when he alleged that they were enclosing land belonging to the vill of Kilburn. Roger de Mowbray, patron of Byland, came to their assistance, and when Daiville and the monks had made peace Mowbray constructed a ditch to the west of the abbey, which was then at its third site at Stocking (*Mon. Ang.* V, 351–2). This is evidently the ditch below 'Midelberg' mentioned here.

117   *Notification to all present and future of the agreement between the monks of Byland and John de Daiville by which, if the animals of John or his heirs or his villeins of Kilburn cross these boundaries (as no. 116), they are to be returned without complaint so that they (John and his men) shall not enjoy common pasture, nor make any claim against the monks beyond those bounds, saving the free right of the tenants of Kilburn. [c. 1186 x c. 1210].*
Hiis testibus Nigello de Luvetoft', Galfrido Fossard, Hugone de Munford', Gilkello (*sic*) de Smedtona, etc.

Marginal note: ob ante 10 R. Jo, written in a later hand. This seems to refer to the first witness, whose Christian name has been underlined.
Pd: *EYC* IX, no. 139.
Dating: as no. 116.
Note: Farrer (*EYC* III, 4) and Clay (*EYF*, p. 56) note that Nigel de Luvetot the younger, son of Richard, died in 1219.

118   *Rubric: Quitclaim by Robert son of Leolf of his common within the boundaries written above.*

119   *Rubric: Bond by Thomas Le Noble for himself and his heirs concerning all the common and pasture, as much as belongs to him.*

120   *Rubric: Quitclaim by Thomas Le Noble of his common within the boundaries written above.*

121   *Rubric: Chirograph agreement between the monks and the prior of Newburgh, concerning common pasture in* Calvecotedale, *for which common the monks have granted the prior common pasture pertaining to one carucate in Kilburn, from the great spring below Cam to the north and west. The canons later claimed this common, and the monks in turn claimed the homage and service of the prior of Newburgh for the land and for 7 bovates which were formerly held of Ralph son of Alan of Leake, concerning*

which a chirograph was levied in the king's court. Note to search for this
chirograph in the Newburgh bundle. [4 Feb. 1219].

Text: MS Dodsworth 91, fol. 74r–v, no. 7. Final concord between the
abbot and monks of Byland and the prior and canons of Newburgh
concerning common pasture in 'Calvecotedale' about which a
lawsuit had been brought. The abbot and convent granted common
pasture, as above; the canons are to have the common pasture freely
and without impediment, and the monks are not to make meadow
nor restore the buildings and hedges which have been torn down, nor
the ditches which have been destroyed, without the licence of the
canons. Sealed with the seals of both houses. Facta est autem hec
concordia coram H. decano Ebor' anno ab incarnatione domini
M°CC°octavo decimo die lune proxima post purificationem Beate
Marie. Hiis testibus magistro Roberto de Wynt', canonico Ebor',
Willelmo de Erdena, magistro Roberto de Rue, magistro A. de Clayton', Willelmo Darel, Adam de Boltebi, Hugone de Upsale, Roberto
de Kerebi, Stephano de Blabi et aliis.

Dating: From transcript. The first witness, Robert of Winchester, first occurs as
canon of York in 1217; he was prebendary of Fridaythorpe by 1218/19, then prebendary of Fenton (by 1230) and finally precentor of York (by 1235); he appears to
have resigned, probably by Mar. 1240: *Fasti York*, pp. 15, 71, 74.

Note: Stephen de Blaby also attests nos 415, 422, 602, 606, 816 and 1042 below.
Adam of Boltby attests nos 379, 444, 598, 602, 611, 618, 623, 624, 816, 1042 below.
See no. 731 below, which cross references this rubric as a fuller version.

[fol. 17v]

COXWOLD (SE5377), township and parish in the wapentake of
Birdforth (NR). Coxwold lies on the southern edge of the Hambledon
Hills, and includes the townships of Byland Abbey, Oulston, Yearsley,
Angram Grange, Wildon Grange, Thornton on the Hill and Baxby.
Coxwold was held by the Coleville family, who became benefactors
of Byland.

122   *Confirmation, addressed to all the sons of holy mother church who will*
see or hear this writing, by Thomas de Coleville, knight and lord of Coxwold,
to God and St Mary and to the abbot and convent of Byland, of all the lands
which they have of the gifts of his ancestors. Grant of all his meadow of
Elfrykholm *by the boundaries by which the door-keeper of the house first*
held it at farm, with his body for burial. Grant of free entry and exit for their
men, their draught animals, carts, oxen, and horses, and licence to pasture
their animals whenever they wish. Grant also of licence to enclose the
meadow from 17 kal. Apr. (16 Mar.) until the hay is brought in, saving to

him and his heirs and his free men common of the meadow in the time when it is not enclosed, and saving also the tithes of Elfrykholm *to the canons of Newburgh. Pledge to warranty. Sealed with the donor's seal.* [York; 1326]. [Hiis testibus dominis Rogero de Mow]bray domino meo, Iohanne de Eyvil, Willelmo de Buscy, Ricardo Mansel.

Copy: MS Top. Yorks. e. 7, fols 122v–123r (old pp. 192–3), from which the date and the readings in square brackets are supplied. The witness list continues: Thoma Maunsel, Willelmo de Wyvil, Willelmo Darel, Gaufrido de Upsal, Willelmo de Staingrive, Iohanne de Cancefeld, Symone de Lilling et aliis. Also noted in MS Top. Yorks. d. 11, fol. 265r–v.

Note: There is a rubric for the charter entered at no. 676 below.

123 *Notification by letters patent by the official of York of the case heard between the prior and convent of Newburgh, appropriators of the church of Coxwold by master Ralph, and the abbot and convent of Byland by brother John of Gilling, relating to tithes.* The consistory court of York, York Minster, Wed. before St Peter's Chair [22 Feb.] 132[ ]

Note: This is largely illegible. In MS Top. Yorks. d. 11, fol. 265r–v (old pp. 495–6), no. 122 is followed by a charter of Thomas de Coleville concerning meadow called 'Esebrigge' which the monks may enclose, and for which they are to pay tithes to the canons of Newburgh. Testibus dominis Olivero de Buscy, Marmaduco Darell. There is a cross reference to old fol. 116, an agreement between the monks and Thomas de Coleville, 1389: . . . communem? in Cukewald cum metis et via de Wildon ad abbatiam cum nova conventione de silibus (?) repunitis vide fol. 116 ubi mete inter monachos et dom(inum) Tho de Coleville militem. Test' Tho de Coleville et Iohanne militibus, Tho de Etton. Dat apud Byland 1389.

[folios lost to old fol. 119 inclusive]

SESSAY (SE4575), parish in the wapentake of Birdforth (NR); see MS Top. Yorks. d. 11, fol. 265v. The grants in Sessay originated with the Darel family in the early 13th century (for confirmations see below nos 678–81).

CATTON, High Catton (SE7153) and Low Catton (SE7053), in the parish of Low Catton and wapentake of Harthill (ER); for charters contained in this section see MS Top. Yorks. d. 11, fol. 265v. Henry III confirmed Catton, as it had been confirmed by Henry II and Richard I (no. 527). It is clear from nos 668–9 that the original donor of lands in Catton was Agnes de Percy. The Percy family also held land in Catton in the parish of Topcliffe (NR), but that Catton near Stamford Bridge was the land conveyed to the monks is clear from *KI*, p. 86: the abbot held 24 carucates of Percy lands which had been exchanged for lands in Seamer.

[fol. 18r, old fol. 120r]

CLIFTON (SE5953), in the parish of Overton and the wapentake of Bulmer (NR). Clifton lies on the river Ouse to the NW of the city of York. The abbot held the manor of Clifton and no. 127 contains measurements of the messuage there. In 1271 the king ordered that his justices should hear pleas at the abbot's court at Clifton rather than Sutton (no. 529 below). Clifton was a major centre for the collection of wool from the Yorkshire Cistercian houses by Italian merchants, for transport down the river Ouse to Hull for export (Waites, *Monasteries and Landscape*, p. 191).

124 *Grant and confirmation, addressed to all the faithful in Christ present and future, by the abbot and convent of St Mary, York, with the consent of their chapter, to the abbot and convent of Byland of half the toft which Reginald Corbelarius held of them next to that of the monks of Jervaulx in Clifton, in the valley, with that small portion of land which Osbert the cook held of them outside the said toft towards the north, in a straight line as far as the selion at the head of the crofts, to hold in perpetual farm and to enclose as they wish and to do within the enclosure whatever they wish. The monks are to pay an annual rent of 3s., half at Whitsuntide and half at St Martin in Winter (11 Nov.). They are to claim no rights in the common of Clifton except for free entry and exit for themselves, their men, carts and ploughs. Confirmation of all the land which they have of the abbot and convent of Jervaulx lying next to the said land towards the river Ouse, to enclose as they wish and do there whatever they wish. They have a charter of the abbot and convent of Jervaulx concerning the same land (no. 125). Sealed with the chapter's seal.* [1224 x 1251].

Hiis testibus Roberto de Skegnesse tunc senescallo Sancte Marie Ebor', magistro Iohanne de Hamerton', Roberto de Auford', etc.

Dating: contemporary with or later than no. 125. The first witness attests, without title, after 1227 and into the 1230s: *Chs Vicars Choral*, I, nos 152–3, 157. A John of Hammerton, son of Alan son of Elias de Hou, occurs between 1190 and 1203. There was also a John of Hammerton, son of Fulk, who was dead by 1202. The witness here seems to be John son of Henry, who died soon after 1251 (*EYC* I, no. 516, and p. 416, II, 81–2).

125 *Notification, addressed to all the faithful in Christ seeing or hearing this present writing, by Abbot Eustace and the convent of Jervaulx, of their grant and confirmation, with the consent of the chapter, to the abbot and convent of Byland, of that land which lies to the north of the donors' house in Clifton outside the enclosure of the messuage, which they, the donors, hold of the abbey of St Mary, York. The abbot and convent of Byland are to render*

30d. yearly, half at Whitsuntide and half at St Martin (11 Nov.). The abbot and convent are to hold the land under the same conditions as the donors hold it of St Mary's Abbey. Pledge to warranty. [1221 x 1254].

Hiis testibus Henrico priore de Bellalanda, etc.

Dating: Abbot Eustace of Jervaulx was elected in 1221 and his last recorded occurrence is in 1254 (*HRH* II, 286). His grave slab survives (see W. H. St John Hope and Harold Brakspear, 'Jervaulx Abbey', *YAJ*, XXI (1910–11), 301–44 (p. 319); *VCH Yorks.*, III, 142).

126 *Notification to all present and future by Walter son of Hugh of Clifton of his remission and quitclaim, for himself and his heirs, to the abbot and convent of Byland and their successors, of whatever he and his heirs claim as their own right in their enclosure in Clifton, that is, recognition that he made a claim by writ of novel disseisin on the enclosure. Sealed with the donor's seal.* York; 1240.

Hiis testibus [dominis] Roberto de Lexyngton', Radulfo de Sulleng, Willelmo Culeworth, etc.

Note: The rubric calls the donor Walter 'aurifaber'. The witnesses were royal justices. For final concords made in their presence at York see no. 258 below (Jan. 1241), no. 722 (July 1240), no. 927 (June 1240) and no. 1003 (July 1240).

127 *Boundaries and measurements of the messuage of Byland in Clifton: in length from the common road of Clifton to the ditch called* le Engedik *towards the north; and in width between the land of St Mary's, York on the one side and the river Ouse on the other.*

The length of the hall of Clifton, 53 feet and its width 62 feet, which are 8 rods, 86 feet.

The length of the white chamber, 66 feet, its width 40 feet, which are 6½ rods, 40 feet.

The length of the other chamber, 60 feet, its width 41 feet, and it comes to 6 rods and 60 feet.

The length of the corner of the same, 51 feet, in width 10 feet, and they make 1 rod and a quarter and 10 feet.

The length of the larger private chamber, 24 feet, the width 20 feet and it makes 1 rod and 80 feet.

The length of the other private chamber is 13 feet and the width 13 feet, and it makes a quarter of a rod and 80 feet.

There is there one corner which is estimated to contain 1 rod.

Total number of rods is 24 and three quarters of one rod

No witnesses.

[fol. 18v]

CARLTON MINIOTT (Carlton near Thirsk, SE3981), township in the parish of Thirk, and the wapentake of Birdforth (NR), approximately 2 miles west of Thirsk. The monks acquired minor pieces of lands here, initially 2 bovates from William son of Ralph Frankelayn (no. 128), which were confirmed by William of Carlton (no. 129) and demised by Abbot Henry (no. 130).

128 **Original:** *Grant and confirmation in free alms, addressed to all the faithful in Christ present and future, by William son of Ralph Frankelayn of Carlton, to God and St Mary and the abbot and monks of Byland, of 2 bovates in the region of Carlton with their toft/s and croft/s and appurtenances, liberties and easements inside and outside the vill, far and near. To hold of him and his heirs free from all secular service for the salvation of the donor's soul and of his ancestors and heirs. Pledge to warranty. Sealed with his seal. [c. 1235 x 1250].*

Hiis testibus Willelmo de Karletona, Willelmo filio Willelmi de Ebor', Thoma de Syltona, Roberto de Auford', Willelmo Arundel, Willelmo de Foxholes, Alano de Leke, Willelmo de Mandevill, Serlone de Faldingtona, Ricardo Mainild', Gamello forestario, Thoma clerico de Suttona, Philippo filio Philippi de eadem villa et aliis.

Location: BL Egerton charter 2160; endorsed: Tresk B i xi (Thirsk, first bundle, 11); C. Willelmi filii Rad' Frankelyn de duabus bovatis terre sui in Karletona iuxta Tresk; seal: large black seal, now broken into 3 fragments.

Dating: The first four witness also attest no. 130, which dates from the office of Abbot Henry of Battersby. William of Carlton, son of Ivo, was a tenant in Carlton Miniott in 1209 when he was granted 5 carucates and 2 bovates by Roger of Carlton. Roger's son, William, probably the first witness, was tenant in Carlton in the reign of Henry III, and had been succeeded by his son, Henry, by 1250 (*VCH NR* II, 64–5). William son of William of York attests a charter of Nicholas de Stuteville II of ?1224 x 1233 (*EYC* IX, no. 60).

Note: The cartulary copy has the first 3 witnesses only, and a marginal note: B. Thresk. The grant is confirmed in no. 129.

129 *Rubric: Confirmation of the same [2 bovates] by William of Carlton.*

Original: *Grant and confirmation, addressed to all the faithful who will see or hear this writing, by William of Carlton, to God and St Mary and the abbot and convent of Byland, of the grant made by William son of Ralph Frankelayn of Carlton of 2 bovates in the region of Carlton (no. 128), to hold freely, quit of all secular service. Pledge to warranty. Sealed with his seal. [c. 1235 x 1250].*

Hiis testibus domino Philippo de Batheresby tunc persona de Billingtona (*recte* Rillingtona), Willelmo filio Willelmi Ebor', Thoma

de Siltona, Roberto de Auford, Willelmo Arundel, Willelmo de
Foxhol', Alano de Leke, <Wil>lelmo de Mandevil', Serlone de
Faldingtona, Ricardo Maynild', Gamello forestario, Thoma clerico de
<Su>ttona, Philippo filio Phillippi de Suttona et aliis.

Location: BL Stowe charter 437; endorsed: Tresk B i xii (Thirsk, first bundle, 12);
Confirmatio Willelmi de Karletona de donatione Willelmi filii Rad' Frankelayn de
duabus bovatis terre in villa de Karletona; cut for seal tag; no seal or tag.
Dating: as no. 128.
Note: The first witness was rector of a moiety of Rillington from 29 Aug. 1235 until
1267: *Fasti Parochiales*, V, 34.
Marginal note: b(aculus) i Thresk.

130 *Demise and confirmation, addressed to all the faithful in Christ
present and future, by Abbot Henry and the convent of Byland, to William of
Boltby and his assigns of 2 bovates in the region of Carlton with their toft
and croft and appurtenances inside and outside the vill; to hold of the abbot
and convent free from all service except for 12d. paid yearly at St Martin in
Winter (11 Nov.). Pledge to warranty. Sealed as a chirograph.* [1230 x 1268].
Hiis testibus Willelmo de Carletona, Willelmo filio Willelmi de Ebor',
Thoma de Siltona, Roberto de Auford', etc.

Dating: An Abbot Henry professed obedience in 1300 and occurs in 1301; Henry of
Battersby occurs as abbot between 1230 and 1268. The attestation of no. 124 by the
last witness suggests the earlier period. See also note to no. 128.

131 *Notification to all present and future by William son of Ralph of
Carlton, of his grant and confirmation to Henry his brother, of a piece of his
toft, measuring forty feet wide, in Carlton towards the western part of the
donor's toft, and the whole croft from the highway up to the end of the same
croft, 1 perch on* Wynbelbergh *and 1 perch on* Ridersty. *To hold of the
donor and his heirs for homage and service and for 2d. paid yearly to the
abbot and convent, 1d. at Christmas and 1d. at Easter. Pledge to warranty.*
[?1231 x 1250].
Hiis testibus Willelmo de Carleton', etc.

Dating: probably the same time as nos 128–130; these all relate to the same
property.

132 *Rubric: Agreement made in the king's court between the monks and
William of Carlton concerning 2 bovates in the same [Carlton].*
Marginal note: lxv in quat'.

[fol. 19r, old fol. 121]
COATHAM (NZ5925), in the parish of Kirkleatham and wapentake of
Langbargh East (NR). Much of the northern part of the parish is salt

marsh, and there were many salt pits in the Middle Ages; Byland
Abbey was only one of several monastic houses to acquire land and
saltpans in Coatham, others including Guisborough Priory (*Cart.
Guis.*, II, 113–24), Newburgh Priory and Ellerton Priory. East
Coatham in the 12th century became a port in which the Brus family
had an interest (*VCH NR* II, 371–2); for quittance of toll, see below,
nos 139–40.

133   *Grant in free alms by William of Kilton, addressed to the archbishop of
York and the whole chapter of St Peter (York) and all the sons of holy church
present and future, to God and the monks of St Mary of Byland, of a toft and
croft in Coatham which used to belong to Reinbald son of Reynald, with the
houses built thereon nearest to Edmund son of Franc towards the east. Grant
also of the saltpan which Jordan held of the donor; those plots* (areas)
*between the great bridge and the wall of the saltpan of Robert son of Bernolf
on each side of the watercourse, which plots used to belong to the donor; that
plot which William Broun held of the donor's father Ilger nearest to the
bridge which is called* Lenebrigg *towards the east; 3 acres of profitable land
on the butts towards the east of* Lenebrigg *in the region of Kirkleatham; 1
acre at* Graistan; ½ *acre in the east part of* Adelwaldkeld; *and ½ acre
between* Westbec *and the croft of Alden of West Coatham. To hold free from
all service for the salvation of the soul of the donor and of all his ancestors
and heirs. Pledge to warranty.* [c. 1196 x 1206].
Hiis testibus Alano de Wylt', Willelmo Warde, etc.

Pd: *EYC* II, no. 725.
Dating: The donor had succeeded his father by 1196 (*EYC* II, 99); the witnesses
occur in the late 12th and early 13th centuries (see *EYC* I–III, *passim*).
Note: Alden of West Coatham appears as Walden or Walder of East Coatham in the
rubric. Edmund son of Franc of East Coatham granted a toft there to Alden's son,
Walter (*Cart. Guis.*, II, 122). This charter mentions the great bridge, and there is a
reference in no. 136 below to the first bridge. Bridges are mentioned as topographical features in Guisborough charters relating to Coatham: 'the bridge towards the
south', and the old bridge and the new bridge (*Cart. Guis.*, II, 117, 121–2).

134   *Grant in free alms, addressed to all the sons of holy mother church to
whom this present writing shall come, by Roger son of Ilger of Kilton, with
his body, to God and the monks of St Mary of Byland, of that toft with the
house built on it which Hugh son of Isabel held of him in Coatham. Grant
also of 3 acres of his demesne in Kirkleatham to the west of* Westdiutus [?]
*whose heads touch on the boundaries between Kirkleatham and Coatham,
and of 1½ acres in* Grenehill. *To hold of the donor and his heirs free from all
service to do there as they wish, for the salvation of the soul of the donor and*

of all his ancestors and heirs. Pledge to warranty. [late 12th or early 13th cent.].

Hiis testibus Petro Warde, Osberto de Setun, Willelmo de Coco, Regynaldo Rosell', etc.

Dating: The grantor was a brother of the donor of no. 133. Peter Ward, clerk, was instituted to the church of Kirkleatham by Archbishop Geoffrey between 1189 and 1212; the second and third witnesses attest in the late 12th and early 13th centuries.

135 *Agreement between the abbot and convent of Byland and John son of Roger of East Coatham concerning timber work* (meryne) *and a wall in East Coatham. With the assent of both parties these are to be located in equal proportions on the land of the abbot and convent and of the said John. From henceforth these shall remain with the abbot and convent. Sealed with John's seal.* Byland; Wed. after the Annunciation [30 Mar.] 1344. French.

[fol. 19r–v]

136 *Grant in free alms, addressed to all the sons of holy mother church present and future, by Ralph parson of Kirkleatham, to God and the monks of St Mary of Byland, of Henry clerk of Coatham and his heirs with the whole tenement that he held of the donor in Coatham, and of a saltpan in the same between the house of Robert son of Bernolf and the first bridge, and ½ acre of uncultivated land which lies near the same saltpan towards the south. The grant is made free from all service to do there as they wish, for the salvation of the soul of the donor and of all his own.* [c. 1189 x 1212].

Hiis testibus Willelmo de Kiltona, Alano de Wiltona, Adam de Setona, etc.

Dating: On the death of Ralph, parson of Kirkleatham, Archbishop Geoffrey instituted his clerk Peter Ward, who witnessed no. 134. Ralph therefore died some time during the office of Archbishop Geoffrey.

[fol. 19v]

137 *Notification to all present and future by William of Kilton of his grant and confirmation in free alms, to God and St Mary of Byland and the monks serving God there, of 1 toft in Coatham which Henry the clerk once held, with 1½ acres belonging to the same toft, and 1 saltpan to the west of* Lenebrigg, *to hold freely as is contained in the charter which the monks have of Ralph, brother of the donor, formerly parson of Kirkleatham (no. 136).* [c. 1190 x 1212].

Hiis testibus Henrico filio Conani, Osberto persona de Hynderwell', Alexandro de Cotum, etc.

Dating: probably after no. 136. Henry son of Conan witnessed William's grant of Kirkleatham church to Guisborough Priory in 1195 x 1206 (*Cart. Guis.*, II, 96; *EYC*

II, no. 724); Farrer (*ibid.*, no. 891 and p. 237) noted that he was the heir of Robert de Liverton, and was living in the time of King John and Henry III. He was the son of Conan son of Torphin son of Robert son of Copsi (for whom see above, nos 47–52). Note: No. 137 confirms the relationship between William and Ralph of Kilton.

138   *Grant, addressed to all who will hear or see this charter, by Adam de Brus, to the monks of St Mary of Byland, of quittance of toll on all the fish purchased for the use of the monks and for the needy of the house, within his lands at Coatham. The grant is made for the love of God and the salvation of the soul of the donor. [c. 1165 x 1176].*

Hiis testibus Waltero de Stam', Willelmo de Percy, Galfrido filio com(itis), Gerardo de Lac', etc.

Pd: *EYC* II, no. 657.

Dating: the majority of the donor and the death of the second witness.

139   *Rubric: Charter of Peter de Brus concerning quittance of toll in Coatham.* [1196 x 1222].

Marginal note: Gaterich' b(aculus) ii.

Dating: the succession and death of the donor, the son of Adam de Brus II.

140   *Confirmation in free alms, addressed to all the sons of holy mother church present and future who will see or hear this writing, by Peter de Brus, to God and St Mary and the abbot and convent of Byland and their successors, for the love of God and for the salvation of his soul and of all his ancestors and heirs, of all lands and tenements with their appurtenances which the abbot and convent hold within his fee. Grant also of freedom from toll for themselves and their servants throughout his fee.* [1196 x 1222].

Hiis testibus Adam de Setuna, Marmeduco de Theng, Roberto de Estre, Ricolfo de Gamettona, etc.

Pd: *EYC* II, no. 670.

Dating: the succession and death of the donor, the son of Adam de Brus II.

Note: The rubric describes this as a general confirmation of all lands and tenements held within his fee, and concerning toll.

[fol. 20r, old fol. 122]

CAYTON (TA0583), township and parish in the wapentake of Pickering Lythe (NR). Lands in Cayton were closely associated with those in Deepdale (nos 158–204) and Osgodby (nos 855–76). The monks' interests in Cayton originated with William son of Henry of Cayton (nos 141–2, 144–5) who confirmed to Byland all the lands in Deepdale which the monks had of the grant of his great-grandfather, Durand de Cliffe (no. 180). The monks' property in Cayton comprised small portions of land.

141   *Notification to all present and future by William son of Henry of Cayton, of his grant in free alms to God and St Mary of Byland and the monks serving God there, for the salvation of his soul and of his ancestors, of 1 toft with a croft in the vill of Cayton, and land 1 perch in width in the region of Cayton, that is, in* Hovenhandris *next to* Engmar, *nearest to the south, except for 2 perches, that is the perch and toft and croft which Philip used to hold of the donor. Pledge to warranty.* [late 12th or early 13th cent.].

Hiis testibus Rogero filio Haldani, Roberto Fareman, Roberto filio Symonis de Angotby, etc.

Dating: Donor said to be alive in 1202 (*EYC* I, no. 366), but see also the occurrence noted in 1208 (*ibid.* XI, 235); for the witnesses see *EYC* I, no. 364 note, no. 366 note, no. 616; III, no. 1311.

Note: William's father was Henry, son of Henry son of Durand of Cayton, also called Durand de Cliffe, who was a joint holder in 1166 of a knight's fee in Deepdale, Killerby, Osgodby and a small portion of Cayton (*EYC* XI, 233–5).

142   *Grant in free alms, addressed to all who see or hear these letters, by William son of Henry de Cayton, to God and the monks of St Mary of Byland, of 1 toft and croft in Cayton, 6 rods in width, next to the toft which Thankard held towards the east, and in length the same as the other croft. Grant of free entry and exit. This grant is made free from all service for the salvation of the soul of the donor and of all his ancestors and heirs, to enclose as the monks wish. Pledge to warranty.* [late 12th or early 13th cent.].

Hiis testibus Gilberto de Aetona, Roberto, etc.

Dating: as no. 141. First witness attests throughout the period from 1157 to 1215 (*EYC* I, nos 381–2, 391–2, 395, 402, 644 etc., II, no. 996 note).

143   *Notification to all present and future by the monks of Byland of their remission to Richard Hericius of all the toft and croft which they have of the grant of William son of Henry (nos 141, 142), which Philip held, and 1 rood which the same Philip held next to* Engmar. *To hold rendering to the monks 6d. yearly, 3d. at St Michael (29 Sept.) and 3d. at Easter. Pledge to warranty.* [late 12th or early 13th cent.].

Hiis testibus Willelmo de Angotby, etc.

Dating: by reference to nos 141–42.

144   *Grant in free alms, addressed to all who see or hear these letters, by William son of Henry of Cayton, to God and the monks of St Mary of Byland, of that bovate in the region of Cayton which Robert son of Wuluine held, with the toft and croft which Geoffrey Hanche held next to the toft of Ralph the smith, with all its meadows, pastures, easements and appurte-*

nances inside and outside the vill. The grant is made for the salvation of the soul of the donor and of all his ancestors and heirs, for the performance of forinsec service on the bovate where 12 carucates make a knight's fee. Pledge to warranty. [late 12th or early 13th cent.].

Hiis testibus Gilberto de Aetona, Willelmo de Osgotby, Roberto de Irtona, Olyvero de Croum, etc.

Dating: for donor see no. 141 and note; the second witness attests no. 143.

[fol. 20r–v]

145 *Notification to all present and future by William of Cayton of his demise to the monks of Byland of 2 acres with a perch of 18 feet in the enclosures* (oftnames) *in Cayton towards the west, to hold free from secular service for 10 years, according to the agreement made between them concerning 5 acres of land, until they are able to recover the 5 acres in Deepdale which R(ichard) de Percy withheld from them. When they do recover the land the 2 acres are to revert to William and his heirs, saving the term of 10 years. Pledge to warranty the 2 acres until the land in Deepdale is recovered.* [1198 x 1244; probably earlier in the period].

Hiis testibus Gilberto de Atona, Willelmo de Osgotby, Roberto de Hirton, Olyvero de Croum, etc.

Dating: A date of late 12th or early 13th century is suggested for nos 141–2 and 144 but see note below.

Note: This charter, and no. 197 below, are likely to relate to the disputes between Richard de Percy, mentioned here, and his nephew, William de Percy III. On the partition of the Percy lands after the death of William de Percy II in 1175 the knight's fee in Osgodby, Deepdale and Killerby was assigned to Jocelin of Louvain, husband of Agnes de Percy. Their son, Henry, died between 1197 and Michaelmas 1198, during the lifetime of his mother, who died between 1201 and 13 Oct. 1204. Henry's son, William de Percy III, who attained his majority before 1214, was the heir of his great-grandfather. However, he enjoyed possession of only part of the barony, a large portion having been assigned by Agnes to her younger son, Richard de Percy. There was a long dispute between William and his uncle until Richard's death in 1244: see *EYC* XI, 6–7; *EYF*, p. 71. See no. 197 below. The word 'offnama' or 'oftnama' is glossed by the *Revised Medieval Latin Word List* as 'intake' or 'enclosure'.

[fol. 20v]

146 *Grant in free alms, addressed to all who see or hear these letters, by John son of William of Ayton, to God and the monks of St Mary of Byland, of all the land he had in the region of Cayton between the croft of Richard of Rillington and the ditch of Killerby to the east of Cayton, to do with as they wish. To hold free from all service for the salvation of the donor's soul and of all his ancestors and heirs. Pledge to warranty.* [before 1211].

Hiis testibus Baldewyno de Alvestain, Alano Bucell', Roberto de
Irtona, Willemo de Osgotby, etc.

Dating: The second witness was dead by 1211 (*EYC* I, 295–6).

[fol. 21r, old. fol. 123]
WEST CLAYTON (SE2610), in the parish of High Hoyland and
wapentake of Staincross (WR). The monks' land centred on Brans
Croft, which cannot now be located (*West Yorks.*, II, 343).

147   *Grant in free alms, addressed to the archbishop of York and the whole
chapter of St Peter's (York) and all the sons of holy mother church who will
see or hear these letters, by Robert son of Hugh of Clayton, to God and the
monks of St Mary of Byland, of a half bovate in Brans Croft in the region of
Clayton which Simon son of Caschim held of the donor, for which the monks
are to perform forinsec service. Grant also of 8 acres of his demesne in
Clayton, that is a toft with 3 acres which Richard Surays held of the donor, 1
acre and 3 perches in* Milnefeld, *2 acres and 1 perch in* Baredrode, *and 1
acre in* Estfeld. *The monks are to hold the land of the donor and his heirs quit
of all service, to do with as they wish; they are to render 40d. yearly, 20d. at
Whitsuntide and 20d. at St Martin (11 Nov.). Pledge to warranty.* [late
12th or early 13th cent.].
Hiis testibus Iohanne de Byrki', Gileberto de Notton', Willemo filio
Ade, etc.

Dating: witnesses (see *EYC* III, *passim*).

148   *Rubric: Quitclaim by Thomas the falconer* (putor) *and Petronilla his
wife, of 20d. annual rent which the monks used to render for a tenement in
Clayton.* [early to mid 13th cent.].
Marginal note: B(aculus) i.
Dating: before no. 149, by which time Thomas was dead.

149   *Quitclaim, addressed to all the faithful in Christ who see or hear this
charter, by Petronilla, widow of Thomas the falconer, in her lawful power, to
God and St Mary and the abbot and convent of Byland, of 25d. annual rent
which the abbot and convent used to render to her ancestors and to her for all
lands and tenements which they have in the vill and region of Clayton of the
grant of her ancestors, as their charters witness. This quitclaim is made in
free alms, for the salvation of the soul of the donor, and of her father and
mother and all her ancestors and heirs, and for a certain sum of money which
the monks have given her. Undertaking to make no further claim to the rent.
Pledge to warranty. Sealed with the donor's seal.* [early to mid 13th cent.].

Hiis testibus dominis Iohanne de Hoderod, Ricardo de Thornhill', Roberto de Denby militibus, etc.

Dating: witnesses. Richard son of Jordan of Thornhill occ. ?1210 x 1220; John of Hodroyd occ. as steward of Pontefract possibly as late as the mid 13th century (*EYC* III, no. 1540, note; VIII, 248).

150 *Grant in free alms, addressed to all the sons of holy mother church to whom the present charter shall come, by William de Lisours for himself and his heirs, to the abbot and convent of Byland or their assigns, of an annual rent of 5d. and quitclaim of a half bovate in Clayton. The grant is made free from all secular service. Pledge to warranty. Sealed with the donor's seal.* [late 13th cent.].

Hiis testibus domino Willelmo filio Thome, Iohanne de Horbery, militibus, Thoma de Dromfeld,' etc.

Dating: William de Lisours occ. 1251 (*Cart. Monk Bretton*, pp. 51–2).
Note: The identity of the donor is uncertain. William de Lisours does not occur in accounts of the family. William fitz Godric, who was dead by 1194, married Aubreye de Lisours, and their son was William fitz William (see *EYF*, p. 28). Described as William son of Aubreye de Lisours he confirmed a grant to Hampole Priory, and he died in 1219 x 1224 (*EYC* VIII, 20). However this is almost certainly too early for the grantor of the present charter, and the attestation of the second witness suggests a date before 1302. Clay notes (*ibid.*, 184) that the family of Dronsfield (Dransfield) held interests in West Bretton and Cumberworth from the middle of the 13th century.

[fol. 21r–v]
151 *Letters patent of Thomas de Bilham of Clayton granting and confirming to Dom. Henry of Pontefract, clerk, an annual rent of 9d. to be taken from the abbot and convent for the half bovate which the abbot and convent hold in Brans Croft in Clayton, with the service of the said abbot and convent. Pledge to warranty. Sealed with the donor's seal.* Byland; Ascension [5 May] 1345.
No witnesses.

[fol. 21v]
152 *Letters patent of Thomas de Bilham of Clayton quitclaiming for himself and his heirs all right and claim to 9d. rent and all services due from the abbot and convent for a half bovate in Brans Croft in Clayton. Pledge to warranty to the abbot and convent and their successors. Sealed with the donor's seal.* Byland; Friday after St John the Baptist [2 Sept.] 1345.

In presentia Marmeduci Darell, Iohannis de Ryllyngton' et Iohannis de Upsall.

Dating: There are two feast days associated with St John the Baptist, his birth (24

June) and his beheading (29 Aug.). Since in 1345 24 June fell on a Friday, the second feast must be intended.

[fol. 22r, old fol. 124]

NORTH CAVE (SE8932), township and parish in the wapentake of Harthill (ER). The land granted in North Cave (no. 153) was far removed from the majority of the abbey properties, and this may account for the lease of the land to a tenant (no. 155).

153 *Grant in free alms, addressed to all the sons of holy mother church, by Roger de Mowbray, to God and St Mary of Byland and the monks serving God there, of a half carucate and 5 acres, with toft and croft, in North Cave, with all appurtenances and with easements of the vill and the surrounding area, in meadows, pastures, water and moor. The grant is made free from all service for the salvation of the soul of the donor and of his father and mother and heirs. Pledge to warranty. No other men of religion to be received in the vill, to the injury of the monks, by the donor and his heirs.* [1138 x 1147].
Testibus Sampsone de Albeneio, Herberto de Cunibergh, Roberto de Dayvilla, Rogero de Flamavilla, etc.

Copy: MS Dodsworth 91, fols 114v–115r, where the witness list omits 'etc' and continues: Roberto de Belcamp' et aliis multis clericis et laicis.
Pd: *EYC* III, no. 1827; (calendar) *Mowbray Charters*, no. 41.
Dating: *EYC* dates to 1145 x 1160; however, as pointed out in *Mowbray Charters*, the Byland *Historia Fundationis* dates the grant of land in North Cave to 1147 or before, and it was confirmed by Pope Hadrian IV in 1154 (*PUE* III, no. 96).

154 *Notification by Roger de Mowbray to the archbishop of York that when he granted land to God and the monks of St Mary of Byland, which the monks hold in North Cave, he also granted and confirmed the liberties which pertained to the land. This he did for the salvation of his soul and of the souls of his ancestors. Order that they should have the said liberties in free alms.* [1154 x 1186].
Testibus Ricardo priore de Novoburgo, Roberto de Molbray, etc.

Pd: *EYC* III, no. 1828; (calendar) *Mowbray Charters*, no. 62.
Dating: office of the first witness (not 1160 x 1175, as *EYC*).

155 *Grant, addressed to all the faithful who will hear or see this writing, by Abbot Henry and the convent of Byland, to Simon son of Simon of North Cave and his heirs, for homage and service, of a half carucate and 5 acres in North Cave. Simon is to hold the land with the toft there of the abbey in fee and hereditary right, and to render an annual rent of 1 silver mark, ½ mark at Whitsuntide and ½ mark at St Martin (11 Nov.). The land is to be held* *free from all service, except for making suit of court three times a year, at the first pleas after the feasts of Michaelmas, Christmas, and Easter. Sealed as chirograph.* [1230 x 1268].

Hiis testibus Waltero tunc priore de B(ellalanda), Henrico suppriore, Willelmo cellerario, etc.

Dating: Prior Walter and William the cellarer also attest nos 796, 799 and 1038. Roger the subprior witnesses no. 796; Henry the subprior witnesses no. 1038, for which a date of mid 13th century is suggested. This would place no. 155 in the period of office of Abbot Henry of Battersby.

[fol. 22r, old fol. 124]

CROSSLEY (now Crossley Hall, SE1333) in the parish of Bradford and wapentake of Morley (WR).

156 *Rubric: Charter of Thomas of Crossley concerning all the land, meadow and woodland which he had in the region of Crossley by the boundaries laid down in the charter.* [early to mid 13th cent.]

Text: MS Dodsworth 91, fols 72r–73r, no. 5. Notification to all the sons of holy mother church who see or hear this writing, by Thomas of Crossley, of his confirmation to God and the monks of St Mary of Byland, of all the land, meadow and woodland which the monks have in Crossley as contained in these boundaries: as the sike falls from 'Brokewellrode' towards 'Kayselflatsyk' and from there as far as the road which runs to Bradford, and from the road to the ditch between Thomas's house and 'Kayselflat'. All this ditch is to remain with the monks to do with as they wish. From the ditch the boundary runs to 'Caldewellesyke' to 'Kyrkesty' and ascends from 'Kyrkesty' to the land of Thomas of Idle and across Thomas's land to 'Brokewellesyk'. The monks are to enclose the land and meadow and wood with a ditch, wall or hedge whenever and however they wish, and the ditch, wall or hedge may be on their land or Thomas's land. If Thomas or his heirs are unable to warranty the land they will give an exchange. Sealed with his seal. Hiis testibus domino Iohanne de Hoderode, tunc seneschallo domini comitis Lincolnie, Roberto de Stapilton, Richardo de Thornhill, militibus, Henrico persona de Normanton, Roberto de Bolling', Hugone de Brodecroft, Thoma de Meyingham, Hugone de Wyndhill et aliis.

Marginal note in cartulary: Whitacr' B(aculus) i.
Dating: as no. 149.

157 *Writ of novel disseisin from King Edward I to the sheriff of Yorkshire to order Joseph (Chauncy), prior of the Hospital of St John of Jerusalem in*

England, to restore to Abbot Adam of Byland 3 acres of land, 6 acres of meadow, and 4 acres of woodland in Crossley, which the abbot claims to be the right of the church of Byland, and into which the prior has no entry except by the disseisin made by Robert de Maunby, formerly prior of St John of Jerusalem in England to Abbot Henry of Byland, predecessor of the said abbot, after the first crossing of the sea by King Henry, the grantor's father, into Brittany, as he says, and he claims that the prior ejected him. If the prior does not do it and if the abbot gives surety for his claim, the case is to be heard at the next sitting of the justices. Westminster; 20 Oct. 2 Edward I [1274].

Marginal note: Whitacr' B(aculus) i.

Note: Added to letter: Abbas noluit prosequi quia prior fuit thesaurarius regis. Joseph Chauncy was treasurer of Edward I from 2 Oct. 1273; his successor occurs in 1280: *Handbook of British Chronology*, p. 100.

[fol. 22v]

DEEPDALE (TA0682), in the parish of Cayton, and wapentake of Pickering Lythe (NR). Deepdale was part of a cluster of Byland estates comprising Deepdale, Cayton (nos 141–6) and Osgodby (nos 855–76). The Deepdale section of the cartulary is an extensive one, with 47 documents. An early benefactor was Durand de Cliffe (nos 158, 159) and Durand's sons William and Henry confirmed his grants and supplemented them (nos 161–4); other sons, Robert (no. 164) and Richard (no. 188), and grandson Henry (no. 164) assented to them. William son of Durand, also called William of Cayton, granted the monks the church of Rillington (nos 930–1), a grant confirmed by William's nephew, Henry, and Henry's son William (nos 932, 933). Other benefactors in Deepdale included Angot of Osgodby and his descendants (nos 166–8), Ralph de Hallay (no. 165), and the family of Simon de Cliffe (nos 172–7). Deepdale was in the Percy fee, and between *c.* 1160 and 1166 William de Percy confirmed the monks' properties (nos 189, 667). The abbey holdings in Deepdale were extensive, including the manor (no. 159, 162) and pasture land (nos 158, 159), as well as *culture* (nos 163, 167, 168, 176, 187), cultivated land (nos 164) and open fields (165, 166). Some of the land was used for sheep farming (nos 158–9, 175, 178, 183, 194) and there was a grange there by the late 12th century (nos 174, 176, 183, 185, 194).

158 *Grant in free alms, addressed to the archbishop of York and all the sons of holy mother church, by Durand de Cliffe, to God and the monks of St Mary of Byland, of 44 acres in the region of Deepdale and common pasture for 400 sheep and for their other animals throughout the territory of*

*Deepdale, Osgodby, and Cayton, with easements belonging to the vills. To
hold free from all service except for 5s. annual rent to be paid to him and his
heirs when socage rent is due. Pledge to warranty. [c. 1160 x 1166].*

Hiis testibus Ricardo decano de Semar, Willelmo filio meo, Ricardo
sacerdote, etc.

Dating: William de Percy confirmed all the grants of Durand de Cliffe and his heirs
in Deepdale, and those of Angot of Osgodby and his heirs in Osgodby between *c.*
1160 and 1166: see below no. 189 and no. 667, from where printed in *EYC* XI, no. 22.
Farrer suggested a date fairly late in the lifetime of William de Percy.

Note: Byland is also recorded as having houses in Deepdale in the period 1147 x
1167 (below, no. 988; *Cart. Riev.*, no. 243 (p. 178)). With Richard son of Angot and
Geoffrey son of Robert, the donor held a knight's fee in Deepdale, Killerby and
Osgodby (Cayton): *EYC* XI, 233–5. For grants by William and Henry, sons of
Durand, see nos 161–64.

159 *Grant in free alms, addressed to the archbishop of York and all the sons
of holy mother church, by Durand de Cliffe, to God and the monks of St
Mary of Byland, of his manor of Deepdale and 44 acres with the appurtenances of the manor, and common pasture for 400 sheep and other animals
throughout Osgodby and Cayton. The land is to be held free from all service
except the payment of 6s. annual rent to the lord Percy when socage rent is
due. Pledge to warranty. [c. 1160 x 1166].*

Hiis testibus Ricardo decano de Semar, Willelmo filio meo, Ricardo
sacerdote, etc.

Pd: *EYC* XI, no. 189.
Dating: The witnesses suggest the same date as no. 158.

160 *Rubric: Confirmation by Henry of Folkton (ER) of the grant of
Durand de Cliffe.* [late 12th cent.].

Dating: Henry de Floctona is more likely to be Henry of Folkton, south west of
Scarborough, than Flockton (WR). He was married to Alice of Cayton (see below,
no. 178). He witnessed Rievaulx charters dated by Farrer to between 1162 and
c. 1175 (*EYC* II, nos 1246, 1250).

161 *Rubric: Charter of William son of Durand concerning the grant by his
father.* [late 12th cent.].

Dating: William son of Durand made a grant to Byland (no. 930 below) which
Farrer dated to between 1180 and 1190.

162 *Rubric: Confirmation by Henry son of Durand de Cliffe concerning
the grant by his father of the manor of Deepdale (no. 159).* [late 12th cent.].

Marginal note opposite nos 160–62: b(aculus) i.
Dating: as no. 161.

163   *Grant in free alms, addressed to all the sons of holy mother church, present and future, by William of Cayton, to God and St Mary and the monks of Byland, of those 2 bovates in his* culture *in the region of Deepdale lying nearest to the* culture *of Ralph of Osgodby. The monks are to hold these of the donor and his heirs with all easements, free from all service, for the salvation of the soul of the donor and of his ancestors and heirs. To secure this, the monks have granted the donor 2 houses in Scarborough, one in Sand Gate, and the other in Baxter Gate, which the donor gave with his niece Alice as her marriage portion when she married Ralph de Pallyng. Pledge to warranty. The monks will render 12d. yearly to him and his heirs, and will acquit the land of the socage due to the king and others. They are to do with the land as they wish.* [late 12th or early 13th cent.].

Hiis testibus Radulfo Bardolf, Willelmo de Atun, Guarino de Hallay, etc.

Pd: *EYC* XI, no. 191, where dated *c.* 1180 x 1190.

Dating: The donor granted the church of Rillington to Byland in the late 12th century (no. 930). The first witness occurs in a court case of 1210–1212: *Curia Regis Rolls*, VI, 48, 309, 393; *EYC* XI, 217. The second witness may be the William son of Gilbert who attests no. 164, and the son of Gilbert son of Langus (no. 172). The third witness, Warin de Hallay, held 3 carucates in Covenham (Lincs.) of Richard de Percy in 1212: Clay suggested that he was a son of Robert and brother of Ralph (grantor of no. 165); see *EYC* XI, 208–9. Warin also witnessed a general charter of Richard de Percy which can be dated to between 1204 and 1210 (*ibid.* XI, no. 87). The Ralph of Osgodby mentioned in this charter may be the grandson of Angot, son of Richard, and brother of William, grantor of no. 167.

Note: Baxter Gate, the street of the bakers of the town of Scarborough, is mentioned in 1246 (*VCH NR* II, 553). According to David Crouch and Trevor Pearson (*Medieval Scarborough: studies in trade and civic life*, Yorkshire Archaeological Society Occasional Paper no. 1 (Otley, 2001), p. 109) it had been renamed by the 15th century.

[fols 22v–23r]

164   *Grant, addressed to all who read or hear these letters, by William of Cayton son of Durand, to God and the monastery of St Mary of Byland and the brothers of the said monastery, of land 40 perches in length, partly cultivated and partly not cultivated, in his dole* (portion) *of* Hordehov *with the full width of the land. The measurement of the land begins at the end of the dole towards the south and stretches northwards. The grant is made free from all secular service for the salvation of the soul of the donor and for the souls of all his ancestors and heirs. Pledge to warranty against all men except the king. The donor's brother Robert and nephew Henry have agreed to the same; sealed with their seals as well as that of the donor.* [late 12th cent.].

Hii sunt testes Ricardus de Semar decanus, Willelmus filius Gilberti de Atun, etc.

Dating: The donor also granted no. 163. Clay (*EYC* XI, 240) suggested that Robert might be an error for Richard, brother of William, on whom see nos 181, 188; however, Robert occurs in nos 862, 863, and 930. Henry, nephew of the donor, was son of Henry, son of Henry, son of Durand. Richard, chaplain of William de Percy, rector of Seamer and rural dean of Dickering received the church of Seamer in the period 1145 x 1153 (*ibid.*, no. 9) and witnesses in the second half of the 12th century (for example, *ibid.*, nos 71, 75, 78; and above, nos 158–9 and below nos 165, 186, 492, 637, 855, 930). William son of Gilbert of Ayton attests in the period 1170 x 1190 (*EYC* XI, no. 196); see note to no. 163 and no. 172.

[fol. 23r, old fol. 125]

165   *Grant in free alms, addressed to the archbishop of York and the whole chapter of St Peter (York) and all the sons of holy church, by Ralph de Hallay, to God and the monks of St Mary of Byland, of 4 acres of meadow in his fee of (East) Ayton in the open fields* (wandayl), *in the northern part. The grant is made free from all secular service for the salvation of the soul of the donor and of all his ancestors and heirs. Pledge to warranty.* [1175 x c. 1212, possibly 1175 x 1181 or 1191].

Hiis testibus Helia filio Walteri, Ricardo decano de Semar', etc.

Pd: *EYC* XI, no. 175.

Dating: The donor succeeded his father, Robert, who occurs as tenant of the Hallay fee in 1166 and 1175. The earliest date for Ralph's succession is therefore 1175, and he had evidently himself been succeeded by Warin, probably his brother, by 1212 (*EYC* XI, 208–9). Clay dated the charter to 1175 x 1181 or 1191 x c. 1200, on the grounds of the address to the archbishop of York. Although the latest date suggested here is that provided by the succession of Warin to the Hallay fee it is possible that the attestation of Richard, dean of Seamer, would place the charter nearer to 1200 than 1212.

166   *Rubric: Charter of Richard son of Angot concerning a* cultura *in Deepdale, between the enclosures* (oftnames) *and* Witegat *nearest to the boundaries of Seamer.* [late 12th or early 13th cent.].

Dating: The donor, the son of Angot of Osgodby, witnessed a charter of 1185 x 1211: *EYC* I, no. 382. For a further grant by him see below, no. 855.

Note: The monks were granted land in the 'oftnames' in Cayton in no. 145 above.

167   *Rubric: Charter of Ralph son of Richard of Osgodby concerning a* cultura *in Deepdale in* Hordhoudayla *next to the grange of Deepdale.* [late 12th or early 13th cent.].

Dating: A Ralph of Osgodby, without further description, occurs in a charter as the holder of *culture* in Deepdale, 1180 x 1190 (no. 163 above). Ralph represents the third generation of the family of Angot of Osgodby. He had a brother named William, who occurs in no. 168.

168 *Grant in free alms, addressed to all the sons of holy mother church, by Ralph son of Richard of Osgodby, to God and St Mary and the monks of Byland, of 2* culture *in his demesne in the region of Deepdale, of which one lies between 4 hows* (hogas) *and the other nearby to the south. The* culture *begin at the syke* (a sirco *for a* sicco) *which comes from Deepdale and stretch as far as the boundaries of Seamer. The grant is made free from secular service for the salvation of the soul of the donor and of his father and mother and all his ancestors and heirs. Pledge to warranty. His brother and heir, William, attests and agrees the grant.* [late 12th or early 13th cent.].
Hiis testibus etc.

Dating: as no. 167.

169 *Grant in free alms, addressed to all the sons of holy church who will see or hear these letters, by Geoffrey son of G. of Osgodby, to God and the monks of St Mary of Byland, of that bovate in the region of Deepdale which lies between the land of William of Osgodby and that bovate which the donor previously granted to the monks in free alms. The monks are to hold the land free from all secular service, to do there whatever they wish, for the salvation of the soul of the donor and of his ancestors and heirs, and for the performance of forinsec service of the king. Pledge to warranty.* [early 13th cent.].
Hiis testibus Willelmo filio Ricardi de Angotby, Henrico fratre eius, Roberto de Hirton', etc.

Dating: The first witness approved the grant of his brother, Ralph (no. 168). The father of the donor, whose name is here abbreviated to G., may be Gilbert of Osgodby who attests a charter of Elias, brother of Theobald of Dalton, between 1182 and *c.* 1210 (*EYC* XI, no. 232).
Note: The rubric locates the bovate near to the land of Daniel.

170 *Rubric: Charter of the same [Geoffrey son of G.] concerning another bovate in Deepdale, for the performance of forinsec service.* [early 13th cent.].
Dating: as no. 169.

171 *Rubric: Charter of the same [Geoffrey son of G.] concerning a half acre in Deepdale to the north of* Blakow. [early 13th cent.].
Dating: as no. 169.

172 *Grant in free alms, addressed to the archbishop of York and the whole chapter of St Peter (York) and all the sons of holy church, by Simon de Cliffe, to God and the monks of St Mary of Byland, of 1* cultura *in Deepdale, nearest to the land of Seamer. The grant is made quit of all claim and of all secular service for the salvation of the soul of the donor and of his father and* *mother and all his own. Pledge to warranty. Sealed with the donor's ring because he does not have a seal. [c. 1145 x 1170].*

Hiis testibus Osberto Arundell, Gilberto filio Langus, etc.

Copy: MS Dodsworth 91, fol. 90v, no. 33, where the witness list omits 'etc' and continues: et Willelmo filio eius, Richardo presbitero de Caituna, Roberto filio capellani.

Pd: *EYC* XI, no. 193, where the dating is based on the occurrence of the first witness in Whitby charters in the period 1140 x 1166; as Clay notes, this may be the Osbert Arundel who as a canon of Beverley occurs in the same period and as late as *c.* 1170 x 1177; see also *Beverley Minster Fasti*, ed. Richard T. W. McDermid (YASRS, 149 (1993 for 1990), p. 14.

Note: Any relationship between Simon and his son Robert and Durand de Cliffe and his sons William, Richard and Henry, is not clear. Gilbert son of Langus may be the father of William son of Gilbert of Ayton (no. 164) who also attests as William of Ayton (no. 163), and grandfather of Gilbert son of William (no. 183, as Gilbert of Ayton, nos 180, 186, 187, 195).

173   *Rubric: Confirmation by Robert son of Simon of the grant of his father (no. 172).*   [late 12th cent.].

Dating: Robert son of Simon witnesses a charter of William son of Durand in the period *c.* 1180 x 1190: see *EYC* XI, no. 190 and below, no. 186.

174   *Rubric: Charter of the same Robert concerning 1* cultura *at* Fourhus *which stretches from the grange up to the boundaries of Seamer.* [late 12th cent.].

Dating: For the grantor see no. 173.

175   *Rubric: Charter of the same Robert concerning 2* culture *of his land in Deepdale in free alms, one of which is nearest to the monks' sheepfold.* [late 12th cent.].

Dating: For the grantor see no. 173.

[fol. 23v]

176   *Rubric: Charter of the same Robert concerning his* cultura *in Deepdale which is nearest to our* cultura *from the east part of the grange.* [late 12th cent.].

Dating: For the grantor see no. 173.

177   *Rubric: Charter of the same Robert concerning 2* culture *in Deepdale at the 4 hows.* [late 12th cent.].

Dating: For the grantor see no. 173.

178   *Rubric: Charter of Alice of Cayton, wife of Henry of Folkton, that neither she nor her heirs will impound the monks' flocks in* Whitecliva *or in*

*other places belonging to them, and concerning 1 pound of wax to be
rendered yearly to the monks.* [late 12th cent.].

Note: Henry of Folkton confirmed the grant of Durand de Cliffe (above, no. 160).

179 *Rubric: Confirmation by Henry son of Henry of Cayton concerning 2
bovates in Deepdale rendering 12d. yearly.* [early 13th cent.].

Note: The donor was a grandson of Durand de Cliffe: see *EYC* XI, 235.

180 *Confirmation, addressed to all the sons of holy mother church present
and future, by William son of Henry of Cayton, to the monks of St Mary of
Byland, of all the grants which Durand de Cliffe and William his son made,
of land, meadow and pasture, in the region of Deepdale, Osgodby and
Cayton, as their charters show. This confirmation is made for the salvation of
his soul and of all his ancestors and heirs, to hold free from all service except
an annual payment of 6s. as contained in their charters. Pledge to warranty.*
[early 13th cent.].

Hiis testibus Gilberto de Aetona, Iohanne de Aetona, Alano de
Collum, etc.

Dating: John of Ayton witnesses in the 1190s and the early 13th century: see *EYC* I,
nos 381, 413, 644. Alan de Collum witnesses between *c.* 1180 and 1195 (*ibid.* II no.
1077). For Gilbert of Ayton see note to no. 172. In 1208 the donor gave 100s. for
keeping Richard of Cayton to an agreement made between Richard's brother,
William, and Henry, the donor's father: *EYC* XI, 235.

Note: The rubric calls the donor the 'true heir' of Cayton.

181 *Rubric: Confirmation by Richard son of Durand of the homage of
Theobald.* [late 12th to early 13th cent.].

Dating: The donor was party to a final concord in 1200 and occurs in 1208: see note
on the dating of no. 180.

182 *Grant, addressed to the archbishop of York and the whole chapter of St
Peter (York) and all the sons of holy mother church, by Robert son of Simon
of Osgodby with the consent and good will of William his son and heir, to
God and the monks of St Mary of Byland, of 1 bovate of his demesne in the
region of Deepdale, that is the bovate lying furthest to the south and next to
the land of Ivetta daughter of Daniel of Irton. Whatever is lacking from this
bovate the donor will make up from his higher* cultura *at* Fourehoues *which
lies on* Depedalebek *to the western part of* Sumendeshou. *This grant is
made for the salvation of his soul and of all his ancestors and heirs. To have
and to hold of the donor and his heirs, quit of all secular service. Pledge to
warranty by Robert and William.* [late 12th cent.].

Hiis testibus Willelmo de Caytona, Willelmo de Angotby, Willelmo Maucuvenant, etc.

Marginal note: b(aculus) ii.

Dating: On the donor see note to no. 173. With his brother, Ralph, Daniel of Irton (pa. Seamer) witnesses a Whitby charter of date before 1160 (*EYC* XI, no. 10, and p. 273). The first witness is William, son of Durand de Cliffe, and the second probably William son of Angot of Osgodby, who was buried at Whitby (*ibid.*, no. 185). This suggests a date late in the 12th century. The third witness may be an ancestor of Laurence and Robert de Maucuvenant, who held a quarter of a knight's fee in Little Carlton (Lincs.) of the Percy fee in 1242–3 (*ibid.*, p. 213).

183 *Grant in free alms, addressed to all the sons of holy mother church present and future, by Robert son of Simon of Osgodby, to God and the monks of St Mary of Byland, of 7* culture *in the region of Deepdale. Of these, one, which the donor's father, Simon, gave, is nearest to the land of Seamer; another is nearest to the monks' sheepfold towards the south; the third lies next to the spring of Pagan; the fourth is near to the monks'* cultura *to the east of their grange; and 3 lie in* Fourhous. *Grant also of 2 bovates nearest the south next to the land of Ivetta daughter of Daniel of Irton. Whatever is lacking from the bovates in these places the donor will make up from* Symundeshou. *To hold of the donor and his heirs with all appurtenances quit of all secular service for the salvation of his soul and of all his ancestors and heirs. Pledge to warranty.* [late 12th or early 13th cent.].

Hiis testibus Galfrido Maucuvenant, Gilberto filio Willelmi de Aetona, Warino de Hauleya, etc.

Dating: For the Maucuvenant family see note to no. 182; for Gilbert of Ayton, see nos 180, 186, 187, 195; for Warin de Hallay, see note to no. 163.

184 *Rubric: Confirmation by William son of Robert of the same 7* culture. [early to mid 13th cent.].

[fol. 24r, old fol. 126]

185 *Rubric: Charter of Ivetta daughter of Daniel concerning a part of her land in the region of Deepdale beginning at the road which runs from Seamer in front of the gate of the grange towards Cayton.* [2nd half of the 12th cent.].

Dating: Ivetta is mentioned in nos 182–83. Daniel of Irton was brother of Ralph of Irton, father of Baldwin. He attests charters of 1130 x 1138 and 1142 x 1154 (*EYC* I, no. 372 and II, no. 1202). This would suggest a date for no. 185 of the second half of the 12th century.

186 *Rubric: Charter of William son of Durand concerning 2 acres in Deepdale called* Bramlidayles. [*c.* 1180 x 1200].

Text: MS Dodsworth 7, fol. 101v. Grant in free alms, addressed to all present and future, by William son of Durand of Cayton, with the goodwill and assent of Richard his brother and heir, to God and the monks of St Mary of Byland, of 2 acres of profitable land called 'Bramlidailes' in Deepdale, to do there whatever the monks wish. This grant is made for the salvation of his soul and of all his ancestors and successors. Pledge to warranty. Hiis testibus Ricardo persona de Semare, Stephano de Alost, capellano, Gileberto de Atona, Iohanne de Atona, Roberto de Yrtona, Roberto filio Simonis, Willelmo de Osgotebi, Willelmo de Kilverdbi.

Pd: *EYC* XI, no. 190; Clay's dating.

187 *Grant in free alms, addressed to all the sons of holy mother church present and future, by William son of Durand de Cliffe, to God and the monks of St Mary of Byland, of all that* cultura *in the region of Deepdale called* Hordhaudailt *and the butts which stretch towards* Depedalesiic *and all the land which the donor had next to the boundary of Seamer, and all* Hofidlandailt *stretching towards* Depedalesiic, *and all the* cultura *nearest to* Fourhows *towards the north, and 2 acres of cultivated land at* Bramlaidailes. *The grant is made free from all secular service for the salvation of the soul of the donor and of all his ancestors and heirs. Pledge to warranty the said lands with pasture belonging to 1 bovate in Deepdale.* [c. 1180 x 1209].

Hiis testibus Alano Bucel, Gilberto de Atona, Iohanne de Atona, etc.

Dating: The first witness can be identified as Alan Buscel II who succeeded his father, Alan I, *c.* 1170 and died in 1211 (*EYC* I, 296). The charter seems to have been issued before no. 188.

188 *Confirmation, addressed to all the sons of holy church present and future, by Richard son of Durand of Cayton, to the monks of St Mary of Byland, of all the grants and confirmations made by his father, Durand, and his brother, William, in Deepdale, Osgodby, Cayton and Killerby, as contained in their charters. This confirmation is made for the salvation of his soul and of all his ancestors and heirs. Pledge to warranty as in the charters of his father and brother (nos 159, 164, 187).* [1204 x 1209].

Hiis testibus Roberto Walensi tunc vic(ecomite) Ebor', magistro Laurentio de Wilt', Ricardo de Wydevilla, etc.

Marginal note: (in a later hand) 'vic inter 8 & 11 Jo'. The name of the first witness has been underlined.

Pd: *EYC* XI, no. 192.

Dating: tenure of first witness, the undersheriff of Yorkshire in the time of Roger de Lacy, sheriff: see *Lord Lieutenants*, pp. 52–3.

189 *Confirmation, addressed to the archbishop of York and the whole chapter of St Peter (York) and all the sons of holy mother church, by William de Percy, to God and St Mary and the abbot and convent of Byland and their successors, for the salvation of his soul and of all his ancestors and heirs and successors, of all the grants of Durand de Cliffe and his heirs in Deepdale, and the grants of Angot of Osgodby and his heirs in Osgodby, and of all lands, rents, possessions and tenements which the abbot and convent have of his fee in whatever places. The monks are to hold these free from all secular service, and do with them whatever they wish without hindrance on the part of William and his heirs. Sealed with his seal. [c. 1160 x 1166].*

Testes sunt Radulfus de Iretona, Marmeduk, Reynaldus Basset, etc.

Pd: from no. 667 (fol. 73v below) in *EYC* XI, no. 22.

Dating: as *EYC*: Ralph of Irton had been succeeded by his son, Baldwin, by 1166.

Note: In the *Historia Fundationis* grants of land in Deepdale and Cayton are ascribed to William de Percy: *Mon. Ang.* V, 352.

190 *Rubric: Confirmation by William de Percy of the grants of Durand de Cliffe and Angot of Osgodby.* [before Easter 1175].

Dating: Possibly as no. 189, but in the absence of text this can only be dated to before the death of William de Percy.

191 *Rubric: Charter of Geoffrey son of Pain of Osgodby concerning 1 acre, and confirmation of the grant made by his father.*

192 *Rubric: Charter of William son of Robert of Osgodby concerning 3* culture *in Deepdale.* [late 12th or early 13th cent.].

Dating: William, son of Robert, son of Simon of Osgodby assented to his father's grant of 1 bovate: see no. 182 above.

193 *Rubric: Charter of William son of Henry of Cayton by which the guardian of Deepdale paid ½ mark on his behalf at Seamer.* [early to mid 13th cent.].

194 *Rubric: Chirograph agreement between the monks and Thomas de Anlacby (Anlaby, pa. Kirk Ella) concerning the exchange of 8 sellions in Deepdale which the monks have of Thomas, of which 4 lie next to the sheepfold and the other 4 next to the wall of the grange of Deepdale.* [? late 13th cent.].

Marginal note: B(aculus) iii.

Note: Clay discusses two narrative accounts of the Anlaby family, both preserved among the Dodsworth manuscripts. According to these Thomas was one of three sons of William, who was granted land in Seamer by his father and he granted these to William de Percy in exchange for lands in East Ayton. It is not clear how the family acquired an interest in Seamer, but by 1284/5 a member of the family named Thomas was holding 13 bovates in Deepdale (*EYC* XII, 25–7; *KI*, p. 139).

[fol. 24r–v]

195 *Grant in free alms, addressed to all the sons of holy mother church present and future, by William son of Henry of Cayton, to God and the monks of St Mary of Byland, of 2½ bovates in the region of Deepdale, that is, all the land which came to the donor when the holding of his ancestors in Deepdale was divided between the donor and Richard of Rillington. The monks are to hold the land freely and do with it what they wish, for the salvation of the soul of the donor and of all his ancestors and heirs. Pledge to warranty.* [before 1211].

Hiis testibus Gilberto de Atona, Baldwino de Alvestain, Alano Bucel, Iohanne de Atona, etc.

Dating: Alan Buscel II died in 1211 (*EYC* I, 296). Baldwin of Allerston occurs in the late 12th and early 13th century (*ibid.* I, nos 389–90). Gilbert and John of Ayton witness together in *c.* 1180 x 1190, and Gilbert son of William of Ayton and Alan Buscel attest together in 1170 x 1190 (*ibid.* XI, nos 190 (above, no. 186), 196).

[fol. 24v]

196 *Rubric: Charter of Rose, wife of Richard of Osgodby, concerning 2 bovates in Deepdale. Surrendered.* [?late 12th cent.].

Note: If this is the wife of Richard son of Angot a date in the late 12th century is likely.

197 *Rubric: Chirograph of William of Cayton concerning 2 acres for another 2 acres in Deepdale from which Richard de Percy ejected us.* [1198 x 1244, probably earlier in the period].

Note: William demised land to Byland until the monks should recover the land in Deepdale that Richard de Percy withheld from them (no. 145 above, and note).

198 *Rubric: Charter of William son of Richard of Osgodby concerning a* cultura *near the sheepfold in Deepdale.* [13th cent.].

Note: The grantor was the grandson of Angot of Osgodby.

199 *Rubric: Confirmation of the same William of the grants of his grandfather, father and brother.* [13th cent.].

Note: This is a confirmation of the grants of his grandfather, Angot, his father, Richard, and his brother, Ralph (nos 166, 167, 168; also nos 189, 190).

200 *Rubric: Charter of William son of Richard of Osgodby concerning harvest service.* [13th cent.].

201 *Confirmation and quitclaim, addressed to all the sons of holy mother church present and future, by Henry son of Richard of Osgodby for himself and his heirs, to God and St Mary and the abbot and convent of Byland, of all the grants, lands and possessions with their appurtenances which the abbot and convent have of his fee and by the grant of his ancestors. The confirmation is made for the salvation of the soul of the donor and of all his ancestors and heirs. Pledge to warranty. Sealed with the donor's seal.* [before c. 1260]. Hiis testibus dominis Galfrido de Upsal', Willelmo filio eius, Alano de Lek', etc.

Dating: Geoffrey of Upsall the elder occurs in 1244 and held a knight's fee in Kilvington in 1282 (*EYC* IX, 180–1); he had been succeeded by his son, Hugh, by 1284–5 (*KI*, pp. 97–8). The attestation of Alan of Leake suggests a date before *c.* 1260 (see nos 31, 121, 128, 129, 494–6, 509, 515, 616, 848, 852, 998, 1146). The donor would appear to be a later descendant of the line of Angot of Osgodby.

202 *Rubric: Confirmation of John of Eston of all the lands which the monks have in Deepdale, Cayton, Osgodby, Killerby and Rillington. Look among the confirmations.*

Note: A text of the confirmation by John of Eston of the manor of Rillington and the monks' lands in Osgodby and Cayton, is included in the cartulary at no. 960 (under Rillington).

203 *Rubric: Remission by William son of Henry of Cayton of 18d. yearly for the farm of the socage of Deepdale.* [13th cent.].

204 *Rubric: Quitclaim by Henry of Folkton (ER) of the same 18d.* [late 12th cent.].

Marginal note beside nos 203 and 204: b(aculus) iiii.
Dating: Henry was married to Alice of Folkton (no. 178 above) and confirmed a grant by Durand de Cliffe (no. 160); for other occurrences see no. 160, note.

[fol. 25r, old fol. 127]
DENBY, in the township of Upper Whitley and the parish of Kirkheaton, and BRIESTWISTLE, in the parish of Thornhill, both in the wapentake of Agbrigg (WR). The headings to fols 25–27 include both place names. The only significant settlement in Briestwistle is now Briestfield (SE2317); the lost vill of 'Alwoldley' appears to have been the eastern side of Briestwistle, and may have been depopulated by the monks (*West Yorks.*, II, 442–3, III, 795–6). Lower Denby lies at SE2416 and Upper Denby at SE2316. This is one of the most extensive sections of the cartulary; even without taking into account two missing folios of Denby charters (old fols 130–1) there are fifty docu-

ments and rubrics copied into the cartulary. There has also been a remarkable survival of original charters, now BL Add. charters 7409–82 (see Appendix I), and a fragment of a charter roll, preserved in MS Dodsworth 76, contains copies of some Denby charters. The accumulation of lands was due to the steady acquisition of property from a range of benefactors in the vill. The families of Henry of Thurstonland, Michael of Briestwistle, Swane of Denby, and Osbern of Denby, laid the foundations of Byland's territorial expansion. One of the earliest acquisitions was a modest one, one acre of land and a spring (no. 205), and the rent due on this was the subject of a further set of charters (nos 206–10, 214). From the late 12th century onwards the monks acquired land described as profitable land and pasture land (see for example, no. 225), and mining rights (no. 228). There were evidently controversies over certain issues, among them the extension of arable and the use of pasture (nos 244, 250). There was a road linking the grange of Denby with Bentley (no. 210)

205   Original: *Grant in free alms, addressed to the archbishop of York and the whole chapter of St Peter (York) and all the sons of holy church, by Henry of Thurstonland, to God and the monks of St Mary of Byland, of 1 acre in the region of Denby, that is, all his part around* Stockeswella *and the spring itself, and all that part at the head of the sike of* Pilatecroft *to complete the acre. If there is more than 1 acre there he grants it to the monks. The grant is made free from all secular service for the salvation of the soul of the donor and of all his ancestors and heirs, to do there as the monks wish. Pledge to warranty.* [1184 x 1191 or 1191 x 1194].
Hiis testibus Waltero filio Hugonis vicecomite, Henrico clerico, Adam filio Orm, Michaele de Breretuisil, Roberto de Silfleia, Willelmo filio Helie, Unfrido de Laceles, Willelmo filio Morker, Simone de Dala, Osberto de Stodleia.

Location: BL Add. charter 7415; endorsed: Denebi I B I (Denby, first bundle, 1); C. Henrici de Turstanland de una acra terre. Pur. Nota; seal: red wax, round; SIGILL HENRICI DE THVRSTAINLAND. Second charter: BL Add. charter 7414; endorsed: Denebi I B i altera melior est; C. Henrici de Turstaintland de una acra terre.
Pd (from original): *EYC* III, no. 1813; (calendar) *Yorks. Deeds*, VI, 51–2, no. 169.
Dating: in *EYC* 1184 x 1191, with no explanation. However Farrer dated another charter (*ibid.*, I, no. 221), also attested by the first witness, to between 1184 and 1191, on the grounds that the sheriffs from 1191 are well attested, and therefore Walter son of Hugh must have been sheriff before that date. In the cartulary copy (where the name of the first witness is William) the word *vicec'* is suspended; in both originals it is expanded to *vicecomite*. However, if this is an error for *vicecomitis* the first witness may be Walter son of Hugh Bardolf, who was sheriff from 1191 to

1194, although Hugh died without direct heirs in 1194, his heir being his brother Robert (*Lord Lieutenants*, p. 51). The grantor attests a charter of 1202 x c. 1210 (*EYC* VIII, no. 90). Humphrey de Lascelles attests between c. 1196 x 1210 and c. 1200 x 1212 (*ibid.*, nos 152, 155). William son of Morker attests c. 1189 (*ibid.*, 226).

Note: The cartulary copy has the first 3 witnesses only and ends 'etc'. The first witness is given as 'Willelmo'. There are minor textual variants between BL Add. charter 7414 and 7415, and the cartulary text is closer to the latter. The cartulary rubric states that the charter has been copied ('duplicatur').

206   Original: *Grant in free alms, addressed to all the sons of holy church present and future, by Henry of Thurstonland, to God and the monks of St Mary of Byland, of 4 bovates in the region of Denby with tofts and crofts etc. inside and outside the vill. The grant is made free from secular service to do with whatever they wish, for the salvation of the soul of the donor and of all his ancestors and heirs, to hold for the performance of knight service as pertains to a half carucate, where 12 carucates make a knight's fee. Pledge to warranty.* [1204 x 1209].

Hiis testibus Roberto Walensi tunc vic(ecomite) Ebor', Ricardo Malebis, Willelmo de Percy, Willelmo de Corneburgo, Gikello de Smedtona, Gaufrido Fossard, Thoma de Lasceles, Iordano de Hetona, Iordano de Floctona, Rogero de Tornet', Thoma de Tornet', Adam de Mirefeld, Iordano de Denebi.

Location: BL Add. charter 7410; endorsed: Denebi i B ii (Denby, first bundle, 2); seal: as no. 205.

Marginal note in cartulary: (in a later hand) '6. R. Jo.'. The word 'vic' in the text has been underlined.

Pd (from original): *EYC* III, no. 1814; (calendar) *Yorks. Deeds*, V, 52, no. 170.

Dating: as *EYC* (no explanation); tenure of first witness.

Note: The cartulary copy has the first five witnesses only and ends 'etc'. William of Cornborough and Gikel of Smeaton attest no. 116 above.

207   Original: *Notification by the monks of St Mary of Byland that they owe Henry son of Henry of Thurstonland 20s. annual rent paid to him and his heirs at St Oswald (5 Aug.) for a half carucate which his father, Henry, gave them in Denby. They shall pay this farm faithfully as long as his father and his heirs warranty the land.* [1199 x 1214].

Hiis testibus Symone decano Ebor', magistro Willelmo archidiacono de Notingham, Hamone thesaurario, magistro Willelmo de Sciendebi, magistro Gregorio, Constantino priore de Bell(al)ande, Gaufrido suppriore, Waltero cellerario, Ricardo subcellerario, Roberto infirmario, Gikello monacho, fratre Willelmo grangiario de Elmeda.

Location: BL Add charter 7431; endorsed: Denebi i B iii (Denby, first bundle, 3); Carta Henrici filii Henrici de xx sol.; seal: black wax, round, legend recorded in

Yorks. Deeds as SIGILL HENRICI FIL'I HENRIC, but no longer visible.
Pd (calendar): *Yorks. Deeds*, VI, 52, no. 171.
Dating: first three witnesses.
Note: The cartulary copy has the first, second and fourth witnesses only and ends 'etc'. This is an unusually complete list of the obedientiaries of Byland; the reference to the granger of Emley indicates the existence of a grange there by the early 13th century.

208   Original: *Undertaking, addressed to all the sons of holy mother church present and future, by Gilbert of Croft, secured by his seal, that he will only exact 1 silver mark from the monks of St Mary of Byland from the farm of 20s. which they owe Henry of Thurstonland annually at St Oswald (5 Aug.) for land which they hold of Henry in the region of Denby. Sealed with Henry's seal at Gilbert's request.* [1216 x 1240].

Hiis testibus Henrico Walense tunc ballivo domini Iohannis de Lasci, Henrico de Scelflai, Henrico de Thurstainland', Mattheo de Thurstaineland, Nicolao de Birton', Roberto de eadem villa.

Location: BL Add. charter 7436; endorsed: Denebi B i iiii (Denby, first bundle, 4); C. Gilberti de Crofto de i m. redd. eidem; seals: (i) red-brown wax, round; SIGILL GILEBERTI DE CROFTE (ii) as no. 207.
Pd (calendar): *Yorks. Deeds*, VI, 53, no. 173.
Dating: Henry Waleys was steward of John de Lascy, constable of Chester (d. 1240) from 1216. Henry of Thurstonland and Matthew of Thurstonland attest together with Robert de Birton (Kirkburton) in 1202 x *c.* 1210 (*EYC* VIII, no. 90), suggesting a date earlier in the period. No. 213 may have been issued on the same occasion.
Note: The cartulary copy has the first three witnesses only and ends 'etc'.

209   *Rubric: Charter of Henry son of Henry concerning 1 mark of the said 20s. which he sold to Gilbert of Croft. Surrendered.*
Original: *Sale and quitclaim, addressed to all the sons of holy mother church present and future, by Henry son of Henry of Thurstonland, to Gilbert son of Hugh of Croft and his heirs and assigns, of 1 silver mark from the yearly farm of 20s. which the monks of Byland were accustomed to render to Henry for all his land in Denby, at St Oswald (5 Aug.). Sealed with his seal. For greater security he has shown this to the monks.* Byland [1216 x 1240].

Hiis testibus Thoma tunc priore de Bellaland', Willelmo subpriore, Willelmo cellerario, Hugone mercatore, Iohanne de Beverlaco, monacho, et capitulo de Bellaland', Henrico Walensi tunc senesc(allo) domini Iohannis de Lascy, Henrico de Schelflay, Mattheo de Turstanland, Nicholao de Birton', Roberto de Birton', Petro de Birton', clerico, et aliis pluribus.

Location: BL Add. charter 7449; endorsed: Denebi i B v (Denby, first bundle, 5); C. Henr' filii Henr' de i marca; seal: round, red wax; SIGILL' HENRICI FILI

HENRICI.
Pd (calendar): *Yorks. Deeds*, VI, 52–3, no. 172.
Dating: see no. 208.

210   Rubric: *Quitclaim by Michael of Briestwistle of an annual rent of 1 mark, and also of 2s. for the road between Denby and Bentley.* [c. 1260]
Dating: as no. 214.

[fol. 25r–v]
211   Original: *Grant in free alms, addressed to all the sons of holy mother church present and future, by Henry son of Swane of Denby, to God and the monks of St Mary of Byland, of all his land in Denby except for 3 acres which he has granted to the Hospital of (St John of) Jerusalem. The monks are to hold the land with all its appurtenances free from all secular service, and do with it what they wish, for the salvation of the soul of the donor and for the souls of his father and mother and of all his ancestors and heirs. For this the monks initially gave him 100s. and in recognition of the grant will give him and his heirs 7s. 6d. annually within the octave of Whitsuntide. Pledge to warranty.* [1191 x 1194].

Hiis testibus Radulfo de Novavilla domino meo, Hugone Bardolf tunc vicecomete (*sic*), Hugone de Boeby, Rogero de Bavent, Sampsone filio Hervei, Roberto filio Dolfini, Wymundo de Mirefeld, Roberto de Chambord, Willelmo Datona, Waltero Dathelingflet, Yvone fratre eius.

Location: BL Add. charter 7416; endorsed: Denby B i (Denby, first bundle); C. H. filii Swani de Denby; seal: red wax, round; SIGIL' ENRICI F. SVAINI F.
Copies: MS Dodsworth 76, fol. 146r, damaged (omits first witness); MS Dodsworth 8, fol. 84r; MS Dodsworth 94, fol. 59r, no. 1.
Pd (from original): *EYC* III, no. 1807; (calendar) *Yorks. Deeds*, VI, 47–8, no. 158.
Dating: second witness. The cartulary copy has only the first three witnesses and ends 'etc'.
Note: Although the endorsement indicates only that the charter was in the first Denby bundle its location in the cartulary between no. 210 (charter 6) and 212 (charter 8) suggest that this was charter 7 in the first bundle. In the right hand margin of the cartulary (fol. 25r), in a later hand, is a family tree showing the descent from Swane of Denby, though his son, Henry, to Henry's son Jordan (ante 6 R1), and from Osbert of Denby, through his son William, to William son of William (temp. H3). Another scribe has added a second son of Henry son of Swane, ?Swane son of Henry.

[fol. 25v]
212   Rubric: *Confirmation by Jordan son of Henry of Denby of all his land in Denby except the 3 acres noted above.*
Original: *Confirmation in free alms, addressed to all the sons of holy mother*

church present and future, by Jordan son of Henry of Denby, to God and St Mary of Byland and the monks serving God there, of the grant made by Henry his father, that is, all the land of Denby except for 3 acres. The monks are to hold the land with all its appurtenances, liberties and easements inside and outside the vill, free from all service, to do there whatever they wish, for the salvation of the soul of the donor and of his father and mother and all his own. The monks are to render to him and his heirs 7s. 6d. at the grange of Denby within the octave of Whitsuntide for all service. Pledge to warranty. [before 1219].

Hiis testibus domino Hugone de Novavilla domino meo, Hugone filio Walteri, Matheo filio Hugonis de Sepelaya, Adam filio Philippi, Alano de Whytelay, Iordano filio Mathei de Flokketon', Petro clerico de Wymund' de Mirefeld, et toto wapentaco de Wakefeld'.

Location: BL Add. charter 7464; endorsed: B. primus 8 (first bundle, 8); Confirmatio Iordani de Deneby filii Henrici de Denby; seal: oval, red wax; SIGILL' IORDANI FIL' HENRICI DE DENEBI.
Copies: BL Add. charters 7470, 7474.
Pd (calendar from BL Add. charter 7464): *Yorks. Deeds*, VI, 48, no. 159.
Dating: Death of grantor (9 Feb. 1219). In 3 Henry III Mary, widow of Jordan of Denby, claimed against Henry le Waleys a third part of 2 bovates in Denby and 'Harelawe' as her dower. She also brought a claim against the abbot of Byland: *Yorks. Fines 1218–1231*, p. 21 and note.
Note: A later marginal note in the cartulary reads 'tempore R I' against 'Confirmatio Iordani'. This is entirely consistent with the date of no. 218, also issued by Jordan son of Henry of Denby.

213 *Rubric: Charter of Henry son of Henry of Thurstonland concerning 1 mark. Surrendered.*
Original: *Sale and quitclaim, addressed to all who will see or hear this charter, by Henry son of Henry of Thurstonland, to the abbot and convent of Byland and their successors, of that half silver mark from the annual farm of 20s. which the monks of Byland were accustomed to render to him at St Oswald (5 Aug.) for Henry's land in Denby. Of this 20s. he sold 1 mark to Gilbert son of Hugh of Croft and his heirs, and quitclaimed it to the abbot and convent so that Gilbert shall return to the monks the charter which Henry gave him concerning the mark which he sold him. This quitclaim is made in free alms for the salvation of his soul and of all his ancestors and heirs, notwithstanding the previous chirograph agreement between him and the monks concerning the 20s. to be rendered to him and his heirs, which from now on shall no longer be paid.* [1216 x 1240].

Hiis testibus Henrico Walensi, tunc senescallo domini Iohannis de Lascy, Henrico de Scelflay, Mattheo de Turstainland, Nicholao de Birton', Roberto de Birton', clerico, et aliis.

Location: BL Add. charter 7413; endorsed: Quieta clamatio Henrici de; seal: round, green wax; SIGILL' HENRICI FILI HENRICI.
Pd (calendar): *Yorks. Deeds*, VI, 53, no. 174.
Dating: see no. 208.

214   Rubric: *Remission by Michael of Briestwistle of 1 mark which the monks were accustomed to render to Gilbert of Croft and of 2s. which they rendered to William son of Jordan of Flockton for a road between Bentley and Denby.*
Original: *Quitclaim, addressed to all the faithful in Christ seeing or hearing the present charter, by Michael of Briestwistle for himself and his heirs or assigns, to God and St Mary and the abbot and convent of Byland, of that mark of annual rent which the abbot and convent used to render to Gilbert of Croft at the feast of St Oswald (5 Aug.) for land in Denby, which mark Michael received from them in Gilbert's name. Quitclaim also of 2s. annual rent which they rendered to Jordan of Denby and his heirs for a path running between their grange of Denby and Bentley, which Michael received from them in the name of Gilbert of Croft or William of Flockton, son and heir of Jordan of Flockton, by the charters of Gilbert and William which Michael has surrendered to the abbot and convent. If any claim is made against the monks for the money or annual rent by Gilbert of Croft or William of Flockton or their heirs or assigns Michael and his heirs will bear the monks' expenses. Sealed with the seal of the grantor. Pledge to warranty. [c. 1260].*
Hiis testibus dominis Thoma filio Willelmi, Iohanne de Hoderod, Radulpho de Horbyri, Willelmo de Wath, militibus, Ricardo le Normaund, Willelmo de Beumont, Iohanne de Crancewyk, Henrico de Byry, Iohanne de Byry, et aliis.
Location: BL Add. charter 66799; endorsed: Deneby B i vi (Denby, first bundle, 6); C' M. de Brertuysel de remissione unius marci quam consuevimus reddere Gilberto de Croft et de ii solidis quos reddidimus Willelmo filio Iordani de Flocketun pro via inter Benetelay et Deneby; seal: oval, red wax; legend not visible.
Pd: *Yorks. Deeds*, V, 29, no. 59, from the original then in the possession of Lord Allendale of Bretton Park, Wakefield.
Dating: see no. 242, which is related to this quitclaim.
Note: For the grant by Jordan of Flockton see no. 241 below.

215   *Sale and quitclaim, addressed to all who will see or hear this charter, by Henry son of Henry of Thurstonland, to the abbot and convent of Byland and their successors, of ½ silver mark from the 20s. farm which the monks were accustomed to render to him annually at St Oswald (5 Aug.) for the donor's land in Denby. Of the 20s. the donor has sold one silver mark to Gilbert son of Hugh of Croft and his heirs. He now quitclaims that silver mark to the abbot and convent so that Gilbert will give them the donor's* *charter concerning the same mark (no. 209). This quitclaim is made for the salvation of the soul of the donor and of his ancestors and heirs, notwithstanding a chirograph charter drawn up between himself and the monks concerning the 20s. due to him and his heirs, which they shall no longer pay.* [1216 x 1240].

Hiis testibus Henrico Walensi tunc senescallo domini Iohannis de Lascy, Henrico de Schelflay, etc.

Dating: as no. 208.

216 *Rubric: Quitclaim by Daniel son of Daniel the clerk, of all his right in 3 acres which Henry son of Swane granted to the hospital.*

Original: *Remission, addressed to all who will see or hear these letters, by Daniel son of Daniel the clerk for himself and his heirs, to God and the monks of St Mary of Byland, of all right which he and his ancestors had in 3 acres with appurtenances which Henry son of Swane granted to the Hospitallers of Jerusalem in the region of Denby. Pledge on oath that neither he nor his heirs will bring any claim against the monks or against the Hospitallers concerning the 3 acres.* [1191 x 1194].

His testibus Roberto Walensi, Iordano de Floctona, Henrico de Turstainland, Willelmo de Sothil, Rogero de Tornetona, Thoma de Tornetona, Iordano de Denebi, Swano de Brett', Willelmo filio Willelmi de Denebi.

Location: BL Add. charter 7435; endorsed: Denebi i B ix (Denby, first bundle, 9); C. Daniel' filii Danielis de remissione iuris in tribus acris de Denebi; seal: red-brown wax, round; SIGILL' DANIEL' FIL' DANIEL' CL'I.

Pd (calendar): *Yorks. Deeds*, VI, 55, no. 181.

Dating: For the grant by Henry son of Swane see no. 211. This may have been issued on the same occasion.

Note: The word for clerk in its genitive form, *clerici*, makes it clear that it was Daniel senior who was the clerk, not the grantor of this charter.

217 *Rubric: Charter of Simon son of Henry concerning 1 carucate in the region of Denby, rendering to him 2s. yearly.*

Original: *Grant in free alms, addressed to all the sons of holy mother church present and future, by Simon son of Henry of Denby, to God and St Mary of Byland and the monks serving God there, of 1 carucate with its appurtenances in the region of Denby which Henry his father gave him for homage and service. He grants this to the monks with the assent and goodwill of Jordan, his brother and his lord, free of service, to hold of the donor and his heirs, with tofts and crofts and assarts, and all its appurtenances, liberties and easements inside and outside the vill, for the performance of forinsec service on 1 carucate where 12 carucates make a knight's fee, and for 2s.*

paid yearly to him and his heirs, 12d. at Whitsuntide and 12d. at St Martin (11 Nov.) for all the service due to them. The grant is made for the salvation of his soul and those of his father and mother and all his ancestors and heirs. Pledge to warranty. Because he does not have a seal, the charter is sealed with the seal of his brother Jordan. [1190 x 1198].

Hiis testibus Iordano et Helia fratribus meis, Symone filio Symonis de Claitona, Rogero fratre eius, Suano de Brettona, Adam de Hoiland, Iordano de Floctun.

Location: BL Add. charter 7423; endorsed: Denebi i B x (Denby, first bundle, 10); C. Symonis fil' Henrici de Denebi de una carr' terre in Denebi faciendo forinsecum servitium; seal: oval, red wax; SIGILLUM IORDANIS FIL <HEN>RICI DE DENEB. Second charter: BL Add. charter 7447: endorsed: C. Symonis fil' Henrici de Denebi de una carr' terre in Denebi; seal: oval, red wax; SIGILL IORDANIS FIL . . . EBI.

Copy: MS Dodsworth 76, fol. 146r.

Pd: *EYC* III, no. 1811 (from MS Dodsworth 76); calendar, from original: *Yorks. Deeds*, VI. 48, no. 160.

Dating: *EYC* gives 1190 x 1219, but the charter was issued before no. 218.

218 Rubric: *Confirmation by Jordan son of Henry of Denby of the said carucate, which Simon his brother granted the monks rendering 1 pound of pepper for all service.*

Original: *Grant and confirmation, addressed to all the sons of holy mother church present and future, by Jordan son of Henry of Denby, to God and the monks of St Mary of Byland, of 1 carucate in the region of Denby which Simon his brother granted them in free alms, to hold free from all secular service of him and his heirs, with tofts and crofts and assarts and all appurtenances, liberties and easements inside and outside the vill, in woodland, plain, land and water, meadow and pasture, moor and marsh, turbaries, ways and paths and all other easements, rendering forinsec service to the lord king on 1 carucate where 12 carucates make a knight's fee. For the rent of 2s. which Simon his brother was accustomed to render to Jordan the monks will give Jordan and his heirs 1 pound of pepper within the octave of St Martin for all service that belongs to him and his heirs. This confirmation is made for the salvation of his soul and of his father and mother and all his ancestors and heirs. Pledge to warranty.* [1194 x 1198].

His testibus Rogero de Bavent tunc vicec(omite) Eborac', Alexandro de Baiocis, Waltero de Bovingtona, Willelmo de Corneburch, Alano de Sinderbi, Petro de Meteleia, Adam de Mirefeld, Henrico de Selfleia, Symone fratre meo, Willelmo de Breretuisel, et comitatu Eboracensi.

Location: BL Add. charter 7437; endorsed: Denebi i B. xi (Denby, first bundle, 11); Conf' Iordani filii Henrici de Denebi de donatione 1 carrucata de Simone fratre

eius; seal: oval, red wax, damaged; SIGILL IORDANI FILI <HENRICI> DE DENEBI.
Pd (calendar): *Yorks. Deeds*, VI, 48–9, no. 161.
Dating: first witness.

219 Rubric: *Remission by Jordan son of Henry of 2 pounds of pepper for 1 pound of cumin.*
Original: *Quitclaim, addressed to all the sons of holy mother church who will see or hear these letters, by Jordan son of Henry of Denby for himself and his heirs, to God and the monks of St Mary of Byland, of 2 pounds of pepper which the monks were accustomed to render to him yearly, 1 pound for the carucate in Denby which he granted them, with its appurtenances, with his brother, Simon, and the other pound for the bovate they held of him in Allerton, for 1 pound of cumin paid to him yearly within the octave of St Oswald. Forinsec service is due to Jordan's lords from the lands which they hold of him, without interference, as his charters attest. Pledge to warranty.* [before 1219].
Hiis testibus Roberto de Mohaud, Radulfo de Normanvill', Samsone de Wridlesford', Hugone de Swinlingtun, Hugone de Hortun, Adam de Mirefeud, Iohanne filio Hugonis de Tornetun.
Location: BL Add. charter 7418; endorsed: Denebi i B xii, forinsecum (Denby, first bundle, 12, forinsec); Iordani filii Henrici de redditu ii libris piperis; seal: oval, brown wax; SIGILL IORDANI FILI HENRICI DE DENEBI
Copy: MS Dodsworth 76, fol. 146r, where marginal note also indicates no. 12.
Pd (calendar): *Yorks. Deeds*, VI, 49, no. 162.
Dating: death of the donor; see also nos 212, 217, 218.

220 Rubric: *Remission by the same [Jordan son of Henry] of 1 pound of cumin.* [1209 x 1212].
Text: MS Dodsworth 76, fol. 146r; MS Dodsworth 8, fol. 83v.
Quitclaim, addressed to all the sons of holy mother church present and future, by Jordan son of Henry of Denby, to God and the monks of St Mary of Byland, of 1 pound of cumin which the monks were bound to render annually to him for that carucate which he gave in alms with his brother Simon, and quitclaim of all that he had had against the monks up until this time. Hiis testibus Henrico Reddeman tunc vicecomite Ebor', Hugone de Magneby, Hugone clerico de Alverton', Thoma de Thorneton', Rogero le Scot, Ada tunc priore Belleland', Gikello cell(erario).
Dating: first witness.
Note: A marginal note in Dodsworth 76 indicates that this is charter 13.

221 *Rubric: Chirograph agreement between the monks and John son of Harding of Shepley concerning a third part of* Osmundesmait.

Original: *Agreement between the abbot and monks of Byland on the one part and John son of Harding and Matthew of Shepley on the other relating to all the complaints which had been brought by the monks against John and Matthew in 1202, both in the king's court and in the court of the archbishop. John has quitclaimed to the abbot and monks a third part of* Osmundesmait *which the abbot and monks had claimed belonged to a carucate which they held in alms in Denby, to have and use as their own as they wish without impediment by John and his heirs, provided that it should not be assarted on either side nor a house built there without the consent of either party. The monks are to have free right of way for themselves, their animals and their wagons as they have need along the road lying between John's barn towards the west and his little tower* (thuriolum), *so that there shall be no more constraints on the road than there were when this agreement was made. For this quitclaim the monks have given John 10s. and they have remitted to John and Matthew all complaints against them, especially the alleged violence done to their brother, Richard of Stodley.* [after 1202].

His testibus magistro Stephano de Melsa, magistro A. domini archiepiscopi capellano, magistro R. de Melsambi, magistro Ricardo de Turre, magistro Nicholao de Wlrunhamtun, Ieremia de Torhil, Rogero de Ledesham, Iohanne Talenax, Hugone de Silkestun', Radulfo de Ecclesfeud et multis aliis.

Location: BL Add. charter 7463, one half of a chirograph; endorsed: Denebi i B xiiii (Denby, first bundle, 14); Compo' pacis inter Bell' et Iohannem filium Harding; de via estimo quod thuriolum ponitur pro le kylne ('concerning the road – I think that the tower means the kiln'), words which also appear on a vellum tag, attached, with 'suspicor' for 'estimo'; seal: red wax, oval; SIGILL IOHANNIS FIL ARDING. Pd (calendar): *Yorks. Deeds*, VI, 54, no. 177.

222 *Rubric: Chirograph between the same John [son of Harding] and the monks concerning an exchange of lands.*

Original: *Agreement, addressed to all who will see or read these letters, between the monks of St Mary of Byland and John son of Harding concerning an exchange by which the monks have given John 9 acres in the region of Denby for 7 acres in the same region which he has granted to the monks. Of the 7 acres which John grants to the monks 4 lie above the long furlongs nearest to the houses of the monks, another 2 are in Castlegate on the southern side, and 1 lies above* Stockewelle *furlangs. If anything is lacking John will make it up from* Pilatecroft *nearest to the houses of the monks, and if there is more he grants it to them for his soul and his wife and* *his ancestors and heirs. Of the 9 acres which John has received in exchange from the monks 8 lie above the long furlongs towards the north, and the ninth where Alvive's house was, and if there is more there he shall have it all. The last acre, at Alvive's house and at the exit of* Pilatecroft, *shall be the monks' boundary unless more shall be granted to them in free alms.* [before Michaelmas 1189].

His testibus Hugone filio Harding, Matheo filio eius, Michaele de Breretuisel, Henrico de Turstainland, Roberto de Solvelai, Willelmo filio Helie, Simone de Emelei, Suano de Kirkebi, Huvieto de Emmelei.

Location: BL Add. charter 7480, one half of chirograph; endorsed: Denebi i B xv (Denby, first bundle, 15); Compositio inter nos et Iohannem filium Harding de escambio terre in Denebi; seal: red wax, round; SIGILLVM IOHANNIS FILII HARDING.

Pd: *EYC* III, no. 1812; (calendar) *Yorks. Deeds*, VI, 54, no. 176, from the original.

Dating: The first witness died between Michaelmas 1188 and Michaelmas 1189 (*EYC* VIII, 246).

Note: The second witness is also known as Matthew of Shepley (*EYC* VIII, 246).

223 Rubric: *Charter of William of Soothill* (Sothell) *concerning the same.* [late 12th or early 13th cent.].

Dating: William of Soothill occurs in the early 13th century (*EYC* VIII, no. 133) but the charter may be near in date to no. 222.

[fols 25v–26r]

224 Original: *Grant in free alms addressed to the archbishop of York and the whole chapter of St Peter (York) and all the sons of holy church, by William son of Osbert of Denby, to God and the monks of St Mary of Byland, of 24 acres of profitable land in the region of Denby, that is in* Pilatecroft *and in the long furlongs and in the tofts and at the head of the tofts towards the north. Grant also of the whole* cultura *which the donor had nearest to the monks'* cultura *which they had of Henry son of Swane. If there is anything lacking from the 24 acres the donor will make it up from his own* culture *to the easement of the monks. Grant also of common pasture of the vill for 200 sheep and 20 animals and 2 horses wherever he, his heirs and his men graze their animals beyond the corn and meadow. Grant also of all his iron stone throughout Clover Leys* (Claverlay) *to mine freely and to use as the monks wish, with rights of entry and exit to transport the mineral across his land. William and his heirs are to have their own enclosure in Clover Leys, that is, whatever is contained within the ditch to the west of his house as far as the boundaries of Flockton, from the beginning of May until the hay is brought in. Thereafter the monks are to have common pasture throughout Clover*

Leys. The grant is made free from all secular service for the salvation of the soul of the donor and of all his ancestors and heirs. Pledge to warranty. The monks are to render 3s. yearly in recognition in the octave of Whitsuntide. [c. 1170 x 1186].

His testibus Roberto decano Ebor', Hamone cantore, Geroldo, Alano, Mainerdo canonicis, Alfredo, Alano, Willelmo de Buun, Alexandro vicariis sancti Petri, Petro de capella archiepiscopi, Gervasio filio Romundi, Roberto de Sigillo, magistro Matheo, Thurstano Galien, Hugone filio Willelmi cellararii, Ernaldo primebred.

Location: BL Add. charter 7432; endorsed: Denebi i B xvi (Denby, first bundle, 16); C. Willelmi fil' Osberti de xxiiii[or] acris terre; seal: round, red wax; legend recorded in *Yorks. Deeds* as SIGILL' WILLELMI DE DENEBI; no longer visible.

Pd (from original): *EYC* III, no. 1808; (calendar): *Yorks. Deeds*, VI, 46–7, no. 155.

Dating: first two witnesses. The number of members of the chapter and vicars choral who attest indicates that this charter was issued at York.

Note: The cartulary copy has the first five witnesses and ends 'etc'. The printing in *EYC* erroneously gives the penultimate witness as 'Hugone filio Willelmi cellarario'.

[fol. 26r, old fol. 128]

225 *Rubric: Charter of the same William [son of Osbert of Denby] concerning 12 acres in the region of Denby and 1 acre of meadow opposite, rendering 18d.*

Original: *Grant in free alms addressed to the archbishop of York and the whole chapter of St Peter (York) and all the sons of holy church, by William son of Osbert of Denby, to God and the monks of St Mary of Byland, of 12 acres in the region of Denby, that is, 8 acres in the long furlongs and 4 in* Stokewellefurlangas. *If there are not 12 acres in these places the donor will make them up from* Scortebuttes. *Grant also of 1 acre of meadow opposite the west part of Clover Leys within the dyke. If there is more than 1 acre there, the donor grants it for the love of God and for the salvation of his soul and of his wife and his children, and for the souls of his father and mother and all his ancestors. The grant is made free from all secular service. The monks are to render 18d. to the donor and his heirs yearly within the octave of Whitsuntide. Pledge to warranty.* [c. 1170 x 1186].

His testibus Roberto Butevilain decano ecclesie Sancti Petri Ebor', Stephano canonico, Alano canonico, Roberto Schire, Germano persona ecclesie de Thornil, Fulcone capellano decani, Alano de Sancto Wilfrido, Roberto nepote decani, Thoma fratre eius, Symone de Emmelaie, Suano de Kirkebi, Willelmo filio Arkilli de Emmelaie, Henrico coco de Austona, Adam clerico de Eppelbi nepote Murdaci decani, Ailsi de Brett' filio Ade forest'.

Location: BL Add. charter 7427; endorsed: Denebi i B. xvii (Denby, first bundle, 17); C. Willelmi filii Osberti de Denebi de xii acris terre (twice); seal: round, brown wax; SIGILL WILLELMI DE DENEBI.

Pd (from original): *EYC* III, no. 1809; (calendar): *Yorks. Deeds*, VI, 47, no. 156.

Dating: The witnesses suggest that the charter was issued in the same period as no. 224.

Note: Stephen, canon of York, is probably Stephen the Roman, who occurs as canon of York, 1164 x 1174, before 1173, and 1158 x 1181 (*Fasti York*, p. 129). He attests nos 395, 491, 594, 1156 below.

226 *Rubric: Charter of the same William [son of Osbert of Denby] concerning 7 acres in Denby, rendering 12d. at the Assumption (15 Aug.).*
Original: *Grant and confirmation, addressed to the archbishop of York and the whole chapter of St Peter (York) and all the sons of holy church, by William son of Osbern of Denby, to God and the monks of St Mary of Byland, of 7 acres of his land in the region of Denby, that is, those acres which lie between Longley and the sike which is the boundary between Denby and the land of* Alwoldley. *If there are more than 7 acres there he grants the whole to the monks and if there are fewer than 7 acres he will make them up from his land in Denby for their easement. The grant is made with the goodwill and concession of Jordan, his son and heir, to hold of him and his heirs in perpetual alms, quit of all secular service, for the salvation of the donor's soul and of his father and mother, and of all his ancestors and heirs. The monks are to render to him and his heirs in recognition 12d. yearly at the Assumption (15 Aug.) at Denby. Pledge to warranty by him and Jordan. [c. 1200 x 1227].*

His testibus Iohanne de Birkine vicecomite, Hugone de Dranefeld, Ricardo filio Iordani de Tornhil, Adam filio Philippi de Sitlingtona, Ieremia persona de Tornhil, Henrico de Turstaineland.

Location: BL Add. charter 7455; endorsed: Denebi i B. xviii (Denby, first bundle, 18); Carta Willelmi filii Osberni de vii acris terre in Denebi; cut for seal tag; no tag or seal.

Pd (from original): *EYC* III, no. 1817; (calendar): *Yorks. Deeds*, VI, 47, no. 157.

Dating: Adam son of Philip of Shitlington attests in the period *c.* 1180 x 1212 (*EYC* VIII, 212). The first witness is not known to have exercised the office of sheriff or undersheriff. He died in 1227 (*EYF*, p. 6)

227 *Grant, addressed to all the sons of holy mother church present and future, by William son of William of Denby, to God and the monks of St Mary of Byland, of all his meadow in Clover Leys which lies between the wood and the grange of Denby, to hold of the donor and his heirs quit of all secular service, to do there as the monks wish, for 2 silver marks which the monks gave him in his great need. Pledge to warranty. [before 1218].*

Hiis testibus Willelmo filio Willelmi de Emelay, Thoma de Horbiry, Iordano de Heton', etc.

Copy (abbreviated): MS Dodsworth 133, fol. 139v ('in certayne transcripts of evidence taken out of St Maries Tower in Yorke under the hand of Hen. Sandwith clerke her copye for Sir Ric Beaumont. in tergo rotuli'), which omits 'etc' in the witness list and continues: Matheo de Scepley, Ada de Mirefeld, Iordano filio Mathei, Iordano filio Liulfi, Eustachio de Horbiry.

Dating: Thomas of Horbury was steward of the earl of Warenne and died not later than 1218 (*EYC* VIII, 212–13). Jordan de Heton (Kirkheaton) occurs in the first two decades of the 13th century (*ibid.*, nos 89, 90, 108, 137 etc).

228 *Rubric: Chirograph agreement between the monks and William son of William son of Osbert concerning the monks' right in the stone minerals in Clover Leys.*

Original: *Agreement, addressed to all the faithful of Christ who will see or hear this writing, between Abbot Robert and the convent of Byland on the one part and William son of William son of Osbert of Denby on the other, by which the abbot and convent have remitted and quitclaimed to William and his heirs all their right to mine stone* (minaria petre) *in Clover Leys. For this quitclaim William has granted to the abbot and convent in free alms all his land with its woodland in the place called* Buttis *which touches on the 10 acres which they hold to the north. He quitclaims to the monks all the right to mine ore* (minaria lapidis) *throughout the land which the monks hold of him and others in the region of Denby, also saving to the abbot and convent the pasture of Clover Leys and of all Denby, and common easements according to their charters. Pledge to warranty for himself and his heirs, and the abbot has promised the same for himself and his convent. For greater security both parties have sealed the agreement.* [early 13th cent.].

Hiis testibus Rogero decano de Ledesham, Ieremia persona de Torenhil, Adam persona de Hetun, Willelmo de Brettun, Willelmo de Sothhil, Petro de Birtwait, Adam de Holand, Roberto de Hoderesfeld, Swayno de Brettun'.

Location: BL Add. charter 7434, cut as chirograph; endorsed: Denebi i B xx (Denby, first bundle, charter 20); Carta Will' fil' Will' fil' Osberti; seal: round, red-brown wax; SIGILL' WILL<ELM>I . . . DE DENEBI (see also no. 244).

Pd (calendar): *Yorks. Deeds*, VI, 50, no. 164.

Dating: This was probably issued at the same time as no. 244, which settled all controversies between the monks of Byland and William of Denby up to the year 1220. Adam, parson of Kirkheaton, and Jeremiah of Thornhill attest together in the early 13th century (*EYC* VIII, no. 154).

Note: The monks of Rievaulx were also active in the West Riding, and an agreement dated 1170 allowed the monks of Byland to take ore and charcoal for their forges in Emley from Emley, Bretton, Shitlington, Denby, Briestwistle and Thornhill: see no. 988 below.

229   *Rubric: Charter of William son of William of Denby concerning all his land in* Krokedelandes *that is 4 acres.*
Original: *Grant and confirmation, addressed to all those who will see or hear these letters, by William son of William of Denby, to God and the monks of St Mary of Byland, of all his land in* Crokedelandes, *that is 4½ acres. If there are more than 4½ acres there he grants it all, and if there are fewer he will make up the land elsewhere, to the easement of the monks. To hold free from all service, for the salvation of his soul, and of his father and mother and all his ancestors and heirs. Pledge to warranty.* [early 13th cent.].
His testibus Adam de Mirefeld, Adam persona de Heton', Adam clerico de Emmeleia, Alano de Witteleia, Swano de Brett', Iordano filio Henrici de Denebi.
Location: BL Add. charter 7429; endorsed: Denebi i B xxi (Denby, first bundle, 21); Crokeland; seal (damaged): oval, red-brown wax; SIGILL' WILL<ELMI DE DENEBI>.
Pd (calendar): *Yorks. Deeds*, VI, 50, no. 165.
Dating: as no. 228.

230   *Confirmation, addressed to all the sons of holy mother church present and future who will see or hear these letters, by William son of William son of Osbert of Denby, to God and the monks of St Mary of Byland, of all the grants, agreements, liberties and customs contained in his father's charters, which the monks have, that is, 43 acres of profitable land in the region of Denby and 1 acre of meadow in Clover Leys, by the boundaries and places contained in the charters. Grant and confirmation of free entry and exit for themselves, their men and their animals, and wagons for transport through-out his lands. Further grant and confirmation of 4 acres in Bradley which his father demised at the point of death. Pledge to warranty. The grant and confirmation are made in free alms for the salvation of his soul and of all his ancestors and heirs. The monks are to render yearly in recognition of this confirmation 5s. 6d., that is 4s. 6d. within the octave of Whitsuntide and 12d. at the Assumption (15 Aug.), at Denby.* [before 1218].
Hiis testibus Thoma de Horbiry, Iordano fratre eius, Adam filio Philippi, Ricardo de Thornyll, Ieremia persona de Thornyll', etc.
Dating: death of first witness; see no. 227.

231   *Rubric: Quitclaim by William of* Aldwoldley *of his right in an assart in the wood of Denby.*
Original: *Quitclaim, addressed to all present and future, by William of* Aldwoldley, *to the house of St Mary of Byland and the monks serving God there, of the claim which he brought against the monks concerning an assart*

in the wood of Denby which Dolfin son of Godwin held of the house of Byland. Undertaking for himself and his heirs to bring no further claim. [1190 x 1210].

Hiis testibus Iurdano filio Ricardi, Elya de Wlfleia, Adam de Mirefeld, Adam filio Philippi, Adam de Holand', Roberto fratre suo, Rogero de Scardeclive.

Location: BL Add. charter 7454; endorsed: Denebi B ii xxiiii (Denby, second bundle, 24); C. Willi de Edwal' de quieta clamatio' clami sui; no sign of sealing.
Pd (from original): *EYC* III, no. 1815; (calendar): *Yorks. Deeds*, VI, 55, no. 179.
Dating: as *EYC*.

232 *Rubric: Charter of William son of Assolf concerning 10 acres in the region of Denby, rendering 4d., and remission of his right in the wood of Denby.* [early 13th cent.].

Marginal note: B(aculus) ii.
Dating: The donor made a grant (no. 233), for which a date of *c*. 1200 x 1220 is suggested.
Note: Assolf was the ancestor of the Tong family, who had sons Jordan, Richard and John. William is not recorded, although Assolf had a grandson named William (*EYC* VIII, 206).

[fol. 26r–v]

233 **Original:** *Grant in free alms, addressed to all who will see or hear these letters, by William son of Assolf of* Aldwoldley, *to God and the monks of St Mary of Byland, for the salvation of his soul and of his father and mother and of all his ancestors and heirs, of 14 acres in* Aldwoldley *which Robert son of Godwin held of him within these boundaries: from* Caldwelle Rode *as far as* Stainclif *and from there as the road goes to Thornhill and from there to the orchard which stands next to the house of Adam, and from there to* Edwin Welle *and thus as far as the monks' land which stretches to* Grosmunt. *The monks are to do with the land whatever they wish. Remission and quitclaim of a rent of 4d. which the monks paid yearly in recognition of the 10 acres concerning which the monks have the donor's charter (no. 232). Pledge to warranty.* [c. 1200 x 1220].

Hiis testibus Willelmo de Sot Hil, Ada de Hoylanda, Willelmo de Bretton', Gordano filio Liolf, Ada de Mirefeud, Suain filio Matildis de Bretton, Toraud' filio Ade, Petro de Bretton', Willelmo de Bredwisil, et aliis.

Location: BL Add. charter 7451; endorsed: Denebi ii B. xxvi (Denby, second bundle, 26); c. W. de Alwald' de xiiii acris; seal: round, brown wax; SIGILL' WILL'I DE AVELVALDELEIE.
Pd (from original): *EYC* III no. 1816; (calendar) *Yorks. Deeds*, VI, 164–5, no. 543.

Dating: as *EYC*; the witnesses occur also in nos 227, 228, 229, 235, 236.
Note: The cartulary copy has first three witnesses only and ends 'etc'.

[fol. 26v]
234 *Rubric: Chirograph agreement between the monks and Thorald of Bretton concerning the said 14 acres, rendering to the monks 2s. yearly.* [early to mid 13th cent.].
Dating: The grantor attests no. 244, dated after 1220.

235 *Rubric: Charter of John son of Richard of Batley and Margaret his wife concerning the whole of their meadow in Denby in the place called Clover Leys.*
Original: *Grant and confirmation in pure alms, addressed to all the sons of holy mother church who will see or hear these letters, by John son of Richard of Batley and Margaret his wife, to God and St Mary of Byland and the monks serving God there, of all their meadow in the region of Denby in the place called Clover Leys, and ½ ucre in* le Crokedelandis *towards the west, and 1 perch there towards the south. To hold free from secular service for the salvation of their souls and for the souls of their ancestors, successors and heirs. Pledge to warranty. Sealed with their seals.* [before 1218].
Hiis testibus domino Thoma de Horbiri, Willelmo de Breton, Ada de Mirfeld, Michele de Brerethuisil, Reinero de Wambewelle, Willelmo de Deneby, Willelmo filio Iordani de Floketon' et Willelmo filio Alani de Wytteley et multis aliis.
Location: BL Add. charter 7428; endorsed: Denebi ii B xxix (Denby, second bundle, 29); C. Iohannis de Bateley et Margarete uxoris eius de toto prato suo in Deneby; pur'; seals: (i) yellow-brown wax, round; SIGILL' IOHIS DE BATLL' (ii) yellow-brown wax, pointed oval; SIGIL' MARGARETE.
Pd (calendar): *Yorks. Deeds*, VI, 56, no. 183.
Dating: death of first witness; see no. 227.
Note: MS Dodsworth 8, fol. 90r, contains a copy of a grant by John of Batley (grantor of no. 235), son of Richard of Batley, with the consent of Richard his son and heir, of 1 acre in a field called Bradley in the region of Denby, 2 roods of land and woodland, 1 called 'Holrode' and the other called 'Robertrode', for the salvation of his soul and that of Mariota his late wife. Because the land was of Mariota's inheritance her son Richard has confirmed the grant in his full age.

236 **Original:** *Grant in free alms, addressed to all the sons of holy church present and future, by William of Soothill, to the monks of St Mary of Byland, for the salvation of his soul and of all his ancestors and heirs, of all that* cultura *called* Twychel *in the region of Denby and all the lands which John son of Harding granted to the monks and exchanged with them in the region of the said vill. The monks are to hold the land free from service and to do there whatever they wish.* [1204 x 1209].

Hiis testibus Roberto Walensi tunc vicec(omite) Ebor', Laurentio de Wiltona, clerico, Ricardo de Metdeleia, Thoma de Thorint', Rogero de Thorint', Iordano filio Henrici et multis aliis.

Location: BL Add. charter 7417; endorsed: Denebi ii B xxx (Denby, second bundle, 30); C. Will' de Sothil de cultura; pur'; seal: red wax, oval; SIGILL WILL'I DE SOTHIL.

Pd (calendar): *Yorks. Deeds*, VI, 55. no. 180.

Dating: first witness; see note to no. 188.

Note: The cartulary copy has the first 4 witnesses only and ends 'etc'. The name of Robert le Waleys is underlined, and a marginal note, in a later hand, reads 'ab anno 6 ad 12 R. Jo.' indicating what was thought to be his period of office as sheriff of Yorkshire.

237 *Rubric: Charter of Margery, widow of John, concerning the said* cultura *and lands.*

Original: *Grant in free alms, addressed to all the sons of holy church present and future, by Margery, formerly wife of John son of Harding, in her widowhood, to the monks of St Mary of Byland, for the salvation of her soul and of her husband and all her heirs, of all the* cultura *called* Twychel *in the region of Denby, and of all the lands which John her husband had granted and exchanged with the monks there. To hold free from all service and to do there as they wish.* [1204 x 1209].

Hiis testibus Roberto Walensi tunc vicec(omite) Ebor', Iohanne de Birkin, Rogero fratre eius, Iordano de Hetona, Henrico de Turstainl', Adam de Miref' et multis aliis.

Location: BL Add. charter 7441; endorsed: Denebi ii B xxxi (Denby, second bundle, charter 31); C. Mariorie de cultura Twich'; seal: red-brown wax, oval; SIGILL' MARGERIE DE DENEBIE. On reverse of seal tag: omnibus sancte ecclesie . . .'.

Pd (calendar): *Yorks. Deeds*, VI, 55, no. 178.

Dating: first witness; see note to no. 188.

238 *Grant, addressed to the archbishop of York and the whole chapter of St Peter (York) and all the sons of holy mother church present and future, by William son of Michael of Briestwistle, to God and the monks of St Mary of Byland, of all the land of Healey in the region of Briestwistle and whatever is contained within these boundaries: between the sike which is between Healey and* Osmundesmait *and between the other sike which comes from* Barstainwell *and flows between Healey and the region of Briestwistle. The monks may enclose the land with a ditch and hedge by the said boundaries wherever they wish. Undertaking that neither the donor nor his heirs will seek common within these boundaries. Further grant of that half bovate with a messuage and toft and croft which Richard son of Waltheof held of the donor in the same vill, and 4 assarts which the countrymen called roods; the* *monks may enclose these as they wish. Waltheof of Cheshire held one of these of the donor; Elias the smith held another; part of the third, which lies towards Whitley, was held by Richard son of Waltheof; and the fourth was held by Mariota, the donor's mother's sister. Grant also of a messuage with 2½ acres and half a perch which Dolfin held of the donor in the same vill, and 3 acres in* Milnerode *and in* Orpitcis *between the old forge and the land of Alexander. The grant is made in free alms to hold of the donor free from all secular service, to do with these lands whatever the monks wish, for the salvation of the soul of the donor, and those of his father and mother and of all his ancestors and heirs. Pledge to warranty. The donor and his heirs are to hold his capital messuage in Briestwistle and the meadow in which the chapel is towards the north of his house.* [early 13th cent.].

Hiis testibus Rogero de Ledesh' tunc decano de Pontefracto, Gilberto de Nottura, Iohanne de Birkin, Rogero fratre eius, etc.

Marginal note: Brertwisell.

Dating: first witness. John and Roger of Birkin attest together *c.* 1188 x 1202 (*EYC* VIII, no. 167).

Note: BL Add. charter 7445 is a grant by the same donor, addressed to the archbishop of York and the whole chapter of St Peter and all the sons of holy mother church present and future, to God and the monks of St Mary of Byland, of all his land of Healey and whatever is contained within specified bounds. It is endorsed: omnia que hic continentur . . . mult' melius habentur in aliis cartis nostris et si hec ostenderetur magis obesset quam prodesset. Healey (SE231169) is in Briestwistle.

[fol. 27r, old fol. 129]

239 *Rubric: Charter of John son of Michael concerning all the right which he had in Healey which the monks have of the grant of William his brother.*

Original: *Remission and quitclaim, addressed to all the sons of holy church present and future, by John son of Michael of Briestwistle for himself and his heirs, to God and the monks of St Mary of Byland, of all right and claim which he and his ancestors had in the land of Healey by the boundaries contained in the charter of his brother, William, which the monks have (no. 238). The monks are to do there as they wish, for 8s. which they have given him. Pledge that he and his heirs will not infringe the quitclaim.* [early 13th cent.].

Hiis testibus Roberto de Mohaud, Adam de Mirefeud, Ricardo de Tornhil, Henrico de Turstaineland, Willelmo de Brerdtuisil fratre meo, Willelmo filio Thome de Tornhil.

Location: BL Add. charter 7422; endorsed: Denebi ii B xxxiiii (Denby, second bundle, 34); C. Iohannis fil' Michaelis de Hegleis; seal: round, red wax; SIGILL IOHANNIS FIL MICHEL.

Pd (calendar): *Yorks. Deeds*, VI, 25, no. 79.

240 *Rubric: Quitclaim by Matthew of Shepley, Eustace of Horbury and Thomas de Mohaut of all their right in Healey.*
Original: *Remission and quitclaim, addressed to all who will see or hear these letters, by Matthew of Shepley, Eustace of Horbury, and Thomas de Mohaut for themselves and their heirs, to God and the monks of St Mary of Byland, of all right which they had or might have between the 2 water courses in Healey which are on either side of the land, as far as the hedge that is between Healey and the land to which the monks established their title against Adam of Healey. The monks are to do there whatever they wish and enclose at will, for the exchanges which William of Briestwistle made with them elsewhere in his land. The donors and their heirs are to have pasture for their flocks with the flocks of the monks between the said watercourses after the corn and hay have been gathered. Pledge to warranty. [before 1218].*
His testibus Radulfo de Normanvill' et Roberto de Mohaud, tunc baillivis de Westtridhing, Thoma de Horbiri, Adam filio Philippi, Ricardo de Tornhil, Willelmo filio Iohannis de Tornhil, Willelmo filio Thome de Tornhil, Adam de Mirefeud, Willelmo de Brerdtuisil, Iordano filio Henrici, Iohanne fratre Willelmi de Brerdtuisil.
Location: BL Add. charter 7439; endorsed: Denebi B ii xxxv (Denby, second bundle, 35); C. Mathei de Sepeley et Eustacii de Horbyri et Thome de Mohaud de remissione iuris in Denebi; three seals; brown wax, 2 oval, 1 round; faded.
Copy (abbreviated): MS Dodsworth 76, fol. 146v, where marginal note also indicates no. 35.
Pd (calendar): in *Yorks. Deeds*, VI, 25, no. 80.
Dating: death of the third witness.

241 Original: *Grant in free alms, addressed to the archbishop of York and the whole chapter of St Peter (York) and all the sons of holy church, by Jordan of Flockton, to God and the monks of St Mary of Byland, of a road sufficient for themselves, their men and their goods, across his lands from their forge at Bentley as far as Denby, and common throughout his land of Flockton for their flocks from Denby. The grant is made free from all secular service, for the salvation of the soul of the donor, and those of all his ancestors and heirs. The monks are to render 2s. yearly for all service, 12d. at Whitsuntide and 12d. at St Martin (11 Nov.). Pledge to warranty. [before 1218].*
Hiis testibus Thoma de Horebiri, Adam filio Philippi, Thoma de Thornet', Reinaldo clerico de Bradef', Simone de Ferseleia, Henrico Scotto de Pugkesei, Thoma Scotto de Neut'.
Location: BL Add. charter 7456; endorsed: Denebi ii B xxxvi (Denby, second bundle, 36); C. Iordani de Flock' de via & de communa per totam terram suam de Flocketon etc; puratur per cartam vi; seal tag; no seal.
Copy (abbreviated): MS Dodsworth 76, fol. 146v.
Pd (calendar): *Yorks. Deeds*, VI, 72–3, no. 248; *ibid.*, VIII, 58, no. 162, from a second

original then in the possession of Lord Allendale.

Dating: death of the first witness.

Note: The cartulary copy has the first three witnesses only, and ends 'etc'. This was an important grant, that provided the monks with a road linking their property at Denby, where they mined, to the grange of Bentley where their forges were located (*West Yorks.*, III, 774–5). The meaning of the third endorsement seems to be that the grant is made in free alms by charter no. 6, that is, no. 214 above.

242 **Original:** *Quitclaim, addressed to all the sons of holy mother church who will see or hear the present charter, by Michael of Briestwistle, knight, for himself and his heirs, to God and St Mary and the abbot and convent of Byland, of 3s. 4d. annual farm remaining from that annual farm of 1 mark which he bought from Gilbert of Croft (no. 214), from which mark he has granted to the abbot and convent 10s. for two pittances annually, for the salvation of his soul and of all his ancestors and heirs, as contained in his charter. Further quitclaim of 2s. annual farm which he bought from William of Flockton and which the monks were obliged to render for a road which they have across his lands from Bentley going to and returning from Denby. To hold freely and to do with these lands whatever they wish. Surrender of all muniments concerning the same to the monks. Pledge to warranty. Sealed with the donor's seal.* Within the octave of Epiphany, [6–13 Jan.] 1259 [1260].

Hiis testibus dominis Thoma filio Willelmi, Radulfo de Horrebiry, Iohanne fratre eius, Willelmo de Wath, militibus, Ricardo le Normaund, Willelmo Beumont, Iohanne de Deneby, Rogero de Wambwell, Iohanne de Wlveley, Symone de . . . Henrico filio Rogeri, Henrico de Kyrkeby, Roberto de Wyteley et aliis.

Location: BL Add. charter 7444; endorsed: Deneby B ii xxxvii (Denby, second bundle, 37); C. M. de Brertwysel de vs. iiiid; seal: green wax, oval; blurred.

Copy (abbreviated): MS Dodsworth 76, fol. 146v.

Pd (calendar): *Yorks. Deeds*, VI, 53, no. 175.

Note: The cartulary copy has the first three witnesses only, and ends 'etc'. The sum of 5s. 4d. noted in the endorsement refers to both quitclaims.

243 *Rubric: Charter of William of [Denb]y concerning a* cultura *in* Haukinsclif *in exchange for another* cultura, *reserving for the monks a certain road, etc.*

Original: *Grant, addressed to all the sons of holy mother church present and future, by William of Denby, to God and the monks of St Mary of Byland, of his* cultura *of Haukenisclif lying towards the north, in exchange for the monks'* cultura *lying near the boundaries of Flockton and extending east to the wood of Shitlington, saving to the monks their road which lies on the* *western side of the* cultura *and extends to the road which they have of Jordan of Flockton and his heirs, namely a perch 20 feet wide, towards their house at Bentley. Pledge to warranty.* [c. 1220].

Hiis testibus Rogero de Byrkeng, Ieremya de Thorney, Roberto clerico de Huderisfeld', Iordano de Floketon', Iohanne de Wythel', alio Iohanne de eadem villa et multis aliis.

Location: BL Add. charter 7453; endorsed: Denebi ii B xxxviii (Denby, second bundle, 38); C. Willelmi de Denebi de escambio i cultura; marked for cutting for seal tag.
Copy (abbreviated): MS Dodsworth 76, fol. 146v.
Pd (calendar): *Yorks. Deeds*, VI, 73, no. 249.

244 *Rubric: Chirograph agreement between the monks and William of Denby concerning controversies and complaints which have been laid to rest. The monks have both parts.*
Original: *Agreement between the monks of St Mary of Byland and William of Denby settling all the claims and controversies which had existed between them up to 1220, in particular on the part of William concerning 300 wethers which the monks pastured in the region of Denby and which used the pasture of Whitley. William now grants for himself and his heirs that the monks may have, in addition to the animals of their tenants in Denby and as far as the pasture can sustain them, 300 wethers within the region of Denby. They are also to have entry and exit across the common pasture inside and outside the vill as far as their pasture of Whitley, or the pasture of other vills within 2 leagues of Denby where they may have pasture. Grant also of a suitable right of way for them, their men, horses, wagons and carts over his land between Denby and Flockton. Both parties are to have wood growing on their own parcels of land in the common of Denby, saving common rights of herbage. William has withdrawn the complaint he made concerning the extension of ploughing towards the common pasture of Denby on the south side of Castlegate. Both parties promise to uphold this agreement, and William has sworn an oath to do so.* [after 1220].

Hiis testibus Rogero decano de Ledesham, Ieremia de Thornhil, Adam persona de Hetona, Rogero de Birking, Willelmo de Sothil, Thoma de Horebiri, Alano de Withele, Thoma de Moald, Swano de Brettona, Thoraldo de Bretton' et aliis.

Location: BL Add. charter 7442, cut as chirograph; endorsed: Denebi ii B xxxix (Denby, second bundle, 39); Conf' Willelmi de Denebi de querelis motis et sopitis inperpetuum; seal: round, red-brown wax; SIGILL WILL'I F'L WILL'I DE DENEBI.
Copy (abbreviated): MS Dodsworth 76, fol. 146v.
Pd (calendar): *Yorks. Deeds*, VI, 49–50, no. 163.

245 *Notification to all present and future by William son of Michael of Briestwistle of his grant in free alms to God and the monks of St Mary of Byland, of a half bovate in Briestwistle, free from all secular service, with all its appurtenances, which Roger son of Peter held. Grant also of 3 acres in* Milneroda *and in* Orpictis *between the old forge and the land of Alexander. The grant is made for the salvation of the soul of the donor and of his father and mother and all his ancestors and heirs. Pledge to warranty.* [early 13th cent.].

Hiis testibus Ieremia de Thornyl, Rogero decano, Adam de Myrefeld.

Copy (abbreviated): MS Dodsworth 76, fol. 146v.

Dating: The first witness is the parson of Thornhill who attests nos 226 (*c.* 1200 x 1227), 228, 230 (before 1218), 243 (*c.* 1220) and 244 (after 1220); he occurs as Germanus, parson of Thornhill, in no. 225, and attests without title in no. 221. The second witness, described as dean of Ledsham, attests nos 46, 228, 244, and as dean of Pontefract, no. 238; he occurs without title in nos 221, 248. Adam of Mirfield witnesses nos 42–4, 206, 218, 219, 227, 229, 231, 233, 235, 237, 239, 240.

246 *Rubric: Quitclaim by William son of Michael of all right which he had in the woodland between Briestwistle and Denby.*
Original: *Remission and quitclaim, addressed to the archbishop of York and the whole chapter of St Peter (York) and all the sons of holy mother church, by William son of Michael of Briestwistle for himself and his heirs, to God and the monks of St Mary of Byland, of all the right which he or his ancestors had or could have in the wood between Briestwistle and Denby, to do there as they wish. This quitclaim is made for the salvation of his soul and of his father and mother and all his ancestors and heirs.* [before 1218].

His testibus Hugone de Lelai, Thoma de Horbiria, Iordano fratre eius, Henrico de Turstaineland, Willelmo filio Osberni de Denbi, Iordano et Willelmo filiis eius, Matheo filio Henrici de Turstaineland.

Location: BL Add. charter 7425; endorsed: Denebi ii B xli (Denby, second bundle, 41); Cart' util' et necessaria; C' Willelmi de Brertwis' de bosco iuxta denebi; seal: round, red wax; SIGILL WILLELMI FILII MICAHELIS.
Pd (calendar): *Yorks. Deeds*, VI, 24, no. 77.
Dating: death of the second witness.

247 *Rubric: Charter of William son of Michael concerning land from the spring called* Barstainwell *through the sike of the said spring as far as* Healey.
Original: *Grant, addressed to the archbishop of York and the whole chapter of St Peter (York) and all the sons of holy mother church present and future, by William son of Michael of Briestwistle, to God and the monks of St Mary of Byland, of all the land and whatever is contained within these boundaries: from the spring called* Barstainwelle *through the sike of the spring to the*

land of Healey and across the land of Healey up to the sike which flows
between Healey and Denby wood, and again through the sike westwards
towards the house of Ailric as far as the moor. The grant is made to God and
the said monks, to hold of him and his heirs freely and to do there whatever
the monks wish. This is done for the love of God and for a quitclaim of the
complaints which the monks had against him and his men of Briestwistle
concerning the injuries which they did to them, for which injuries William
was compelled by ecclesiastical censure to make peace with them. William
and his men of Briestwistle are to have pasture for their animals with those of
the monks within the said boundaries after the harvest and after the hay has
been carried away. Pledge to warranty. [before 1218].

Hiis testibus Hugone de Lelai, Thoma de Horebiri, Iordano fratre
eius, Henrico de Turstainland, Willelmo filio Osberni de Denebi,
Iordano et Willelmo filiis eius, Matheo filio Henrici de Turstainlanda.

Location: BL Add. charter 7424; endorsed: Denebi ii B xlij (Denby, second bundle,
42); C. Willelmi de Brert' de terra a Bar . . . welle usque Hegleis; seal: round, brown
wax; SIGILLUM WILL'MI FILII MICAELIS.

Copy (abbreviated): MS Dodsworth 76, fol. 146v.

Marginal note: in a different hand from the main cartulary hand: nota utrum
licitum est ad claud'.

Dating: The latest date is provided by the death of the second witness. The
witnesses suggest that nos 246 and 247 were issued on the same occasion.

[fol. 27r–v]

248 *Chirograph agreement between the monks of St Mary of Byland and
William son of Michael of Briestwistle that all quarrels and controversies
which had arisen between them in 1220 shall be completely laid to rest, and
especially that all the lands and messuages of the monks in Briestwistle shall
remain free in the same way and in the same measure as is contained in the
monks' charter. William and his heirs undertake to make no further claim.
Sealed by both parties. 1220.*

Hiis testibus Rogero de Ledesham decano, Germano de Thornhill,
Ada persona de Hetona, Willelmo de Sothill, Willelmo de Denby, etc.

Marginal note: by opening of charter, in later hand, '5H3'.

[fol. 27v]

249 *Rubric: Charter of William son of Michael concerning the land called
Mariot rode; in free alms.* [early 13th cent.].

Text (abbreviated): MS Dodsworth 76, fol. 146v. Grant by William son
of Michael of Briestwistle to God and the monks of Byland of all that
land called Mariotrode in Briestwistle in width from the western part
to the . . . and in length from the . . . as far as the path which runs from
Briestwistle to the church of Thornhill.

250   *Rubric: Charter of William son of Michael of Briestwistle concerning the sentence of excommunication he would undergo should he presume to injure the monks in any way.*

Original: *Undertaking on oath, addressed to all the sons of holy church who will see or hear these letters, by William son of Michael of Briestwistle in the hand of Roger, dean of Pontefract, that whenever he or his heirs shall in any way transgress against the charters which the monks of St Mary of Byland have of him, or against any agreement which he confirmed with his seal, or seize or cause to be seized their animals, particularly their sheep in the pasture where they ought to go, and two of their brothers shall say this* in verbo veritatis *and their shepherd shall swear to it, they will subject themselves to the sentence of excommunication, until such time as whoever is responsible shall pay ½ silver mark to the dean and make full restitution to the monks.* [1195 x 1214].

Hiis testibus Bernardo persona de Normantun, Roberto persona de Sandala, Adam persona de Hetun, Roberto persona de Fedherstan, et capitulo de Pontefracto.

Location: BL Add. charter 7433; endorsed: Denebi B ii xlv (Denby, second bundle, 45); C. Willelmi de Bretwisel de sententia excommunicationis subeundo; seal: red wax, round; SIGILL' WILLMI FILII MICAHELIS.
Pd (calendar): *Yorks. Deeds*, V, 24–5, no. 78.
Dating: This is related to no. 251.

251   *Rubric: Attestation by Simon, dean of York, that W(illiam) of Briestwistle will not bring any claim concerning lands which the monks have of him.* [1195 x 1214].
Dating: Dean Simon of Apulia.

252   *Rubric: Attestation by Roger, dean of Pontefract, that W(illiam) of Briestwistle should undergo the sentence of excommunication if he shall do anything against his writings.* [1195 x 1214].
Dating: This is related to nos 250–1.
Note: Roger, dean of Pontefract, also attests as Roger of Ledsham, or dean of Ledsham: see, for example, nos 221, 228, 238, 244, 248, and as Roger, dean, in 245.

253   **Original:** *Grant in free alms, addressed to all the sons of holy mother church present and future who will see or hear this charter, by Michael son of John of Denby, to God and St Mary and the abbot and convent of Byland, of 1 carucate and the whole tenement which he had or could have by hereditary right, with* Holroda *and* Roberts rode, *with woods, meadows, mineral rights, and all other things belonging to the land in the vill and region of Denby, to do there whatever the monks wish. This grant is made for the* *salvation of his soul and of his father and mother and all his ancestors and heirs, to hold of him and his heirs free from all secular service. Pledge to warranty. Sealed with the donor's seal.* [mid 13th cent.].

Hiis testibus dominis Willelmo filio Thome de Emeley, Iohanne de Hetona, Iohanne de Hoderod, Iohanne de Horebiry, militibus, Symone de Chyveth, Ricardo de Breretwysel, Willelmo de Swynton', Iohanne de Bretton', Willelmo de Edwaldley, Iohanne de Batteley, Willelmo de Mirefeud, Roberto de Mirefeud, Willelmo de Stokesley, Thoma de Ettona.

Location: BL Add. charter 7446; endorsed: Deneby iii B. liii (Denby, third bundle, 53); purus; C. Mychaelis filio Iohannis de Deneby de una carrucata terre in eadem villa; seal: oval, red-brown wax; S. MICHAEL' DE DENBI.

Marginal note in cartulary: Bac(ulus) iii.

Pd (calendar): *Yorks. Deeds*, VI, 51, no. 167.

Dating: The witnesses are consistent with a date in the mid 13th century. The second, third, fourth and fifth witnesses attest together in 1269: *Yorks. Deeds*, VI, 56, no. 184.

Note: The cartulary copy has the first four witnesses only and ends 'etc'.

254 Original: *Grant and quitclaim, addressed to all the sons of holy mother church present and future who will see or hear this charter, by William son of Thomas of Emley, to God and St Mary and the abbot and convent of Byland, of the grant which Michael son of John of Denby made, that is, 1 carucate and the whole tenement which John of Denby, Michael's father, formerly held of Thomas son of William of Emley in fee and hereditary right in the vill and region of Denby, with all* Holroda *and* Roberts rode *with their appurtenances, to do with as they wish, as contained in Michael's charter (no. 253). This grant is made for the salvation of his soul and of all his ancestors and heirs, to hold free from all secular service. Undertaking to make no further claim. Sealed with the donor's seal.* [early to mid 13th cent.].

Hiis testibus dominis Iohanne de Heton', Iohanne de Hoderod, Iohanne de Horebiry, militibus, Symone de Chyveth', Iohanne de Bretton', Willelmo de Edwaldley, Iohanne de Bateley, Willelmo de Mirefeld, Roberto de Mirefeld, Willelmo de Stokesley, Thoma de Etton' et aliis.

Location: BL Add. charter 7419; endorsed: Deneby iii B. liiii (Denby, third bundle, 54); purus; Conf' Willelmi filii Thome de Emmeley de una carrucata terre in Deneby quam habemus ex dono Michaelis filii Iohannis de Deneby; seal: oval, brown wax. Second charter: BL Add. charter 7468; no medieval endorsements; seal: oval, brown wax.

Copy: MS Dodsworth 8, fol. 90r.

Dating: as no. 253.

Note: The cartulary copy is incomplete, due to loss of folio.

[2 folios lost, old fols 130–31]. Fol. 130 contained copies of Denby charters, some of which survive as originals: see Appendix I.

DALTON (SE4376), in the parish of Topcliffe and the wapentake of Birdforth. MS Top. Yorks. d. 11, fol. 131, suggests that grants of land here were associated with the families of Coleville and Buscy.

[fol. 28r, old fol. 132]
DALE TOWN (SE5388), in the parish of Hawnby and wapentake of Birdforth (NR), on the North Yorkshire Moors. The provision of a road around the spring for the monks' animals from Murton (no. 257) suggests that the two properties were closely linked and that Dale was associated with Murton Grange, which lies ½ mile to the south of Dale.

255   *Grant in free alms, addressed to the archbishop of York and the whole chapter of St Peter (York) and to all the sons of holy church, by Ralph del Turp, to God and the monks of St Mary of Byland, of a spring in Dale called* Wdekelda *and a suitable road around the spring for their flocks from the grange of Murton.* [1170 x *c.* 1190].
Hiis testibus Murdaco decano de Westmerland, Theobaldo nepote eius, magistro Godwyno cementario, Alano clerico de Halmeby, etc.
Pd: *EYC* III, no. 1839.
Dating: The donor witnessed a charter of William Engelram (Ingram) in favour of Rievaulx Abbey of 1178 x 1181 (*EYC* II, no. 716); the first witness occurs in the second half of the 12th century. A Godwin, mason, also attests in the latter part of the century (*ibid.* I, no. 84; II, no. 991). Peter Fergusson (*Architecture of Solitude* (Princeton, 1984), pp. 72, 169, 171), notes the occurrence of Godwin in this document, and suggests that he was a secular master mason.
Note: Before 1200 Ralph's daughter, Ymaine, confirmed land in Dale, which her father granted as her marriage portion, in exchange for land in Marton in Cleveland (BL Add. charter 70694; printed from MS Dodsworth 45, fol. 71r, in *EYC* III, no. 1841). Farrer noted that Ymaine may have married William Engelram (and see no. 257 below). The spring called 'Wdekelda' is tentatively identified in *VCH NR* II, 31, as 'probably the spring in the wood called Plumpton Wood, from which a path leads south-west to the grange of Murton, on the high ground between the Dale and Sledhill Beck, the northern boundary of Old Byland'. The text of no. 255 is very faint.

256   **Original:** *Quitclaim, addressed to all who see or hear these letters, by Ralph del Turp, to God and the monks of St Mary of Byland, of all the right which he and his ancestors had beyond the bottom of the valley of* Sprohesdala *which is nearer to Dale to the west, that is as the cliff* (clefsti) *descends towards the higher head of West* Sprohesdala *and along the valley bottom in a straight line as far as the middle of the Rye. This grant is made in pure alms, free from all secular service, for the salvation of his soul and of his father and mother and Walter Engelram his brother and of all his ancestors and heirs.* [1147 x 1186].

Hiis testibus Rogero de Molbrai, Nigello et Roberto filiis eius, Roberto de Daivill', Hugone Malab(issa), Toma de Colevill', Henrico de Riparia, Radulfo de Beau', Hamone Beler.

Location: NYCRO, ZDV I 25 (MIC 2894/2377–8); endorsed: C. Rad' de turp de quieta clamatione totius iuris sui ultra fundum vall' de sprohesdale; Mortona B. i. x (Murton, first bundle, 10).

Pd (calendar): *HMC Various Collections*, II, 5–6 (no. 6).

Dating: the attestation of Roger de Mowbray's sons and his own departure on crusade.

Note: The endorsement suggests that the cartulary compiler has interfered with the original order by entering this charter under the heading of Dale rather than Murton. The cartulary copy, which is much damaged, has only the first four witnesses. This charter establishes that Ralph del Turp was a brother of Walter Engelram. The name of their father is not known, but he was a younger brother of William Engelram, who occurs in the reign of Henry I. Walter, whose mother was named Maud and whose wife was Holdeard, was a benefactor of Guisborough Priory and Rievaulx Abbey (*EYF*, pp. 47–8). He was succeeded by his son, William: see no. 257.

257   Original: *Grant, addressed to the archbishop of York and the whole chapter of St Peter (York) and all the sons of holy mother church present and future, by William Engelram, to God and the monks of St Mary of Byland, of a spring called* Wdekelde *in the region of Dale, and a suitable road around the spring for their men and their flocks from Murton. The grant is made free from all secular service, for the salvation of the soul of the donor and those of all his ancestors and heirs. Pledge to warranty.* [c. 1180 x 1212].

His testibus Willelmo de Lasceles, Thoma de Colevill', Gaufrido Fossard, Ernaldo de Uppesala, Gilberto de Meinil de Angotebi, Waltero filio eius, Gilberto de Meinhil de Thurkilbi, Stephano filio eius.

Location: NYCRO, ZDV I 25 (MIC 2894/2382); endorsed: Carta Will' Engeram de fonte; Mortona B. i ix (Murton, first bundle, 9); see note to no. 256.

Pd: *EYC* III, no. 1840 from the cartulary copy, which includes the first five witnesses only; (calendar) *HMC Various Collections*, II, 6 (no. 7).

Dating: William Engelram, son of Walter, is here confirming the grant of his uncle, Ralph del Turp. William appears to have succeeded his father by 1184 x 1188, when he confirmed his father's grants to Guisborough Priory (*EYC* II, no. 717; *EYF*, p. 48). Farrer and Clay noted that he was still living in 1206 when he held Dale of William Malebisse, but he occurs between 1209 and 1212 in nos 259 and 260 below. He may have married Ymaine, daughter of Ralph del Turp, his cousin: see note to

no. 255 above.
Note: Gilbert de Meinil of Osgoodby and his son, Walter, who attest here, were
donors of land in Osgoodby (nos 743–4, 746–52, 782).

258 Original: *Final concord made in the king's court of York, Hilary term
25 Henry III, in the presence of Robert of Lexington, Ralph de Sules,
William of Culworth, J<olland> de Neville and Warner Engayne, justices,
between Abbot Henry and the convent, plaintiffs, and Robert Engelram,
defendant, concerning a spring in Dale. The abbot claimed that Robert had
not allowed him sufficient passage to drive his animals from the abbey
grange nor those of his men of Murton to the spring, and other easements
which the abbot ought to have under a charter of Robert's father, William,
concerning which a plea had been brought in court. Robert has granted for
himself and his heirs to the abbot an adequate way to the spring, and all other
easements. Further grant of 4 acres in length and width around the spring,
which the abbot and convent may enclose as they wish without interference
by Robert or his heirs. Robert and his heirs and their men of Dale may,
however, have free access to the pasture of Dale and to water their animals at
the spring. The abbot has received Robert and his heirs into all the good deeds
and prayers of his house. Notification that the abbot and convent will not
enclose the ancient entry and exit to the pasture of Dale, and will ensure that
Robert, his heirs and his men, have sufficient access to the spring.* York;
octaves of St Hilary 25 Henry III [20 Jan. 1241].
Location: NYCRO ZDV I 25 (MIC 2894/2381), sewn to lower edge of no. 257.
Copy: PRO CP 25/1/264/35, no. 8.
Pd (calendar): *HMC Various Collections*, II, 6 (no. 8); *Yorks. Fines 1232–1246*, pp. 98–9
(from PRO copy).
Note: Robert was the son of the donor of no. 257. For the abbot's summons of
Robert on 24 June 1240, and his complaints against him, see *Curia Regis Rolls*, XVI,
143. For Robert of Lexington and William of Culworth as justices, see above, note
to no. 38. The cartulary has a marginal note, in a later hand: 23 H 3. The name of the
fourth justice is abbreviated to J. de Neville, and a later hand has written
'Jollandus' in the margin; Jolland also occurs in the cartulary at nos 488, 722, 841,
927, 1003. A sketch shows the relationship between William Engelram 'dominus
de Dale 15 Jo' and his son Robert Engelram 'dominus de Dale filius Willelmi 25
H 3'.

[fol. 28v]
259 Original: *Notification of the agreement between the monks of St
Mary of Byland and William Engelram by which William and his heirs will
receive no men or women of religion, nor their flocks, within the vill and
pasture of Dale, except the monks of Byland and their flocks. Pledge to
warranty. Sealed with the seals of Abbot Walter and William Engelram.*
[1209 x 1212].

Hiis testibus Henrico Redem' tunc vicecomite Ebor', Ada de Stavel',
Willelmo de T[am]eton', [Roberto Enge]ra[m], Philippo de Colevill',
Hugone de Magnebi, Hugone de Uppessale, Henrico de Munfort,
Rogero de Carlton, Stephano de Meinil.

Location: NYCRO, ZDV I 25 (MIC 2894/2384–5). This is the upper half of a
chirograph, indented; endorsed: B. i xvii (first bundle, 17).

Pd (calendar): *HMC Various Collections*, II, 6 (no. 10).

Dating: Walter, abbot of Byland, and the first witness, who was undersheriff of
Yorkshire for Gilbert Fitz Reinfrid, sheriff in the period 1209–1213 (*Lord Lieutenants*, p. 53).

Note: There is some damage to the charter, and the name of Robert Engelram has
been conjectured from no. 260, where all the witnesses occur in the same order. The
cartulary copy has only the first three witnesses. The rubric reads: 'Contra
Willelmum Engeraum de non recipiendis aliis infra Dalam'.

260   Original: *Grant in free alms, addressed to all the sons of holy mother
church present and future, by William Engelram, to God and the monks of St
Mary of Byland, of common pasture in Nettle Dale in front of the gate to
their grange of Murton. The grant is made to hold free from secular service
for the salvation of his soul and of all his ancestors and heirs. Pledge to
warranty.* [1209 x 1212].

Hiis testibus Henrico Redem' tunc vicecomite Ebor', Ada de Stavele,
Willelmo de Tamton', Roberto Engeram, Philippo de Colevill',
Hugone de Magnebi, Hugone de Uppessale, Henrico de Munfort,
Rogero de Carlton, Stephano de Meinil.

Location: NYCRO, ZDV I 25 (MIC 2894/2386–7); endorsed: C. Will' Engeranni de
communa pastura in Netteldal; Mortona B i xi (Murton, first bundle, 11).

Pd (calendar): *HMC Various Collections*, II, 6 (no. 9).

Dating: as 259.

Note: The cartulary copy has the first four witnesses only. W. Brown calendared an
original charter then (1914) in his own possession, now NYCRO ZFL 3 (MIC
1289/40), by which Abbot Walter and the convent of Byland released to William
Engelram all right in 2 bovates in Dale which the monks had of the grant of
Richard Malebisse. The witnesses were Thomas, prior of Byland, Gikel the cellarer,
Adam his colleague (*socius*), Ingeler, keeper of the work of the church, Gilbert
master of the *conversi*, Henry de Redeman, sheriff of Yorkshire, Hugh de Magnebi,
Henry of Silton, Robert the sheriff's clerk (*Yorks. Deeds*, II, 58, no. 144). The
witnesses suggest a date roughly contemporary with nos 259–60.

[fol. 29r, old fol. 133]

YORK: The York section of the cartulary is badly damaged. Few of the
charters were copied out, the compiler choosing to render most
entries as rubrics. The evidence suggests that Byland was not a major
property owner in the city, and the abbey's tenements lay in Coney

Street, Ousegate, Patrickpool, and King Street. There were separate cartulary sections for the abbey properties in Bootham and Gillygate, outside the city walls, and Clifton.

261 *Rubric: Charter of Bertram de Bulmer concerning 3 tofts in York in Coney Street, on the River Ouse.* [before 1166].

Dating: death of the grantor. This may be related to the charter by which Bertram de Bulmer granted to John and his wife to hold of Stephen, Bertram's son, the toft which they took in exchange for a toft which they quitclaimed to the monks of Byland, that is the toft which Bertram had granted them: *EYC* I, no. 250, from the cartulary of St Leonard's Hospital, York (BL MS Cotton Nero D iii, fol. 122).

262 *Rubric: Confirmation by Emma de Humez of the same tofts for 6s. yearly.* [before 1208].

Dating: death of grantor. Emma de Humez was the daughter of Bertram de Bulmer. She married twice (i) Geoffrey de Valoignes, who died in 1169, and (ii) Geoffrey de Neville, who died in 1193.

263 *Rubric: Quitclaim by William of 1 of 3 of the tofts in Ousegate.*

264 *Rubric: Charter of Gerard of Stokesley concerning all the land in Coney Street with the buildings on it, of that land which his father held of the monks of Durham in Ousegate . . . of the hospital of St Nicholas.*

Original: *Surrender, addressed to all the sons of holy mother church present and future, by Gerard of Stokesley, to God and the house of Byland, of himself. Grant and confirmation, with his body for burial there, to God and St Mary of the same house and the monks serving God there, of all his land in Coney Street in the city of York, which his father held of the monks of St Cuthbert, Durham, with all the buildings on it. He makes this grant contemplating the salvation of his soul, to hold of him and his heirs in free alms for 1 pound of cumin yearly at St Martin (11 Nov.), saving the rent due to the king and the monks of Durham. The grant is made for his own soul, and for the souls of his father, Lewin, and his brother, Hugh, and all his ancestors and heirs. Pledge to warranty. Sealed with the donor's seal.* [c. 1190 x 1210].

Hiis testibus magistro Laurentio de Wiltona, Petro constabulario, Petro presbitero de Richemund, Gaufrido Fossard, Gikello de Smitheton, Gilberto de Thorni, Gilberto de Thurkebi, Stephano filio eius, Willelmo Fairfax tunc preposito Ebor', Alexandro de Baiocis, Philippo filio Baldewini, Thoma filio Iol, et aliis.

Location: Durham Cathedral Muniments, 5 The College, Durham, 4.1.Sacr.18;

endorsed: 4ª.1ᵉ.sacrist. S. I. Ebor. C. Gerardi de Stokell' de annuo redditu de terra in Kunigstrete soluto priori et conventui Dunelm.

Pd: *EYC* I, no. 245.

Dating: witnesses.

Note: The grantor is to be identified as Gerard son of Lewin, who was granted the church of Stokesley for life by Abbot Clement of St Mary's, York, *c*. 1170 x 1184 (*EYC* I, no. 563). He was an important York citizen and probably a money lender. He granted land in Coney Street to Paulinus son of William son of Gilbert between 1185 and 1205, and to St Peter's Hospital between 1193 and 1203 (*ibid.* I, nos 239–40, from BL MS Cotton Nero D iii, fol. 102v). St Nicholas's Hospital, mentioned in the rubric, was located outside Walmgate Bar.

265 *Rubric: Charter of Gerard concerning the whole of his land in Coney Street which the monks of Durham have.* [late 12th or early 13th cent.].

Dating: see no. 264.

Note: This may refer to Durham Cathedral Muniments 4.1.Sacr.13, a grant to the prior and monks of Durham of land in Coney Street which Gerard's father held of them: *EYC* I, no. 246.

266 *Chirograph between the monks and Paulinus de Mowbray concerning all the land and houses which the monks have of the grant of Gerard in Ousegate for the service of 3s. and there is in this a certain addition by which in the course of time the rent may be increased.*

Text illegible. [early 13th cent.].

Hiis testibus Tho<ma> . . . . . . suppriore, Ada. . . .

Note: Paulinus de Mowbray witnessed a charter of William Fairfax (1204 x 1220) quitclaiming to Durham Cathedral Priory a house in Coney Street formerly of Hugh son of Lewin (*EYC* I no. 247, dated 1204 x 1220). As bailiff of York he attested in the early 13th century, and probably after 1217: *Chs Vicars Choral*, I, no. 371.

267 *Chirograph of Aubrey de Mowbray concerning 5s. rent for booths in Ousegate. And when the plea 'cessavit' etc they gave 1 mark.* [1276/7].

Hiis testibus Roberto de . . . holme maiore, Willelmo de Stokes'.

Dating: The first witness is likely to be Robert de Bromholm, mayor of York. He attests charters as mayor in 1276/7 and 1277 (*Chs Vicars Choral*, I, nos 302, 494).

Note: The text of the charter is illegible. The canons of Bolton held houses in York of Aubrey de Mowbray in 1287–8, 1288–9 and 1291–2 (Ian Kershaw and David M. Smith, ed., *The Bolton Priory Compotus 1286–1325, together with a priory account roll for 1377–1378*, YASRS, 154 (2000), pp. 37, 41, 43).

268 *Rubric: Charter of Gerard son of Lewin . . . Lambert Whit'*

269 *Rubric: Charter of Thomas . . . Lambert . . . in Ousegate which he granted to the said Lambert.*

[fol. 29r–v]

270 *Grant and confirmation under his seal, made by the promptings of love and for the salvation of the souls of his ancestors and heirs, by Hugh son of Lambert Whitfor, to God and St Mary of Byland and the monks serving God there, of all the land which his father, Lambert, held behind the booths in Ousegate which belonged to Hugh son of Lewin and Thomas son of <Lewin>, to have all the solars on the said <land>.*

Hiis testibus . . . Sperry, Henrico Blundo aurifabro . . .

Note: Much of the text, especially at the top of fol. 29v, is illegible.

[fol. 29v]

271 *Rubric: Charter of Alan, priest of St Wilfrid of York.*

272 *Rubric: Confirmation by Henry de Neville of all the land . . .*

273 *Rubric: Confirmation by Ralph, son of . . . of land . . .*

274 *Rubric: Confirmation by Emma de Humez of the land of Alan . . .*

275 *Rubric: Quitclaim by Robert son of Elias of the grant . . .*

276 *Rubric: Charter of Robert son of Elias of the grants . . .*

277 *Rubric: Chirograph between . . . . . . Robert son of Elias.*

278 *Rubric: Charter of Henry cordwainer concerning 1 toft in . . .*

279 *Rubric: Charter of the same concerning 2s.*

280 *Rubric: Charter of the same.*

281 *Rubric: Confirmation by Juliana, wife of . . .*

282 *Rubric: Confirmation by William son of . . .*

283 *Rubric: Charter surrendered.*

284 *Rubric: Charter of William Mast and his wife concerning 1 messuage in Patrickpool between the land of St Andrew of Fishergate, and the land of Hugh Broun, and concerning land in Gillygate. [? early 13th cent.].* Text illegible.

Dating: William Mast's land in Patrickpool is mentioned in a charter, which he attests, of the vicars choral of York in the early 13th century, probably after 1217: *Chs Vicars Choral*, I, no. 371.

Note: In another charter, which can be also dated to the early 13th century, William son of Emma Mast and his wife, Helewise, quitclaimed to Robert Sakespei, priest, land held of the monks of Byland lying between the land of the canons of St Andrews, which Andrew Biscop holds, and that which James the glover holds, rendering 2s. to the monks of Byland and paying husgable: *Chs Vicars Choral*, I, no. 372. The grant by William Mast and his wife is recorded in the Gillygate section of the cartulary (below, no. 368) and a further confirmation of his wife (no. 369) gives her name as Emma. Thus there were two William Masts, father and son, and it seems from nos 368–9 below that William Mast the elder was the grantor of no. 284 (rubric at no. 368). The land of the Gilbertine canons may be that in the parish of St Sampson and St Benet which they are recorded as holding by *c.* 1230: PRO E135/25/1, discussed by J. E. Burton, 'Historical Evidence', in *The Church and Gilbertine Priory of St Andrew, Fishergate*, ed. Richard L. Kemp and C. Pamela Graves, *The Archaeology of York*, 11, *The Medieval Defences and Suburbs*, fasc. 2 (Council for British Archaeology for the York Archaeological Trust, 1996), p. 53.

285 *Rubric: Confirmation of Emma his wife.*

286   *Rubric: Charter of Gilbert of Fenton . . . concerning the same.*
Note: Gilbert of Fenton attests charters of 1247 x 1262: *Chs Vicars Choral*, I, nos 406–7. See below no. 370.

287   *Rubric: Charter of Richard, earl of Cornwall, concerning a boat on the river Ouse.*
Note: Much of the text is illegible and only part of the address and the warranty and sealing clauses can be deciphered. There is a rubric at no. 533 below, noting the licence granted by King Edward III to have a boat, granted by Richard, late count of Poitou and Cornwall, on the Ouse between York and Boroughbridge (1328).

[fol. 30r, old fol. 134]
288   *Rubric: Confirmation by the king of the said grant of a boat on the water of Ouse.*
Note: There is a further rubric concerning this at no. 533 below.

289   *Rubric: Charter of Bertram P<ellirarius> (skinner) . . . with houses built on in . . . rendering . . . Nicholas his brother.*
Note: The donor may be Bertram, skinner, who made a grant to Byland of a house in the parish of St Martin, Coney Street, in the reign of King John (PRO E/35/25/1; inquest of *c.* 1230), or Bertram Parmunter (furrier) of no. 290.

290   *Rubric: Charter of Alexander de . . . of the enfeoffment of Bertram Parmunter; surrendered.*

291   *Charter of Nicholas son of Robert son of Simon, for the abbot and convent of St Mary of Byland, concerning a house in the street called Cargate between the house of Paulinus the goldsmith and the house of Alan son of Samson, to hold in free alms.*
Text illegible.
Marginal note: Kergat.
Note: Alan son of Samson occurs in 1195 x 1215 (*EYC* I, no. 321) and in 1255 or 1256 (*Chs Vicars Choral*, I, no. 294, and 1247 x 1262, *ibid.*, nos 406, 407). Paulinus the goldsmith occurs in ?1269: *ibid.*, no. 268. Cargate or Kergate is modern King Street near Ouse Bridge.

292   *Chirograph of Roger Salter concerning a booth which the monks have of the grant of Nicholas, rendering to the monks 6s. yearly.*
Text illegible.

293   *Rubric: Chirograph of William.*

294   *Rubric: Charter of William of Fryton.*

295   *Rubric: Chirograph between . . . and Henry de . . .*

[fol. 30v]
AIRYHOLME (Erghum) (SE6773), in the parish of Hovingham and wapentake of Ryedale (NR), approximately 1½ miles south of Hovingham. Other abbey properties in this area included Scackleton (nos 1104–43).

296   *Grant in free alms, addressed to the archbishop of York and all the sons of holy church, by Roger de Mowbray, to God and the monks of St Mary of Byland, of land in Airyholme lying near to Howthorpe by these boundaries, namely from* Braydestamkelde *as far as* Thrispol. *Further grant for the salvation of his soul and of all the faithful of the* cultura *of* Deneshous *which lies between the fields of Coxwold and Kilburn.* [c. 1140].
Testibus Willelmo de Wyvill', Rogero de Cundy, Willelmo de Muntpincun, Willelmo de Curcy, Radulpho Beler, etc.
Pd: *Mowbray Charters*, no. 34.
Dating: According to the *Historia Fundationis* Roger granted Airyholme to the monks in 1140 (*Mon. Ang.* V, 350). The charter was copied into the *Historia* (MS Dodsworth 63, fols 13v–14r) but not printed in *Mon. Ang.* The description of the recipients as the monks of Byland is clearly an anachronism, marking a later interpolation or modification, since in 1140 the monks were still at Hood.

297   *Notification that the land of Airyholme . . . which are in the bundle of the lords of Mowbray, and confirmations and charters under the heading of Scackleton. Also in the chirograph charters of William de Mowbray under the heading of Fawdington. Moreover . . . to William . . . 20 marks for . . .*
Note: This entry is very faded and cannot be viewed under ultra violet light because of the coloured initials and rubrics. For disputes between the abbot and convent and Nicholas de Yeland and his wife, Eustacia, concerning land in Airyholme (1225–6) see *Curia Regis Rolls*, XII, 2, 39, 284–5, 293, 423, and for a final concord of 18 Nov. 1226 see *Yorks. Fines 1218–1231*, p. 80.

[fol. 31r, old fol. 134]
EGGLESTONE, Premonstratensian Abbey (NR). This section of the cartulary concerns Startforth (NZ0416) in the township and parish of Gilling West (NR) near Barnard Castle, where the monks held a small amount of land. Egglestone Abbey (NZ0615) lies approximately 1 mile SE of Startforth, and nos 298–9 represent a rationalization of monastic property.

298   *Final concord between the church of Byland of the Cistercian order under the presidency of Abbot Henry, and the church of Egglestone of the Premonstratensian order under the presidency of Abbot Hamo, by which the former have demised to Hamo and the church of Egglestone all right which they have in Startforth near to Barnard Castle, which the monks held of the grant of Matilda de Vipont (Veteri Ponte), John the merchant and Roger his son, Thomas de Burgh, Gilbert de Turribus and Geoffrey his son, Thomas son of the parson, Thomas de Richebergh and John son of Arthur. The abbot and convent of Egglestone are to hold the land of the abbot and convent of Byland with all its easements within and outside the vill, according to the contents of the charters of the donors which the monks have, and rendering to the monks of Byland and their successors 4 silver marks yearly, 2 marks each at Easter and St Martin in Winter (11 Nov.). Sealed with the seals of both houses.* Around the Purification of the B. V. M. [*c.* 2 Feb] 1235 [1236].
[Hiis testibus Richero tunc priore et] conventu de Bellal' et Waltero tunc priore et conventu de Eglestun'.
Marginal note: (in later hand) '1235 19 H3'.
Note: The portions of the witness list in square brackets are supplied from no. 299. In 1086 land in Startforth, in Gilling West, was held by Ernisan Musard, and by Bodin (*EYC* V, 83, 198). In the early years of the 13th century Helen de Hastings, daughter of Torphin of Allerston and wife of Hugh de Hastings (d. 1208), granted the patronage of Startforth church to the canons of Egglestone; Jervaulx Abbey also held land there, granted by Aveline, widow of Roger of Gatenby (*ibid.*, no. 313 and note). Thomas de Burgh is to be identified as Thomas, son of Thomas de

Burgh, steward of Countess Constance of Brittany and Richmond (*EYC* V, 165–6). On 18 July 1231 at York a final concord was reached between Adam son of Simon and Matilda his wife, plaintiffs, and Abbot Henry, defendant, concerning ½ carucate in Startforth about which an assize of mort d'ancestor had been brought. Adam and Matilda acknowledged the land to be of the right of the abbot, to hold of them, and the heirs of Matilda, for 1 pound of cumin or 3d. yearly at Christmas, for all service saving forinsec service. For this the abbot gave 20s. sterling: see *Yorks. Fines 1218–1231*, p. 161, from PRO CP 25/1/262/24, no. 74. The grant by Byland of its land in Startforth may represent rationalization of interests in the face of acquisitions by the canons of Egglestone.

299 *Memorandum by Abbot Henry and the convent of Byland of the lands and rents in Startforth near Barnard Castle demised at farm to Hamo, abbot of Egglestone and the convent, around the Purification 1235 [1236], that is, the half carucate with 3 tofts, 2 crofts, and 1 croft next to the church of St Michael towards the north and the* cultura *called* Crokesti *with its appurtenances, of the grant of Matilda de Vipont, and 4 acres and 1 toft granted by Thomas son of Alan, parson. The rents are from Thomas son of Thomas Foster and his heirs, 16s. with homage, and from Guy son of Roger 1 pound of pepper for the service on land held of the grant of Thomas de Burgh. All this was granted by Abbot Henry and the convent to the abbot and convent of Egglestone, as contained in a chirograph (no. 298). Sealed by both convents. Pledge to warranty for the service contained in the chirograph.* [*c.* 2 Feb. 1235 [1236]].

Hiis testibus Richero tunc priore et conventu de Bellal' et Waltero tunc priore et conventu de Eglestun'.

Copy: MS Dodsworth 7, fol. 146v.
Dating: as no. 298.

[fol. 31v]

ARDEN (Erden), Benedictine Priory of nuns (NR), founded by Peter of (Sand) Hutton, and confirmed by Roger de Mowbray (*Mowbray Charters*, no. 20). Greenway notes that Peter was probably the same man as Peter of Thirsk, a sub-tenant of Malebisse, who also granted land near Arden to Rievaulx Abbey (*ibid.*, no. 240) and who was Roger's constable of Thirsk in the 1140s (*ibid.*, p. lx). Arden is now represented by Arden Hall (SE5190), which lies some 7 miles to the NW of Byland Abbey and 3 miles from Old Byland. It is situated to the south of the River Rye, just under 1 mile from its confluence with Wheat Beck, mentioned in nos 300–301. Arden Great Moor lies between the Rye to the south and Wheat Beck to the north, and the area north of Wheat Beck, referred to in no. 300, is Snilesworth Moor.

300   *Final concord in the king's court in the presence of G(eoffrey), bishop of Ely, and J(ohn), bishop of Norwich, and Ranulph Glanvill, justices of the king, and other justices, H(ubert), dean of York, R(ichard), treasurer of the king, G(odfrey) de Lucy, Hugh Bardolf, and other faithful men, between the abbot of Byland and the nuns of Arden through Prioress M(uriel) and brother S(tephen), then guardian of the nuns, concerning land and woodland in Arden which the nuns claimed and about which there had been a plea between them in the king's court: namely, all the lands which the nuns had deraigned by a recognition of novel disseisin against the abbot and convent in the king's court are to remain with the nuns [that is all the lands towards the south as far as the highway leading to Cleveland through the Wheat Beck* (Witebec) *to the Rye], as perambulated [by the wapentake of Birdforth. All the land to the north beyond the Wheat Beck which by right belongs to the nuns shall be held by the abbot and convent for 10s. annually and the nuns are to warranty the land. For this agreement the abbot has given the nuns 20 marks].* Westminster; Tues. after All Saints 33 Henry II [3 Nov. 1187].

Copy: MS Dodsworth 91, fol. 99r–v, no. 47, from which the text in square brackets is supplied.

Pd: *English Lawsuits from William I to Richard I,* ed. R. C. Van Caenegem, 2 vols, Selden Society, 106–7 (1990–91), II, 634–5, no. 591, from MS Dodsworth 91, although it is stated that the document is copied from the Byland cartulary.

Note: Sally Thompson, *Women Religious: the founding of English nunneries after the Norman Conquest* (Oxford, 1991), p. 233, notes the occurrence of Prioress Muriel in 1187, 1189, and 1212; see also *HRH* I, p. 207. Geoffrey de Ridel, bishop of Ely, and John of Oxford, bishop of Norwich, were two of three bishops appointed by Henry II as justices in 1179, at the same time as he appointed Godfrey de Lucy (Turner, *English Judiciary,* pp. 21–2).

301   *Quitclaim by Prioress Muriel and the nuns of Arden of all right which they had in land in Arden [on the north side of Wheat Beck up to the boundary between them and the monks, in accordance with the chirograph between them in the king's court (no. 300). [c. 1187].* Teste priore et capitulo de Novoburgo].

Pd (calendar): *HMC Rutland,* IV, 75, from the original in the possession of His Grace the Duke of Rutland, Belvoir Castle.

Note: The readings in square brackets are supplied from no. 300.

302   *Settlement of a dispute between Abbot Roger and the monks of Byland and Prioress Muriel and the nuns of Arden. At the request of the dean and chapter of York and Jeremiah, archdeacon of Cleveland, the abbot and monks have pardoned the nuns all damages caused by impounding of animals, striking of their men and lay brethren and other enormities inflicted on them, and have undertaken to pursue no further the action which they have begun* *against the nuns. The prioress and nuns have granted to the abbot and monks and their successors free transit through their lands by road and path over the nuns' land. Both chapters have unanimously agreed that neither party shall proceed to judgement, secular or ecclesiastical, against the other nor annoy nor distrain the other. If either err, the matter is to be settled by amicable agreement.* coram Ieremia archidiacono et multis aliis. Hawnby church; St Margaret 35 Henry II [? 20 July 1189].

Marginal note: '1189' and '35 H 2'.

Pd: *HMC Rutland*, IV, 75–6, from the original in the possession of his Grace the Duke of Rutland, Belvoir Castle. The chirograph part of the original has been torn, and the date 1189 is written under the fold.

Dating: Jeremiah, archdeacon of Cleveland, died shortly before Henry II's death (6 July 1189), and *Fasti York*, p. 37 notes this appearance in 1189 as his last occurrence. The date of this document, the feast day of St Margaret Virgin and Martyr (20 July) 1189, is therefore problematic.

303 *The boundaries between the monks and the nuns of Arden.*
There are only two lines on fol. 31v (old. fol. 134). These are the boundaries of the land . . . by which the nuns of Arden . . . that is, through Wheat Beck towards the west as far as . . .

[1 folio lost, old fol. 135]
This seems to have contained charters relating to Emley and Fawdington.

[fol. 32r, old fol. 136]
FAWDINGTON (SE4372), township in the parish of Topcliffe and wapentake of Birdforth (NR). Fawdington lies on the east bank of the river Swale; Thornton Bridge, mentioned in nos 305 and 306, lies about a mile downstream. Of the charters and rubrics in the surviving portions of this section, nos 304–6 relate to fishing rights in the Swale; and nos 307–9 relate to a chantry, possibly financed by rent from Fawdington.

304 end of witness list: . . . testibus Ricardo priore de Novoburgo, Thoma de Colevill', Hugone Malebys, Galfrido de Sutton', Gilleberto de Rampothna.

Note: It is clear from the rubric to no. 305 that no. 304 related to a fishery on the Swale.

305 *Grant in free alms, addressed to all the sons of holy mother church present and future, by John de Daiville, to God and the monks of St Mary of*

Byland, of licence to strengthen and repair their fishery on the Swale as far as the bank on the donor's side towards Thornton (Bridge), with beams and nails as seems fit, without any interference by John and his heirs. The fishery is to have 2 bays, each 10 feet wide, whereby the backs of the fishing weirs (caude kedellorum) *are to be extended. The grant is made free from secular service for the salvation of the soul of the donor and of his father and mother and all his ancestors and heirs. Pledge to warranty.* [before 1243; probably before 1235].

Hiis testibus Thoma de Lascell', Galfrido Fossard, Stephano de Meinill de Thirkilby, Thoma de Cressy, etc.

Dating: death of the donor, but probably before the concord between John and the abbot and convent, reached before 1235 (see note below).

Note: The rubric identifies the donor as John son of Robert de Daiville. Between 1186 and 1190 Nigel de Mowbray restored to John the land which his father had held of Nigel's father, Roger de Mowbray (*Mowbray Charters*, no. 361). John married Matilda, daughter of Jocelin of Louvain and Agnes de Percy, and died before 1242–3 when his son, Robert, was holding knights' fees of the Mowbrays in Yorkshire (*EYF*, pp. 23–4). On 17 Jan. 1235 a final concord was made at York between Abbot Henry, plaintiff, and Robert de Daiville by Robert de Munford his attorney, defendant, concerning a fishery in the river Swale: (text at no. 488 below, pd in *Yorks. Fines 1232–1246*, pp. 32–33, from PRO CP 25/1/263/28, no. 51).

306 *Quitclaim for himself and his heirs, addressed to all the sons of holy mother church, by Richard de Riparia, to God and the monks of St Mary of Byland, of all right which he and his heirs have or might have in the enclosure* (haia) *of Fawdington which the monks have strengthened . . . of water towards Cundall and Thornton (Bridge).* [before 1243].

Hiis testibus Iohanne Dayville, Olyvero de Buscy, ... Mayn. . . Galfrido Fossard, Hugone de Upsale, etc.

Dating: Certainly before the death of the first witness, but Hugh of Upsall witnesses before 1212 (nos 259, 260) and before 1217 (no. 611).

Note: It is possible that this is the Richard de Riparia who, with others, allegedly took advantage of a vacancy at Byland to destroy a ditch near the abbey grange at Fawdington, root up a hedge, and attack the doors. See the writ, 10 Sept. 1254, to the sheriff of York to investigate: *Cal. Inq. Misc. (Chancery)*, I, 67–8, no. 199. Oliver de Buscy was a frequent witness of Byland charters (see also nos 411, 412, 420, 421, 424, 425, 445, 602, 606, 618, 834, 837, 997, 1027, 1044, 1053, 1069) and quitclaimed to the monks forinsec service on land they held in Osgoodby (no. 684). His relationship to William de Buscy (nos 116, 414, 651, 701, 712, 752, 776, 793, 831, 832, 836, 849), son of Robert (nos 414, 728, 781, 831, 888) and nephew of Oliver de Buscy (nos 323, 737, 1104, 1105) who died in 1166 is not known.

306A *Rubric: Charter of William de Mandeville to Robert de Shupton' of the* cultura *called Stocking.* [mid 13th cent.].

Note: William de Mandeville granted to the monks all his land next to the road leading from their grange towards Fawdington, and reached a final concord with them in 1251–2 concerning 2 carucates in Fawdington: MS Dodsworth 91, fols 119r–120r, nos 73–4.

307 *Memorandum that . . . of Dom. Adam of Husthwaite sold to the dean and chapter for 5 marks annually for the maintenance of a chaplain for the soul of Master Thomas de <Wyth>ene and received from them. . . .*

Note: This relates to no. 309. Dom. Adam of Husthwaite was abbot of Byland, and occurs in 1272, 1279, 1280, 1282 and 1283, and again in 1309 x 1310.

308 *Rubric: Letter or exhortation, copied, of William Melton, archbishop of York, concerning the said 5 marks to be paid faithfully each year. 7 Oct. [1333].*

Note: Much of the the the text is faded and difficult to read. This is related to the chantry established by no. 309. There is reference to Dom. John of St Clement, vicar choral of St Peter, York. The date is the non. Oct. in Melton's 17th year [1333]. I have been unable to locate this document in the register of Archbishop Melton (York, Borthwick Institute of Historical Research, Reg. 9).

[fol. 32r–v]

309 *Notification by Abbot Adam and the convent of Byland, of their grant with the full consent of the chapter, to Master Thomas de Wythen, archdeacon of Nottingham, and his heirs and assigns, of an annual rent of 5 marks, to be paid in the church of St Peter, York, half within the week of Whitsuntide and half at St Martin in Winter (11 Nov.), for the maintenance of a chaplain to pray for Thomas's soul and for all the faithful dead. Bond to pay under penalty of 20s. to the fabric of the church of St Peter; the abbot and convent place themselves under the jurisdiction of the dean and chapter, who may compel them under threat of ecclesiastical censure. Similar bond to the mayor and city of York for 20s. for the construction of Ouse Bridge and another 20s. at their discretion. [1268 x 1277].*

Hiis testibus domino Willelmo decano Ebor', domino Willelmo de Wykewan', cancellario Ebor', Thoma de Stokes, Roberto de Bromholme, etc.

Copies: BL Add. ch. 20546, late 14th-century copy, endorsed 'obligatio periculosa qua obligamur cantarie altaris sancti Thome archiepiscopi in ecclesia Beati Petri Ebor' pro quolibet termino non soluto', 'baculo abbatum ponatur', and in a later hand, 'Roger Dodsworth 115', from where copied in MS Dodsworth 91, fols 139v–140r, no. 115, which repeats the first two endorsements of BL Add. ch. 20546. After the second witness BL Add. ch. 20546 continues: Thoma de Ludham et Stephano de Sutton canonicis Ebor', dominis Iohanne le Spicer tunc temporis maiore Ebor', Waltero de Stokes, Roberto de Bromholme et Symone le Grant, magistris Thoma, Iohanne de Aselby, Symone de Haplestorp, Iohanne de Wyten, et multis aliis.

Dating: Thomas de Wythen was archdeacon of Nottingham by 1262, and archdeacon of York by 1277. William Wickwane first occurs as chancellor in 1264. Abbot Adam's predecessor, Henry of Battersby, was still in office in 1268 (*HRH* II, pp. 269–70).

Note: The chantry of Thomas de Wythen, canon of York, at the altar of St Thomas of Canterbury on the north side of the north-west pillar of the lantern is noted in a chantry survey of York Minster: see J. Raine, ed., *The Fabric Rolls of York Minster*, SS, 35 (1859 for 1858), p. 302. The date of foundation is given as 1280 and the endowment of the chantry by the abbot and convent of Byland with 5 marks annually is noted.

[fol. 33r, old fol. 137]

FAWCETT FOREST (Fawcett Bank, SD6894, Fawcett Lees, NY5673), Kendal (Westm.). The origins of Byland's interest in this area lay in the grant of William II of Lancaster (no. 310), whose father had been enfeoffed of lands by Roger de Mowbray. The extensive lands conveyed to Byland were confirmed by William's heir, Helewise (no. 312), and by her husband, Gilbert son of Roger son of Reinfrid (no. 311), sheriff of Lancashire (1205–15) and of Yorkshire (1209–13). His undersheriff in Yorkshire, Henry de Redman, confirmed grants made by Hugh and Ralph, sons of Robert, son of Sigge (nos 313–15).

310 Rubric: *Charter of William [of Lancaster] concerning all his part of [Borrow]dale by the boundaries contained in his charter.*

Original: *Grant in free alms, addressed to the archbishop of York and the whole chapter of St Peter (York) and to all his men, French and English, and to all the sons of holy church, by William of Lancaster, to God and the monks of St Mary of Byland, of all his part of Borrowdale within these bounds: as the highway goes through Arnstone as far as the pleached hedge (plassicium) which has been made on account of the Scots, and along the hedge as far as* Hovedh Kellan *and from there along the brow of the hill of Bannisdale from that part which is opposite Borrowdale, as far as Bannisdale extends, and from there as far as the head of Borrowdale to the boundaries of Westmorland. The grant is made free from all secular service, with all that belongs to it and all its easements, to do there as the monks wish. It is made for the salvation of the soul of the donor and for the salvation of his wife and his father and mother and all his kin, and for the ending of the quarrel which Wimund, bishop of the Isles, once had against his father. Pledge to warranty, and if it should happen that he and his heirs are unable to warranty the land they will grant an exchange to the same value and convenience.* [1170 x 1184].

Hiis testibus Gilleberto filio meo, Normanno dapifero, Willelmo capellano, Richardo capellano, I. [de Lancastro], Ivone capellano de Appelbi, Willelmo de Pio Monte, Anselmo filio Michaelis, Henrico Fossar[d, Ricardo de . . ., W]illelmo filio Gaufridi, Roberto clerico [de] Kirkebi, Radulfo monacho cellarario [de Bellalanda, Wi . . .] sacrista, fratre Iohanne grangiario, [fratr]e Willelmo sutore, Achardo pres[bitero.]

Location: Bagot MSS, Levens Hall, Kendal, Cumbria, Box A, no. 26.

Pd: Farrer, *Kendal*, pp. 388–9.

Dating: Farrer gives 1175 x 1184 (p. 388) and 1154 x 1189 (p. 231). The dating here is by the succession and death of the donor.

Note: For the charters at Levens Hall (nos 310 etc.) see *HMC, 10th Report, app. iv* (1885, rpt. 1906), pp. 318–23. The charter has sustained rodent damage since printed by Farrer, and readings enclosed within square brackets are from his text. The grantor is William II of Lancaster, son of William son of Gilbert of Lancaster; the elder William was enfeoffed by Roger de Mowbray with lands in Lonsdale, Kendal, and Horton in Ribblesdale (*Mowbray Charters*, no. 370). He was dead by 1170; William II of Lancaster, founder of Cockersand Hospital which later became a Premonstratensian Abbey, died in 1184 and was buried at Furness Abbey (*VCH Lancs.*, I, 357–61). The first witness is his bastard son, who attests a number of his charters (*ibid.*, I, 361, note). William's grant to Byland is recorded in the *Historia Fundationis* (*Mon. Ang.* V, 352). Wimund, bishop of the Isles, was consecrated at York and was deprived of his see in 1138 x 1140. An account of his career is given by William of Newburgh (*Historia Rerum Anglicarum*, Book I, chapters 23–4 (I, 73–6)). According to William, Wimund was professed a monk at Furness Abbey, and was sent with certain brethren to the Isle of Man (possibly for the foundation of a daughter house at Rushen in 1134). He was made bishop of the Isles, and, claiming to be the son of the earl of Moray, he gathered forces around him and attacked parts of Scotland and the isles. The king of the Scots granted him an area around Furness, where Wimund made enemies of the local nobility who eventually captured and blinded him. He retired to Byland, where William of Newburgh claimed to have seen him many times. The quarrel between William I of Lancaster and Bishop Wimund mentioned here probably dates from the period described by William of Newburgh. On Byland's interests in Bretherdale see J. E. Satchell, 'The Bretherdale Wool Weight', *TCWAAS*, 89 (1989), 131–40 (pp. 138–9).

311 *Rubric: Confirmation by Gilbert son of Roger son of Reinfrid of the grant of William of Lancaster.* [*c.* 1189 x 1220].

Dating: Gilbert son of Roger son of Reinfrid occurs between *c.* 1189 and 1219 when he undertook to pay rent to St Mary's Abbey, York, for land in Barton in Richmondshire; he married Helewise, daughter of William II of Lancaster by Helewise de Stuteville (see no. 312) between 1184 and 1189, and succeeded in the right of his wife. They had a son, William III of Lancaster (*EYC* V, 81, and no. 184; Farrer, *Kendal*, 1–2; *VCH Lancs.*, I, 357–66 (especially pp. 361–3)). Gilbert was steward of Henry II and Richard I, sheriff of Lancaster from 1205 to 1215 and sheriff of Yorkshire from 1209 to 1213 (*Lord Lieutenants*, p. 53). He died in 1220 (Farrer, *Kendal*, 6).

312   *Rubric: Confirmation by Helewise daughter of William of Lancaster of*
the grant of her father. [before 1194].

Text: MS Dodsworth 91, fol. 79v, no. 18. Notification by Helewise,
daughter of William of Lancaster the younger, in her lawful power, of
her confirmation of the grant of her father to God and St Mary and
the abbot and convent of Byland and their successors, of land in
Borrowdale, by the boundaries contained in his charter (no. 310).
Confirmation also of the grant of land in Kendal which is of her fee by
Hugh and Ralph, son of Sigge (no. 314). The monks are to hold the
land in free alms and do there as they wish. Pledge to warranty. Hiis
testibus Torfino filio Roberti, Thoma filio Cospatrici, Radulfo de
Arundel, Anselmo de Furneis, Romfaro de eadem, Gikello dapifero
meo et Hugone presbitero, Alano filio Benedicti et aliis.

Dating: Death of first witness.

313   *Rubric: Charter of Robert son of Sigge given to his two sons, Hugh*
and Robert (recte Ralph). [late 12th or early 13th cent.].

Dating: see no. 314.

Note: In no. 314 the sons of Robert son of Sigge are given as Hugh and Ralph, and
Robert may here be an error.

314   *Grant by Hugh and Ralph, sons of Robert son of Sigge, of all the land*
in Kendal which they held of H(enry) de Redman by specified boundaries,
rendering to Henry 10s yearly.

Fabricated original or copy: *Grant in free alms, addressed to all the sons*
of holy mother church present and future, by Hugh and Ralph, sons of
Robert son of Sigge, to God and the monks of St Mary of Byland, of all their
land in Kendal which they held of Henry de Redman, by these boundaries:
from Brough as the public road goes from Westmorland towards Kendal as
far as Bannisdale Beck and from Bannisdale Beck to Dowdyrigg (between
Fawcett and Whinfell) and to the head of Dowdyrigg, and from there in a
straight line across to Brough. Whatever is within these bounds they grant
free from all service, to do there as the monks wish, for the salvation of their
souls and of all their ancestors and heirs. The monks are to render annually
to Henry de Redman and his heirs 10s., 5s. at Easter and 5s. at St Michael
(29 Sept.). Pledge to warranty. [late 12th x early 13th cent.; after 1188].

Hiis testibus Thoma filio Cospatrici, Gilberto de Loncastro senescallo
de Kendala, Gervasio de Aincurt, Radulfo de Bethhom, Anselmo de
Stainton', Iohanne Aleman' vicecomite de Eppelby, Thoma de
Hellebec, Willelmo de Askeby, Willelmo de Furnais, Willelmo de

Cornburgh', Willelmo de Braidewath', Matheo Gernet, Sampsone de Wynfell'.

Location: Bagot MSS, Levens Hall, Kendal, Cumbria, Box A, no. 23.
Pd: Farrer, *Kendal*, pp. 389–90.
Dating: Farrer gives Michaelmas 1197 x Michaelmas 1198 on pp. 389–90, and 1198 x 1200 on p. 231, with no explanation. John Alemann, or Laleman, accounted for revenues in Cumberland in 1199/1200 and Westmorland in 1200/1201 (*Pipe Roll 1 John*, p. 210, and *2 John*, p. 33). Henry de Redman (Redmayne) was the son of Norman de Yealand, to whom William I of Lancaster granted Levens in the time of Henry II. Henry had succeeded to Levens by 1188 and granted land to Cockersand Abbey *c.* 1200 (*VCH Lancs.*, VIII, 175). Henry de Redman occurs as steward of Kendal in 1199/1200 and 1200 x 1209 (Farrer, *Kendal*, p. 4); he was undersheriff of Yorkshire for Gilbert Fitz Reinfrid from 1209 to 1213 (*Lord Lieutenants*, p. 53).
Note: The charter is written in a late 14th- or early 15th-century hand, and has a blob of wax for a seal. Much of the witness list is not visible in the cartulary. The cartulary rubric calls this a charter of Hugh and Ralph sons of Sigge. The last witness quitclaimed all right he had in the pasture of Hugh and Ralph (no. 318 below).

315 *Confirmation by Henry de Redman of no. 314.* [late 12th or early 13th cent.].
Fabricated original or copy: Hiis testibus Thoma filio Gosp(atrici) . . . scallo de Kendala, Gervasio de Aincurt, Radulfo de B<ethom, Anselmo de> Stainton', Iohanne Aleman' vicecomite de Eppelby, Thoma de <Hellebec, Willelmo de> Askeby, Willelmo de Furnais, Willelmo de Corneburgh', Willelmo <de Braidewath, Matheo> Gernet, Sampsone de Wynnefel'.

Location: Bagot MSS, Levens Hall, Kendal, Cumbria, Box A, no. 24.
Dating: as no. 314.
Note: The charter, which is very faded, is in the same hand as no. 314, and the witnesses suggest that they were issued at the same time, or that they represent forgeries with the witnesses taken from the same charter.

316 *Notification by Matthew de Redman of his confirmation to God and the monks of Byland of all the land which the monks have of the fee of his father, as the charter of his father, Henry, attests. Pledge to warranty.* [mid 13th cent.].
Hiis testibus Willelmo de Hyreby, Henrico de Suleby, Radulfo de Aincurt, Thoma filio Iohannis, etc.

Copy: MS Dodsworth 94, fol. 23v, no. 30, which omits 'etc' in the witness list and continues: Alano de Wardecop, Iohanne de Ormesheved, Willelmo filio Simonis, Radulpho de Tibbay.
Dating: Matthew de Redman was the son of Henry son of Norman. In 1242 he held part of the manor of Yealand Redmayne of William III of Lancaster. Matthew was sheriff of Lancashire between 1246 and 1248. His son, Henry, occurs in 1267 (*VCH*

Note: The Levens Hall collection includes an original of the confirmation of nos 315 and 316 by Richard de Redman, Matthew's brother.

[fol. 33v]

317 *Confirmation, addressed to the archbishop of York and the whole chapter and all the sons of holy mother church, by Gilbert son of Roger son of Reinfrid, to God and St Mary and the monks of St Mary of Byland, of all the land which the monks hold of Henry de Redman, that is, the land which they have of the grant of the sons of Robert son of Sigge (boundaries as no. 314). Licence to enclose the land as they wish. This confirmation is made for the salvation of his soul and of his wife and all his ancestors and heirs, to hold in free alms as Henry's charter attests. [c. 1189 x 1220].*

Hiis testibus . . . to de Busse, Willelmo de Wynleshores, Gilleberto de . . . ra.

Dating: see no. 311.

318 *Rubric: Quitclaim by Sampson of Whinfell of all the right he had in the land and pasture held of Hugh and Ralph, sons of Robert.*

Text illegible.

Note: The grantor witnesses nos 314, 315.

[fol. 34r, old fol. 138]

FOREST OF GALTRES, a royal forest covering most of the wapentake of Bulmer stretching from the gates of York 20 miles north to Crayke. A number of Byland's properties lay within the royal forest (no. 321).

319 *Boundaries of the demesne of the lord king in the forest of Galtres.*

Text illegible. ?28 Edward I.

[fol. 34r–v]

320 *Boundaries of the whole forest of Galtres.* ?10 Aug.

Text illegible.

[fols 34v–35r]

321 *Inquisition into the boundaries of the Forest of Galtres in the presence of John de Segrave, the king's keeper of the forest beyond Trent, by writ of the lord king sent to the said John. The abbot of Byland demonstrated to the king that he, the abbot, against the charters of his predecessors the kings of England, had been distrained to find maintenance for the king's foresters and other royal ministers of the forest of Galtres at his granges of Fawdington and Boscar, which are within the bounds of the forest, and that this was* *against his liberties. Sworn testimony to this effect.* York; Wed., eve of St Nicholas [5 Dec.] 7 Edward II [1313].

Note: F. Drake, *Eboracum* (London, 1736), pp. xxxviii, prints an inquisition, taken at York on Mon. 3 May 9 Edward II [1316] following a perambulation of the forest of Galtres (translated in *EYC* I, 330–1).

[fol. 35r–v, old fol. 139]

322 *Inquisition in the presence of John de Crombwell, keeper of the forests of the king and Gregory de Thorneton, knight of the said John, into certain articles pertaining to the state of the forest of Galtres, by jurors Thomas de Ryvere . . . de Boulton', knights, John de Thorneton, John . . . . . .by, Thomas Blaunkfront, Robert of Malton, Peter de . . . Thomas le Harpur, Thomas son of William of Shipton, Peter son of Walter of the same, Stephen . . .pson', Gervase de Roucliff', John of Clifton, Robert de Thorneton, John of Foston, wardens, William Cust, William Lovell, agisters of the forest, and other faithful men, concerning both the forest and what was outside the forest. The abbot of Byland, John of Myton, was attached by pledges outside the attachments of the forest at the forest court in the presence of the said keeper of the forest, for failing to provide maintenance at his granges of Fawdington and Boscar against the assize of the forest. He appeared in person and said expressly that he was not bound to receive the steward of the forest or any other ministers of the forest or provide maintenance for them at his granges, under royal charter. The jurors testified to the abbot's claim and he was quit. Sealed by the jurors and by John de Crombwell.* Mon. before [ ] Virgin 1 Edw. III [25 Jan. 1327 x 24 Jan. 1328].

[1 folio lost, old fol. 140]

FELIXKIRK (SE4684), a parish and township in the wapentake of Birdforth. The Knights Hospitaller had a preceptory at Felixkirk: see MS Top. Yorks. d. 11, fol. 267r, which indicates that the charters entered in this section related to the advowson of the church. For agreement reached between Byland and the vicar of Felixkirk, see below, nos 1055–6, 1057, 1059.

[fol. 36r, old fol. 141]

THORPE LE WILLOWS ('Graunt Thorpe', now Thorpe Grange, SE5777), in the parish of Coxwold and the wapentake of Birdforth (NR). Thorpe Grange lies roughly 1 mile south of Ampleforth and just over 2 miles SE of Byland Abbey. Yearsley lies about 2 miles to the S/SE of Thorpe Grange. Land in Thorpe was acquired from 1147, the principal donor being William de Wyville, who some years before he became steward of Roger de Mowbray granted the monks the whole vill of Thorpe (no. 323). His grant was confirmed by his son Richard, who added his newly-won forest (nos 324–5). At around the same time another important Mowbray tenant, Thomas de Coleville, confirmed the monks in possession of land and woodland around Thorpe and Coxwold (nos 327–8), which was later a cause of dispute between Byland and Newburgh Priory (see no. 728). Byland had established a grange at Thorpe by 1181 (no. 728) and by 1190 had built houses below the grange (no. 330). 'Graunt Thorpe' was probably so called to distinguish it from 'Petithorpe', Thorpefield near Thirsk. The name Thorpe le Willows is a corruption of 'Woolhouse'; it was at Thorpe that the monks had an important woolhouse which by the late 13th century was being used by the nuns of Arden. See *Select Cases concerning the Law Merchant AD 1270–1638*, ed. C. Gross, 3 vols, Selden Society, 23 (1908), 46 (1929), 49 (1932), II, 69–71.

323   Fabricated original: *Notification by William de Wyville of his grant in free alms to God and the monks of Byland and their successors of all that is written below: the whole vill of Thorpe with all its appurtenances, common of the wood between Thorpe le Willows and Yearsley* (medium contra medium), *by the road which goes through the centre of* Thursedena *to Hovingham and towards Coxwold, and the woodland between Oxendale (in Coxwold) and the ancient way which descends from* Heriehou *and goes through* Ulfisthweith *as far as the water course, and from there to the north as the water course flows to* Sighederesbrigga *to the north of* Whiteker *as* Mikilbek *falls to* Whiteker *and from there to the boundary of Ampleforth; the whole land with woodland pertaining to it and the pasture which is between the millpond and Thorpe le Willows and 20 acres in the wood between Thorpe le Willows and Yearsley, with common pasture in the wood and dead wood for their own uses at Thorpe le Willows, and 60 pigs in the time of pasturing quit of pannage. Grant also of the land which the grantor had to the south of the river. The monks are to hold all this of the grantor and his heirs free from all secular service as he held it and his [brother] before him. Pledge to warranty by him and his heirs for the salvation of their souls.* [1147 x 1157].

Hiis testibus Rogero de Molbrai de quo omnia predicta teneo, Olivero Busci, Hugone Malabissa, Ada Luvel, Ada del Archis, Gregorio de Insula, Radulfo Naturel, Gikello capellano.

Location: NYCRO, ZDV I 5 (MIC 1352/401–411).
Pd (calendar): *HMC Various Collections*, II, 4–5 (no. 4).

Dating: The grantor does not occur after 1157 (*Mowbray Charters*, p. 240). For two confirmations by Roger de Mowbray see *Mowbray Charters*, nos 50 and 51 (no. 326 below), and for one by Henry II in 1164 see MS Dodsworth 7, fol. 105r.

Note: The handwriting suggests a date later than 1200. This is one of three 13th-century copies of a supposed original. The cartulary copy has the first three witnesses only. The unpublished catalogue of monastic records at NYCRO notes that a significant variant between the 'original' and the cartulary copy is that the former has the reading *pater* (father) for *frater* (brother), and suggests that as William de Wyville succeeded his brother, Ralph, rather than his father, the cartulary copy may preserve the original reading. That Ralph and William were brothers is confirmed by no. 325 below. The water course referred to may be Holbeck, which runs to the north of Thorpe Grange. Oliver de Buscy who attests here and nos 737, 1104 and 1105 below was dead by 1166, when he had been succeeded by his brother, Robert, who was the grantor of land in Osgoodby (no. 831). Hugh Malebisse was steward of Roger de Mowbray between *c.* 1147 and 1154; he attests no. 326 below. Members of the Malebisse family were benefactors in Murton (nos 578–95).

324   *Grant and confirmation in free alms for himself and his heirs, addressed to all the sons of holy mother church present and future, by Richard son of William de Wyville, to God and the abbot and monks of Byland and their successors, of Thorpe near Ampleforth (Thorpe le Willows) with all appurtenances inside and outside the vill. Pledge to warranty.* [after *c.* 1157].

Hiis testibus Rogero de <Molbray, Radulfo de> la Haye, Symone de Staingriva, Roberto de Surdevals, <Willelmo de> Hayrum, W<illelmo Dod, Ricardo Si>lvam.

Dating: The witness list is damaged, but what remains suggests that the charter was issued at the same time as no. 325. Richard (nos 324–5) is generally said to have succeeded his father William by 1166, but William's last occurrence is in 1157. See note to nos 323 and 325.

Note: The rubric states that the charter has been copied.

325   *Rubric: Confirmation by the same Richard of forest which Roger de Mowbray granted to Ralph, Richard's uncle.*
Original: *Grant and confirmation in free alms, addressed to the archbishop of York and the whole chapter of St Peter (York) and all the sons of holy church, by Richard de Wyville, to God and the monks of St Mary of Byland, of Thorpe le Willows with all its appurtenances and the newly-won forest which Roger de Mowbray granted first to Richard's uncle, Ralph, and then to his father, William, by the boundaries set down in Roger de Mowbray's charter and that of William, Richard's father (no. 323). The grant is made free from all secular service, for the salvation of the soul of the donor and of all his ancestors and heirs. Pledge to warranty.* [*c.* 1157 x 1186].

Hiis testibus Rogero de Molbrai, Radulfo de Lahai, Simone de Stainegriva, Roberto de Surdevals, Willelmo de Hairum, Willelmo Dod, Ricardo Silvam, Herberto fratre eius, Ricardo de Dalt', Gerardo stabulario, Walkelino Trussevilain.

Location: NYCRO ZDV I 5 (MIC 1352/412–15); endorsed in contemporary hand: conf' Ric' de Widevill' de Torp. G'thorp' B. i ii (Thorpe le Willows, first bundle, 2). Marginal note in cartulary: B(aculus) i.

Pd: *EYF*, p. 116, no. 16; (calendar): *HMC Various Collections*, II, 6–7 (no. 11).

Dating: See no. 324. *EYF* dates to *c.* 1160 x 1186, possibly *c.* 1176 when five of the witnesses attest together (*EYC* IX, no. 160). Ralph de Wyville last occurs *c.* 1147 and had been succeeded by his brother, William (no. 323) by 1154 at the latest and William does not occur after 1157.

326 *Confirmation in free alms, addressed to the archbishop of York and the whole chapter of St Peter (York) and all the sons of holy church, by Roger de Mowbray, for the salvation of his soul and of all his own, of the grant which William de Wyville made to God and the monks of St Mary of Byland, of the whole land of Thorpe le Willows, by the boundaries by which Roger granted it to Ralph de Wyville and William his brother, that is common of the wood between Thorpe le Willows and Yearsley* (medium contra medium) *by the road which runs through the centre of* Thursedene *to Hovingham and thus to Coxwold, the wood between Oxendale and the ancient road which descends from* Hesthou *and runs through to the watercourse, and from there to the north as the the water course flows to* Sighe<desbrigga> *and from there to the north of* Whiteker *as* Mychelbec *falls into* Whiteker *and thus to the boundary of Ampleforth.* [1147 x 1157/1164].

Hiis testibus Roberto de Dayvill', Rogero de Flamavill', Hugone Malebissa, etc.

Marginal note (in later hand): 'Wm Wyvile ante 20 H 2', 'Ricardus filius Wm' and 'Rad'us W. frater'.

Pd: *Mowbray Charters*, no. 51, where it is pointed out that the terminal date is provided by the confirmation by Henry II in 1164.

Dating: William's grant (no. 323) was made before 1157 and it is possible that this confirmation was issued during his lifetime. See note to no. 323.

Note: The boundaries in this charter should be compared with those of no. 323. The rubric states that the charter has been copied.

[fol. 36v]

327 *Confirmation, addressed to the archbishop of York and all the sons of holy mother church, by Thomas de Coleville, to God and the monks of St Mary of Byland, of whatever the monks hold in the land and woodland which lie between Oxendale and the boundaries of Gilling below the highway on the northern side which runs through the centre of* Thursedena *towards*

Hovingham. Neither the donor nor his heirs nor his men will assart nor cause to be built on nor plough the said land, nor will they grant nor sell to anyone, except for the grant or sale of wood. [1155 x 1186].

Hiis testibus Rogero de Molbray, Ricardo priore et capitulo de Neuburgo, Willelmo de Colavilla, magistro Roberto Magno, etc.

Dating: second witness. The charter was issued at Roger de Mowbray's Augustinian house of Newburgh.

Note: Both this grant and the following quitclaim (no. 328) may have been made earlier than the date of the charter suggests. The *Historia Fundationis* implies that they date from around the time Roger de Mowbray granted the third site of the abbey in 1147: *Mon. Ang.* V, 351.

328 *Quitclaim for himself and his heirs, addressed to the archbishop of York and the whole chapter of St Peter (York) and all the sons of holy church present and future, by Thomas de Coleville, to God and St Mary of Byland, of land and woodland pertaining to it between the monks' millpond and Thorpe le Willows, and the whole of* **Berscliva** *and* **Burtoft** *and whatever belongs to the vill of Coxwold on the northern side of* **Whiteker**. *Grant also of 20 acres in the wood between Thorpe le Willows and Yearsley and common pasture there for all their animals as the men of Thorpe have, and free entry and exit for themselves, their men, animals and carts. Grant also of the right to take dead wood for the use of their place in Thorpe, as well as pasture for 40 pigs in the time of pasturing, quit of pannage. The monks are to do with the land whatever they wish. Pledge to warranty.* [c. 1162 x 1173].

Hiis testibus <magistro> Swayno de hospitali Sancti Petri, Symone de Sigillo, magistro Roberto . . .

Dating: The witness list in damaged. The first witness does not occur until after 1162, and had been succeeded by Paulinus of Leeds by 1186 (*EYC* XI, 170; *Mowbray Charters*, p. 193). Simon de Sigillo was a canon of York and prebendary of Langtoft, who first occurs in 1143 x 1153 and last *c.* 1170 x 1186; however, he is noted (*Fasti York*, p. 84) as having been succeeded in his prebend by John son of Letold by 1173. See note to no. 327.

329 *Confirmation, addressed to the archbishop of York and the whole chapter of St Peter, York, <and all his men English> and French and all the sons of holy mother church, by Roger de Mowbray, to God and the monks of St Mary of Byland, of the grant made by Thomas de Coleville (as in no. 328). The confirmation is made for the salvation of his soul and those of his father and mother <and of all his ancestors and heirs>. Further grant and confirmation of a road between the abbey and Wildon, as attested in the chirograph between them and Thomas de Coleville.* [1177 x 1186].

Hiis testibus Roberto de Bucy, Warino <?filio Simonis>, etc.

Pd: *Mowbray Charters*, no. 68. The charter is partly illegible because of damp.

Dating: The agreement contains a reference to a road between Wildon and the new abbey; Greenway suggests this is the fourth abbey site occupied in 1177, and that this accordingly provides the earliest date for Coleville's grant.

[fol. 36v–37r]

330   *Rubric: Chirograph charter of Thomas de Coleville concerning houses below the grange.*

Original: *Agreement between the convent of Byland and Thomas de Coleville, that the houses which the monks have built below their grange of Thorpe le Willows to the south may remain without any claim by Thomas and his heirs. The monks are not to make any settlement (***herbergiamentum***) beyond the ditch nearest to the houses towards the south without the permission of Thomas and his heirs. They shall build a conduit in the said ditch so that whenever they need it they may divert the flow of water for their own use.* [before 1190].

Hiis testibus Hugone persona de Rudeb', Roberto de Daivilla et Gaufrido nepote eius, Willelmo filio Meldredi, Alexandro nepote Thome de Colevill', Roberto de Wirecestre.

Location: NYCRO, ZDV I 5 (MIC 1352/392–393), cut as chirograph; endorsed: Thom' de Collevill' de grangia de Torp de domibus subtus Grang' (12th century); C' T' de Colvill de domibus subtus Grang' carta secunda (13th century); Graunt Thorp' v' ir' vj; seal: pendant, dark wax, long figure holding staff or sword.
Pd (calendar): *HMC Various Collections*, II, 3 (no. 1).
Dating: Robert de Daiville had been succeeded by his son John by 1186 x 1190 (*EYF*, p. 24).
Note: Fol. 37 (old fol. 142) has been torn away; only the first full line of this agreement remains on fol. 36v, but there is sufficient to identify this with the original, of which there is also a 13th-century copy at NYCRO. The text of the first full charter on fol. 37r has been badly damaged. Its rubric appears to read: Carta Thome de.

[fol. 38r, old fol. 143]

331   . . . *of our beloved in Christ the abbot of Byland, who has suggested that he and his predecessors had before the 20th year of E. king of England son of king H. (i.e. 20 Edward I, Nov. 1291 x Nov. 1292) possessed their grange of Thorpe le Willows and paid tenths on it as a spiritual holding, and pay tenths as such and not as a lay fee. Therefore in the last grant in the county of York they should have paid for Yearsley pasture as clergy. However collectors have been asking for tenths as from the laity. The abbot has complained . . .*

Note: The first part of the document is missing from damaged fol. 37v.

332 *Rubric: Agreement between the monks and <the canons of Newburgh> concerning Oxendale and Gilling. Look in the Newburgh bundle.*

Note: The text of this agreement is given at no. 728 below.

333 *Rubric: Confirmation of John . . . Thorpe, wool merchant. Look in the second bundle among the confirmations.*

334 *Rubric: Agreement between the monks and the canons of Newburgh made in the church of Coxwold concerning various matters and concerning places in Thorpe le Willows which are not subject to tithe. Look in the first Newburgh bundle.*

Note: The text of this agreement is given at no. 732 below.

[fol. 38v]

GAYTERYG, a lost place name, recorded in Middlesbrough, wapentake of Langbargh West (NR). The property in 'Gayteryg' was the outlet which the monks of Byland enjoyed on the river Tees. The grant, by William de Acklam, the genealogy of whose descendants is included on fol. 41r (no. 367), of his fishery with licence to fish in the Tees, together with common pasture and rights of free entry and exit, was confirmed by his lords, Peter and Adam de Brus, and by his son (nos 335–8). Other benefactors included Geoffrey of Ayresome and his family (nos 339–41) and Roger Cosin (343–51 etc.).

335 *Grant in free alms, addressed to the archbishop of York and the whole chapter of St Peter (York) and all the sons of holy church, by William of Acklam, to God and the monks of Byland, of his fishery below* Gayteryg *as he and his ancestors held it, and the site of the said fishery with 9 acres, or more if there is more land there. Grant also of licence to fish in the Tees with a net where others draw their nets, and to erect their timber and prepare their hurdles and dry their nets on the banks below the fishery. Undertaking that the donor and his heirs will not construct another fishery between this one and the one that he built below Ayresome nor will they allow anyone else to construct a fishery. Grant also of common pasture where his men of Acklam have it, for 4 oxen and 2 horses and for other animals bringing wood to the fishery, for two nights if they have reason to stay, and of free entry and exit by the road which they have and which the donor granted them as far as their lodge and their fishery. The grant is made for the salvation of the soul of the donor and that of his wife Margery and of all their children and all their ancestors and heirs. The monks have received him, his wife and their children in full confraternity of their house. Pledge to warranty.* [before 1196].

Hiis testibus R. . . . . . Marton, Ricardo filio Symonis de Mikelby, Radulfo le Graunt.

Pd: *EYC* II, no. 703.

Dating: *c.* 1170 x 1180 in *EYC*, without explanation; for a confirmation by Adam de Brus (d. 1196) see no. 336A.

Note: The charter is illegible in places. The grantor confirmed to Whitby Abbey the grant of his mother, Cecilia: *Cart. Whitby,* I, 102 (no. 125); *EYC* II, no. 705, where dated 1170 x 1180. The *Historia Fundationis* notes the grant of land in 'Gayteryk' by William of Acklam in the time of Abbot Roger: *Mon. Ang.* V, 352. The rubric states that the charter has been copied.

336   *Rubric: Confirmation by Peter de Brus of the said fishery etc.*

Marginal note: B(aculus) i.

Note: This could be Peter de Brus I (d. 1222) or Peter de Brus II (d. 1240).

336A   *Confirmation, addressed to all who will see or hear these letters, by Adam de Brus, to God and the monks of St Mary of Byland, of the grants of William of Acklam, as contained in William's charter (no. 335). The confirmation is made for the salvation of Adam's soul and of his wife and of all his ancestors and heirs.* [before 1196].

Hiis testibus Rogero de Conniers, Galfrido de Thorp', Roberto clerico, etc.

Copy: MS Dodsworth 94, fol. 16r, no. 16 (transcribed from the original in St Mary's Tower). This omits 'etc' in the witness list and continues: de Martona, Willelmo filio Fulconis de Malteby, Roberto de Lascels et Gerardo fratre eius, Alano de Flamvilla, Stephano de Rosell', Ricardo de Hilton, Willelmo filio Rogeri, Simone de Tholebut, Turstano Berghebi, Roberto Ingeranni, Iohanne Esturmi, Roberto capellano, Ricardo de Crathorne. 'The seale faire on horseback'.

Pd: *EYC* II, no. 773, from MS Dodsworth 94.

Dating: death of the grantor.

[fols 38v–39r]

337   *Confirmation in free alms, addressed to the archbishop of York and the whole chapter of St Peter (York) and all the sons of holy church, by Roger son of William of Acklam, to God and the monks of St Mary of Byland, of the grant made by his father of his fishery in* Gayteryg *and of land and pasture which they have there, with all their appurtenances in lands, meadows and pastures, in roads and paths and all other easements, as contained in the charter of his father. Grant of pasture for 60 sheep to the north of Acklam where his men of Acklam have it, the lambs of which were with their mothers in that pasture up to St John the Baptist. The grant is made for the salvation of the soul of the donor and those of his wife and his ancestors and heirs, and the monks have received him and his wife and children in full confraternity of the house. Pledge to warranty.* [before 1231].

Hiis testibus Roberto de Mauteby, Willelmo de Staynesby, Willelmo filio Odonis, etc.

Dating: Donor dead by 1231: *EYC* II, 52.

[fol. 39r, old fol. 144]

338   *Grant, addressed to all the sons of holy mother church present and future, by Roger son of William of Acklam, to God and the monks of St Mary of Byland, of the land which he has in* Florum *containing 1½ acres next to the bovate which the monks have in perpetual alms of the carucate of Roger Cosin, between the carucate and the small marsh towards . . . in width and from the small marsh as far as* Fulehousic *in length. The monks are to hold the land free from secular service and are to cultivate it and enclose it as they wish. The grant is made for the souls of Roger's father, mother, his ancestors, his wives, and his children. Pledge to warranty.* [before 1231].

Hiis testibus Roberto persona de Marton', Willelmo filio Odonis et Gregorio filio eius, etc.

Marginal note: Florum.
Dating: as no. 337.

339   *Grant in free alms, addressed to the archbishop of York and the whole chapter of St Peter (York) and all the sons of holy mother church, by Geoffrey of Ayresome, to God and the monks of St Mary of Byland, of 4 acres next to the* cultura *which they have above* Gayteryg. *The grant is made free from secular service for the salvation of the donor's soul and those of all his ancestors and heirs. Pledge to warranty.* [late 12th cent.].

Hiis testibus Willelmo et Nicholao de Midelburgh monachis . . . Petro presbitero, Iordano clerico, etc.

Pd: *EYC* II, no. 704.
Note: The grantor is likely to be the Geoffrey of Ayresome, son of Matilda, who granted land in Middlesbrough to Whitby Abbey (*Cart. Whitby*, I, 101, no. 123); see no. 341. The two monks were presumably monks of Whitby Abbey's cell at Middlesbrough. The rubric states that the charter has been copied.

340   *Rubric: Charter of Geoffrey of Ayresome concerning the same 4 acres.*

341   *Confirmation, addressed to the archbishop of York etc, by Baldric son of Matilda of Ayresome, to God and the monks of St Mary of Byland, of the grant made by Geoffrey of Ayresome [his father,* recte *brother] of 4 acres in* Gayteryg *as the charter of Baldric's father attests. Pledge to warranty.* [late 12th cent.].

Hiis testibus Hugone Morand' monacho de Whitby, Iordano diacono de Midlesburgh, Roberto clerico de Acclum, Rogero Cosyn, etc.

Date: The last witness is the grantor of no. 343.

Note: In the rubric of the charter Baldric is described as Geoffrey's brother. Jordan, deacon, also attests Geoffrey's charter for Whitby (see no. 339 note), and may be the Jordan *clericus*, who attests no. 339. For a grant by Baldric to Whitby Abbey see *Cart. Whitby*, I, no. 135; this is witnessed by William son of Odo and Gregory son of William (see no. 338 above). The rubric states that the charter has been copied.

342   Rubric: *Charter of Geoffrey [   ] of Linthorpe concerning 1 acre of land*
. . .

[fol. 39r–v]

343   *Grant, addressed to the archbishop of York etc, by Roger Cosin and Emma his wife, daughter of Maleth, to God and the monks of St Mary of Byland, of a toft in Linthorpe which is to contain 1½ acres, and all their* cultura *in* Gateryg *which is nearest to the river Tees, and whatever the donors have in land and water as far as their land stretches from the water channel of Ayresome to the west. The monks may make fisheries and construct buildings and do here as they wish. Further grant of all easements. These grants are made free from all secular service, for the souls of the donors, their fathers and mothers and all their ancestors. Emma confirms that the land is of her hereditary right, and both donors pledge to warranty in full chapter. The monks have received them in confraternity and will perform service for them at their death. If Roger ever wishes to convert his life the monks will receive him.* [1160 x 1170].

Hiis testibus Willelmo de Herlesey decano, et capitulo de Whitby, Roberto presbitero de Lithe et Willelmo fratre suo.

Marginal note: (opposite opening of text) Levynthorpe; (at foot of folio) iiii.

Pd: *EYC* III, no. 1851.

Dating: Roger Cosin granted to Whitby Abbey a bovate in Linthorpe lying next to the bovate of the monks of Byland: *Cart. Whitby*, I, 109, no. 138; *EYC* III, no. 1852, where dated 1160 x 1180.

Note: Malet, man of Roger de Mowbray in Linthorpe, occurs in a Whitby charter of 1130 x 1139 (*Cart. Whitby*, I, 214–16, no. 271). William de Herleseie attests, without title, three charters of Robert de Liverton in favour of Whitby Abbey (*Cart. Whitby* I, 76 (no. 80), 86 (no. 97), 187–8 (no. 229); also *EYC* II, nos 892–3, dated by Farrer 1165 x 1175 and 1170 x 1180).

[fol. 39v]

344   Rubric: *Confirmation by Roger de Mowbray of the grant of Roger Cosin.* [*c.* 1160 x 1170].

Dating: see no. 343.

345 *Rubric: Charter of Roger Cosin and Emma his wife concerning a bovate in Linthorpe towards . . . and 1 carucate which they have of the fee of Roger de Mowbray, rendering forinsec service etc.* [*c.* 1160 x 1170].
Dating: see no. 343.

346 *Confirmation, to all the sons of holy mother church present and future, by William son of Roger Cosin of the grant of his father to God and St Mary of Byland and the monks serving God there (no. 343). Pledge to warranty for the salvation of his soul and of all his ancestors and heirs.* [late 12th or early 13th cent.].
Hiis testibus Willelmo fratre eius . . . Roberto de Mauteby . . . And(rea) de Thormodeby, Ricardo de . . .
Note: The text is faded and damaged.

347 *Confirmation in free alms, addressed to all the sons of holy mother church <present and future>, by Roger of Acklam, son of William, to God and the monks of St Mary of Byland, of the grant of Roger Cosin and Emma his wife of 1 bovate in Linthorpe (no. 343). Pledge to warranty for the salvation of his soul and of all his ancestors and heirs.* [before 1231].
Hiis testibus . . . fratribus meis, Roberto persona de Mart', Roberto . . .
Dating: death of the grantor.
Note: The text is faded and damaged.

348 *Rubric: Charter of William son of Roger Cosin.* [late 12th or early 13th cent.].

349 *Rubric: Charter of William son of Lyne . . . for their carts . . .* Gildemoor . . . Kirkegate *towards . . . throughout the whole land.* [late 12th cent.].
Note: William son of Line of Linthorpe issued a charter in favour of Whitby Abbey in which he describes himself as the nephew of Geoffrey of Ayresome (*Cart. Whitby*, I, 113–14, no. 145). It was witnessed by Gregory of Linthorpe (no. 353 below). Geoffrey of Ayresome was the grantor of nos 339–40 above, of late 12th-century date.

350 *Rubric: Charter of William son of Lyne concerning 3 acres <in Lin>thorpe in the eastern part . . . and the road called* Kirkgate. *These [nos 349, 350] are bound together.* [late 12th cent.].

[fols 39v–40r]
351 *Confirmation, addressed to all the sons of holy church present and future, by William of Ayresome, to God and the monks of St Mary of Byland,*

of 4 acres which he had in Gayteryg *before the gates of the place which they hold in free alms, to hold free from secular service and to do with as they wish. The confirmation is made for the salvation of the soul of the donor and of his father and mother, his wife, and all his ancestors and heirs. Pledge to warranty.* [before 1231].

Hiis testibus Rogero de Acclum, W . . . de Staynsby, W. filio Odonis, etc.

Marginal note: Gayteryg.
Copy: MS Top. Yorks. e. 8, fol. 107r (old p. 178), where the grantor is called William Ruffus of Ayresome. The Christian name of the second witness is missing; the witness list omits 'etc' and continues: Gregorio filio eius, Willelmo fratre eiusdem Gregorii, Roberto de Stainesbi, Rogero de Boscehala, Andrea de Turmodebi, Roberto de Wassan.
Dating: The death of the first witness (see no. 337).

[fol. 40r, old fol. 145]
352   *Rubric: Charter of Roger Cosin concerning 1 bovate which he gave with Richard his son, performing forinsec service.*

353   *Rubric: Charter of Gregory of Linthorpe concerning 1 acre in* Florum *lying towards the south and east.*

Marginal note: b(aculus) ii.
Note: A Gregory of Linthorpe witnessed a charter of Alan of Wilton after 1215: *EYC* II, 124. However another occurs in 1301: *Cart. Guis.* I, 167–8.

354   *Rubric: Charter of William son of Osaius concerning 2½ acres and ½ rood in Linthorpe.*

355   *Rubric: Charter of William son of Lyne concerning 6 acres in Linthorpe lying above* Gildermor *and below the road called* Kirkgate *and concerning common pasture in Linthorpe for their flocks from* Gayterigg. [late 12th cent.].

Dating: see no. 349.
Note: The place names 'Gildhusmor' and 'Kirkgate' in Linthorpe occur in *Cart. Whitby*, II, 371 (no. 409) and 373 (no. 413).

356   *Confirmation, addressed to all the sons of holy mother church present and future, by William son of Richard son of William son of Lyne, to God and St Mary and the monks, of 6 acres in the region of Linthorpe, that is, 2 lying nearest to* Gildemora *towards the west, 2½ at the head of Linthorpe lying on the eastern part below the road called* Kirkgate *towards the channel of Marton and 1½ <next to> the house of the prior of Guisborough between* Gildusdic *and the marsh, and common pasture . . . in* Gaytryg *throughout*

Linthorpe. *This confirmation is made free from all service for the salvation of the soul of the donor and of <his ancestors> and heirs. Pledge to warranty.* [mid 13th cent.].

Hiis testibus Willelmo de Tampton', . . . E. . . de Laisethorpe . . . Henrico Rufo, Waltero filio Andree, etc.

Dating William son of Lyne, grandfather of the donor, occurs in the late 12th century: see nos 349, 355 above.

357 *Grant, addressed to all the faithful present and future, by Roger son of William of Middlesbrough, to God and the monks of St Mary of Byland, of 3 acres in the region of Linthorpe which he had of the grant of William son of Lyne, free from all service except for 1 pound of pepper at St Michael as laid down in the charter of <William son of Lyne> (? no. 355). Pledge to warranty.*

Hiis testibus Ingeramo . . . (rest obscured)

357A *Rubric: Charter of William . . . concerning . . . acres of land.*

358 *Grant and confirmation, addressed to all who will see or hear this writing, by William le Retur de Caldenesby, son and heir of Beatrice, daughter of Richard Lyne, of all land, pasture, and rents which the abbot and convent have in Linthorpe, Ayresome and* Gaterygg *and anywhere in his fee of the grant of his ancestors. This grant is made for the love of God, to God and St Mary and to the abbot and convent and their church of Byland and their successors. Pledge to warranty against the prior of Guisborough and all other men. Sealed with his seal.* [?mid to late 13th cent.].

Hiis testibus Stephano Gower, Iohanne filio eiusdem, [Willelmo] de Malteby, Willelmo Boye.

Copy: MS Dodsworth 91, fol. 95r, no. 40, from which readings in square brackets are supplied. The witness list continues: Willelmo de Faiceby, Willelmo de Thormotby et aliis multis.

Dating: The third witness attests in the mid to late 13th century: see nos 361, 365, 720.

359 *Rubric: Charter of Gilbert son of Geoffrey of Linthorpe concerning a small parcel of land which Gilbert granted to John Rusche <son of> John Carham. The monks have the charter, which has been returned, and it is bound with a charter of the same Gilbert.*

Marginal note: B(aculus) iii.

[fol. 40v]

360 *Notification to all the faithful in Christ present and future of the*

chirograph agreement between the abbot and convent of Byland and Margery, widow of Middlesbrough, that Margery in her widowhood has exchanged with the abbot and convent 10 acres in Linthorpe for 6 acres in 'Suterflatt' and 4 in 'Hordpittes'. For these 10 acres the abbot and convent have granted another 10 acres in various places. Of these, 2 selions lie at Peslandes *in the carucate of Cosyn, 2 selions lie at* Mordailes *in the same carucate, 2 lie near* Gorm' *and 3 abut the eastern marsh above* Hungerschotes *in the same carucate and 2 lie above* Wlfeholes. *The abbot and convent pledge to warranty the exchange.* [29 Aug. 1235 x Feb. 1267].
Hiis testibus domino Honorio tunc priore de Bellalanda, Hugone suppriore, Willelmo cellerario, Iohanne socio eius.
Dating: see no. 361.

361 *Rubric: Confirmation by Ralph her son concerning the same 10 acres.* [29 Aug. 1235 x Feb. 1267].
Text: MS Top. Yorks. e. 9, fol. 56r (old p. 85). Confirmation by Ralph son of William of Middlesbrough of 10 acres, 6 in the *cultura* called 'Suterflat' and 4 at 'Hordpittes' which his mother, Margery, exchanged with them for another 10 acres. Pledge to warranty. Hiis testibus domino Willelmo de Mauteby, Henrico filio Radulfi, Willelmo Loreng, Gilberto de Mauteby, Galfrido Cusyn, Philippo persona de Rillingtona, Ada de Batheresby, Willelmo Lave, Willelmo filio Osanne, Gilberto le Fraunceys.
Dating: sixth witness.

362 *Rubric: Charter of Roger of Middlesbrough concerning 2½ acres in the fields of Linthorpe which the monks have of the grant of William son of Lyne rendering to William and his heirs 1d. yearly. The monks have a returned charter of the same William son of Lyne and a charter of Richard his son.*

363 *Rubric: Confirmation in the form of a chirograph of Geoffrey Cosyn concerning all the land which the monks have of his fee in Linthorpe. He has 1 acre of the monks.*

364 *Rubric: Charter of John son of Roger son of Siward concerning a toft at the head of . . .*
Marginal note: B(aculus) ii.

365 *Confirmation, addressed to all who will see or hear these letters, by Simon de Vere, to the abbot and convent of Byland, of all lands and tene-*

ments in his fee in Thormodby and Linthorpe and elsewhere. [*c.* 1229 x 1287].

Hiis testibus Roberto de Wausand, W[illelmo de Malte]by, Roberto de Laysyngby, H[ingelramo] de [Boyngton], Nicholao de Acclum.

Copy: MS Dodsworth 7, fol. 98v, from which the readings in square brackets are supplied. The witness list continues: Symone persona de Bildesdal, Ricardo de Rus et aliis.

Marginal note in cartulary: B(aculus).

Dating: The grantor appears to be the younger Simon de Vere. His father, Simon, son of Walter de Vere, succeeded as a minor in 1205. He was dead by 1213 and his son, Simon, also succeeded as a minor. He was of age in 1229 and was still alive in 1287 (*EYC* III, 61–2).

[fols 40v–41r]

366 *Confirmation, addressed to all the faithful who see or hear this writing, by Thomas of Boynton, knight, of all lands. He has carefully heard the charter which the monks of Byland have of William of Acklam his ancestor concerning a fishery on the Tees (no. 335), and the confirmation of Roger of Acklam, William's son (no. 337), as well as the charter of Roger of Acklam confirming land of Roger Cosin in Linthorpe and Emma his wife, daughter of Maleth (no. 347), and the confirmation of Roger of Acklam of all the monks hold of his fee (no. 338). Confirmation and quitclaim of the above in free alms for the salvation of his soul and the souls of his ancestors and heirs. Pledge to warranty.* Byland; Friday after St Denis [11 Oct.] 1392.

Hiis testibus domino Thoma de Colvell', milite, Henrico filio meo et herede, Thoma de [Etton] etc.

Marginal note: (in later hand) 13 R 2.

Copies: MS Dodsworth 94, fol. 15r–v, no. 15, from the original in St Mary's Tower, and MS Dodsworth 63, fol. 63r, from cartulary fol. 146 (*sic*). Dodsworth 94 omits 'etc' from the witness list and continues: Willelmo de Sproxton, Roberto de Newton, Iohanne de Baxeby, Willelmo Barkesworth, Stephano Dayvill et aliis. There is a sketch of the seal.

[fol. 41r, old fol. 146]

367 *Genealogy of William of Acklam. William had a son Roger. Roger had two daughters, one of whom married Ingelram of Boynton. The other died, and the whole inheritance therefore came into the hands of Ingelram. By his wife Ingelram had a son, William. William had a son, Ingelram. Ingelram had a son, Walter, who succeeded his father in 1320. Walter had a son, Thomas, and another named Walter, and Thomas succeeded his father. Thomas had a son, Thomas, who was a knight in the reign of Richard II, and who is still alive. He had a son, Henry.*

Copy: MS Dodsworth 63, fol. 63r. from cartulary fol. 148 (*sic*).

[fol. 41v]

GILLYGATE, the street of St Giles, lying just outside the city walls of York, on the road leading north to Sutton on the Forest and Helmsley.

368 *Rubric: Charter of William Mast and his wife concerning 1 messuage in Patrickpool (York) and the lands which the monks have in the street of St Giles (Gillygate). Look under the heading 'York' in the second bundle.* [? early 13th cent.].

Note: The charter was entered at no. 284 above, but is illegible.

369 *Rubric: Confirmation of Emma his wife concerning the same messuage and land.* [? early 13th cent.].

Note: The rubric also appears at no. 285 above.

370 **Spurious:** *Grant in free alms, addressed to all the sons of holy mother church, by Gilbert de Camera of Fenton, to God and St Mary and the abbot and convent of Byland, of the land which he had in the street of St Giles outside the walls of York, that is, the land which lies nearest to the land which the abbot and convent have of the grant of William Mast and Emma his wife towards the north. This grant is made for the salvation of his soul and of his wife, and of all his ancestors and heirs. The monks are to hold the land free from secular service and to do there whatever they wish. Sealed with the donor's seal.* [? mid 13th cent.].

Hiis testibus domino Helya de Fentona, subthesaurario tunc Ebor' ecclesie, domino Willelmo de Fenton', vicario dicte ecclesie, Philippo de Fenton', etc.

Dating: Gilbert de Camera of Fenton may be the same as Gilbert of Fenton who attests in 1247 x 1262 (see above, no. 286). William of Fenton occurs, without title, in the mid 13th century (*Chs Vicars Choral*, I, no. 329) but there is no record of him as a vicar of St Peter's, and the witness list may be corrupt.

Note: The rubric ends 'conliguntur', i.e. that nos 369 and 370 were tied together.

371 *Rubric: Letters of attorney of the same Gilbert [de Camera] by William de Crawm his attorney to release to the monks seisin on the land.*

372 *Memorandum concerning a charter of Reiner de Daiville relating to ½ silver mark from 1 toft with houses in the street of St Giles. Note that he has quitclaimed whatever is contained in this charter, except for the said toft, to William son of Robert of Reedness (pa. Whitgift, WR) and his heirs, by a charter which the monks have and for which he paid a sum of money. The monks returned to him the charter of Nicholas son of Ranulf concerning 7s. 8d. and the charter of Robert son of Fulk concerning a half bovate in*

Reedness which is mentioned in the charter. By this charter, made in 1240, a grant was made of 1 toft with a house which the same Reiner had in the street of St Giles, York. 1240.

373 *Grant in free alms, addressed to all who see or hear these letters, by Reiner de Daiville, to God and the monks of St Mary of Byland, for the salvation of his soul and of his wife and all his ancestors and heirs, of ½ silver mark for making a pittance on Palm Sunday from the rent which the donor and his heirs have in Reedness of Robert son of Fulk. The donor and his heirs will be answerable to the monks for the rent, and they will not grant nor sell nor alienate it without the consent of the chapter. The monks will be in the service of* (stabunt mecum) *the donor and his heirs for the said land. Grant also of a toft with a house which he has in the street of St Giles, free from all service except for 2d. to the king paid at York yearly at the feast of St Peter ad Vincula (1 Aug.). This grant is made for the building of the new church. Pledge to warranty.* [1240].

Hiis testibus Iohanne de Dayvill et Nicholao fratre eius, Waltero de Dayville et Eudone et Roberto <fratribus> eius.

Dating: The charter would appear to be roughly contemporary with no. 372. John de Daiville died before 1242/3: *EYF*, p. 24.

Note: The reference to the building of the new church is not clear. The abbey church was little altered after its completion around 1195. In the 1230s the mosaic tile floors, which survive in the presbytery and south transept, were laid. See David Robinson, ed., *The Cistercian Abbeys of Britain* (London, 1998), p. 82.

374 *Grant in free alms, addressed to all who will read or hear these letters, by Reiner son of William the clerk of Adlingfleet, to God and the monks of St Mary of Byland, of his house in York in the street of St Giles and the land belonging to it, free from all secular service. The grant is made for the salvation of his soul and those of his wife and all his ancestors and heirs, to provide a pittance on Palm Sunday after the donor's death. For the land the monks are to render 2d. to the king at St Peter ad Vincula (1 Aug.).* [c. 1154 x 1186].

Hiis testibus Rogero de Molbray et Roberto filio eius cum omni frequentia eorum, Waltero persona de Athelingff', Ricardo clerico de Huseflete.

Dating: Robert de Mowbray began to attest his father's charters *c.* 1154: *Mowbray Charters*, p. xxix. Walter, clerk of Adlingfleet, occurs in 1164 x 1177 (*EYC* I, no. 487). William, clerk of Adlingfleet, and his son William attested a charter of Marmaduke Darel of Sessay between 1170 and 1180 (*ibid.* II, 294).

Note: Adlingfleet was held by the Daiville family of the Honour of Mowbray: *Mowbray Charters*, p. xlvi, and p. 264.

[fol. 42r, old fol. 147]

375 *Grant in free alms, addressed to all the faithful of Christ who will see or hear this present charter, by John Spicer (Speciarius, grocer), son of William son of Agnes, citizen of York, to God and St Mary of Byland and the monks serving God there, of land in the street of St Giles. The land lies in length and width between the land of the monks on one side and the land which belonged to Richard of Skelton, and from the king's highway in front to the wall behind, rendering husgable. The grant is made for the salvation of the soul of the donor and of his wife and of his ancestors and heirs. Pledge to warranty. Sealed with the donor's seal.* [1260s or 1270s].

Hiis testibus Waltero de Stokes tunc maiore Ebor' . . . Iohanne de Sutton'.

Dating: Walter de Stoke(s) was mayor of York in 1269, 1272 and 1278 (*Chs Vicars Choral*, I, nos 67, 170, 173, 268, 329, 377 and notes). There were two John Spicers, the elder attesting in the mid 13th and the younger in the later 13th and early 14th centuries. Both were mayor of York (*ibid., passim*).

376 *Quitclaim, addressed to all who will see or hear this writing, by John de Holme, citizen of York, to the abbot and convent of Byland, of all rights that he claims or might claim in a messuage in the street of St Giles in the suburb of York which the monks have by the grant of John Spicer, citizen of York. Pledge to make no further claim. Sealed with the donor's seal.* [1280s or 1290s].

Hiis testibus Iohanne Sampson tunc maiore Ebor', Nicholao de Selby, Petro de Saunton', etc.

Dating: John de Holme and Alice his wife made a grant of land in Micklegate in 1276/7 (*Chs Vicars Choral*, I, no. 302); John Samson occurs as mayor in 1280 or 1281 and 1299–1300 (*ibid.*, nos 28n, 82, 424; he attests a charter with Nicholas of Selby and Peter of Sancton (ER) in 1280 or 1281 (*ibid.*, no. 424).

[fol. 42v]

HOOD (SE5082), in the parish of Kilburn and wapentake of Birdforth (NR). Hood Grange lies about 1½ miles to the east of Sutton under Whitestonecliffe, and was the first site of the abbey, occupied between 1138 and the move to Old Byland in 1142. The site of Hood was then granted by Roger de Mowbray to Augustinian canons who came from Bridlington to establish a monastery there; the canons moved to Newburgh Priory in 1145 and Hood became a grange of Newburgh. The documents entered into this section of the cartulary relate to agreements with Newburgh.

377 *Grant in free alms, addressed to the archbishop of York and the whole chapter of St Peter (York) and all the sons of holy church, by Roger de Mowbray, with the consent of Robert d'Aunay and the monks of Whitby, to Abbot Gerald and his convent and their successors, of Hood by the boundaries which he showed them. This grant is made for the salvation of his soul and of all his ancestors and heirs. [1138 or 1139].*

Hiis testibus Sampsone de Albeneyo, Rogero de C<undy>, Gundrea matre Rogeri de Molbray, Helya de Sancto Martino, etc.

Pd: *EYC* XI, no. 115; (calendar) *Mowbray Charters*, no. 32.

Dating: The *Historia Fundationis* dates the grant of Hood to 1138 (*Mon. Ang.* V, 349). John of Hexham notes the foundation before Christmas. As Greenway (*Mowbray Charters*) points out, the charter making the grant may be slightly later.

Note: At the time of the foundation the site of Hood was occupied by Robert d'Aunay, a relative of Gundreda d'Aubigny and a monk of Whitby. The rubric describes this as the first charter of Roger granting Hood and its appurtenances. The first witness was a cousin and chaplain of Roger de Mowbray; he granted several churches to Newburgh Priory, and ended his life as a canon there (*Mowbray Charters*, nos 196–7).

378 *Grant and quitclaim, addressed to all the faithful of the church, by Roger, abbot of Byland and the monks, to the canons, of Hood as Roger de Mowbray granted it to them. [1142 x 1143].*

Dating: The site of Hood was granted to canons from Bridlington on the removal of the convent to Old Byland. For Roger de Mowbray's confirmation see *Mowbray Charters*, no. 194.

Note: In this much abbreviated charter, which has the rubric 'transcriptum carte per quam dedimus canonicis de Novoburgo dictum locum de Hode cum pertinentiis', Roger is described as 'servus servorum dei de [Beghlande]'. The canons moved from Hood to Newburgh in 1145.

379 *Notification, addressed to all who will see or hear these letters, by Hugh, bishop of Durham, of the end of the controversy between the canons of Newburgh and Adam Fossard concerning Hood and certain boundaries. The case had been committed to him by the lord pope, and in the bishop's presence and that of Robert de Stuteville and his son, William, an agreement was reached. Adam has demised and granted in free alms to the church of St Mary, Newburgh, the place of Hood where the church stands, with land and marsh by the boundaries which they have made, that is on the south side of the church along the bank called* Haithwait, *on the western side, from the same bank northwards along the boundary which they have made as far as the brow of the next hill where the boundary clearly turns the corner which they have made and stretches towards the east as far as a certain bank. The boundary then crosses the new road which the monks have made and drops* *down to the* cultura *of the canons and then climbs along the bank to the new road and as it climbs stretches along the road itself first to the east and then turning to the north to that place where the boundary between them runs eastwards to the highest point of the moor. These boundaries were defined and perambulated in a friendly manner by Adam Fossard and the canons together with a large number of worthy men. The canons have acknowledged Adam as patron of the place [and quitclaimed] all right which belonged to them. The canons are to have no common in the land of Adam Fossard outside the boundaries which have been named without the consent of him or his heirs, nor shall Adam and his heirs share anything in common with the canons within these bounds. [1174 x 1183].*

Hiis testibus Willelmo [archidiacono Dunelmen'], Hugone fratre ipsius, Symone camer(ario), magistro Willelmo Blesensi, etc.

Copy: MS Dodsworth 7, fol. 149r, from the original in St Mary's Tower, York, from which readings in square brackets are supplied; the witness list omits 'etc' and continues: magistro Ricardo de Coldingham, Gaufrido magistro monialium de Duua, Willelmo Hansard, Willelmo filio arch(iepiscopi), Waltero de Wiverthorp, Ada de Warrum, Iohanne de Hovingham, Simone de Kirkebi, Willelmo de Stutevilla, Nicholao de Stutevilla, Iohanne de Stutevilla, Ricardo Croera, Reginaldo de Capetot, Ada de Boltebi, Willelmo Was(celin), Michaele filio Brien, Willelmo filio Ingel[rami], Gilberto de Meinil, Iohanne de Herford, Waltero de Creic, Philippo, Toma nepote prioris, Willelmo Albo, . . . de Ulvestun, Ingelero de Torp. There is a note at the foot of fol. 149r: in dorso carta de divisis inter Sutton et Hod.

Pd: *EEA* XXIV, no. 102, from cartulary and from MS Dodsworth 7 (the folio reference is given incorrectly as fol. 147); *EYC* IX, no. 121, from MS Dodsworth 7; *Mon. Ang.* VI, 322–3 from BL MS Cotton Cleop. C III, fol. 301 (where the name of the bishop appears as Henry).

Dating: Clay dated the confirmation to 1166 x 1183, basing the date on the succession of Adam to the fee held by Geoffrey Fossard in 1166 and the death of Robert de Stuteville III. However, as G. V. Scammell (*Hugh du Puiset, bishop of Durham* (Cambridge, 1956), p. 85) and Martin Snape (*EEA* XXIV, p. 89) point out, the earliest date of issue is provided by the attestation of the bishop's son, William du Puiset, as archdeacon (of Northumberland): see *Fasti Monastic Cathedrals*, p. 40.

Note: The second witness, Hugh du Puiset, like William a son of Bishop Hugh, attests with his brother in *c.* 1180 x 1185, and is likely to have been the Hugh du Puiset who was chancellor of France (Scammell, *Hugh du Puiset*, pp. 257, 312). Simon the chamberlain was one of Bishop Hugh's most important officials, and parson of the monastic church of Billingham (*ibid.*, pp. 146, 235). The fourth witness, William of Blois, witnessed charters of Hugh du Puiset (*ibid.*, pp. 255, 257–9, 261–2). He became subdean, then precentor, and finally bishop of Lincoln (1203–6). William son of the archbishop may be the son of Archbishop William Fitz Herbert (d. 1154), on whom see *EEA* XXIV, p. xli, and Scammell, *Hugh du Puiset*, p. 237, or the son of Roger de Pont L'Evêque, noted in *Fasti York*, p. 4. Master Richard of Coldingham was rector of Elvet and of Bishop Middleham (both

County Durham) (*ibid.*, p. 146). The nunnery of 'Dove' of which Geoffrey was master is the priory of Keldholme (NR).

380   *Rubric: Memorandum that Adam Fossard confirmed Hood to [the canons of Newburgh] by indenture. Look in the Newburgh bundle.*
Note: Confirmations by Adam's son, Robert, and by William de Stuteville, are printed in *Mon. Ang.* VI, 322; for the latter, see also *EYC* IX, no. 24.

381   *Confirmation by Thomas Fossard of the boundaries of Hood: by the great ditch through the middle of* Swynesailes *to Sleights and through the centre of Sleights to the small river called* Litilclifsyde *and from there along the highway which runs below* Cronochowe *to the water which runs from the canons' house and then westwards to the ditch called* Crendyke. *Look under Newburgh.* [after 1227].
Dating: This is probably the Thomas Fossard who had succeeded his brother, Robert, son of Adam Fossard, by 1227.

[fols 42v–43r]
382   *Chirograph between the abbot and convent of Byland and the prior and convent of Newburgh at the termination of the controversy concerning 2 parks in the region of Sutton. The abbot and convent grant and quitclaim to the canons the higher park which is nearest to the field of Hood to do there whatever they wish, saving the rights of the free tenants of Sutton as far as common rights of entry and exit are concerned. The abbot and convent will not have common in the canons' park and the canons will not have common in the monks' park which is next to the wood of Balk. Moreover the prior and canons shall no longer keep goats in the region of Sutton. The prior and convent grant for themselves and their men licence to strengthen the 2 mill-ponds of the vivaries, as contained in a chirograph made in the king's court between the abbot on the one part and Robert de Daiville and Thomas de Coleville on the other. The abbot and convent will reserve to the prior and convent indemnity of damage which they may have as a result of the said millponds. Pledge to warranty. Sealed by both parties.* Letare Sunday [6 March] 1238 [1239].
Hiis testibus domino Symone tunc priore de Marton . . . Ada de Hilton', Radulfo de Frydeby, etc.
Marginal note: (in later hand) '23 H 3'.
Note: The text is entered into the cartulary at no. 1065 below.

[fol. 43r, old fol. 148]
383   *Rubric: Chirograph concerning common pasture for animals in the new park. Look in Sutton, second bundle.*

Note: This may refer to no. 1068, but see no 385, where the rubric appears to match no. 1068 more accurately.

384 *Notification, addressed to all to whom the present writing shall come, of the ending of the quarrel between Abbot H(enry) and the convent of Byland and Prior J(ohn) and the convent of Newburgh. The abbot and convent concede . . . in* Langker *above Hood, and they shall not retain the water there . . . Robert Fossard . . . was accustomed, and common pasture. They have conceded to the prior and convent that portion of land below* Cronokh *towards the west about which a plea had been brought. They further concede to the prior and convent licence concerning a secular chaplain. The prior and convent for their part have conceded the right to have a mill pond above Sutton and to strengthen it as seems best and most useful to them.* Mon. . . . 1251.
Teste utriusque parte capitulorum.

Marginal note: B(aculus) iii; (in later hand at end of text) '35 H 3 1251'.

Note: There were two priors of Newburgh named John whose periods of office coincided with that of Henry of Battersby as abbot of Byland (1230–68). This is Prior John of Skipton (occ. 1251, 1256); see *HRH* II, 428.

385 *Rubric: Agreement between the monks and Richard Malebisse concerning a mill pond and meadow in Sutton and a watercourse below Reins. Look under Sutton, third bundle.*

Note: The text is included in the cartulary at no. 1068 below.

[fol. 43v]

HOVINGHAM (SE6675), township and parish in the wapentake of Ryedale (NR); the parish also includes Airyholme, Howthorpe, Coulton, Fryton, and Scackleton. No. 387 indicates that land in Hovingham was among the early endowments of Byland. Hovingham was part of Gundreda de Gournay's dowry (*Mowbray Charters*, p. 143) and she granted land here both to Byland (no. 387) and to Newburgh Priory (*Mowbray Charters*, no. 201). Hamo Beler (no. 388) was a Mowbray knight, who was enfeoffed with land in Burton Lazars (Leicestershire) and a mill in Thirsk; Philip of Billinghay (no. 392) was enfeoffed by Mowbray with land in Hovingham (*Mowbray Charters*, nos 341, 349). Both added to the monks' lands here.

386 *Rubric: Charter of Roger de Mowbray concerning Scackleton and Airyholme and common pasture throughout the whole forest of Hovingham where his animals graze. Look under Scackleton, in the first bundle.*

Note: The text is entered into the cartulary at no. 1104 below.

387 *Grant in free alms, addressed to the archbishop of York and all the sons of holy church, by Gundreda (d'Aubigny) mother of Roger de Mowbray, to God and the monks of St Mary of Byland, of her meadow in Hovingham, that is, the osier bed* (salcetum) *on the south side of* Tuf' *as* Hardyngcroc *goes, and the whole meadow from the northern side* (plaga) *of* Tuf *as far as the meadow of the church. The grant is made free from all secular service for the salvation of her soul and of her father and mother and all the faithful.* [1147 x c. 1154].

Hiis testibus Willelmo de Wydavylla, Adam Lovell', Ernaldo de Vilers, etc.

Pd: *Mowbray Charters*, no. 47.

Dating: terminal date provided by death of donor.

388 *Grant in free alms, addressed to the archbishop of York and the whole chapter of St Peter (York) and all the sons of holy church, by Hamo Beler, to God and the monks of St Mary of Byland, of 10 acres of meadow in Hovingham near the spring which flows from Hovingham towards Fryton near to the* cultura *called* Holover *as encompassed by the ditch which the monks have constructed. The grant is made free from secular service for the salvation of the soul of the donor and of all his ancestors and heirs. Pledge to warranty.* [1154 x 1181].

Hiis testibus <Rogero de Molbray> et Nigello et Rogero filiis eius, Ricardo priore de Neubergh', etc.

Dating: the office of Richard, prior of Newburgh; the address to the archbishop of York suggests a date before the death of Archbishop Roger in 1181. It is possible that the second 'Roger' of the witness list is an error for Robert, who with his brother Nigel attests no. 390, also with Prior Richard of Newburgh.

Note: Hamo Beler was enfeoffed by Roger de Mowbray by 1153, and held 1 knight's fee in 1166 (*Mowbray Charters*, nos 61, 322, 341). He witnesses as late as *c.* 1186 (*ibid.*, nos 26, 31). The warranty clause suggests a date later in the period.

389 *Rubric: Confirmation by Robert Beler of the grant of Hamo.* [1154 x 1186].

Marginal note: Skakilden B(aculus) i.

Dating: Robert Beler, brother of Ralph, first occurs after 1154 (*Mowbray Charters*, nos 204, 240). He was a frequent witness to the charters of Roger de Mowbray, as late as 1186 (*ibid.*, nos 28, 69, 84).

Note: A charter of Nigel de Mowbray, 1163 x 1169, noted that Robert Beler had granted the monks of Rievaulx land in 'Hoveton' for 2 silver marks yearly (*ibid.*, no. 251).

390   *Confirmation in free alms, addressed to the archbishop of York and the whole chapter of St Peter (York) [and all the sons of holy church], by Roger de Mowbray, to [God and St Mary and the monks] of Byland, of the grant of Hamo Beler of 10 acres of meadow in Hovingham, as in no. 388. The confirmation is made for the salvation of his soul.* [1154 x 1181].

. . . presente Nigello filio meo qui testis et concessor est huius rei et Roberto [fratre eius et Ricardo priore de Neubergh', etc.].

Pd: *Mowbray Charters*, no. 61.

Dating: see no. 388.

Note: The text of the charter is illegible in places due to damage to the folio, and lacunae are supplied from no. 388.

391   *Rubric: Confirmation by Nigel de Mowbray of the same 10 acres.* [before 1190].

392   *Rubric: Charter of Philip of Billinghay concerning meadow in Hovingham towards Fryton.* [after 1184].

Dating: Philip of Billinghay succeeded to the fee of his brother Peter after Peter's death in 1184 (*Mowbray Charters*, no. 349, note). He attests earlier than this date, but the confirmation probably dates to after his succession.

393   *Memorandum that a charter of Roger de Mowbray and Gundreda his mother granted common pasture throughout the forest of Hovingham wherever <their animals or> those of their men pasture. Look in Scackleton.*

Note: This may refer to nos 1104–5 below.

394   *Rubric: Notification that the abbot and convent granted to William de Mowbray a toft in . . . which touches on* Spenl' *and ½ mark in the mill and 5 acres in* Spenl', *as appears under the heading 'Nidderdale'.* [c. 1204].

Dating: This grant was part of the agreement of 1204 which terminated the controversy between William de Mowbray and the monks (no. 695 below). The toft and 5 acres are there specified as being in Hovingham.

ORMSIDE (Westm.). At the foot of fol. 43v, following the Hovingham charters, is the place name of Ormside, followed by a note: Plures cartas inde habemus et evidenc(ias) set nichil omnino nobis conferunt.

[fol. 44r, old fol. 149]

SHAP (NY5615) (Westm.). Byland's property in Shap originated with the grants of Thomas son of Cospatrick. Detailed boundaries are given in nos 395, 397 and 399, but damage to the cartulary makes these difficult to read in places. The manor which Byland held within Shap was Wasdale and Hardendale (Nicolson and Burn, *Westmorland*, I, 480). Much of Byland's land comprised pasture land (see nos 395, 396, 400) and woodland and moorland (no. 397). There is a reference to the charges for straying animals (no. 398) and a description of the making of boundaries (no. 399). Byland's lands in Fawcett Forest and Borrowdale lay to the south of the holdings in Shap.

395   *Grant, addressed to the archbishop of York and the whole chapter of St Peter (York) and all the sons of holy church, by Thomas son of Cospatrick, to God and the monks of St Mary of Byland, of all his part of Shap within these boundaries: from* Slegiliterna *as far as* Traneterna *(?Trantrams in Thrimby) and from there as far as Bleatarn and from Bleatarn up the sike as far as the head of the sike and from there by the boundaries which he has perambulated with the monks: from the west part of* Tri . . . fel *along the bottom of* Lasikerdac *to the ford of* Thornerebec *and from there to the ditch in which the hawthorn* (alba spina) *stands, and from the western side of Wraynsete as far as the western side of Shaphow and to the nearest path on the east of* Wytcast' *and along the path to Blea Beck and as far as the green open space beyond the spring . . . to Blea Beck, and from there as the water falls into Wasdale and Sleddale as far as . . . All this is granted to the monks. Also across the same from* Ierles' *as far as the head of* Haropes . . . *lasts across westwards as far as the great rock, and from there across the brow of the mountain as far as . . .* Borghra *and across* Borghra *to the great <road> that comes from Kendal to Westmorland, and by the same road to Wasdale Beck . . . and across through Wasdale Beck to the lower head of Wasdale Beck . . . between Shap and Crosby [Ravensworth] to <Ka>ldegata. All this is to be held free and quit of service to him and his heirs, with all appurtenances. Grant also of common pasture in* Withcastilgila *between the path and the highway which crosses . . . dale to the western head of* Withcastilgata, *with free entry and exit for their animals to the pasture. The donor and his heirs are not to build on the land but it is to remain in common between them. Grant also of timber and other necessities for their house throughout the wood of* Ragarthscogh'. *Pledge to warranty. [c. 1177 x 80].*
Hiis testibus Roberto <decano Ebor, magistro> Widone magistro scholarum, Geroldo canonico, Meinardo, Stephano de Roma, canonicis . . . . . . Noblet, Alano capellanis, etc.
Dating: earliest date by second witness; occurrences of Gerard, Maynard and Stephen the Roman, canons of York.
Note: The grantor was the founder of Shap Abbey for Premonstratensian canons, established in the 1190s at Preston Patrick, which moved to Shap before Thomas's death in 1201 (*MRH*, p. 191; H. M. Colvin, *The White Canons in England* (Oxford,

1951), pp. 168–9). His grant to Byland is recorded in the *Historia Fundationis* (*Mon. Ang.* V, 352). There is an abbreviated copy of the charter in MS Dodsworth 63, fol. 70r.

[fol. 44r–v]

396 *Notification, addressed to all who will read or hear these letters, by Thomas son of Cospatrick that he has demised to the monks of St Mary of Byland, 10 acres of cultivated land in the region of Shap in Long Rigg to the north of* Castelgata *<and common pasture> for 500 sheep throughout his fee wherever his animals and those of his men of Shap pasture. He has also demised free entry and exit to the pasture. If Thomas has cultivated land which is nearer and more suitable for the said sheep to use the said pasture, and the monks and Thomas do not wish to put their folds there, the land shall be manured. However, if the monks wish to put their animal folds on the cultivated land they can do so in a suitable place, or they may put them wherever they wish in the pasture. Thomas and his heirs are not to plough nor otherwise intrude any further than they did of old. The monks are to hold this land free from all secular service as pure alms until he or his heirs shall deliver to the monks the land he granted them by charter and which Matilda de Vipont claimed, that is the land between* Caldegata *and* le Scupandstan. *When Thomas or his heirs deliver this land to the monks, as contained in his charter, Thomas or his heirs shall retain the said pasture of Shap and 10 acres free and quit from the monks, and the monks will remove their buildings which they have constructed within the 10 acres, and any crops they may have sown, and their folds with their sheep. Pledge to warranty in the hand of William, constable of Appleby.* [before 1201].

Hiis testibus Willelmo constabulario, Murdaco decano, Galfrido nepote Willelmi constabul(arii).

Dating: Death of the grantor: see no. 395.
Note: Matilda de Vipont's daughter, Joan, married Thomas, son of Thomas son of Cospatrick: Colvin, *White Canons in England*, p. 169.

[fols 44v–45r]

397 *Final concord in the king's court at Appleby before Roger Bertram, R[obert] de Ros, William of York, and <Robert> of Lexington, justices, and other faithful men of the king then present, between Henry, abbot of Byland, plaintiff, through his monk, brother Robert, and Patrick son of Thomas, defendant, concerning 300 acres of woodland and appurtenances in Borrowdale and Wasdale and 500 acres of moor and 10 acres and pasture for 500 sheep in Shap and in Howe. Patrick acknowledges all this to be the right of the abbot and his church, which they have of the grant of Patrick's father, Thomas son of Cospatrick, whose heir he is. The boundaries are: from*

Slegisterne *to* Traneterne *(Trantrams in Thrimby) and from there to Bleatarn, from Bleatarn over the sike to the head of the sike, from there through the boundaries on the western side of Tongue Rigg* (Tungefel) *though the bottom of* Lankesclac *to the ford of* Thornerebec *and to the ditch in which the hawthorn stands, from there from the west side of Wraynsete to the west part of Howe and to the nearest path from the east [from* Withcastelgile*] and along that path to Blea Beck, and from there up to the green open place [beyond the spring of Blea Beck] and as the water falls from* Museyon *between Wasdale and Sleddale, as far as* Ier[lesete *and from there by the brow of]* Ierlesete *as far as the head of* Harhopes *and* Grenhopes *and as far as the valley [lasts towards the west] as far as the large rock, and from there across the brow of the mountain to the highest head of* Borghra *and through* Borghra *to the highway that runs from Kendal to Westmorland, and along the road to Wasdale Beck and along Wasdale Beck to the lower head of the same, and from there along the boundaries between Shap and Crosby to* Caldegate, *and through* Caldegate *to the north to the great stone, and from there though the great stones and along the bottom of the valley to* Slegisiterne, *except for the land between* Caldegate *and le* Stupendstayn *that Matilda de Vipont claimed. Moreover Patrick conceded all the land called* Ierlesete *and all the common pasture in* Withcastilg<il> *between the path and the highway which crosses towards Kendal at the western head of* Withcastilgil, *with free entry and exit to the pasture, and with estovers of the wood from* Ragarscodh *to* Hardendale, *to burn, enclose or build on, as is the right of the abbot and his church. The abbot and his successors are to hold the land of Patrick and his heirs freely in perpetual alms free from all secular service. Neither the abbot and his successors nor Patrick and his heirs are to build within the said bounds, that is, between the path and the highway which crosses towards Kendal at the western head of* Withcastilgile *but this shall remain in common between them. If Patrick and his heirs shall have any cultivated ground which is nearer or more suitable for the 500 sheep the abbot and convent shall be allowed to construct folds there if they wish, but Patrick and his heirs are to have all that land manured. Neither Patrick nor his heirs nor his men are to sow or make meadow any further than they did of old. Patrick and his heirs are to warranty the land. For this concord the abbot has given Patrick 40s. sterling.*
Appleby; octave of St Philip and St James, 19 Henry III [May 1235].

Copies: PRO CP 25/1/249/3, no. 16, from which damaged portions have been supplied; this is endorsed: et abbas de Hep appon' clamum suum in predicta pastura inter le stupendestem et Shapesbec et preterea in aliis pasturis ratione ecclesie de Hep; MS Dodsworth 63, fol. 70r.
Pd: (with translation, from PRO C25/1/249/3, no. 16) F. W. Ragg, 'De Culwen', *TCWAAS*, ns 14 (1914), 343–432 (pp. 393–5).

Note: The king's justices Roger Bertram, Robert de Ros and William of York sat in assize at York in Jan. 1235 (for another final concord made during this assize see no. 488 below). William of York was a clerk at the Bench. He served as an itinerant justice in Cumberland (1227), and in 1234 he became the second highest justice; in 1231 he became a member of the court *coram rege* (Turner, *English Judiciary*, p. 196). Patrick was the younger son of Thomas son of Cospatrick and succeeded his older brother, Thomas. For an assize of novel disseisin brought by Joan de Vipont, Alexander of Shap, Roger de Hoton, Robert son of John and Roger de Barewell, against the abbot of Byland and Patrick son of Thomas in 1236, see *Cal. Pat. R. 1232–1247*, p. 162.

[fol. 45r, old fol. 150]

398   *Final concord made in the king's court at York the day after mid Lent [20] Henry III in the presence of <William> of York, justice, appointed on the order of the king, between the abbot of Byland and Alexander of Shap, Roger de Hoton, and Robert <son of> John and Roger de Barwell, by which they recognised for themselves and their heirs the agreement reached in no. 397. Neither they nor their heirs are to make any claim to the said pasture. If their horses are found within the said boundaries once, twice or three times in the year, they may be retrieved without any claim being made by the abbot and convent. Beyond this, any horses or oxen are to be charged 1d. per 12 oxen, 1d. per 12 horses and 1d. per 100 sheep.* York, 10 Mar. 1236.

Dating: see note to no. 397. Mid-Lent Sunday is the fourth Sunday in Lent, which in 1236 fell on 9 Mar.

Note: The rubric states that this has been extracted from the rolls of the justices according to the chirograph between them and Alexander of Shap, Roger de Hoton and certain others concerning that pasture which is contained in the same chirograph (see no. 397 note). There is an instruction to look in quire 37.

[fol. 45r–v]

399   *Grant and confirmation, addressed to all the sons of holy mother church present and future, by Thomas son of Thomas of Shap, to God and the monks of St Mary of Byland, of the grant made by his father of lands and pastures in the region of Shap, with all easements, liberties and appurtenances as laid down in the charter of his father. Thomas makes known the boundaries about which there has been dispute between him and the monks: from Bleatarn through the sike in which a plough was drawn* (factus fuit tractus carruce) *as far as the head of . . . and from there through the ditches and piled stones to the head of* Biglandes *towards . . . and by the ditches made by the drawing of a plough to* Laubeslac *and through the middle of . . . towards the ford of* Thornerbec *to the west of the great pile of stones to where the white [hawthorn] stood, and along the slope to the great Wraynesete and from the slope through the middle of the turbary and* *through the ditches made with piled stones as far as the gulf* (vorago) *to the south of the turbary, and so from the other great gulf in a straight line to Howe. This confirmation is made by the boundaries laid down by his father's charter, free from all secular service, to do with as the monks wish, and for the salvation of the donor's soul and those of his father and all his ancestors and heirs. Pledge to warranty.* [early to mid 13th cent.].

Hiis testibus Gwydone de Hellebec, Henrico de Crendala, Alexandro de Wistour, etc.

Note: The grantor was the son of Thomas son of Cospatrick (nos 395–6), and brother of Patrick (nos 397, 400), who succeeded him. He married Joan de Vipont.

[fol. 45v]

400 *Rubric: Chirograph charter of Patrick son of Thomas concerning 10 acres and pasture for 100 sheep in the pasture of Howe and Shaphow, that we shall have 100 sheep in the said pasture.* [early to mid 13th cent.].

Marginal note: B(aculus) i.

HARDENDALE (NY5814), BORROWDALE (NY5603), and WASDALE (Wasdale Beck, NY5608, Wasdale Head, NY5408), all in Shap (Westm.).

401 *Notification in the form of a chirograph, by Thomas son of Thomas son of Cospatrick, of his grant and confirmation, in the presence of neighbours of the countryside, to the monks of Byland and their successors in perpetual alms, of his own land and land held in severalty within these bounds: from* Slegisterne *to . . .* panstayn *and from there . . .* hterkelde *and to* Sandpitt' *and from there as far as* Ryngandkeld *in* Withsite *and along the path to the head of . . . by the same path as far as* Gaitbusk *and across Blea Beck and from there by the path to S . . . ishow and from there to* Wreynsete *. . . to* Wetherbryg *and through* Scalberghhrik *. . . Grant to the same monks of common pasture for their sheep . . . as far as the water of Lowther as they were accustomed to have in the lifetime of his father. Pledge to warranty.* [early to mid 13th cent.].

Hiis testibus Gw<ydone de Hellebec> . . . de Rossegyll, Gilberto de Asteby, Ada fratre eius.

Marginal note: Hardenesdale.

402 *Rubric: Assize against the abbot of Shap concerning common pasture in the same.*

402A *Rubric: Note other assizes against Gilbert de Dale concerning 20 acres of moorland and pasture in Wasdale . . . Look under in the book of. . . .*

403 *Rubric: Quitclaim by John le Fraunsays of his moor in Bretherdale.* [Ascension, 1279].
Text: MS Dodsworth 63, fol. 66v, from cartulary fol. 85v. Hiis testibus domino Gilberto de Curwen, domino Roberto de Yomenwith, domino Iohanne de Rosegill, militibus, Willelmo Pynkniche etc. Dodsworth was here copying from the Asby section of the cartulary, which suggests that the full text was entered there.
Note: Robert de Vipont, son of Ivo, granted the manor of Milburn to John le Fraunceys in 27 Henry III (1242/3): Nicholson and Burn, *Westmorland*, I, 302.

404 *Rubric: Chirograph . . . de Curwen . . . in a straight line as far as the king's highway from Kendal. Shap. First bundle.*

405 *Rubric: Quitclaim by Simon son of Adam of Milburn (Westm.) of his [land] in Bretherdale and meadow belonging to it. Look in Shap, first bundle.* [Ascension [11 May] 1279].
Text: MS Dodsworth 63, fol. 66v, from cartulary fol. 85v. Testibus domino Roberto Hengleys, domino Henrico de Stanlay, domino Roberto de Souleby, militibus, Thoma Buel', Iohanne de Hormesheved, Andrea de Merton, Nicholao de Musegrave, etc.

406 *Rubric: Chirograph agreement between the monks and Ivo de Vipont (Veteriponte) [concerning certain claims (exactiones) which the monks had made against him. Among other things, Ivo conceded to the monks free transit for themselves and their wagons, packhorses to all necessary places in Westmorland and in Kendal, without hindrance].* [before 1242/3].
Text: MS Dodsworth 63, fol. 70r, from cartulary fol. 150.
Dating: Ivo had been succeeded by his son Robert by 27 Henry III: see note to no. 403.

407 *Chirograph agreement with the abbot of Shap . . . in the second bundle of the abbots.*

408 *Rubric: Judgement between the monks and Thomas de Hastings.*
Note: This may be the son of Hugh de Hastings (d. by 1203) and his wife, Helen; he confirmed to Egglestone Abbey the patronage of Startforth church (*EYC* V, 221).

[fol. 46r, old fol. 151]

ISLEBECK (SE4577), a detached portion of the parish of Kirby Knowle, in the wapentake of Birdforth (NR), about 3 miles SE of Thirsk. It is now marked on maps as Islebeck Grange, to the north of Isle Beck. The Islebeck charters are of interest for the number of lost field names they contain. The grants comprise very small pieces of land: meadow, pasture, profitable land, and *culture*. A summary of the monks' holdings was added in a later (medieval) hand (no. 431).

409 *Grant in free alms, addressed to the archbishop of York and the whole chapter of St Peter (York) and all the sons of holy mother church present and future, by William de Mowbray, to God and the monks of St Mary of Byland, of all his meadow near Islebeck to do with as they wish. Roger son of Walter of Carlton had given the meadow to William for a debt which he owed him, as is contained in Roger's charter (no. 410). The monks are to hold the land of William and his heirs free from all service for the salvation of the soul of the grantor and of his father and mother and all his ancestors and heirs. Pledge to warranty.* [1191 x 1199].
Hiis testibus Roberto de Moubray avunculo meo, Roberto et Philippo fratribus meis, etc.

Marginal note: B(aculus) i.
Dating: The donor was the eldest son of Nigel de Mowbray, eldest son of Roger de Mowbray. William was born *c.* 1171 and died in 1224 (*Mowbray Charters*, p. 261). His uncle, Robert, who attests here, died after 1199. Roger of Carlton inherited the fee from his father, Walter, between 1154 and 1166 (*ibid.*, no. 353). In no. 410 below, which appears to be contemporary with the present charter, William de Mowbray is described as Roger's lord, which suggests a date after the death of William's father, Nigel (1191).

410 *Grant and quitclaim, addressed to all present and future, by Roger son of Walter to his lord, William de Mowbray, of all his meadow near Islebeck for 20s. silver which he owed him for acquittance of the account of his stewardship.* [1191 x 1199].
Testibus Roberto de Moubray avunculo domini mei, Philippo de Moubray, Roberto fratr(ibus) eius.

Dating: as no. 409.

411 *Rubric: Charter of Walter of Islebeck . . .*
Original: *Grant, addressed to all present and future, by Walter of Islebeck, to God and St Mary and the abbot and monks of Byland, for the salvation of his soul and of all his ancestors and heirs, of 3 acres of meadow with appurtenances in Islebeck, that is, 1 acre with the meadow adjoining at* Emmyng

croft *near the monks' land on the eastern side, 1 acre in the* cultura *called*
Bagby Acre in the eastern part of the cultura, *½ acre with meadow adjoining*
at Staynwath *near the monks' land on the eastern side, and ½ acre in*
Brotes, *also near the monks' land to the east. The monks are to hold this land*
free from secular service. Quitclaim for himself and his heirs of all right he
had or could have in meadow in Islebeck which the monks had of the grant of
William de Mowbray. Pledge to warranty. Sealed with the grantor's
seal. [probably before 1224].

Hiis testibus dominis Thoma de Colevyl', Olivero de Buscy, Waltero
de Meynil, militibus, Willelmo de Carletona, Willelmo filio Willelmi
de Ebor', Willelmo de Maundevyl, Serlone de Faldingtona, Willelmo
de Foxoles et aliis.

Location: Leeds, YAS, DD 94/10; endorsed: Cᵃ Walt'i de Isyrbek de tribus . . . terre.
Isirbek. B. i. iii (Islebeck, first bundle, 3); this is consistent with its position in the
cartulary.
Pd (calendar): *Yorks. Deeds*, II, 95, no. 249, from the original charter then in the possession of Sir Ralph Payne-Gallwey, bart.
Dating: If the charter was issued in the lifetime of William de Mowbray the latest
date would be 1224. The witnesses are consistent with a date in the first quarter of
the 13th century: William son of William of York and William of Foxholes attest
together 1224 x 1233 (*EYC* IX, no. 60). Many members of the Coleville family took
the name of Thomas and they are difficult to distinguish (see for instance attesta-
tions of nos 29, 382, 417, 422, 466, 479, 505, 507, 509, 580, 584, 592, 658, 672, 796 etc.).
Note: The rubric is very faint. Walter of Islebeck is probably not Walter of Carlton,
father of Roger (nos 409, 410), who was dead by 1166. It seems that the monks'
interest in this part of Islebeck originated with Roger, and this is likely to be the
charter of a later Walter. Walter of Carlton witnessed charters of 1174 x 1175
(*Mowbray Charters*, nos 110–12). Walter may be the same man as Walter son of
Nigel, grantor of no. 417 below.

412 *Charter of Gilbert son of Walter concerning meadow which he*
quitclaimed, and confirmation of all their lands. Grant in free alms of <all
his lands> in the vill and region of Islebeck, for the salvation of his soul and
of all his ancestors and heirs, and confirmation of all they have there, with
appurtenances in land, meadow, common, pastures, rents and other things.
Undertaking to make no further claim. For these, the monks have received
Gilbert into confraternity of their house and have promised him burial.
Pledge to warranty. Sealed with the donor's seal. [? *c.* 1252].

Hiis testibus dominis Ricardo Malebys, Olyvero Buscy, Willelmo
Burdona, Ivone de Etton, militibus.

Dating: see below, no. 428.
Note: The text is much damaged. The rubric reads: 'Carta Gilberti filii eiusdem
Walteri de eodem prato quod nobis quietum clam' et confirmat omnes terras
nostras ibidem'.

[fol. 46v]

413 *Memorandum that in a court held at Carlton near Thirsk (Carlton Miniott) in the presence of Walter, lord of Carlton, and John of Kilvington, his steward, through brother John of Gilling, certain charters concerning lands and meadow which the monks had in Islebeck and Carlton were upheld.* Eve of the Nativity of the B. V. M. [7 Sept.] 1319.

414 *Rubric: Charter of Roger of Carlton concerning 4 acres of meadow which Roger de Mowbray granted.*
Original: *Grant and confirmation, addressed to the archbishop of York and the whole chapter of St Peter (York) and all the sons of holy church, by Roger son of Walter of Carlton, to God and the monks of St Mary of Byland, of 4 acres of meadow next to Islebeck, as Roger de Mowbray granted in free alms. The grant is made free from all service, for the salvation of his soul and of all his ancestors and heirs. The monks may do there as they wish. Pledge to warranty.* [1184 x 1187].
Hiis testibus Reinero vicecom(ite) Ebor', Rogero de Bavent, Roberto de Lamara, constabul(ario), Alano de Sinderbi, Thoma de Colevill', Willelmo de Corneburg', Hamone Beler, Roberto de Busci, Adam Luvel, Roberto Beler, Gisleberto de Angoteb', Gisleberto de Turkillebi, Thoma filio Petri, Iukelo de Smitun', Willelmo de Busci, Ada de Karletun'.

Location: BL Egerton charter 2161; endorsed: Ca' Rogeri de Carletona de iiii acris prato iuxta Isirbek'; Isirbek', B(aculus) i iiii (Islebeck, first bundle, 4); seal: round, yellow wax; SIGILLVM ROGERI DE CARELTUNA.
Pd (calendar): *Yorks. Deeds*, II, 93–4, no. 242, from the original then in the possession of Sir Ralph Payne-Gallwey, bart.
Dating: Reiner de Waxham was deputy sheriff of Yorkshire from 1184 to 1187. Robert de Buscy, who attests here and nos 728 and 888 was the grantor of land in Osgoodby (no. 831); William de Buscy was his son, and a frequent witness of Byland charters (nos 116, 651, 701, 712, 752, 776, 836, 849).

415 *Rubric: Charter of Ernald of Islebeck concerning a toft and 5 acres in various places, and pasture for 10 sheep and 4 animals and 4 pigs and 1 horse.*
Original: *Grant, addressed to all who will see or hear these letters, by Ernald of Islebeck, to God and the monks of St Mary of Byland, of the toft of ½ acre in Islebeck held of him by Adam, with a perch of 18½ feet and 5 acres in the region of the vill, each in their own place, on the south side, that is, 1 acre in* Eringwatdala, *1 acre in* Stainwatflat, *½ acre in* Wandaila, *½ acre in* Sunnolfdala, *½ acre in* Stockebriggedale, *3 roods in* Yleker, *and 3 roods in* Braidebuttis; *also pasture for 10 sheep, 4 animals, 1 horse and 4*

pigs through the common of the vill, with free entry and exit. The monks are to hold this free from secular service for the salvation of his soul and of all his ancestors and heirs. Pledge to warranty. [late 12th or early 13th cent.].

His testibus Gaufrido Fossard, Thoma de Lasceles, Waltero del Menil, Gilberto de Torny, Drogone de Hairum, Gilberto de Turkilby, Stephano filio eius, Stephano de Blabi, Gaufrido de Ampilford, Waltero filio Gille, Roberto filio Petri, Adam fratre eius.

Location: Leeds, YAS, DD 94/10; endorsed: Isirbec. B. i. v. (Islebeck, first bundle, 5); C. Arnaldi de quin. Yserbec; seal: green wax, oval; fleur de lys; SIGILL ARNOLD DE ISELBEC.

Pd (calendar): *Yorks. Deeds*, II, 94, no. 243, from the original charter then in the possession of Sir Ralph Payne-Gallwey, bart.

Dating: Geoffrey Fossard was succeeded by his son Adam some time after 1166. However, the other witnesses are more consistent with a date in the late 12th or possibly early 13th century, suggesting that this is the Geoffrey Fossard who occurs *c.* 1208 (no. 618 below). Gilbert de Meinil of Thirkleby and his son Stephen were grantors in Osgoodby, and frequent witnesses of Byland charters.

416 *Rubric: Charter of Adam of Islebeck son of Hugh of Dale concerning 1 toft and croft at the head of the vill and ½ acre. The charter has been surrendered.*

417 *Rubric: Charter of Walter son of Nigel of Islebeck concerning the meadow called* Le Crok *and a small piece of land at* Le Withes. *In triplicate.*

Original: *Grant in free alms, addressed to all the faithful in Christ, by Walter son of Nigel of Islebeck, to God and St Mary of Byland and the monks serving God there, for the salvation of his soul and of all his ancestors and heirs and with his body, of all his meadow called* Le Crok *at* Wilthebusc *which Walter of Dale once held of him for a term. Grant also of a parcel of land lying at the head of the monks' land at* Wilthebusc *and a parcel lying at the head of their land at* Brothes *abutting onto* Sunnolfdale *dykes, and a parcel at the head of the monks' land at* Withes. *Pledge to warranty. Sealed with the donor's seal.* [? early 13th cent.].

Hiis testibus domino Thoma de Colevill', domino Willelmo de Harum, Willelmo de Neuby, Willelmo de Maundevill', Willelmo de Stokisley, Willelmo de Foxholis, Philippo Pile Brakan, Iohanne filio Ace, Willelmo filio Gamelli de Suttona et multis aliis.

Location: three copies of this charter survive as Leeds, YAS, DD 94/10: (i) endorsed Ca. Walteri de Isirbec de prato et terra; B. i. vii; Crok'; (ii) endorsed: C Walteri de Isirbec; b. i; with variant 'Iohanne filio Ace de Baggeby'; (iii) endorsed: C. Walteri filii Nigelli de quodam prato in Yserbec; Isirbek' B. i vii; with variant as (ii).

Pd (calendar): *Yorks. Deeds*, II, 95–6, no. 250, from the original charter (iii above)

then in the possession of Sir Ralph Payne-Gallwey, bart. Brown notes minor differences in spelling.
Note: The three copies are noted in the rubric.

418   *Rubric: Charter of Gilbert son of Ernald of Islebeck concerning 5 acres and ½ acre of meadow in* [erased] *and pasture for 6 <animals>, 2 horses, 20 sheep and 2 pigs.*

419   *Rubric: Charter of the same Gilbert [son of Ernald of Islebeck] concerning 1½ acres which lie at the exit of the vill.*

420   *Rubric: Charter of the same [Gilbert son of Ernald of Islebeck] concerning a park <in the east?> and all the meadow which lies at the head of that acre which he granted for pits.*
Original: *Notification to all present and future by Gilbert son of Ernald of Islebeck of his grant in free alms and confirmation, made for the salvation of his soul and of all his ancestors and heirs, to God and the monks of St Mary of Byland, of 1 acre in the region of Islebeck, that is ½ acre on* Bawedebusch *and ½ acre at* Wilghebusch, *with its adjoining meadow. The grant is made free from all secular service. Grant also with the said acre of all the meadow that lies at the head of that acre which he granted them for pits. Further grant of whatever remains of the other ½ acre which his father granted in* Hemmingcrofst, *in meadow and profitable land, with all common easements and liberties belonging to the land inside and outside the vill. Pledge to warranty.* [early to mid 13th cent.].
Hiis testibus Olivero de Bosci, Hugone de Magnebi, Stephano de Meynil de Turkelbi, Roberto de Auford, Henrico de Silton', Nicholao de Heton', Simone de Marthebi, Philippo de Sutton', Olivero de Heton'.
Location: BL Egerton charter 2162; endorsed: Ca Gilb'i fil' Arnaldi de i acra terre et prato adiacente; Isirbek' B. i. x (Islebeck, first bundle, 10); seal: oval, red-brown wax; SIGILL' GILBERTI D DALTVN.
Pd (calendar): *Yorks. Deeds*, II, 94, no. 244, from the original then in the possession of Sir Ralph Payne-Gallwey, bart.
Dating: The witnesses suggest the early 13th century, certainly in the first half of the century. The first three and the fifth attest together in no. 1053 below, dated 1225, and in nos 421, 424.

421   *Rubric: Charter of Gilbert concerning 1 acre which lies at* St[ain]wath *and at* Her[ing]wath.
Original: *Grant in free alms, addressed to all the sons of holy mother church to whom the present writing shall come, by Gilbert of Islebeck, to God and the monks of St Mary of Byland, of 1 acre in the region of Islebeck to do with*

as they wish, that is ½ acre in Stainwar *and ½ acre in* Heringwar. *The grant is made for the salvation of his soul and of all his ancestors and heirs. Pledge to warranty.* [early to mid 13th cent.].

Hiis testibus Marmeduco Darel, Olivero de Buscy, Stephano de Meynil, Iohanne de Langebergh, Willelmo de Laceles, Roberto de Auford, Waltero de Yserbec, Olivero de Hetom' et aliis.

Location: Leeds, YAS, DD 94/10; endorsed: Ca. Gilb(ert)i de i acra t(er)re; Isirbek B. i. xi (Islebeck, first bundle, 11).

Pd (calendar): *Yorks. Deeds*, II, 95, no. 248, from the original then in the possession of Sir Ralph-Payne Gallwey, bart.

Dating: as no. 420. The first witness is not likely to be the Marmaduke Darel who died by 1203 but his grandson, who occurs in 1246.

Note: There is a difference in the field names between the rubric and the original.

422 *Rubric: Charter of the same [Gilbert son of Ernald of Islebeck] concerning 1½ acres in* Northoftis.

Original: *Grant in free alms, addressed to all who will see or hear these letters, by Gilbert son of Ernald of Islebeck, to God and the monks of St Mary of Byland, of 1 acre in* Brotis *and ½ acre in the north part of* Northofthes. *Pledge to warranty.* [early to mid 13th cent.].

Hiis testibus Roberto de Dayvill, Henrico de Silton', Stephano de Thurkilby, Thoma de Colevill, Rogero de Stapelton', Willelmo de Karleton', Stephano de Blaby, Willelmo clerico de Dauton', Waltero de Hyserbech et multis aliis.

Location: Leeds, YAS, DD 94/10; endorsed: C. Gilb(ert)i fil(ii) Arnald(i) de j ac(ra) t(er)re et dimid'; Isirbek'. B. i. xii (Islebeck, first bundle, 12).

Pd (calendar): *Yorks. Deeds*, II, 95, no. 247, from the original then in the possession of Sir Ralph Payne-Gallwey, bart.

Dating: as no. 420. The first witness is probably Robert son of John de Daiville, who succeeded his father in 1242/3.

423 *Rubric: Charter of the same [Gilbert] concerning 1 acre . . . equal*

424 *Rubric: Charter of the same [Gilbert] concerning 1 acre.*

Original: *Grant in free alms, addressed to all present and future, by Gilbert son of Ernald of Islebeck, to God and the monks of St Mary of Byland, for the salvation of his soul and of all his ancestors and heirs, of 1 acre of profitable land in the region of Islebeck, that is ½ acre and 14 perches at* Heringwarpet *and ½ acre and 14 perches at* Brotes. *Pledge to warranty.* [early to mid 13th cent.].

Hiis testibus Olivero de Buscy, Hugone de Magneby, Stephano de Meynil de Turkelby, Roberto de Auford, Henrico de Silton', Nicholao de Hetton', Simone de Martherby, Philippo de Sutton'.

Location: Leeds, YAS, DD 94/10; endorsed: C. Gilb(ert)i fil(ii) Arnald(i) de j ac(ra)
t(er)re lucrabilis; Isirbek'. B. i. xiiii (Islebeck, first bundle, 14).
Pd (calendar): *Yorks. Deeds*, II, 94, no. 245, from the original then in the possession
of Sir Ralph Payne-Gallwey, bart.
Dating: as no. 420.

425 *Rubric: Charter of the same [Gilbert] concerning 1 acre at*
With<erane>.
Original: *Grant in free alms, addressed to all present and future, by Gilbert
son of Ernald of Islebeck, to God and the monks of St Mary of Byland, for the
salvation of his soul and of all his ancestors and heirs, free from all secular
service, of 1 acre in the region of Islebeck at* Wytherane *near to the monks'
land. Pledge to warranty.* [early to mid 13th cent.].
Hiis testibus Olivero de Buscy, Hugone de Magneby, Stephano de
Meynil de Turkelby, Henrico de Silton', Simone de Matherby,
Philippo de Sutton', Waltero de Yserbec, Gamello forestario.
Location: Leeds, YAS, DD 94/10; endorsed: C. Gilb(ert)i fil(ii) Arnald(i) de j ac(ra)
t(er)re apud Wytherane; Isirbek'. B. i. xv (Islebeck, first bundle, 15).
Pd (calendar): *Yorks. Deeds*, II, 95, no. 246, from the original then in the possession
of Sir Ralph Payne-Gallwey, bart.
Dating: see no. 420.

426 *Rubric: Charter of Gilbert concerning . . . akepith. Copied.*

427 *Rubric: Chirograph <of Wa>lter of Islebeck.*

428 *Final concord [held at York in the presence of Silvester, bishop of
Carlisle, Roger of Thirkleby, Hugh, abbot of Selby, Gilbert de Preston, Adam
of Hilton, justices, and other faithful men of the lord king then present],
between Henry of Carlton, plaintiff, and Gilbert son of Walter of Islebeck,
concerning 4 bovates, except for 4 acres and 3 roods, in Islebeck; between the
same Gilbert, called to warrant by Walter of Dale and Agnes his wife as to 3
acres; between the same Gilbert whom John of Hoby has called to warrant as
to 1 acre of meadow; between the same Gilbert whom Abbot Henry of Byland
has called to warrant as to 3 roods; and between the same Gilbert whom
Osanna, formerly wife of Walter of Islebeck has called to warrant as to 2
bovates. Henry quitclaims to Gilbert all the above, and all right in a bovate
and 12 acres of meadow which the abbot holds of Gilbert at the time the fine
was levied. Gilbert has given Henry 5 silver marks in recognition.* York; the
morrow of the Purification of the B. V. M. 36 Henry III [3 Feb. 1252].
Marginal note: (in medieval hand) 'exceptis iiii acris et iii rodas'; (in later hand) '36
H 3'.
Copy: PRO CP 25/1/264/43, no. 27, from which the missing portions have been

supplied.
Pd: *Yorks. Fines 1246–1272*, pp. 74–5 (from PRO copy).

[fols 46v–47r]
429 *Notification by John of Islebeck son and heir of John of Islebeck of his quitclaim, for himself, his heirs and assigns, to God and St Mary and all the saints, and to the abbot and convent of Byland and their successors, of all right which he had or might have in lands and tenements, and in 18 acres of meadow, with their appurtenances, which the monks have in the region of Islebeck. Remission of all quarrels he and the monks had for a suit of non plevin which John had pursued before the justices of the Bench. The monks are to hold the land in free alms, quit of all secular service. Undertaking for himself and his heirs to make no further claim under a suit of non plevin. In return for the quitclaim the abbot and convent have received John into the fraternity of their house, so that he will participate in all the good deeds of the house and of the order. Sealed with the donor's seal.* St Barnabas [11 June] 1334.
Hiis testibus dominis <Willelmo> Darell, Willelmo Malbys, Iohanne Colvyll, Iohanne Mynyot militibus, Iohanne de Kilvington, Marmaduco Darrel.
Copy: Leeds, YAS, DD 94/10. This is not the original document. There are interlineations, and the notice of confraternity is written on the dorse.
Pd (calendar): *Yorks. Deeds*, II, 96, no. 251, from the charter then in the possession of Sir Ralph Payne-Gallwey.
Note: In 1252 Henry of Carlton quitclaimed land to Gilbert son of Walter of Islebeck (no. 428). In 1284–5 Gilbert held the land of John of Carlton. In the early fourteenth century the land was in the hands of John son of Gilbert of Islebeck. John had two sons, William, whose mother was Scottish, and John (the grantor of no. 429) whose mother was English. A writ close of 4 Nov. 15 Edward III (1341) ordered the sheriff of York to enquire touching lands in Islebeck forfeit because of William of Islebeck's adherence to the Scottish cause. The inquisition held at York the following January found that William became an adherent of the Scots on the Thurs. before All Saints 18 Edward II (31 Oct. 1324). In 2 Edward III (1328–9) John son of John of Islebeck claimed to be the true heir on the grounds that William was illegitimate. An inquisition of 11 Edward III (1337–8) found that John Moryn, his son and his wife, were then in possession of the manor. A further inquisition of 1344 found that William had been seised of the manor on the death of his father, but that he had forfeited it because of his adherence to the Scottish cause. See *Cal. Pat. R. 1343–5*, pp. 311–15, *VCH NR* II, 48. The name of the first witness is conjectured from no. 430. The cartulary has the first four witnesses only. The final clause of the cartulary copy is on the dorse of the original.

430 *Quitclaim, addressed to all who will see or hear this writing, by John Moryn, knight, for himself and his heirs and assigns, to the abbot and convent of Byland and their successors, of all right he had or might have, in* part or in whole, in places in Islebeck written below, that is all that meadow to the west of Islebeck. It is called Le Crok and it lies at the head of the arable land of the abbot and convent. The meadow extends the width of the arable land and in length from the arable land to the water course which is the boundary between Islebeck and Dalton. Quitclaim also of the meadow on the same side of Islebeck at the head of the profitable land of the abbot and convent which . . . acres are at þe Cartgapp as it extends the width of the land and in length to the said water course. Also all that meadow to the eastern part which is called Crinigleat as it lies at the head of the profitable land of the abbot and convent and stretches <across> the said land in length as it goes in a straight line from the head of the said land to the large meadow of the abbot and convent. All that meadow which lies above the profitable land of the abbot and convent at Northostes the width of the land and as it stretches in length as far as the stone that the donor placed there as a boundary between him and the abbot and convent, and all that meadow that touches on the profitable land of the abbot and convent called Hemyngcroft are quitclaimed to the abbot and convent. This quitclaim is made to God and St Mary and the abbot and convent of Byland and their successors in pure alms. Sealed with the donor's seal. [c. 1338 x 1345].

Hiis testibus dominis Willelmo Malbys, Willelmo Darell, Iohanne de Colvyll, Iohanne Minyot, militibus, etc.

Dating: John Moryn had obtained the manor of Islebeck from John son of John of Islebeck by c. 1338 (see note to no. 429). In 1342 William son of John of Islebeck was found to be legitimate, and John Moryn and his son, John, were ordered to pay 100s. for every year they had held the manor. In 1343 the king granted it to Simon Symeon; the Moryns refused to relinquish it, but were forced to do so, and quitclaimed it in 1345 when Simon granted it to Thomas Ughtred. It was at Thomas's request that the inquisition of 1344 was held (Cal. Pat. R. 1343–5, pp. 311–15).

Note: The rubric calls this a quitclaim by John Moryn of meadow in Islebeck lying in various places; it has been copied and the other copy is among the confirmations of the magnates.

431 Added in later (?15th-century) hand: extent of the holdings in Islebeck.

The monks have in the vill of Islebeck 2 tofts, one in the northern part of the vill with 4 adjacent crofts near Islebeck Tonge towards the north 5 perches in width, and the second in the western part of the vill with 3 crofts towards the west, 3½ perches in width. The perches are 21 feet in length. In the field to the east between the meadow and Le Hedeland reckoning from Le Outgange which is the highway towards the east there are 2 selions in the demesne of the vill and then the monks have 4 selions, then 12 in demesne and 4 held by the monastery, then 12 in demesne and 4 held by the monas-

tery, and 7 more in demesne and 4 held by the monastery, 15 in demesne and 5 of the monastery, 10 of the demesne and 3 of the monastery. The first stretches from the meadow to the moor, and between 2 others there is a gore (strip of land) towards the meadow. In the same fields in the cultura *which abuts onto* Le Westpot *reckoning from the moor towards the west there are 7 [selions] in demesne and 3 held by the monastery. In the same fields between* Le Hedeland *and the moor reckoning from the king's highway there are 10 in demesne and 2 held by the monastery, 16 in demesne and 2 of the monastery, 6 in demesne and 4 of the monastery. In the western fields reckoning from* Le Croft *towards the west there are 13 in demesne and 1 held by the monastery, and 47 in demesne and 4 held by the monastery whose boundaries are included towards the south within the meadow. The monastery likewise has 15 acres of meadow lying together near the waterfall. Note that the tofts and the selions and the meadow are marked with stones.*

Note: The inquisition of 1344 found that the abbot held 2 tofts with crofts, 18 acres of land and 18 acres of meadow. See note to no. 429.

[fol. 47v]
YARM (NZ4112), township and parish in the wapentake of Langbargh West (NR). The parish is bounded to the north and west by the river Tees and on the north and east by the river Leven. There were many monastic houses with property in Yarm in the Middle Ages, including Guisborough, Fountains, Healaugh Park, and Mount Grace (*VCH NR* II, 319–23).

432   *Rubric: Charter of Arnold son of Richard son of Gode of a toft with the houses built on it, and all its lands and appurtenances, that is from the church of St Mary Magdalene.*
Marginal note: Gaytrig B(aculus) ii.

433   *Rubric: Charter of Arnold the Fleming (Flandrensis) concerning land in Yarm with the house on it which he will buy from Richard Parvus, and in which the monks will receive him honourably. He and his heirs are to hold it for 6d. yearly, paid to the abbot and convent.*

434   *Grant in free alms, addressed to all the faithful in Christ present and future, by Stephen of Yarm, clerk, to God and St Mary and the abbot and convent of Byland, of a messuage with appurtenances in Yarm between the dwelling of Jordan de Lester' and the house of William brother of Raynald. The grant is made for the salvation of his soul and of his father and mother and all his ancestors and heirs, to do with as the monks wish, rendering [2]d.*

annually for husgable at the feast of St Peter ad Vincula (1 Aug.) for all other secular service. Pledge to warranty. [early to mid 13th cent.].

Hiis testibus domino Iordano de Lester', domino Honorio tunc priore Bellel', Willelmo cellerario, Willelmo portario, etc.

Dating: second witness.

Note: Jordan de Lestre witnesses a Guisborough charter and occurs in a court case of 1240: *Cart. Guis.* II, 42, and note.

435   *Confirmation in the form of a chirograph, addressed to all the faithful in Christ present and future, by Adam, abbot of Byland and the convent of the same place, of the agreement between them and Hugh de Fenwyk of Yarm, namely that they grant to Hugh that messuage in Yarm which they have of the grant of Stephen of Yarm, clerk, lying between the dwelling formerly of Jordan de Lester' and the house of William brother of Raynald. Hugh is to hold the messuage in fee and hereditary right rendering 2s., 12d. each at Whitsuntide and the feast of St Martin in Winter (11 Nov.), and gavelkind. Pledge to warranty. Hugh and his heirs are not to sell or in any way alienate the property without the consent of the monks. Sealed with the seals of both parties.* [last quarter of 13th cent. or early 14th cent.].

Hiis testibus dominis Edmundo tunc priore, Willelmo suppriore, Rogero de Gyr . . . magistro conversorum, Ada de Cundale granatore, etc.

Dating: Abbot Adam of Husthwaite who occurs between 1272 and 1283, and in 1309 x 1310, and 1315: *HRH* II, 270.

436   *Rubric: Chirograph of Thomas son of Hugh concerning 1 toft rendering to the monks 18d.*

437   *Rubric: Chirograph of Robert le Felter concerning a house which the monks have of the grant of Arnold for 2s. a year.*

438   *Rubric: Charter of Henry the tanner concerning a toft in Yarm.*

439   *Rubric: Charters of Agnes of Linthorpe; surrendered.*

[fols 47v–48r]

440   *Indenture of remission and quitclaim by the abbot and convent of Byland, for themselves and their successors, to John Alayn of Yarm and his heirs and assigns of all right and claim which they have or might have in 2 messuages in Yarm which John has of the grant and enfeoffment of Dom. Henry of Pontefract, chaplain, rendering to the abbot and convent for 1 of* *the said messuages, which was formerly held by Agnes of Linthorpe, 2d. yearly at St Martin in Winter (11 Nov.). John agrees for himself and his heirs that if they fail to pay the rent in whole or in part, the abbot and convent may distrain in the said messuage until it is paid. Sealed by both parties.* Annunciation [25 Mar.] 1347.

[fol. 48r, old fol. 153]
441   *Rubric: Chirograph of the canons of Guisborough concerning the exchange of 1 acre of land which the monks had of the gift of . . . of Acklam for that acre near to the monks' curtilage, which they have of the same canons.*

[fol. 48v]
COLD KIRBY (SE5384), in the parish of Old Byland and wapentake of Birdforth (NR). Cold Kirby lies about 2½ miles to the SW of Tylas Farm, in Old Byland, the abbey tile house on the site of the second abbey. The Knights Templar held the manor of Cold Kirby, and there were disputes over lands which the abbot claimed to belong to his manor of Sutton under Whitestonecliffe, to the SW of Cold Kirby.

442   *Agreement, addressed to all the sons of holy mother church who will see or hear these letters, between Roger, abbot of Byland and the monks of the same place and Richard Croyer concerning land in* Scheperlage *which had been in dispute between them. Roger, on the advice of his monks and chapter, Robert d'Aunay, Robert de Daiville, William Wildfar and Godric a conversus, quitclaims all the land to Richard. Neither Roger nor his monks, present and future, will make any claim on the land, under the agreement by which Richard has given the monks the corn which was on the land when the compromise was reached. Of the land at* Scheperlage *Richard grants the monks, for the term of his life, 100 acres which lie nearest to Old Byland in the open land at Cold Kirby; after his death the monks are to restore the land to his heir and to the men of Cold Kirby.* York; [Jan. 1151 x 22 Jan. 1153].
. . . facta in capitulo Sancti Petri Ebor' coram archiepiscopo Henrico Murdac et coram decano <Roberto> Butevilayn et coram thesaurario Hugone et coram Thoma de Ramavill', etc.

Pd: *EYC* IX, no. 76.
Dating: Archbishop Henry Murdac did not enter York until January 1151; terminal date provided by election of Hugh du Puiset to the bishopric of Durham.
Note: As Clay points out, the second witness did not become dean until 1158, and he suggested that 'decano' was an error for 'archidiacono', a post which Robert Butevilain held until 1157. However, the dean in 1151 x 1153 was Robert de Gant, and it is possible that 'decano' is correct and that a copyist inserted 'Butevilain' in error. Robert Butevilain is generally called Robert the dean (nos 26, 27, 47, 56, 58,

59, 224, 395, 887, 924, 1156) but appears in the cartulary once as 'Robert Butevilain, dean of the church of St Peter, York' (no. 225) and once as 'Robert II dean' (no. 491). On Richard Cruer (Croyer) who was, at a date later than this charter, enfeoffed of land in Cold Kirby by Robert de Stuteville III, see *EYC* IX, 6 and note 5, 76, 146. The rubric gives his name as Richard Crowell and the place name as 'Scheperdlage'. He attested no. 379, an act of Bishop Hugh du Puiset concerning the end of a controversy between the canons of Newburgh and Adam Fossard about the boundaries of Hood.

443   *Final concord reached in the king's court in the presence of Simon of Pattishall, James of Potterne, Henry de Pont-Audemar, Richard de Mucegros, justices, and other faithful men of the lord king then present, between brother Emericus, master of the Knights Templar in England, plaintiff, through brother William de Fauflor, and Herbert, abbot of Byland, defendant, through Walter his monk, concerning a* cultura *called* **Karebyflatt** *which Emericus claimed to belong to his manor of Cold Kirby, and the abbot claimed to belong to his grange of Old Byland. On the order of the king 12 knights were summoned to make a perambulation and testify on oath whether the* cultura *belonged to the manor or the grange. The abbot has acknowledged this to be the right of Emericus and the Knights of the Temple, and for this recognition Emericus has granted the abbot and convent the said* cultura *to hold of Emericus and other brethren of the Temple for 4s. yearly, 2s. at Easter and 2s. at St Michael (29 Sept.). The brethren of the Temple are not to have common for their animals in the said* cultura *or in any other pasture belonging to Old Byland, whether the pasture be in profitable land or moorland or other land, without the assent of the abbot and his successors, and the abbot and his successors are not to have common within the pasture of the brethren belonging to the manor of Cold Kirby without their good will and consent.* Woodstock; the quindene of St Martin, 11 John [11–25 Nov. 1209].

Copy: PRO CP 25/1/261/12, no. 205.
Pd: *Yorks. Fines John*, pp. 160–1 (from PRO copy).

[fols 48v–49r]
444   *Final concord, place and date as no. 443, between Emericus, master of the Knights Templar in England, plaintiff, through brother William de Fauflor, and Robert Fossard, defendant, concerning all the pasture between the highway that runs to Cleveland and the brow of the cliff in width and in length and the boundaries made between Robert Fossard and Adam of Boltby up to the boundaries of Kilburn. Emericus claimed this to belong to his manor of Cold Kirby, and Robert to his manor of Sutton under Whitestonecliffe. On the order of the king 12 knights were summoned to make*

perambulation and to testify on oath whether the pasture belonged to the manor of Cold Kirby or that of Sutton. As a result Emericus has acknowledged the pasture to belong to the right of Robert. For this recognition Robert has granted Emericus common pasture within the said boundaries for all his animals of Cold Kirby and for those of his men, to hold of Robert for 10s. yearly, 5s. at Whitsuntide and 5s. at St Martin (11 Nov.). One of the men of the brethren at Cold Kirby, Robert son of Thredrec, and his heirs shall pay Robert and his heirs 3s. at the said terms, and the brethren and their other men of Kirby shall pay the remaining 7s. Neither Robert nor anyone else is to create profitable land from the pasture without licence and assent of the brethren or their successors. Woodstock; the quindene of St Martin, 11 John [11–25 Nov. 1209].

Copies: PRO CP 25/1/261/12, no. 195; (partial): MS Dodsworth 63, fol. 69v, from cartulary fol. 153v.

Pd: *Yorks. Fines John*, p. 160 (from PRO copy).

[fol. 49r, old fol. 154]

445 *Quitclaim, addressed to all the faithful in Christ who will see or hear this charter, for the salvation of his soul and for the souls of his father and mother and of all his ancestors and successors, by Robert Fossard to St Mary and the brethren of the Knights of the Temple of Solomon in Jerusalem of 7s. which the brethren and their men of Cold Kirby are accustomed to render for pasture in Sutton. They shall continue to pay 6d. at Whitsuntide, and shall have free pasture as is contained in no. 444. Robert and his heirs will bring no further claim. Pledge to make no further claim and to warranty. Sealed with the donor's seal.* [c. 1209 x 1227].

Hiis testibus Philippo filio Iohannis, Olyvero de Buscy, Stephano de Maynyll', etc.

Copy: MS Dodsworth 63, fol. 71r, from cartulary fol. 154.

Pd: *EYC* IX, no. 85.

Dating: clearly after no. 443; donor was dead by 1227.

446 *Notification to those present and future by Robert Fossard of his quitclaim, for himself and his heirs, to Robert of Cold Kirby and his heirs of the annual rent of 3s. which Robert was accustomed to render as part of the rent of 10s. which the Templars and their men of Cold Kirby pay yearly for common pasture in Sutton (under Whitestonecliffe) which is between the highway which goes to Cleveland and another road, in accordance with the agreement made in the court of King John between Robert Fossard and the Templars and the men of Cold Kirby (no. 444). Robert Fossard will make no demand on Robert of Cold Kirby beyond the 6d. silver he owes yearly at*

Christmas. For this quitclaim Robert has paid to Robert Fossard 10 silver marks. [c. 1208 x 1211 or 1216 x 1224].

Hiis testibus W. abbate de Ryevalle, etc.

Pd: *EYC* IX, no. 84, where dated 1216 x 1224.

Dating: Robert Fossard had succeeded his father, Adam, by 1208. The dating in *EYC* is based on the identification of the witness as Abbot William of Rievaulx. However, if the charter is contemporary with, or slightly later than, no. 445 the witness is Abbot Warin of Rievaulx (occ. 1208, died 1211; *HRH* I, 140).

[fol. 49v]

447 *Rubric: Plea between the monks and the men of Cold Kirby concerning the new enclosure at Whitestonecliffe. Look in the book of pleas.*

448 *Rubric: Pleas before the lord king at Thirsk, with assize on our behalf.* 19 Edward [. . .]. *These are to be sought in the book of pleas.*

449 *Rubric: Quitclaim by Richard Champion of the same pasture. Look under Sutton in the third bundle.*

450 *Rubric: Quitclaim by the same Richard Champion to us and our servants. Look under Sutton, as above.*

451 **Original:** *Quitclaim, addressed to all the faithful in Christ to whom the present writing shall come, by Brother Imbert de Peraut, master of the Knights Templar in England, on the advice and with the consent of the chapter meeting at Easter in London, to the abbot and convent of Byland, of all right they have or might have in the future in the pasture which the abbot and convent recently enclosed next to their sheepfold of Whitestonecliffe. This quitclaim is made by the master and brethren for themselves and their heirs. If any of the animals belonging to the Templars or their men of Cold Kirby shall enter the enclosure because it is defective they shall not be impounded, but may be redeemed, notwithstanding this quitclaim. Sealed with the seal of the chapter.* [Easter 1270 x March 1272].

Hiis testibus fratre Radulfo capellano, fratre Ricardo filio Iohannis, fratre Willemo le Englys, fratre Rogero de Akeny, fratre Roberto Scropp', fratre Ranulfo de Bremesgrave, fratre Willemo de Merden tunc preceptore Ebor'.

Location: Leeds, YAS, DD 146/18/6.

Pd (calendar): *Yorks. Deeds,* IX, 167–8, no. 440, from an original at Farnley Hall (MSS no. 70), in the custody of YAS. Also pd (calendar): *Yorks. Deeds,* I, 161–2, no. 447, from an original then (1909) in the possession of Frederick Fawkes of Otley; endorsed: Sutton; seal: green wax.

Dating: Imbert de Peraut occurs as master of the Knights Templar in England between March 1270 and 13 June 1271; his successor was in office by 10 March 1272: M. Gervers, ed., *The Cartulary of the Knights of St John of Jerusalem in England, Secunda Camera, Essex* (British Academy Records of Social and Economic History, ns 6, 1982), p. 46 (no. 77) and p. 568.

Note: The cartulary copy omits the last three witnesses.

[fol. 50r, old fol. 155]

SOUTH KILVINGTON (SE4284), parish in the wapentake of Birdforth (NR), approximately 2 miles north of Thirsk. Upsall and Thornbrough, also mentioned in the documents in this section, are in the same parish. Byland's acquisitions in South Kilvington came fairly late, beginning with Geoffrey of Upsall's grant of rent to make pittances (no. 452), later converted to a chantry (no. 455).

452   *Grant in free alms, addressed to all the faithful of Christ present and future, by Geoffrey of Upsall (South Kilvington), to God and St Mary and the abbot and monks of Byland, of 5 marks' annual rent from his water mill in Kilvington for making 2 pittances yearly, 1 at St Mary Magdalene (22 July) and the other at St Cuthbert (20 Mar.), throughout the donor's life; after his death the pittance at St Cuthbert shall be his anniversary. If, because of flooding or for any other reason, the mill shall be moved, or if the monks are prevented in any way from taking the rent, then they are to have it from the donor's farm in Kilvington, in equal portions at St Martin in Winter (11 Nov.) and Whitsuntide. The grant is made for the salvation of the soul of the donor and of all his ancestors and heirs. Pledge to warranty. Sealed with the donor's seal.* [before 1279].

Hiis testibus dominis Nicholao de Meynyll, Iohanne de Eyvyll, Ada de Eyvill, Willelmo de Roseles, militibus, etc.

Copies: MS Dodsworth 91, fols 77v–78r (no. 15) and 117v (no. 70); the witness list of no. 15 has 'domino' for 'dominis', omits 'etc', and continues: Yvone de Etton, Nicholao Talenaces, Thoma de Etton, Willelmo de Bec, Willelmo le Playdour et aliis; both copies have a sketch of a seal; MS Top. Yorks. e. 7, fol. 123r (old p. 193), which has 'Salvato' [underlined] for 'Talenaces'; Top. Yorks. e. 8, fol. 182r–v (old pp. 328–9) (witness list incomplete).

Dating: On 15 Feb. 1416 the king ordered his escheator in Yorkshire to meddle no further in the rent of 5 marks which the monks had in the vill of Kilvington, which rent an inquisition found to have been granted by Geoffrey of Upsall before the Statute *De Religiosis* (*Cal. Cl. R. 1413–1419*, p. 256). This reference to the Statute of Mortmain indicates a date before 1279.

Note: Geoffrey of Upsall held a knight's fee in Upsall and South Kilvington of Baldwin Wake in 1282; in 1284–5 Geoffrey's son, Hugh of Upsall held 4 carucates in Upsall of the heirs of Baldwin Wake and in turn of Roger de Mowbray (*EYC* IX, 180; *VCH NR* II, 41; *KI*, p. 97). Nicholas de Meinill of Whorlton was summoned to

Parliament from 1295 to 1299: *EYF*, p. 60. John de Daiville is to be identified as the chief justice, keeper of the forests north of the Trent from 1257 to 1261, who died before 1291: *ibid.*, p. 24. Thomas of Etton was a frequent witness of Byland charters, and there were clearly several members of the family with the name of Thomas. It is not easy to distinguish between them.

453 *Confirmation, addressed to all the faithful in Christ present and future, by Hugh of Upsall son of Geoffrey of Upsall, to God and St Mary and the abbot and convent of Byland, of 5 marks' rent from his mill of Kilvington, to make 2 pittances yearly, as contained in his father's charter (no. 452). Sealed with the donor's seal. [after 1282].*
Hiis testibus dominis Nicholao de Meynill, Iohanne de Eyvill, Ada de Bartona, militibus, Radulfo de Thornetona rectore ecclesie de Brandesby, etc.
Copies: MS Dodsworth 91, fol. 117r, no. 69, where the witness list has 'domino' before 'Radulfo', omits 'etc' and continues: domino Willelmo rectore capelle de Couseby, Iohanne de Thorntona, Wydone de Kylvyngton, Iohanne de Helbeke, Willelmo Stedeman, Roberto coco de Thornton et aliis. Also MS Top. Yorks. e. 9, fol. 45r (old p. 63).
Dating: Hugh was recorded as holding 4 carucates in Upsall of Roger de Mowbray in 1284–5, indicating that he had succeeded his father some time between 1282 and 1284.

454 *Assise held in the presence of John de Insula, H. de Scrope and John of Doncaster, justices of the lord king, to inquire into whether Geoffrey of Upsall and Stephen of Kilvington unjustly disseised the abbot of Byland of a free tenement in South Kilvington and 5 marks rent. Geoffrey and Stephen failed to appear but sent their bailiff, William Fairbairn, who said that they had done no injury to the abbot and convent. Witnesses said under oath that the abbot, as his predecessors, had been seised of the tenement until he was unjustly disseised by Geoffrey and Stephen. The abbot recovered seisin, and Geoffrey and Stephen were amerced 10 marks.* York; day after St Thomas, martyr, 4 Edward II [30 Dec. 1310].
Marginal note: (in later hand) '4 E 2'.
Note: The grantor is Geoffrey of Upsall the younger, tenant in Upsall, South Kilvington and Thornbrough in 1316 (*EYC* IX, 180). A note in the right hand margin, in a later hand, indicates that 'Hugh Upsall' was the son of Geoffrey Upsall.

[fol. 50r–v]
455 *Indenture between the abbot and convent of Byland and Geoffrey of Upsall, knight, by which Geoffrey quitclaims for himself and his heirs, to the abbot and convent and their successors, all manner of pittances which the abbot and convent and their predecessors made. For this quitclaim the abbot*

and convent agree to find a monk chaplain to celebrate every day in the chapel of St Mary Magdalene outside the gates of the abbey (sic) *for the souls of Geoffrey and his ancestors and heirs except on certain feast days, that is, the Circumcision, Epiphany, the Purification of the B. V. M., St Benedict, abbot, the Annunciation, the second and third weekly mass in Passion week, Easter, St Philip and St James, the Ascension, the Invention of the Holy Cross, the second and third weekly mass at Whitsuntide, St John the Baptist, St Peter and St Paul, the Assumption of the B. V. M., St Bernard, abbot, the Nativity of the B. V. M., the Exaltation of the Holy Cross, St Michael, All Saints, the Nativity, St Stephen the protomartyr, St John the Evangelist, the Holy Innocents, the dedication of the said chapel and all Sundays throughout the year. On these days the monk chaplain may celebrate if he wishes with the mass of the day by saying a collect for the souls of Geoffrey and his ancestors and heirs. The abbot and convent quitclaim to Geoffrey all annual pensions and the rent of 5 marks, saving the 5 marks which were the subject of the assize of novel disseisin (no. 454). The two pittances mentioned in earlier writings (nos 452, 453) are now converted to the celebration in the chapel outlined above. The abbot and convent concede that Geoffrey and his heirs may retain the rent of 5 marks when the chantry is in arrears until the arrears are paid in full. The abbot and convent reserve the rents, dues and customs which Geoffrey owes for lands which he hold in Over Silton, as contained in a document. Sealed with the seals of both parties.* Byland; 14 May 1311.

Marginal note: (in later hand) '4 E 2'.

Note: Both Hugh of Upsall, who held the manor in 1284–5, and his brother, William, died without issue. William was succeeded by 1294 by his brother, Michael, who in turn was succeeded by his son, Geoffrey, grantor of this charter. The reference, in this charter, to the celebration of mass in the chapel of St Mary Magdalene outside the gates of the abbey must be an error for the chapel of St Mary Magdalene, Upsall: on 23 Aug. 1316 Geoffrey had licence to alienate in mortmain a messuage and 8 bovates in Thornbrough and Upsall for a chaplain to celebrate divine service in the chapel of St Mary Magdalene, Upsall, for his soul and those of his ancestors and heirs (*Cal. Pat. R. 1313–1317*, p. 536). In 1327 Geoffrey sold the manor to the Scropes of Bolton (*VCH NR* II, 41–2). For further charters of Geoffrey, one dated 1326, which may have appeared on fol. 156, see MS Dodsworth 91, fols 135r–136r, nos 110–11. On 7 Feb. 1341 [1342] Henry le Scrope, son of Geoffrey le Scrope, confirmed to Byland an annual rent of 5 marks which the abbot and convent received from the mill of Kilvington (MS Dodsworth 91, fol. 81r, no. 21).

[1 folio lost, old fol. 156]

KEPWICK (SE4690), in the parish of Over Silton, and the wapentake of Birdforth. MS Top. Yorks. d. 11, fol. 268r, notes a confirmation by Roger de Benton of pasture for 200 sheep.

[fol. 51r, old fol. 157]
KIRKBY MALZEARD (SE2374), parish in the wapentake of Lower Claro (WR). The grants received by Byland from the Mowbray family included easements, wood, iron ore and lead mines in the forest of Nidderdale, and this became an important asset to the monks. There was a Mowbray castle at Kirkby Malzeard, which was razed after the participation of Roger de Mowbray and his son Nigel in the rebellion of the Young King in 1173/4. The interests of Fountains Abbey in Nidderdale led to conflicts between the two houses; for one instance, see below, no. 707.

456 *Grant in free alms, addressed to the archbishop of York and all the sons of holy mother church, by Roger de Mowbray, to God and the monks of St Mary of Byland, of 2 bovates in Kirkby Malzeard with all their appurtenances and common easements in his forest of Nidderdale, namely iron, a tithe of the lead mines and a salt spring, pasture and other necessities for their house.* [1147 x 1153].
Hiis testibus Sampsone de Albaneio, Hereberto de Moravilla, Ricardo Burdet, etc.
Marginal note: Nidderd' B. ii.
Pd: *Mowbray Charters*, no. 48.
Dating: as *Mowbray Charters*, on the grounds that this was probably made after the general grant of easements in Roger's forests (below, no. 643) and before no. 689.
Note: The rubric states that the charter had been copied. The marginal note suggests that it was copied from the second Nidderdale bundle or section. Arthur Raistrick notes that this charter provides the earliest evidence, after the Roman period, for mining on Greenhow Hill, Nidderdale: *Lead Mining in the mid-Pennines: the mines of Nidderdale, Wharfedale, Airedale, Ribblesdale and Bowland* (Truro, 1974), p. 18. For further discussion of Byland's mining activities in Nidderdale, see below, note to no. 707.

457 *Grant in free alms, addressed to the archbishop of York and the whole chapter of St Peter (York) and all the sons of holy mother church, by Roger de Mowbray, to God and the monks of St Mary of Byland, of a toft in Kirkby Malzeard which was held by Gamel of Nidderdale lying in the north of the vill; 3 acres between* Epedecros *and Kirkby Malzeard which touch on the road between Kirkby and Laverton; 4 acres between* Morthwayt *and Kex Beck* (Kesebek) *around the assart of Roger the priest; and common rights and easements throughout the whole region of the vill, including free and* *convenient entry and exit for themselves, their men and the animals they have there. The monks are to hold the above free from all secular service. Pledge to warranty for the salvation of the soul of the donor and of all his ancestors and heirs. [c. 1170 x 1186].*

Hiis testibus Nigello de Molbray filio meo, Philippo de Muntpinzun, Roberto de Bello Campo, etc.

Pd: *Mowbray Charters*, no. 67.

Dating: as *Mowbray Charters*, on the grounds that Philip of Montpincon does not occur before *c.* 1170 (see *ibid.*, no. 376 note).

Note: Kex Beck flows to the north of Kirkby Malzeard.

458   *Grant in free alms, addressed to the archbishop of York and all the sons of holy mother church, by Roger de Mowbray, to God and the monks of St Mary of Byland, of his man Alfnaf of Kirkby Malzeard with his toft and the neighbouring toft towards the east, and a* cultura *of 3 acres in the field of Kirkby Malzeard called* Bywrtreflath. *To hold of the donor and his heirs free from all secular service. [c. 1170 x 1186].*

Hiis testibus Herberto filio Ricardi, Alano de Limesia, Rogero filio Aye, Iohanne de Crevequer, etc.

Pd: *Mowbray Charters*, no. 66.

Dating: as *Mowbray Charters*, on the grounds that the second and third witnesses do not occur before *c.* 1170.

459   *Rubric: Confirmation of Nigel de Mowbray of the same with tofts and the* cultura *aforesaid.* [before 1190].

Marginal note: B(aculus) ii Niderdale.

Dating: the death of Nigel de Mowbray.

460   *Rubric: Charter of Nigel [de Mowbray] concerning 4 acres in Kirkby Malzeard above Kex Beck.* [before 1190].

Text: MS Top. Yorks. e. 8, fol. 137v (old p. 239). Grant and confirmation in free alms, addressed to the archbishop of York and the whole chapter of St Peter (York) and all the sons of holy church, by Nigel de Mowbray, to God and the monks of St Mary of Byland, of 4 acres in Kirkby Malzeard above Kex Beck at the assart of Roger Veteranus, priest. The assart is to be reckoned with the 4 acres. The grant is made free from all secular service for the salvation of his soul and of all his ancestors and heirs, Pledge to warranty. Hiis testibus Roberto de Molbraio fratre meo, Philippo de Muntpinzun, Nicholao de Belum, Roberto Beler, Henrico de Lubeham, Gaufrido Coco, Ernaldo dispensatore.

Dating: as no. 459.

461 Rubric: *Charter of Thurstan de Belvoir concerning 3 acres in Carr House (in Kirkby Malzeard) with a perch of 20 feet.*

462 Rubric: *Chirograph of Geoffrey Myses concerning 2 acres lying in Wulwynriddyng' nearest the river.*

463 *Grant in free alms, addressed to the archbishop of York and the whole chapter of St Peter (York) and all the sons of holy mother church present and future, by Philip of Billinghay, to God and the monks of St Mary of Byland, of all the land which he had between the monks' land in Kirkby Malzeard to the west and the toft which Godwin held nearest to that land towards the west, and from the road which runs through the centre of the vill to the sike at the head of the crofts. The grant is made free from all secular service and for the salvation of the soul of the donor and of all his ancestors and heirs. Pledge to warranty.* [c. 1184 x 1190].
Hiis testibus Roberto senesc(allo), Sampsone de Malasart, Ricardo Noel, etc.

Dating: Philip of Billinghay succeeded his brother Peter by 1184. He was a benefactor of Malton Priory and witnessed charters of Roger de Mowbray between 1170 and 1186 (*Mowbray Charters*, nos 82, 179–80, 349 note). For his charter concerning land in Hovingham see above, no. 392.

[fol. 51v]
464 *Notification to all present and future by William Drury of Sproxton of his grant in free alms, for the salvation of his soul and of all his ancestors and heirs, to God and St Mary and the abbot and convent of Byland, of 6 acres in Kirkby Malzeard, with their appurtances and with toft and croft, meadows and pastures and all other easements belonging to the land, inside and outside the vill, which the abbot and convent first held of him at farm. They are to render to William and his heirs 1 pound of cumin yearly at the first fair of Ripon and knight service for ½ bovate where 18 carucates make a knight's fee. Pledge to warranty. Sealed with the donor's seal.* [Aug. 1235 x Feb. 1267].
Hiis testibus Gocelino Noel, Gocelino de Braythewath, Willelmo filio Willelmi de Ebor(aco), Philippo persona de Ryllyngtona, etc.

Copy: MS Top. Yorks. e. 8, fol. 182v (old p. 330), which omits 'etc' from the witness list and continues: Willelmo de Foxhole, Willelmo de Maundevil, Serlone de Faldington, Philippo filio Philippi de Suctona, Roberto de Queneby, Stephano Gery, Willelmo de Waldo, Willelmo de Bildesdale.
Dating: Philip, parson of Rillington, was instituted in Aug. 1235 and had resigned by Feb. 1267 (*Fasti Parochiales*, V, 34).
Note: The rubric states that the cumin may be paid to William Drury or to Goscelin of Braithwaite (Baywathe), the second witness.

465   *Rubric: Charter of Goscelin Vehilethen concerning the said 6 acres. Surrendered.*

Note: Goscelin of Braithwaite confirmed to Fountains Abbey all its possessions which were granted by his ancestors, including the land granted by Goscelin Veyllechen and other grants which the monks had received by 1256: *Cart. Fountains*, I, 144 (no. 9).

466   *Notification to all present and future by Goscelin of Braithwaite of his grant and confirmation in free alms, for the salvation of his soul and of all his ancestors and heirs, to God and St Mary and the abbot and convent of Byland, of 6 acres granted by William Drury in Kirkby Malzeard, lying at the head of the vill towards Azerley, that is to the south side of the road. Pledge to warranty. Sealed with the donor's seal.* [c. 1241 x 1266].

Hiis testibus domino Thoma de Colvyll', Rogero de Stapilton', Willelmo de Midelton' tunc senescallo Rogeri de Mowbray, etc.

Dating: Reference to the steward of Roger de Mowbray. The donor witnessed no. 464.
Note: Azerley lies approximately 1½ miles east of Kirkby Malzeard.

467   *Rubric: Charter of William Drury concerning all his land in Kirkby Malzeard rendering 1 pound of cumin.* [mid 13th cent.].

Dating: as no. 466.

468   *Rubric: Quitclaim by Goscelin of Braithwaite of the said 1 pound of cumin.* [mid 13th cent.].

Dating: as no. 464.

469   *Rubric: Charter of Uviet of Kirkby Malzeard concerning 5 acres there.* [late 12th cent.].

Text: MS Top. Yorks. e. 7, fol. 144r (old p. 235). Grant, addressed to all the sons of holy church present and future, by Uviet of Kirkby Malzeard, to God and St Mary of Byland and the monks serving God there, of 5 acres in Kirkby Malzeard, that is, 3 acres between 'Fulgata' and 'Therverdsic' and 1 acre on either side of 'Crembelsic', to hold in free alms and to do there as the monks wish, for the salvation of his soul and of all his own. Pledge to warranty. Hiis testibus Roberto de Butei, Alano filio Romundi, Roberto de Kerebi, Radulfo filio et herede meo, Willelmo filio Radulfi, Willelmo Galopin, Rogero fratre eius, Ricardo de Witewrd et Benedicto fratre eius.

Dating: Uviet witnessed a charter of Roger de Mowbray in favour of Fountains Abbey, *c.* 1181: *Mowbray Charters*, no. 137; *Cart. Fountains*, I, 307 (no. 18).

470 Rubric: Confirmation by Ralph son of Uviet of the same. They (pre-sumably 469 and 470) are bound together.

Dating: Nos 470–76 are likely to date from the late 12th or early 13th century.
Note: Ralph son of Uviet granted land in Kirkby Malzeard to Fountains Abbey: *Cart. Fountains*, I, 409 (no. 4).

471 Rubric: Charter of the same [Ralph son of Uviet] concerning 1 acre with a perch of 20 feet in Bessekeldcroft.

472 Rubric: Charter of the same [Ralph son of Uviet] concerning 1 acre in 2 places. These are bound together.

Note: This seems to imply that the land is in two half-acre strips.

473 Rubric: Charter of the same [Ralph son of Uviet] concerning ½ acre and 16 perches.

474 Rubric: Charter of the same [Ralph son of Uviet] concerning various lands in small portions.

475 Grant in free alms, addressed to all the sons of holy mother church present and future, by Ralph son of Uviet, to God and the monks of St Mary of Byland, of that bovate in Kirkby Malzeard which Torbrand son of Quene held, with all its appurtenances inside and outside the vill, except for the croft which Torbrand held, for which Ralph had granted them the croft called Durandesherth and 1½ perches at the standing stone (standandstayn) below Stainmore. The grant is made to hold free from secular service, rendering to Ralph and his heirs 2s. yearly, 12d. at Whitsuntide and 12d. at St Martin (11 Nov.). Pledge to warranty. [late 12th or early 13th cent.] Hiis testibus etc.

Dating: as no. 470.
Note: Ralph was the grantor of 6 charters not entered in the cartulary (nos 470–74, 476) and his father was presumably the grantor of no. 469.

[fol. 52r, old fol. 158]

476 Rubric: Charter of the same [Ralph son of Uviet] concerning 3 acres with 1 perch of 20 feet, granted so that the monks render to the lord Mowbray 20d. and the remaining 4d. to him.

Note: In no. 475 the annual rent for the land is specified as 2s.

477 Rubric: Charter of Walter the forester of Coverdale (Brogden) concerning the said 4d.

478   *Rubric: Charter of Uctred Kyrkeman of Kirkby Malzeard concerning 1 rood in the same.*

479   *Notification to all present and future by Richard Neville of his grant in free alms to God and St Mary and the abbot and convent of Byland, of 2 acres and 3½ roods in Kirkby Malzeard, namely 2 acres in* Gillebria *ridding nearer the south, and ½ acre in* Cokescote *and 1½ roods in* Dynandeyorthe. *The grant is made to hold freely for the salvation of the soul of the donor and of all his ancestors and successors, to do there whatever the monks wish. Pledge to warranty. Sealed with the donor's seal.* [c. 1241 x 1266].

Hiis testibus domino Willelmo de Midelton' tunc senescallo Rogeri de Moubray, Rogero de Stapilton', Thoma de Colavilla, Alano de Audefeld', Gocelino Noel, etc.

Dating: Reference to the steward of Roger de Mowbray. The first three witnesses attest no. 466 and the last witness attests no. 464.

480   *Rubric: Confirmation by Matilda daughter of Odo of the said 2 acres and 3½ roods.*

481   *Rubric: Charter of Odo and Amice concerning the same. Surrendered.*

482   *Rubric: Confirmation of Matilda daughter of Odo concerning the same. Surrendered.*

Note: A note states that nos 481 and 482 were not displayed.

483   *Rubric: Charter of the same Matilda concerning 1 acre. Copied.*

484   *Quitclaim by letters patent by John de Mowbray, lord of the Isle of Axholme and of the honours of Bramber and Gower, for himself and his heirs to the abbot and convent of Byland, of 1 pound of pepper in annual rent which the monks used to render for lands held in the manor of Thirsk and 2s. annual rent for lands held in the manor of Kirkby Malzeard. Pardon of arrears. Sealed with the donor's seal.* Epworth; Sunday after the Exaltation of the Holy Cross, 19 Edward III [18 Sept. 1345].

Note: In 1322, following his father's hanging for his part in the siege of Tickhill castle, John de Mowbray was imprisoned in the Tower of London. His inheritance was restored in 1327. No. 484 is cross referenced below at no. 661. In 1349 John granted a moiety of the advowson of Bubwith church, with licence to appropriate (no. 106) for the soul of his first wife, Joan. He died on 4 Oct. 1361: *CP* IX, 380–83.

485 *Rubric: Agreement between the monks of Fountains and those of Byland concerning Nidderdale and various lands in Kirkby Malzeard. Abbatum Baculo secundo,* 'in the second bundle of the [records of the] abbots'.

[fol. 52v]
KILBURN (SE5179), parish and township in the wapentake of Birdforth (NR). The parish of Kilburn included Hood, Birdforth, Byland Abbey, Cams Head, Wass, Newstead, Ousey Carr, Rose Hill, Stocking, Oldstead, and Cold Cam. Many of Byland's lands were concentrated in this area. Kilburn was held of Roger de Mowbray by Robert de Daiville, his constable, and in 1186 x 90 land there was restored by Nigel de Mowbray to Robert's son, John (*Mowbray Charters*, no. 361). No. 486 provides evidence for colonization in the area.

486 *Notification of the chirograph agreement by which the monks of St Mary of Byland demise to Robert de Daiville a fishery with a millpond between Kilburn and* Middleberga *and the field around the fishpond for his men to fish. Licence to assart from the bottom of the valley where the arable land touches on the road, in a straight line as far as* Rauthekeldsic *towards Kilburn. Robert demises to the monks land from the spring next to the garden of Wildon by the boundaries which they have perambulated as far as Ousey Carr and the whole of Ousey Carr and from there in a straight line along the road at the head to the north of Ousey Carr to the head of the assart of* Ketelburne *and from there in a straight line up over again to the profitable land of Wildon. The monks are to do with this as they wish. The whole of the woodland of Rose Hill from the head of the assart of* Ketelburne *to the west as far as the highway which goes from Carlton to Kilburn shall not be assarted but shall remain as common pasture by the boundaries which have been perambulated. From the highway to the corner of* Dritrarneker *towards the west by the boundaries which they have perambulated and from there to the corner of* Dritrarneker *on the north and from there to the profitable land shall remain with Robert as meadow and corn, and after the harvest it shall be common pasture. Robert shall assart outside Trencar as he wishes as far as the road from Kilburn towards Osgoodby to the north of Trencar. He may sow these assarts and lands annually as he wishes and if he wishes he shall make a fishery between Kilburn and Hood. The monks may enclose 15 acres to do with as they wish in* Caldecothedala *and they shall have full common pasture throughout Kilburn for their flocks from Wildon and Stocking, and free entry and exit for their flocks and their men through*

Robert's land. Each year Robert shall have an enclosure for his oxen and horses at his own judgement and that of the grangers of Wildon and Stocking. [*c.* 1147 x 1186, with later interpolations].

Hiis testibus Rogero de Molbray, Hugone Malabisse, Hugone iuniore Malebisse, etc.

Copy: MS Dodsworth 94, fol. 31r–v, no. 41, which omits witnesses.

Pd: *EYF*, pp. 108–10, no. 4 (from MS Dodsworth 94, fol. 31r, with variants from the cartulary copy).

Dating: the disputes between the grantor and the monks and the departure of Roger de Mowbray on crusade.

Note: The *Historia Fundationis* of Byland records that Robert de Daiville was one of the knights of Roger de Mowbray who around 1147 came into conflict with the monks, and that after the resolution of the dispute agreements were reached (*Mon. Ang.* V, 351–2). It is likely that there was a written agreement, probably dating to shortly after 1147. However, the detailed boundary clauses make it likely that this charter has been interpolated; Clay suggests the time of the abbot of Byland's case against John de Daiville in 1224 (below, no. 487).

[fols 52v–53r]

487 *Final concord in the king's court in the presence of Martin of Pattishall, Thomas of Moulton, Stephen of Segrave, Thomas of Heydon, Robert of Lexington, Geoffrey le Sauvage and other justices, between Abbot Robert, plaintiff, through Ingelram his monk, and John de Daiville, defendant, concerning 80 acres of common pasture in Kilburn about which a plea of warranty has been made. John acknowledges and concedes to the abbot common pasture throughout the region of Kilburn for 600 sheep by the long hundred, with all their lambs until the time of separation, and pasture for 95 oxen, 2 bulls and 30 cows from the two abbey granges of Stocking and Wildon; the abbot and convent may use the pasture for the animals of both or either of the granges as they wish. John and his heirs reserve the right to have an enclosure for their oxen, horses and all other cattle in the field of Kilburn, that is the whole field of winter sowing* (hivernagium) *or the whole field of* Tramese *by view of the grangers of Wildon and Stocking, from the time of corn and hay harvest until St Martin (29 Sept.). After this time the abbot and his successors are to have common pasture in that field for the said cattle as in the other areas of the vill. Grant also by John of a road through the centre of Scencliffe Grange for driving 200 sheep from Stocking grange to the pasture of Coxwold and back without impediment. The abbot and convent are to hold this of John and his heirs in free alms, quit of all secular service. Pledge to warranty by John and his heirs. The concord is made saving to the abbot and convent all the matters contained in the charter of Robert de Daiville, John's father, which the abbot had on the day on which the agreement was reached. The abbot has received John and his heirs into all the* *good deeds and prayers offered at the house of Byland. All matters mentioned in Robert's charter which are treated in this fine are cancelled, and all things not mentioned there are reserved for the abbot and convent.* Westminster; three weeks from Easter, 8 Henry III [5 May 1224].

Marginal note: (in later hand) '8 H 3'.
Copies: PRO CP 25/1/262/17, no. 8; (abbreviated): MS Dodsworth 63, fol. 73v, from cartulary fol. 158v.
Pd: *Yorks. Fines 1218–31*, pp. 55–6 (from PRO copy).
Note: In 1222 the abbot appeared in court against John de Daiville, who failed to appear. The abbot appointed either Brother Nicholas de Stanford or Roger of London, his attorneys. A few months later, in Hilary term 1223, he appointed as his attorney his monk Engelram, or brother Reginald. See *Curia Regis Rolls*, X, 313–14; XI, 84, 87. At Michaelmas 1242 the abbot appeared in court against Robert de Daiville for not holding to a fine in the king's court at Westminster between Abbot Robert and John, Robert's father, concerning common pasture for 200 sheep and 76 oxen, 13 cows and 2 bulls, and a fine made in the king's court at York between the abbot and Robert himself concerning 2 fisheries in the Swale and a fishpond in Kilburn. The first of these is the above fine, and the second refers to no. 488 below (*Curia Regis Rolls*, XVII, 526).

[fol. 53r–v, old fol. 159]

488   *Final concord in the king's court in York in the presence of Roger Bertram, Robert de Ros, Adam de Novo Mercato, William of York, Jolland de Neville, itinerant justices, and other faithful men of the lord king then present, between Abbot Henry of Byland, plaintiff, and Robert de Daiville, defendant, through Robert de Munford, his attorney, concerning a fishery on the Swale about which a plea of warranty had been brought. Robert acknowledges the fishery to be the right of the abbot and convent, as the grant of Robert's father, John. He also acknowledges all the river Swale as far as mid-stream to be the right of the abbot as far as the abbot's land extends on the side of Fawdington. Robert grants for himself and his heirs that the abbot and his successors may strengthen a fishery on Robert's land in the region of Cundall above Fawdington mill without hindrance, that is, between the said mill and the water called* Lowebeck. *The fishery may have one bay 10 feet wide, without a net, and another 2 bays or one to fish, according to the wish of the abbot. Robert concedes that the abbot and his successors may strengthen, raise or repair the pond of the fishery as they wish on the land of Robert lying opposite Cams Head, that is, the Cams Head nearest opposite Wildon grange, with a sufficient way around the vivary to fish and draw nets on Robert's side of the land. The pond shall have at its head – if the abbot and convent so wish – 6 perches with a perch of 20 feet from the bottom of the valley across Robert's land towards Kilburn, and on the land of the abbot, as much as they wish. The abbot and his successors may assart as far as the* *water of the pond rises, in length and width between the pond and the road which leads from the abbey to Kilburn. If the water rises above the road the abbot and convent shall repair the road. Robert grants as much land and woodland as far as the ditch of the abbot lasts between the head of Kilburn and Ousey Carr, that is, as much as Juliana de Munford acquired of the abbey. The monks are to hold all this in free alms. In return for this grant, warranty, fine and agreement the abbot and convent quitclaim to Robert all right and claim in the covert* (coopertus) *of* Melclyve *(for Scencliffe Grange), that is, from the highway which comes from Thirsk by the straight boundaries between Osgoodby and Kilburn as far as the land of the vill of Hood and then by the brow of the hill below Hood Castle, and in all the covert on the west side as far as the said road from Thirsk, reserving a sufficient road in winter and summer for the abbot and his monks and his men, carts and horses, throughout Kilburn. If the animals of the abbot are found within the aforesaid boundaries they shall be returned to their own nearest pasture without hindrance. The abbot and convent also reserve all matters contained in the final concord between Abbot Robert and John de Daiville (no. 487). As a result of this concord the abbot shall not have the right of way which he was accustomed to have before the agreement between the exit of Osgoodby and Kilburn, as far as the covert lasts. Here Robert and his heirs shall make for them a sufficient way for their carts, both for the abbot, monks and men of Byland as for those of their granges.* York; Wed. after St Hilary [18 Jan.], 19 Henry III [1235].

Marginal note: (in later hand) '19 H 3'. There is a sketch showing the descent from 'Robert Deyvile sen' to 'John Deyvile' to 'Robert filius Iohannis Deyvile 19 H 3 35 H 3'.

Copy: PRO CP 25/1/263/28, no. 51.

Pd: Yorks. Fines 1232–1246, pp. 32–3 (from PRO copy).

Note: The king's justices Roger Bertram, Robert de Ros and William of York heard no. 397 above at Appleby in May 1235. The spelling 'Melclyve' for Scencliffe in nos 488, 489, 732, 760, may result from the confusion of the beaver-tailed capital S with capital M; see note to no. 39 above.

[fols 53v–54r]

489 *Final concord reached in the king's court before Silvester, bishop of Carlisle, Roger of Thirkleby, Hugh, abbot of Selby, Gilbert de Preston, and Adam de Hilton, itinerant justices and other faithful men of the lord king then present, between John de Daiville, plaintiff, and Henry, abbot of Byland, defendant, concerning 86 acres of woodland in Kilburn about which an assize of mort d'ancestor had been brought. The abbot acknowledges the 86 acres to be John's right, and has restored them to him. Moreover the abbot has conceded that John and his heirs may enclose the whole of their woodland*

of Rose Hill except for 60 acres of land and woodland, which are to remain the possession of the abbot and his successors. They may similarly enclose the whole of Holestorth *from the boundaries between Thirkleby and Kilburn as far as the meadows and ploughed lands belonging to Kilburn and Osgoodby. If the animals of the abbot or his successors cross within the woodland of Rose Hill and* Holestorth *through the default of enclosure they shall not be seized but may be reclaimed without hindrance. When the wood has been enclosed John and his heirs will maintain the enclosure so that the animals shall not stray, and if they do stray John and his heirs may drive them back without hindrance. For these concessions and acknowledgements John has granted to the abbot 60 acres of woodland in Rose Hill, that is 7 acres of wood lying nearest to the road next to the ditch of Ousey Carr towards the west, and 53 acres on the western side of the cultivated ground of the abbot in Wildon near the king's highway which runs from Coxwold towards Thirsk, which road is 50 feet wide. The abbot and his successors may enclose, assart, or do whatever they wish with the 60 acres. John also grants common pasture throughout Scencliffe Grange for all the flocks which they have in Wildon under the fine levied between Robert, former abbot of Byland, predecessor of Abbot [Henry] and John de Daiville, grandfather of the present John, whose heir he is, except that John may cut down a fourth part of the wood of* Melclyve *(for Scencliffe Grange) every fourth year and to enclose it if he wishes, so that the flocks of the abbot and his successors may not enter there. If they do so enter they shall not be impounded but may be redeemed. After the fourth year of cutting the enclosure shall be destroyed and the other three parts shall remain as pasture. Every fourth year John and his heirs shall enclose a fourth part of of the said wood if they wish, and the other three parts shall remain enclosed as pasture. John concedes for himself and his heirs that the abbot and his successors shall have their flocks at Osgoodby if they wish within the whole pasture of* Melclyve *and Kilburn, except the enclosure of Rose Hill and* Holestorth *which they ought to have in Wildon under the said fine between Abbot Robert and John de Daiville, grandfather of the present John. If they do not have oxen they may place cattle there if they wish without hindrance. The abbot and his convent are to hold all the above in free alms, quit of secular service. John pledges to warranty, saving to both parties articles not contained in this agreement but covered by the fine between Abbot Robert and John de Daiville as well as that between Abbot Henry and Robert de Daiville, John's father. The abbot has received John into all the good deeds and prayers of the church of Byland.*
York; octave of St Hilary 36 Henry III [20 Jan. 1252].

Marginal notes: (in later hand) on fol. 53v opposite line 2 of text, '36 H 3' and opposite line 22 of text, 'Iohannes Davile'; on fol. 54v a sketch shows the descent of

'Robertis Deyvile pater Iohannis' to 'Iohannes filius Roberti de Ayvil', to 'Robertus filius Iohannis Deyvile', to 'Iohannes filius Roberti Deyvile 36 H 3'.
Copy: PRO CP 25/1/264/43, no. 22 (damaged).
Pd (calendar): *Yorks. Fines 1246–1272*, pp. 57–8 (from PRO copy).

490 *Rubric: Confirmation by John de Daiville of the above.* [*c.* 1252 or 1278].

Note: There are two charters of John de Daiville copied from originals in St Mary's Tower: MS Dodsworth 91, fol. 102r–v, no. 51, a memorandum of a confirmation by John de Daiville of licence to have, in place of the 600 sheep with lambs, which they have of his predecessors in the pasture of Kilburn another 600 sheep called wethers ('multones'). Further grant that their tenants may use common pasture within their boundaries with free entry and exit as often as they wish to the grange of Stocking and Wildon. Test' domino Roberto de Hovyngham priore de Novoburgo, dominis Willelmo de Buscy, Willelmo Darel, militibus, Ricardo de Malebys, Willelmo Froste, Thoma de Etton, Willelmo de Stokesley, Willelmo Pledur et aliis. Byland; Mon. after St John *ante portam latinam* [9 May] 1278; MS Dodsworth 94, fol. 32r–v, no. 42, an inspeximus by John de Daiville of charters and chirographs made in the king's court and elsewhere by his predecessors. Hiis testibus domino Roberto de Hovingham priore de Novoburgo, dominis Willelmo de Buscy, Willelmo Darel militibus, Ricardo de Malebisse, Willelmo Frost, Thoma de Etton, Willelmo de Stokeslay, Ada de Eyvill, et Goscellino nepotibus meis et aliis. Byland; eve of the Assumption [14 Aug.] 1270.

[fol. 54v]
KILLERBY (TA0682), in the parish of Cayton and the wapentake of Pickering Lythe (NR). The charters contained in the cartulary are those of Richard son of Siward and his family, Siward having entered the religious life at Byland (no. 491). There is evidence of benefactions of three generations of the family (no. 493).

491 *Grant and confirmation in free alms, addressed to the archbishop of York and the whole chapter of St Peter (York) and all the sons of holy church, by Richard son of Siward of Killerby, to God and the monks of St Mary of Byland, of 2 bovates in Killerby. Further grant of another 4 bovates in the same vill of his fee, of which 2 were granted by his father Siward and 2 by his brother Ralph when the monks accepted them into the religious life. For the tofts of this land Richard has granted in exchange land in the west part of Killerby in his nearest* cultura *and because he was not able to grant enough in that* cultura *he has granted more in* Keldhill. *Moreover he has granted 1 acre of his land* sur le fulledaile *in* Keldehill. *He has granted all this to hold free from secular service, save for the performance of forinsec service. Pledge to warranty for himself and his heirs, for the salvation of their souls and of all their ancestors and heirs.* [1158 x 1181].

Hiis testibus Roberto secundo decano, Alano, Meynardo, Stephano de Roma canonicis Sancti Petri Eboraci, etc.

Pd: *EYC* XI, no. 194.

Dating: The first witness, on whose title see above, no. 442 note, and the death of Archbishop Roger de Pont L'Evêque, after which there was a vacancy until 1189. Stephen the Roman, canon of York, occurs 1164 x 1174, before 1173, and 1158 x 1181 (*Fasti York*, p. 129), and nos 225, 395, 594 and 1156. The common formula of the warranty clause suggests a date later rather than earlier in the period.

492 *Confirmation, addressed to the archbishop of York and the whole chapter of St Peter (York) and all the sons of holy mother church, by William son of Richard of Killerby, to God and the monks of St Mary of Byland, of 6 bovates in the region of Killerby, that is, 2 which the monks have of the grant of Siward his grandfather, 2 which they have of the grant of Ralph his uncle, and 2 of the grant of Richard his father as his charter (no. 491) witnesses. Grant and confirmation of the exchange which his father made for the tofts of the said land and 1 acre which he granted above* le fulledaile *of Keldhill. To hold of William and his heirs in free alms, quit of secular service as his father's charter witnesses, performing forinsec service as it pertains to the land. Pledge to warranty.* [late 12th cent.].

Hiis testibus Ricardo persona de Semar', Willelmo de Caytona, Henrico filio Henrici, etc.

Copy: MS Top. Yorks. e. 7, fos 121v–122r (old pp. 190–91), which omits 'etc' from the witness list, and continues: Willelmo de Angotebi, Roberto filio Willelmi de Hirtona, Roberto filio Simonis de Angotebi.

Dating: first witness. The copy in MS Top. Yorks. e. 7 has a note that 'this was made before 1236'.

493 *Confirmation in free alms, addressed to all the sons of holy mother church to whom the present charter shall come, by William son of Ralph the clerk of Killerby for himself and his heirs and assigns, to God and St Mary and the abbot and convent of Byland, of 6 bovates in the region of Killerby, of which they have 2 of the grant of Richard his great-grandfather, 2 of the grant of Siward, Richard's father, and 2 of the grant of Ralph, brother of Richard the donor's great-grandfather. Confirmation also of the exchange which his great-grandfather made (no. 491). To have and to hold of William and his heirs free from secular service. Pledge to warranty against the lords of Pickering, Seamer and Topcliffe and against all men and women, [against all demands for suit of court, wapentakes, scutages and all other customs and services belonging to the 6 bovates, with the exchange made with them for the tofts of the said 6 bovates and 1 acre on* Le Fuldays *of Keldhill. The donor has handed this charter to the abbot and convent, sealed with his seal.]* [day after All Saints [2 Nov.] 1270].

Text breaks off.

[Hiis testibus Thoma de Anlakby, Willelmo de Morepad, Willelmo de Cresaker, Waltero de Kayton, Willelmo de Hirton, Henrico de Osgotby, Bartholomeo de Scaklbi, Ricardo ad fontem de Dalton et aliis].

Copy: MS Dodsworth 91, fols 149v–150v, no. 125, in a later inspeximus of Walter of Killerby (27 Apr. 1390), from which the missing portions of the text, the witness list and date are supplied. The following folio also contained deeds relating to Killerby (MS Top. Yorks. d. 11, fol. 268v).

[1 folio lost, old fol. 161]

[fol. 55r, old fol. 162]

LAYSTHORPE (SE6378), in the parish of Stonegrave and wapentake of Ryedale (NR), lying 1½ miles to the NW of Stonegrave and less than a mile SE of Oswaldkirk. This section of the cartulary is of interest because of the way in which the abbey property can be seen to have developed from grants by small land holders, operating in concert with one another, and from grants in which husband and wife were associated. Charters of individuals of modest social status were attested by men of high standing.

494 *Grant and confirmation in free alms, addressed to all the faithful of Christ who will see or hear the present charter, by John de Cresacre, for the salvation of his soul and of his heirs and all his ancestors, to God and St Mary and the abbot and convent of Byland, of the homage and service of Adam de Vermelys and his heirs for 3 bovates and 1 acre with 2 tofts in the region and vill of Laysthorpe. To have and to hold free from secular service. Pledge to warranty. Sealed with the donor's seal.* [before 1301; probably mid. 13th cent.].

Hiis testibus dominis Galfrido de Upsall', Alano de Leek, Waltero de Staynesby, militibus, Iohanne de Blaby, Iohanne de Crauncewich, etc.

Copy: MS Dodsworth 91, fols 82v–83r, no. 24, which omits 'etc' in the witness list and continues: Thoma de Ettona, Hugone preposito de Laysthorpe, Willelmo filio Gamelli de Sutton, Sampsone clerico, Willelmo le Playdur, Rogero Pinkeney de Kyrkeby, Gilberto Cutt' et aliis.

Dating: John de Blaby was either the son of Amice and Stephen de Blaby, or their grandson, who died in 1301 and whose heirs were six daughters (*VCH NR* II, 47). John of Cranswick occurs in 1268 and Walter of Stainsby in 1284–5 and 1303 (*ibid.*, 88, 297). The first witness is therefore probably to be identified as Geoffrey of Upsall the elder who had been succeeded by 1284/5. Adam de Vermenles occurs in the mid 13th century (no. 495), and Alan of Leake witnesses before the late 1260s (nos 31, 121, 128, 129, 201, 509, 515, 616, 848, 852, 998, 1146). No. 494 is likely to date from the same period. Thomas de Etton, probably a member of the family of Etton of Gilling, is a frequent witness to Byland charters. There were clearly a number of members of the family with the name Thomas, and it is difficult to distinguish between them. Thomas de Etton and his wife Felicia were enfeoffed with land in Laysthorpe by the abbot and convent (nos 508–9 below).

Note: The rubric identifies the donor as John son of John de Cresacre.

495 *Grant and quitclaim, addressed to all the faithful in Christ who will inspect or hear the present writing, by Adam de Vermenles, with the assent and goodwill of Albreda (Aubrede) his wife, to God and St Mary and the abbot and convent of Byland, of the homage and service of Reginald de Hotton and his heirs for 2 bovates in Laysthorpe. Sealed with the seal of Albreda and with that of Adam. Pledge to warranty.* [*c.* 1240 x 1259].

Hiis testibus domino Rogero de Thurkilby iusticia domini regis, Ada de Hilton', Alano de Leek, militibus, Willelmo de Stokeseya clerico, etc.

Copy: MS Dodsworth 91, fol. 103r, no. 53, which omits 'etc' from the witness list and continues: Moyse serviente de Sutton, Gilleberto Chut, Philippo forestario, Willelmo filio Gamelli, et aliis.

Dating: The first witness was a clerk of William of Raleigh, chief justice *coram rege* (who became bishop of Norwich in 1239), before acting as a justice between *c.* 1240 and 1259 (Turner, *English Judiciary*, p. 217); he occurs in the cartulary in 1244, 1247, 1252 and 1258 (nos 489, 841, 905, 947, 1090, 1201). It is worth noting his attestation of a charter of a fairly minor individual.

Note: In 1266 the abbot of Byland brought a plea against Adam de Vermenles and Albreda his wife to warrant 2 messuages and 2 bovates in Laysthorpe: Baildon, *Monastic Notes*, I, 29.

496 *Rubric: Charter of Thomas de Anlacby concerning 1 bovate, 1 toft, 1 acre and 1 rood in the vill and region of Laysthorpe.* [mid 13th cent.].

Text: MS Top. Yorks. e. 9, fols 25v–26r (old pp. 24–5). Grant, addressed to all the <sons> of holy church, by Thomas de Anlackeby, to the church of Byland, of 1 bovate with a toft, 1 acre and 1 rood in Laysthorpe (MS Haysthorpe), that is, the bovate which John de Neuton gave with his daughter, Albreda (Aubrede), in marriage. Sealed with the donor's seal. Hiis testibus dominis Galfrido de Uppesal, Roberto de Sproxeton, domino Alano de Lek, militibus, Iohanne de Neuton, Henrico de Laton, Thoma de Etton, Iohanne Burdon, Sampsone de Laisthorp et aliis.

497 *Grant, addressed to all the sons of holy mother church, by Samson of Laysthorpe, to God and St Mary and the abbot and convent of Byland, of the homage and service of Roger son of Alexander of Ryton (Kirby Misperton) for 1 bovate in Laysthorpe which Roger formerly held of Samson and Emma,* *that is, 3s. annual farm, half received at St Martin in Winter (11 Nov.) and half at Whitsuntide, and forinsec service. The grant is made with the assent and goodwill of Emma his wife for the salvation of their souls and of all their ancestors and heirs and for 10 marks which the monks have given them in their great need. To have and hold of the donors and their heirs in fee alms, quit of secular service, to do there as they wish. Pledge to warranty. Sealed with Samson's seal and with Emma's seal.* [mid 13th cent.].

Hiis testibus dominis Willelmo de Wydevill, Willelmo de Stayngreve, Willelmo de Barton, militibus, Iohanne de Crauncewik', Thoma de Etton', etc.

Dating: see no. 505.

498 *Rubric: Quitclaim by William son of Roger of Carlton of 1 bovate in Laysthorpe with the homage and service of the said Roger son of Alexander.* [late 13th cent.].

Text: MS Dodsworth 91, fol. 96v, no. 43. Quitclaim, addressed to all the sons of holy mother church who will see or hear this writing, by William of Carlton son of Roger of Carlton, to God and St Mary and the abbot and convent of Byland, of 1 bovate in Laysthorpe with the homage and service of Roger son of Alexander of Ryton for 1 bovate and 1 toft in the same vill. Grant also of 3s. annual farm from the said bovate together with 3 acres and meadow in Laysthorpe. The grantor holds all this of the abbot and convent for 1 pound of white incense, as is contained in chirograph charters which he has of them and which he has surrendered. The monks are to do with this grant as they wish. Sealed with the donor's seal. Hiis testibus dominis Iohanne Ingram, Gaufrido de Uppesal, Willelmo filio eius, Willelmo de Barton, Iohanne de Iarkynvill, militibus, Iohanne de Stayngrive, Rogero Rabot, Roberto Barne, Thoma de Etton, Ada de Aynderby, et aliis. Also MS Top. Yorks. e. 9, fol. 26v (old p. 26).

499 *Rubric: Charter of John son of William son of Hugh of Laysthorpe concerning 12d. annual farm to be taken from Henry of Scackleton.*

500 *Rubric: Quitclaim by Hugeline Percehay of Roger son of Fulk formerly her villein with his family and chattels.*

[fol. 55v]

501 *Rubric: Chirograph of the same Hugeline concerning 1 toft in Laysthorpe rendering 2s. to her.*

502 *Rubric: Charter of John Burdon, John his son, Samson of Laysthorpe and others quitclaiming the said 2s.*

503 *Rubric: Quitclaim by Hugeline of Laysthorpe of Ralph son of William son of Fulk of Laysthorpe, her villein, and his family and chattels.*

504 *Rubric: Small chirograph of Ralph son of W[illiam] son of Fulk concerning ½ pound of wax to be paid yearly at St Andrew the Apostle (30 Nov.).*

505 *Rubric: Charter of Emma daughter of Hugeline of Laysthorpe concerning a toft and croft at the exit of the vill and various parcels of land. Confirmation of other lands and rents in the vill and region of Laysthorpe.* [1261 x 1263].
Text: MS Dodsworth 91, fol. 101v, no. 50. Memorandum that Emma of Laysthorpe, daughter of Hugeline of Laysthorpe, granted to God and St Mary and the abbot and convent of Byland, 1 toft and croft at the exit of the vill of Laysthorpe next to the cross, 1 selion in 'Ryskhow' towards Stonegrave, ½ acre in the field near the vill, 1 selion at 'Howsholme', 1 at 'Mylneholm' and 3 acres and 3 roods in the same *cultura* called 'Mylnholm', and 1 selion on 'Le Beryg' towards Oswaldkirk with the meadows lying adjacent. Grant also to the abbot and convent of 1 bovate nearest on the south to the 2 which Hugeline her mother formerly held, and which she and her husband, Samson of Laysthorpe, granted to the monks, and the homage and service of Roger son of Alexander of Ryton and his heirs on 1 bovate, and 3s. annual farm and forinsec service on the same, half at St Martin in Winter (11 Nov.) and half at Whitsuntide (no. 497). Grant also of her share of 2s. annual rent which the monks were accustomed to render to John Burdon and John his son, and to John of Laysthorpe formerly her husband and herself, and to Adam Vermenles and Albreda his wife. Testibus dominis Petro de Percy tunc vicecomite Ebor', Iohanne de Eyvill, Willelmo Malebys, Thoma de Colevill, Willelmo de Buscy, Willelmo de Stayngrave, Willelmo de Barton, militibus, Willelmo de Sproxton, Petro de Ros, Thoma de Etton, Waltero de London de Ampleforth, Iohanne Burdon, Willelmo le Pledour, Gilberto Cutter et aliis.
Dating: first witness.

506 *Rubric: Charter of Samson of Laysthorpe and Emma his wife concerning 1 bovate in Laysthorpe.* [1250s].
Text: MS Top. Yorks. e. 8, fol. 181r–v (old pp. 326–7). Grant, addressed

to all the sons of holy mother church present and future, by Samson of Laysthorpe and Emma his wife, to God and St Mary and the abbot and convent of Byland, of 1 bovate in Laysthorpe lying to the south of the 2 bovates which Lady Hugeline once held. What is lacking in the 2 bovates they will make up from the 7 acres which they hold of the abbot and convent there. To hold of them and their heirs and assigns with all liberties and appurtenances, with free entry and exit and all easements belonging to the land. As 1 bovate is of Emma's inheritance she has sworn on the gospels, for herself and her heirs, to make no further claim, under penalty of 5 marks. She places herself under the jurisdiction of the abbot of Peterborough. Sealed with their seals. Pledge to warranty. Hiis testibus domino Petro de Wakesand, Gaufrido tunc decano de Bulmer . . . de Blabi, Henrico de Thornetona, Iohanne de Burdun, Ada de Wermour, Willelmo filio Gamelli, Willelmo Holeghe et aliis. There is a sketch of a seal with the legend S. EMME FIL. IULIANE, and a note: 'first seal is wanting'. Emma was the daughter of Hugeline of Laysthorpe, and the name 'Juliana' in the sketch of the seal may be an error.

Note: Abbot John of Peterborough was justice in Yorkshire in the 1250s: as such he occurs in nos 548, 550, below. Adam de Wermour is probably Adam de Vermenlys (Vermelys).

507 *Chirograph charter, addressed to all the faithful of Christ who will see or hear the present charter, of Abbot Henry and the convent of Byland notifying that they grant and confirm to Thomas de Etton 2 bovates with two tofts in the region and vill of Laysthorpe, namely those bovates and tofts which William le Champiun otherwise William of Byland once held of the abbey. Thomas and his heirs are to hold the land for homage and service with all its easements inside and outside the vill, rendering 1 silver mark, half at Whitsuntide and half at St Martin in Winter (11 Nov.) for all service. The first payment is due at Whitsuntide 1268. Pledge to warranty. Sealed with the seals of both parties.* [1268].

Hiis testibus dominis Galfrido de Upsall, Thoma de Colvill', Willelmo de Buscy, Richero de Wausand', Thoma de Clarvaus, Willelmo de Barton', militibus, Petro de Stayngreve, etc.

Marginal note: B(aculus) ii, and (in a later hand) '1269'.
Copy: MS Dodsworth 91, fol. 102v, no. 52, which omits 'etc' from the witness list and continues: Willelmo de Sproxton, Iohanne de Blaby, Willelmo de Staynnesby, Roberto Barne de Gillinge, Waltero de Colton', Ada de Vermel<nes> et aliis.

508 *Chirograph charter, addressed to all the faithful of Christ who will see or hear the present charter, of Abbot H(enry) of Byland and the convent noti-*

fying that they grant and confirm to Thomas de Etton and Felicia his wife, for homage and service, 1 toft with croft at the exit of the vill of Laysthorpe near the cross, and 1 selion in Riskhow *towards Stonegrave and ½ acre in the same field near the vill, 1 selion in* Howstholm, *and 1 selion in* Milneholm *and 1 selion in* Le Berigh *towards Oswaldkirk, with the meadows lying next to the lands along the whole field of Laysthorpe, all of which lands the monks have of the grant of Emma of Laysthorpe daughter of the late Hugeline of Laysthorpe. Thomas and Felicia are to hold the lands with all their easements. If Thomas dies before Felicia, she is to hold all the above without hindrance for the rest of her life, saving her dowry and a third portion of Thomas's goods and chattels. They are to render 1 pound of cumin at Whitsuntide for all service. Pledge to warranty. One part of the chirograph, sealed with the abbey seal, is to remain in the hands of Thomas and Felicia, and the other, sealed with Thomas's seal, is to remain with the abbot and convent. [c. 1268].*

Hiis testibus dominis Richero de Wausand, Willelmo de Barton', militibus, Iohanne de Neuton', Waltero de Colton', etc.

Dating: as no. 507.

[fol. 56r, old fol. 163]

509 *Chirograph charter, addressed to all the faithful of Christ to whom this present writing shall come, of Abbot Henry and the convent of Byland notifying that they grant to Thomas de Etton for homage and service 3 bovates in the region and vill of Laysthorpe, 1 which they had of the grant of Thomas de Anlacby with a croft (no. 496), 1 with 2 tofts which Henry Bareth formerly held, and 1 with 1 toft which they had of the grant of Walter of Gilling with his body, and 1 toft which they had of the grant of the same Walter to complete the rent of 1 mark. Thomas is to hold the lands of the abbot and convent with all their easements and appurtenances, rendering yearly 15s. sterling, half at Whitsuntide and half at St Martin in Winter (11 Nov.) and 1 pair of spurs on Easter Day, and performing forinsec service. Thomas is not to sell or in any way alienate these 3 bovates and 5 tofts without the assent of the abbot and convent. Pledge to warranty. Sealed with the seal of both parties. [c. 1268].*

Hiis testibus dominis Galfrido de Upsal, Thoma de Colvyll, Roberto de Sproxton', Willelmo de Barton', Alano de Leek, militibus, etc.

Marginal note: (in later hand) '1268', '53 H 3'.
Dating: With reference to no. 507.

510 *Rubric: Chirograph of Roger de Hetona concerning 1 bovate in Laysthorpe and the homage of Roger son of Alexander of R<yton> and* concerning an annual farm of 3s., doing forinsec service and rendering a pound of white incense at Christmas.

511   Rubric: Chirograph of William son of Roger of Carlton concerning 3 acres and meadow in the vill and region of Laysthorpe; we receive nothing for this land.

512   Rubric: Chirograph of John de Bulmer concerning making suit at the court of the abbot and convent.

513   Rubric: Chirograph between the monks and Roger son of Fulk concerning 1 toft with appurtenances in Laysthorpe which Lady Hugeline granted; rendering to the abbot and convent 2s. and ½ pound of wax.
Marginal note: B(aculus) iii.

514   Rubric: Chirograph between the monks and Walter Percehay concerning 2 bovates with appurtenances which Walter of Gilling and Amice his wife conveyed to the monks for an annual farm of 1 mark.

515   Rubric: Transcript of John Burdon and his son, and Samson of Laysthorpe and Adam Vermenles concerning 2 bovates for homage and service in Laysthorpe. [c. 1230 x 1260].
Text: This is probably the charter copied from the original in St Mary's Tower in MS Dodsworth 91, fols 107v–108r, no. 61. Quitclaim, addressed to all the sons of holy mother church to whom the present writing shall come, by John Burdun and John his son, Samson of Laysthorpe and Emma his wife, and Adam de Vermelis and Albreda his wife, to God and St Mary and the abbot and convent of Byland, of 2s. annual rent which the abbot and convent render for a toft in Laysthorpe which they have of the grant of Hugeline. This quitclaim is made for the salvation of their souls and of their ancestors and heirs in free alms, free from service. If any of them wishes to bring a claim or plea, the abbot and convent are allowed without hindrance to enter and recognize as their own fee 2 bovates, 3½ acres, and 1 messuage in Laysthorpe which they have granted to the donors. Pledge to warranty. Sealed with their seals. Testibus domino Alano de Lek, Gaufrido decano de Bulemer, fratre Willelmo magistro de Monte, Rogero de Otrington, Ricardo de Thresk, Waltero de London, Willelmo filio Gamelli, Willelmo Holegh et aliis.
Dating: The first three witnesses attest together in the period 1231 x 1268 (no. 848); the second and the last two attest together in no. 506.
Note: A John Burdon occurs in Hovingham in 1298: VCH NR I, 482.

[fol. 56v]

LIBERTIES

This section contains the royal charters for Byland Abbey from Henry II to Richard II; these were evidently stored in the chest (*scrinium*), and nos 516–27 were marked with the letters A–L. These charters both confirmed lands granted to the abbey and granted liberties and exemptions.

516   *Rubric: Great confirmation of King Henry II of all lands granted to the monks or to be granted in the future. Copied in triplicate and marked with 'A'.*

517   *Notification by Henry [II], by the grace of God king of England, duke of Normandy and Aquitaine, and count of Anjou, to his archbishops, bishops, deans, earls, barons, justices, sheriffs, ministers, reeves of his towns and boroughs and seaports, and all the faithful of England and Normandy, that the abbey of Byland, the abbot, monks and the brethren serving God there, their lands, men and goods and possessions are under his protection. Wherefore the abbot and monks should hold their lands and goods, ecclesiastical and lay, freely, in woodland and plain, meadow and pasture, lands and waters, ponds and fisheries, marshes and forests, millponds and mills, tofts and crofts, roads and paths, and all other easements and customs. Freedom for themselves and their men in cities and towns, in markets and fairs, wherever they travel throughout England and Normandy and all his lands, from toll and pontage, passage, pedagium, lastage and from all gelds, danegeld, horngeld, scutage, hidage, carucage, shires, assizes, pleas, lawsuits, summonses, amercements and suits of shire, wapentake and tithing, and all common assizes and fines belonging to murder and theft, and from customary payments to sheriffs and their bailiffs, and all other aids, assarts, rewards, waste and pleas of waste, and from all secular service and demand. Grant also of liberty of their court over all their tenants, with soc and sac, tol and theam and infangantheof and utfangantheof and all forfeits pertaining to themselves, their lands and all their men, whether they are judged in their own court or elsewhere. The king prohibits them from being impleaded or having to answer concerning any holding except in the king's presence or before his chief justices. No-one is to injure the abbot and monks against their charters of liberty on pain of £10 penalty. The grant is made for the soul of King Henry his grandfather, for the salvation of his own soul, and those of his predecessors and successors.* Westminster; [14 Dec. 1175 x 6 Sept. 1181].

Testibus Ricardo Wynton', Galfrido Eliensi, Iohanne Norwic'

episcopis, magistro Waltero de Coust', magistro Iohanne Cumin, Ricardo de Lucy, Willelmo filio Radulfi, Reginaldo de Curtenay, Willelmo de Laumal, Thoma Basset apud Westmonasterium.

Pd: *Mon. Ang.* V, 343–4.

Dating: The consecration of John of Oxford as bishop of Norwich and the election of John Cumin to the bishopric of Dublin.

Note: The rubric notes that this charter has not been copied, and therefore must be kept very carefully; this may mean that the charter from which the text was transcribed into the cartulary was the only copy preserved at the abbey. The rubric further states that it was marked with 'B'. As a full copy was entered in the cartulary (unlike no. 516) this must mean that there was no other copy of the confirmation. No. 516 had been copied three times, and was not entered in the cartulary.

518 *Rubric: Protection of the same King Henry [II] in which he forbids them to be impleaded; and freedom of suit of the shire court.* [1154 x 1189].

519 *Rubric: Charter of the same [King Henry II], addressed to the sheriffs and ministers of the whole of England and to the keepers of the ports, concerning freedom from toll, pontage, passage etc. Copied and marked with 'D'.* [1154 x 1189].

520 *Rubric: Confirmation by the same [King Henry II] of Asby and grant of Bretherdale, rendering to him 6s. Marked with 'E'.* [1154 x 1189].

Text: No. 520 may refer to the text copied into the cartulary at no. 568 below. There is an abbreviated charter of Henry II relating to Moreville's grants in Asby and Bretherdale in MS Dodsworth 63, fol. 66v: Confirmation by King Henry [II], son of the Empress, of all the land in Asby which Hugh de Moreville granted. In this he grants and confirms the whole of Bretherdale. 'Ista confirmatio duplicatur sub diverso tenore unde in una carta eiusdem domini regis bene et expresse specificantur mete et divise de Bridesdale' (? no. 521).

521 *Rubric: Confirmation by the same [King Henry II] of the said Asby and 3 tofts in York. Marked with 'F'.* [1154 x 1189].

522 *Rubric: Confirmation by the same [King Henry II] of all the lands which Torphin son of Robert, Walleve de Berford, and Robert son of Torphin etc. granted in Warcop. Copied and marked with 'G'.* [1154 x 1189].

523 *Rubric: Confirmation by the same [King Henry II] of the grant of William de Wyville of land in Thorpe (le Willows) and other lands which have been granted. Marked with 'H'.* Clarendon [1155 x 1172].

Text: MS Dodsworth 7, fol. 105r. Notification by Henry II, king of England, duke of Normandy and Aquitaine and count of Anjou, addressed to his archbishops, bishops, justices, earls, barons, sheriffs, ministers and all his faithful of England, of his confirmation to God and the abbey of St Mary of Byland and the monks of the Cistercian order serving God there, for the salvation of his soul and of his wife, and for the soul of his grandfather, King Henry, and of all his predecessors, of the grant of William de Wyville, that is, of Thorpe (le Willows) as his charter attests. The monks are to hold the land, and their grants given by other men, freely, with sac and soc and toll and team and infangentheof and utfangentheof. They are to be quit of themantala and danegeld and secular pleas. Testibus Ricardo de Camvill, <Simone> filio Petri, Iohanne Malduit apud Claredun.

Dating: Before the introduction of the *dei gratia* clause. See Nicholas Vincent, 'The Charters of Henry II: The Introduction of the Royal *Inspeximus* Revisited', in Michael Gervers, ed., *Dating Undated Medieval Charters* (Woodbridge, 2000), pp. 97–120.

524   Rubric: *Confirmation by the same [King Henry II] of the land which Amfrey de Chauncy granted in Skirpenbeck. Marked with 'I'.* Poitou [*c.* 1166 x 1172].

Text: BL MS Egerton 2827 (Easby cartulary), fols 256v–257r (from where printed in *EYC* II, no. 837). Notification by Henry II, king of the English, duke of Normandy and Aquitaine and count of Anjou, addressed to the archbishop of York, and to his barons, justices, sheriffs, and ministers, and to all his faithful of Yorkshire, of his confirmation of the grant of land in Skirpenbeck made by Amfrey de Chauncy, as his charter attests (no. 1156). Testibus Ricardo de Humez conest', Ricardo de Lucy et Willelmo de Caynco apud Pictaviam.

Dating: Farrer's dating to *c.* 1160 x 1167 is not explained. Amfrey succeeded to Skirpenbeck *c.* 1164. Henry left England in Mar. 1166, and the *dei gratia* clause was introduced in 1172.

525   Rubric: *Charter of commendation concerning the common laws of England, granted by King John and called Runnymede.*
Note: This refers to Magna Carta.

526   Rubric: *Confirmation by King Richard [I] of all the lands which the monks have or may have in the future, and of various liberties which he granted. There is no copy of the charter and it must be kept carefully. Marked with 'K'.*

[fol. 57r, old fol. 164]
A note at the head of the folio states that the monks had no general
charter of confirmation of their lands and liberties from King John.

[fol. 57r–v]
527   *General confirmation by King Henry [III], by the grace of God king of
England, lord of Ireland, duke of Normandy and Aquitaine and count of
Anjou, addressed to all his archbishops, bishops, abbots, priors, earls, barons,
sheriffs, ministers, and bailiffs, and all his faithful, to <the abbey of Byland>
and the monks serving God there in perpetuity, for the salvation of his soul
and the souls of his ancestors and heirs, of all the donations written below, as
confirmed by his grandfather, Henry II, and his uncle, Richard I, namely, the
abbey of Byland, with granges, lands and possessions, specifying: Old
Byland, Murton, Snilesworth, Cam, Oldstead, Thorpe (le Willows), Wildon,
Rose Hill, Osgoodby, Sutton and its appurtenances, Bagby, Thorpe near
Thirsk (Thorpefield) with pasture in Moskwith, Fawdington with moor and
pasture, Boscar, Scackleton, Catton with lands, meadow and pasture in
Skirpenbeck, Deepdale with lands in Osgodby, Cayton, Killerby and
Scarborough, Sledmere, Bentley with lands and pasture in Denby and Wind
Hill,* Merschagh *with lands in Whitley and Bradford Dale, the granges of
Bleatarn, Asby and Shap, with lands in Hardendale, Bretherdale,
Borrowdale, Fawcett Forest, Warcop, and of all the pasture and wood they
have in Nidderdale, and pasture in Kirkby Malzeard, Thirsk, Thirkleby,
Islebeck, Ampleforth, Cave, Ottringham, and land in York and Clifton with
lands and meadow in Thorpe near York,* Gayterigg *with a fishery and lands
in Acklam, Marton, Stainsby, Hovingham and lands in Baxby, Rillington,
and Bolton (on Swale), with all appurtenances, sheepfolds, houses, buildings, men, rents, servants, lands, meadows and pastures, woodland and
plain, heathland, millponds, water, ponds, fisheries, mills, saltpans, forests,
tofts and crofts, roads and paths, entries and exits, and all other possessions,
liberties and customs, as contained in the charters or chirographs of the
grantors. Grant of free transit of bridges and across the sea throughout his
lands. Grant of freedom of toll in towns and markets, crossings and bridges,
in seaports and all places throughout his land, and of toll, pontage, passage,
lastage, and all gelds, danegeld, hornegeld, scutage, assizes, pleas, lawsuits,
summonses, amercements, suits of wapentake, tithing, and those pertaining
to murder and theft, and aids to sheriffs and bailiffs, custodies, armies,
castleworks, walls, ditches, bridges, and causeways, and wardpenny,
averpenny, tithingpenny, hengwith, flemwith, blodwite, leirwite, flemes-
frith, grithbreche, forestall, hamsoken, haymfayr, frankpledge, tallage,
carriage, pannage and other exactions that belong to the king, and common*

assarts, rewards, wastes, pleas of the forest and all secular exactions, and sac and soc, toll and team, infangenthef and utfangenthef. All pleas concerning the abbot and monks are to be heard by the justices in the county of York and pleaded at their manor of Sutton (under Whitestonecliffe) within the liberty of the abbot and convent in the same way as in the liberty of St John of Beverley, and within the county of Westmorland at Warcop. By the king's hand. Windsor; 20 Feb. 31 Henry III [1247].

Hiis testibus [Ricardo] comite Cornubie fratre nostro, Ricardo de Clara, comite Gloucest' et [Hereford'] Petro [de Saband'], Radulfo filio Nicholai, etc.

Pd (calendar): *Cal. Ch. R.* I, 314.

Dating: obscured here, but supplied from the copy recited in no. 543, as are the obscured portions of the witness list, which there continues: Bertramo de Cryoll, Paulino Peymer, Roberto de Mustegros, Ricardo de Grey, Iohanne de Grey, iusticiario Cestr', Bartholomeo Peche, Roberto Walerand, Galfrido Childwith et aliis. The word 'Hereford' is supplied from Oxford, Bodleian Library Douce charter 25, on which see note below.

Note: The rubric calls this the great confirmation, confirming all the grants and confirmations by the king's grandfather, Henry II, and uncle, Richard I. It further notes that this was copied four times and sealed with the old seal. The rubric is followed by the letter L. The witness Paulinus Peymer, who appears as Paulinus Peiner or Peuier in no. 528, is Paulinus Peuire (Peyur), who occurs in *Pipe Roll 27 Henry III*, pp. 112, 290, 293, 301–2 (1241–2). On 23 Feb. 1247 the monks paid for the enrolment of the king's confirmation of the charters of his grandfather and uncle: *Cal. Cl. R. 1242–1247*, p. 501. A charter of Henry III (Oxford, Bodleian Library Douce charter 25), taking the abbot and convent into his special protection, has the same place, date and witness list as no. 527 and as the text recited in no. 543. There is no copy in the charter rolls.

[fol. 57v]

528 *Grant by King Henry [III], by the grace of God king [of England, lord of] Ireland, duke of Normandy and Aquitaine and count of Anjou, addressed to his archbishops, [bishops], abbots, priors, counts, barons, justices, sheriffs, provosts, ministers and bailiffs, to Henry, abbot and the convent of Byland and their successors, of free warren in all his demesne lands outside the bounds of the royal forest. No-one is to enter the warren to flee there, or to take anything belonging to the warren without the assent of the abbot, on forfeit of £10 to the king. By the king's hand.* [Windsor; 5 June 1246].

Hiis testibus Petro de Sa[bundia, Willelmo de Eboraco preposito Beverl'], Iohanne Hansello (*sic*) cancellario Sancti Pauli London', Radulfo filio N[icholai, Bertrammo de Cryoil, Paulino] Peuier', Iohanne de Lexyngtona, etc.

Pd (calendar): *Cal. Ch. R.* I, 294.

Copy: MS Top. Yorks. d. 11, fol. 251r (old p. 439), from which the readings in square brackets are supplied. This copy correctly reads 'Mansello' for the third witness, omits 'etc' and continues: Roberto de Muscegros, Richardo de Clifford, Galfrido de Childewyk et aliis. John Maunsell became chancellor of St Pauls, London, in 1243, and his last occurrence was in 1261 (*Fasti London*, p. 26). The cartulary text is faded, and of the date only the regnal year, 30 Henry III, is visible.

Note: On 4 June 1246 the monks offered 50 marks for the king's confirmation of certain lands and liberties, and the king ordered his barons of the Exchequer to acquit them of payment: *Cal. Cl. R. 1242–1247*, p. 429.

529   Rubric: *Charter of King Henry III under his new seal [extending the abbey liberties and removing the justices from Sutton] to Clifton. [? West-minster; 13 Nov. 56 Henry III [1271]].*

Copy of rubric: MS Top. Yorks. d. 11, fol. 269r (old p. 503). The cartulary copy is faded.

Note: It is possible that this refers to *Cal. Ch. R.* II, 178, an inspeximus and renewal 'under the seal now in use' of the king's charter of 20 Feb. 1247 (no. 527). By this charter the king's justices, who had been accustomed to sit in the abbot's court at Sutton under Whitestonecliffe, were ordered to sit from henceforth in the abbot's manor of Clifton. This location, just outside York, would have been more convenient for the justices. No. 544 below, a list of the claims to liberties made by Byland, includes a reference to the removal of the court to Clifton.

530   Rubric: *Two letters concerning merchandise; sealed with the half seal [cum pede sigilli] . . . against the visit of aliens. Look . . . 1326.*

Note: This may refer to the letter, dated 20 July 20 Edward II (1326) addressed to the sheriff of Yorkshire, taking all foreign merchants under the king's protection, but forbidding the entry of any merchant from France, except from Flanders and Brittany: see Rymer, *Foedera*, II, 162.

531   Rubric: *Confirmation of King Edward II of the grant of Adam of Ruston of 2s. annual rent from Scarborough [per processum legis]. Look as above in the royal chest (in scrinio R.). [5 June 1309].*

Pd (calendar): *Cal. Pat. R. 1307–1313*, p. 161.

Dating: The rubric gives the regnal year, 2 Edward II, only. The full date is supplied from the patent roll. This was a licence for alienation in mortmain by Master Adam of Ruston of a yearly rent of 2s. in Scarborough. No. 1217 below is the grant by Adam of Ruston of a rent of 2s. from his tenement in Scarborough.

[fols 57v–58r]

532   *Notification in letters patent by King Edward [III], king of England, lord of Ireland and duke of Aquitaine, to all to whom the present writing shall come, that his father, Edward [II], had by letters patent granted licence to acquire lands etc. up to the annual value of £20 to hold notwithstanding the Statute of Mortmain. The king grants licence to Richard de Allerton of York to alienate to the abbot and convent 1 messuage in Bootham, to John son* of Henry of Clifton to alienate 1 messuage in the same, to William de Quiherd to alienate 1 acre in Thorpe Underlees [Thorpefield], all of which are not held in chief and which are valued at 27s., as found by inquisition of the king's escheator beyond the Trent, Simon de Grymmesby, which was returned to the chancery. These lands are to be held in partial fulfilment of the £20, saving the services due to the capital lords of the fees. York; 16 Aug. 1 Edward [III] [1327].

Teste me ipso.

Note: The rubric called this *allocatio Edwardi secundi post Conquestum*, and in the text neither King Edward is identified. However, it is clear from *Cal. Pat. R. 1327–1330*, p. 146, dated 16 Aug. 1327, that the king who granted this licence for alienation was Edward III not Edward II. The attribution to Edward II in the rubric seems to have been an error on the part of the compiler of the cartulary, an error apparently repeated in no. 533. The calendar has the reading 'le Quilter' for 'de Quiherd'.

[fol. 58r, old fol. 165]

533   *Rubric: Licence from King Edward [III] to have a boat, granted by Richard, late count of Poitou and Cornwall, on the River Ouse between Boroughbridge and York.* [9 Mar. 1328].

Note: A note states that the charter was 'in scrinio' (in the chest). The rubric describes this as a licence from Edward II, and the date is given as his second regnal year; however, it is clear from *Cal. Pat. R. 1327–1330*, p. 249, dated 9 Mar. 1328, that the king who issued this licence was Edward III not Edward II. See also no. 532. The original grant was made by Richard, earl of Cornwall and king of the Romans, the younger son of King John, who died in 1272. There is a rubric for this document at no. 287 above, in the York section of the cartulary.

534   *Letters patent of King Edward [II], by the grace of God king of England, lord of Ireland, and duke of Aquitaine, addressed to all to whom the present writing shall come, granting licence, for himself and his heirs, for his beloved in Christ the abbot and convent of Byland to appropriate the church of Rillington, which is in the monks' advowson, and convert it to their own uses. This grant is made without hindrance by him or his heirs notwith-standing the statute of Mortmain.* Newburgh; 5 Nov. 10 Edward II [1316].

Teste meipso.

Copy: MS Top. Yorks. e. 8, fol. 140v (old p. 245).
Pd (calendar): *Cal. Pat. R. 1313–1317*, p. 560.
Note: For the appropriation of Rillington church see below, nos 971–87. There is a rubric for no. 534 at no. 971.

535 *Rubric: Licence from King Edward II to acquire lands to the value of £20. Look under the heading 'Ampleforth'.*
Note: An interlineation, which seems to relate to this entry, notes that it was by writ under the privy seal. For damaged portions of the cartulary to which this rubric refers see above, nos 14–17; see also *Cal. Pat. R. 1317–1321*, p. 322, a general licence to acquire lands in mortmain, dated 20 Mar. 1319.

536 *Rubric: Charter of King Edward II concerning various liberties.*
Note: It is possible that this refers to the inspeximus and confirmation (dated at York, 22 Mar. 1318) of Henry III's charter of 13 Nov. 1271, confirming his charter of 20 Feb. 1247 (no. 527): *Cal. Ch. R.* III, 406.

537 *Rubric: Grant and confirmation of liberties by King Edward III. Look in the royal chest.* [30 May 1359].
Pd (calendar): *Cal. Ch. R.* V, 159. This is an inspeximus of royal charters of 1247, 1271 and 1318. The regnal year (33E/20F Edward III) only is given in the rubric.
Note: It is noted that there is only one copy ('simplex habetur').

538 *Rubric: Licence from King Edward III to accept lands in Ampleforth notwithstanding the Statute [of Mortmain] with the whole legal process and circumstances. It is copied out under the heading 'Ampleforth'.* 39 Edward III [25 Jan. 1365 x 24 Jan. 1366].
Note: See *Cal. Pat. R. 1364–1367*, p. 85, for licence dated 4 Feb. 1365 for alienation in mortmain by John de Salesbury, vicar of Ampleforth, and Richard of Cundall, in satisfaction of 40s. of the £20 yearly the monks are allowed to acquire, of 1 messuage, 8 tofts, 4 bovates, 20 acres and ½ acre of meadow in Ampleforth. For damaged documents in the Ampleforth section, see above, nos 12, 14, 15. Above the first line of this rubric and bracketed with it is a note to look in the chest.

539 *Rubric: Inspeximus by King Edward III, under the great seal, of the inquisition held at Howden into the right of the lord king to present to a moiety of Bubwith church. In favour of the monks.* Westminster [15 May 1370].
Pd (calendar): *Cal. Pat. R. 1367–1370*, pp. 408–9.
Note: The rubric here gives the date only by the regnal year, 44 Edward III. The inquisition was held at Howden on 22 Apr. 44 Edward III [1370] before Thomas de Musgrave, escheator, and 12 named jurors who swore that the king had no right of presentation.

[fol. 58r–v]
540 *Confirmation in letters patent by King Edward [III], king of England and France, and lord of Ireland, addressed to all to whom these present letters shall come, to his beloved in Christ the abbot and convent of Byland,*

of a moiety of the church of Bubwith which is appropriated to them. Westminster; 18 April, 45E/32F Edward III [1371].
Teste meipso.

Pd (calendar): *Cal. Pat. R. 1370–1374*, p. 65.

[fol. 58v]
541 *Rubric: First confirmation by King Richard II of various liberties.* [Westminster; 1 Feb. 1378].

Pd (calendar): *Cal. Pat. R. 1377–1381*, p. 119, an inspeximus dated at Westminster 1 Feb. 1378, of the royal charters of 1247, 1271, 1318 and 1359. Note: The rubric gives the regnal year, 1 Richard II, only.

542 *Rubric: Licence from the same King Richard [II] to create a park.* [Westminster; 5 Feb. 1380].

Pd (calendar): *Cal. Pat. R. 1377–1381*, p. 433, a licence at the request of Henry de Percy, lord of Northumberland, for the monks to enclose 100 acres of land and pasture adjacent to the abbey and not within the boundaries of the forest, in order to create a park. The rubric gives the regnal year, 3 Richard II, only.

[fols 58v–60r]
543 *Inspeximus with clause 'licet' by King Richard [II], by the grace of God king of England and France, and lord of Ireland, addressed to his archbishops, bishops, abbots, priors, dukes, earls, barons, knights, justices, sheriffs, reeves, bailiffs, ministers, and his other faithful, of letters patent dated 1 Feb 1 Richard II (no. 541) confirming the charter granted to the abbot and convent of the church of St Mary of Byland, by Edward III (no. 537), reciting the confirmation by King Edward II (no. 536?) of the charter of Henry III (no. 527, recited). The abbot and convent have petitioned the king, claiming under royal charters that from time immemorial they have received all goods and chattels of felons attainted or outlawed within their lands, that they have their own coroner and other franchises in their lands. These are granted by the king. Given in the hand of the king.* Westminster; 7 May 16 Richard II [1393].

Hiis testibus venerabilibus patribus W. Cantuar' totius Anglie primate, Thoma Ebor' Anglie primate cancellario nostro, archiepiscopis, W. Wynt', I. Sarum thesaurario nostro episcopis, Iohanne duce Aquit' et Lancastr', Edmundo duce Ebor', Thoma duce Glouc', avunculis nostris carissimis, carissimo fratre nostro Iohanne de Holand', Huntynd camerario nostro, Willelmo Sarum comitibus, Ricardo le Scrope, Thoma de Percy, senescallo hospitii nostri, Edmundo de Stafford', custode privati sigilli nostri et aliis.

Pd (calendar): *Cal. Ch. R.* V, 335.

Note: This was under the privy seal. There is a note at the foot of the folio that this was enrolled in the memoranda of the Exchequer among the records of Michaelmas Term 17 Richard II by the Lord Treasurer's Remembrancer; for this see PRO E 368/166, mm 7r–d, headed: carta abbatis et conventus ecclesie beate Marie de Bellalanda de diversis libertatibus eis per regem et progenitores suos concessos irrotulatos. The cartulary rubric calls this 'nova concessio sive ratificatio eiusdem Ricardi secundi de libertatibus nostris in specialiter etc'. The first four witnesses are William Courtenay, archbishop of Canterbury, Thomas Arundel, archbishop of York, William of Wykeham, bishop of Winchester, and John Waltham, bishop of Salisbury.

[fols 60v–61r]

CLAIMS OF THE LIBERTY OF BYLAND. This section comprises 34 documents and rubrics that relate to the Liberty of Byland and uphold claims to various liberties and exemptions. It begins with a glossary of legal terms. The inclusion of this document seems to be related to the abbot's claims (Easter Term 1294), made when, summoned to answer to the king *quo warranto*, he claimed to have gallows in Sutton under Whitestonecliffe; free warren in all his demesne lands in Sutton and Bagby, Marderby, Osgodby, Wildon, Stocking, Old Byland, Murton, Snilesworth, Scackleton, Thorpe le Willows, Wilsden, Wind Hill, Bentley, Denby, 'Whitacres', Thorpefield, Cam, Angram, Deepdale, Catton and Felixkirk; infangentheof and utfangentheof; return of the king's writs; the right to have a coroner; his own amercements and those of his men amerced in the king's courts, amercements for the escape of thieves; waifs; deodands; chattels of his fugitive men and of condemned felons; amends of breaches of the assize of ale in the above places and also Fawdington, Thornaby, Otterington, Laysthorpe and Skirpenbeck; freedom for himself and his men of the said places from tolls, pontage, carriage, pannage, common fines and amercements of the county and suits of county and wapentake courts; to plead pleas of withernam; that the king's justices in eyre and those holding assizes, should plead at the abbot's manor at Clifton all pleas concerning the abbot and his men (*Yorkshire Hundred and Quo Warranto Rolls*, ed. Barbara English, YASRS, 151 (1996 for 1993 and 1994), pp. 248–50). On this occasion the charters of Henry III of 5 June 1246 (no. 528 above, concerning free warren) and 13 Nov. 1271 (no. 529 above, concerning the extension of the abbey liberties and the removal of the justices from Sutton to Clifton) were displayed. For an earlier summons relating to the abbot's claim to have his own coroner, gallows, return of writs, estreats, pleas of withernam, amends of breach of the assize of bread and ale, see *ibid.*, pp. 178–9. Much of this section of the cartulary relates to *quo warranto* proceedings.

544 *Claims of the liberty of the monastery of Byland, with an explanation of certain words* (clam' libertatis monasterii de Bell' cum declaratione quorundam vocabulorum). **De theloneo:** *The abbot claims that he and his men are quit of the payment of toll in all markets, and on all goods bought and sold.* **Item de pontagio:** *They are free from giving aid towards the repair of bridges, and of passage and pedage.* **Item de lestagio:** *They are free from certain customs exacted at fairs and markets.* **Item de** omnibus **geldis, danegeldis:** *They are quit of all geld and danegeld, that is from certain customs at one time levied against the Danes in England.* **Item hornegeldis:** *They are quit of horngeld, that is free from the custom exacted by tallage throughout the land, that is on horned beasts.* **Item de scutagiis et de hidagiis:** *They are quit of scutage and hidage, that is free if the lord king taxes the whole land by hides.* **Item de carucagiis**: *They are quit of carucage, that is free if the lord king taxes the whole land by ploughs.* **Item de schiris, assis', placitis, querelis, summonitionibus, misericordiis, sectis com(itatus), wapentak':** *They are quit of shires, assizes, pleas, lawsuits, summonses, amercements, suits of county court and wapentake, that is free from suit at the hundred which is also called the wapentake.* **Item de sectis trithing(orum) et de omni iure et communi assisa et de pecunia que ad murdrum et latrocinium pertinet et de auxiliis vicecom(itum) et ballivorum suorum et de omnibus ad eos pertinent(ibus) et de omnibus auxiliis aliis et custodiis exercitibus operationibus castellorum murorum vallorum vivariorum stagnorum pontium calcearum et aliarum clausurarum:** *They are quit of the suit of tithings, and of all common assizes, fines for murder and theft, the aids of sheriffs and their bailiffs, and all other aids, custodies, military service, repair of castles and walls, ditches and millponds, bridges and causeways.* **Item de wardepeny:** *They are quit of the custom of* wardescam. **Item de averpeny:** *They are quit of averpenny, that is, giving pence for the lord's herds.* **De thetingpeny:** *They are quit of tithingpenny, that is giving pence or customary payment to the reeve of the hundred.* **Item de hengwith. Item de flemewith:** *They are free from amercements for harbouring wrongdoers, and they are to hold pleas in their own court and have the amercements proceeding from them.* **Item de blodewite:** *They are quit of amercements for the shedding of blood, and they are to hold pleas in their court and have the amercements proceeding from them.* **Item de leirewite:** *They may take amercements and compensation from one who takes a villein woman without licence.* **Item de flemfrith:** *They may take* *the chattels or amercements of a fugitive.* **Item de grithbreck:** *that is the breaking of the king's peace, because 'grith' in English is 'pax' in Latin and 'pees' in French* (romane). **Item de forstall:** *that is they are quit of amercements of cattle taken within their lands, and they are to hold pleas in their court.* **Item de hamsoken:** *that is they are quit of amercements for the violent entry of houses, against the peace of the lord king. They are to hold pleas concerning this crime in their own court.* **De haymfare et de francopleg', tallagiis, cariagiis, pannagiis et de omnibus aliis occasionibus que ad ipsum regem pertinent et de omnibus assign', rewardiis, vastis, et placitis foreste et de omni servitio et exactione seculari:** *that is of hamfare, frankpledge, tallage, carriage, pannage and all other taxes which belong to the king, and all assarts, regards, wastes, and pleas of the forest, and all secular service and demand.*

The abbot claims by the same charter to have liberty of his court over his tenants, with **soke,** *that is suit from his men in court according to the custom of the kingdom;* **sac,** *that is pleas and compensation from his men in his court;* **toll** *(concerning which see above, under 'toll');* **team,** *that is they have all the produce of their villeins with the households and chattels wherever they may be in England, except that if any villein shall stay free for a year and a day in any town with a charter and shall have been received into a gild, he shall remain free;* **infangentheof,** *that is that men taken on his demesne or in his fee for theft shall be judged in his court;* **utfangentheof,** *that is that thieves taken outside his land shall be returned to his court and judged there.*

Item omnimoda forisfacturam, *that is all forfeit of themselves and their lands and men wherever they shall be judged, whether in the king's court or in another, and that they may have all their goods and possessions freely as any church on the king's lands.*

The abbot claims by the same charter that all pleas determined or to be determined both in the presence of itinerant justices and justices assigned to hold an assize touching the abbey, the monks or their men, within the county of York, shall be heard in his manor of Clifton outside York, which is in his liberty, as in the liberty of St John of Beverley. Westminster 13 Nov. 56 (Henry III, 1271, no. 529).

The abbot *claims by virtue of a clause relating to the liberty of Beverley aforesaid and particularly by a charter of the lord king concerning flemfrith, return of writs, pleas of prevention of distress* (vetiti namii), *to have his own coroner, prison and measures, custody of thieves, gallows, the right to seize waif (masterless men), right of wreck, deodand, the chattels of fugitives and felons. See the gloss to this text, that is, that they may take chattels or amercements of a fugitive man.*

The abbot claims to have free warren in all his demesne lands outside the bounds of the king's forest, with all liberties belonging to the same, so that no-one can enter or take what belongs to the free warren without the assent of the abbot, on penalty of £10 forfeit to the lord king. This is claimed under the charter granted at Westminster 5 June 30 Henry III (1246, no. 528).

See the claims of the archbishop of York about the liberty of Beverley as evidence of our liberties.

Articles (capitula) *pertaining to this word:* de francoplegio vid. in primis: *If all free tenants come as they are summoned.*
If anyone is in the Liberty who now impleads another outside the Liberty.
If any malefactor is summoned for theft or fire or robbery or any other crime against the peace.
If any receiver (receptator) *shall be such as etc.*
If anyone shall be found to counterfeit money or clip coin.
If blood is shed by anyone.
If any encroachment shall take place in the Liberty.
If any road should be obstructed or . . . etc.
If anything is turned off course.
If measures are as they should be, as in gallons, bushels, ullage (shortfall of liquid in a cask), measures of the mill.
If a butcher sells against the assize.
If the assize of bread and ale is kept.
If anyone brews against the assize.
If any malefactors in parks, fisheries, or warrens, or any other lands or waters.
If there is a suit of court all who ought to be present should be present.
If there are ale testers how they should fulfil their office.
Concerning ministers: how they should conduct themselves in their offices.
Concerning villeins who remain outside the Liberty.
Concerning deodands of the chattels of felons and fugitives.
Concerning houses pulled down or built to the harm or injury of anyone.
Concerning seizure of wreck and waif.
Concerning entry of a customary tenant and all forfeits.
According to some frankpledge is called 'skirresterne' *or* 'lyte'.

Articles pertaining to the crown of the lord king.

Concerning hue raised and not followed as ordered by the justice.
Concerning a wife or daughter taken by force against the peace of the lord king.

Concerning backflows (from mill dams) other than they ought to be or were accustomed to be, to the harm etc.

Concerning those who do not have a right of way as they ought to have or were accustomed to have.

Concerning assizes not kept, as in ale, ells, measures etc.

Concerning evildoers in fisheries and parks.

Concerning thieves and those who harbour them or where they sold and bought.

Concerning treasure found and concealed against the crown.

Concerning men removed from before the justices and afterwards coming to their own land.

Concerning the pleas of the crown that are not terminated in the presence of the justices.

Concerning the pleas of the crown that are concealed by those etc.

Concerning a man who has been killed and buried without the view of the coroner.

Concerning ditches and walls or other constructions made recently by which harm might come to someone.

Concerning defaulters who do not come when summoned.

Concerning armed men riding against the order of the lord king.

Concerning vigils observed as they ought to be and are accustomed to be.

Concerning ladies and daughters whose marriage ought to be in the right of the lord king.

Concerning masterless men (**wayphis**) whom no-one ought to have but the king or those to whom he gives such liberties.

Instruction to look at: a writ with a chirograph relating to Sutton, with a foot of fine sent to the itinerant justices concerning the removal of the court from Sutton to Clifton (no. 529); the writ **vetiti namii** etc.; the plea 'quo warranto' and gallows etc.; extracts of amercements; a letter of William of Soham on behalf of the monks; a bundle of returnable writs; a completed writ concerning the liberty of the abbot at Clifton in the time of King Edward, with a bundle bound together.

Note: The rubric describes this document as claims of the liberty of the monastery of Byland, with an explanation of certain words; for these, see N. Neilson, *Types of Manorial Structure in the Northern Danelaw, Customary Rents*, Oxford Studies in Social and Legal History, ed. P. Vinogradoff, vol. II, (Oxford, 1910). The first letter of the rubric, the 'D' of 'De' is a red and blue, five-line initial. The names of the liberties, that is, those words which are glossed, are underlined in red, and here given in bold. William of Soham occurs as a justice in eyre in Cumberland and Westmorland in 1278 and as a king's justice in Yorkshire in 1279–80 (*Cal. Cl. R.*

1272–79, pp. 504, 544–5; English, ed., *Yorkshire Hundred and Quo Warranto Rolls*, p. 2) and between 1280 and 1286 (*Cal. Cl. R. 1279–88*, pp. 17, 20, 38, 103, 266, 441). He was associate justice to John de Vaux in *Quo Warranto* proceedings in 1279: Donald W. Sutherland, *Quo Warranto Proceedings in the Reign of Edward I 1278–1294* (Oxford, 1963), p. 51n. He received a petition presented on behalf of the abbot (below, no. 553).

[fol. 61v]

545   Rubric: *Pleas of liberty in Warcop in the county of Westmorland.* 40 Henry III [28 Oct. 1255 x 27 Oct. 1256].

546   Rubric: *Pleas of the crown at the same term. Look in the roll for Westmorland.*

547   Rubric: *Pleas of liberty in Warcop in the presence of William of Soham and John of Mettingham, with completed writs.* [c. 1278].
Note: William of Soham and John of Mettingham were appointed, along with John de Vaux, Geoffrey of Lewknor and Thomas of Soddington, justices in eyre in Cumberland, Westmorland and Northumberland, in 1278 (Sutherland, *Quo Warranto*, p. 194). They occur together in 1280 (*Cal. Cl. R. 1279–88*, p. 17).

548   Writ of King Henry III addressed to the abbot of Peterborough, Henry de Laton and their fellow justices in Westmorland. Since by charter he has granted to the abbot and monks of Byland several liberties in their lands in Yorkshire and Westmorland, which the itinerant justices in Yorkshire cannot act on, he orders that the charter be read and these liberties contained in it be observed. 40 Henry III [28 Oct. 1255 x 27 Oct. 1256].
T' etc.
Note: The abbot of Peterborough was John de Caux, elected in early 1250, who died in 1263; he was the king's envoy to Scotland in 1257 and Treasurer of England from 1260 to 1263 (*HRH* II, p. 58). In no. 506 above Emma, wife of Samson of Laysthorpe, swore to make no further claim to land of her inheritance which she and her husband had granted to Byland, and placed herself under the jurisdiction of the abbot of Peterborough.

549   Writ of the king, addressed to his justices in Yorkshire, notifying them of his grant to the abbot of St Mary of Byland of licence to have his own coroner within the liberty of St Mary of Byland. The coroner is to be chosen in the court of the liberty from among the more prudent and law-worthy knights or servants of the court, and is to take the oath of coroner. Order that they should hear the pleas presented by the said coroner, as is the custom and law of the kingdom. 26 [Henry III?] 28 Oct. 1241 x 27 Oct. 1242].
Note: The name of the king is not given. In *Quo Warranto* proceedings in 1279–81

the abbot claimed, among other liberties, to have his own coroner. He failed to show special warrant, and was held to be in contempt and an enquiry was ordered (English, ed., *Yorkshire Hundred and Quo Warranto Rolls*, pp. 178–9).

550 *Mandate from Abbot John of Peterborough, Henry de Laton and their fellow justices in Westmorland to the bailiff of the liberty of Byland to cause to be brought before them on the Friday before St Martin all writs of the king that he has concerning the liberties of the abbot of Byland and all attachments of the pleas of the crown concerning the same liberty, so that on that day the pleas relating to the liberty shall not remain unheard for default of justice. They are to bring this writ.* 14 Nov. 42 [Henry III] [1257].
Note: The rubric calls this 'another writ concerning the same'.

551 *Writ of King Henry III ordering the abbot of Peterborough, Henry de Laton and their colleagues in the county of York not to trouble the abbot and convent or their men on their next visitation, against their liberties which they have under his charters.* 42 Henry III [28 Oct. 1257 x 27 Oct. 1258].
Note: The rubric states that this is the third writ of the lord king, suggesting that no. 549, where the king is not named, is also a writ of Henry III. The writ is followed by a note to look for a chirograph reached in the court of Byland at Sutton in the same year.

552 *Writ of King Edward [I] to his justices in the next visitation of the county of York to observe the liberties claimed by the abbot and convent of Byland under the charters of his predecessors, according to the form of the Statute.* 7 Edward [I] [20 Nov. 1278 x 19 Nov. 1279].

[fols 61v–62r]
553 *Petition by J(ohn) of Reigate to William of Soham, justice of the king, on behalf of his beloved friend the abbot of Byland for the maintenance of their liberties as granted by the charters of the kings of England, which he has seen in the presence of Roger of Thirkleby and others.* [*c.* 1278 x 1279].
Note: John of Reigate was escheator north of the Trent in the 1270s: *Cal. Cl. R. 1272–1279*, pp. 1–5, 59, 313, 400. He was chief justice in southern England in the *Quo Warranto* proceedings of 1278–80 (Sutherland, *Quo Warranto*, pp. 42, 73). Roger of Thirkleby was a royal justice until 1250: on his career as justice see above, no. 495, note.

[fol. 62r, old fol. 169]
554 *Writ of Edward [I], by the grace of God king of England, lord of Ireland and duke of Aquitaine, to John de Vaux and his fellow itinerant justices in the county of York. The abbot claims to have charters of previous kings concerning his liberties. Mandate to investigate and to allow him to*

use them according to the statute lately provided. Westminster; 5 June 8 Edward [I] [1280].

Teste me ipso.

Note: No. 555 suggests that no. 554 is a writ of Edward I. For John de Vaux, see note to no. 547 above.

555 *Writ of Edward I, by the grace of God king of England, lord of Ireland, and duke of Aquitaine, to his justices at York stating that the abbot and monks of Byland claim by charter of his father Henry III that all pleas concerning them and their men of Sutton are heard by the king's justices at Sutton or Clifton, and that all coroners' pleas are heard by their own coroner in the presence of the justices and heard and determined by the justices according to the law of the land. Order to investigate.* Westminster; 6 June 8 Edward I [1280].

Teste me ipso.

556 *Rubric: Removal of our regalian rights from Sutton to Clifton, and from Warcop to Appleby, by the charter of Henry III sealed with his new seal and not with the old.*

Note: In 1247 pleas concerning the abbot and monks were heard at Sutton and Warcop by the king's justices (no. 527); in 1271 pleas were to be heard at Clifton (no. 529).

557 *Rubric: Roll of pleas and oaths of assizes and of the crown at Clifton within the liberty of the abbot of Byland in the presence of John de Vaux, William of Soham and their fellow itinerant justices. In the month after the feast of St John the Baptist.* 8 Edward I [June 1280].

Note: This rubric is followed by two notes: look for the bundle of returnable writs sent to the sheriff of York; look for the bundle of completed writs pertaining to the liberty of Byland annexed to the said rolls.

[fol. 62r–v]

558 *Notification that on 4 non. Apr. (2 Apr.) 1282 an inquisition was held between the lord king [Edward I] and the abbot of Byland concerning amercements, by the following jurors, Ivo de Etton, William Lovell, William de Habeton, Walter of Coulton, Roger Rabot, Richard Marshall (de Marescale), Walter de Habeton, William de le Bek of Ampleforth, John de Neuby, Robert Olyver of Dalton, John Mansell of Birdforth, Michael de Berenby, Thomas Mansell of Heton, Robert Bigod of the same, William Purying, Thomas of Etton, Hugh of Carlton, and Robert son of Drogo of Wombleton, who swore that after the making of the charter of Henry III, father of the present king, the abbot and his men were accustomed to have* *their amercements and their men who were amerced before justices in the abbot's court, and that the abbot or his attorney received tolls of their amercements and those of their men after pleas had been heard.* 2 Apr. 9 Edward I, 1282.

Marginal note: (in later hand) '10 E 1'.

Note: William Lovell, William de Habeton (Halberton) and Roger Marshall were jurors in *quo warranto* proceedings in Yorkshire, 1279–81: English, ed., *Yorkshire Hundred and Quo Warranto Proceedings*, pp. 135, 173.

[fol. 62v]

559 *Writ of King Edward, by the grace of God etc., addressed to his justices in the next visitation of the county of York. He has granted to his beloved in Christ the abbot of Byland that during their next visitation he may use and enjoy the liberties which he claims to have under the charters of his predecessors, the kings of England, as he has been accustomed to do. These are to be maintained according to the Statute unless the king orders otherwise.* Quenington ['Queynton'], Glos.; 22 Mar. 7 Edward [I] [1279]. Teste me ipso.

560 *Similar writ addressed to his treasurer and barons of the Treasury. His beloved in Christ the abbot of Byland claims by charters of his predecessors, the kings of England, to have amercements for himself and his men wherever they shall happen to be amerced. Not wishing to injure the abbot he orders them to allow the abbot to have amercements as he claims under the charters of the king's predecessors.* Westminster; 2 Sept. 9 Edward [I?] [1281]. Teste me ipso.

561 *Writ of King Edward [I] to his sheriff of Westmorland. In his parliament at Westminster it was proclaimed that all who claimed to have liberties under the charters of his predecessors should produce them for examination on a fixed day. Order to allow the abbot of Byland and others in the county to enjoy their liberties until his next coming to the county or the next visitation of the justices.* Woodstock; 22 Apr. 9 Edward [I] [1280]. Teste meipso.

Note: This refers to the statute *De Quo Warranto*, the Statute of Gloucester of 1278.

562 *Writ of King Edward [I] to his itinerant justices in Lincolnshire. The abbot of Byland claims under charters of the king's predecessors to have liberties within the county of York. The abbot is to show by what warrant he claims the said liberties. Not wishing the abbot to be injured he orders his justices to return to him the charters when they have been examined.* Westminster; 2 Sept. 10 Edward [I] [1281].

Teste me ipso.
Note: See *PQW*, p. 437.

[fol. 63r, old. fol. 170]
563 *Writ of King Edward, addressed to the sheriff of Yorkshire, concerning wrongdoing not being unpunished. The abbot and convent claim by virtue of charters of his predecessors to have their own amercements and those of their men. The king recently decreed that, in order to prevent any wrongdoing from going unpunished by their neglect, he has reserved amercements for himself. Wishing to spare the abbot and convent the amercements of his predecessors before this statute, he orders the sheriff that the demands which he made of the abbot and convent for contempt should be relaxed until the next parliament.* Newburgh; 12 Apr. 19 Edward [I?] [1291].
Teste me ipso.

564 *Writ of King Edward [II] addressed to the treasurer and to the barons of the Exchequer, notifying them that Edward his father, former king of England, had in his tenth year of his reign by letters patent pardoned all the people of his realm their amercements from the beginning of the reign of his predecessor. Mandate to apply this to Byland.* York; 3 June 1 Edward [? II] [1308]
Teste me ipso.

[fol. 63v]
The folio is headed: 'Claims of the Liberty of Byland [heard] in the presence of Hugh of Cressingham and his colleagues'. Hugh occurs as a justice in eyre in Yorkshire in 1293 and 1294 (*Cal. Cl. R. 1288–96*, pp. 294, 310, 337, 350–1 etc.). He heard *quo warranto* proceedings in 1292–4 in Lancashire, Yorkshire, Cumberland, Westmorland and Northumberland: *PQW*, pp. 203, 226; Sutherland, *Quo Warranto*, pp. 68, 108.

565 *Letter of attorney, addressed to all the faithful who will inspect the present letters, issued by Abbot John and the convent of Byland to Brother John of Fenton their fellow monk and John Cort to plead in their name and for the liberty of Byland in the presence of Hugh of Cressingham and other itinerant justices of the lord king in York for their liberties in all cases brought and to be brought touching them, their monastery and their men.* Byland; Mon. after St Barnabas [15 June] 1293.
Note: On 13 June 1292 the abbot of Byland nominated John of Fenton and William de Wynkeburne his attorneys until St Martin; the abbot had licence to go overseas: *Cal. Pat. R. 1281–1292*, pp. 494–5.

[fols 63v–64r]

566 *Plea de quo warranto heard in the presence of Hugh of Cressingham and his fellow itinerant justices at York. The abbot of Byland was summoned to reply to the lord king under the plea de quo warranto concerning his claims to have gallows* (furcas) *in Sutton, free warren in all his demesne lands in the said vill and in Bagby and Marderby, Osgoodby, Wildon, Stocking, Old Byland, Murton, Snilesworth, Scackleton, Great Thorpe (Thorpe-le-Willows), Wilsden, Wind Hill, Bentley, Denby, Whitacres, Little Thorpe (Thorpefield), Angram, Cam, Deepdale, Catton and Felixkirk, and infangentheof, utfangentheof, and return of all writs of the king; claim also to have his own coroner and amercements of his own men in all royal courts where they are amerced, amercements of escaped thieves, waifs, deodands, and chattels of all his fugitives and condemned felons and fines for breach of assize in the aforesaid vills and Fawdington, Thorpe, Thornaby, Ampleforth, Otterington, Laysthorpe and Skirpenbeck, and to be free for himself and his men of these vills from tolls, pontage, passage, carriage, pannage, common fines and amercements of the shire and from suit of shire and wapentake courts, and pleas of vetiti namii. Claim also that justices should hear pleas touching them and their men in his manor at Clifton and take the profits.*

The abbot appeared and as to the gallows at Sutton and infangentheof and utfangentheof he produced a charter of King Henry III to substantiate his claims (56 Henry III (1271), no. 529). As to infangentheof and utfangentheof and free warren he produced a charter of the said king issued in his 30th year (5 June 1246, no. 528), and granted to Abbot Henry; general charter of liberties of Henry III etc.

Roger of Hegham appeared for the lord king and gave testimony concerning infangentheof and utfangentheof. He claimed that the abbot had abused his powers by going outside his liberties etc. He takes, condemns, and judges persons for wrongdoing committed outside his liberty and his power. He often takes men outside the liberty and brings them back into the liberty and judges them there. As to free warren he says that by the authority of his charter the abbot has lands not his own in warren. As to the claim that the king's justices should go to Clifton to hear pleas, he says that the abbot cannot claim this by virtue of the present clause. This liberty does not exist in the liberty of St John of Beverley in that the justices are appointed by the archbishop of York to hear pleas in the presence of justices. The liberties which the abbot claims do not accord with those of St John of Beverley.

As to the claim to have return of writs, chattels of felons and his own coroner and other liberties by the same clause (clausula) *none of these liberties are contained implicity or explicitly in the clause, and so the said*

abbot has not shown any warrant for the said liberties and he seeks indem-
nity for the lord king. York; quindene of Trinity [7 Jun.] 21 Edward I
[1293].
Marginal note: opposite mention of Henry III's charter of 1271: 'patris domini R.
nunc datis a(nno) r(egni) sui quinquag' vi quam profert et que testatur quod idem
H. rex'.
Pd: *PQW*, p. 223 (from *quo warranto* roll 20d). See also English, ed., *Yorkshire
Hundred and Quo Warranto Rolls*, pp. 248–50.
Note: Roger of Hegham represented the king in the *Quo Warranto* proceedings of
1293–4: Sutherland, *Quo Warranto*, pp. 68, 110, 232–3.

[fol. 64r, old fol. 171]
567 *Writ of Edward [I] addressed to Hugh of Cressingham and his fellow
itinerant justices in the county of York. The abbot of Byland has claimed
certain liberties under charters issued by the king's predecessors. The king
has ordered the abbot to appear before them to show by what right (quo
warranto) he claims the said rights. These charters are to be exhibited and the
abbot granted his liberties.* Newcastle; 15 June 21 Edward I [1293].
Teste me ipso.

[fol. 64v]
CLAIMS TO LIBERTY IN WESTMORLAND

568 *Grant and confirmation by Henry [II], by the grace of God king of
England, duke of Normandy and Aquitaine, and count of Anjou, addressed
to all his archbishops, bishops, earls, barons, justices, sheriffs, and other
ministers, and all his faithful, for the salvation of his soul and of his father
and mother and his grandfather, King H(enry I), and for the souls of all his
predecessors, to God and the abbey of St Mary of Byland and the monks of
the Cistercian abbey serving God there, of all that land in Asby which Hugh
de Moreville granted in free alms for 2 marks of silver yearly. Confirmation
of the whole of Bretherdale to hold of the king for the service of 5s yearly.
Wherefore the monks should hold the said lands freely with sac and soc, toll
and team, infangentheof and all other liberties, and that they be free of
tenmantale, danegeld and other secular exactions.* Westminster; [6 Oct.
1174 x 1183].
Testibus Ricardo Wynt', Hugone Dunelm', Galfrido Elien' episcopis,
magistro Waltero de Coust', Ricardo de Lucy, Thoma Basset, Roberto
de Stuteville, Bertranno de Verdun', Radulfo filio Stephani.
Dating: Consecration of first and third witnesses and death of Robert de Stuteville
III.

Note: Tenmantale (themantale) was a land tax levied on a carucate. There is a rubric for this charter at no. 520 above.

569   Rubric: *Liberties of Byland within the county of Westmorland, both in warren and in pleas and juries.*

570   Rubric: *Writ of King Henry III to his justices in the next visitation concerning the charter of liberties to be read on behalf of the abbot and convent.* 52 Henry III. [28 Oct. 1267 x 27 Oct. 1268].

571   Rubric: *Writ of the same King Henry [III] sent to the sheriff of Westmorland to protect the rights and liberties of the monks.* 54 Henry III [28 Oct. 1269 x 27 Oct. 1270].

572   Rubric: *Writ of King Henry [III] to conduct an inquiry into the names of those who have fled and who have taken <wild beasts> in the warren of the abbot and convent.* 55 Henry III [28 Oct. 1270 x 27 Oct. 1271].

573   Memorandum *that the abbot and convent have the chief rolls of the pleas and juries settled at Warcop with the pleas of the crown held on Wed. after St Peter and St Paul [29 June] in the presence of Nicholas de Hanlon, justice of the king.*
Note: No regnal year is given.

574 Rubric: *Pleas of our liberty of Warcop heard in the presence of William of Soham and John of Mettingham, concerning pleas and juries, as above.* Wed. in the week of Whitsuntide 7 Edward I [24 June 1279].
Note: William of Soham and John of Mettingham, justice, occur together in 1280 (*Cal. Cl. R. 1279–88*, p. 17), and above, no. 547.

575   Memorandum *that the abbot and convent had their liberties fully in Westmorland for the whole time of Robert de Vipont the elder, but Robert de Vipont the younger disturbed them greatly, by cutting down their gallows* (furcas) *and committing other atrocities, as in explained in their bursars' accounts* (in bursario nostro). *At last peace was made between them, as follows,* Omnibus etc. *However, the concord was never sealed by either party, but seisin has been continued in some articles.* [early 13th cent.].
Note: The opening words only are recorded. There is a copy in MS Dodsworth 63, fol. 61v. Robert de Vipont the elder was the son of Matilda de Vipont and brother of Ivo (see above, no. 406). He occurs in 1203, when he paid for the marriage of Matilda, daughter of Torphin son of Robert and widow of Hugh son of Jernegan, as a justice in 1218 (*EYC* V, 43, 93) and in 1226 (*Cart. Guis.* I, 277). A general confirmation by Robert de Vipont to the monks of Byland of their lands in Westmorland

survives among the Edenhall of Musgrave collection at the Cumbria Record Office, Carlisle (uncatalogued).

576 *Rubric: The pleas heard in the presence of Henry of Cressingham and his fellow justices in the county of Westmorland are in the treasury* (in bursar').

Note: See *PQW*, pp. 786–7, 789–90. The abbot of Byland was summoned to show by what warrant he claimed free chase in Tebay and lands in Asby: octave of Michaelmas, 20 Edward I, 6 Oct. 1292. Henry appears to be an error for Hugh.

577 *Rubric: Memorandum that the abbot and convent now have a new charter of King Richard II with a prohibition (clausula) 'de licet'. The abbot and convent of St Mary, York, by virtue of their permission 'de licet' use their liberties there.*

[fol. 65r, old fol. 172]
MURTON (SE5388), in the parish of Hawnby and the wapentake of Birdforth (NR). The parish covers a large stretch of moorland between the Cleveland Hills on the north and the Hambledon Hills on the SW. Murton lies roughly one mile SW of Hawnby and north of Old Byland, and Murton Grange just to the south of Byland's property in Dale Town, with which it was closely associated (see above, nos 255–60). The main benefactors were members of the Malebisse family, tenants of the Honour of Mowbray. Although the *Historia Fundationis* suggests that the original endowment in Murton and Snilesworth (below nos 1076–84) came from Hugh Malebisse I, who was steward of Roger de Mowbray between *c.* 1147 and 1154, the earliest charter appears to be that of his son, Hugh II (no. 578), whose own son, Hugh III, may have quitclaimed Murton (no. 579). Hugh III died without heirs in 1206. His cousin, Richard Malebisse of Acaster Malbis (son of William, the brother of Hugh II) founded the Premonstratensian abbey of Newbo (Lincs.) No. 578 indicates that the monks of Byland held the vill of Murton for an annual rent of 40s., and this evidently passed to the canons of Newbo; the rent is the subject of nos 580–91, confirmations and quitclaims by Richard's grandson William (son of John), and William's son Richard. Nos 593–6 relate to tithe arrangements with the parish church.

578 *Grant in free alms, addressed to the archbishop of York and the whole chapter of St Peter (York) and all the faithful of holy church, by Hugh Malebisse, for the salvation of his soul and of all his own, to God and the monks of St Mary of Byland, of all his vill of Murton with all its appurtenances. To hold of the donor and his heirs free from all secular service,*

rendering yearly 40s. to him and his heirs, 20s. at Whitsuntide and 20s. at
St Martin (11 Nov.). Quitclaim of whatever claim he and his ancestors had
in Byland on the Moor [Old Byland]. Pledge to warranty. [c. 1170 x 1186].
Hiis testibus Rogero de Molbray, Roberto filio eius, Hugone filio meo,
Roberto de Belcaup, etc.

Marginal note: B(aculus) i.

Copies: MSS Dodsworth 94, fol. 18r (abbreviated); Top. Yorks. e. 8, fols 137v–138r
(old pp. 239–40); Top. Yorks. e. 9, fol. 24r (old p. 21); NYCRO ZDV I 1 (Sandwith's
Exscripta). These last three copies omit 'etc' in the witness list and continue:
Philippo de Muntpinzun, Roberto Beler, Henrico de Lobbeham, Iohanne
capellano, Roberto de Auverl, Willelmo le Blund. MS Top. Yorks. e. 9 omits
'Hugone filio meo', and has 'Anners', underlined, for 'Auverl'.

Pd: *EYC* III, no. 1836; no explanation of date (1165 x 1185).

Dating: Philip de Montpincon does not occur before *c.* 1170 (*Mowbray Charters*, nos
25, 376 and note); the latest date is that of Roger de Mowbray's departure on
crusade. The common formula in the pledge of warranty may suggest a date later
rather than earlier in the period.

Note: The rubric states that the rent was quitclaimed by the abbot of Newbo; see
no. 580. The *Historia Fundationis* assigns the grant of Murton and Snilesworth to
Hugh Malebisse I, who had been succeeded as steward by 1154 (*Mon. Ang.* V, 351).
These grants later led to disputes (*ibid.*, 352). Roger de Mowbray confirmed the
grant of Murton and Snilesworth in 1147 (*Mowbray Charters*, no. 44). It is clear from
the witnesses that this is a grant by his son, Hugh II, who succeeded before 1166
and was dead by 1188 (*EYC* III, 456).

579   *Rubric: Quitclaim by Hugh Malebisse of Byland and Murton for the*
payment of 40s. due to him. Copied. [before 1206].

Dating: The grantor could be Hugh II (d. by 1188) or his son (d. before 1206).

580   *Quitclaim, addressed to all the sons of holy mother church present and*
future, by Abbot Luke and the convent of Newbo, of 40s. annual rent which
they customarily demanded of the abbot and convent of Byland, that is, 20s.
annual rent which Thomas son of Adam of Arncliffe had granted to Newbo
out of charity and which he was accustomed to receive from the monks from
the grant of Richard Malebisse, and 20s. which William Malebisse granted
to Newbo in perpetual alms, and which the monks of Byland were bound to
pay William in hereditary right for their grange of Murton, as William
asserted. This quitclaim is made for 26 marks sterling which the monks have
paid into their hand in their great need. Pledge to warranty. [1243 x *c.*
1257].

Hiis testibus domino Willelmo Malbys, domino Thoma de Colvyll,
Waltero capellano, Willelmo de Stokeslaya, etc.

Dating: The predecessor of Abbot Luke of Newbo, Matthew, occurs in 1243 (*HRH*
II, 507); Abbot Luke himself is recorded in 1249, and he had been succeeded by

William by 1257 (*ibid.*; Colvin, *White Canons*, p. 411). It is likely that the William Malebisse mentioned here is the grandson of Newbo's founder, and son of John Malebisse; Farrer noted occurrences in 1233 and 1258 (*EYC* III, 456); however he was still alive in 1267 when William Malebisse claimed against the abbot of Byland the manors of Byland, Balk and Murton except for 40s. rent in Murton: Baildon, *Monastic Notes* I, 30, from *Curia Regis Rolls* 180, Hilary 51 Henry III, m. 10d. See nos 583–4.

Note: Newbo was founded in 1198 by Richard Malebisse, lord of Acaster Malbis. He also held land of the honour of Eye, and it was on these lands that the abbey was founded; Colvin, *White Canons*, pp. 165–8. During the case of 1267 the abbot of Byland claimed that his predecessors had paid 40s. as service for the manor of Murton, and that the abbot of Newbo was at that time seised of the said 40s. by assignment of the ancestors of William Malebisse. The rubric states that the charter was copied.

581   *Rubric: Charter of Thomas of Arncliffe concerning 20s. Surrendered.*

582   *Rubric: Charter of Richard Malebisse concerning the same 20s. Surrendered.* [late 13th cent.].

Note: This is likely to be Richard, son of William Malebisse, who was holding Hawnby of Roger de Mowbray in 1284/5 and who occurs in 1301. He was the son of the grantor of nos 583, 584.

583   *Rubric: Quitclaim by William son of John Malebisse of 20s.* [before *c.* 1257].

Note: For the grantor see no. 580 and no. 584.

584   *Grant, confirmation and quitclaim, addressed to all the faithful in Christ present and future, by William Malebisse son of John Malebisse, out of the impulse of charity and for the salvation of his soul and of all his ancestors and heirs, to God and St Mary and the convent of Byland and their successors, of 40s. which the abbot and convent of Newbo granted and quitclaimed to the abbot and convent of Byland by their charter (no. 580). William and his ancestors were accustomed to receive the 40s. in hereditary right from the abbot and convent of Byland for the grange of Murton, and he and Thomas son of Adam of Arncliffe then granted them by charter to Newbo. To have and to hold in free alms quit of all secular service. Pledge to warranty. Sealed with the donor's seal.* [1243 x *c.* 1257].

Hiis testibus Thoma de Colavill', Willelmo de Harum, Adam de Hilton', Willelmo de Midelton', Adam de Nereford, Rollando de Renegyle, Iohanne de Reigate, Willelmo de Stokesleya, Ricardo Malebysse fratre meo.

Copies: MS Dodsworth 94, fols 17v–18r, no. 20; NYCRO ZDV I 1 (Sandwith's *Exscripta*); in these the witness list continues: Iohanne de Kereby, Willelmo de

Maundevill, Philippo filio Philippi de Suitona, et multis aliis.
Dating: as no. 580.

[fol. 65v]
585   Rubric: *Charter of John Malebisse for the canons of Newbo concerning 20s. rent. Surrendered to the monks.* [1214 x mid 13th cent.].
Text: MS Dodsworth 94, fol. 17r–v, no. 19. Grant, addressed to all the sons of holy mother church who see or hear this writing, by John Malebisse, to God and the church of St Mary of Newbo and the canons of the Premonstratensian order serving God there, of 20s. rent from Murton Grange which Thomas of Arncliffe had of the grant of John's father, Richard, to be taken from the monks of Byland at 2 terms, 10s. at St Martin (11 Nov.) and 10s. at Whitsuntide. Hiis testibus domino Briano filio Alani, Hugone Malebisse, Ricardo le Maunsel, Roberto de Acaster, Roberto Haget, Willelmo Paumes, Radulfo Malebisse, Thoma de Acastra, Thoma de Arneclive, Ricardo Maunsello, Henrico Noie, Willelmo de Mortun, Radulfo Buchard, Willelmo filio Willelmi, filio Hugonis, Roberto archidiacono. 'The seale a man on horseback'.
Dating: The grantor is the son of Richard Malebisse, founder of Newbo (d. 1210).
Note: The word 'Iohannis' is repeated in the cartulary rubric. The final witness may be an archdeacon in the diocese of Lincoln, in which Newbo was situated. Robert of Hailes, for instance, attests Lincoln episcopal acta as archdeacon of Huntingdon from 1214, and as archdeacon of Lincoln from 1225 to 1234: see *The Acta of Hugh of Wells, bishop of Lincoln, 1209–1235*, ed. D. M. Smith, Lincoln Record Society, 88 (2000), nos 12, 14–18, 234–5, 431.

586   Rubric: *Charter of the same [John Malebisse] appointing Thomas of Arncliffe to receive 20s. from the monks.* [1214 x mid 13th cent.].

587   Rubric: *Charter of William Malebisse concerning the remaining 20s. Surrendered.*

588   Rubric: *Quitclaim by Richard Malebisse of Murton, Snilesworth and Byland. Look in the Byland bundle.*
Note: The grantor is likely to be Richard son of William Malebisse. He was still alive in 1301.

589   Rubric: *Quitclaim by William Malebisse of 20s. which he granted to the abbot of Newbo.*

590   Rubric: *Quitclaim by William Malebisse of John Caipun his villein.*

591 *Rubric: Letter of Richard Malebisse assigning 20s. to Gramar formerly wife of Hugh Malebisse the younger. [c. 22 Sept. 1206].*

Note: This relates to a final concord, dated 22 Sept. 1206, between Robert de Luttrington and Constance his wife, plaintiffs, through John Gramaticus in place of Constance, and Richard Malebisse, defendant, concerning the dower which appertained to Constance from her late husband, Hugh Malebisse, in Hawnby and Scawton and the service of William Engelram in Dale. Robert and Constance renounced all claim in the dower to Richard and his heirs, and for this Richard granted to Robert and Constance the annual rent of 20s. from the abbot and convent for the grange of Murton. Constance was to receive this rent for life in the name of her dower, 10s. at St Michael (29 Sept.) and 10s. at Whitsuntide (*Yorks. Fines John*, p. 108, from PRO CP 25/1/261/8, no. 48). The name 'Gramar' in the rubric refers to Constance's attorney. Richard Malebisse was the son of Constance and Hugh.

592 *Confirmation in free alms, addressed to all the faithful in Christ present and future, by Richard Malebisse, for the love of God and for the salvation of his soul and of all his ancestors and heirs, to God and St Mary and the abbot and convent of Byland and their successors, of all the lands and possessions which the monks have in various places in his fee, free of all secular service. Pledge to warranty. Sealed with the donor's seal.* Scawton; St Edward, king [6 Jan.] 1280 [1281].

Hiis testibus domino Rogero Mowbray, domino Thoma de Colvyll, Willelmo de Barton', Iohanne de Iarpenvyle militibus, Waltero le Graunt, etc.

Marginal note: (in later hand) '9 E I'.

593 **Original:** *Notification to all who hear or see these letters of the agreement between the church of St Mary, Byland, and the church of Hawnby in the time of Abbot Roger, Jeremiah, archdeacon of Cleveland, Robert, dean of Helmsley, and Alexander, dean, that the church of Byland shall render yearly to Hawnby church 20s. for the tithes of Murton, 10s. at Whitsuntide and 10s. at St Martin (11 Nov.).* [1170 x 1181].

Hiis testibus Ieremia archidiacono, Roberto decano, Alexandro decano, Radulfo capellano archid(iaconi), Ricardo clerico de Scaltun et toto capitulo de Cliveland'.

Location: BL Add. charter 70693; chirograph, cut straight across; endorsed: compo' cy. de xxs.; Mortona B ii xviii (Murton, first bundle, 18); seals: (i) brown wax, oval; SIGI . . . ARC . . . DE CLIVELAND (ii) red wax, oval, smaller than (i), faded.
Pd (plate, with comment): *The British Museum Quarterly*, VII (1932), 39–40.
Dating: The first witness was in office by 1170; terminal date is that of no. 594. The cartulary has the first four witnesses and ends 'etc'.

594 *Inspection, addressed to all his officials and all the sons of holy mother church, by Roger, archbishop of York and legate of the apostolic see, of the agreement between the churches of Byland and Hawnby, reciting no. 593, with witnesses as in no. 593.* [1177 x 1181].

Hiis testibus Roberto decano, Hamone cantore, magistro Wydone, etc.

Copy: NYCRO, ZDV I 1 (Sandwith's *Exscripta*), which omits 'etc' from the witness list and continues: Radulfo archidiacono, Ieremia archidiacono, Gilberto abbate de Seleby, Ricardo priore de Novoburgo, Roberto preposito Beverlac', Stephano canoni[c]o, Adamo de Thorn'.

Pd: *EYC* III no. 1838 (from the cartulary), where dated 1164 x 1176; *EEA* XX, no. 9 (from Sandwith), where dated 27 Sept. 1177 x 1181, probably after 30 Oct. 1177.

Dating: Farrer's dating not explained in *EYC*. Hamo became precentor *c*. 1170 x 1174; Archbishop Roger died in 1181. It is not clear whether Dean Robert who attests here is dean of York, or the rural dean of Helmsley who attests no. 18. However the other witnesses suggest the dean of York. The dating here follows Lovatt (*EEA* XX), who suggests that the position of Guy as third witness might indicate a date after 1177 when he became master of the schools, his predecessor having drowned on 27 Sept. that year. The fourth witness was vice-archdeacon of Richmond. Stephen, canon, is Stephen the Roman, canon of York, who occurs in 1164 x 1174, before 1173, and 1158 x 1181 (*Fasti York*, p. 129). He attests nos 225, 395, 491 above, and no. 1156 below. Robert is noted as provost of Beverley between 1181 and 1201, but the latest recorded occurrence of his predecessor, Geoffrey, is no later than 1177 (*Beverley Minster Fasti*, ed. Richard T. W. McDermid (YASRS, 149 (1993 for 1990), pp. 4–5).

595 *Memorandum that in a bull Pope Hadrian IV confirmed specifically Murton and the agreement concerning tithes with the consent of the said <arch>bishop and archdeacon. Sealed by 12 cardinals.* Lateran; 23 Nov. 1156.

Text: MS Dodsworth 63, fols 36v–38r. Bull of Pope Hadrian IV addressed to Roger, abbot, and the brethren of Byland present and future, confirming the site of the abbey, as contained in the charter of Roger de Mowbray, lands in Old Byland, Murton, Wildon, Scackleton, Fawdington, Boscar, Cam, and Snilesworth, liberties granted by Henry, king of the English, the privileges of the Cistercian order, and freedom from the payment of tithes. Lateran, by the hand of Roland, cardinal priest and chancellor, 9 kal. Dec. [23 Nov.] in his second year [1156].

Pd: *PUE* III, no. 116.

Note: This suggests that the agreement predated the confirmation in no. 593. The papal chancellor, Roland Bandinelli, cardinal priest of San Marco, is the future Pope Alexander III (no. 596). He was chancellor in the last weeks of Pope Eugenius III and under popes Anastasius IV and Hadrian IV: I. S. Robinson, *The Papacy 1073–1198: Continuity and Innovation* (Cambridge, 1990), p. 94.

596 *Memorandum that Pope Alexander III similarly confirmed Murton and the agreement concerning tithes. Sealed by 12 cardinals.* Tours; 1163.

597 *Summary of a bull of Pope Alexander IV, addressed generally to archbishops, bishops, abbots, priors, deans, archdeacons etc. If there are any agreements of peace between the Cistercians and others, reached with the consents of both parties, they are to be kept firm and inviolable for all times.* Anagni; in the first year of his pontificate. [1254 x 1255].

[fol. 66r, old fol. 173]
MARDERBY, in the parish of Felixkirk and the wapentake of Birdforth (NR). Marderby Grange (SE4783) lies roughly one mile to the NW of Sutton under Whitestonecliffe and the same distance to the south of Felixkirk and the preceptory of the Knights Hospitaller at Mount St John. The monks acquired land from the early 13th century, the principal benefactors being the Fossard family and their tenants. No. 598 contains a number of place names which have disappeared.

598 *Grant in free alms, addressed to all the sons of holy mother church present and future, by Robert Fossard, to God and St Mary and the monks of Byland, of 12 bovates in the region of Marderby with their appurtenances inside and outside the vill, which they held of him at farm. Grant also of 30 acres of profitable land in the* cultura *called* Hestkeld *towards the north, 10½ acres of profitable land on* Crossebergh *in the region of Sutton, 4½ acres on either side of the watercourse of Sutton near Balk, 6 acres of meadow in* Northaskeholme, *3 acres of meadow in* Witheker *and 2 acres called* Iokenewath. *To hold of him and his heirs free from all secular service except for forinsec service on 12 bovates where 10 carucates make a knight's fee. Pledge to warranty.* [*c.* 1208 x 1219].
Hiis testibus Eustachio de Stutevill', Willelmo de Scipwith, Iohanne de Melsa, Roberto de Hesell', etc.

Marginal note: B(aculus) i.
Copy: MS Top. Yorks. e. 7, fols 145v–146r (old pp. 238–9), which omits 'etc' in the witness list and continues: Thoma de Ettona, Thoma le Chen, Adam de Boltebi, Hugone de Uppesale, Waltero de Saurebi, Matheo parsona de Kirkebi, Adam de Chottingham, Willelmo de Redburn, magistro Laurentio clerico, Willelmo Takel, Hugone clerico de Alvertona.
Pd: *EYC* IX no. 86.
Dating: The donor is said to have succeeded his father between 1200 and 1209 and he died by Jan. 1227 (*EYC* IX, 152–3); however, he had succeeded by 1208: see below, no. 618. As pointed out in *EYC*, if the fourth witness in no. 598 is the individual who died before 1219 the terminal date can be pushed back from 1226. The

first witness would then be Eustace, son of Robert de Stuteville III.
Note: See no. 611, where the same witnesses attest.

599   *Rubric: Charter of the same [Robert Fossard] concerning 3 bovates
with tofts and crofts in the same. [c. 1208 x 1227].*
Dating: succession and death of the grantor.

600   *Rubric: Charter of the same [Robert Fossard] concerning 1½ roods in
Northsthow and all the meadow which Geoffrey the priest held. [c. 1208 x
1227].*
Dating: succession and death of the grantor.

601   *Rubric: Charter of the same [Robert Fossard] concerning 5½ acres and
1 rood in Northshow and the . . . which Ralph son of Margaret held. [c.
1208 x 1227].*
Dating: succession and death of the grantor.
Note: There is damage to the manuscript at this point.

602   *Rubric: Quitclaim by Simon of Marderby of Northstow and assarts
in the region of the vill. [before 1227].*
Text: MS Top. Yorks. e. 7, fol. 144r–v (old pp. 235–6). Quitclaim,
addressed to all the sons of holy mother church present and future by
Simon of Marderby, to the monks of St Mary of Byland, of all right
and claim that he and his heirs ever had in 'North Shcoe' and other
assarts which the monks have in the region of Marderby of the grant
of Robert Fossard of Sutton, saving common pasture for himself and
his heirs when the hay is brought in. Pledge to make no claim. Hiis
testibus Roberto Fossard, Ada de Boutheby, Olivero de Busci,
Stephano de Neill, Henrico de Siltona, Roberto de Auford, Stephano
de Blaby. Sketch of seal with legend SIGI SIMONIS FIL' WILL'
BVLDEL
Dating: death of Robert Fossard.

603   *Rubric: Charter of Robert Fossard concerning lordship in Marderby*
sub minori forma. [c. 1208 x 1227].
Dating: succession and death of the grantor.

604   *Confirmation and quitclaim, addressed to all the sons of holy mother
church present and future, by Thomas Fossard, brother of Robert Fossard of
Sutton, to God and the monks of St Mary of Byland, of all the grants in
Marderby and Sutton which they have of the grant of his brother Robert, to*

do there as they wish, as contained in Robert's charters which the monks have. Pledge to warranty. [1227 x 1233].

Hiis testibus domino Nicholao de Stutevill', Willelmo de Thamptona, Waltero de Saureby, etc.

Dating: Thomas, son of Adam Fossard, succeeded his brother, Robert, by 1227 (*EYC* IX, 153). This confirmation may have been issued shortly after his succession. The first witness, Nicholas de Stuteville II, the son of Nicholas de Stuteville I, died in 1233. Walter of Sowerby was his steward, who occurs in 1205 x 1218 and 1219 (*EYC* IX, 19 and no. 52).

605 *Rubric: Charter of Robert Fossard concerning 3 acres of land and meadow in the assart called* Ravenyldriddyng. [*c.* 1208 x 1227].

Dating: succession and death of the grantor.

606 *Grant in free alms, addressed to all those who will see or hear these letters, by William de Redburna, to God and the monks of St Mary of Byland, of 3 bovates in Marderby, that is, those which are furthest from the south of that carucate of land called* le Plouland *and 3 tofts lying together, that is, the tofts held by Geoffrey of Catton, Uctred son of Paynot, and William Drury, with all their easements and appurtenances inside and outside the vill. To have and to hold of the donor and his heirs in perpetuity in exchange for 2 bovates and the service on a further 5 bovates in Oulston for the performance of forinsec service on 3 bovates where 10 carucates make a knight's fee. Pledge to warranty.* [before 1224].

Hiis testibus domino Willelmo de Mowbray, Rogero de Mowbray, Iohanne de Dayvill', etc.

Copy: MS Top. Yorks. e. 7, fol. 121v (old p. 190), which omits 'etc' from the witness list and continues: Thoma de Lasceles, Gaufrido Fossard, Roberto filio eius, Olivero de Buscy, Hugone de Uppesale, Stephano de Menil, Stephano de Blaby, Gileberto de Meinil de Thurkilby, Gilberto et Nicholao filiis eius, Gaufrido de Ampelforda, Gaufrido filio Columbe.

Dating: William de Mowbray died in 1224, and Roger who attests with him here was his younger brother.

Note: William de Redburn occurs in 1190 x 1210 (*EYC* IX, no. 78), and was granted land in Little Edston by Matthew de Benefield; he was succeeded by his son, another William, who quitclaimed land to Malton Priory in 1241 (*VCH NR* II, 491). No. 606 was confirmed by Robert Fossard (MS Top. Yorks. e. 7, fol. 145r (old p. 237)). Stephen de Meinill was the eldest son of Gilbert de Meinill of Thirkleby, who also attests here with his other sons Gilbert and Nicholas. This charter confirms that Nicholas son of Gilbert de Meinill who occurs in nos 767 and 817 was the son of Gilbert the elder, and brother of Stephen and Gilbert.

[fol. 66r–v]
607 *Grant and confirmation, addressed to all the sons of holy mother church present and future, by Abbot Walter and the convent to William de*

Redburna of 2 bovates in Oulston which they have of the grant of Adam of
Baxby in demesne with Elias son of Edward who remains on the land, and
the homage and service of William of Gilling on 2 bovates which he held of
the abbot and convent in the same vill, that is, 3s. silver yearly, with forinsec
service. Grant also of the homage of William of Baxby on 2 bovates which he
held of the abbot in the same vill, that is, 1 pound of pepper yearly, with
forinsec service, and the homage and service of Ralph of Leake for 1 bovate in
the same vill, that is, forinsec service. William is to hold all this of the abbot
and convent and their successors in fee and hereditary right for forinsec
service on 7 bovates where 17 carucates make a knight's fee in exchange for 3
bovates in Marderby which William had of the grant of Robert Fossard.
Pledge to warranty. [before 1224].

Hiis testibus domino Willelmo de Molbray, Drogone de Harum,
Willelmo filio eius, Galfrido Fossard, Roberto filio eius, etc.

Dating: as no. 606.

608 *Rubric: Charter of Robert Fossard concerning his own grant of the*
said 3 bovates. [c. 1220 x 1227].
Text: MS Top. Yorks. e. 8, fols 181v–182r (old pp. 327–8). Grant and
confirmation, addressed to the archbishop and the whole chapter of
St Peter (York) and all the sons of holy mother church present and
future, by Robert Fossard, to the monks of St Mary of Byland, of 3
bovates in Marderby, that is the bovate held by Peter de F. . . .thwaite
[obscured by tight binding], and the 2 held by Walter son of Oswald
of Thirsk, free from all service except for forinsec service where 10
carucates make a knight's fee. The monks are to do there as they wish.
The grant is made for the salvation of the soul of the donor and of all
his ancestors and heirs. Pledge to warranty. Hiis testibus magistro
Rogero tunc decano Ebor', magistro Gaufrido de Norwic, magistro
Iohanne Romano canonico, Iohanne de Daivill, Thoma de Lacel,
Willelmo de Tamton, Stephano de Menil de Thurkelbi, Roberto
Fossard filio Gaufridi Fossard, Roberto de Auford, Thoma Fossard
fratre meo.

Dating: The earliest date is provided by the first witness and the latest by the death
of the grantor.

609 *Rubric: Charter of Robert Fossard concerning 2 tofts and crofts and*
the whole of Hovingham and 5 acres and 1 rood. [c. 1208 x 1227].
Dating: succession and death of the grantor.

610 *Rubric: Case settled between the monks and Master Hugolinus concerning having a path for the parishioners of Felixkirk between Marderby and the church.* [before 1222].

Note: Hugolinus is to be identified as Ugo de Comite, a papal nominee to the living of Felixkirk, who was succeeded in 1222 by Oddo Bobonis, papal subdeacon and chaplain; in 1244 yet another papal nominee, Conrad, canon and proctor of Ivrea, was provided to Felixkirk: *Reg. Giffard*, p. 176n; *CPRL* I, 88, 206; J. E. Sayers, *Papal Government and England during the pontificate of Honorius III* (Cambridge, 1984), p. 188. Throughout the period the church was served by a vicar: for Geoffrey, who was vicar in the time of Archbishop Walter de Gray, see nos 1055–6. On 16 Feb. 1276 Archbishop Giffard issued notice that there had been a controversy between the abbot of Byland and the Knights Hospitaller as to whether Conrad (Corrado), who at one time held the living of Felixkirk, had been presented by the Knights. He declared that a certain Hugolinus (Ugo) had held the living on the authority of the pope, and had held it until he was promoted to a bishopric overseas. Conrad had been appointed by a papal legate, and there was no record in the archives of the church of York that Conrad had been presented by the Knights (*Reg. Giffard*, p. 296). However, the Hospitallers presented in 1233 (*Reg. Gray*, p. 60).

611 *Rubric: Confirmation by Nicholas de Stuteville of the exchange with William de Redburne and of certain other lands.* [before 1217].

Text: MS Top. Yorks. e. 7, fol. 122r (old p. 191). Confirmation, addressed to all the faithful of Christ present and future, by Nicholas de Stuteville, to God and the monks of St Mary of Byland, of 3 bovates with tofts and crofts in Marderby, with all appurtenances and easements inside and outside the vill, which he had by exchange with William de Redburn for land in Oulston by confirmation of Robert Fossard. Confirmation also of 2 tofts in Marderby of the grant of Robert Fossard which Cuthbert the smith held, with all the intake, 1 toft which Nicholas held, 4 acres, 3 of which lie between (blank) and the house of the parson and one which Walter son of Elwin held, and 15 acres in Sutton, as contained in the charters which the monks have of Robert Fossard and William de Redeburne (no. 606). The grant is made in free alms, quit of secular service, for the salvation of his soul and of all his ancestors and heirs. Hiis testibus Eustachio de Stutevil, Willelmo de Scipwhic, Iohanne de Melsa, Roberto de Hesel, Thoma de Ettona, Thoma de Chen, Alano de Boltebi, Hugone de Uppesale, Waltero de Saurebi, Mattheo [MS monacho] parsona de Kirkebi, Adam parsona de Cottingham, Willelmo de Redburne, magistro Lawrentio clerico, Willelmo Takel', Hugone clerico de Cliftona.

Dating: This could be Nicholas de Stuteville, who died *c.* 1217, or his son, who died in 1233. The attestation of Robert of Hessle suggests the former; see note to no. 598, where the witness list is the same as that in no. 611.

Note: The witness list, which here reads 'Walter of Sowerby, monk, the parson of Kirkby' is an error for 'Walter of Sowerby, Matthew, parson of Kirkby', as in no. 598. Walter was steward of Nicholas de Stuteville: see note to no. 604. In no. 598 the last witness appears as Hugh, clerk of Allerton.

612 *Rubric: Charter of Robert Fossard concerning licence to assart all downs and thickets which are harmful to the monks. [c. 1208 x 1227].*
Dating: succession and death of the grantor.

613 *Rubric: Charter of John son of Simon concerning 2 bovates with assarts. [before 1268].*
Dating: Before no. 616, when the land granted to Eleanor by her brother, John, and by Eleanor to the monks of Byland, was regranted by them to Robert Peitevin.

614 *Rubric: Quitclaim by the same [John son of Simon] of the same. [before 1268].*
Dating: as no. 613.

615 *Rubric: Charter of Eleanor daughter of Simon concerning all the land which she had in <Marder>by with a toft. This land had been granted to Robert Peitevin, part of whose land lies at* Keldekeldsike. [before 1268].
Dating: as no. 613.

616 *Grant and confirmation, addressed to all the sons of holy mother church present and future to whom this present charter shall come, by Abbot Henry and the convent of Byland to Robert Peitevin for homage and service, of their land which they had in Marderby of the grant of Eleanor daughter of Simon of Marderby, that is, the smaller assart which lies to the western part of* Kaldekeldsic *with the small parcel lying next to it, and 2 selions lying between the land of the Hospitallers and the monks' land as it stretches from the vill of Marderby as far as* Hestkeldeflat *with an adjacent toft. Eleanor had all this by the grant of her brother John, and granted and quitclaimed it to the monks in full court at Sutton by her own charter (no. 615) and that of her brother, which the monks have (613 or 614). Robert is to have and hold this of the abbot and convent and their successors in fee and hereditary right, for homage and service, rendering 2d. yearly at St Martin in Winter (11 Nov.) for all service. Pledge to warranty. In the form of a chirograph. Sealed with the seal of both parties. [1231 x 1268].*
Hiis testibus domino Galfrido decano de Bulmer, domino Alano de Leec, Waltero de Staynesby, Willelmo le Breth', etc.
Dating: This seems to belong to the earlier Abbot Henry.
Note: Alan of Leake witnesses nos 31, 121, 128, 129, 201, 494–6, 509, 515, 848, 852,

998, 1146, and Rievaulx charters: *Cart. Riev.*, pp. 207, 234 (nos 292, 331); William Breth witnesses in the time of Abbot Adam of Rievaulx: *ibid.*, p. 230 (no. 325).

617 *Rubric: Chirograph agreement between the monks and William Arundel and Joan of Sutton concerning 3 bovates and 4 acres, rendering to William and Joan 21s., to hold for their lifetime only, as contained in the said charters. The period specified in the said charters is past* (preteritus). [1227 x 1240].

Dating: Joan was the widow of Robert Fossard, and in 1227 was a party to fines concerning her dower in Sutton (*Yorks. Fines 1218–1231*, pp. 104, 114; *EYC* IX, 153). She married William Arundel, and in 1240 she was party to a fine with the abbot of Byland (below, no. 1046, note).

[fols 66v–67r]

618 *Notification to all present and future by Robert Fossard, son of Adam Fossard, lord of Sutton under Whitestonecliffe, of his grant and confirmation in free alms, to God and St Mary and the monks of Byland, of all his lordship in Marderby, Felixkirk, Laysthorpe, Hood and Otterington and whatever right he had in these vills, that is, homage, services, rents, freemen and villeins, custodies, right of giving in marriage, wardships, reliefs, escheats etc, with advowsons of churches, suit of court and all other services, customs, aids and demands. Further grant in free alms of the homage and service of the prior of the Hospital of St John of Jerusalem for lands which he holds of the donor, the homage and service of Geoffrey Fossard for land which he holds of the donor in Sutton, the homage and service of Simon of Marderby and his heirs for land which they hold of the donor in Marderby and the homage and service of William the chaplain and his heirs, Philip son of Philip of Sutton and his heirs and the other homage and service for the land they hold of the donor in Sutton. This is granted for the salvation of his soul and of all his ancestors and heirs to do there whatever the monks wish. Pledge to warranty.* [c. 1208].

Hiis testibus domino Nicholao de Stutevilla, Hugone de Upsale, Ada de Boltby, Olyvero Buscy, etc.

Dating: Robert Fossard succeeded his father, Adam, by 1208 and was dead by 1226. He had an uncle named Geoffrey, who was the brother of Adam Fossard. In view of the case brought against the Knights Hospitaller of Mount St John in the parish of Felixkirk in 1208 (no. 619) it is likely that Robert made his grant of the manor on his succession to the fee, and that his claim against the Knights followed shortly after. Nicholas de Stuteville II confirmed the grant of the manor of Marderby, but his charter cannot be dated more precisely than 1224 x 1233 (no. 624). For the Buscy family as benefactors of Byland see nos 683–4.

[fol. 67r, old fol. 174]

619 *Final concord reached in the king's court at Woodstock in the presence of the king and Simon of Pattishall, James of Potterne, Henry de Pont-Audemar, Robert de Aumari, and Richard de Mucegros, his justices, between Robert Fossard, plaintiff, and Robert, prior of the Hospital of St John of Jerusalem in England, defendant, concerning the customs and services which Robert demanded from the prior for the free tenement which he holds of Robert Fossard in Marderby and Felixkirk near Sutton under Whitestonecliffe, that is, 1 carucate with appurtenances. Robert demanded that the prior do homage for the land and make suit at Robert's court at Sutton every three weeks, but he had refused to recognize this service, and so a plea had been instituted. The prior now acknowledges the service due to Robert, and in return Robert remits the claim from the day of this agreement. And in the court the prior did homage to Robert.* Woodstock; Mon. after the Nativity of the B. V. M. 12 John [8 Sept. 1210].

Marginal note: (in later hand) '12 Jo.'.

Note: Simon of Pattishall was a noted justice under Richard I and King John; Henry de Pont-Audemar was active in administration in Normandy and joined the court *coram rege* in 1207; Robert de Aumari began his career as a justice on the eyre of 1208–9 and until the end of 1211 was a judge *coram rege*; Richard de Mucegros also sat *coram rege*, and served on eyre in 1208–9 and until 1211 (Turner, *English Judiciary*, pp. 8, 128, 132–3, 136).

[fol. 67r–v]

620 *Indenture made between the abbot and convent of Byland on one part and the prior and brethren of the Hospital of St John of Jerusalem in England on the other, at the termination of a dispute which had arisen because the abbot and convent had exacted from the prior homage, fealty and suit of court at Sutton under Whitestonecliffe every three weeks, and scutage, for the lands and tenements which the prior and brethren hold of the abbot and convent in Marderby and Felixkirk. The prior and brethren acknowledge that they owe fealty to the abbot of Byland and suit of court at Sutton every three weeks, as owed to the predecessors of the abbot and convent time out of mind, and undertake to perform such fealty and suit of court to the abbot of Byland and his successors, and the abbot and convent remit homage and scutage for the said lands for themselves and their successors. Sealed with the seals of both parties.* [before 1271].

Hiis testibus dominis Radulfo de Nevyll', Alexandro fratre eius, Willemo de Dayvill, Willemo Malbys, Iohanne de Colvyll', Iohanne Minyot, militibus, Iohanne de Multon', Roberto de Stay<nes>by, etc.

Dating: Before the removal of the court from Sutton to Clifton (no. 529, above).

[fol. 67v]

621 *Memorandum that on 29 Oct. 1335 Philip de Thame, prior of the Hospital of St John of Jerusalem in England, did fealty to Walter of Yarm, abbot of Byland, in the abbey church of St Mary, York, for lands in Marderby and Felixkirk in the presence of John de Killing, seneschal of the abbot, William of Topcliffe . . . of the same, John of Upsall, his attorney and many others, monks, hospitallers and seculars.*

Marginal note: (in later hand) '1335'.

621A *Rubric: Letter of attorney of the said prior for making the said suit of court faithfully.*

622 *Memorandum that Arnold, lord of Upsall, and Adam Fossard, lord of the whole estate of Sutton near Felixkirk, lived in the time of Henry II, son of the Empress Matilda; both of them were knights and their land and pasture were coterminous. These were the boundaries between the lands of the said Arnold and Adam: from the moor called Middlemoor as now shown by the small sike and by an ancient ditch through the middle of Burtonholme as far as Fossarddyk, and from there ascending along the watercourse which is called Holbeck as far as the field of Kirby Knowle. Within these boundaries a wood called Killingwith was enclosed towards the vill of Marderby. In that wood neither Arnold nor the men of the vill ever had common pasture except by straying when Adam Fossard did not know. But the men of Sutton and Marderby peacefully used the pastures and common in the wood and beyond the said boundaries as far as the watercourse which is called Thenesdalebek. Often there arose great discord between Arnold and Adam both over the common of Killingwith and about the cutting down of trees growing in Middlemoor, which was then beautiful and fair. At length with the mediation of friends and relatives of both men a final agreement was reached, namely that Arnold should marry Adam's sister, Juliana, and that there should be peace and concord about Middlemoor; moreover to complete the marriage Adam should concede to Arnold and the men of Upsall common pasture in Killingwith but without the right to fell trees. They lived in peace and harmony for the rest of their lives. And the said Adam Fossard made part of the manor of Sutton and of the great hall of Marderby, as appears by an old register about the timber of the moor of Middlemoor and Killingwith, and according to the said register it is called Middlemoor because the land and pasture of Marderby and Upsall lie next to each other.* [c. 1183 x 1203].

Copy: MS Dodsworth 63, fol. 74r, from cartulary fol. 175b (*sic*).
Pd: *EYC* IX, no. 81 (from cartulary copy).

Dating: *EYC* dates to between 1183 and 1203 (the succession and the death of the first witness to no. 623).

[fol. 68r, old fol. 175]

623 *Notification of the agreement reached at the conclusion of the controversy between Adam Fossard, lord of Marderby, and Arnold of Upsall, lord of Upsall, concerning the cutting down and taking away of trees growing in Middlemoor, which lies between their respective lands and pastures, which had been reached through the mediation of their friends. It was agreed that both parties could use the wood for building materials, but neither was to sell or give it away without the consent of the other.* Middlemoor; [*c.* 1183 x 1203].

In presentia Willelmi de Stutevill', Ade de Boltby, Hugonis de Malbys, Iohannis de Dayvill', Gilberti de Meynill' militum, et aliorum multorum tunc ibi presentium.

Copies: MS Dodsworth 63, fol. 74v (from cartulary fol. 175) and MS Dodsworth 118, fol. 81v (apparently from the original). The latter has 'Stephani', dotted for deletion, for 'Gilberti', and a sketch of a seal with legend SIGILL' ARNALDI DE VPPESAL. There follows a copy of no. 624, with the marginal note 'bothe thes charters seeme to be in one hand'.
Pd: *EYC* IX, no. 82, from MS Dodsworth 118.
Dating: see no. 622.

624 *Rubric: Confirmation by Nicholas de Stuteville of the grant of Robert Fossard son of Adam Fossard of the manor of Marderby with its appurtenances in Felixkirk and of the agreement made between Adam Fossard and Arnold of Upsall (nos 622, 623).*

Original: *Confirmation, addressed to all who see or hear this charter, by Nicholas de Stuteville, to God and the monks of St Mary of Byland, of the grant of Robert Fossard, as in rubric, and also of the agreement between Adam Fossard and Adam of Boltby and others. This confirmation is made for the salvation of his soul and of all his ancestors and heirs according to the contents of the charters and agreements which the monks have.* [?1224 x 1233].

Hiis testibus domino Henrico de Baton', Helya de Cumbe tunc vice(comite) Ebor', Stephano Menyll', Hugone de Uppesall, Willelmo de Percy de Kildall', Rogero de Stapilton, Ada de Hilton, Willelmo de Bartona, Willelmo filio Willelmi de Eborac', Willelmo de Salcoke, Willelmo de Foxoles, et aliis.

Location: BL Stowe charter 443; endorsed: Martherby B. i (Marderby, first bundle); seal and tag missing.
Copies: MS Dodsworth 94, fol. 21r–v, no. 26 (from original); MS Dodsworth 118, fols 81v–82r; MS Top. Yorks. e. 9, fol. 25r–v (old pp. 23–4); (brief summary from

cartulary fol. 175) MS Dodsworth 63, fol. 74v.

Pd: *EYC* IX, no. 60, from MS Dodsworth 118.

Dating: Clay points out that this could have been issued by Nicholas I (d. by 1217) or Nicholas II (died in 1233). However, the first two witnesses, Henry de Baton (Bathonia) and Elias de Cumbe, described as sheriff of Yorkshire, held office as sheriff and undersheriff respectively from 1242 and 1244 (although Elias is not mentioned in *Lord Lieutenants*). Clay suggests an unrecorded tenure by Elias at a date before 1233.

Note: The copy in MS Dodsworth 94 has a note: Libr' B. fol. 174 [recte fol. 175], a cross reference to the cartulary.

625   *Notification by Robert Fossard of Sutton under Whitestonecliffe of his grant in free alms to Abbot Henry and the convent of Byland of 2 bovates and 3 messuages in Sutton and 40 acres of woodland in* Gildusdale, *that is all the <land> between the arable land of* Gildusdale *and the pasture of Marderby called Middlemoor. Grant also of pasture in Sutton for 80 sheep with their offspring up to three years, 6 cows with the same, 6 mares with the same, 6 sows with the same, 40 goats with the same and 4 oxen. To have and to hold of the donor and his heirs free of all service, with licence to enclose the woodland as they wish. Pledge to warranty.* [1241 x 1243].

Hiis testibus Iohanne de Dayvill, Thoma de Lascel', Willelmo de Tampton, etc.

Dating: The occurrence of Abbot Henry of Battersby suggests that the donor was Robert, son of Thomas Fossard, who succeeded by 1241 (see below, no. 1000). The first witness died in 1242/3.

A note is added that a fine was levied in the court of king H. and it is in the register of pleas of Byland.

[fol. 68v]

KIRBYMOORSIDE (SE6986), township and parish in the wapentake of Ryedale (NR). This section of the cartulary is headed **MIDDLETON**, a manor held by the Wake family, heirs of the Stutevilles through the marriage of Hugh Wake to Joan, daughter of Nicholas de Stuteville II.

626   *Grant, addressed to all the sons of holy mother church who will see or hear this writing, by Baldwin Wake, to God and St Mary and the abbot and convent of Byland, for the salvation of his soul and of his father and mother and his ancestors and heirs, of 100s. annual rent to be taken from the manor of Middleton by the hand of Nicholas Wake during his lifetime, and after his death by whoever holds the said manor. The monks are to receive half at Whitsuntide and half at St Martin in Winter (11 Nov.) in order to make pittances as follows: in the first free day in the first month after Easter in commemoration of the souls mentioned above, 20s; in the first free day in the first month after St Michael (29 Sept.) for the commemoration of the same,*

20s; the remaining 60s. are to be divided among 9 pittances for the commem-
oration of the said souls in perpetuity. To hold of the donor and his successors
with no interference. Only the proctor of the convent may receive it. Pledge
to warranty. Sealed with the donor's seal. [1276 x 1282].

Hiis testibus domino Nicholao Wake fratre meo, Hugone Wak,
Iohanne de Horbiry, etc.

Copy: MS Top. Yorks. e. 7, fol. 123v (old p. 195), which omits 'etc' in the witness list
and continues: Alberico de Wythsbyre tunc senescallo, Roberto de Wyleby,
Galfrido . . . Ricardo le Rus, militibus, Nicholao Druval, Willelmo filio Walteri,
domino . . . Nicholao de Runghetona.

Dating: the succession and death of the donor. Hugh Wake married Joan, elder
daughter of Nicholas de Stuteville II (d. 1233), before 1229. Hugh died on crusade
before 18 Dec. 1241, and Joan lived until 1276. At the time of her death Middleton
was held of her by Nicholas Wake. Her heir was her son, Baldwin, grantor of this
charter. He was dead by 1282 when he was succeeded by his son, John. At the time
of Baldwin's death Middleton was still held by Nicholas Wake. The third witness
married Elizabeth, daughter of Baldwin Wake by his first wife, Ela, one of the three
daughters of William de Beauchamp; he died *c.* 1302: *EYF*, pp. 43, 85. For the family
of Wake, see *CP* XII, part II, 295–305.

627   *Bond issued by Nicholas Wake and addressed to all the faithful in*
Christ who will see or hear this writing, to pay 100s. yearly to the abbot and
convent of Byland at 2 terms, as specified in no. 626. He himself was obliged
to pay Baldwin Wake 100s. for lands he held of him in Middleton, Wrelton,
Aislaby and Cawthorn, and which Baldwin has nominated him to pay.
Sealed with his seal. [before 1282].

Hiis testibus dominis Baldewyno Wak, Iohanne de Steyngreve,
Albrido de Whittelbyr, Iohanne de Iarpenvyle, Willelmo Malecak,
militibus etc.

Dating: death of first witness.

[fol. 68v–69r]

628   *Confirmation, addressed to all the faithful in Christ to whom the*
present writing shall come, by John Wake son of Baldwin Wake, to God and
St Mary and the abbot and convent of Byland, of all grants which they have
or might have in his fee, and of the annual rent of 100s. which was accus-
tomed to be rendered by the hand of Nicholas Wake from the manor of
Middleton, to make pittances, as contained in his father's charter (no. 626).
The confirmation is made for the salvation of his soul and of his father and
mother, and all his ancestors, heirs and successors. Pledge to warranty.
[1289 x 1300, possibly 1290].

Hiis testibus dominis Hugone Wak' tunc senescallo, Iohanne de
Steyngreve, Iohanne de Horbyry, Henrico de Appilby, Willelmo de
Harum, militibus, Waltero de Louthorp', Thoma de Etton' et aliis.

Copies: MS Dodsworth 91, fols 138r–139r, no. 114; MS Top. Yorks. e. 8, fol. 109r (old p. 182).

Dating: John succeeded his father in 1282, and took seisin of his lands in 1289; he died in 1300. See no. 626. In a further document which is not entered into the cartulary John ordered his provost to pay to the abbot and convent and their successors 100s. for their pittances from his manor of Middleton; the witnesses are the same as no. 628, and the letter is dated St Michael (29 Sept.) 1290: MS Dodsworth 91, fols 151v–152r, no. 126.

[fol. 69r, old fol. 176]

629 *Inquisition held in the presence of Robert Wodehous, king's escheator beyond Trent, by Jordan of Hovingham, Henry Hagett, R. Stut<eville>, John Aspelon', W[illiam] Monk, W[illiam] de Wath, Walter of Skewsby, J. de Middleton, Nicholas of Fadmoor, W. of Howthorpe, Robert de Nevill and Bernard de Bergh, jurors, who swore on oath that the abbot of Byland took 100s. yearly from the manor of Middleton by the grant of Baldwin Wake and the confirmation of John Wake his son and heir from the time of the grant. They swore further that the abbot is now prevented from taking the rent by John Thwait, bailiff of the queen, who wishes to authenticate the abbot's muniments before he allows it. They say that the manor is held in chief of the king for homage and service. Sealed with their seals.* Kirbymoorside; Friday before St Mark, 5 Edward II [21 Apr. 1312].

Copy: MS Top. Yorks. e. 9, fol. 24v (old p. 22), from which the extensions in square brackets are supplied. The transcript is followed by a note: 'the seals in brown wax except þe 10 & 12 are yet appendant to þe deed'.

Note: For the writ ordering the inquisition see *Cal. Inq. Misc. (Chancery)*, II, 28, no. 122 (6 Mar. 1312).

630 *Letter of Isabella, by the grace of God queen of England, lady of Ireland and duchess of Aquitaine, to John de Thweyt, her bailiff of Cottingham and Cropton, ordering that he should cause to be paid to the abbot and convent the 100s. annual rent from the manor of Middleton which they have of the grant of the ancestors of Thomas Wake, and the arrears.* York; 3 June 5 Edward II [1312]. French.

631 *Rubric: Similar letter from Thomas de Holand to his bailiff of Cropton, present and future, to pay the arrears.* [c. 1312].

[fol. 69v]

MARTON IN CLEVELAND (NZ5115), parish in the wapentake of Langbargh West (NR). Marton lies in present day Middlesbrough, and the nearest abbey lands were those in 'Gateryg', Linthorpe and

Thornaby on Tees. The Malebisse family, also benefactors in Murton and Snilesworth, were the main donors here.

632   *Grant in free alms, addressed to the archbishop of York and the whole chapter of St Peter (York) and all the sons of holy church, by Hugh Malebisse, at the request and grant of Matilda his wife, to God and the monks of St Mary of Byland, of a toft in Tollesby 8 perches in width and 40 in length, and 20 acres in the region of Marton, that is 10 acres on one side of the vill in* Munkflat *and the wandale of* Crossebidaila *and 10 acres on the other side of the vill, that is* Wutskereflat *and the* cultura *of Marketgate from the east of the valley. Grant also of common pasture in Marton for 100 sheep and other animals which they keep in the toft for tilling the ground. As has been stated, the grant is made at the request and with the permission of the donor's wife, Matilda, whose dower it is, for the salvation of the soul of the donor and of his wife, their fathers and mothers, their children and their ancestors. Pledge to warranty.* [1170 x 1186].

Huius donationis sed et petitionis et concessionis predicte Mathilde sponse mee testes sunt rogatu eiusdem Mathildis Ricardus prior de Neubergh, Rogerus decanus de Foston, Gamaliel de Kylvyngton', etc.

Pd: *EYC* III, no. 1849.

Dating: Farrer gives 1170 x 1188. However, the latest date is provided by the first witness.

Note: The mention of the donor's wife, Matilda, identifies this as a grant of Hugh Malebisse the younger, who occurs in 1166 and was dead by 1188. The charter three times makes the point that the grant is made with the consent of Matilda.

633   *Rubric: Charter of Hugh Malebisse concerning a* cultura *called* Hovydlandflat *in the region of Marton. Look under* Gaterygg *in the first bundle.* [before 1188].

Dating: If this is the same donor as no. 632 then the terminal date is his death.

Note: This is a cross reference to the 'Gaterygg' section of the cartulary, but the charter is not apparently entered there.

634   *Confirmation, addressed to all the sons of holy mother church present and future, by William Malebisse, to God and the monks of St Mary of Byland, of the toft which Walter the miller held in Marton in exchange for the toft granted by William's father, Hugh, in Tollesby (no. 632). However much land is lacking in Walter's toft he has granted from the land on the other side of the road. This exchange is made in free alms for the salvation of his soul and of all his ancestors and heirs until he or his heirs are able to hand over their toft in Tollesby. Pledge to warranty the toft in Marton in order that they shall recover the toft in Tollesby.* [before 1206].

Hiis testibus Waltero de Meinil, Gilberto de Thurkilby, Stephano filio eius, Willelmo de Buggedena, etc.

Dating: The attestation of Gilbert de Meinill of Thirkleby and his son, Stephen, suggests a date in the late 12th century; the first witness is probably Walter de Meinill of Osgodby, who occurs in the same period. This would suggest that the grantor is to be identified as William Malebisse, son of Hugh the younger, who was still living in 1206.

Note: In 1201 Richard Malebisse, son of William Malebisse, subinfeudated Marton to his cousin, William son of Hugh Malebisse. In 1206 William son of Hugh granted it to Constance, widow of his brother, Hugh, and her second husband Robert de Luttrington (*EYC* III, 456–8). The charter (no. 634) is followed by a note that the chirograph charter of John de Blaby, which is in the third bundle, should not be transcribed because they have the other part handed over by his heir. John de Blaby was the son of Amice, daughter of Hugh and sister of William Malebisse, and Stephen de Blaby (occ. 1227, 1234); John's son and heir, John, died without male issue in or around 1301 (*VCH NR* II, 47, 265; *EYC* III, 456). He was succeeded by six daughters, one of whom occurs in no. 635.

635 *Order from Simon Ward, sheriff of Yorkshire, on behalf of the king to the bailiff of Birdforth to cause a jury of 12 knights to appear before John of Doncaster at York on Mon. the day after the Sun. after Easter to enquire into claims concerning the rights the abbot had in a messuage and 20 acres in Tollesby and Marton which the abbot has recovered in the king's court against Adam de Hurworth and Joan his wife, and others, by default, and concerning which of the predecessors of the abbot was seised of the land. In the meantime the land is to be taken into the king's hands. The chief lord of the fee is to be informed. Further order to summon a similar jury at the same time and in the same place to enquire into the right of the abbot in 1 bovate in Fawdington, which he has recovered in the king's court against Lawrence of Topcliffe, through Lawrence's default. In the meantime the land is to be taken into the king's hands.* Westminster. [1315 x 1317 or May–Nov. 1318 or 1318 x 1323].

Dating: Simon Ward as sheriff of Yorkshire, for whose career see *Lord Lieutenants*, pp. 64–5.

Note: John de Blaby the younger, son of John de Blaby and grandson of Stephen, died without male heirs in or around 1301 and was succeeded by six daughters, the eldest of whom was Joan, who married Adam de Hurworth. She occurs as a widow in 1345 (*VCH NR* II, 47, 265).

636 *Rubric: Plea concerning 1 toft and 20 acres in Marton. Bound with the charter (no. 635).*

Note: There is a catchword at the foot of folio 69v, in the same hand as the cartulary: 'Carta Agnetis de Percy'.

[fol. 70r, old fol. 177]
MOSKWITH, in the parish of Topcliffe (NR).

637 *Grant in free alms, addressed to the archbishop of York and the whole chapter of St Peter (York) and all the sons of holy church present and future, by Agnes de Percy in her widowhood, to God and the monks of St Mary of Byland, of pasture in Moskwith for 38 cows and their calves up to one year. The grant is made for the soul of her husband Jocelin, for her own soul and for the souls of all her ancestors and heirs. Pledge to warranty.* [1180 x 1181 or 1191 x 1198].

Hiis testibus Ricardo decano de Semar', Galfrido sacerdote, Roberto sacerdote, Rogero filio Radulfi, etc.

Copy: MS Top. Yorks. e. 7, fol. 141r (old p. 229), which omits 'etc' from the witness list and continues: Henrico de Edbrictona, Ricardo diacono, Ricardo Perio . . . Radulfo filio Ketelli.

Pd: *EYC* XI, no. 75.

Dating: Agnes de Percy, daughter and co-heir of William de Percy (d. 1175), married Jocelin of Louvain (d. 1180). Agnes herself died between 1201 and 1204. As her charter is addressed to the archbishop of York it may date from the last year of Roger de Pont L'Evêque or to after the enthronement of Archbishop Geoffrey. Agnes's grant was confirmed by her son before 1198: see no. 638.

638 *Confirmation, addressed to all the sons of holy mother church to whom this writing shall come, by Henry de Percy, out of the impulse of divine love and for the souls of his father and mother and of all his ancestors, kinsmen and friends, no less for the salvation of his own soul and of his wife and their children, to God and the monks of Byland, of the grant made by his mother, as her charter attests (no. 637).* [1180 x 1181 or 1191 x 1198].

Hiis testibus Petro de Brus, Henrico de Putheaco, Philippo filio Roberti, Galfrido de Percy, Roberto de Altaripa clerico, etc.

Copies: MS Dodsworth 7, fol. 133v, and MS Dodsworth 91, fol. 125v, no. 88, where the witness list has 'Willelmo Pictavensi' after the third witness, omits 'etc', and continues: Gilberto de Levint', et Udardo et multis aliis.

Dating: Henry de Percy died in his mother's lifetime, before Michaelmas 1198: *EYC* XI, 6. See no. 637.

Note: This is followed by a note to the effect that a confirmation of the same Henry which is under the heading 'Catton' is better. This concerns the said pasture in Moskwith among other rights. There is an instruction to look there.

639 *Rubric: Schedule of the abbot to the Lord Percy for using common in Moskwith often* (frequentanda).

MERSCHAW (lost). No. 639 is followed by an instruction to look for 'Merschaw' under Windhill (now Wind Hill Gate and Wood) and Woolley. Land in 'Mershaw' was granted by Isabel, mother of Henry de Byri, and confirmed by Henry III (see no. 527). Woolley (SE 3213) is in the parish of Royston and the wapentake of Staincross (WR). The Woolley section of the cartulary occupied old fols 241–3, the final section of the cartulary.

MICKLEY (SE2576), in the parish of Kirkby Malzeard and wapentake of Lower Claro (WR).

640 *Grant in free alms, addressed to all the sons of holy church present and future, by Thurstan de Belvoir, to God and the monks of St Mary of Byland, of 3 acres of his land in Carr House with a perch of 20 feet, that is, those 3 acres which lie in* Wulwynriddyng *nearest to the river and which begin at the southern head of the same ridding. The monks are to hold this land free from all service, to do with as they wish, for the salvation of the soul of the donor and of all his ancestors and heirs. Pledge to warranty. [c. 1170 x 1184].*
Hiis testibus etc.

Note: Carr House (now Carr House Farm) lies less than one mile to the south east of Mickley. 'Wulwynriddyng' occurs in no. 462, in a Kirkby Malzeard charter. The river referred to in this charter is the Ure, which runs to the north of Mickley. Roger de Mowbray restored to Ralph de Belvoir 1 carucate in 'Kerhae' in increment of his other fee in Mickley between *c.* 1170 and 1184 (*Mowbray Charters*, no. 346, where the identification of Carr House is suggested). No. 640 is followed by a note that the surrenders ('dimissiones') of Mickley only mention 2 acres, rendering 12d. yearly.

[fol. 70v]
MOWBRAY CHEST. This contained the charters of the patrons of Byland Abbey, from Roger de Mowbray and his mother, Gundreda de Gournay, to John de Mowbray, who died in 1361. The charters of the Mowbray family are to be found both in this and in the topographical sections of the cartulary; some, such as no. 646, are cross referenced by the compiler of the cartulary. Those of Roger de Mowbray, founder of Byland, included in this section, are general charters of confirmation (nos 641–5). Roger left England for the Holy Land in 1186, and died there in 1188. His elder son, Nigel, was closely associated with his father's grants, and he and his brother, Robert, witnessed their father's charters from an early date. Nigel issued confirmations in his father's lifetime and after his death, in the short

period before Nigel's own crusade, in December 1189 (nos 648–50, 662). Nigel's son and heir, William (d. 1224) was involved in a dispute with Byland over land in Middlesmoor (nos 653–5) and issued general charters of confirmation (nos 651–2). William's elder son, Nigel, died without heirs in 1230, and was succeeded by his younger brother, Roger. Roger issued general confirmations for the abbey (nos 656–7), as did his son, Roger, who succeeded his father in 1266 (nos 658–9). Roger's son, John de Mowbray, confirmed the monks' rights in Nidderdale, which had earlier been a source of conflict (no. 660). He was hanged at York in 1322. John's son, another John, had his inheritance restored in 1327. He quitclaimed rent from land in Kirkby Malzeard (rubric at no. 661, with text at no. 484) and issued an inspeximus of the charters of his predecessors (no. 664). He was the grantor of a moiety of Bubwith church (no. 106). With the exception of no. 662 the Mowbray charters, the originals of which were stored in the Mowbray chest, are presented in chronological order of donors.

641   *Rubric: Charter of Roger de Mowbray concerning all our lands. Copied.* [before 1186].

Dating: Roger's departure from England on crusade.

Note: The rubric is followed by a note that this charter is better than all his other charters; it is marked with an A; look under Oldstead. The Oldstead charters occupied old fols 63–66, and were transcribed in MS Dodsworth 63, fols 34–35. This may be the charter printed from there in *Mowbray Charters*, no. 69.

642   *Rubric: Charter of the same [Roger de Mowbray] concerning the same lands, which is almost identical. Three copies.* [before 1186].

Dating: as no. 641.

643   *Grant in free alms, addressed to the archbishop of York and the whole chapter of St Peter (York) and all the sons of holy church present and future, by Roger de Mowbray, to God and the monks of St Mary of Byland, of all common easements in pasture, materials, ways, paths and waters, throughout all his forests of Nidderdale, Coxwold, Bagby, Balk, Hovingham and Scackleton. Grant also of free entry and exit for themselves, their men and their flocks, and quittance of pannage. The grant is made free from all secular service for the salvation of his soul and of all his ancestors and heirs. Pledge to warranty.* [1142 x 1147].

Hiis testibus Sampsone de Albaneyo, Willelmo de Arches, Radulfo de W<yvil>l, etc.

Pd: *Mowbray Charters*, no. 42.

Dating: As *Mowbray Charters*, where it is pointed out that the Byland *Historia*

Fundationis suggests a date before the move to the third conventual site of Stocking. The grant of easements in the forests was confirmed by Pope Hadrian IV, by the hand of Roland, papal chancellor, in 1154, the first year of his pontificate (*PUE* III, no. 96). Greenway further indicates that the witnesses (and the third witness, partially obscured by damage to the MS, may be Ralph de Wyville) are consistent with that date, although the warranty clause may be an interpolation.

644   *Grant in free alms, addressed to the archbishop of York and the whole chapter of St Peter (York) and all the sons of holy church present and future, by Roger de Mowbray, to God and the monks of St Mary of Byland, of freedom from the payment of fees for the use of his and his heirs' seals, for donations and confirmations. The freedom is granted for the salvation of his soul and of all his ancestors and heirs. [c. 1170 x 1186].*
Hiis testibus Ricardo priore et capitulo de Neuburgh, Roberto de Molbray filio meo, Philippo de Muntpinzun, etc.
Pd: *Mowbray Charters*, no. 64.
Dating: As *Mowbray Charters*; Philip de Montpincon begins to attest *c.* 1170, and the donor left on his final journey to the Holy Land in 1186.

645   *Notification by Roger de Mowbray to Eustace Fitz J(ohn) and all his ministers and men in Yorkshire, French and English, that he has granted licence for the monks of Byland to exchange lands, inhabited or uninhabited, for land which may be nearer or more useful to them. The grant is made for the salvation of his soul. [c. 1147].*
Testibus Sampsone, Willelmo de Arches, Roberto de Dayvill, etc.
Pd: *Mowbray Charters*, no. 45.
Dating: The same witnesses attest *Mowbray Charters*, nos 43 and 44, which Greenway has dated to *c.* 1147. The first witness is Samson d'Aubigny.

646   *Rubric: Confirmation by the chapter of York of the grants of Roger de Mowbray. Look under the heading Old Byland.*
Note: The Old Byland section of the cartulary is missing.

647   *Rubric: Confirmation of William de Stuteville of the site of the abbey. Look under the heading Oldstead. [before 1203].*
Text: MS Dodsworth 63, fol. 35r, from a lost portion of the cartulary, fol. 64, under the heading Oldstead. Grant, addressed to all the sons of holy mother church who will see or hear these writings, by William de Stuteville, to God and the monks of St Mary of Byland, of the site of the abbey which is founded on his patrimony and of whatever the monks have of his fee and inheritance, in free alms for the salvation of his soul and of his father and mother and of all his ancestors and heirs. Hiis testibus Willelmo de Cottingham, Roberto de Melsa,

Benedicto de Sculcot', Galfrido Wacel, Galfrido de Bosco, Willelmo Will(elmi) de Furn', fratre Richardo de Furnes, Bartholomeo de Stuttevill', Ricardo clerico de Dancestr'.

Note: The grantor was the son and heir of Robert de Stuteville III. He was king's justice, and died in 1203. He was succeeded by an under-age heir, Robert de Stuteville IV, who died still a minor in 1205.

648 *Grant and confirmation, addressed to all the faithful of holy church, by Nigel de Mowbray, to the abbot and monks of Byland and their successors, for the salvation of his soul and of his father, Roger, and all his ancestors and heirs, of their new abbey, and of all the lands of his fee, wherever they are, which they have of the grant made by his father, Roger, and others. Pledge to warranty.* [1177 x 12 Dec. 1189].

Testes sunt Robertus Dayvill', Willelmus frater eius, Hugo de Malabestia, Robertus Bellocamp', Hamo Beler.

Pd: *Mowbray Charters*, no. 70.

Dating: The transfer to the final conventual site of New Byland and the departure of Nigel de Mowbray on crusade.

Note: The rubric to this charter calls it Nigel's 'short confirmation' (cf no. 649) sealed with sign 'th' (illustrated).

649 *Rubric: Great confirmation by the same [Nigel de Mowbray], word for word that of his father. It is good. Look under the heading Oldstead.* [before Dec. 1189].

Dating: Nigel's departure on crusade.

650 *Rubric: Confirmation by the same [Nigel de Mowbray] of Cam, Thorpe and Ampleforth.* [before Dec. 1189].

Dating: as no. 649.

[fol. 71r, old fol. 178]

651 *Confirmation, addressed to all his men, Norman, French and English, and all the faithful of holy church, by William son of Nigel de Mowbray, for the love of God, to God and the abbot and monks of Byland and their successors, of all the lands, pastures and tenements with their appurtenances, which the monks have of his fee or may have in the future, to hold in free alms quit of all secular service. Pledge to warranty. Made and sealed in the chapter of St Peter, York, in the presence of Simon the dean, and Hamo the treasurer, the donor's judges, Master William, archdeacon of Nottingham and other canons there present. York;* [1199 x Oct. 1210, possibly *c*. 1204].

Testes sunt magister Gregorius, Robertus dapifer meus, Ricardus

Malebisse, Philippus filius Iohannis, Willelmus de Corneburgh, Willelmus de Buscy, Rogerus de Fontibus.

Dating: Simon of Apulia became dean in February 1195, and was consecrated bishop of Exeter on 5 October 1214. Hamo first occurs as treasurer in 1199. Richard Malebisse died in 1210. If this confirmation was issued in the wake of the settlement concerning Middlesmoor then the date would be nearer to 1204. See nos 653, 695 below, and no. 701 which is attested by the same witnesses as no. 651.

Note: At Michaelmas 1209 the abbots of Fountains, Rievaulx and Byland rendered account for £100 for consideration of the king's court as to whether they should give aid to William de Mowbray to acquit him of the fine due to the king when William was impleaded by William de Stuteville concerning lands which he claimed against him. See *Pipe Roll 1209*, Pipe Roll Society, ns 24, p. 139.

652 *Rubric: Great confirmation by the same [William de Mowbray] of all lands, and concerning other matters.* [before Mar. 1224].

Marginal note: beside nos 651 and 652, in the same hand as the cartulary, 'N'.
Dating: the death of William son of Nigel de Mowbray (*CP* IX, 374).

653 *Rubric: Settlement in the form of a chirograph between the same William [de Mowbray] and the monks concerning the agreements by which the monks have Middlesmoor and the confirmation which William made.* [? c. 1204].

Note: Middlesmoor lies in Nidderdale, and was apparently granted to Byland by Roger de Mowbray in 1172 for 10 years to hold in mortgage for 300 marks (see *Mowbray Charters*, no. 54 and note). In 1204 Innocent III appointed Simon, dean, and Hamo, treasurer of York, papal judges delegate, to decide the dispute between William de Mowbray and the monks of Byland concerning Middlesmoor (*ibid.*, p. 42); text at no. 695 below. It is possible that the confirmation in no. 651 was issued after the settlement.

654 *Rubric: Agreement in the form of a chirograph between the same two parties, made through the dean and chapter of York, concerning Middlesmoor. Look in the first Nidderdale bundle (no. 695).*

655 *Notification, addressed to the archbishop of York and the chapter of St Peter (York) and all his men, French and English, by William son of Nigel de Mowbray that he has received from the abbot and monks of Byland 300 silver marks which they were bound to pay him for the forest of Middlesmoor in Nidderdale, according to an agreement reached recently at York, and a further 20 marks paid by the monks on William's behalf to the sheriff of Yorkshire under the same agreement. William now quitclaims the money, as the abbot and convent have pardoned him 100 silver marks which he was bound to pay them under a loan in exchange for making his confirmation of all their lands. They have also restored to him the men who held anything of them in*

Thirsk, that is William son of Ernisius, William nephew of Ingeler, Roger Hakesmal, Jordan Bacun, Robert de Barra, and Adam his brother, all of whom now hold of him, William, as they did of the monks, and they have also restored to him 1 toft and 5 acres in Hovingham and ½ mark from the mill there, and 15 acres of meadow in Fryton and all they had in the Isle of Axholme. [c. 1204].

Hiis testibus Symone decano Ebor', Hamone thesaurario, magistro Willelmo archidiacono Notingham', Ricardo Malbisse, Willelmo de Corneburgh, Roberto dapifero, etc.

Dating: The agreement to which this refers (no. 695 below) is dated 1204.

[fol. 71r–v]

656 *Notification, addressed to all the sons of holy mother church, by Roger son of William de Mowbray that he has inspected, heard and examined at Byland all the charters which the abbot and monks have of his ancestors, that is, Roger de Mowbray his great-grandfather and first founder of Byland, Roger's son Nigel, his grandfather, and Nigel's son William, his father. Confirmation of all these charters concerning the site of the abbey, and all granges, manors, lands, rents, pastures etc. The confirmation is made in free alms for the salvation of his soul and of all his ancestors and heirs and all the faithful dead, and in fulfilment of an oath by which he was bound. Pledge to warranty. Sealed with the donor's seal.* [1241 x 1266].

Hiis testibus domino Willelmo de Ireby, domino Iohanne Haunsard, domino Willelmo de Mideltona, domino Waltero de Eglisclyve.

Dating: The donor's father, William, died by Mar. 1224, and was succeeded by his elder son, Nigel, who died without heirs in 1230. Roger then succeeded as a minor, and took livery of his lands from the king on 20 May 1241, which is taken as the earliest date for the issue of this confirmation. Roger died around Nov. 1266: *CP* IX, 374–6.

657 *Rubric: Agreement in the form of a chirograph between the same Roger [de Mowbray] and the monks, with 7 seals, concerning acres [sic] of woodland etc. by which he made the confirmation written above. This was replaced in the small box (pix) on account of the fragility of the seals.* [1241 x 1266].

Dating: as no. 656.

658 *Confirmation as chirograph, addressed to all who will see or hear this charter, by Roger son of Roger de Mowbray, for the love of God, to God and the abbot and monks of Byland and their successors, of all lands, pastures and tenements which the monks have throughout his fee, to hold in free alms*

quit of secular service. Pledge to warranty. Sealed with the donor's seal.
[1278 x 1297].

Hiis testibus dominis Rogero de Lascels, Radulfo filio Willelmi, Milone de Stapilton', Thoma de Colvill, Ricardo de Malbys, etc.

Dating: Roger de Mowbray was still a minor at the time of his father's death around Nov. 1266. The king took his homage in 1278. By 1296 he was Lord Mowbray, and he died before 21 Nov. 1297: *CP* IX, 376–7.

659 *Rubric: Confirmation by the same [Roger son of Roger de Mowbray] of the boundaries of Middlesmoor. Look in the first bundle of Nidderdale.* [1278 x 1297].

Dating: as no. 658. Text at no. 700 below.

660 *Confirmation and quitclaim, addressed to all who will see or hear this writing, made by the promptings of love, by John son and heir of Roger de Mowbray for himself and his heirs, to the abbot and convent of Byland, of all right he claimed or might ever claim in all the pasture in Highfield, Ramsgill and Middlesmoor, and especially the pasture for wild and domestic pigs. Pledge to make no further claim. Grant of all his pigs in Nidderdale at the time this document was issued, for the assistance of the sick of the said house. Sealed with the donor's seal.* Kirkby Malzeard; Palm Sunday [12 Apr.], 1321.

In presentia domini Nicholai de Hewyk, Willelmi Russell, Willelmi de Sunygys, Willelmi de Brathwayte, et aliorum plurimorum.

Copy: MS Dodsworth 7, fol. 112r; sketch of seal.

Note: John son of Roger de Mowbray was born *c.* 1286 and knighted in 1306. His marriage to Aline de Braose (1298) brought him the lordships of Bramber and Gower. In 1312 he was keeper of the city and county of York. He was banished in July 1321 but pardoned in Aug. In Jan. 1322 he took part in the siege of the king's castle at Tickhill and was hanged at York on 23 Mar. 1322: *CP* IX, 377–9. No. 673 is another deed of John de Mowbray made on the same occasion. 'Hirefeld' is identified in *EPNS WR*, V, as Heathfield, but Highfield lies immediately to the south.

661 *Rubric: Quitclaim of John son of John de Mowbray of 1 pound of pepper and 2s. annual rent. Look under the heading Kirkby Malzeard.* [Epworth, 18 Sept. 1345].

Note: The full text is given at 484. In 1322 as a result of his father's activities John was imprisoned in the Tower of London, and his inheritance was restored in 1327. For a general confirmation issued in 1345 see no. 664. In 1349 he granted a moiety of the advowson of Bubwith church, with licence to appropriate (no. 106) for the soul of his first wife, Joan. He died on 4 Oct. 1361: *CP* IX, 380–83.

[fols 71v–72r]

662 *Confirmation, addressed to all the sons of holy church who will see or hear these letters, by Nigel de Mowbray, to God and the monks of Byland, of ½ carucate in Cave and Fawdington according to the agreements which have been made between the monks and Humphrey de Mandeville and Walter de Riparia and their heirs. Confirmation also of 12 bovates in Thorpe near Thirsk (Thorpefield), which the monks have of the grant of Matilda of Stonegrave and her son Simon, and quitclaim of the hose of scarlet cloth which the monks were obliged to give the donor and his heirs yearly for all service. Confirmation of the agreements made between the monks and William, nephew and heir of Ingelram of Thirsk concerning land in Thorpe[field], 1 bovate in Bagby and 3 bovates in Thirsk which Ingelram his uncle granted and confirmed by his charter. Confirmation of the service of William son of Hucce and his heirs, and the grant which he made them in Bagby, as his charter attests, and 1 toft in Thirsk which was held by Geoffrey Harpin and another which Roger son of Walter Harkesmall and Jordan his companion held. All this is confirmed in free alms for the salvation of the soul of the donor and of his father and mother and all his ancestors and heirs. Pledge to warranty.* [1186 x Dec. 1189].

Hiis testibus Roberto fratre meo, Willelmo filio meo et herede, Galfrido Hagat, Ricardo de Widevilla, Hamone Beler, etc.

Pd: *Mowbray Charters*, no. 73.

Dating: after the departure of Roger de Mowbray for the Holy Land, and before Nigel himself left England for the final time.

[fol. 72r]

663 *Rubric: Mandate sent by John de Mowbray to his bailiffs to defend the monks' lands and privileges.*

Note: It is not clear if this is John son of Roger de Mowbray (d. 1322) or his son John (d. 1361).

[fols 72r–73r, old fols 179–180]

664 *Notification by John son and heir of John de Mowbray, Lord of the Isle of Axholme and of the honours of Gower and Bramber, addressed to his stewards, vassals, foresters, bailiffs, provosts, and all his other ministers and all the faithful of Christ, of his inspeximus of all the grants, confirmations and quitclaims made by his ancestors, that is, Gundreda de Mowbray, her son Roger de Mowbray, Roger's son Nigel de Mowbray, Nigel's son William de Mowbray, William's son Roger de Mowbray, Roger's son Roger de Mowbray and Roger's son John de Mowbray and others, to God and St Mary and the abbot and monks of Byland. He confirms all lands, tenements,* *rents, services both of free men and villeins, meadows, moors, pastures, marshes, woods, roads, paths, etc. far and near, and especially Middlesmoor and Ramsgill by the boundaries specified in the grants. He makes all these grants and confirmations from the promptings of love and for the salvation of his soul and of his father and mother and all his ancestors and heirs. He grants that the abbot and monks, and their men and their tenants within the liberty, shall be quit of suit of John's court at Sutton. They shall also be quit of toll for themselves and their men throughout the liberty of Byland, and have free entry and exit across his lands. Confirmation of all the liberties which they received in the past from the lord king and his predecessors, and especially freedom from pleas in his court of Sutton.* Byland; St Margaret the Virgin [20 July] 1345.

Hiis testibus dominis Willelmo Darrell, Willelmo Mancoys, Rogero de Weston', Iohanne de Colvyll', Iohanne de Waxand militibus, Marmeduco Darell, Iohanne de Kylvyngton, Iohanne de Baxeby, Iohanne de Upsale, Roberto Buscy, et aliis.

Marginal note: (in later hand) '29 Ed. 3'.

Note: The original charter, BL Stowe charter 436, is much damaged. There is a reference here to the abbot's court at Sutton, even though in 1271 it had been ordered that the royal justices hear pleas at Clifton rather than Sutton (see no. 529). It is possible that the court met at Clifton only on those occasions when the king's justices were present.

[fol. 73v]

BUNDLE OF THE MAGNATES (*Magnatum Baculus*). This section, of 22 charters and rubrics, brings together various confirmation charters. Some were issued by tenants in chief who either granted land themselves, or confirmed grants by their tenants: the Lacy earl of Lincoln, holder of the Honour of Pontefract (no. 665), the earl of Warenne (no. 666), the families of Percy (nos 667–9), Ros (nos 670–1), and Wake (nos 674–5). However the 'magnates' also include prominent knightly families, such as Coleville (no. 676), Darel (nos 678–81), Buscy (nos 683–4), Percehay (no. 685) and Wyville (no. 686). The reason for the inclusion of two Mowbray charters here (nos 672–3) rather than in the previous section is not clear, nor is the rationale behind the entry of nos 670–1, which relate specifically to Ampleforth, nos 678–80, which relate to Sessay, and no. 685 (Scackleton) here rather than in the relevant topographical section.

665   *Rubric: Confirmation by the earl of Lincoln of Denby and of all the monks' lands in Elmet which are of his fee.*

Note: There are two originals which could be intended here: (i) BL Add. charter

7465 (calendared in *Yorks. Deeds*, VI, 59, no. 192) and (ii) BL Add. charter 7438 (calendared *ibid.*, no. 193). (i) is a grant and confirmation by John, earl of Lincoln and constable of Chester, of all the monks' lands in Denby, Briestwistle, Clayton, Flockton, Allerton, Crossley, West Bretton, Wilsden, 'Whiteacres', Wind Hill, Woolley, Moorhouses, 'Mereschaw' and elsewhere in his fee. (ii) is a similar confirmation by Henry de Lacy, earl of Lincoln and constable of Chester.

666 Rubric: *Confirmation by the earl of Warenne of Bentley and Emley.*

667 *Confirmation by William de Percy, addressed to the archbishop of York and the whole chapter (of York) and all the sons of holy mother church, for the salvation of his soul and of all his ancestors and heirs, to God and St Mary and the abbot and convent of Byland and their successors, of all the grants made by Durand de Cliffe and his heirs in Deepdale and elsewhere in William's fee, and of all the grants of Angot of Osgodby and his heirs in Osgodby and elsewhere in William's fee. Confirmation also of all other lands and rents which the monks have of his fee, to do with as they wish without any hindrance by William and his heirs. Sealed with the donor's seal. [c. 1160 x 1166].*
Testes sunt Radulfus de Irtona, Marmedocus, Reynaldus Basseth, Willelmus filius Gwery, etc.
Pd: *EYC* XI, no. 22.
Dating: The grantor here is William de Percy II, who died in 1175. The first witness had been succeeded by his son, Baldwin, by 1166 (*EYC* XI, 273).
Note: The rubric states that the charter has been copied, and there is a copy at no. 189 above.

668 Rubric: *Confirmation by Richard de Percy of land in Catton which his mother granted. Copied.* [before 1244].
Note: The donor can be identified as the grandson of William de Percy II, a younger son of Agnes de Percy and Jocelin of Louvain. It is clear from this charter that Agnes was donor of land in Catton, but no charter survives in the cartulary. Richard died before August 1244 (*EYC* XI, 7).

669 Rubric: *Confirmation by Henry de Percy of Catton, Deepdale, etc. Copied. Look under the heading Catton.* [before 1198].
Text: MS Dodsworth 7, fols 102v–103r. Grant and confirmation, addressed to all the faithful in Christ who see or hear this charter, by Henry de Percy, for the salvation of his soul and of all his ancestors and heirs, to God and St Mary and the abbot and convent of Byland and their successors, of the sites of their granges of Deepdale by Seamer, and Catton, with free entry and exit. Confirmation also of grants in Deepdale, Osgodby, Cayton, Killerby and Catton, and of the

grant of his mother, Agnes, in Moskwith. Further confirmation of the exchange which Richard de Percy his brother made with them of certain arable land in Catton. The monks have received him and his heirs into all the prayers and good works made in their house, and he pledges to warranty the grant. Hiis testibus Petro le Brus, Iohanne filio Roaldi, Willelmo Peitevyn, Gilberto del Mund', Simone de Spoford, Galfrido de Perci, Nigello de Camera, et Augero filio Richerii.

Note: Henry de Percy was the elder son of Agnes de Percy and Jocelin of Louvain, and thus the brother of the donor of no. 668. Henry died before his mother, by 1198. His son, William III, inherited the barony of William de Percy II, although this was disputed by his uncle, Richard (*EYF*, p. 71). For the exchange of land between Richard de Percy and the monks of land in Catton see T. Martin, ed., *The Percy Cartulary*, SS, 117 (1911), pp. 93–4.

670 *Confirmation in free alms, addressed to the archbishop of York and the whole chapter of St Peter (York) and all the sons of holy mother church, by Robert de Ros, to God and the monks of St Mary of Byland, of the grant of Ralph de Surdeval of lands, tenements and pastures in the vill and region of Ampleforth, and of other grants which the monks have received in his fee. Further grant of an adequate road for the monks and their men with carts, wagons, pack horses and animals without any contradiction or hindrance as his own and his liege men have, except over certain meadows in time of enclosure and corn. Grant of freedom from all customs for the monks and their brethren buying and selling in the town and market of Helmsley which might be exacted by his bailiffs. Pledge to warranty.* [1190 x 1226].

Hiis testibus Drogone de Harum, Willelmo filio eius, Alexandro de Neyvill', Symone de Staingrive, etc.

Marginal note: Helmsley.
Pd: *EYC* X, no. 95.
Dating: The rubric identifies the donor as Robert de Ros *senior*, that is Robert de Ros II. He entered his inheritance in 1190, retired to join the Knights Templar before 23 December 1226, and was dead by July 1227.

[fols 73v–74r]

671 *Confirmation and quitclaim for himself and his heirs, addressed to all the sons of holy mother church who will see or hear this writing, by Robert de Ros, son of William de Ros, to God and St Mary and the abbot and convent of Byland and their successors, of all lands, rents, pastures and tenements which the abbot and convent have of his fee, both in the vill of Ampleforth and elsewhere, to hold of the donor and his heirs in free alms, quit of all secular exactions. Affirmation and ratification of the confirmations which* *the monks have of his grandfather Robert de Ros, for the salvation of the soul of the donor and all his ancestors and successors. Pledge to warranty. Sealed with the donor's seal.* [before 1285].

Hiis testibus dominis Petro de Ros fratre nostro, Gilberto de Cukeryngton, Iohanne de Melsa, Ricardo de Malbys, etc.

Copy: MS Dodsworth 94, fol. 54v, no. 69, which omits 'etc' from the witness list and continues: Iohanne de Staingreva, militibus, Galfrido de Holbek, Iohanne de Helpiston, Thoma de Etton, Willelmo de Bek, Hugone de Carleton, Waltero de London et aliis.

Dating: The rubric identifies the donor as Robert de Ros *iunior*. He died in 1285 (*EYC* X, 29).

672 *Notification, addressed to all the sons of holy mother church who will see or hear the present charter, by Roger son of William de Mowbray, of his* inspeximus *and examination at Byland of all the charters and confirmations which the abbot and monks have of his ancestors, that is, Roger de Mowbray his great-grandfather, first founder of the house, Roger's son Nigel, the grandfather of the grantor, and Nigel's son William, the father of the grantor, of the site of the abbey and all granges, manors, lands, rents, possessions, pastures and tenements wherever they are on his fee, with all their appurtenances above and below ground, far and near, and confirmation of the same. This confirmation is made in free alms for the salvation of his soul and of all his ancestors and heirs and all the faithful dead, and also in respect of his promise and the preservation of a certain oath to make this confirmation by which he was bound in the presence of certain noble men. Grant and quitclaim of freedom from toll for the monks and their men and tenants buying and selling in the vill and market of Thirsk and throughout his land and fee, and of freedom for the monks and their men of Thirsk and in all other vills and elsewhere in Roger's fee from the repair of bridges, ponds, causeways and roads and from suit of oven or mill, from amercements under the assize of bread and ale, and if they wish they may have orchards and furnaces within their own houses throughout his fee. Pledge to warranty. Sealed with the donor's seal.* [1241 x Nov. 1266].

Hiis testibus domino Willelmo de Ireby, domino Iohanne Haunsard, domino Willelmo de Midelton', domino Waltero de Eglisclyve, domino Thoma de Colvylle, Willelmo de Harum, Rogero Rawth', etc.

Marginal note: Thresk.

Dating: Roger took livery of his lands from the king in 1241 and died around Nov. 1266.

[fol. 74r–v, old fol. 181]

673 *Confirmation in free alms, addressed to the archbishop of York and the whole chapter of St Peter (York) and all the sons of holy mother church, by John de Mowbray, son and heir of Roger de Mowbray, for the love of God, to God and St Mary and the abbot and convent of Byland and their successors serving God there, of whatever the monks have of his fee, free from all secular service, and freedom from all service, suits of court, secular demands on both cultivated and uncultivated lands, meadows, pastures, moors, marshes, roads, paths, forests, woods, scrub lands, groves, turbaries, lead and iron mines, quarries, waters, millponds, fishponds, fisheries, mills, commons and all other things, far and wide, above and below ground. Grant also of freedom from tolls, as in the charter of his grandfather, Roger. Licence to acquire, alienate, and exchange lands. The abbot and convent have pardoned John 100 silver marks which he owed them under a certain bond which they have returned to him. Pledge to warranty. Sealed with the donor's seal.* Kirkby Malzeard; Palm Sunday [12 Apr.] 1321.

Datum apud Kyrkebi Malsard die dominica in Ramis Palmorum in presentia domini Nicholai de Hewyk, Willelmi Russell, Willelmi de Sunynges, Willelmi de Brathewath et aliorum plurimum.

Marginal note: Duplicatur.

Note: No. 660 above is another deed of John de Mowbray, made on the same occasion.

[fols 74v–75r]

674 *Quitclaim and confirmation, addressed to all the sons of holy mother church who will see or hear the present charter, by Baldwin Wake, for himself and his heirs and successors, to God and St Mary and the abbot and convent of Byland, of whatever the monks have of the fee of Thomas Fossard in Sutton, Marderby, Laysthorpe, Felixkirk and Hood with a chief messuage in Sutton, with all liberties, easements and appurtenances in all places far and wide, in demesne lands, meadows and pastures, in woods, waters, mill ponds, mills, fisheries, fishponds, in lands held by villein tenure, holdings of free tenants, marriages, reliefs, wardships, escheats, and all other services, customs, aids, and suits of court belonging to the donor and his successors. Quitclaim also of an annual rent of 60s. which the abbot and convent were accustomed to render to the donor's father, Hugh Wake, and to his mother, Lady Joan de Stuteville, as is contained in the chirograph between them. The confirmation and quitclaim is made for the salvation of his soul and of his father and mother, and all his ancestors and heirs, free from all secular service and suits of court and scutage. Pledge to warranty. Sealed with the donor's seal.* [1276 x 1278].

Hiis testibus dominis Alexandro de Kyrketon' tunc vicecomite Ebor',
Nicholao Wak fratre meo, Iohanne de Stayngreve, Hugone Wak, Ada
de Barton', etc.

Dating: The earliest date is provided by the death of Joan de Stuteville and the
succession of Baldwin Wake: see no. 626. The first witness held office between 1274
and 1278: *Lord Lieutenants*, p. 60.
Note: The rubric states that the charter was copied. There is a rubric cross referencing no. 674 at no. 1050 below.

[fol. 75r, old fol. 182]

675   *Confirmation and quitclaim by Baldwin Wake, addressed to all the
sons of holy mother church who will see or hear the present charter, for the
love of God and the salvation of his soul and of his father and mother and of
all his ancestors and heirs, to God and St Mary and the abbot and convent of
Byland and their successors, of all lands which the monks have of his fee,
with all liberties and easements, free from all secular exaction. Pledge to
warranty. Sealed with the donor's seal.* [1276 x 1278].

Hiis testibus dominis Alexandro de Kyrketon' tunc vicecomite Ebor',
Nicholao Wak fratre meo, Hugone Wak, Iohanne de Stayngreve, etc.

Marginal note: (in later hand) 'vic. Ebor 3456 Edw'. The name of the first witness
has been underlined.
Copy: MS Dodsworth 91, fos 84v–85v, no. 27, which omits 'etc' and continues the
witness list: Adam de Barton, Thoma de Coleville, militibus, Albredo tunc
seneschallo meo, Roberto Tackell tunc receptore meo, Alano de Sutton, clerico,
Thoma de Ettona, Radulfo de Thornton tunc ballivo domini regis, Willelmo del
Beck de Ampilford et multis aliis.
Dating: This was probably issued on the same occasion as no. 674.
Note: The rubric calls this 'confirmatio Baudewyn Wak optima de omnibus terris'.

676   *Rubric: Confirmation by Thomas de Coleville of meadow in*
Helfrikeholm *and all lands etc. Look under the heading of Coxwold.*
Note: The text is entered into the cartulary at no. 122 above.

677   *Rubric: Confirmation by Hugh de Neville of Denby and other lands in
his fee. Look under Denby.*
Note: There are three charters of Hugh de Neville in favour of Byland: (i) BL Add.
charter 7443, endorsed 'Denby B iii lxv' (calendared in *Yorks. Deeds*, VI, 58, no. 189);
(ii) BL Add. charter 7421, endorsed 'Conf. B i xi'; (iii) BL Add. charter 7467 (calendared in *Yorks. Deeds*, VI, 58, no. 190). (i) is a quitclaim of all right in lands and tenements which the monks had of his fee in Denby. (ii) is very similar, but the lands
specified are of Hugh's fee in Denby and elsewhere. (iii) is a release to the monks
of all distraint for his fee pertaining to the grange of Denby. The content, and the
endorsement, makes it likely that the rubric no. 677 refers to (ii) and the cross reference of (i) is to a missing folio of the Denby section.

678 *Rubric: Confirmation by William Darel of lands in his fee and of free movement over the moor. Look under Sessay.* [1203 x 1226].

Note: The Sessay section of the cartulary is missing. The donor is probably the William Darel who succeeded his father, Marmaduke I, by 1203: *EYC* XI, 336–7. It is possible that it was his grandson, who succeeded by 1260 and was still living in 1278/9, but no. 681 below suggests that the original donor of lands in Sessay was William Darel I.

679 *Rubric: Confirmation by Marmaduke Darel of the same. Look as above.* [Byland; Nativity of the B.V.M. [8 Sept.] 1344].

Text: MS Dodsworth 7, fol. 133r. Notification by Marmeduke Darel, lord of Sessay, addressed to all whom the present writing shall reach, of his inspeximus of the charters and confirmations of his ancestors which are held by the abbot and convent of the monastery of Byland. Confirmation of the same in free alms, and pledge to warranty. Hiis testibus Thoma de Etton, Roberto de Sproxton, Iohanne Darel fratre meo, Iohanne de Multon, Roberto Buscy, Ada Dese et multis aliis. Place and date.

680 *Rubric: Confirmation by William Darel the younger of the same. Look as above.*

Note: The grantor may be William Darel who succeeded his father, Marmaduke, in 1260, and was still living in 1278/9, or his grandson, who succeeded in 1301 and died *c.* 1344. The witnesses to no. 681 suggest the former.

681 *Rubric: Confirmation by William Darel of the same. As above.* [1260 x 1278/9].

Text: MS Dodsworth 94, fol. 23r–v, no. 29: Headed: Confirmatio Willelmo Darell iunioris. Confirmation by William Darel, son of Marmaduke Darel, of all the land which the monks have of the grant of William Darel his grandfather, and free transit over his moor at Sessay, as in the charter of William the elder (no. 678). Pledge to warranty. Sealed with his seal. Hiis testibus Marmeduco Darell filio meo milite, Nicholao Talenate de Tresky, Baldewino de Schipton, Radulfo de Thorneton, Thoma Maunsell de Hedon, Roberto filio Margarete, Willelmo filio Gamelli de Sutton, Roberto de Foxholis de eadem, Willelmo le Pledur et aliis.

Dating: William Darel, son of Marmaduke II, had succeeded by 1260 and was still living in 1278/9. This suggests that the monks' interests in Sessay dated back to the time of William Darel I, who succeeded by 1203.

Note: The first witness is Marmaduke Darel III, who was tenant in 1284/5.

682 *Rubric: Attestation by the chapter of St Peter, York, of the grants of Roger de Mowbray. Look under Old Byland.*

[fol. 75r–v]
683 *Confirmation and quitclaim, addressed to all the sons of holy mother church present and future, by Oliver de Buscy for himself and his heirs, to God and St Mary and the abbot and monks of Byland, of all forinsec service on all the land the monks hold in Osgoodby, as much as belongs to 3 carucates where 10 carucates make a knight's fee; this service belonged to Oliver and his heirs by hereditary right. The quitclaim is made in free alms, for the salvation of his soul and of all his ancestors and heirs. He binds himself and his heirs by this writing and by an oath to acquit the service on his tenement in Thirkleby, and pledge to warranty. [before 1243].*
Hiis testibus Iohanne de Ayvill', Roberto de Percy, Henrico de Ferlyngton', etc.

Copies: MS Dodsworth 94, fol. 9v (no number), which omits 'etc' from the witness list and continues: Willelmo de Teniton, Stephano de Maynill de Thurkelby, etc; MS Dodsworth 45, fol. 72v, which has witnesses as MS Dodsworth 94, and continues: Cutebarto fratre eius, Nicholao fratre eius, Henrico de Silton, Nicholao de Heton, Olivero de Heton, Galfrido de Ampleford etc. This copy is headed 'ex carta originali' and ends 'fol. 169b'. There is a genealogy of the Meinill family on fol. 73r.

Dating: Oliver de Buscy frequently attests Byland charters between *c.* 1208 and *c.* 1252 (see nos 306, 411, 412, 424, 425, 445, 602, 606, 618, 834, 837, 997, 1027, 1044, 1053, 1069); a later Oliver de Buscy, son of William, was tenant in Thirkleby in 1284/5 (*VCH NR* II, 43, 56; *KI*, p. 95; see no. 959 below). If the first witness is John son of Robert Daiville, who died in 1242/3, this suggests the donor was the earlier Oliver. In 1224 the first three witnesses were ordered to hold an assize of novel disseisin: see note to no. 1086.

684 **Original:** *Notification, addressed to all the sons of holy mother church present and future, by William de Buscy, knight, son of Oliver de Buscy, of his inspeximus of the charters and enfeoffments of his ancestors, and confirmation and quitclaim in free alms to God and St Mary and the abbot and convent of Byland and their successors, of whatever right he had in Osgoodby. Pledge to make no further claim. Sealed with the donor's seal. The market place of Thirsk, Mon. after St Agatha 1315 [18 Feb. 1316].*
Hiis testibus domino Iohanne de Barton de Friton', Thoma de Colevill, Iohanne Malbys, Roberto de Colevill', militibus, Iohanne de Hamby senescallo dictorum abbatis et conventus, Roberto de Foxholes, William Wysbarne et aliis.

Location: Leeds, YAS DD 146/18/6.
Pd (calendar): *Yorks. Deeds*, IX, 130–1, no. 330, from the original from Farnley Hall,

in the custody of the Yorkshire Archaeological Society.

Note: The cartulary copy omits the last witness and the place and dating clause. The grantor was the son of Oliver de Buscy who held Thirkleby in 1284/5, on whom see no. 683 note.

685 *Confirmation and quitclaim, addressed to all the sons of holy mother church present and future, by Walter de Percehay, knight, for the salvation of his soul and of his father and mother and of all his ancestors and heirs, to God and St Mary and the abbot and convent of Byland and their successors, of all right and claim which he has or could have in lands which the abbot and convent have in Scackleton on the day on which this document was drawn up. The monks are to hold all the lands and tenements with appurtenances, liberties and easements within the vill of Scackleton and outside in free alms, quit of all secular exactions. Pledge to make no further claim, and pledge to warranty. Sealed with the donor's seal. In return for this the monks have received Walter into all the spiritual good deeds of their house.* Byland; St Benedict, abbot [21 Mar.] 1299 [1300].

Hiis testibus dominis Iohanne de Barton', Ivone de Ettona, Thoma de Colvile, militibus, Iohanne de Bordesden', Willelmo de Skipton, Roberto de Colton', Hugone de Calveton', et aliis.

Marginal note: (in later hand) '27 E 1'.

Copy: MS Dodsworth 63, fol. 71r, from cartulary fol. 192b (*sic*).

[fols 75v–76r]

686 *Confirmation and quitclaim, addressed to all the faithful in Christ present and future, by John de Wyville, son and heir of William de Wyville, for the salvation of his soul and of all his ancestors and heirs, to God and the abbot and convent of St Mary of Byland and their successors, of all lands which the monks hold of his fee, to hold free of all secular exaction. Undertaking to make no further claim, and pledge to warranty. Sealed with the donor's seal.* Byland; day after St Andrew [1 Dec.] 1299 [28 Edward I]. Hiis testibus dominis Waltero de Taye, Milone de Stapilton', Ivone de Etton', Waltero Percehay, etc.

Copy: within an inspeximus by Ralph Hastings son and heir of Ralph Hastings, MS Dodsworth 91, fols 89r–90r, no. 32, where the witness list omits 'etc' and continues: militibus, Hugone de Calveton, Iohanne de Butterwyke, Willelmo del Bek, Hugone de Carleton et aliis. The date is given as St Andrew 1299. The inspeximus is dated at Byland, Sat. before the Nativity of the B. V. M. 39 Edward III [6 Sept. 1365]. Sketch of seal.

Note: There is a further copy of this charter at no. 1197 below.

[fol. 76v]

NIDDERDALE, an extensive area of moorland, which included abbey lands in Kirkby Malzeard, and the mining areas which are the subject of this section. Fountains Abbey was also a major landholder in this area, being, like Byland, the recipient of grants from Roger de Mowbray. A number of agreements had to be negotiated of which one is included in the cartulary (no. 707). The boundaries described in nos 688, 689, and 700 show that the area granted to Byland was extensive, from Brown Ridge on Masham Moor to the north, to Heathfield (approximately 2 miles north west of Pateley Bridge) to the south and along the west bank of the Nidd between Ramsgill and Middlesmoor. To the west their lands stretched as far as Whernside (no. 700). The ditch mentioned in no. 700 as the boundary between the lands of Byland and Fountains would appear to have run to the east of the Nidd and to have separated the Byland lands from Fountains Earth. It is clear from no. 707 that both houses were also exploiting the area of Nidderdale to the west of Pateley Bridge.

687 *Rubric: Charter of Roger de Mowbray and Nigel his son concerning a certain part of their forest of Nidderdale within certain boundaries.* [*c.* 1160 x 1172].

Fabricated original: *Notification, addressed to the archbishop of York and the whole chapter of St Peter (York) and all the faithful in Christ, present and future, by Roger de Mowbray and his son, Nigel, of their grant to the monks of St Mary of Byland, of part of their forest of Nidderdale by the following boundaries (much illegible). In the said pasture they may have 30 sows and 5 boars but all pigs are to be removed 15 days before the Nativity of St John the Baptist (24 June).*

His testibus Roberto de Daivilla, Hugone Malebis, Thoma de Colevilla, Hamone Beler, Radulfo de Beuvair, Rogero filio Gaufridi, Nicholao de Bellun, Roberto filio Rogeri, Rogero filio Hugonis, Roberto clerico.

Location: Halton Place, Yorke deeds, no. 57.

Pd: *Mowbray Charters*, no. 53. The endorsement of the charter, 'Nidd. B. i. j.' indicates the first charter in the Nidderdale bundle, and the first in the cartulary section.

Dating: See *Mowbray Charters*.

Marginal note: B(aculus) i.

Note: Greenway noted that both the grant and the witness list are probably genuine, but the handwriting belongs to the late 12th or early 13th century, and the detailed clauses also suggest a period later than the 1160s.

688 **Original**: *Grant in free alms, addressed to the archbishop of York and the whole chapter of St Peter (York) and all the sons of holy church, by Roger de Mowbray, to God and the monks of St Mary of Byland, of all that part of his forest of Nidderdale within these boundaries: as* Higherfeldebec *comes from the boundaries of Craven and falls into the river Nidd and through mid-stream of the Nidd as far as the water of* Magna Stenes *(?How Stean Beck) and from the water of Stean* (Stenes) *as far as the boundaries of Craven and from there along the boundaries of Craven to the boundaries opposite* Higherfeldebec. *Within these boundaries the monks may build, assart and plough wherever they wish. Roger and his heirs will keep nothing within these boundaries except wild beasts and fowl which they take else-where. The monks shall have everything else there, above and below ground, to do with as they wish. The monks are to have free and adequate entry and exit for themselves and for their men, for their animals and packhorses, and for their carts to their places throughout Roger's land and forest. Roger's foresters are not to enter within these boundaries for any purpose except to take the wild beasts and fowl. They may not go and return to the places of the monks except for one entrance which the monks shall assign, and may only take from the brethren of that place what they wish to give. The grant is made in free alms, quit of all secular service; pledge to warranty. The grant is also made for the salvation of his soul and of his father and mother and of all his ancestors and heirs.* [c. 1173 x 1180].

Hiis testibus Roberto abbate de Fontibus, Ricardo priore et capitulo de Neuburgh, Nigello et Roberto filiis, Hugone Malebissa, Radulpho de Beuver, Willelmo de Daivilla, Philippo de Muntpinzun, Hamone Beler, Adam Luvel, Nicholao de Belum, Radulfo clerico de Insula, et Petro clerico, Roberto Beler, et Rogero de Daivilla, Roberto de Daivilla, Thome de Colevilla.

Location: Halton Place, Yorke deeds, no. 58; endorsed: Rogeri de foresta inter Higerfeldebec et Stenes. Nidderdale. B'. i. ii (Nidderdale, first bundle, 2); seal: identified by Greenway as Roger de Mowbray's seal no. 3.
Pd: *Mowbray Charters*, no. 56 (from original).
Dating: between the mortgage arrangement of 1172 (*ibid.*, no. 54) and the death of the first witness. The cartulary copy has witnesses up to and including Ralph de Belvoir.
Note: Fountains Abbey, whose abbot witnesses here, had extensive interests in Nidderdale: see below, no. 707. The rubric states that the charter has been copied. The watercourse here called 'Magna Stenes' may be How Stean Beck, which joins the Nidd above Stean (SE0973), which lies to the west of the Nidd about a mile from Middlesmoor (SE1074). 'Higherfeldebec' is probably related to the name of Highfield (SE1367), immediately south of Heathfield, which lies 5 miles SSE of Middlesmoor, with Ramsgill (SE1171) mid way between the two.

689 **Original:** *Confirmation in free alms, addressed to the archbishop of York and the whole chapter of St Peter [York] and all the sons of holy church, by Nigel de Mowbray, to God and the monks of St Mary of Byland, of the grant made by his father, Roger, of that part of his forest of Nidderdale which is contained within the boundaries between* Higherfeldbec *and Stean from the river Nidd as far as the boundaries of Craven, free and quit as his father's charter attests. The confirmation is made for the salvation of his soul and of his father and mother, his wife Mabel, and all their ancestors and heirs. Pledge to warranty. [c. 1173 x 1180].*

Hiis testibus Rogero de Molbr' patre meo et Roberto fratre meo, Ricardo priore et capitulo de Neuburgh, Roberto abbate Font', Hogone Malab(is)sa, Radulfo de Beuver, Willelmo de Daivilla, Philippo de Muntpinzun, Hamone Beler, Adam Luvel, Nicholao de Bellun, Radulfo clerico, Petro clerico, Roberto Beler, Rogero de Daivilla.

Location: Halton Place, Yorke deeds, no. 59; endorsed: Carta Nigelli de Molb' de confirmatione Highefeld et Stenes. Nidderdale. B'. i. iii; seal: identified by Greenway as seal no. 1. of Nigel de Mowbray.
Pd: *Mowbray Charters*, no. 57 (from original).
Dating: This was made on the same occasion as no. 688. The cartulary copy has witnesses up to and including Hamo Beler.

[fols 76v–77r]
690 **Fabricated original:** *Notification by Roger de Mowbray to his bailiffs, reeves, foresters and ministers and all Christians, of his grant in free alms to God and the monks of St Mary of Byland, of 2 stags and 3 hinds to be taken each year from his forest of Nidderdale for the use of the sick monks. Licence for the monks' brethren, shepherds and guardians of their pasture in Nidderdale to have within the monks' pasture wild mastiffs in chains, hunting horns and weapons, but no harm shall be done by men carrying arms or their dogs to the beasts reserved by Roger and his heirs. If anyone does any such harm the abbot shall expel him from the valley and from his service. The brethren of the monks residing in Nidderdale shall give nothing to Roger's foresters except what they wish to give of their own free will. Pledge to warranty. [before 1154].*

Testes sunt Gundrea mater mea, Nigellus et Robertus filii mei, Hugo Malabestia dapifer meus, Georgius de Sancto Martino, Willelmus de Widvilla, Thomas de Colevilla, Walwannus de Insula, et alii.

Location: Halton Place, Yorke deeds, no. 56; endorsed: Carta Rogeri de Molbrai de canibus habendis et cornubus in valle et aliis contentis. Nidderdale, B'. i. iiij. pur; seal: identified by Greenway as Roger de Mowbray seal no. 3.
Pd: *Mowbray Charters*, no. 49 (from original).

Dating: as Greenway points out, this charter may have been fabricated to supply the details which not do appear in the original grant (*Mowbray Charters*, no. 60, not entered in the cartulary). The witness list may be taken from a genuine charter of date before 1154, by which date Gundreda d'Aubigny was dead and Hugh Malebisse had ceased to be steward. The hand of the fabricated original is of the early 13th century.

The witness list in the cartulary copy ends after William de Wyville.

[fol. 77r, old fol. 184]

690A   *Rubric: Charter of the same [Roger de Mowbray] concerning the same, and concerning having dogs and carrying arms.*

691   *Confirmation in free alms, addressed to the archbishop of York and the whole chapter of St Peter (York) and all the sons of holy church, by Nigel de Mowbray, to the monks of St Mary of Byland, of 2 stags and 3 hinds to be taken yearly from his forest of Nidderdale for the use of the sick monks. This confirmation is made for the salvation of his soul and of all his ancestors and heirs. The monks may take these beasts at whatever time of the year and by whatever means they wish, having forewarned Nigel's foresters. Grant also of free use of his seal, as is contained in his father's charter (no. 644). Pledge to warranty. [c. 1186 x Dec. 1189].*

Hiis testibus Roberto de Moubray fratre meo, Willelmo et Roberto filiis meis, Rogero de Sancto Martino, Rogero de Dayvill', Radulpho clerico, etc.

Pd: *Mowbray Charters*, no. 71.

Dating: probably after Roger's de Mowbray's departure for the Holy Land, and before Nigel left England. See also no. 690.

692 *Rubric: Charter of the same [Nigel de Mowbray] concerning 3 stags and 4 hinds and freedom of his seal etc. It is good. [c. 1186 x Dec. 1189].*

693   *Rubric: Agreement in the form of a chirograph between the monks and William de Mowbray.* York; Mon. after the Invention of the Holy Cross [3 May], no year.

694   *Rubric: Quitclaim by William de Mowbray of 300 marks, 20 marks and certain lands which the monks paid him for the forest of Middlesmoor. Copied. One copy is in the Mowbray chest and the other under Kirkby Malzeard.*

Note: For the copy in the Mowbray chest see no. 655. Middlesmoor (SE1074) is in Stonebeck Up, in the parish of Kirkby Malzeard.

[fol. 77r–v]

695 *Notification, addressed to all the faithful in Christ, by Simon, dean, and Hamo, treasurer, of York of the termination of the dispute between William de Mowbray and the abbot and monks of Byland concerning the forest of Middlesmoor in Nidderdale, settled at York on the Tuesday after the feast of St Peter ad Vincula (1 Aug.) 1204. The dispute had been committed to them by Pope Innocent III. The abbot and monks have given William 300 silver marks in order to possess the forest in perpetuity, and William has confirmed the forest to them, and all the grants and possessions which his grandfather and father granted to them and confirmed by their charters. For this concession the monks have remitted to William 100 silver marks which they used to demand, and moreover have given him 20 silver marks for 1 carucate in Airyholme which they will hold in perpetuity. They have conceded to him the men who held land of them in Thirsk, so that they will hold land of William under the same conditions as they held of the monks. They have further granted to William 1 toft and 5 acres in Hovingham, and ½ silver mark from the mill there, licence to assart, grant or sell from the wood of Hovingham without impediment on the part of the monks. Finally they have restored to William all they had in the Isle of Axholme of the grant of Roger de Mowbray, and for the meadow of Hovingham which the monks are to retain they have given him land in exchange, that is 15 acres of meadow in Fryton. Pledge with an oath to observe all the above. York; 3 Aug. 1204.*

Hiis testibus Symone decano, Hamone thesaurario Ebor', magistro Willelmo archidiacono de Notyngham, magistro Gregorio, Ricardo Malbys, Willelmo de Corneburgh, etc.

Copy: MS Top. Yorks. e. 8, fols 107v–108r (old pp. 179–80) (omits witnesses).

Note: For the papal mandate to the judges delegate see C. R. Cheney and Mary Cheney, eds, *The Letters of Pope Innocent III concerning England and Wales (1198–1216)* (Oxford, 1967), no. 554; and see above, no. 653. Jane Sayers points out that it is surprising that William de Mowbray brought the case against Byland to an ecclesiastical court rather than the king's court, which would have been the 'obvious forum for so influential a layman'. She suggests that a clerical adviser suggested to William that he take his complaint to the pope. See Jane Sayers, *Papal Judges Delegate in the Province of Canterbury 1198–1254* (London, 1971), p. 218. At the foot of fol. 77r are two columns, headed 'Firma ten' in Niderdale', giving lists of rents from the following places: Ang', Westh' (?West House Farm, SE1072), Inge, Wherynsidhous, Haythencarr', Scarhous (Scar House, SE0677), Wulsell, Newhous (New House, SE0149), Lymley, Midelesmour (Middlesmoor, SE1074), Stene (Stean, SE0973), Morhous (Moorhouse, SE0872), Regalehous (Rayhill House, SE1170), Ramesgyll (Ramsgill, SE1171), Colthous (Colt House, SE1269), Goldwhayt (?Gouthwaite Farm, SE1268), Herfeld (Heathfield or Highfield, SE1367), Esthfald, Blaschawhous. This may be in the same hand as no. 431.

[fol. 77v]

696 *Rubric: Attestation by the same [dean and treasurer] concerning the men who held of the monks in Thirsk, and other matters.* [1204].

Dating: as no. 695.

697 *Rubric: Great confirmation by William de Mowbray of the above agreements.* [1204].

698 *Rubric: Chirograph drawn up in the king's court between Roger son of W[illiam] de Mowbray and the monks concerning the forest of Middlesmoor; it is in the chest.* [Westminster; 3 weeks from St Michael, 33 Henry III [Oct. 1249]]

Text: PRO CP 25/1/264/41, no. 33. Final concord made in the king's court at Westminster 3 weeks from St Michael 33 Henry III, in the presence of Roger of Thirkleby, Gilbert de Preston, John de Cobham, Alan of Wassand, William of Wilton, and other faithful men of the lord king then present, between Henry, abbot of Byland, plaintiff, and Roger de Mowbray, defendant, as to the forest of Middlesmoor in Nidderdale, with its appurtenances. Roger acknowledged this to be the right of the abbot, above and below ground, of the grant of William father of Roger. The abbot has licence to assart in the forest and plough and build where he wishes, saving to Roger the wild beasts of the forest. They can hunt in the forest to take all manner of wild beasts in whatever way they wish and may have just one forester in the forest to guard their hunting within the forest of the abbot and his successors. The abbot and his successors can hunt as they wish within the forest and no-one is to disturb their hunting. They can hunt outside their forest of Middlesmoor as far as the forest of Roger and his heirs, and are allowed to call back their dogs by mouth and by horn to the bounds of the forest of Middlesmoor. Roger grants woodland, with its appurtenances above and below ground by the following boundaries: as 'Hyrefeldbek' comes from the boundaries of Craven and falls into the Nidd and up through the middle of the Nidd as far as the water of 'Magna Stene' (? How Stean Beck) and so to the boundaries of Craven and from there to 'Hyrefeldbec' (see nos 688, 689 above). Roger further granted suitable rights of way for their men, cattle, pack animals, and carts through the forest of Kirkby [Malzeard] as far as Nidderdale. A house has been assigned to Roger's foresters outside the abbey grange of Ramsgill, and whenever Roger or his heirs come to Nidderdale the abbot will find them suitable lodging in the grange, and 5 cartloads of

hay yearly. They will demand no more of the abbot, his successors
and the lay brethren staying in the grange.

Pd: *Yorks. Fines 1246–1272*, pp. 11–12.
Note: The cartulary rubric is followed by the letter B.

699 *Remission, release and quitclaim, addressed to all who see or hear this
writing, by Roger son of Roger de Mowbray under the impulse of charity, to
the abbot and convent of Byland and their successors, of all right and claim
which he ever had or might have in all his pasture and also in common
pasture for any breed of pigs, wild boar or domestic pigs, in Highfield,
Ramsgill and Middlesmoor. Neither Roger nor his heirs, nor anyone in their
name, ministers or tenants, will demand or claim anything in the said places
or any others places belonging to his fee and lordship in Nidderdale, of which
the said abbot and convent are enfeoffed. He further grants all wild boars in
Nidderdale for the maintenance of the sick of their house. Sealed with his
seal. [1278 x 1297].*

Hiis testibus dominis Willelmo de Colvill', Roberto de Furneys,
Milone de Stapilton', militibus, etc.

Dating: see no. 658.

700 *Confirmation by Roger son of Roger de Mowbray, addressed to all the
faithful in Christ to whom the present writing shall come, for the love of God
and for the salvation of his soul and of his father and mother and of all his
ancestors and heirs, to the abbot and convent of Byland and their successors,
of all lands, possessions and tenements, confirmations and quitclaims, and of
all liberties within his fee, which had been granted by kings, or by his ancestors or by any of his feoffees. This is granted in free alms, quit of all service
and suits of court. The conflict which had existed between Roger on the one
part and the abbot and convent on the other concerning the boundaries of the
forest of Middlesmoor has been settled in this way, that Roger has conceded
for himself and his heirs all the said forest both below and above ground
within these boundaries: as the water course called* Magna Stene *(?How
Stean Beck) falls into the river Nidd and along the Stean to its source and
from there as far as* Menhou *which is also called* Brimhou, *and from there
along the boundaries of Craven as far as Whernside, and from there to*
Roulandsete *and from there to* Wolvedalehede *and to* Niderhou *and
from* Niderhou *along the boundaries of Mashamshire as* Brunrig *(? Brown
Ridge) goes as far as the head of the ditch which is the boundary between the
monks of Byland and those of Fountains, and then following the said ditch to
the Nidd and along the Nidd to the place where the Stean (How Stean Beck)
falls into the Nidd. The abbot and convent are to hold all that is contained*

within these boundaries of Roger and his heirs, to do as they wish, in free
alms in perpetuity. Pledge to warranty. [1278 x 1297].

Hiis testibus dominis Rogero de Lascels, Radulfo filio Willelmi,
Milone de Stapilton', Thoma de Colvill', Ricardo Malbys milit(ibus),
etc.

Dating: Roger de Mowbray was still a minor at the time of his father's death
around Nov. 1266. The king took his homage in 1278. By 1296 he was Lord
Mowbray, and he died before 21 Nov. 1297: *CP* IX, 376–7.

[fol. 78r, old fol. 185]

701   *Grant, confirmation and quitclaim, addressed to all the sons of holy*
mother church present and future, by William de Mowbray for himself and
his heirs, to God and St Mary and the abbot and convent of Byland and their
successors, of the forest of Middlesmoor in Nidderdale, with all its appurte-
nances above and below ground, in free alms, quit of all secular service.
Grant also of free entry into and exit from his lands, for themselves and their
animals and carts without any interference, except sown land and meadow
in the close season. This grant and quitclaim is made for the salvation of his
soul and of all his ancestors and heirs and for a certain sum of money which
the abbot and convent have given him for this quitclaim, that is, 300 silver
marks, in the presence of Simon, dean of York, and Hamo, treasurer of York,
who are his judges, and other canons of St Peter, in their chapter. The grant
is made in free alms, as any alms made to religious men by their advocates
and patrons within the kingdom of England. Pledge to warranty. Sealed
with the donor's seal in the presence of Dean Simon and Hamo the treasurer
in their chapter house. York. [1204].

Hiis testibus Ricardo Malabissa, Willelmo de Corneburgh, Roberto
dapifero, Philippo filio Iohannis, Willelmo Buscy, Rogero de
Fontibus, etc.

Dating: see no. 695.
Note: The witnesses also attest no. 651 which relates to the same business. The first
two also attest no. 695.

702   *Rubric: Quitclaim by Alice, widow of Richard Dikeman de Hirfeld of*
all her right in Hirfeld.

703   *Notification, addressed to all the sons of holy mother church present*
and future who will see or hear this writing, by John de Eston, knight, that if
any of the animals of the abbot and convent in Nidderdale shall stray, or for
any reason cross into the pasture of Appletreewick in Craven and be found
there, John and his heirs are not to be allowed to impound the animals –
unless they are kept under forest watch (wardefactum) *– but they are to be*

restored without harm or claim to their own pasture of Nidderdale. Sealed
with the donor's seal. [late 13th cent.].

Hiis testibus dominis Nicholao Punchardon', Marmeduco Darell',
Ricardo de Malebys, Ivone de Ettona, militibus, Willelmo de
Greyndorg, Roberto de Eston, fratre meo, etc.

Dating: The grantor held in chief in 1284–5 (*KI*, pp. 51, 144–5). The first witness was
tenant of Kepwick and Ivo de Etton was tenant in Gilling in Ryedale at the same
date (*ibid.*, pp. 97, 112, 116, 118; *VCH NR* I, 480–1, II, 54).

Note: The rubric states that the charter has been copied. Appletreewick lies to the
south of the areas granted to Byland.

704 *Rubric: Charter of his brother, Robert, concerning the same.*

705 *Rubric: Charter of Walter the forester concerning 4d. annual rent*
which the monks were accustomed to render to him.

706 *Rubric: Quitclaim by Goscelin of Braithwaite of 1 pound of cumin.*
[mid 13th cent.].

Note: Goscelin of Braithwaite witnesses charters in favour of Fountains Abbey
(see, for example, *Cart. Fountains*, I, 19 (nos 21, 25), 25 (no. 12), 25–6 (no. 13), 88 (nos
4–5), 101 (no. 49)), and occurs as Jocelin son of Philip, grantor of lands in
Braithwaite to Fountains Abbey. In 1256 he confirmed grants made by his ancestors, including Gocelin Veyllechen (*ibid.*, I, 144, no. 9). He also occurs in 1257 (*ibid.*,
I, 307, no. 20). See also above, nos 464–6 and 468.

[fol. 78r–v]

707 *Notification, addressed to all the sons of holy mother church present*
and future, by the Abbots R(obert) of Furness, R(oger) of Rievaulx and
A(cius) of Beaulieu that investigation of the dispute between the abbots of
Fountains and Byland concerning mineral rights in Nidderdale had been
committed to them by the General Chapter, and that at their request an
agreement had been reached under the following terms. The abbot and
convent of Fountains have granted to the abbot and convent of Byland two
mine shafts (grovas) *in Highfield Hill* (Hirefeldebergh) *successively*
within the boundaries of the monks of Fountains; and, for the term of 7 years
beginning at the Purification (2 Feb.) 1226, two mine shafts in Cold Stones
in common with them, so that during the said term the monks of Fountains
and Byland shall divide all the expenses and all the mineral of those mine
shafts except for what belongs to the king. At the end of the said term the
monks of Byland shall withdraw from the 2 mine shafts at Cold Stones
whether there has been profit or not. Moreover the monks of Byland shall
have that mine shaft at Cold Stones with the monks of Fountains in which

they previously worked together until the same shaft has been profitable, according to the bounds of the mine, with appropriate entry and exit and rights of carriage throughout the pasture and wood of Fountains without hindrance. For this concession the abbot and convent of Byland have renounced all right of possession and use which they ever had or might have within the boundaries belonging to the monks of Fountains by reason of their charters, and at the end of the 7 years they will make no claim except in the two mine shafts in Highfield Hill, and the monks of Fountains will make no claim within the lands of Byland without their licence. The monks of Byland will make no claim within the boundaries of the monks of Fountains in respect of the charter concerning common easements throughout Nidderdale which they displayed, unless Fountains should recover the forest which they lost to William de Stuteville. Both parties have agreed in good faith that they will seek nothing from the king or from the lord of the land or anyone else which might hinder or impede the right, use or possession of either party. Any such claim is null. If any monk or lay brother of either house is found guilty of making such a claim and thus infringes this agreement he shall undergo the punishment laid down in the previous agreement between the two houses, and be every sixth day on bread and water. All previous quarrels are now settled and original agreements are to be held to. The present agreement was reached on 24 Jan. in the said year with the assent of both chapters, in the time of Abbot J(ohn of Kent) of Fountains and R(obert) of Byland, in the presence of N(icholas II), former bishop of the Isles, abbots R(obert) of Rufford, W. of Stanley in Arden, H(enry) of Kirkstead, W. of Sallay, R(alph) of Kirkstall, E(ustace) of Jervaulx, whose seals have been attached, along with the seals of the judges. 24 Jan. 1226.

Pd (calendar): from BL MS Add. 40009, pp. 41–3, in *Cart. Fountains*, I, 216–17 (no. 35), with minor differences in place names (e.g. 'Le Feldeberg' for 'Hirfeldeberg'). Note: This is the only document entered in the surviving portions of the Byland cartulary relating to the disputes between Byland Abbey and Fountains Abbey over boundaries and mining rights in various parts of Nidderdale. Between 1151 and May 1155 Roger de Mowbray had granted the monks of Fountains mining rights in his forest of Nidderdale (*Mowbray Charters*, no. 103); between 1147 and 1153 he made a grant to Byland of iron and a tithe of his lead mines, also in Nidderdale (above, no. 456). It is clear that tensions arose as a result of the acquisitions made by both houses. An agreement between Roger de Mowbray and the monks of Fountains (1174 x 1175, printed in *Mowbray Charters*, no. 111 from the original, BL Harley charter 83 C 38) stated that if the monks of Fountains should lose any of the forest which Roger had granted them, either for common, or as a result of interference, and he was unable to warranty the forest, then the monks of Byland were to be free to return to the monks of Fountains the earlier charter which they had agreed to preserve. The monks of Fountains were to use the easements of the forest until they had been given land in exchange, and when they did so, they were once again to place the charter in the keeping of Byland. No. 707, which concerns the working of mines, contains a reference to an earlier composition between the two abbeys. Two such compositions are contained in the cartulary of Fountains. On 8 Mar. 1184 Abbots William of Fountains and Roger of Byland reached an arrangement concerning the partition of lands in Kirkby Malzeard, Winksley and Studley about which there had been dispute; the lands were to be divided equally and mention is made of a bridge to be built across the Nidd by the monks of Byland (*Cart. Fountains*, I, 215, no. 33). This may be the agreement referred to in no. 485 above. In 1198 a further agreement arranged for the partition between the two abbeys of lands between 'Bacstenebec' and 'Beckermot' according to their value, with the part towards 'Bacstenebec' remaining with Fountains, and the part nearer 'Beckermot' remaining with Byland, and rights of way for cattle, wagons and packhorses. The occurrences in this agreement of the names Ramsgill, Highfield and Middlesmoor, which also occur in no. 707, locate the area in dispute in Nidderdale. The punishment of monks or lay brethen infringing the conditions laid down in the agreement was that they should go on foot to the other abbey to give satisfaction; if anyone persisted in his contumacy he was to be sent to another house and not return except by permission of the General Chapter (*Cart. Fountains*, I, 215–16, no. 34).

The 1198 agreement does not occur in the surviving parts of the Byland cartulary, but like no. 485 the original might have been in the *baculus abbatum* and copied on one of the missing folios. In 1225 the Cistercian General Chapter delegated to the abbots of Furness, Rievaulx and Beaulieu investigation of the dispute between Byland and Fountains, adding that in the meantime the monks of Byland were to continue mining: see Canivez, *Statuta*, II, 42 (no. 34). No. 707 represents the outcome of the investigation. The area concerned has been identified by Raistrick, who has argued that both houses mined along their common boundary where the Providence vein crossed Ashfold Gill, from Heathfield Moor to Cold Stones: Raistrick, *Lead Mining*, pp. 18–19. 'Hirefeldebergh' is not recorded in *EPNS WR*, but the medieval form 'Hirefeld' for Heathfield and Highfield (SE1367) is well attested. Heathfield Moor is at SE1167.

There was a further dispute which was settled in 1260: *Cart. Fountains*, I, 217. The initial of the name of the abbot of Stanley, W, must be an error for S, that is, Stephen of Lexington who is recorded as abbot from 1223 until he became abbot of Savigny in 1229. The abbot of Sallay is Stephen of Eston.

[fol. 79r, old fol. 186]

EAST NESS (SE6978) and WEST NESS (SE6979), in the parish of Hovingham and the wapentake of Ryedale (NR). East and West Ness lie approximately 3 miles NE of Hovingham on the south bank of the river Rye, and on the northern edge of the Howardian Hills. Odo de Balliol and his wife Agnes held lands here of Robert de Stuteville and Robert de Gant, who both confirmed grants to Byland. These consisted of small pieces of land and rights of entry and exit. The grants were later confirmed by the Stonegrave family, benefactors in Thorpefield.

708 *Grant and confirmation in free alms, addressed to the archbishop of York and the whole chapter of St Peter (York) and all the faithful in Christ, by Odo de Balliol and Agnes his wife, for the love of God and the salvation of their souls and of all the faithful, to God and the monks of St Mary of Byland, of 16 acres of meadow in the region of Ness, that is, 10 acres of the fee of Robert de Stuteville between the two watercourses, and 6 acres of the fee of Robert de Gant in Waterholme, free from all secular service, with free entry and exit for themselves, their men, animals and wagons across their land. Pledge to warranty.* [1166 x 1181, probably 1166 x 1175].

Hiis testibus Willelmo de Staingriva, Symone filio eius, Odone de Boltby, etc.

Pd: *EYC* VI, no. 56.

Dating: 1166 x 1181 (*EYC*), where it is, however, noted that the first witness was probably dead by soon after 1175; the see of York was vacant between 1181 and 1191.

Note: *EYC* identifies Ness as West Ness; however, no. 710 locates the meadow in East Ness. Waterholme lies about ½ mile east of East Ness. The two watercourses are the river Rye to the north of East Ness, and Holbeck to the south.

709 *Rubric: Quitclaim by the same Agnes of the same meadow; look under Scackleton in the first bundle.*

Note: The reason for the reference to Scackleton is not clear; the text does not appear in the Scackleton section of the cartulary.

710 *Confirmation, addressed to all the sons of holy mother church present and future, by Robert de Stuteville, son of William de Stuteville, to God and St Mary and the abbot and convent of Byland, of the grant of Odo de Baillol and Agnes his wife of 10 acres of meadow between the two water courses in region of East Ness (no. 708). Grant and confirmation also of free entry and exit for themselves, their men, animals, carts and wagons into the meadow from the highway, 1 perch in width where the ancient narrow path* (semita) *was, across the profitable land towards the south. Further confirmation of the agreement reached with his father, that is, that every year they should place a gate at the entry which they have from the said highway towards the south to their meadow until they shall have transported their hay there. When they have transported the hay they shall raise an embankment where they made the gate so that the men of the vill do not cause damage. If any men do knock down the embankment and cause any damage the abbot and convent will not be to blame, and Robert and his heirs will go to the men and compel them to mend it suitably. The abbot and monks have all this of Robert and his heirs free from all secular service, for the salvation of the soul of Robert and of his father and mother and all his ancestors and heirs. Pledge to warranty. Sealed with the donor's seal.* [1265 x c. 1272].

Hiis testibus dominis Nicholao de Boltby, Willelmo de Stayngr', Galfrido de Upsall, Petro de Wausand', etc.

Dating: The succession of the grantor, and the death of the first witness.

Note: The grantor can be identified as Robert, the son of William de Stuteville, members of the family of Stuteville of Cowesby (Yorks.) and Gressenhall (Norfolk) which descended from Osmund de Stuteville (d. 1192), a younger son of Robert de Stuteville III (*EYC* IX, 34–7). In 1166 Osmund held two-thirds of a knight's fee of Robert, comprising lands in Cowesby, East Ness, Stillingfleet, Riplingham and Brantingham (*ibid.*, 142). Osmund's successor, who may have been underage at the time of his father's death, was William de Stuteville, who appears in no. 712 as William son of Osmund. He was a knight of William de Warenne in 1216, was a benefactor of Rievaulx Abbey, and confirmed grants to Fountains Abbey. Clay suggested that he was probably the William de Stuteville who was sheriff of York-shire between 1229 and 1232, and may be the same William de Stuteville who married Margery, daughter and heiress of Hugh de Say, and widow of Hugh de Ferrers and Robert de Mortimer. William de Stuteville of Gressenhall died in 1259 and by 1265 his son, Robert, grantor of no. 710, was in possession of his estates. Robert died before 20 Aug. 1275. He was succeeded by Jordan Foliot, son of his sister. The first witness, Nicholas of Boltby, was dead by 31 Oct. 1272 (*EYC* IX, 164).

711 *Confirmation in free alms, addressed to all who will see or hear these letters, by Robert de Gant, to God and the monks of St Mary of Byland, of the 6 acres of meadow which Odo de Balliol and Agnes his wife granted in Waterholme. The confirmation is made for the salvation of his soul and of all his own, free from all secular service. Mandate to all his friends to maintain and protect this grant for the monks, as the charters of the donors state.* [1166 x c. 1175].

Hiis testibus Willelmo clerico, Willelmo de Staingriva, Symone et Olyvero filiis eius, Roberto de Staingriva, etc.

Pd: *EYC* VI, no. 57.

Dating: as no. 708.

[fol. 79r–v]

712 *Confirmation, addressed to all the sons of holy church present and future, by William son of Osmund de Stuteville, to the monks of St Mary of Byland, of the grant of Odo de Balliol and Agnes his wife of 10 acres between the two water courses in the region of East Ness, as attested in their charter and the charter of his grandfather, Robert de Stuteville. Grant of free entry and exit as in no. 710. The monks are to hold this land of William and his heirs free from all secular service, for the salvation of his soul and of all his ancestors and heirs. Pledge to warranty.* [c. 1202 x 1226].

Hiis testibus Galfrido Fossard, Willelmo de Buscy, Gilberto de Gorny, Drogone de Harum, Iohanne de la Mara, etc.

Marginal note: genealogy showing the descent of the Stuteville family from Robert

de Stuteville through his son Osmund son of Robert, his grandson, William son of Osmund, to his great-grandson Robert son of William (fol. 79r, in later hand).
Dating: The coming of age and death of the first witness.
Note: On the grantor see no. 710 note.

[fol. 79v]
713 *Rubric: Chirograph of the same William [son of Osmund de Stuteville] concerning the gate and the embankment (see no. 710); look under Scackleton, as above.* [c. 1205 x 1265].
Dating: The coming of age and death of William de Stuteville; see no. 710.
Note: The reason for the reference to Scackleton is not clear; the text does not appear in the Scackleton section of the cartulary.

714 *Rubric: Confirmation by Robert son of William of the same; as above.* [c. 1265 x 1275].
Dating: as no. 710.

715 *Grant and confirmation in free alms, addressed to the archbishop of York and the whole chapter of St Peter (York) and all the sons of holy church, by Matilda of Stonegrave, to God and the monks of St Mary of Byland, of 5 acres of meadow in* Roulandwra *in Waterholme in the region of West Ness, free from secular service, for the salvation of her soul and of all her ancestors and heirs. Confirmation of 6 acres in Waterholme granted by Odo de Balliol and Agnes his wife, as contained in their charter (no. 708). Pledge to warranty the said meadow, with free entry and exit across her land in West Ness.* [c. 1175 x 1181].
Hiis testibus Symone et Olivero filiis meis, Ingelrana Hairun, Willelmo de Swynton', Willelmo capellano de Nunyngton, Gamello preposito, etc.
Copy: MS Dodsworth 94, fol. 55v, which has the first five witnesses.
Pd: *EYC* VI, no. 58 (from cartulary).
Dating: between the death of William, Matilda's husband (c. 1175) and the vacancy in the see of York following the death of Roger de Pont L'Evêque.

716 *Grant and confirmation in free alms, addressed to the archbishop of York and the whole chapter of St Peter (York) and all the sons of holy church, by Simon of Stonegrave, for the salvation of the soul of his mother, Matilda, and for the salvation of his own soul, and of all his ancestors and heirs, to God and the monks of St Mary of Byland, of 5 acres of meadow in* Roulandwra *in Waterholme in the region of West Ness, granted by his mother, and of 6 acres of meadow granted by Odo de Balliol and his wife, Agnes, with free entry and exit as their charters attest. Pledge to warranty.* [c. 1175 x 1181].

Hiis testibus Matilda matre mea, Olyvero fratre meo, Willelmo de Swynton', Ingelrano Hairun, etc.

Copy: MS Dodsworth 91, fol. 105v, no. 58, which omits 'etc' from the witness list and continues: Odone de Boltebi, Waltero filio Hugonis, Walkelino Trussevilain, Willelmo filio Radulfi.

Dating: as no. 715.

717 *Grant and confirmation in free alms, addressed to all the sons of holy mother church present and future, by Simon son of William of Stonegrave, for the salvation of his soul and of all his ancestors and heirs, to God and the monks of St Mary of Byland, of 5 acres of meadow in* Roulandwra *in Waterholme in the region of West Ness, which they have of the grant of his great-grandmother, Matilda of Stonegrave. Confirmation also of the grant of 6 acres of meadow by Odo de Balliol and Agnes his wife, to hold as their charters attest. Pledge to warranty.* [1226 x 1229].

Hiis testibus Roberto de Cokefelde tunc vicecomite Ebor', Ricardo de Riparia, Alano de Flamvyll', Willelmo de Barton', Iohanne Pulayn, Willelmo Haket, Waltero fratre eius, Martino clerico de Maltona, etc.

Dating: office of first witness.

Note: Matilda is described here as 'attava', but she was the great-grandmother of Simon, not his great-great-grandmother. Her son, Simon, who was living in the time of King John, was the father of William (who died before 1226 x 1229), father of the grantor of his charter. Simon son of William, who married Beatrice, daughter of Jordan Foliot, was still living in 1257. This confirmation appears to have been issued at or shortly after his succession.

[fols 79v–80r]

718 *Confirmation and quitclaim in free alms, addressed to all the sons of holy mother church who will see or hear this charter, by Peter of Stonegrave, knight, son of Simon of Stonegrave, knight, with his body, to God and St Mary and the abbot and convent of Byland, of all the grants which they have of his predecessors. This is made for himself and his heirs for the salvation of his soul and of his father and mother and all his ancestors and heirs. The land is to be held of Peter and his heirs free from all secular service, with free entry and exit across his lands. Pledge to warranty. As he did not have his seal ready, he has affixed his private seal, together with that of William de Lascels, knight.* [1254 x 1260 or 1266 x 1267].

Hiis testibus domino Willelmo de Latymer tunc vicecomite Ebor', Galfrido de Upsall', Iohanne de Raygath', Iohanne de Oketon militibus, magistro Ricardo de Clifford, tunc escaetore domini regis, magistro Alano de Esyngwald', etc.

Marginal note: (in later hand) '39 H 3', referring to the first year of office of the first witness; 'tunc vicecomite Ebor' has been underlined in the text of the document.

There is also a genealogy showing the descent from William of Stonegrave and Matilda, 'attava Simonis et mater Oliveri', through their son Simon son of William, to Peter son of Simon, knight 39 H 3, to Peter's son (unnamed), his son William, and Simon son of William. A second hand adds that John of Stonegrave married Ida. This refers to John of Stonegrave who died in 1295 and who married Ida, a daughter of Baldwin Wake.

Copy: MS Dodsworth 91, fol. 106r–v, no. 59, which omits 'etc' from the witness list and continues: Richardo de Vescy, Iohanne de Neuton, Thoma de Etton, Iohanne de Blaby, Waltero de Colton, Willelmo de Thorny, Iohanne de Holthorpe, Willelmo del Becke de Ampleford', Roberto le Barne, Willelmo de Etton, Waltero le Romaine et aliis.

Dating: period of office of first witness. The donor died in 1267/8 (*EYC* VI, 122).

[fol. 80v]

NUNTHORPE (NZ5413), township in the parish of Great Ayton and wapentake of Langbargh West (NR). Nunthorpe lay just to the south of abbey properties in Ormesby and Marton in Cleveland. The abbey appears to have held only 2 bovates. Nunthorpe was a former site of the nunnery of Baysdale, and this explains the rent due to the prioress and nuns (no. 722). The priory was originally founded at Hutton Lowcross by Ralph de Neville, and the second site, at Nunthorpe, had been granted to the nuns by 1170. The final site, at Baysdale, was granted by Guy de Bovingcourt between 1190 and 1204 (Janet Burton, *The Monastic Order in Yorkshire 1069–1215* (Cambridge, 1999), p. 131).

719 *Rubric: Charter of William Schetling concerning 2 bovates in Nunthorpe. Surrendered.*

720 *Rubric: Charter of Walter de Skeeftlinge concerning the same 2 bovates. Surrendered.* [1240].

Text: MS Dodsworth 91, fol. 121r, no. 77, from the original in St Mary's Tower, York. Grant, addressed to all the faithful in Christ present and future, by Walter de Skiflings, parson of Kildale, to God and the abbot and monks of St Mary of Byland, of 2 bovates in Nunthorpe which he has of the grant of William de Scifling his brother. The monks are to do there as they wish, and to hold the land free from all service except for the payment of 2s. yearly at St Martin in Winter (11 Nov.) to the nuns of Baysdale. The grant is made for the salvation of the soul of the donor and for an annual pittance at Christmas. Pledge to warranty. Hiis testibus Iohanne de Bulemer, Willelmo de Malthebi, Engeram de Bovigton', Gaufrido de Piketon, Willelmo de Lohareng, Henrico clerico, Gaufrido Cusin, Adam fabro, Radulfo de Middelburge et aliis.

Pd: *Mon. Ang.* V, 347.

Dating: This is related to the final concord of 1240 (no. 722 below).

721 *Rubric: Charter of the nuns of Baysdale concerning the same. Surrendered.*

722 *Final concord levied in the king's court in the presence of Robert of Lexington, Ralph de Sulleng, William of Culworth, Jolland de Neville, Robert de Haya, Simon de Hales, Warin Engayn, itinerant justices, and other faithful men of the lord king then present, between Abbot Henry of Byland, plaintiff, and Walter de Skeftlyng, defendant, concerning 2 bovates with their appurtenances in Nunthorpe, about which a plea of warranty had been brought. Walter acknowledged the whole of the said land to be the right of the abbot and church of Byland, as granted by himself, to be held by the abbot and his successors in free alms rendering 2s. sterling yearly to the prioress and church of Baysdale at St Martin in Winter (11 Nov.) for all service. Pledge to warranty. The abbot has received Walter and his heirs into all the good deeds and prayers of the monks which are offered in the church of Byland.* York; three weeks from St John the Baptist 24 Henry III [15 July 1240].

Marginal note: (in a later hand), showing William de Sceftlinge as the father of Walter de Sceftlinge 20 H 3.

Copies: PRO CP 25/1/264/34, no. 177; (much abbreviated) MS Dodsworth 91, fol. 121v, no. 78.

Pd (calendar): *Yorks. Fines 1232–1246*, p. 76 (from PRO copy).

723 *Grant and confirmation, in the form of a chirograph, addressed to all the faithful who will read or see these letters, by Abbot Henry and the convent of Byland to Stephen Russell of 2 bovates in Nunthorpe, which they have of the grant in free alms of Walter de Skeftling; to be held by Stephen and his heirs free of all service except for 2s. and 1 pound of cumin yearly at St Martin in Winter (11 Nov.). Pledge to warranty. Sealed as a chirograph with the seals of both parties.* [c. 1230 x 1268].

Hiis testibus domino Honorio tunc priore de Bellal', Willelmo cellarario, Ada de Hiltona, Waltero de Moubray, etc.

Dating: Adam de Hilton was collector of the fortieth in the NR in 1232 and a justice in eyre in 1252 (*VCH NR* II, 238) and this suggests the earlier Abbot Henry, Henry of Battersby.

724 *Memorandum that in the third year of King Edward, son of King Edward (Edward II, 1309/10) Abbot Adam received 1 pound of cumin from Robert Greteheved for 2 bovates in Nunthorpe. In 1279 he received 3 . . . as rent for the said pound of cumin, as appears in various rentals.*

[fol. 81r, old fol. 188]

NEWBURGH PRIORY (SE5476) (NR), an Augustinian priory founded by Roger de Mowbray from Bridlington Priory. The convent initially occupied the site of Hood, vacated by the monks when they moved to Old Byland. The canons remained there for two years (1143–5) before moving to Newburgh Priory, SE of Coxwold. Newburgh Priory lies 1½ miles south of the final site of Byland Abbey (SE5478). The two houses held lands in the same area and these were a source of contention, particularly lands in the region of Wildon and Thirsk, as well as Hood itself (no. 725). In addition Newburgh's appropriation of the church of Coxwold necessitated negotiations about tithes and other church dues (nos 729–35, 737–8).

725 *Agreement reached between the monks of Byland and the canons of Newburgh relaxing all claims and complaints made by both sides. On the part of the monks these were claims relating to Hood, Little Wildon, 1 carucate in Thirsk, land and woodland to the south of* Whitaker *between Deepdale and Oxendale, and the grange which the canons have constructed above* Wlveshou. *The grange may remain in place but with this proviso, that the canons shall not build a vill there, nor have men living there with their wives, nor more than 3 women living there. They may have servants as necessary and keep as much livestock as they wish, but the livestock is not to graze in* Berstlyna *nor anywhere else in the pasture of the monks without their permission. The livestock belonging to the monks is not to graze in the pasture of the canons without their permission. The canons are to construct no buildings between the grange and the boundaries of the monks. If for any reason there are buildings of the canons around* Wluestewayt *they are to be 2 furlongs away from the houses which the monks have previously built there, wherever the canons wish to build on their land; and the flow of water is not to be impeded. In the same way all complaints and claims made by the canons have been laid to rest, especially those concerning 1 carucate in Wildon, the assarts which the monks have made around their abbey and their granges, the tithes of Cam, the assarts of Acca and William, the land and woodland lying to the north of Whitaker, and concerning* Grafclint *which the canons have granted to the monks in perpetuity. For this the monks have granted the canons 1 toft in Thirsk and 2 bovates in Kirkby Malzeard, and Roger de Mowbray has granted them 4s. yearly from the mill of Thirsk until such time as he shall grant them that ½ carucate in Brignall or elsewhere (see no. 738). Also, Roger has granted the canons 12d. from the said mill for the tithes of the assarts of Acca and William. The boundaries between the monks and the canons are: the road nearer* Whitaker *that comes from Brink Hill*

(Coxwold) and goes to Grafclint *and from there as the road runs below* Grafclint *as far as the nearest watercourse on the east, and from there across the watercourse through the middle of* Pilethewayt *as far as the great watercourse below* Wluesthewayt *by the boundaries and boundary marks which they themselves made in the presence of the men of the province, and by the same watercourse to the other watercourse from Oxendale which is the boundary between them. It has been agreed that if the monks acquire any cultivated land within the parishes of the canons they shall pay tithes without dispute, and if the canons have any land they shall lose nothing because of the monks. All these agreements are to be kept firmly. If any of the brethren, on the part of the monks, shall unlawfully seize anything within the boundaries of the canons he is to restore it and receive one punishment in chapter and remain on bread and water for one day. If a hired labourer does the same he is to lose 4d. from his wages. The same is to apply to the brothers and hired labourers of the canons. With the assent of both chapters.* [1154 x 1157].

Hiis testibus domino Rogero Ebor' archiepiscopo, Rogero de Molbray, Nigello filio eius, Roberto de Dayvilla, Waltero de Riparia, Hugone Malebis, Thoma de Colevilla, Iohanne de Crevequer, etc.

Pd: Janet E. Burton, 'The Settlement of Disputes between Byland Abbey and Newburgh Priory', *YAJ*, 55 (1983), 67–71 (pp. 71–2).

Dating: after the consecration of the first witness and in the same period as the issue of nos 737–8. See also no. 729, issued before 1157.

726 *Rubric: Confirmation by Roger de Mowbray of the same agreement.*

727 *Rubric: Transcripts of charters made from the register of the canons of Newburgh concerning the tithes of Wildon and the crofts of Acca and William, for 1 carucate of land in Thirsk. Look under Newburgh, in the first bundle.*

Note: This may refer to nos 737–8 below.

[fol. 81r–v]

728 Original: *Chirograph agreement, addressed to all the sons of holy mother church, between the monks of Byland and the canons of Newburgh, that the canons shall have nothing, by grant or purchase, in that wood and land between Oxendale and the boundaries of Gilling below the highway on the north side which runs through the middle of* Thursedene *towards Hovingham. The monks have, and are to have, 20 acres in the woodland to do with as they wish, and common pasture for their livestock of the grange of Thorpe (le Willows) as the men of Thorpe (le Willows) used to have. They are* *also to have dead wood from Thorpe for their needs. In the season of grazing they are to have 40 pigs without pannage, and if they have more there in the season of pannage they are to pay pannage if Thomas de Coleville so wishes. The monks are to acquire no more than this by purchase or grant. Neither the monks nor the canons are to have anything in Yearsley either by purchase or grant. Both the monks and the canons are to be allowed to buy or receive through grants wood for their use from the woodland which lies to the south of the said road, if Thomas de Coleville or his heirs wish to grant or sell it to them.* [1177 x 1181].

His testibus domino Rogero Ebor' archiepiscopo, capitulo Ebor', capitulo Rievall', capitulo de Font', capitulo de Brell', capitulo de Gisebur', Rogero de Molbr', Willelmo de Colavilla, magistro Roberto Ebor', Roberto capellano, Hugone Malab', Hamone Bel', Roberto de Burci'.

Location: (1) BL Egerton charter 585; chirograph, cut through; endorsed: N<e>wburgh B. i. iii (Newburgh, first bundle, 3); compositio inter canon' de Novoburgo de terra et bosco inter Oxedala et Gilling; six seal tags, five seals, one with legend visible: SIGILL ABBATIS DE FONTIBUS. Seals formerly identified as those of Roger de Mowbray, the chapter of York, the abbot of Fountains, William de Coleville, the chapter of Newburgh. This is the Byland half of the chirograph. (2) NYCRO, ZDV I 5 (MIC 1352/396–7); endorsed 'inter nos et monac' de bellad de Oxedal', indicating that the surviving original was the Newburgh copy; tags for 5 pendant seals. Minor variants in witness list: 'Eb' for 'Ebor', 'H' for 'Hug'.
Pd (calendar): *HMC Various Collections*, II, 4 (no. 2), from the copy now in NYCRO.
Dating: Thomas de Coleville's grant, which was confirmed by Roger de Mowbray (no. 329 above), can be dated after 1177 by the reference to the new abbey. The witness list in the cartulary copy ends with William de Coleville.

[fol. 81v]
729 *Agreement between the canons of Newburgh and the monks of Byland by which the canons quitclaimed to the monks their tithe of Wildon for a certain carucate in Thirsk, and similarly the tithe of Cam.* [1154 x 1157].

Hiis testibus Sampsone de Albeneyo, Rogero de Moubray, Roberto filio Baldwini Brun, Radulfo de Witvill', Waltero de Brandesby, etc.

Pd: Burton, 'Settlement of Disputes', 72.
Dating: the first witness ceases to attest *c.* 1157. Ralph de Wyville was succeeded by his brother, William, who does not occur after 1157.
Note: The rubric calls this an *cy(rographum) antiquum cum sigillis*. There is an instruction that it is to be well looked after.

730 *Agreement between the monks of St Mary of Byland and the canons of St Mary of Newburgh concerning the tithes of Scackleton Grange, namely that the monks of Byland will pay 2 silver marks yearly to the canons of Newburgh, 1 at St Martin (11 Nov.) and 1 at Whitsuntide, in recompense* *for the tithes on the lands which they cultivate in Scackleton, counting in the 2 marks the 4s. which the monks pay yearly to the canons for remitting the right which they have to woodland in the region of Bagby. Sealed with the seal of both chapters. [?1219 x 1234].*

Hiis testibus abbate et conventui . . . vall, Willelmo priore et conventui <de K>yrkeham.

Dating: There is a flaw in the manuscript; the first witnesses could be the abbot and convent of Rievaulx or Jervaulx. The 'K' of Kirkham is obscured, and a later hand has written 'Kyrkham' at the end of the witness list. If the prior of Kirkham is William de Muschamp then this would give a date between his first occurrence and that of his successor, Richard.

731 *Rubric: Chirograph between the monks and the canons of Newburgh concerning* Caldecotdale, *concerning which fuller mention is made under the heading Cam.*

Note: This refers to no. 121 above.

[fols 81v–82r]

732 *Agreement reached in the church of Coxwold on Friday before Pope Gregory (12 Mar.) 1233 after the dispute between Prior John and the convent of Newburgh on the one part, and Abbot Henry and the convent of Byland on the other, namely on the part of the prior concerning the tithe of 1 bovate in Scackleton; the tithe of 2½ acres in Barleycroft in the field of Osgoodby; <the tithe of> 1 acre in the same field near the stone bridge to the south of it which used to be held by of Hugh of Hood; concerning other places turned into meadow in the same field; tithes of hay from 2 acres in the assart which belonged to Gilbert the baker next to* Toc enge, *4 acres on the north side of Thirkleby mill (MS* Gurquilby*) between the two rivers of Hood and Sutton flowing down from the said vills; other places turned into pasture near the place called* Gamldekelde; *the tithes of the crofts of Ackeman and Geoffrey son of Columbe, and the assart of Carlton; a great* cultura *in the upper field of Osgoodby opposite* Meleclyve; *9 houses with their gardens and orchards in the same vill; 4 acres in the field of Thorpe in the place called* Coltelayes, *and ½ acre in* Skynnerenges *and 5 acres in* Scynnerbuttes; *2 acres in* Sovolvetre, *a* cultura *in* Rigwayande *and the great* cultura *which lies in front of the grange of Thorpe le Willows, and another* cultura *lying in the northern part between the ditch of the cultivated land of the monks and the woodland called* Thorpesgate; *6 acres turned into meadow in the place called* Gudewynholme. *The dispute had arisen on the part of the abbot and convent of Byland because of the disturbance to their alms in the vill of Sutton by fishing in Gormire Lake by their servants against their liberties; the cutting down of their woodland in the same vill; the construction of*

houses and making of enclosures in Yearsley against the agreement made
between them; the disturbance to their alms in their grange of Cam by their
sheep; the assault on their servants by the servants of Newburgh at Coxwold,
both in the presence of the judges delegate, that is, the archdeacon of Durham
and his co-judges, the precentor of York and his co-judges, the prior of St
Mary's, York and his co-judges, the archdeacon of Cleveland acting on ordi-
nary authority on the part of the prior and convent, and in the presence of the
abbot of Cockersand and his colleagues, and the abbot of Egglestone and his
colleagues on the part of the abbot and convent. A friendly agreement was
reached by all parties as follows. The prior and convent remitted to the abbot
and convent all the disagreements which they caused, as rehearsed above,
except the tithe of 1 bovate in Scackleton about which there had been dispute,
and the tithe of Barleycroft, which the monks are to pay annually to the
canons, and except the tithe of the great cultura *in the field of Osgoodby*
opposite Meleclyve *(Scencliffe). If at any time* Scynnerbuttes *shall be*
brought back into cultivation, then the tithe is to be paid to the canons. An
oath was taken by trustworthy persons that the prior and convent took the
said tithes of 1 bovate in Scackleton and from the cultura *of Barleycroft. The*
disputes on the part of the abbot and convent were relaxed, except for the
agreements reached by both sides concerning Caldecotdale *and Yearsley.*
For this peace agreement the abbot and convent have given the canons 100s.
sterling. Sealed with the seal of the archdeacon of Cleveland and of both
parties. Coxwold; Friday before Pope Gregory 1233 [10 Mar. 1234].
Hiis testibus magistro S. archidiacono Clivel', domino Ricardo de la
Ryver', Roberto persona de Kilvingtona, Iohanne Bovario capellano,
etc.

Marginal note: (in later hand) '17 H 3'; catchwords (in the cartulary hand) at the
foot of fol. 81v.

Note: Hood Beck and Sutton Beck meet just north of Thirkleby mill. The first
witness is Master Serlo [?de Sunninges], whose first and last occurrences as archdeacon of Cleveland are in 1230 and 1238. On the form 'Meleclyve' for Scencliffe
see above no. 488, note.

[fol. 82r–v, old fol. 189]

733 Original *Settlement of the disagreement which had arisen between*
the prior and canons of Newburgh of the order of St Augustine in the diocese
of York, appropriators of the church of Coxwold, and the abbot and convent of
Byland of the Cistercian order in the said diocese, concerning the mortuary
fees, tithes and offerings of the servants and secular hired workmen of the
abbot and convent of Byland, which the canons claim to belong to them and
the church of Coxwold, and which the monks denied. The controversy was
settled by the intervention of friends in this way: the prior and convent

might bring actions and proceedings against all their secular parishioners, whether they be servants within the abbey or outside in granges, or hired workmen or others, just as they believe by right that they should render mortuary fees, tithes and oblations to the church without any impediment on the part of the monks of Byland, who are not to assist them in any way against the prior and convent. The canons shall not take any further action against the abbot and convent nor any monk, novice or lay brother with respect to the mortuaries and oblations, or induce anyone else to bring such an action. In cases where any monk or lay brother is an executor of a parishioner of Coxwold or administrator of their goods if they die intestate, the abbot and convent shall faithfully render what is due to the canons in terms of mortuaries. The prior and convent have sealed with their common seal the part of the chirograph going to Byland and the abbot and convent have sealed the part going to Newburgh. Brink Hill (Brynk) Grange; id. Sept. [13 Sept.] 1314.

Location: BL Stowe charter 439; cut as chirograph; damaged; no medieval endorsements; no sign of sealing.

Marginal note: (in later hand) '8 Ed 2'.

Note: Brink Hill is in the parish of Coxwold, and was a grange of Newburgh Priory. A confirmation, not in a surviving portion of the cartulary, was issued at Brink Grange by Prior John of Newburgh and Abbot John of Byland on 29 Sept. 1315; this treated a number of issues and among other agreements confirmed no. 732 (MS Dodsworth 91, fols 85v–86v, no. 28). Prior John of Newburgh is John of Foxholes (1304–18); Abbot John of Byland is John of Winkburn, whose first recorded appearance is noted in *HRH* II as 22 April 1316, with his predecessor, Adam of Husthwaite, occurring on 21 Sept. 1314 (*HRH* II, 270).

[fol. 82v]

734 *Agreement with the canons of Newburgh of the order of St Augustine in the diocese of York, appropriators of the church of Coxwold, plaintiffs, and the abbot and convent of Byland of the Cistercian order, defendants, concerning the levying and payment of tithes of coppice wood at* Midelesbergh *within the said parish of Coxwold and belonging to Byland. An agreement has been reached by the mediation of friends that whenever the abbot and convent or their men sell or demise anything to any secular persons within the parishes of the canons, the canons shall be allowed to claim tithes of all kinds of trees except oaks and what in English are called maples, of whatever age and size, and ash of the width of one quarter of an ell in the place where they are cut down. They can enter the wood to take tithe except for certain species of trees which from ancient times have not been subject to tithe. Sealed with the seals of both convents.* For the prior and convent, at Newburgh, in the chapter; Thurs. after St Margaret the Virgin [21 July], 1334.

Hiis testibus magistris Philippo de Nassyngton', Iohanne de
Towthorpe, Ricardo de Snoweshull, Iohanne de Burton', Willelmo de
Derlyngton' cleric(o), et aliis.

Note: *MED* mapel (n.) is glossed as 'any of the European maples; esp. the common
maple (Acer campestre)'.

[fols 82v–83r]

735   *Notification by William de Ferriby of the agreement between the abbot
and convent of the monastery of Byland of the Cistercian order in the diocese
of York on the one part, and the prior and canons of Newburgh of the order of
St Augustine in the same diocese on the other, appropriators of the church of
Coxwold, concerning the levying and payment of tithes on the produce of
certain granges and places, namely, Wildon, Angram, Oldstead, Newstead,
Cam and Osgoodby, belonging to the abbot and convent, and lands
belonging to these granges or places within the parish of Coxwold which
have recently been let at farm to certain secular persons by the abbot and
convent and about which there has been discord. At length in order to reach
an agreement the abbot and prior and their convents appointed Masters
William de Langton, John de Norton, Geoffrey de Langton and Hugh de
Fletham as arbitrators. If these four mediators or arbitators are unable to
reach an agreement they wish that the issuer of this document, William de
Ferriby, archdeacon of Cleveland, be called in to arbitrate on his own and
decide, and the religious have granted him full power to do so.*
*The four negotiators discussed the matter but were unable to secure an
agreement among themselves and the case was referred to the archdeacon.
After many delays and consultations with men learned in the law the archdeacon summoned both parties to his presence. The prior and convent
appeared by their proctor, Henry Hayholm, and the abbot and convent did
not appear. The decision of the archdeacon was that the abbot and convent
were for all time to have the tithes of sheaves and hay in the grange called
Oldstead and places belonging to it, in the name of the prior and convent and
their church of Coxwold and were to pay them yearly 4 silver marks for the
said tithes, in equal portions at Whitsuntide and St Martin in Winter (11
Nov.). The parties are to agree to this within two months. As to the other
places, Wildon, Angram, Newstead, Cam, Osgoodby and the place called
Oldstead, if it does not please the abbot and convent to have the tithes of
Oldstead rendering 4 marks yearly, the prior and convent and the church of
Coxwold shall take from the grange and the places mentioned all the tithes,
complete, real and personal tithes from now on, as was the custom previously. If this arrangement is unsatisfactory to the abbot and convent the
prior and convent and the church of Coxwold shall demise at farm the tithe of*

the granges and the places belonging to them, and take all the personal tithes.
The consistory court of York; Apr. 1369.

Date: The text gives two dates: 6 Apr. and the feast of St Vitalis (28 Apr.). There is clearly some error in the dating clause, possibly as a result of the process of copying.

Note: At the foot of fol. 83r, in the same hand as no. 431, is a note that Master John Norton required the sentence of Dom. William de Ferriby, archdeacon, written above. He asserted that it was not *de iure*, citing his reasons for questioning the validity of the agreement, including that only one of the two parties was present. William de Ferriby was archdeacon of Cleveland from 1355 to 1379.

[fol. 83r–v, old fol. 190]

736 *Grant, addressed to all the sons of holy mother church, by Thomas Fossard, son of Adam Fossard of Sutton, to the canons of Newburgh, for the salvation of his soul, of licence to have – if they wish – another 40 animals in his pasture of Sutton, in addition to the 20 cows and their offspring for one year with one bull which they have of the gift of Robert Fossard, the donor's brother, as Robert's charter indicates. These animals can be of any kind whatsoever, and may be placed in the same pasture without hindrance by Thomas and his heirs. Pledge to warranty.* [before 1227].

Hiis testibus etc. *Know that the agreement between us and the canons concerning 2 parks excludes goats.*

Dating: the death of the grantor.

Note: This rubric indicates that the charter was copied from the register of Newburgh Priory.

[fol. 83v]

737 *Notification, addressed to all the faithful of holy mother church present and future, by Roger de Mowbray, that Bartholomew Gigator has restored to him his land, namely, Little Wildon, which Roger has now granted in free alms, with the consent of his son, Nigel, to Prior Augustine and his (Roger's) canons of Newburgh. He has also granted a carucate in Thirsk, which they, with the consent of Roger and Nigel, have granted to Bartholomew and his heirs to hold for a pound of incense or 12d.; Roger grants this carucate to acquit the monks of Byland of the tithe of Great Wildon. Grant also of all the assarts which their men of Kilburn had assarted, and confirmation of all the grants which his men have made and may make in the future.* [c. 1147 x c. 1154].

Hiis testibus Gundrea matre mea, Aleliz uxore mea, Sampsone de Albaneyo, Rogero abbate et capitulo de Bellalanda, Radulpho de Wynclyva, Hugone Camino, Willelmo de Stutevylla, Olyvero de Buscy, Roberto de Dayvyll', Odone de Newsom, Willelmo filio Hengeleri, Waltero de Carleton', Petro de Hotona.

Pd: *EYC* IX, no. 165; (calendar) *Mowbray Charters*, no. 200.
Dating: occ. of Nigel de Mowbray and death of first witness.
Note: This is preceded by a rubric stating that it, and no. 738, were copied from the register of Newburgh.

738 *Grant, addressed to all the sons of holy church, by Roger de Mowbray, to God and St Mary and his canons of Newburgh of 4s. yearly in his mill of Thirsk for acquittance of the monks of Byland, until he shall grant them ½ carucate in Brignall or elsewhere in free alms. Further grant of 5s. from the same mill to acquit the monks of the tithes of the assarts of Acca and William. These 5s. are to be given by whoever shall hold the mill at farm at those times when the farm of the mill is rendered. [c. 1147].*
Hiis testibus Rogero abbate de Bellal' cum monachis suis, Nigello filio meo, Waltero de Ryparia, etc.

Pd: *Mowbray Charters*, no. 198.
Dating: Greenway suggested that this is related to Roger's grant, to Byland, of licence to make exchanges of land, which was addressed to Eustace Fitz John (see no. 645 above, *Mowbray Charters*, no. 45), and which she dated *c.* 1147. Both Roger and Eustace had interests in Brignall.
Note: This is followed by a note stating that the monastery of Guisborough has this carucate of land in Thirsk and holds it of the monastery of Newburgh. Its house (*mansio*) is at the ?furthest part of the vill of Thirsk.

[fol. 84r, old fol. 191]
OSGOODBY (SE4980) in the parish of Thirkleby and the wapentake of Birdforth (NR). Osgoodby lies in the region of other estates of Byland, at Thirkleby to the south, Bagby and Balk to the west, Sutton under Whitestonecliffe to the north and Kilburn to the east. The Osgoodby section is one of the largest in the cartulary, with 101 entries, of which only 18 contain full texts, with 83 rubrics only. Osgoodby was held by the Meinill family as a subtenancy of the Buscys, who themselves held of Roger de Mowbray. The first recorded member of the Meinill family is Walter de Meinill of Osgoodby, who was granted the 2 carucates that had been held by his father and a third carucate from his demesne by Roger de Mowbray; this was made with Ascelina his wife (*Mowbray Charters*, no. 374). The first member of the family to become a benefactor of Byland was Walter's son Gilbert (nos 739, 743, 744, 747, 782, 784). Gilbert's son, Walter, was associated with his father in no. 743, and was the grantor of nos 746, 749–52, 756, 759, 776, 778–9, 783 and 794. Walter had a brother, Thomas de Meinill, who appears to have succeeded him, and who issued grants and confirmations (nos 763–64, 773–5, 803–5); Thomas had a son, Gilbert (no. 807). Walter de Meinill had a daughter, Alice (no. 755).

There was also a Meinill family of nearby Thirkleby. Gilbert de Meinill of Thirkleby granted and quitclaimed land to Byland (no. 786), sometimes in association with his son, Stephen (nos 761, 762, 816). A charter surviving as an original that may have been copied into the (now lost) Thirkleby section of the cartulary indicates that Stephen was Gilbert's eldest son and heir, that Gilbert's wife was Idonea, that she had a brother named Philip, and that Gilbert himself had a brother named Peter (Leeds, YAS DD 146/47, a grant by Gilbert of land in Thirkleby). Gilbert had another son, Gilbert (nos 796, 797, 816, 826), and a daughter named Alice, who granted 2 bovates given to her as her marriage portion when she married Henry Holey (Holeghe), with whom she was associated in grants and quitclaims to the monks (nos 798–800, 816–17). This branch seems to have held a tenancy of Thomas de Meinill, son of Gilbert de Meinill of Osgoodby, who quitclaimed to the monks the homage and service of Gilbert de Meinill of Thirkleby (no. 817), as well as that of Alice and her husband, Henry Holey, Nicholas de Meinill, and Geoffrey Fossard (no. 817). Geoffrey's Fossard's tenancy of the family of Meinill of Osgoodby is confirmed by nos 771–2, and he witnessed nos 752, 754.

In addition the cartulary reveals the interaction of a number of lesser families in the building of the abbey estate in Osgoodby. Roger son of William of Osgoodby (nos 745, 795, 815, 830) may have been the son of William son of Langus, who occurs in no. 739. He married Ivetta (no. 789), who held 2 bovates in dower, and they had sons Stephen (no. 789) and Gilbert (nos 769, 816, which indicates that the name of Gilbert's wife was Julietta). Gilbert had daughters Anabel (no. 808), Joan (no. 809), Ivetta (no. 810–4), and sons Walter and Thomas (no. 813). Ivetta married Simon of Boltby (nos 810, 811) and had a son, Walter (no. 812). She issued a charter concerning 2 bovates that she received as her marriage portion (no. 790). It appears that the dower of Ivetta, wife of Roger, became the marriage portion of Ivetta, her granddaughter; it is not certain whether Gilbert son of Ivetta (no. 791) was the son of Ivetta the elder or the younger. If the 2 bovates were conveyed to the abbey by Ivetta the younger (no. 790), then it may well have been her son.

Other benefactors of the abbey included Geoffrey son of Arthur de Torp and his father and brother (nos 739–41), Henry son of Gamaliel (nos 757–8) and Geoffrey son of Columbe (nos 816–19, 821–3), his wife, Alice (nos 819, 824) and their son, Reyner (nos 820, 825). Alice is a name that occurs in the Meinill family, but whether Alice, wife of Geoffrey de Columbe, was also a Meinill, is not clear. The Buscy family, from whom the Meinills held the tenancy in Osgoodby, makes only a few appearances in this section. Robert de Buscy made a small grant to the monks and released them from rent due to him (no. 831), which was confirmed by his son, William (no. 832), who also witnessed nos 752, 776. William confirmed the grants of Gilbert and Walter de Meinill of Osgoodby (no. 793). Oliver de Buscy and William de Buscy also confirmed the monks' holdings in Osgoodby (nos 834, 835; full texts at nos 683, 684 above). William son of Nigel de Mowbray issued a confirmation of lands the monks held in Osgoodby, below Hood castle (no. 836).

This series of grants, confirmations and quitclaims seems to have brought the monks the entire region of Osgoodby, and the boundaries given in no. 743 suggest that as early as 1198 the monks' land stretched as far as Thirkleby and Balk to the west. Many of the field names (such as 'Tocenge' or 'Tockengh' (no. 752)) have been lost, possibly because of depopulation, or because the whole area became a monastic estate. The monks' consolidation of this estate was helped by the relinquishment of rights by, and exchanges with, Newburgh Priory (nos 754, 780–1, 802, 816, 828).

739   *Grant in free alms, addressed to the archbishop of York and the whole chapter of St Peter (York) and all the sons of holy church, by Gilbert de Meinill of Osgoodby, to God and the monks of St Mary of Byland, of 4 bovates in Osgoodby, 2 of which belonged to William son of Langus and 2 of which lie nearest to them to the north, and 1 toft in the same vill 6 perches in width which belonged to Gerbod. Grant also of a right of way through his wood and field in a straight line from Hood Beck as far as the highway which runs from Osgoodby to Kilburn, that is, from the south of Osgoodby, and of all the land, woodland and meadow contained between the watercourse running from his mill of Osgoodby as far as Balk Beck, and from the highway running between Osgoodby and Thirkleby in a straight line by that new road which the monks made as far as Hood Beck and from the monks' road as far as the place where the same rivers meet above Thirkleby mill. Outside these boundaries he grants his whole lordship between the water of Sutton and the water of Osgoodby. Remission and quitclaim of whatever right and claim he and his ancestors had in the land and woodland between the watercourse which comes from Hood and that watercourse which comes from Sutton, and in the ½ carucate which they have in Osgoodby of Geoffrey son of Arthur. To construct houses if they wish they may take materials from his wood for their needs as much as pertains to the 4 bovates. This grant is made in free alms, quit of all secular service, for the salvation of the donor's soul* *and of his wife and of all his ancestors and heirs. Pledge to warranty.* [1180 x 1199].

Hiis testibus Radulfo priore de Giseburna, Roaldo canonico eius, Alano presbitero, Garino de Vescy, etc.

Marginal note: B(aculus) i.

Dating: The first witness occurs in 1180 and had been succeeded by Roald (possibly the second witness) by 1199.

Note: The Geoffrey son of Arthur mentioned in this charter is probably the Geoffrey son of Arthur de Torp to whom Abbot Roger granted ½ carucate in Ampleforth. Greenway suggests this was an exchange (*Mowbray Charters*, p. 250, referring to MS Dodsworth 91, fol. 120r, *recte* fol. 120v, no. 76). At a date before 1154 Roger de Mowbray restored to Arthur son of William de Torp the land which his father held of Roger's father, Nigel, that is ½ carucate in Osgoodby (*Mowbray Charters*, no. 390). This is presumably the land subsequently granted to Byland by Arthur's son, Geoffrey, which is referred to in no. 739. The grants was confirmed by his brother (nos 740, 741); the Arthur of no. 742 may be their father or a later generation of the family.

740 *Rubric: Confirmation by Adam brother of Arthur of the same ½ carucate in Osgoodby.* [*c.* 1180 x 1199].

Dating: as no. 739.

741 *Rubric: Charter of the same Adam. Surrendered.* [*c.* 1180 x 1199].

Dating: as no. 739.

742 *Rubric: Charter of Arthur concerning the same; sealed by the Lord Mowbray. Surrendered.* [*c.* 1180 x 1199].

Dating: as no. 739.

743 *Grant in free alms, addressed to the archbishop of York and the whole chapter of St Peter (York) and all the sons of holy church, by Gilbert de Meinill of Osgoodby, with the goodwill and consent of Walter his son and heir, to God and the monks of St Mary of Byland, of all the assart of Gamel and all the assart of Hugh from the south of* Stainbrigge *in the region of Osgoodby, and all the land between* Stainbrigge *and the bridge which the monks built opposite Thirkleby, and between the sike which falls from* Stainbrigge *on the eastern side of the assarts of Gamel and Hugh and the land towards Bagby which he formerly granted and confirmed to the monks in alms by charter. Further grant of all the land and meadow which belonged to 13 bovates between the water which falls to the millpond of Thirkleby and Balk Beck and all that land which he had between the watercourses. The*

monks are to hold all this free from secular service, to do there as they wish.
Pledge to warranty. [1194 x 1198].

Hiis testibus Rogero de Bavent, vic(ecomite) Ebor', Thoma de
Colvill', Willelmo Darell, Willelmo Malbisse, etc.

Marginal note: 'Bavent' has been underlined in the text and a later hand reads: 'vic
8 9 10 Ric'. There is a genealogy showing the descent from Gilbert de Meinill of
Osgoodby and Thirkleby, to his sons Walter, Gilbert and Stephen, to Thomas son of
Gilbert, Gilbert son of Thomas, and Gilbert son of Gilbert.

Dating: The first witness was undersheriff of Yorkshire from Easter 1194 to
Michaelmas 1198: *EYC* I, 184; *Lord Lieutenants*, p. 51.

[fol. 84v]

744   *Grant in free alms, addressed to the archbishop of York and the whole*
chapter of St Peter (York) and all the sons of holy mother church present and
future, by Gilbert de Meinill of Osgoodby, to God and the monks of St Mary
of Byland, of 30 acres with a perch of 20 feet and the woodland above his
wood of Osgoodby near to the monks' wood, that is, along the road towards
the north which leads from Osgoodby towards Bagby. The monks are to hold
the 30 acres of Gilbert and his heirs free from all secular service, and to do
there as they wish, for the salvation of his soul and of all his ancestors and
heirs. The monks may enclose the land with a ditch and hedge if they wish
and are to have free entry and exit as necessary. Pledge to warranty. [before
1203].

Hiis testibus Willelmo de Estutevill, Willelmo de Kernetby tunc
agente vices vicecomitis, Roberto de Moubray, Nigello de Plumpton',
etc.

Dating: The first witness, William de Stuteville, son of Robert III and a king's
justice, died in 1203. He was sheriff of Yorkshire from 1200 to 1202 (*EYC* IX, 9–13).
A charter issued by him in favour of Fountains Abbey, with his body, between 1201
and 1203 was witnessed by William of Carnaby and Nigel of Plumpton (*ibid.*, no.
33). William of Carnaby is not listed as an undersheriff; William's undersheriff was
William Brito (*Lord Lieutenants*, p. 52). Robert de Mowbray could be the son of
Roger or his grandson, son of Nigel de Mowbray.

745   *Rubric: Quitclaim by Roger son of William of Osgoodby of the same*
30 acres of land and woodland.

Note: Roger son of William granted a further charter, no. 765 below.

746   *Rubric: Confirmation by Walter son of Gilbert de Meinill of the same.*
[late 12th or early 13th cent.].

Dating: Walter was the elder son of Gilbert, and occurs in the late 12th and early
13th century.

747 *Rubric: Confirmation by Gilbert de Meinill of 1 acre in Osgoodby which belonged to Alkeman.* [late 12th or early 13th cent.].
Dating: as no. 746.

748 *Rubric: Charter of Walter de Meinill concerning 2 bovates in Osgoodby for the land which lies above North Middleburgh and South Middleburgh.* [late 12th or early 13th cent.].
Dating: as no. 746.

749 *Rubric: Charter of the same Walter [de Meinill] concerning another 2 bovates in Osgoodby which Hugh and Gerbod held, and concerning all the land in* Hubustromar' *and* Gildeflatt *and concerning the land which Robert Smyth held. Copied.* [late 12th or early 13th cent.].
Dating: as no. 746.

750 *Rubric: Charter of the same [Walter de Meinill] concerning 2 bovates which Robert and Reynald the carpenter held. Copied.* [late 12th or early 13th cent.].
Dating: as no. 746.

751 *Rubric: Charter of the same [Walter de Meinill] concerning an assart in the region of Osgoodby between the assart of Byland and the assart of Sutton.* [late 12th or early 13th cent.].
Dating: as no. 746.

752 *Grant in free alms, addressed to the archbishop of York and the whole chapter of St Peter (York) and all the sons of holy mother church present and future, by Walter de Meinill son of Gilbert of Osgoodby, to God and the monks of St Mary of Byland, of all that land he had in West Riding below* Sunnescogh *in the region of Osgoodby, and of all that land called* Gibbut *in* Kilburnewra. *Further grant and quitclaim of all common which he had within their land by the following boundaries: from the road which starts on the western side of Osgoodby towards the watercourse of that vill, and from the land of Stephen towards the south which touches on* Ellerbust *as far as the donor's meadow called* Tokcengh. *The monks may enclose all this land with a ditch or hedge by the said boundaries as they wish, and do there whatever they wish. They may also if they wish make a causeway between the common gate of the vill and their land below the road, in such a way, however, that they put another enclosure between the said causeway and the donor's meadow called* Tockengh *because of their animals. From there they may conduct the water through their land as they wish and at their conve-*

nience, as long as the same water returns to its old channel. This grant is made quit of all service, for the salvation of his soul and of all his ancestors and heirs. Pledge to warranty. [late 12th or early 13th cent.].

Hiis testibus Willelmo de Buscy, Thoma de Lascell', Ernaldo de Upsala, Gaufrido Fossard, Gikello de Smydheton', etc.

Dating: The first and fifth witnesses attest together in 1185 x *c.* 1210, and the fourth and fifth together in the same period (see above, nos 116, 117, 206, 264; *EYC* IX, nos 138–9). The second and fourth attest together between 1204 and 1210 (*ibid.* IX, no. 122).

753 *Rubric: Charter of the same [Walter de Meinill] concerning 37 acres of land and woodland above.* [late 12th or early 13th cent.].

Dating: as nos 746, 753.

[fols 84v–85r]

754 *Quitclaim, addressed to all the sons of holy mother church present and future, by Prior Walter and the canons of Newburgh to the monks of St Mary of Byland of all right which they had or might have in 37 acres which Walter de Meinill sold them near their wood of Balk, that is, towards the north east near to the new assart of the monks. The monks are to enclose the land as they wish and do there whatever they wish, as Walter's charter which the monks have attests.* [*c.* 1205 x 1224].

Hiis testibus Gikello de Smydheton', Ernaldo de Upsall, Galfrido Fossard, Thoma de Lasceles, etc.

Dating: Prior Walter's predecessor occurs in 1202; his first recorded occurrence is in 1205 and his last in 1212; he had been succeeded by Prior Philip by 1224 (*HRH* I, 177, and II, 428).

[fol. 85r, old fol. 192]

755 *Rubric: Quitclaim by Alice daughter of the said Walter [de Meinill] of the same 37 acres and woodland.* [? early 13th cent.].

756 *Rubric: Charter of Walter de Meinill concerning 1 bovate which Robert Beneth held and 1 rood in* West Riddyng. [late 12th or early 13th cent.].

757 *Rubric: Charter of Henry son of Gamaliel concerning 1 bovate which Walter de Meinill granted him for forinsec service to Walter.* [late 12th or early 13th cent.].

Note: As Henry of Osgoodby son of Gamaliel Henry issued no. 779 below.

758 *Rubric: Charter of the same [Henry son of Gamaliel] concerning the same 1 bovate, surrendered.* [late 12th or early 13th cent.].

759 *Rubric: Confirmation of the same by Walter de Meinill.* [late 12th or early 13th cent.].

760 *Rubric: Chirograph agreement reached in the king's court between the monks and John de Daiville concerning 86 acres of land and woodland on Rose Hill and common pasture throughout* Melclyve *(Scencliffe) and Kilburn for all the monks' animals of Wildon and Osgoodby. Look under the heading of 'Kilburn'.*

Marginal note: B(aculus) ii.

Note: The text of this agreement is entered at no. 489 above. For the form 'Melclyve' for Scencliffe see above, no. 488, note.

761 *Rubric: Charter of Gilbert de Meinill and Stephen his son concerning 7 perches of land and 1 toft and croft in Osgoodby.* [late 12th or early 13th cent.].

Note: The donor can be identified as Gilbert de Meinill of Thirkleby. He occurs in the last two decades of the 12th century and his son, Stephen, in the first two decades of the 13th. They were frequent witnesses of Byland charters.

762 *Rubric: Quitclaim by the same [Gilbert de Meinill and Stephen his son] of common from the road which begins on the western side of Osgoodby as far as the watercourse of the same vill towards the west and from the land of Stephen de Meinill as far as* Tockheyng. [late 12th or early 13th cent.].

Dating: see no. 761.

763 *Rubric: Charter of Thomas de Meinill concerning 18 acres above* Quynhousflath *and more if more can be found, and 3 roods and 8 acres in various places.* [early 13th cent.].

Dating: This would appear to be Thomas, younger son of Gilbert de Meinill of Osgoodby, who occurs in the first two decades of the 13th century.

764 *Grant in free alms, addressed to the archbishop of York and the whole chapter of St Peter (York) and all the sons of holy mother church present and future, by Thomas de Meinill of Osgoodby, to God and the monks of St Mary of Byland, of all the profitable land which he had in the region of Osgoodby and all the meadow enclosed within these boundaries: from the river of the good spring through the ditch which ascends as far as* Sunnidkelde *and from there as the river from the spring runs through the ditch as far as* Ulfkelde *and from there across the <river> which descends from* Pipefelde *and from there along the ditch as far as Carlton <and> Stocking and across the head of the meadow as far as* Wandelandesheved *and along the ditch as far as the upper part of* Rughthwayt *and across the headland of*

Rughthwayt *as far as the small meadow and from there along the* culture *of* Rughthwayt *as far as the road which drops down from the north part of Osgoodby towards the south to the watercourse of Osgoodby mill. The grant is made free from all secular service for the salvation of the soul of the donor and the souls of his father and mother and of all his ancestors and heirs, for the monks to do there as they wish. Pledge to warranty.* [early 13th cent.].

Hiis testibus Iohanne de Daivill', Philippo filio Iohannis, Thoma de Lasceles, Willelmo filio Rogeri de Herlesay, etc.

Dating: John de Daiville succeeded his father between 1186 and 1190 and died by 1243. Philip son of John attests in the late 12th and early 13th centuries (*EYC* V, nos 275, 277, 338AB, 346, IX, no. 85).

765   *Rubric: Charter of Roger son of William of Osgoodby concerning 1 acre in the same at* Bradebrotys.

Note: Roger son of William also quitclaimed 30 acres of land and woodland (no. 745 above). His son Gilbert granted nos 766, 769.

766   *Rubric: Charter of Gilbert son of Roger concerning 2 bovates and a toft and croft in Osgoodby.*

767   *Rubric: Charter of Nicholas son of Gilbert de Meinill of Thirkleby concerning all the land he had in Osgoodby of the gift of Thomas de Meinill.*

Marginal note: (in later hand) 'Nicholai'.

Note: The grantor is to be identified as a younger son of Gilbert de Meinill of Thirkleby. No. 606 confirms that he was the son of Gilbert the elder and brother of Gilbert the younger.

768   *Rubric: Charter of the same concerning the same land. Surrendered.*

769   *Rubric: Charter of Gilbert son of Roger of Osgoodby concerning 2 tofts and 2 crofts exchanged for 1 toft in the same vill.*

770   *Rubric: Charter of Agnes of Osgoodby concerning 1 toft and croft, and river meadow* (holmus), *rendering gloves. Her additional charter about the same has been returned.*

771   *Rubric: Charter of Geoffrey Fossard concerning 1 bovate which he holds in Osgoodby of Gilbert de Meinill for forinsec service.*

772   *Rubric: Quitclaim by the same [Geoffrey Fossard] of 1 toft and croft in Osgoodby rendering 2 arrows to Walter de Meinill.*

773   *Rubric: Charter of Thomas de Meinill concerning ½ acre in Osgoodby which he held of the monks. Surrendered.*

[fol. 85v]
774   *Rubric: Charter of the same [Thomas de Meinill] concerning the same land. Surrendered.*

775   *Rubric: Charter of Thomas de Meinill concerning 2 tofts and 2 crofts and 1 meadow between the ditch of Osgoodby and the profitable land of the vill.*

776   *Notification to all present and future by Walter de Meinill of Osgoodby of his grant in free alms to God and the monks of St Mary of Byland, of 33 acres with a perch of 20 feet and woodland above the said land in the region of Osgoodby near to the assart which Gilbert his father granted them near to Balk, that is, towards the north east of the assart (no. 744). The monks are to hold the land of Walter and his heirs free from secular service, and are to do with and enclose it as they wish. Pledge to warranty. [1204 x 1209].*
Hiis testibus Roberto Walensi tunc vice(comite) Ebor', Ricardo Malebys, Waltero de Bovigtona, Willelmo de Corneburgh, Willelmo de Buscy, etc.
Marginal note: (in later hand) 'inter 6 & 11 R. Jo'.
Dating: first witness as undersheriff of Yorkshire.

777   *Rubric: Charter of the same [Walter de Meinill] concerning 37 acres with woodland in Osgoodby near to the assart by Balk for 20 marks which the monks have given to him.*

778   *Rubric: Charter of the same [Walter de Meinill] concerning 33 acres with woodland pertaining to them, for 17 marks.*

779   *Rubric: Quitclaim by Henry of Osgoodby son of Gamaliel of common of 18 acres which Walter de Meinill granted them.*
Note: Henry issued no. 757 above concerning land that Walter de Meinill granted to him.

780   *Quitclaim, addressed to all the sons of holy church present and future, by Prior B(ernard) and the convent of Newburgh to the monks of St Mary of Byland, of all right and all common which they had in 30 acres which the monks have of Gilbert de Meinill of Osgoodby in his wood near the monks'*

wood in Balk, for 2½ acres which the canons have received from Gilbert in his
woodland in exchange for this quitclaim. [1186 x 1199].
Hiis testibus Willelmo decano de Tyveryngton', Ernaldo de Upsala,
Galfrido Fossard, etc.
Dating: grantor.

781 *Notification to all to whom these letters shall come, by Prior B(ernard)*
and the chapter of Newburgh, that Robert de Buscy had granted them an
exchange for land which they held in Milnewra, *for which they remitted the*
said land to Robert and to the monks of Byland. [1186 x 1199].
Hiis testibus Alexandro capellano, Gilberto de Thurkilby, Gilberto de
Angotby, etc.
Dating: grantor.

782 *Rubric: Charter of Gilbert de Meinill concerning 4½ acres with his*
body.
Note: The mention of Gilbert's son, Walter, in the following rubric makes it clear
that this was Gilbert de Meinill of Osgoodby.

783 *Rubric: Confirmation of the same by Walter his son.*

784 *Notification to all present and future by Gilbert de Meinill of*
Osgoodby and Walter his son and heir, of their grant in free alms to God and
the monks of St Mary of Byland, of all the land which they had within their
boundaries among the 30 acres which Gilbert sold them in the region of
Osgoodby whether there be ½ acre or more over and above the 30 acres. The
grant is made free from all secular service, for the salvation of their souls and
of all their ancestors and heirs. Pledge to warranty. [late 12th cent.].
Hiis testibus Thoma de Colevilla, Galfrido Fossard, Willelmo
Bugden'.
Marginal note: B(aculus) iii.
Date: see no. 743.

785 *Rubric: Charter of Alice daughter of Gilbert remitting common of 33*
acres.

786 *Rubric: Quitclaim and remission by Gilbert de Meinill of Thirkleby of*
common of 67 acres of land and woodland.

787 *Rubric: Quitclaim by Stephen of all the common belonging to ½*
carucate and 67 acres, etc.

Note: The grantor was probably Stephen de Meinill, son of Gilbert of the previous charter.

788   *Rubric: Charter of William son of Robert of Osgoodby concerning 2 bovates except the tofts and crofts.*

789   *Rubric: Charter of Stephen son of Roger of Osgoodby concerning 2 bovates which Ivetta his mother held in dower. Copied.*

[fol. 86r, old fol. 193]
790   *Rubric: Charter of Ivetta daughter of Gilbert of Osgoodby concerning 2 bovates which her father gave her as a marriage portion.*

791   *Rubric: Quitclaim by Gilbert son of Ivetta of 2 bovates which his mother granted.*

792   *Rubric: Charter of Gilbert son of Roger of Osgoodby concerning 5 bovates in the same vill.*

793   *Rubric: Confirmation by William de Buscy of 5 bovates and 63 acres which Walter de Meinill and Gilbert his father granted.* [early 13th cent.].
Dating: William de Buscy was the son of Robert de Buscy, a benefactor of Byland in the late 12th century, whose grant William confirmed (nos 831–2 below); he attests nos 116, 414, 651, 701, 712, 752, 776, 836, 849.

794   *Rubric: Charter of Walter de Meinill concerning 1 bovate in Osgoodby and all the land which lies between the meadow of* Huethorn-heyng *and the land of Roger son of William.*

795   *Rubric: Charter of Roger son of William concerning the same. Surrendered.*

796   *Grant in free alms, addressed to all who will see or hear this charter, by Gilbert son of Gilbert de Meinill, to God and the monks of St Mary of Byland, of all the land he had in the vill of Osgoodby, that is ½ carucate with its appurtenances and all the other lands and* culture *which he had in the vill, for which the abbot and convent were accustomed to render to Gilbert yearly 40s. sterling. This grant and quitclaim is made with his body, for the salvation of his soul and of all his ancestors and heirs, for the benefits which the monks had often bestowed upon him, and for a sum of money which they have given him in his great need. To hold free of all service. Pledge to warranty. Sealed with the donor's seal.* [mid 13th cent.].

Hiis testibus domino Waltero tunc priore, Rogero suppriore, Willelmo cellerario, Thoma de Colevilla, etc.

Dating: see no. 155.
Note: The donor was of the branch of Meinill of Thirkleby.

797 *Rubric: Quitclaim by the same [Gilbert son of Gilbert de Meinill] of the said 40s.*

798 *Rubric: Quitclaim by Henry Holey with the consent of Alice his wife of all his right in Osgoodby except for 2 bovates which he received with Alice in marriage.*

[fol. 86r–v]
799 *Grant in free alms, addressed to all the sons of holy mother church present and future who will see or hear this charter, by Alice daughter of Gilbert de Meinill in her independent widowhood, to God and St Mary and the abbot and convent of Byland, of 2 bovates in the region of Osgoodby with tofts and crofts and all appurtenances; these 2 bovates were given with her as her marriage portion by her father to Henry Holeghe (Holey) her late husband, and are to be held of her and her heirs free from all secular service. The grant is made for the salvation of her soul, and of her husband Henry, her father and mother, and all her ancestors and heirs, and for the benefits which the monks had often bestowed on her, and for 1 bovate with toft and croft in Sutton which the abbot and convent have granted to her son William, to hold rendering to the abbot and convent 1 pound of cumin or 6d. at Whitsuntide for all service. Each year for the rest of her life in the octaves of St Martin in Winter (11 Nov.) William shall render for the said bovate 2 bushels of wheat and 2 of oats in their granary at Byland. On her death this service shall cease. Pledge to warranty. Sealed with the donor's seal.* [mid 13th cent.].

Hiis testibus domino Waltero tunc priore de Bellal', Willelmo cellerario, Honorio magistro conversorum, Henrico socio cellerarii, Iohanne de Ripon', Waltero de Bedeford, etc.

Copy: MS Dodsworth 63, fol. 61v, from cartulary fol. 190 (*sic*). This copy is abbreviated and has the first and third witnesses only.
Date: see no. 155.

800 *Rubric: Charter of Alice, widow of Henry Holey, concerning the exchange of a toft which belonged to Reginald.*

801 *Rubric: Charter of Thomas de Meinill concerning 3 bovates in Osgoodby which Alan Lewbatus and Tock held, and other lands.*

802 *Agreement, addressed to all the faithful of Christ who will see or hear this writing, between Abbot H(enry) and the monks of Byland and Prior Simon and the canons of Newburgh, by which the prior and canons granted 2 bovates which they had in the fields of Osgoodby and on which the abbot and monks pay tithes to the prior and convent. For this the abbot and monks have granted in exchange 13 acres and 1 acre for common woodland in the region of Osgoodby above* Milnebergh, *and 1½ roods of meadow in the meadow of Osgoodby between the 2 rivers, and 7 acres in the region of Osgoodby in* Staynowwra. *The prior and convent are to hold this land free from secular service, with free entry and exit.* [1234 x 1246].

Dating: Prior Simon occurs in March 1241. The last recorded occurrence of his predecessor, John, is in 1234 (no. 732) and he had been succeeded by Ingelram by 1246 (*HRH* II, 428).

803 *Rubric: Charter of Thomas de Meinill son of Gilbert de Meinill of all he had in Osgoodby, rendering 4s. yearly.*

804 *Rubric: Charter of the same [Thomas de Meinill] remitting the same 4s.*

805 *Rubric: Charter of the same Thomas [de Meinill] concerning 3 tofts and crofts in Osgoodby.*

806 *Rubric: Charter of the same [Thomas de Meinill] concerning 4 pounds of pepper and 1 pound of cumin, 1 of which Gilbert de Meinill of Thirkleby owes him yearly for ½ carucate in Osgoodby and 1 of which Geoffrey Fossard owes for 1 bovate etc.*

807 *Rubric: Quitclaim by Gilbert son of Thomas de Meinill of the monks' debts.*

808 *Rubric: Quitclaim by Anabel daughter of Gilbert of Osgoodby of all her right in the region of Osgoodby.*

Note: It is likely that the Gilbert of Osgoodby mentioned in this and nos 809, 810 and 812 is not the son of Walter de Meinill. Anabel had sisters Joan (no. 809) and Ivetta (nos 790, 791, 810) and brothers Walter and Thomas (no. 812).

809 *Rubric: Quitclaim by Joan daughter of Gilbert of all her right in the region of Osgoodby.*

Note: Joan's sister, Anabel, granted no. 808.

810   *Rubric: Charter of Ivetta daughter of Gilbert concerning her right in all the land of Osgoodby, saving a part of 4s.*

Marginal note: B(aculus) iiii.

Note: Ivetta's sisters Anabel and Joan granted nos 808, 809. Ivetta was married to Simon of Boltby (no. 811) and had a son Walter (no. 813). She does not appear to be Ivetta who was a party to no. 816, whose husband was Roger and son Gilbert. The charter is noted in MS Dodsworth 63, fol. 61v, with reference to cartulary fol. 190 (*sic*).

811   *Rubric: Charter of Simon de Boltby, husband of Ivetta, concerning the same.*

Note: The charter is noted in MS Dodsworth 63, fol. 61v.

812   *Rubric: Confirmation of Ivetta of all grants made by her father Gilbert and Walter and Thomas her brothers in the region of Osgoodby.*

Note: The charter is noted in MS Dodsworth 63, fol. 61v.

813   *Rubric: Quitclaim by the same [Ivetta] of common in 28 acres of land and woodland which the monks have of Walter her son.*

Note: The charter is noted in MS Dodsworth 63, fol. 61v, with reference to cartulary fol. 190b (*sic*).

814   *Rubric: Confirmation by the same [Ivetta] of a toft which Gamel le Pynder held in Osgoodby and another toft and croft.*

815   *Rubric: Charter of Roger son of William of Osgoodby remitting all his right in common land and woodland which the monks have of Gilbert de Meinill and Walter his son.*

816   *Quitclaim, addressed to all the faithful in Christ present and future, by Walter, prior, and the convent of Newburgh, Gilbert de Meinill, his sons Stephen and Gilbert, Geoffrey son of Columbe, Henry Hole and Alice his wife, daughter of Gilbert, Julietta who was the wife of Gilbert, Ivetta who was the wife of Roger, and Gilbert her son, to the monks of St Mary of Byland, of all common which they had in 8 acres with woodland pertaining to them, which Thomas de Meinill granted to the monks in the region of Osgoodby, to do with as they wish, as Thomas's charter attests.* [1205 x c. 1225].

Hiis testibus Thoma de Laceles, Galfrido Fossard, Adam de Boltby, Willelmo Darell, Hugone de Upsale, Roberto Fossard, Stephano de Blaby, etc.

Copy: MS Dodsworth 63, fol. 62r, from cartulary fol. 190b (*sic*).
Dating: Prior Walter of Newburgh.

Note: This represents grants by the Thirkleby branch of the Meinill family. The rubric notes that this document was sealed with 9 seals. Robert son of Thomas Fossard granted and confirmed to Byland the toft and croft which his father granted him for homage and service, that is, the toft and croft held by Geoffrey son of Columbe.

[fols 86v–87r]

817   Rubric: *Quitclaim by Thomas de Meinill son of Gilbert of Osgoodby of the homage and service of Gilbert de Meinill of Thirkleby and his heirs, Nicholas de Meinill, Gilbert son of Roger of Osgoodby, Geoffrey Fossard, Henry Holley (Holey) and Alice his wife and Geoffrey son of Columbe.* [early 13th cent.].

Note: There is a copy of the rubric in MS Dodsworth 63, fol. 62r, from cartulary fol. 190b (*sic*). No. 606 above confirms that Nicholas de Meinill, who also occurs in no. 767, was the son of Gilbert the elder and brother of Gilbert the younger.

[fol. 87r, old fol. 194]

818   Rubric: *Charter of Geoffrey son of Columbe concerning 1 selion between the mill stream of Osgoodby and the road which runs towards Bagby.* [early 13th cent.].

Dating: with reference to no. 816.

819   Rubric: *Charter of the same [Geoffrey son of Columbe] and Alice his wife concerning 1 bovate in Osgoodby near the fishpond, performing forinsec service.* [early 13th cent.].

Dating: with reference to no. 816.

820   Rubric: *Confirmation by Reyner his son concerning the same, as his charter attests.*

821   Rubric: *Charter of the same Geoffrey son of Columbe concerning 1 toft which Gerald held.* [early 13th cent.].

Dating: with reference to no. 816.

822   Rubric: *Charter of the same [Geoffrey son of Columbe] concerning all the right which he had in common of woodland which Gilbert de Meinill granted the monks.* [early 13th cent.].

Dating: with reference to no. 816.

823   Rubric: *Quitclaim by the same [Geoffrey son of Columbe] of all common which he had in land and woodland which the monks have of Gilbert de Meinill and Walter his son.* [early 13th cent.].

Dating: with reference to no. 816.

824 *Rubric: Confirmation by Alice wife of Geoffrey son of Columbe of all the grants made by her husband.* [early 13th cent.].
Dating: with reference to no. 816.

825 *Rubric: Confirmation by Reyner of all the grants which Geoffrey and Alice his parents made, according to the contents of their charters.*

826 *Rubric: Quitclaim by Gilbert son of Gilbert de Meinill of common within the grange of Osgoodby.*

827 *Rubric: Charter of Stephen de Meinhil and Gilbert his son of common of 4 acres in the region of Osgoodby.*
Note: Stephen de Meinill was the son of Gilbert de Meinill. He attests nos 257, 259, 260, 264, 420, 421, 424, 425 etc. As he was succeeded by his brother, Thomas, his son Gilbert may have predeceased him.

828 *Rubric: Chirograph of Walter, prior of Newburgh, concerning the exchange of 1 selion of land for another.* [1205 x c. 1224].

829 *Rubric: Quitclaim by William Brito of all his right in Osgoodby and Sutton, with appurtenances.* [late 12th or early 13th cent.].
Dating: William Brito, a kinsman of Hugh Malebisse, occurs in 1170 x 1180 and 1175 x 1184 (*EYC* I, no. 48 and II, no. 739).

830 *Rubric: Confirmation by William son of Roger of the grants of Gilbert and Stephen de Meinill.*

831 *Grant in free alms, addressed to the archbishop of York and the whole chapter of St Peter (York) and all the sons of holy church, by Robert de Buscy, with his body, to God and the monks of St Mary of Byland, of 5 acres in the region of Osgoodby lying on the eastern side of the vill towards Hood, and 1 toft lying on the western side of the vill towards Bagby. Remission of 40d. which the monks were accustomed to render yearly for ½ carucate in Osgoodby. This grant is made with the consent and good will of his son William, free from all service, for the salvation of the soul of the donor and of his father and mother, and of all his ancestors and heirs. Pledge to warranty.* [late 12th cent.].
Hiis testibus Roberto de Moubray, Radulfo de Surdevall, Rogero de Carletun, etc.
Marginal note: B(aculus) v.
Copy: MS Dodsworth 63, fol. 62v, from cartulary fol. 194.
Dating: The donor succeeded his brother, Oliver, by 1166 (*Mowbray Charters*, no.

401). The Meinill family held a subtenure of the Buscy family in Thirkleby (*ibid.*, p. 242). Robert de Mowbray could be the son of Roger de Mowbray, who died after 1199, or Robert son of Nigel. Ralph de Surdeval occurs in the reign of Henry II.

832 *Rubric: Confirmation by William his son of the same; confirmation also of that* cultura *which lies to the north of the mill of Thirkleby.*

833 *Rubric: Chapter of the Temple concerning 1 bovate with a toft [and] assart towards Hood and ½ acre of meadow for 1 bovate in Thirsk which the monks have granted them.*
Note: This may refer to a charter issued by the chapter of the Templars.

834 *Rubric: Confirmation by Oliver de Buscy of all the grants which Gilbert de Meinill of Osgoodby and Walter and Thomas his sons granted in Osgoodby. Copied. Look in the magnates' bundle.*
Marginal note: opposite nos 833 and 834, in a later hand, a sketch showing a family tree with Gilbert de Meinill and his two sons Walter and Thomas.
Note: The text is given above at no. 683 in the section called the bundle of the magnates.

835 *Rubric: Confirmation by William de Buscy of lordship of the vill of Osgoodby. Look as above.*
Note: The text is given above at no. 684 in the section called the bundle of the magnates.

836 *Notification, addressed to all men present and future, by William son of Nigel de Mowbray, of his confirmation in free alms to God and St Mary and the abbot and monks of Byland and their successors, of all the grants which the abbot and monks have in Osgoodby below the castle of Hood, with all the men of the vill and all appurtenances; confirmation of all charters which they have of the lords de Buscy. Pledge to warranty.* [Dec. 1189 x 1210].
Hiis testibus Willelmo de Buscy, Philippo filio Iohannis, Galfrido Fossard, Rogero de Carleton', Ricardo Malebisse, Roberto dapifero, et aliis.
Copy: MS Dodsworth 63, fol. 62v.
Dating: the departure of Nigel de Mowbray on crusade and the death of the fifth witness.
Note: This suggests that Hood castle lay in the area marked as Hood Hill, to the NW of Osgoodby grange and the SW of Hood grange.

[fol. 87v]
837 *Grant in free alms, addressed to the archbishop of York and the whole chapter of St Peter (York) and all the sons of holy church, by Stephen son of*

Gilbert de Meinill, to God and St Mary of Byland and the monks serving God there and who will serve there in perpetuity, of all his land in Osgoodby near to Hood, that is 3 carucates with their appurtenances, to do there whatever they wish. The grant is made free from all secular service, and the monks have granted to the donor and his heirs participation in the spiritual good deeds of the house in life and in death. Pledge to warranty. [before 1224].
Hiis testibus domino Willelmo de Moubray, Olyvero de Buscy, Iohanne de Dayvilla, etc.
Marginal note at end of rubric: B(aculus) iiii.
Dating: death of the first witness.

838 *Chirograph notifying the termination of a dispute which had arisen between the abbot and convent of Byland on the one part, and John de Daiville, knight, lord of Kilburn, on the other, concerning the boundaries between the grange of Osgoodby and Kilburn. John has acknowledged that the pit commonly called 'le prestpictes' as far as the two ancient maples which stand on the field of the abbot and convent, and from there in a straight line to the ditch called Stocking dyke is, and will be, the boundary and division between the two. Sealed with the seals of both parties.* Kilburn; the day after St Matthew [25 Feb.] 1280 [1281].
Hiis testibus magistro Roberto de Scarthburgh decano Ebor', domino Olyvero de Buscy, domino Marmeduco Darell, militibus, etc.
Marginal note: (in later hand) '8 Ed. 1'.
Copy: MS Dodsworth 63, fol. 62v, from cartulary fol. 194.

839 *Rubric: Chirograph in the king's court between the monks and John de Eyvill concerning common in Osgoodby. Look in Kilburn.*
Note: A text of a final concord of 1252 which relates to a number of places including Osgoodby is entered in the cartulary at no. 489 above.

[fol. 88r, old fol. 195]
SOUTH OTTERINGTON (SE3787), township in the parish of North Otterington and the wapentake of Birdforth (NR), 4 miles south of Northallerton. From 1086 to the 17th century the manor was divided into moieties, one of which was granted to Robert de Brus in the late 11th century.

840 *Confirmation, addressed to all who are or are to come, by Adam de Brus (II), to Geoffrey Fossard of all his holding in Otterington which his father Geoffrey granted him except for the service he owes Adam, that is half in demesne and half for service, in mills, meadows, pastures, ways, paths,* *waters, and free customs, to hold of the heirs of Geoffrey's father in fee and hereditary right for the service of ½ knight's fee. [c. 1180 x 1196].*

Hiis testibus Willelmo Baart, Galfrido Baart, Rogero de Rosel, etc.

Copy: MS Dodsworth 7, fo. 167v (from the original formerly in St Mary's Tower), which omits 'etc' in the witness list and continues: Willelmo Engeram, Roberto Engeram, Waltero de Staynesby, Roberto de Malteby, Willelmo de Wylton', Rycolfo de Galmton, Michaele de Tocotes, Radulfo de Nevill, Roberto de Esturmi, Radulfo Talbot, Willelmo de Staynesby, Ricardo clerico, Iohanne de Briggeham.

Pd: *EYC* II, no. 759, from MS Dodsworth 7.

Dating: The donor died in 1196.

Note: The rubric reads: 'transcript of the confirmation of Adam de Brus which does many times for demonstrating our right in Otterington'.

841 *Final concord in the king's court in the presence of Robert of Lexington, Roger of Thirkleby, Jolland de Neville, Gilbert de Preston and John de Coleham, justices, and other faithful men of the king then present, between the abbot of Byland, plaintiff, and Peter de Brus, defendant, concerning 10,000 haddock which are due to the abbot in arrears from the annual rent of 1000 haddock which Peter owes. The abbot has remitted and quitclaimed all right in the rent, and for this Peter has granted the abbot all the service of ½ knight's fee with its appurtenances in Otterington which Thomas Fossard formerly held of Peter, with homage, service, scutage, wardship, reliefs and escheats, to hold in free alms in perpetuity. Pledge to warranty. The abbot and his successor will surrender any charters and muniments they have concerning the said 1000 haddock.* Westminster; 3 weeks from St Michael, 28 Henry III [20 Oct. 1244].

Marginal note: (in later hand) '28 H 3'.

Copy: PRO CP 25/1/264/37, no. 20.

Pd (calendar): *Yorks. Fines 1232–1246*, p. 119 (from PRO copy).

Note: This was a long standing dispute between the abbey and the Brus family. In 1239 the abbot appointed as his attorney either brother Robert de Pavely his monk, or William *venator* in his plea against Peter de Brus concerning arrears of haddock (*Curia Regis Rolls*, XVI, 113, 143). In 1243 the abbot entered a plea *quare non tenet* concerning the agreement reached before the king's justices in York between the abbot and Peter's father, Peter. Peter failed to attend the court and the sheriff was ordered to distrain on his goods (*ibid.*, XVII, 244). He appeared in court in 1244 and acknowledged the concord which had been reached between his father and the monks. However, he argued that after his father's death an arrangement had been reached whereby he was to pay £40 in respect of the arrears, of which he had paid at least 20 marks, less 2s. It was also agreed that Peter and his heirs would pay 40s. yearly and would surrender to the abbot letters patent stating that as soon as Peter should provide security for payment, the abbot would restore to William of Lancaster a document drawn up between William and the abbot, in Peter's name, releasing Peter from payment of arrears of 10 marks of the £20 remaining (*ibid.*, XVIII, 236–7). The agreement above evidently follows this court case.

842 *Rubric: Writ of the king sent to the escheator after the death of John Malebisse that he not intervene concerning the said homage.* [Westminster; 4 May 1316].

Text: MS Dodsworth 91, fol. 75r–v, no. 9. The king's writ is directed to Robert of Clitheroe, his escheator beyond Trent, who, at the king's request has caused there to be an inquisition into the lands of John Malebisse, deceased, who on the day he died held the manor of Acaster of the honour of Eye for the service of 10s. yearly, and lands in Ayton in Cleveland of the said honour for the service of 40d. yearly, and lands within the liberty of Byland at Otterington and elsewhere for military service. Because he did not hold other lands in chief on the day he died custody of his lands ought to belong to the king. William, John's son and heir, is aged 17. The king orders land in Acaster and Ayton to be retained but not to intervene in Otterington. Westminster, 4 May [marginal note: 9 Edward II].

Note: For related documents, see *Cal. Cl. R. 1313–1318*, p. 282 (25 April 1316); *Cal. Fine R. II, 1307–1319*, p. 273 (8 Mar. 1316), p. 274 (5 Apr. 1316), pp. 276–7 (26 Apr. 1316), p. 279 (15 May 1316). In 1317 Abbot John issued a notification to the effect that as the custody of the lands and tenements of William, son of John Malebisse recently deceased, in Sutton and Otterington ought, by reason of his minority, to be taken by the abbot and convent as chief lords, they have taken them into their custody and held them for a year and a half and received rents and revenues, and have made William an allowance of a sum of money. They have restored, for a sum of money, all the lands etc. to William. Sealed with the common seal on one part, and by William on the other, and with the seal of Richard, rector of Scawton, and Lawrence of Copmanthorpe, steward. Byland, eve of the nativity of the B. V. M. (7 Sept.) 1317. See MS Dodsworth 7, fol. 110r.

843 *Rubric: Order of the escheator sent to his sub-escheator that he should not intervene.* [May 1316]

Note: There is a note that these two are bound together with the said fine (no. 841).

[fol. 88v]
OVER SILTON (SE4593), parish in the wapentake of Birdforth (NR). The parish, which also includes Kepwick, lies on the western edge of the Hambledon Hills.

844 *Grant by letters patent in free alms by Simon Blundy of Leake, son of Malger de Newerk, to God and the monks of Byland and their successors, of a toft and croft, 11 acres of arable and 2 acres of meadow with all their appurtenances, and a water mill with its soke. The abbot and monks or those who hold of them may do whatever they wish, and may strengthen and repair the*

*mill ponds as necessary because of damage by the water, without any
hindrance. Pledge to warranty for the donor and his heirs for the salvation of
their souls.* [late 12th or early 13th cent.].

Hiis testibus Andrea de Magneby, Willelmo de Kirkeby, Laurentio de
Siltona, etc.

Marginal note: Collecta; B(aculus) i.

Dating: When *c.* 1210 Robert son of Adam Fossard granted to the Knights
Hospitaller specified land in Felixkirk he excepted the *cultura* of Simon Blundus
and land bounded by the curtilage of the wife of Robert the hermit (*EYC* IX, no.
83). Andrew of Maunby witnesses in the period 1190 x 1202 and 1183 x 1203 (*ibid.*
III, no. 1860, and IX, no. 93).

845 *Rubric: Confirmation by William Malebisse of the same and of land in
Tollesby.*

Note: The text is entered below at no. 1077. Hugh Malebisse held a tenancy in Over
Silton of the Mowbray honour (*Mowbray Charters*, no. 371).

846 *Rubric: The same in the confirmation by William son of Hugh
Malebisse; in Snilesworth, in the second bundle, and in the first bundle
concerning the same.*

847 *Rubric: Confirmation by Thomas son of Henry of Silton of the same
land and of the inflow* (refullus) *of water. Copied under another wording*
(diverso tenore).

848 *Notification in the form of a chirograph, addressed to all the sons of
holy mother church present and future to whom the present writing shall
come, by Abbot Henry and the convent of Byland, of their grant to Geoffrey
of Upsall for homage and service of the mill of Silton with all its soke as freely
as they were granted it by the charters of Thomas of Silton (no. 847),
Geoffrey his brother and Simon of Leake (no. 844), which they have and
which they will surrender. Grant also of all the land and meadow which they
have in the vill of the grant of Simon of Leake (no. 844) as confirmed by
Thomas of Silton and Geoffrey his brother. Geoffrey and his heirs are to hold
the land of the monks in fee and hereditary right rendering yearly 1 pound of
wax at the high altar of the monks' church on the day of the Purification of
the B.V.M. (2 Feb.). They shall make suit once at the abbot's court of Sutton
annually, that is at the first court after the feast of St Michael (29 Sept.). If
Geoffrey is in remote parts his bailiff shall make suit for him. On a day on
which a thief is to be tried in the court he shall make suit, and also when the
justices are there. If he fails to make suit on any on these occasions he shall
give the abbot 2 talents. On the occasion of that suit he shall not be placed in*

assize or jury or any other inquest. When Geoffrey dies his heir shall give the abbot 2 pounds of wax for relief and do homage to the abbot and receive seisin from him without delay. The abbot is to demand no further service. Sealed with the seal of both parties. [1231 x 1268].

Hiis testibus domino Alano de Lek, domino Galfrido de Hustwayt tunc decano de Bulmer, fratre Willelmo magistro de Monte, Iohanne de Blaby, etc.

Dating: Abbot Henry.
Note: There are two notes added to the document: (i) understand that when the above speaks of the arrival of justices it is to be understood as itinerant justices *ad omnimoda placita* (ii) Geoffrey and his heirs are not to grant or alienate anything of the above without the consent of the abbot and convent. With the above witnesses. A talent, mentioned in this document, was a small sum of money.

849 *Rubric: Charter of Fulk Paynel concerning an annual rent of 12d. in Little [Nether] Silton.* [before 1183 or 1188/9 x 1204].
Text: MS Dodsworth 7, fol. 110r. Grant, addressed to all who read or hear these letters, by Fulk Paynel, to the monks of St Mary of Byland, of the service of Robert son of Henry and his heirs on 1 tenement of 15 acres in Silton, that is, 12d., 6d. at Whitsuntide and 6d. at St Martin. Pledge to warranty. Hiis testibus Andrea de Magnebi, Willelmo de Kerkebi, Laurentio de Silfton', W. capellano eiusdem ville, Willelmo filio Willelmi, Airico de Kepwic, Gillone de Kepwic, Willelmo de Burci. This was copied from the original, as there is a note: in dorso carta Fulconis Painel de servitio Roberti filii Henrici ac heredum eius de Siltona.

Pd: *EYC* VI, no. 43.
Dating: The death of Fulk Paynel I and the loss, by his younger son, Fulk Paynel II, of his English lands.
Note: The grantor could be Fulk Paynel I or II. On the death of William Paynel (*c.* 1145 x 1147) his property was divided between his two sons Hugh I, who obtained West Rasen and Les Moutiers-Hubert in Normandy, and Fulk Paynel I, who obtained Drax and Hambye in Normandy. Hugh's grandson, Hugh II, supported King John and as a result lost Les Moutiers-Hubert to King Philip Augustus of France. Fulk Paynel I died in 1182 or 1183 and was succeeded by his son William II (d. 1184) and by William's infant son, who died in 1188 or 1189. Fulk II succeeded his nephew. He supported Philip Augustus against King John and lost Drax to Hugh II (*EYF*, pp. 68–9; *EYC* VI, 18–27). Andrew of Maunby attests in the early 13th century: *Chs Vicars Choral*, II, no. 107. The first three witnesses are as in no. 844. In 1284–5 Nether Silton is also called 'Silton Paynill': *KI*, p. 98.

850 *Rubric: Chirograph of Geoffrey son of Michael concerning one monk chaplain to celebrate at the gate. Look under the heading of Kilvington.*
Note: This is Geoffrey of Upsall; the full text is included as no. 455 above.

[fol. 89r, old fol. 196]

ORMESBY (NZ5317), parish in the wapentake of Langbargh West (NR). Only one grant is recorded in the cartulary (no. 851).

851   *Grant in free alms, addressed to all the faithful in Christ who will hear or see this charter, by William le Pledur son of Adam of Ormesby, with his body, to God and St Mary and the abbot and convent of Byland, of 1 toft and 6 acres in Ormesby, that is, that toft which lies nearest to the house which belonged to Michael son of William of Ormesby towards the south, and 1 acre in* Neudik, *2 acres at* Rosspole, *1 acre in* Inlandes, *1 acre in Michael's court and at* Swartmod *and 1 acre at* Galacre *below the road which leads to Normanby. To hold rendering 1d. yearly to Alan of Danby and his heirs at Ormesby at Christmas for all service. Pledge to warranty.* [before 1213].

Hiis testibus domino Roberto de Stutevill', domino Roberto de Pothou, domino Waltero de Staynesby, etc.

Copy: MS Top. Yorks. e. 9, fol. 25r (old p. 23), which reads 'Rothou' for 'Pothou' and adds 'domino Ada de Hiltona' as second witness, omits 'etc' and continues: Ricardo de Wauxat, Iohanne de Gousel, Willelmo de Estington, Rogero de Semer, Radulfo de Midelesburg, R'o del Hou, Michale de Estittesley, et aliis. Sketch of seal.

Dating: The first witness is probably Robert de Stuteville V, who died in 1213. The second witness is the earliest recorded member of the Potto family, who held the manor of that name. Robert was party to a deed of 1202: *VCH NR* II, 314–15.

852   *Confirmation and quitclaim in free alms, addressed to all who will see or hear these letters, by William de Percy of Kildale, for himself and his heirs and for the salvation of his soul and for the souls of all his ancestors and heirs, to the abbot and convent of Byland, of whatever they have of his fee in the vills and regions of Thornaby, Ormesby and Battersby and elsewhere. To hold freely as alms given to religious men. Pledge to warranty. Sealed with the donor's seal.* [1230s x 1250s].

Hiis testibus Ada de Hilton', Willelmo Malebys, Galfrido de Upsal, Waltero de Staynesby, etc.

Copy: MS Top. Yorks. e. 9, fol. 52r (old p. 77), which omits 'etc' from the witness list and continues: Alano de Lek, Willelmo de Pykton, Willelmo le Pletur, etc.

Dating: The occurrence of the first witness suggests a date in the 1230s to 1250s.

Note: The manor of Ormesby was held by the family of Percy of Kildale (*VCH NR* II, 278; *KI*, pp. 127, 135–6). William de Percy succeeded his father, Walter, who was still living in 1232, some time before 1243. He died between 1293 and 1295. His younger son, who held Kildale in his father's lifetime, was also called William. See *EYC* II, 90–91; *VCH NR* II, 250–51.

853   *Rubric: Charter of Michael son of William concerning the said toft and 6 acres in Ormesby. Surrendered.*

854 *Rubric: Charter of William le Pledur concerning the same. Surrendered.*

At the foot of this folio is a note: Gatrig b(acul)o iiii°.

[fol. 89v]

OSGODBY (TA 0584), in the parish of Cayton and the wapentake of Pickering Lythe (NR). The abbey lands in Osgodby were part of a group of estates also comprising Cayton (nos 141–6) and Deepdale (nos 158–204). The donors were members of the family of Angot of Osgodby (no. 856); Geoffrey son of Pain, and his son Geoffrey (nos 857–60); William son of Henry of Cayton (no. 861), and his son William (no. 869); Robert son of Durand of Cayton (nos 862–3), and his son, Robert (nos 865–6); land in Osgodby was leased to tenants (nos 870, 872–4).

855 *Grant in free alms, addressed to the archbishop of York and all the sons of holy church, by Richard son of Angot of Osgodby, to God and the monks of St Mary of Byland, of ½ bovate in Osgodby free from all service, for the salvation of his soul and of his father and mother; the other ½ bovate he has granted to the church of Cayton for the soul of his father. The grant and confirmation is made at the request and on the advice of Richard, parson of Seamer.* [c. 1160 x 1181].

Hiis testibus Ricardo decano de Semara, Odone presbitero, Willelmo de Angotby, etc.

Pd: *EYC* XI, no. 195.

Dating: as *EYC*. The donor had succeeded his father by 1166; the latest date is the death of Roger de Pont L'Evêque, archbishop of York, after which the see remained vacant.

Note: The rubric states that the charter has been copied.

856 *Rubric: Charter of Robert son of Simon concerning 1 toft and croft in Osgodby. Look in Deepdale, in the second bundle.*

Marginal note: Depedale: B(acul)us ii.

Note: Robert son of Simon was the son of Simon de Cliffe, a benefactor in Deepdale. Rubrics appear at nos 173–7, and texts of charters at no. 182 (granting 1 bovate in Deepdale) and 183 (granting 7 *culture* in Deepdale).

857 *Rubric: Charter of Geoffrey son of Pain concerning 1 acre in Osgodby. Look as above.*

Note: There is a rubric entered under Deepdale at no. 191, but no text of a charter of Geoffrey son of Pain.

858 *Grant in free alms, addressed to all the faithful in Christ who will see or hear this writing, by Geoffrey son of Geoffrey son of Pain, to God and St Mary and the monks of Byland, of 1 bovate in the region of Osgodby, without a toft, with all its appurtenances inside and outside the vill, that is the bovate of his 2 bovates which lies furthest from the south. Pledge to warranty.* [late 12th or early 13th cent.].

Hiis testibus Gilberto de Aton', Willelmo Ruscel', Henrico de Folketon', Ada Haldan', etc.

Dating: witnesses (see, for example, *EYC* I, 471 and nos 381–2, 390–91, 600, II nos 1246, 1250).

859 *Rubric: Charter of the same [Geoffrey son of Geoffrey son of Pain] concerning all that land called* Paynisdale *and 1 acre in the region of Osgodby and other lands.*

860 *Rubric: Charter of the same [Geoffrey son of Geoffrey son of Pain] concerning 1 toft and croft and ½ acre in the region of Osgodby below* Fulmerhou.

861 *Grant in free alms, addressed to all the sons of holy mother church present and future, by William son of Henry of Cayton, to God and the monks of St Mary of Byland, of that ½ bovate in the region of Osgodby which Raynald son of Osgot held of the donor's father, with toft and croft and all appurtenances inside and outside the vill. To hold free from all service and to do there whatever they wish, for the salvation of the soul of the donor and all his ancestors and heirs. The monks are to perform forinsec service for ½ bovate where 12 carucates make a knight's fee. Pledge to warranty.* [late 12th or early 13th cent.].

Hiis testibus Baldewyno de Alvestain, Iohanne de Atona, Roberto de Irtona, Willelmo de Osgodby, etc.

Dating: Baldwin of Allerston was a benefactor of Malton Priory and Yedingham Priory between the 1180s and *c.* 1214 (*EYC* I, nos 389–90). He attested with the second witness in the 1190s (*ibid.* no. 381).

862 *Rubric: Charter of Robert son of Durand of Cayton concerning 2 bovates in Osgodby for forinsec service.*

863 *Rubric: Charter of the same Robert [son of Durand of Cayton] concerning the same 2 bovates. These 2 charters concern one grant.*

864 *Rubric: Charter of William son of Herbrard and Susanna his wife concerning the same bovates. Surrendered.*

865   *Rubric: Confirmation of Robert son of Robert of the same 2 bovates with toft and croft belonging to them.*

866   *Rubric: Confirmation of Robert of Helperthorpe son of Robert of Cayton of the same 2 bovates. It is good.*

[fols 89v–91r; no fol. 90]
867   *Quitclaim in free alms, addressed to all the sons of holy mother church present and future, by Thomas son of Thomas of Anlaby for himself and his heirs, to God and St Mary and the abbot and convent of Byland, of all right he ever had or might have in that ½ bovate in the region of Osgodby which William son of John Custiby of Cayton gave to Thomas's father for his help, the other ½ of which is held by the abbot and convent by quitclaim and remission of Reginald, brother of the said William son of John Custiby. The quitclaim is made for the salvation of Thomas's soul and of his father, mother and all his ancestors and heirs, and for a certain sum of money which the monks gave into his hands. To hold of Thomas and his heirs free from secular service. Pledge to warranty. Sealed with the donor's seal.* [before c. 1202].
Hiis testibus domino Iohanne de Oketon', domino Willelmo de Boscehaw, Waltero de Caiton', Thoma de Etton', etc.
Marginal note: B(aculus) iii.
Dating: John of Octon was sheriff of Yorkshire (1260–1 and 1265–6) and steward of St Mary's Abbey, York (1255); see *Lord Lieutenants*, p. 58. Another John of Octon occurs in 1197 x 1206, 1195 x 1211, and 1203 x 1216 (*EYC* II, nos 989, 1130, 1263). Thomas of Etton was still living shortly before 1202 (*ibid.*, 399).

[fol. 91r, old fol. 197r]
868   *Rubric: Transcript of the charter of Thomas of Anlaby which he has of the abbot and convent concerning ½ bovate in the region of Osgodby, for homage.*

869   *Quitclaim in free alms, addressed to all the faithful in Christ who will see or hear the present charter, by William son of William of Cayton for himself and his heirs and for the salvation of his soul and of his father and mother and all his ancestors and heirs, to God and St Mary and the abbot and convent of Byland, of the rent of 2d. which his father, William, was accustomed to receive from them yearly, 1d. at Whitsuntide and 1d. at St Martin in Winter (11 Nov.) for ½ bovate with appurtenances in the region of Osgodby which formerly belonged to John de Custiby of Cayton. Undertaking for himself and his heirs not to demand the said rent. Sealed with the donor's seal.* [mid 13th cent.].

Hiis testibus magistro Nicholao de Marton', Willelmo de Stokeslay clerico, Thoma de Etton', Willelmo del Bek de Ampilford, etc.

Dating: William of Stokesley, clerk, attests no. 495 (mid 13th cent.) and without the title of clerk he attests with Thomas of Etton *c.* 1278 (no. 909).

870 *Grant, addressed to all the sons of holy mother church who will see or hear this charter, by Adam, abbot of Byland and the convent of that place, with the consent of the house and chapter, to John called Barde of Butterwick and his heirs of 5 bovates in the region of Osgodby. Of these 3 bovates lie between the land of Rievaulx Abbey on one side and the land of Richard Stanes on the other; John Fox held 1 which lies between the land of John Barde and that of William of Reighton; 1 toft with its croft lies between the chief messuage formerly held by Richard of Osgodby and the toft of William Faukes. Grant also of 5 roods of land which they have by the grant of Geoffrey son of Pain, of which 1 selion lies below* Fulmardhou *to the south between the land formerly of William of Bossall and that of Richard son of John, and another on* Northscotes *which lies between the land of Richard Stanes and that of Richard son of John, and 1 selion near* Scodegate *which lies between the land of John Barde and that of Richard son of John, and 1 selion on* Northscotes *towards the north, saving the rights of the abbot and convent, together with the pasture which they were accustomed to have in the same region. To be held of the abbot and convent rendering 24s. 1½d. yearly, half at Whitsuntide and half at St Martin in Winter (11 Nov.) for all secular service, and homage. Pledge to warranty. In the form of a chirograph, the abbot and convent placing their common seal on the part remaining with John, and John sealing the part which remains with the abbot and convent.* [*c.* 1272 x 1283].

Hiis testibus Nicholao de Hastyng' milite, Thoma de Ebristona, Alano de Everley, etc.

Dating: Abbot Adam of Husthwaite occurs in 1272 and as late as 1283; the grant was made before 1284–5 when John Barde held 4 bovates in Deepdale, and 2 carucates and 5 bovates in Osgodby as well as lands in Cayton (*KI*, pp. 139–40, 145–6).

Copy (abbreviated): MS Dodsworth 63, fol. 67r, from cartulary fol. 197.

871 *Memorandum of the termination of a dispute between the abbot and convent and John Wyville, gentleman. John is to pay 26s. 8d. for rent and arrears of rent on land in Osgodby at St Martin in Winter (11 Nov.) next following, and the abbot and convent shall give John 8s. 10d.* 26 Oct. 18 Henry VIII [1526].

Note: The document has been inserted between folios 89 and 91 and has been counted during modern foliation as fol. 90, although not marked as such.

[fol. 91v]

872 *Notification to all to whom the present writing shall come by John of Butterwick that when he received his land in Osgodby in fee farm from the abbot and convent, he swore on the holy gospels that if he or his heirs were to have any land from the lord king or his successors on which marriage, wardship or relief were owed, which they ought to have of the abbot and convent, then the abbot and convent may resume possession of all the land which he received from them in fee farm, and enter and take possession of it freely without interference by him and his heirs. He will bring no claim of novel disseisin nor any other action of entry or possession. If he does his mobile and his immobile goods may be distrained by any judge and ecclesiastical censure may be used. Bond to observe the above, under pain of ecclesiastical censure, renouncing privilege of court or writ of prohibition, and all other recourse to law, canon or civil.* [late 13th cent.].

Dating: as no. 870.

Note: The rubric calls this a bond by the same that he will not alienate the same land from us.

873 *Grant and confirmation, addressed to all the sons of holy mother church present and future, by Abbot Henry of Byland and the convent of that place, to Thomas of Carlisle of 1 toft and 1 croft in Osgodby which lie between the toft which Thomas himself held and the toft which Ralph the shepherd held in the same vill. To hold in fee and hereditary right, rendering 16d. annually for all secular service, 8d. at Whitsuntide and 8d. at St Martin in Winter (11 Nov.). Pledge to warranty. In the form of a chirograph, sealed with the seal of both parties.* [c. 1231 x 1238].

Hiis testibus Thoma de Annelanby, Roberto de Morpath, Radulfo filio Henrici, etc.

Dating: the succession of Abbot Henry and the death of the third witness, Ranulf son of Henry of Kirkby Ravensworth (*VCH NR* I, 89).

874 *Grant and confirmation, addressed to all the sons of holy mother church present and future, by Abbot Henry of Byland and the convent to Richard Stanes of Osgodby of 1 toft and 1 croft in Osgodby and 1 selion on* le Milnesty, *that is, the toft and croft which the abbot and convent have of the grant of Geoffrey son of Pain, on which toft the cobbler's shop* (sutarium) *of Geoffrey was formerly located. To hold in fee and hereditary right, rendering 20d. yearly for all secular service, half at Whitsuntide and half at St Martin in Winter (11 Nov.). Pledge to warranty. In the form of a chirograph, sealed with the seal of both parties.* [c. 1231 x 1238].

Hiis testibus Thoma de Anelanby, Roberto de Morpath, Radulfo filio Henrici, etc.

Dating: The witnesses suggest that this was issued at the same time as no. 873.
Note: The toft and croft were those confirmed by Geoffrey son of Pain's son,
Geoffrey (no. 860). There is a note added to the effect that the abbot and convent
later recovered the toft and croft and selion by a writ of *cessavit* against Thomas of
Killerby, defendant.

875 *Rubric: Transcript of the charter of William Russell which he has of
the abbot and convent concerning 1 bovate in Osgodby, rendering 12d. to the
monks and 3d. to the church of Cayton.*

876 *Rubric: Transcript of the charter of Robert of Reighton concerning 1
bovate in Osgodby which the monks had of the grant of William son of
Robert; rendering to 12d. to the monks.* [late 13th cent.].
Dating: Robert of Reighton held 1 bovate in Osgodby in 1284–5: *KI*, p. 139.

[fol. 92r, old fol. 198]
PICKERING (SE7984), parish in the wapentake of Pickering Lythe
(NR). The royal forest of Pickering was the largest royal forest in
Yorkshire, and the woodland in 1086 is recorded as 16 leagues by 4
leagues (24 miles by 6 miles): *VCH Yorks.* I, 512. Henry III granted
Pickering to his second son, Edmund, and Edward I granted him the
right to have justices in the Forest of Pickering whenever the king
appointed justices of his forest.

877 *Writ of King Henry [III] to the bailiffs of his son, Edmund, in
Pickering. Since on the king's advice it has been ordained that no one by
reason of his tenements shall be compelled by distraint to make suit at the
wapentake court nor at the court of any lords unless he shall be bound to do
so under the terms of his enfeoffment or if he or his ancestors were accustomed to do so before the king's first crossing into Brittany, he orders them
not to distrain the abbot of Byland to make suit of court at the court of their
lord (Edmund).* The Tower of London; 8 Feb. 56 Henry III [1272].
Testo me ipso.
Note: The rubric reads: Writ of the lord king that no-one should make suit of court
against the statute.

878 *Letter patent of Edmund, son of the king of England, to his bailiffs of
Pickering. The abbot and convent of Byland are known to have been injured
by them many times. He therefore orders them to allow the abbot and
convent freely to enjoy their rights and liberties without injury. They are not
to demand any service of them, which they have not been accustomed to
render and are not bound to do.* Pickering; 20 Oct. 51 [Henry III] [1267].
Copy: NYCRO ZDV I 1 (Sandwith's *Exscripta*).

879 *Memorandum that on Thurs. before St Mark the Evangelist (25 Apr.) 1265 in the wapentake court of Pickering at Snainton in the presence of Osbern of Cornborough, Adam de Daiville, master Robert of London, clerk, in place of John de Daiville, justice of the forest and keeper of the peace and bailiff of Pickering, appointed by the king, a complaint was made by Ralph de Derlyngton, monk of Byland, attorney of his abbot, that Robert del Cliff had committed many grave and unjust distraints against the abbot, claiming that he should make suit of the wapentake court, whereas the abbot has never done it nor has been accustomed to and is free from this under the charters of the lord king. An inquisition was held by 12 jurors of the wapentake, namely, Thomas of Ebberston, Peter le Gayoler, William Malecak, William of Morpath and others, who stated under oath that the abbot never made suit at the wapentake nor ought he to, but should be free from suit at the wapentake, and therefore it was perceived in the wapentake that in future he should not be distrained.* Snainton; 23 Apr. 1265.

880 *Rubric: Similar record in the rolls of the same court, Thursday after the Assumption of the B. V. M. (15 Aug.), 1300, 28 Edward [I].* [18 Aug. 1300].

881 *Rubric: Third record in the same court, 1323, 16 Edward II; look in the magnates' bundle.*
Note: This does not appear in the Magnates section of the cartulary.

[fol. 92r–v]
882 *Memorandum that on Thurs. after the Assumption of the B. V. M. (15 Aug.) 1384, 8 Richard II, the abbot of Byland was accused in the wapentake court held at Pickering. It was said that he was obliged to make suit at the said court and had been amerced many times because he had failed to do so. Richard of Yarm, attorney of the abbot and a monk of Byland, appeared in court and in the presence of the seneschal, Richard de Roucliff, read the charter of King Henry [II] son of the Empress, and other evidences, found in the treasury of Byland, demonstrating that the abbot was not bound to make suit of court. This was corroborated by the seal of Earl Edmund, and by various records of past proceedings of the court as well as by ancient and recent writs and various charters of the kings of England. By order of the seneschal all items and amercements were handed over and destroyed and thus it was enrolled at the end of each judgement 'vacat'. By judgement of the seneschal William de Hawlay who, having seen and heard the charters, records and evidences, judged and decreed that the abbot and convent were not bound to any court. The seneschal ordered in full court that the abbot*

and his successors were not in future to be distrained and were not to make
suit of court to the prejudice of their rights. 18 Aug. 1384.

Note: The rubric reads: final record in the rolls of the said court.

[fol. 92v]

883 *Writ of King Richard [II] addressed to the bailiffs of John, king of*
Castile and Leon, duke of Lancaster, in Pickering. Since by common consent
it has been ordained that no-one by reason of his tenements shall be
compelled to make suit at the court of their lords unless they be specially
bound to do so by the terms of their enfeoffment, or if their ancestors were
accustomed to do so before the first crossing of King Henry son of King John
into Brittany, he orders them not to compel the abbot of Byland to make suit
at the court of their lord in Pickering, against the form of the said provision.
Westminster; 18 June 7 Richard II [1384].

Teste me ipso.

Let a similar writ be sent to the bailiffs of the wapentake of Richmond.

Note: John, king of Castile and Leon and duke of Lancaster, is John of Gaunt, uncle
of Richard II.

[fol. 93r, old fol. 199r]

PETERCORN, the name given to the render of sheaves of corn due to St
Peter's (St Leonard's) Hospital, York. According to tradition, in 936
King Athelstan granted a thrave, or 20 sheaves of corn, from every
plough ploughing in the diocese of York, for the maintenance of the
poor served by the Culdees of St Peter's, York. This grant was said in
the late medieval foundation history of St Leonard's to have been
confirmed by William I at the request of Archbishop Thomas I
(1070–1100). However, Farrer, followed more recently by David Bates,
has suggested that the act, by which King William notified all his men
and lieges of his confirmation to the Hospital of St Peter of the ancient
alms on which the hospital was founded, that is 1 thrave of each
plough working in the diocese of York, was one of William II, not
William I (*EYC* I, no. 166; *RRAN* I, no. 353 (p. 1005)). It may well have
been associated with the removal of the hospital, by William II, to a
site further west, and William's visit to York in 1087 x 1088. The
church was rebuilt under the patronage of King Stephen, when it
became known as St Leonard's. Petercorn led to litigation and
disputes, of which one is represented here (no. 884).

884 *Notification, addressed to all the sons of holy mother church to whom*
the present letters shall come, by Priors William of Kirkham, Philip of

Newburgh and William of St Andrew's (Fishergate, York), that they have
received a mandate from Pope Honorius [III] as follows: the prior and
brothers of the Hospital of St Peter, York, had brought a claim against the
abbots of Fountains, Meaux, Byland, Jervaulx and Kirkstall, of the
Cistercian order, concerning sheaves of corn and other items which they
claim they were obliged to render annually to the hospital, in the presence of
the dean of Lincoln and his fellow judges on the authority of the pope's prede-
cessor I(nnocent III). The judges were in doubt and had sought the advice of
the apostolic see but the plaintiffs did not wait for a response, but had
obtained letters to the judges to the effect that because of disturbances in the
realm of England the matters should be suspended until peace was restored.
If afterwards the parties wished to pursue the claim they should approach the
Roman church. The prior and brothers now wish to take up the case and have
asked the pope to address it. This is referred by the pope to the priors named
above to see if it is so, and if so cite them before the pope, to come by proctor or
in person. Given at the Lateran, 13 kal. Jan. (20 Dec.) in the 9th year of his
pontificate (1224). Acting on this mandate the priors, with the assent of all
parties and of the dean and chapter of York, reached the following settlement.
The abbots and their convents are without deception to pay to the Hospital
tithes on all lands acquired since the Lateran council held by Pope Innocent
III in 1215 or to be acquired henceforth, where the Hospital is accustomed to
receive the said rent of sheaves of corn from each carucate according to the
amount of land and the custom of Yorkshire. For this payment the abbots
shall be free from all burdens, petitions and claims by the same Hospital.
Sealed with the seal of the dean and chapter of York, the seals of all parties,
and the seals of the judges delegate. St Peter, York; the octave of St John
the Baptist [1 July] 1225.

Hiis testibus magistro Rogero de Insula decano, magistro Galfrido de
Norwyz precentore, domino Willelmo thesaurario, magistro Ricardo
Cornub' cancellario Ebor' ecclesie, magistro Waltero de Wisebek'
archidiacono de Estrithing, magistro <Mattheo> archdiacono de
Clyfland, etc.

Note: The heading of the folio is 'Transcriptum cuiusdam compositionis inter nos
et quosdam de ordine ex parte una et fratres hospitalis Sancti Leonardi Ebor' de
garbis'. William of Ely, archdeacon of Cleveland from before 1201 probably died
on 16 Mar. 1223. *Fasti York*, p. 39, notes this as the first recorded occurrence of his
successor, Matthew Scot, 1 July 1225. For the bull of Innocent III, dated 1205, see
C. R. Cheney and Mary Cheney, eds, *The Letters of Pope Innocent III concerning*
England and Wales (1198–1216) (Oxford, 1967), pp. 105–6, no. 635. For the mandate
of Honorius III see *CPRL I, 1198–1304*, p. 100 (which has the date 18 Kal. Jan., 15
Dec.). The mandate of Pope Innocent III to the dean and subdean of York and the
chancellor of Lincoln stated that Ralph, rector, and the brethren of the Hospital of
St Peter, York, had complained that John, abbot of Fountains, and certain others in

the diocese of York, had withheld and refused to pay tithes and other dues. The mandate was also used against Meaux, Byland, Jervaulx, Kirkstall, Easby, Bridlington and Nostell. For comment on the mandates for multiple use such as the one employed in this case, see C. R. Cheney, *Pope Innocent III and England* (Stuttgart, 1976), p. 191. The text is followed by a note to the effect that to Byland's part of the mandate, which was at Fountains, are attached the seals of the chapter of York, of the three judges and of the hospital of St Peter, a total of 5 seals. A second note states that the claims of the master and brothers of the hospital with the pleadings of the abbot and convent are bound with the said agreement.

[fol. 93v]

THORPEFIELD (Petithorpe) (SE4179), in the parish of Thirsk and wapentake of Birdforth (NR), approximately 1½ miles to the SW of Thirsk and SE of the abbey lands in Carlton Miniott. The main benefactors were Matilda of Stonegrave (no. 885) and her son Simon, who with his brother Oliver attested no. 885. They were also benefactors in Ness (above, nos 715–18). Simon evidently withheld part of the land in Thorpefield given by his mother (no. 886) but issued a general charter of confirmation (no. 889). Others who helped to consolidate Byland's holdings in the vill were Robert Belebuche and his son, Adam (nos 889, 890, 892, 893), Nisan son of Odo, his wife, Agnes, and son, Robert (nos 894–7), and the family of Hugh the priest of Thorpefield: his sons Ralph (nos 900, 901, 914, 916), Roger (nos 902, 914, 915), William (no. 914) and John (no. 914), Ralph's son, Robert (no. 914, 905, and, if he is the same man as Robert of Thorpefield, nos 905, 917–919); Robert of Thorpefield had a son, Robert (nos 906, 907, 908, 920). Newburgh Priory had minor interests here, which were surrendered (nos 899, 904). It is clear from no. 909 that the Hospital of St Leonard's, York, was a landholder in Thorpefield, and this may account for the attestation by Master Swane of the Hospital of no. 887, and that a restoration of land to Byland took place in the presence of Master Paulinus and his brethren (no. 892).

885 *Grant in free alms, addressed to the archbishop of York and the whole chapter of St Peter (York) and all the sons of holy mother church, by Matilda of Stonegrave, to God and St Mary and the monks of St Mary of Byland, of 12 bovates in Thorpe near Thirsk (Thorpefield) with their appurtenances, for 10s. silver yearly to her and her heirs for all service, 5s. at Whitsuntide and 5s. at St Martin (11 Nov.), and 1 pair of hose of scarlet cloth rendered yearly to Roger de Mowbray. The grant is made for the salvation of her soul and of all her ancestors and heirs, free from all secular service except the said rent. Pledge to warranty. [c. 1175 × 1181].*

Hiis testibus Symone de Steyngriva et Olyvero filiis meis, Willelmo de Harum et Drogone filio eius, etc.

Copy: MS Dodsworth 7, fol. 165r, where the witness list omits 'etc' and continues: Willelmo sacerdote de Nuningtun', Iordano de Nunington, Willelmo le Surreis, Roberto preposito, Radulfo de Rupe, Roberto filio Gerardi de Harum, Waltero de Nevilla, Willelmo de Nuningtun, et Rainaldo fratre eius. Sketch of seal.

Dating: It is likely that the grant was made after the death of Matilda's husband, William (by 1175); see *Mowbray Charters*, pp. 50–51; the address suggests a date before the death of Archbishop Roger de Pont L'Evêque in 1181, after which the see of York was vacant until 1189.

Note: For the family see *EYC* VI, 122.

886 *Rubric: Chirograph agreement between the monks and Simon of Stonegrave, son of Matilda, concerning 2 of the said 12 bovates.* [1177 x 3 Mar. 1195].

Text: MS Dodsworth 7, fol. 165r–v. Agreement between the monks of Byland and Simon of Stonegrave concerning 2 bovates in Thorpefield which are lacking from the 12 bovates that Simon's mother granted and confirmed by her charter and which Simon also confirmed. Simon will deliver the 2 bovates to the monks before Whitsuntide, and if he fails to do so he will lose 16d. annually from the rent of 10s. which the monks render from the farm of Harome. For the loss of these bovates, that is, for the last 6 years, the rent due at Whitsuntide shall be reduced by 3s. Simon pledges faithfully in the hand of William de Daiville to keep this agreement. When Simon delivers the land he shall keep the said 16d. The agreement was made in the chapter of St Peter, York, on 20 Mar. before the Purification of the B. V. M. when the king's justices held an assize, that is, Bishop Hugh of Durham and William de Stuteville and other justices. At Simon's request the chapter is to impose ecclesiastical censure if the agreement is not observed. Hiis testibus H. cantore, Geroldo canonico, Ada de Thornever, Thoma filio Paulini, Willelmo decano, Roberto de Chambort, Willelmo de Daivill, Radulfo de Surdevall, Patricio de Riedall, Osmundo Cruer, Thoma de Chaltona, Alano de Percehai, Roberto de Vado. Sketch of seal.

Dating: The first witness, Hamo, first occurs as precentor in 1177 x 1181; Hugh du Puiset, bishop of Durham, died on 3 Mar. 1195. As he attests after Gerald, canon, Adam of Thorner was probably still a canon; he was appointed as archdeacon in 1196. The last occurrence of Thomas son of Paulinus, prebendary of Stillington, was in 1191 x 1194. The fifth witness was probably a rural dean.

887 *Confirmation in free alms, addressed to the archbishop of York and the whole chapter of St Peter (York) and all the sons of holy church, by Simon of*

Stonegrave, to God and the monks of St Mary of Byland, of that grant made by his mother, Matilda of Stonegrave, of 12 bovates in Thorpe near Thirsk (Thorpefield), with all appurtenances, as contained in his mother's charter (no. 885). Quitclaim of 10s. silver annual rent due to him and his heirs. The confirmation is made for the salvation of his soul and of all his ancestors and heirs, free from all secular service. Pledge to warranty. If he or his heirs are unable to guarantee the land they will pay the monks 10s. yearly, 5s. at Whitsuntide and 5s. at St Martin (11 Nov.), until they can take possession of the land. [c. 1175 x 1181].

Hiis testibus Roberto decano Ebor', magistro Swano de Hospitali, Gervasio filio Romundi et Alano fratre eius, etc.

Dating: after or at the same time as no. 885.
Note: The second witness was master of the Hospital of St Leonard's, York. He also attests nos 56, 59, 328.

888   *Confirmation, addressed to the archbishop of York and the whole chapter of St Peter (York) and all the sons of holy church, by Roger de Mowbray, to God and the monks of St Mary of Byland, of the grant of Matilda of Stonegrave and Simon her son of 12 bovates in Thorpe near Thirsk (Thorpefield) (nos 885, 887). Quitclaim of the hose of scarlet cloth which the monks were accustomed to receive to him and his heirs yearly for service. The land is to be held free from all service for the salvation of his soul and of all his ancestors and heirs. Pledge to warranty. [c. 1175 x 1181].*

Hiis testibus Roberto de Daivill, Hugone Malabissa, Thoma de Culevilla, Hamone Beler, Radulfo de Beuveyr', Roberto de Buscy, etc.

Copy: MS Dodsworth 7, fols 165v–166r, which omits 'etc' from the witness list and continues: Philippo de Muntpinzun, Roberto clerico filio Willelmi camerarii de Insula.
Pd: *Mowbray Charters*, no. 65, from MS Dodsworth 7.
Dating: *Mowbray Charters* has a terminal date of 1186, but see note to no. 885 above.

889   *Rubric: Charter of Robert Belebuche concerning 1½ bovates.*
Note: For further charters of the grantor see nos 890, 892.

890   *Rubric: Quitclaim by the same [Robert Belebuche] of 1½ bovates which he demanded under the king's writ.*

891   *Rubric: Charter of Richard son of Osmund concerning the same. Surrendered.*

[fols 93v–94r]
892   *Grant in free alms, addressed to all the sons of holy mother church present and future, by Robert Belebuche of Thirsk, with his body, to God and*

the monks of St Mary of Byland, of that bovate in the region of Thorpe near
Thirsk (Thorpefield) which Walter son of Alfred restored to the donor in the
presence of Master Paulinus and the brothers of the hospital of St Leonard,
York, as his own inheritance. The grant is made with all its appurtenances,
to hold of Robert and his heirs free of service rendering 12d. yearly at
Whitsuntide for all the services which he and his heirs were obliged to
perform to the said hospital. In return the monks have discharged all the
donor's debts, namely 20s. to the said Walter for the land and elsewhere 4
marks, 8s. and 9d. Pledge to warranty. [1186 x 1201].

Hiis testibus Roberto clerico de Molbray, Rogero capellano de Thresk,
Willelmo de Lecestria, etc.

Dating: In the period *c.* 1166 x 1186 Roger de Mowbray granted to St Leonard's
William de Leicestria and his tenement in Thirsk (*Mowbray Charters*, no. 312).
Robert, Roger de Mowbray's clerk, attests his charters from 1153 until after 1175
(*ibid.*, pp. lxvi–lxvii, for occurrences). Paulinus, master of St Leonard's, probably
succeeded Swane by 1186, and occurs in 1193 (*EYC* V, no. 334, XI, 170). He died in
1200 or 1201 (*Fasti York*, p. 126). A Walter son of Alvered / Alfred attests a Mowbray
charter of 1142 x *c.* 1154 (*Mowbray Charters*, no. 99).

[fol. 94r, old fol. 200]

893 *Rubric: Confirmation and quitclaim by Adam Belebuche of 4 bovates*
in Thorpefield.

894 *Rubric: Charter of Nisan son of Odo concerning 1½ bovates in*
Thorpefield, that is, those which lie nearest to the land of Richard. [late 12th
cent.].

Dating: The grantor issued a charter which can be dated 1194 x 1198 (no. 895); for
charters evidently issued by his son and his wife/widow, see nos 896, 897.

895 *Confirmation, addressed to all the sons of holy mother church present*
and future, by Nisan son of Odo of the grant made by Robert Belebuche to
God and the monks of St Mary of Byland, that is, 1½ bovates in the region of
Thorpe near Thirsk (Thorpefield) as contained in Robert's charter (nos 889,
890). Quitclaim for himself and his heirs of all right which he or his ances-
tors had in the remainder of 4 bovates in the region of the same vill, for the
salvation of his soul and of all his ancestors and heirs. Pledge to warranty.
[1194 x 1198].

Hiis testibus Rogero de Bavent tunc vicecomite Ebor', Alexandro de
Baiocis subvic(ecomite), Willelmo de Corneburgh, Waltero de
Bovington', etc.

Dating: office of first witness as deputy sheriff of Yorkshire.

896   *Rubric: Confirmation by Robert son of Nisan of the confirmation of his father (no. 895).*

897   *Rubric: Confirmation by Agnes, wife of Nisan, of his grant and confirmation (nos 894, 895).*

898   *Rubric: Confirmation by Hugh de Flamville of the grant of Nisan, that is, 1½ bovates (no. 894).* [late 12th or early 13th cent.].
Dating: by reference to no. 894; Hugh occurs from 1170 and in the early 13th century (*EYC* I, 503, and II nos 750, 790).

899   *Notification by Prior Roger and the convent of Newburgh of their grant and confirmation to Abbot Robert and the convent of Byland of that toft and croft which they had in Thorpefield which Simon Pile held, which lie between the monks' grange and vaccary in the vill of Thorpefield, and the toft with croft in Osgoodby which William Palmer held, which lies within the enclosure of the grange of Osgoodby towards the west. These are granted in exchange for that land which the abbot and convent have in Thorpefield which lies next to the land which belonged to John of Thorpefield on which the canons have their vaccary, as far as the land of John the hunter. Pledge to warranty.* [1220 x 1224].
Teste capitulo nostro.
Dating: Abbot Robert occurs in *c.* 1220, 1223, 1224, 1226, and 1230 and may be the R. recorded in 1219; Robert of Helmsley professed obedience in 1370 and occurs in 1381 (*HRH* II, 269–70). No prior of Newburgh named Roger is recorded at these times. There is a gap between Walter (*c.* 1212 and before 1214) and Philip, first recorded in 1224 (*ibid.*, p. 428; see above, no. 884).

900   *Rubric: Chirograph between the monks and Ralph son of Hugh of Thorpe(field) concerning 6 bovates which he confirmed conditionally.* [*c.* 1180 x 1200].
Dating: As Ralph son of Hugh the priest the grantor issued a quitclaim which can be dated to *c.* 1170 x 1186, probably before 1181 (no. 914).
Note: The grantor had a son, Robert, and brothers Roger, William and John: see no. 914. See also nos 901, 904.

901   *Rubric: Confirmation by the same [Ralph son of Hugh of Thorpefield] of the said 6 bovates, rendering 6d. to the canons of Newburgh.* [*c.* 1180 x 1200].
Dating: as no. 900.

902   *Rubric: Quitclaim by Roger son of Hugh of the said 6 bovates.* [*c.* 1180 x 1200].

Dating: Roger brother of Ralph son of Hugh the priest approved no. 914; he also granted no. 915.

903   *Rubric: Charter of Roger de Mowbray concerning ½ carucate in Thorpefield. Surrendered.* [before 1186].

Note: A general charter of confirmation of Nigel de Mowbray for Byland (no. 662 above; *Mowbray Charters*, no. 73, 1186 x 1190) mentions the agreement reached between the monks and William, nephew and heir of Ingelram of Thirsk concerning land in Thorpefield, but no quantity is specified.

904   *Rubric: Charter of the canons of Newburgh concerning the service of Ralph son of Hugh on 2 bovates for which the monks render 6d. Surrendered.*

Note: Ralph son of Hugh occurs in nos 900, 901, 914, 916.

[fol. 94r–v]

905   *Final concord reached in the king's court in Derby in the octave of St Hilary 42 Henry III in the presence of Abbot John of Peterborough, Roger of Thirkleby, Peter de Percy, John de Wyvill, itinerant justices, and other faithful men of the lord king then present, between Abbot Henry of Byland, plaintiff, by brother Simon de Calveryng, his monk, acting for him, and Prior Richard of Newburgh, whom Robert of Thorpe(field) has called to warranty concerning 2 bovates and 1 toft with appurtenances in Thorpefield about which a plea had been brought in the same court. The prior acknowledged that the land and toft with their appurtenances were of the right of the abbot, and restored them to him in the court, to hold of the prior and his church in perpetuity rendering 6d. yearly at St Michael (29 Sept.) for all service, suit of court, custom and exaction. Pledge to warranty. For this acknowledgement and at the request of the prior the abbot has granted the said 2 bovates to the said Robert to hold of the abbot and his church for 2s. yearly, half at Whitsuntide and half at St Martin in Winter (11 Nov.), and for forinsec service. Pledge to warranty to Robert.* Derby; Jan. 1258.

Note: For Robert of Thorpefield and/or his son Robert, see nos 906–8, 917–21.

[fol. 94v]

906   *Grant in free alms, addressed to all the sons of holy mother church present and future to whom this present writing shall come, by Robert son of Robert of Thorpe Underlees (Thorpefield), to God and St Mary and the abbot and convent of Byland and their successors, of a messuage with its appurtenances in Thorpefield and all the land which the donor had or might have throughout the region of Thorpefield, together with meadows, pastures etc.*

*inside and outside the vill, and with all rights pertaining to it, to do with
whatever they wish. Robert and his heirs will make no further demands on
the land. Pledge to warranty. Sealed with the donor's seal.* [late 13th cent.].
Hiis testibus dominis Ricardo de Malebys, Nicholao Punchard',
Ivone de Etton, milit(ibus), Baldwino de Schiptona, Iohanne
Maunsell de Brudford, etc.

Dating: Nicholas de Punchardon, Ivo de Etton and John Maunsell of Birdforth
were all tenants in 1284/5; the last also occurs in 1301 (*VCH NR* I, 480, II, 17, 54).

907   Rubric: *Charter of the same Robert of Thorpefield concerning 12 acres
in the region of Thorpefield.*

908   Rubric: *Quitclaim by Robert of Thorpefield of 1 messuage and 26 acres
there.*

Note: This is followed by a note that these 3 charters (nos 906, 907, 908) are bound
together.

[fols 94v–95r]

909   *Grant, addressed to all the sons of holy mother church present and
future, by John son of Ivo of Carlton near Thirsk (Carlton Miniott), to God
and St Mary and the abbot and convent of Byland, of that 1 bovate in the
region of Thorpefield which he had and held, with its appurtenances, of the
master of the hospital of St Leonard, York, in fee and hereditary right. The
abbot and convent and their successors or their assigns are to hold this of the
donor and his heirs rendering 3s. silver yearly for 17 years from Christmas
1278, 18d. at St Martin (11 Nov.) and 18d. at Whitsuntide for all service.
Pledge to warranty. Sealed with the donor's seal.* Before Christmas 1278.
Hiis testibus Ada de Boltby, Willelmo de Huppesall, Iohanne de
Iarkyngville, militibus, Ricardo de Malbys, Thoma de Ettona,
Galfrido del Bek', Willelmo le Pledur, et aliis.

Marginal note: (in later hand) '1278 7 E 1'. There is a catchword at the foot of the
folio, in the cartulary hand.

Copy: MS Dodsworth 63, fol. 67r, from cartulary fol. 200b (*sic*) (lacks sixth and
seventh witnesses).

Note: The first witness is Adam of Boltby III, who died between 1279 and 1282
(*EYC* IX, 162); John de Jarpenville held land in Ampleforth in 1284–5 (*VCH NR* I,
462; *KI*, pp. 106, 114–15). William le Pledur and Geoffrey del Bek occur respectively
in no. 5 and no. 8 above.

[fol. 95r, old fol. 201]

910   Rubric: *Quitclaim by William son of Ivo of the said bovate in
Thorpefield with its appurtenances.* [*c.* 1278].

Dating: Probably the same time as no. 909.

911 *Rubric: Quitclaim by Isolda formerly wife of John son of Ivo of the said bovate.* [after *c.* 1278].

Dating: after the death of John son of Ivo.
Note: The rubric is followed by a note that these 3 charters (nos 909, 910, 911) are bound together.

912 *Rubric: Quitclaim by Nicholas son of the said Robert of all his right and of a certain messuage which he sought by writ of the king. Copied.*

Note: 'The said Robert' might refer to no. 908, if the three intervening charters are out of place.

913 *Rubric: Charter of the said Nicholas and the king's writ. Surrendered.*

914 *Grant in free alms and quitclaim, addressed to the archbishop of York and the whole chapter of St Peter (York) and all the sons of holy church, by Ralph of Thorpefield son of Hugh the priest, to God and the monks of St Mary of Byland, of 6 bovates in Thorpefield which he and his ancestors held with all their appurtenances. To hold free from all secular service for the salvation of his soul and of his father and mother and all his ancestors and heirs, except the service due from 2 bovates to the canons of Newburgh, that is 6d. only at St Michael (29 Sept.) for all service on 2 bovates. Pledge to warranty. The following have assented to and secured the grant: Robert his eldest son, and Roger, William and John, the donor's brothers.* [*c.* 1170 x 1186, probably before 1181].
Hiis testibus Roberto decano, Meynardo et Ada de Tornover, canonicis Ebor'.

Dating: The latest date is provided by the death of the first witness, Robert Butevilain. The second witness last occurs in *c.* 1177 x 1181 (*EEA* XX, no. 8) and 1177 x 1186 (*EYC* VI, no. 134); the earliest occurrence of Adam of Thorner as canon is 1177 x 1181 (*EEA* XX, no. 127). He became archdeacon of York in 1196. The address to the archbishop of York suggests a date before the death of Roger de Pont L'Evêque in 1181. This would place nos 900–901 at roughly the same period as no. 914.

915 *Rubric: Quitclaim by Roger son of Hugh of 6 bovates in Thorpefield.* [*c.* 1181 x 1186].

Note: This reflects the assent in no. 914 to the grant of his brother, Ralph.

916 *Rubric: Chirograph against Ralph concerning the said 6 bovates in Thorpefield.*

917 *Rubric: Charter of Robert of Thorpefield concerning 2 bovates there, rendering 2s. yearly to the abbot and convent.*

Marginal note: B(aculus) ii.
Note: This may be the grantor of nos 906–8; see also nos 918–21.

918   Rubric: *Charter of Robert of Thorpefield concerning an exchange of 7 selions in the same vill.*

919   Rubric: *Charter of Robert of Thorpefield concerning 1 messuage and 6 acres which he held of the abbot and convent in fee and afterwards sold to them.*

920   Rubric: *Chirograph of Robert son of Robert of Thorpefield concerning 6 acres in the region of the vill.*

921   Rubric: *Confirmation by R. of Thorpefield concerning 1 acre there.*

922   Rubric: *Charter of Henry son of Robert of Thorpefield of 1 acre there.*

923   Rubric: *Charter of Robert Artays concerning all the land in Thorpefield.*

[fol. 95v]
ST PETER THE LITTLE, YORK. The church lay in Peter Lane to the north of Ousegate and south of Jubbergate. This section contains only 2 documents, both concerned with a transaction by which Byland Abbey undertook to secure provision of a chantry in this small York parish church for residents of Acomb, just to the west of the city.

924   *Grant, confirmation and bond in the form of a chirograph, addressed to all who will see or hear it, by the abbot and convent of the monastery of St Mary of Byland, for a certain sum of money paid to them by Dom. Robert Swetemouth, chaplain, and John of Acomb, executor of the will of John of Acomb, deceased, for the use and convenience of the abbot and convent, to Dom. William of Sherburn, chaplain, and his successors celebrating divine service for the souls of John of Acomb, Helen his wife, Robert and Alice John's deceased father and mother, Robert Swetemouth and John of Acomb their executors, of all brothers and sisters of the deceased, of all those to whom the deceased was bound while he was alive, and for the souls of all the faithful departed, in the church of St Peter the Little, York, at the altar of St John the Baptist there, of a certain annual rent or pension of 6 marks sterling. This is to be paid to William and to the chaplains who succeed him by the abbot and convent or their attorney at York at the Nativity of St John the Baptist (24 June) and St Andrew the Apostle (30 Nov.) in equal amounts, to* *begin at the next feast of St John following this agreement, as is laid down in the ordination of the said chantry on the authority of John (Thoresby), archbishop of York, and others. The abbot and convent commit themselves, their monastery and the church of Rillington which is appropriated to their monastery, under pain of censure, to pay this pension on the occasions and at the place specified. One part of this chirograph, sealed with the seal of the abbot and convent, has been placed in the hands of Dom. William; the other, sealed with William's seal, remains with the abbot and convent.* The chapter house of Byland; Friday 16 Nov. 31 Edward III [1358].

Note: There seems to have been more than one chantry in the church of St Peter the Little connected with the individuals mentioned in this document. On 15 July 1348 John of Acomb paid 6 marks for a licence to alienate 2 messuages and 6s. rent in York and the suburbs for a chaplain to celebrate divine service daily for the grantor during his lifetime and for his soul after his death, and for the souls of Adam de Hedon, John of Nassington and Walter de Yarewell, and on 28 Oct. 1349 he undertook to pay 30s. for licence to alienate a messuage for the same purpose, at the altar of St Mary (*Cal. Pat. R. 1348–1350*, pp. 122, 414). This was John of Acomb the elder, who had died by the time no. 924 was issued. On 14 Oct. 1350 licence was granted, for 60s. paid by Robert Swetemouth of York and William Swetemouth, for the alienation by them of 2 messuages in York for a chaplain to celebrate divine service daily in the church of St Peter the Little for their souls and those of their fathers, mothers, and ancestors (*Cal. Pat. R. 1350–1354*, p. 5), and on 20 Oct. 1356 there is reference to John de Cotheland, warden of the chantry recently established in the church of St Peter the Little by Robert Swetemouth and William Swetemouth (*Cal. Pat. R. 1354–1358*, p. 461). On 30 June 1359 a licence was granted, after inquisition, for 2 marks paid by John of Acomb the younger, for the alienation of land 24 feet long and 23 feet wide, adjacent to the messuage of the chantry of St Margaret the Virgin in the church of St Peter the Little, York, and 9s. rent from a messuage in Goodramgate and Aldwark, for a chaplain to celebrate at the altar of St John the Baptist in the church, for the good estate of Robert Swetemouth, chaplain, and William Swetemouth, and for their souls when they are deceased, and for the souls of John of Acomb the elder and Helen his wife (*Cal. Pat. R. 1358–1361*, p. 240). In 1388 the chantry was said to be at the altar of St Margaret (*Cal. Pat. R. 1385–1389*, p. 424). No mention is made in these records of the part to be played by Byland. The chantry at the altar of St John the Baptist was valued at £4 3s. 4d. in 1535, when the chaplain received a pension of £4 from Byland Abbey (*VE* V, 93), but as noted in *VCH York* neither Acomb chantry is mentioned in 1547 (*VCH York*, 400; see *The Certificates of the Commissioners appointed to survey the Chantries, Guilds, Hospitals etc in the County of York*, ed. W. Page, 2 vols, SS, 91, 92 (1894–5), I, 49–50) but the pension from Byland was attached to the Swetemouth chantry at the altar of St John the Baptist.

925   *Rubric: Transcript of certain letters of indenture concerning the ordination of the chantry in the said church for the soul of John of Acomb and concerning the annual pension of 6 marks, and moreover concerning the taking of an oath by the proctor of the abbot and convent.* [1358].

Note: This is followed by the word 'Quere' ('search', or 'look') but no location is given.

[fol. 96r, old fol. 202]
RYTON (SE7975), in the parish of Kirby Misperton and the wapentake of Pickering Lythe (NR). Ryton lies to the north of the River Rye, just over 2 miles north of Malton and 3 miles from Rillington (nos 930–87 below). The abbey received a grant of 2 bovates from Robert of Gilling and his wife (no. 926–7) and these were granted in fee farm to Walter de Percehay (nos 927A).

926 *Rubric: Charter of Walter son of Robert of Gilling and Amice his wife concerning 2 bovates in Ryton. Copied.* [mid 13th cent.].
Text: MS Top. Yorks. e. 8, fol. 138v (old p. 241). Grant, addressed to all the faithful present and future, by Walter son of Robert of Gilling and Amice his wife, to God and St Mary and the abbot and convent of Byland, of 2 bovates in Ryton, free from secular service, except for 2s. paid to them yearly, 12d. at Whitsuntide and 12d. at St Martin, and a toft which they had exchanged with Walter de Percehay. The grant is made for the salvation of their souls and of all their ancestors and heirs and for all the benefits they have bestowed on them. Pledge to warranty. Sealed with their seals. Hiis testibus Rogero de Stapyltona, Willelmo de Lasceles, Willelmo de Burn', Willelmo Gruer, Waltero Grimet, Iohanne clerico de Newton, Henrico Huic, Willelmo de Foxholes, et aliis. See also MS Dodsworth 63, fol. 67r (copy of rubric).
Dating: This is related to no. 927.

927 *Final concord made in the king's court in the presence of Robert of Lexington, Ralph de Sulleng', William of Culworth, Jolland de Nevill, Robert de Haye, Simon de Hales and Warner Engayn, itinerant justices, and other faithful men of the lord king then present, between Henry, abbot of Byland, plaintiff, and Walter son of Robert and Amice his wife, defendants, concerning 2 bovates and 1 toft with its appurtenances in Ryton, and 1 bovate, 1 toft and 14 acres of woodland in Laysthorpe about which a plea of warranty of a charter had been brought between them in the said court. Walter and Amice acknowledge all the aforesaid to be the right of the abbot and the church of Byland as the grant of Walter and Amice. Moreover they have granted to the abbot the site of a windmill on their land at Laysthorpe so that he or his successors may construct a windmill there as they wish without any hindrance. The abbot and convent are to hold the above in free alms. Pledge to warranty. The abbot has received Walter and Amice and*

Amice's heirs into all the good deeds and prayers which are made in the church of Byland from henceforth. York; day after St John the Baptist 24 Henry III [25 June 1240].

Marginal note: (in later hand) '24 H 3'.

Copies: PRO CP 25/1/263/32, no. 69; MS Dodsworth 63, fol. 67r, from cartulary fol. 202 (abbreviated).

Pd (calendar): *Yorks. Fines 1232–1246*, pp. 61–2 (from PRO copy).

[fol. 96r–v]

927A *Indenture attesting that Walter de Percehay, knight, holds 2 bovates with appurtenances for himself and his heirs in Ryton in fee farm from the abbot and convent and their successors rendering yearly 1 silver mark at St Martin in Winter (11 Nov.) and Whitsuntide in equal portions, as is laid down in an indenture between Henry, former abbot of Byland, and Walter de Percehay, ancestor of Walter, as follows. Recitation of demise by Abbot Henry and the convent of Byland to Walter de Percehay in fee farm of 2 bovates in Ryton, that is, the 2 bovates which Walter of Gilling and Amice his wife granted the abbot in free alms. Walter and his heirs are to hold the 2 bovates in fee and hereditary right of the abbot and convent, rendering yearly 1 silver mark, half at St Martin in Winter (11 Nov.) and half at Whitsuntide for all service. Whenever the rent is not paid within the octaves of these feasts, Walter de Percehay and his heirs shall give ½ silver mark as penalty to the fabric of the church of Byland, and nevertheless pay the farm. Walter concedes for himself and his heirs that the abbot may compel him and his heirs under pain of sentence of excommunication to pay the farm and the penalty, renouncing a writ of prohibition. In the form of a chirograph and sealed by both parties.* [c. 1240].

Hiis testibus dominis Roberto de Lexynton', Willelmo de Culewynt, Roberto de la Haya, etc.

Walter de Percehay has acknowledged that the contents of the above indenture were made by his ancestor, Walter, whose heir he is, and will pay the rent at the due terms. Moreover, Walter, Agnes his wife and William his son have commended themselves to the devotion of the abbot and convent who have received them into their prayers and good deeds. Sealed with the seals of both parties. Byland; All Saints [1 Nov.] 16 Edward III [1342].

Marginal note: (in later hand) '16 E 3'.

Copies: MS Dodsworth 63, fols 67r–68r, and MS Dodsworth 91, fols 148r–149v, no. 124, which omits 'etc' from the witness list and continues: Ioelemo de Nowilla, Radulfo de Suthley, Simone de Hale, Warnero de Engayne, tunc iustic' domini regis itinerantibus apud Ebor'.

[fol. 96v]

928   *Rubric: Charter of Walter de Percehay concerning ½ toft for ½ acre. Surrendered. [c.* 1240 or mid 14th cent.].

Dating: see no. 927A.

929   *Memorandum: We ought to know where to distrain for the farm of Ryton. Let it be known that wherever the lord de Percehay has 8 selions in any* cultura *of all his fields, 7 are his own land towards the west and the eighth is in the abbot and convent's tenement towards the east, and they can distrain on this. The land of William de Cresacres lies next to them, nearest to the south. Walter de Percehay declared this in the year 1342.*

Copy: MS Dodsworth 63, fol. 68r (abbreviated).

[fol. 97r, old fol. 203r]

RILLINGTON (SE 8574), township and parish in the wapentake of Buckrose (ER), approximately 5 miles NE of Malton. Rillington church was one of three churches appropriated to Byland Abbey. There are over 50 charters and rubrics in this section of the cartulary, most of them relating to the grant of the church (originally a moiety of the church) and the process of appropriation and institution of a vicarage. The main benefactors in Rillington were William of Cayton, son of Durand de Cliffe, and his heirs, who were also responsible for grants to the abbey in Deepdale. A moiety of the church was granted by William in the latter part of the 12th century (nos 930–31). This was confirmed by William of Osgodby, son of William after a dispute about the presentation to moieties of the church (nos 935), and by his son, Henry (nos 937, 941). William further quitclaimed his right in the advowson of a moiety in the rural chapter held at Sledmere (nos 945–6). It is clear from nos 940, 943 that Bridlington Priory had some interest in the vill, for Prior Hubert quitclaimed all right in the advowson, as did the count of Aumale, who held a fee in Rillington of the Bigod family (no. 943). In the late 13th century Henry son of William of Osgodby and Cayton cemented the monks' interests in Rillington by granting the manor (no. 949). In 1316 Edward II granted licence for the appropriation of the church (no. 971). Rubrics indicate the existence, in the 'register of charters', of a letter of proxy sent to the papal curia and a petition concerning the appropriation (nos 973–4) and bulls of appropriation (nos 975–7). One of the last holders of the moieties of the rectory, Ralph of Pockthorpe, resigned his post, and possession of the church was taken in the name of the abbot and convent on 30 Nov. 1344 (no. 978). Archbishop William de la Zouche ordained a vicarage in the church on 22 Nov. 1344 (no. 981). The incumbent of the second moiety, John de Sancto Ivone, resigned on 7 Dec. 1345 (no. 982) and the process of appropriation was complete.

930 *Grant in free alms, addressed to all the sons of holy mother church present and future, by William of Cayton son of Durand de Cliffe (Clyva), to God and St Mary of Byland and the monks serving God there, of the church of St Andrew, Rillington, with ½ carucate belonging to it and with all appurtenances inside and outside the vill. This grant is made for the soul of Durand his father and Hilda his mother, and for the salvation of his own soul and of his wife and all his ancestors and heirs. Sealed with the donor's seal. Pledge to warranty. [late 12th cent.].*

Hiis testibus Ricardo persona de Semar, magistris Osberto et Martino fratribus suis, Roberto capellano, Willelmo diacono, Stephano de Alost, etc.

Marginal note: B(aculus) i.
Copy: MS Top. Yorks. e. 9, fol. 26r (old p. 25). This reads 'magistro' for 'magistris', omits the fourth and fifth witnesses, and continues: Roberto et Ricardo fratribus meis, Thoma de Alost, Willelmo de Angotebi, Simone de Alost, etc.
Pd: *EYC* I, no. 622.
Dating: Richard, dean of Seamer, witnessed nos 159–60, issued by the donor's father, Durand de Cliffe and attested by the donor (1160 x 1166). He also witnessed charters of the donor and others relating to Deepdale (nos 164–5, 186), Killerby (no. 492), and Moskwith (no. 637). He requested and advised Richard son of Angot to grant land in Osgodby to Byland (no. 855). He was parson of Seamer, rural dean of Dickering and chaplain to William de Percy.
Note: Osbert and Martin do not appear elsewhere in the cartulary, and the phrase 'fratribus meis' may well be a corruption of the original list. MS Top. Yorks. e. 9 only designates Osbert as *magister*, and this may be master Osbert, canon of York, who occurs in 1159 (*Fasti York*, p. 126). For the family of William of Cayton, see *EYC* XI, pp. 233–5, and for his brothers Richard and Robert see above, nos 164, 172n, 181, 186, 188, 862, 863. For the church of Rillington, see *Fasti Parochiales*, V, 31–6.

931 *Grant in free alms, addressed to all the sons of holy mother church present and future, by William son of Durand de Cliffe (Clyva), prompted by charity, to God and the monks of St Mary of Byland, of the patronage of a moiety of the church of St Andrew, Rillington. This grant is made for the souls of Durand his father and Hilda his mother, and for the salvation of his own soul and of all his ancestors and heirs. Sealed with the donor's seal in order to warranty the grant. [1199 x 26 June 1213].*

Hiis testibus Symone decano Ebor', Hamone thesaurario, magistro Willelmo archidiacono de Notyngham, magistro Radulfo de Kyma, etc.

Dating: Simon de Apulia was received as dean in Feb. 1195 and became bishop of

Exeter in 1214. Hamo occurs as treasurer in 1199, and to 1216. William Testard was archdeacon between 1191 x 1194 and 1214.

Note: This modifies the earlier grant by William (no. 930) in that it specifies the advowson of a moiety of the church. For the rectors presented by the abbot and convent until the creation of the vicarage, see *Fasti Parochiales*, V, 33–4. Ralph de Kyme was official of the archbishop of York in March 1201, when he was appointed archdeacon of Cleveland, although the canons elected Hugh Murdac. He occurs as R. archdeacon of Cleveland in 1207 and 1209; he may have been precentor, and died before 26 June 1213 (*Fasti York*, pp. 15, 38, 115)

932 *Rubric: Ancient chirograph in the king's court between Henry son of Henry and William of Cayton concerning the advowson of the church of Rillington. William son of Henry, his true heir, gave the chirograph when he confirmed a moiety of the church of Rillington granted by William son of Durand de Cliffe (Clyva) (no. 933).*

933 *Rubric: Charter of William son of Henry of Cayton concerning that moiety of the church of Rillington which William son of Durand granted.*
Text (much abbreviated): MS Dodsworth 157, fol. 31r, where the folio is headed 'in baga de Biland'. Confirmation by William son of Henry of Cayton of the advowson of a moiety of the church of Rillington, as granted by William son of Durand of Cayton. Test' Gilberto de Aton, . . . Buscell, Henrico de Folkton.

934 *Rubric: Returned charter of the same William [son of Henry of Cayton] concerning the enfeoffment of William son of William of Osgodby of all his right in a moiety of the church.*

[fol. 97r–v]
935 *Grant and quitclaim, addressed to the archbishop of York and the whole chapter of York and all the sons of holy mother church who will see or hear the present charter, by William of Osgodby son of William of Osgodby, to God and St Mary and the abbot and convent of Byland and their successors, of 1 acre of his demesne land in the region of Rillington with all the right in the patronage and advowson of that moiety of the church there, with 5 bovates of land and meadow and the possessions of the moiety of the church which he had of the grant of William of Osgodby, his father. A controversy had arisen concerning this between Dom. Henry of Battersby, former abbot of Byland, and the convent on one part and William on the other. The dispute concerned to which moiety William had last presented master Adam of Evesham, clerk, who obtained the portion by his presentation and had been canonically instituted. William now renounces any claim he or his heirs*

have or might have in the patronage and advowson of the other moiety, with its 5 bovates of land and meadow and other possessions belonging to the moiety and everything which they have of the grant of William of Cayton son of Durand de Cliffe (Cliva) and other donors, to which moiety the abbot and convent presented Philip of Battersby, clerk, who was canonically instituted. William makes this grant and quitclaim in free alms for the salvation of his soul and of his father and all his ancestors and heirs. The abbot and convent shall be allowed to present to the church whomever they wish or appropriate the church to their own uses without hindrance by him and his heirs. If any further documents concerning the right of patronage shall be found in the possession of William or his heirs and exhibited by them, they shall have no force but be invalid. Pledge to warranty. Sealed with the seal of the chapter of York, the donor's seal, and the seal of Henry of Osgodby his son and heir, who has confirmed all the above. [1264 x 1277].

Hiis testibus domino Willelmo de Langeton' tunc decano ecclesie Sancti Petri Ebor', magistro Thoma de Witham tunc archidiacono de Not', magistro Roberto de Scarburgh tunc archidiacono de Estrithing', Ruffino tunc archidiacono Clyvel,' etc.

Copy (much abbreviated): MS Dodsworth 157, fol. 31r. This has the first witness only.

Dating: The earliest date is provided by the fourth witness and the latest by the first occurrence of Thomas de Witham as archdeacon of York.

Note: Philip of Battersby, clerk, was presented by the abbot and convent to that moiety of the church of Rillington that Robert de Hotham (Ockham) held, saving the vicarage of the church to Lawrence de Wavill, and was instituted on 29 Aug. 1235 (*Reg. Gray*, p. 69). Adam of Evesham, whom the dispute concerned, was dead by 12 June 1268.

936   *Rubric: Charter of William of Osgodby concerning the right of patronage and grant of a moiety of the church. Surrendered.*

937   *Grant and quitclaim, addressed to all the sons of holy mother church who will see or hear the present charter, by Henry of Osgodby son and heir of William of Osgodby, to God and St Mary and the abbot and convent of Byland, of all the grant, quitclaim and confirmation made by his father, William son of William of Osgodby, of the right of patronage of a moiety of the church of Rillington and the grant of the other moiety as contained in his father's charter (no. 935). Henry makes this confirmation in free alms, for the salvation of his soul and of his father and mother and all his ancestors and heirs, to do there whatever they wish. He and his successors will make no claim to the patronage and advowson of the said church. If any further documents concerning the right of patronage shall be found in the possession* *of Henry or his heirs and exhibited by them, they shall have no force but be invalid. Pledge to warranty. Sealed with the donor's seal and those of the abbots of Rievaulx and Jervaulx and of the prior and convent of Newburgh.* [1262 x 1277].

Hiis testibus domino Willelmo de Langeton tunc decano ecclesie Sancti Petri Ebor', magistro Thoma de Witham tunc archidiacono Not', magistro Roberto de Scarbergh tunc archidiacono de Estrithing', etc.

Marginal note: A later hand shows a genealogy of William of Osgodby, his sons Henry (living in the time of Henry III) and William, and William's son Henry.

Dating: see no. 935. If Rufinus of Tonengo, archdeacon of Cleveland, also attested (as in no. 935) then the earliest date would be 1264.

Note: There is what seems to be a much abbreviated copy of this charter in MS Dodsworth 157, fol. 31r, which has the first witness and continues: dominis W. filio Rad(ulfi), W. le Latymer, W. Malebisse, Galfrido de Uppesale, Thoma Colevill, Ricardo Maunsell, W. Barton militibus.

938 *Rubric: Inquisition into the age of the same Henry when he made the confirmation (no. 937).*

939 *Rubric: Charter of the canons of Bridlington concerning their enfeoffment of Rillington. Surrendered.*

[fols 97v–98r]

940 *Quitclaim, addressed to all who will see or hear this charter, by Prior H(ubert) and the convent of Bridlington, to the lord abbot and the convent of Byland, of all right and claim which they had in the patronage and advowson of the church of Rillington, with all its appurtenances inside and outside the vill. They will bring no further claim against the monks concerning the patronage. If any claim* (occasio) *or objection* (cavillatio) *is made against the monks concerning this quitclaim the canons bind themselves to the chapter of York under pain of excommunication to pay 10 marks to the fabric of the church. The canons will bear all the expenses arising from such claims, at the judgement of discreet men. Sealed with the chapter's seal.* [1228 x 1231].

Hiis testibus magistro R. decano Ebor', magistro Galfrido precentore Ebor', magistro Iohanne subdecano et universo capitulo Ebor', etc.

Dating: Roger de Insula became dean in 1220 and last occ. in 1233; Geoffrey of Norwich occ. as precentor between 1220 and 1233; John le Romeyn occ. as subdean in 1228 x 1241. Prior H. is therefore Hubert, who is recorded in 1226 and 1229 and had been succeeded by Thomas by *c.* 1231 (*HRH* II, 345–6). *EYC* I, 490, in referring to this quitclaim, gives the date 1228 or 1229. A quitclaim at this date may be related to the presentation of Robert de Ockham by the abbot and convent to a moiety of Rillington church, saving the right of Lawrence de Wavill, the vicar, that is, a toft in Rillington, with the altarage of the moiety, 1 bovate with a toft in Scampston, and the tithes of corn, hay etc. (*Reg. Gray*, p. 29; *Fasti Parochiales*, V, 33). He was instituted on 30 Jan. 1229.

[fol. 98r, old fol. 204]

941 *Rubric: Quitclaim by H. son of William of Osgodby of all his right in the patronage of a moiety of the said church.*

942 *Rubric: Quitclaim by Richard of Osgodby of the church of Rillington.*

943 *Rubric: Quitclaim by William, count of Aumale, of all his right in the said church.* [*c.* 1228].

Note: For the fee of the counts of Aumale held of the Bigod family in Rillington and other places see *EYC* I, 490–1. On 10 May 1228 justices were appointed to hold an assize of darrein presentment of a moiety of Rillington church between the abbot of Byland, plaintiff, and the prior of Bridlington and the count of Aumale, defendants: *Cal. Pat. R. 1225–1232*, p. 216. The date again suggests that this was related to the presentation in 1229: see note to no. 940.

944 *Rubric: Letters patent of the said count sent to the archbishop concerning his surrender of his right in the said church.* [*c.* 1228].

945 *Grant and quitclaim, addressed to all the faithful in Christ to whom the present writing shall come, by William of Osgodby son of William of Osgodby, to God and St Mary and the abbot and convent of Byland and their successors, or assigns, of 1 acre of his demesne land in the region of Rillington at* Birlestaynes *towards the north, with the right of patronage of the moiety of the church of the vill to which he had presented Master Adam of Evesham, clerk, who has been canonically instituted on his presentation. Undertaking that if he or his heirs or assigns shall seek from the lord king a writ of darrein presentment, or ultra presentatore or quare impedit or quo iure, or a writ of right, or of mort d'ancestor concerning either the moiety or the whole of the church of Rillington, or any other writ, then they shall have no force or value. Undertaking to observe all the above. Sealed with the seal of the chapter of York and his own seal.* [1262 x 1277].

Hiis testibus domino Willelmo de Langeton' tunc decano ecclesie Sancti Petri Ebor', magistro Thoma de Witham tunc archidiacono de Notingham, magistro Roberto de Scarburgh tunc archdiacono de Estriting', etc.

Dating: see note to nos 935, 937.

946   *Memorandum that on Thurs. after St Gregory (12 Mar.) 1261
W(illiam) of Osgodby son of William of Osgodby appeared in the chapter
held at Sledmere in the presence of Robert de Smythton, official of Master
Robert of Scarborough, archdeacon of the East Riding, and Dom. Ralph,
rector of Skirpenbeck and dean of Buckrose. William acknowledged that he
had granted and quitclaimed to God and St Mary and the abbot and convent
of Byland all his right of patronage in a moiety of the church of Rillington to
which moiety he, William, had presented master Adam of Evesham, on
which presentation Adam had been canonically instituted by the archbishop
of York. Nevertheless on the same day he acknowledged in full chapter that he
had no right in the said moiety, but that the advowson of both moieties
pertains to the abbot and convent. Any instruments he might have
concerning the patronage of a moiety of the church were invalid, as demonstrated in a certain charter drawn up about this matter. Sealed with the seal
of the official, together with the seals of the dean and other rectors and vicars
in the said chapter.* Sledmere; 16 Mar. 1261 [1262].

Note: This is the first occurrence of Robert of Scarborough as archdeacon of the
East Riding (*Fasti York*, p. 43). Master Adam of Evesham occurs as rector of a
moiety of the church of Rillington when Stephen de Wiston, canon of Southwell,
was appointed his coadjutor (*Reg. Giffard*, p. 25). As pointed out in *Fasti Parochiales*
(V, 33) the appointment is undated, but is located in Giffard's register between
documents dated Mar. and April 1268. The presentation to this moiety was in
dispute after Adam's death, which had occurred by 12 June 1268 (*Reg. Giffard*, p.
52). This inquisition precedes the final concord below (no. 948).

[fol. 98v]

947   *Final concord in the king's court in the presence of Silvester, bishop of
Carlisle, Roger of Thirkleby, Gilbert de Preston and Adam de Hilton, itinerant justices, and other faithful men of the lord king then present, between
Abbot Henry of Byland, plaintiff, by William of Stokesley his attorney, and
Richard of Osgodby, defendant, concerning the advowson of the church of
Rillington, about which a plea had been brought. Richard has acknowledged
that the advowson of the church pertains to the right of the abbot and his
church, and has restored and quitclaimed it to them. For this acknowledgement and agreement the abbot has received Richard and his heirs into all the
good deeds and prayers offered in his church.* Nottingham; 3 weeks from
Easter, 36 Henry III [21 Apr. 1252].

Copy: PRO CP 25/1/265/45, no. 108.
Pd (calendar): *Yorks. Fines 1246–1272*, p. 81 (from PRO copy).

948   *Final concord in the king's court in the presence of Gilbert de Preston
and John de Wyvill, justices, and other faithful men of the lord king then*

present, between Abbot Henry of Byland, plaintiff, by Brother A(dam) of Husthwaite his monk and attorney, and William of Osgodby, defendant, concerning 1 acre and a moiety of the advowson of the church of Rillington, about which a plea of warranty of charter had been brought. William has acknowledged that the land and moiety of the advowson pertain to the right of the abbot and his church, as granted by William himself, to hold of William in free alms, free from all service. William and his heirs pledge to warranty. Further, William renounces any claim which he may have in the other moiety. The abbot has received William and his heirs into all the good deeds and prayers offered in his church. Westminster; day after St John the Baptist, 46 Henry III [25 June 1262].*

Copy: PRO CP 25/1/265/49, no. 21.
Pd (calendar): *Yorks. Fines 1246–1272*, p. 125, from PRO Case 265, file 49, no. 21.
Note: *Fasti Parochiales* V, 31–2, notes that there was a further case on 26 Mar. 1267, when an inquisition was held before the archdeacon's official, in the rural chapter of Buckrose, into a moiety of the advowson of a moiety of the church which was vacant by the resignation and then the death of Master P., lately rector (see also *Reg. Giffard*, pp. 49–50). The abbot and convent claimed the advowson, as they had presented Master P., but Master P. de Cliffe also claimed to have been presented by Henry, son of William of Osgodby. See also *Reg. Giffard*, pp. 58, 174–5.

949 *Grant and confirmation, addressed to all the sons of holy mother church present and future who will see or hear the present charter, by Henry son of William of Osgodby and Rillington, to God and St Mary and the abbot and convent of Byland and their successors, of all his manor of Rillington with the advowson of the church and all the land which he had in the region of the vill, together with the service of his free tenants, and all other wardships, reliefs, escheats, scutage, exactions, rights and liberties belonging to the manor, church and land. The grant is made for the salvation of his soul and of his father and mother and all his ancestors and heirs, and especially for the good which they have done in finding and providing fuel* (estoveria) *for him and Alice his wife throughout their lives, as is contained in a chirograph of maintenance made between them. The abbot and convent are to hold this in free alms of the master of the Temple rendering annually at the gate of the said manor to the master of* Stukebrig *13d. for all service, half at St Michael (29 Sept.) and half at Easter. Pledge to warranty. Sealed with the donor's seal.* [late 13th cent.].

Hiis testibus dominis Willelmo filio Radulfi, Iohanne de Oketon', Iohanne de Raygate, Adam de Barton', etc.

Copies: MS Dodsworth 91, fol. 73r–v, no. 6, which omits 'etc' from the witness list and continues: Willelmo de Barton, militibus, Thoma de Etton', Thoma de Pokethorp', Gilberto de Ryllington, Waltero de London, Willelmo del Beck de Ampelford, Roberto le Barn, Iohanne de Cnapton', Roberto de Colvill, Willelmo

Pleydur et aliis; MS Top. Yorks. e. 7, fols 124v–125r (old pp. 196–7), which has 'Bonde' for 'London' and 'multis aliis' for 'aliis'.

950   Rubric: *Charter of Henry son of W(illiam) of Osgodby concerning his manor and all the land which he had in Rillington and the advowson of the church.*
Marginal note: B(aculo) ii.

951   Rubric: *Confirmation by the Templars of the grant of the said Henry, rendering to them 4s. yearly.*

952   Rubric: *Confirmation by the Templars of 1 toft and 3 bovates in Rillington.*

953   Rubric: *Quitclaim by Geoffrey son of William, brother of the said Henry [son of William], of all right which he had in Rillington.*

[fol. 99r, old fol. 205]
954   Rubric: *Charter of Adam Noreys concerning 1 bovate with toft and croft which he had of the grant of Ivetta his mother, rendering 12d. to the lord of the fee.* [mid 13th cent.].
Text: MS Top. Yorks. e. 7, fol. 122v (old p. 192). Notification addressed to all present and future by Adam le Norrais of his grant and confirmation in free alms, with his body, to God and St Mary and the abbot and convent of Byland, of that bovate in Rillington with the toft and croft which he had of the grant of his mother, Ivetta, to which he afterwards established title in the presence of justices in York. To hold freely of him and his heirs with all appurtenances, liberties, and easements, and all other things inside and outside the vill, in land and water, meadows and pastures, moors and marshes, mills and all other things, to do with as the monks wish, rendering to the lord of the fee 12d. for all service, 6d. at Whitsuntide and 6d. at St Martin. Pledge to warranty. Hiis testibus dominis Rogero de Stapletona, Thoma de Colevill, Willelmo de Middleton, Willelmo de Leytona, . . . Ebor, Willelmo filio Willelmo de Ebor', Henrico de Pikethorp, Willelmo de Angoteby, Ricardo de Kattona, Rogero de Hyrtona, Alano filio Petri, . . . Adam de Gillington, Iohanne de Grosswans et multis aliis.
Dating: The first three witnesses attest nos 466 and 479, dated *c.* 1241 x 1266. Henry of Pockthorpe occurs in no. 956, dated 1257.

955   Rubric: *Charter of Ivetta concerning the same. Surrendered.*

956 *Rubric: Charter of Henry of Pockthorpe of Rillington concerning the said bovate, toft and croft in free alms. Copied.* [Whitsuntide, 1257].
Text: MS Top. Yorks. e. 11, fol. 71r (old p. 133). Grant, addressed to all the sons of holy other church, by Henry of Pockthorpe of Rillington, to <God> and St Mary and the abbot and convent of Byland, of that bovate with toft and croft which the monks have in Rillington of the grant of Adam le Norays, son of Ivetta of Rillington, to hold freely. Pledge to warranty. H(iis) test(ibus) dominis Willelmo le Latymer tunc vicecomite Ebor', Gaufrido de Hupsale, Willelmo de Latceles, Willelmo Hageth, militibus, R. de Vescy, Willelmo de Stokesley, Thoma de Etton, Willelmo de Etton, Waltero de Coltona et aliis. Whitsuntide, 1257.
Note: This may be the Henry of Pockthorpe who held 1 bovate in Thorpe Bassett and 10½ bovates in Rillington in 1284–5: *KI*, pp. 274–5.

957 *Rubric: Charter of Henry son of William of Osgodby concerning 2 acres of the same bovate.*

958 *Rubric: Writ of the lord king by which Adam le Noreys claimed the said bovate in Rillington of the prior of Malton.*
Note: The Gilbertine priory of Malton established a grange at Rillington; as Golding points out, the possession of the parish church by Byland inhibited the full development of the grange: B. J. Golding, *Gilbert of Sempringham and the Gilbertines c. 1130 – c. 1300* (Oxford, 1995), pp. 406, 415, 418.

959 *Grant and confirmation in the form of a chirograph, addressed to all the faithful in Christ present and future, by Abbot Adam and the convent of Byland to Gilbert son of Robert of Rillington and his heirs for homage and service of 14 bovates in the vill of Rillington. Of these Gilbert holds 7 with his chief messuage in demesne, Roger Strichevals holds 1, Olivia of Scagglethorpe 2, Adam of Langthwaite 4, and Roger Aguilun 1 toft, for which they do service to Gilbert. Gilbert and his heirs are to hold the 14 bovates for forinsec service, that is scutage of the lord king, where 16 carucates make a knight's fee, and are to be free from all suit of court except under writs of right and the trial of a thief taken in the vill of Rillington, and afforcement; they shall perform these suits in the vill of Rillington. Pledge to warranty. Sealed with the seals of both parties.* [late 13th cent.].
Hiis testibus dominis Ricardo de Malbys, Ricardo Walsaund, Olyvero Buscy, Iohanne de Iarkenevyle, militibus, etc.
Copy: MS Dodsworth 157, fol. 31v.

Dating: Gilbert de Rillington and Adam de Langthwaite were tenants in Rillington
in 1284–5: *KI*, p. 72. Richard de Malebisse is the son of William; he was holding
Hawnby of Roger de Mowbray in 1284/5 and was still alive in 1301.

960 *Confirmation in free alms, addressed to all the sons of holy mother
church present and future who will see or hear the present charter, by John de
Eston, knight, for the salvation of his soul and of all his ancestors and heirs,
to God and St Mary and the abbot and convent of Byland and their successors, of his manor of Rillington which the abbot and convent have of the
grant and enfeoffment of Henry son of William of Osgodby, together with the
service of the free tenants (as in no. 949). Further confirmation of the
advowson of the church of Rillington, with its endowment and glebe, and all
other lands which the abbot and convent have in the vills of Osgodby and
Cayton and elsewhere in his fee, by reason of his manor of Thornton in the
vale of Pickering, which manor he holds at present of the fee of the late count
of Aumale. The monks may do there as they please. Undertaking to make no
further claim. Sealed with the donor's seal. [Byland; 6 nones March 1281
[2 Mar. 1282]].*

Hiis testibus dominis Willelmo Lovell, Willelmo Malekak, Iohanne
Ierkenvyle, Ada de Barton', militibus, Henrico de Eligthorp, etc.

Copy: MS Top. Yorks. e. 8, fol. 182v (old p. 329), continued on 186v (old p. 338).
This omits 'etc' from the witness list and continues: Roberto del Clyf, Thoma de
Etton, Galfrido del Beke, Willelmo le Pledur, et aliis. Brief summary in MS
Dodsworth 157, fol. 131r.

Dating: from the text in Top. Yorks. e. 8.

Note: John de Eston held land in Rillington in 1284–5: *KI*, pp. 144–5. A further
confirmation by John, in similar terms and with the same witnesses but preceded
by William Malebisse, was issued at Byland on 7 Mar. 1279 [1280]: MS Top. Yorks.
e. 8, fols 108v–109r (old pp. 181–2). The rubric states that the charter has been
copied.

[fol. 99r–v]

961 *Grant and confirmation in free alms, addressed to all the sons of holy
mother church present and future and sealed with his seal, by William of
Osgodby son of William of Osgodby, to God and St Mary and the abbot and
convent of Byland and their successors, of all right which he had or might
have in the advowson or patronage of the church of Rillington. Further grant
and confirmation under his seal of the homage and service of Gilbert son of
Robert of Rillington and his heirs on 18 bovates in Rillington, of the homage
and service of Matilda daughter of Roger Armiger and her heirs on 2
bovates, of the homage and service of William de Preston and his heirs on 2
bovates, and of the homage and service of Roger Agilun and his heirs on 1*

*toft in the said vill. To hold of the donor free of all secular service, with tofts
and crofts, wardships, reliefs etc. Pledge to warranty.* [1260s x 1280s].
Hiis testibus domino Gilberto de Atona, domino Willelmo Buscell',
domino Iohanne de Atona, Henrico de Angotby, etc.

Dating: William son of William of Osgodby occurs in nos 935, 945, 946, 948, of the
1260s or 1270s.

[fol. 99v]
962   Rubric: *Confirmation by Henry son of the same William of the same.*
On the same line there is a note: 'Carte reddite quatuor sil.'.

963   Rubric: *Report of our presentation and of Henry son of William of
Osgodby; how the candidate presented by the abbot and convent was
admitted; in triplicate with two seals.*

Note: In 1267 Henry son of William of Osgodby and Peter de Cliffe, who claimed
to have been presented to the moiety by William, renounced all claim to the
patronage of a moiety of the church: *Reg. Giffard,* pp. 174–5. However, Henry
claimed the advowson again in 1268 and in the same assize Walter de Grey
claimed rights in the advowson. See *Fasti Parochiales,* V, 36, and PRO Assize Roll
1084, mm. 77, 93.

964   Rubric: *Confirmation by William de Latimer, knight, of lands which
the monks hold in Osgodby, Cayton and Rillington. Look among the confirmation of the magnates.*

Note: The grantor is difficult to identify because successive generations of the
Latimer family took the name of William. William may have been the father of
Robert le Latimer, son of Sir William le Latimer, who on 12 June 1268 was
presented as rector of a moiety of Rillington church by Henry of Osgodby on the
death of Master Adam of Evesham; the archbishop ordered the archdeacon to hold
an inquisition: *Reg. Giffard,* p. 52. William held the office of sheriff of Yorkshire in
1254, 1258 and 1260 and was dead by November 1268. He was succeeded by his
son, William, first Lord Latimer, who died in 1304. His son was William the
younger, who died in 1327. See *CP* VII, 460ff.

965   Rubric: *Chirograph of William Latimer concerning the marriage of the
heir of William of Rillington with the proof of age of John son of William;
with 12 seals.* [1319; 1330].
Text: MS Dodsworth 94, fol. 37r–v, nos 50, 51. Indenture by which the
abbot and convent sold to William Latimer, knight, the marriage and
custody of the body and lands of John son of William of Rillington, to
have until John came of age. William, John's father, held lands of the
abbot and convent for military service. Sealed with the seals of both
parties. York; St Gregory (12 Mar.) 1318 [1319]. *Ibid.,* fol. 37v, no. 51.
Proof of age of John son of William, made at Malton, Sat. before

Ascension (12 May) 1330, in the presence of William de Kirkeby and brother John de Wilmersley, attorneys of the abbot and convent, by John of Butterwick, Robert de Cornwaille, Thomas of Pockthorpe, Henry of Rillington, John of Settrington, William Chaumberleyne, Thomas Chaumberleyne, John Wodecok, William of Burythorpe, Hugh Broune, John Langthwayt, Richard de Bernevill, Thomas, smith of Rillington, jurors. They swore on oath that John was 21 on the eve of the Assumption (14 Aug.) last. Sealed by the jurors.

Note: The party to the first indenture was William the younger, who died in 1327.

966 *Rubric: Charter of Henry son of William of Osgodby concerning 2 acres in the region of Rillington of that bovate which Adam Noreys, son of Ivetta, granted.*

967 *Rubric: Charter of William Latimer, knight, concerning the inquisition held at Rillington relating to certain lands which William son of Gilbert of Rillington held of the abbot and convent.*

Note: For William Latimer see note to no. 964.

968 *Confirmation by Geoffrey, archbishop of York and primate of England, addressed to the archdeacons of Cleveland and the East Riding and their chapters and all the sons of holy mother church, with the assent of the dean and chapter of York whose letters he has received, to the abbot and monks of Byland of the order of Cîteaux and their successors, of 20s. annual pension from the chapel of Scawton which has recently been constructed, and 1 mark from that moiety of the church of St Andrew, Rillington, of which they hold the patronage, which was granted to them by William son of Durand de Cliffe (Clyva) of Cayton. Sealed with his seal.* Ripon; [1 Nov. 1191 x 1204, probably 1203].

Hiis testibus Gilberto priore de Thurgartona, magistro Gregorio, magistro Nigello et magistro Amphredo presentibus omnibus coram nobis apud Ripon' cum multis aliis.

Marginal note: B(aculus) iii.

Copy: MS Dodsworth 91, fols 112v–113r, which omits the third witness and repeats 'presentibus'.

Dating: Archbishop Geoffrey Plantagenet was enthroned at York on 1 Nov. 1191; the office of prior of Thurgarton was already vacant on 30 Aug. 1204 following the death of Prior Gilbert (*HRH* I, 187 and 286). The confirmation is probably related to the final concord of 13 May 1203 (no. 1089 below). Master Gregory may be master Gregory, canon of York (*Fasti York*, p. 121).

Note: For other documents relating to the pension from Scawton chapel see below, nos 1089–1097. The copy in MS Dodsworth 91 is followed by a note: 'Sciendum quod dominus Thomas de Corbrig confirmavit nobis quicquid in ista carta continere distringitur'.

969 *Rubric: Confirmation and inspection by Archbishop Thomas of the said pensions from Scawton and Rillington.*
Note: This may refer to the note in MS Dodsworth 91 (no. 968, note).

[fols 99v–100r]
970 *Indenture between William Latimer, lord of Danby, on one part and the abbot and convent of Byland on the other. For a long time there had been dispute between William, William's ancestors and the predecessors of the abbot concerning issues and profits from the lordship of the vill of Rillington. They have agreed to divide these and between them to appoint a steward to collect the profits of waste and agistments, and to answer for these at 2 courts, 1 after St Michael and 1 after Easter and for all the profits of the lordship of Rillington. Sealed with the seals of both parties.* York; 16 Apr. 3 Richard II [1380].
Done a Everwik lan et iour susditz par ycestes tesmoignes labbe de Ryvaux, monser Rauf' Hastynges, monser Iohanne Bygot, monser Willm' Percehay, etc.
French.
Note: In the course of copying the document into the cartulary a line was omitted; it is written, in the cartulary hand, at the foot of the folio and its position in the text indicated by a caret.

[fol. 100r, old fol. 206]
971 *Rubric: Grant by King Edward II to receive the church of Rillington notwithstanding the statute: look among the royal liberties.*
Note: The text is given above at no. 534 (*Cal. Pat. R. 1313–1317*, p. 560 (5 Nov. 1316)).

972 *Rubric: Form of letters sent by the lord king to the pope for making an appropriation.*

973 *Rubric: [Letter of] Proxy of Brother N. de T., sent to the Roman curia concerning the execution of the said appropriation.*
Note: A note appears beside nos 972 and 973, *ut patet in registro cartarum*, 'as appears in the register of charters'.

974 *Rubric: Form of petition of the abbot and convent to the pope for the said church. Look in the register of charters.*

975 *Rubric: Bull of Pope Gregory confirming the patronage of the said church of Rillington.*
Note: It is not clear if this is Pope Gregory X (1271–6) or XI (1370–78).

976 *Rubric: Copy of the bull of appropriation of Pope Clement [VI]; look among the privileges.* [23 Jan. 1344].
Note: For the bull of appropriation see *CPRL III, 1342–1362*, p. 114 (10 kal. Feb. 1344). The church was said to be valued at 30 marks under the old taxation and 15 marks under the new. A petition had been sent to Clement VI by John de Mowbray, patron of Byland, pointing out the damage which the abbey had suffered from the incursions of the Scots, and requesting the appropriation of Rillington, which was in the patronage of the abbey. The church, which had two rectors, was valued below 32 marks with 10 marks being reserved for the perpetual vicar. The petition was granted on 23 Jan. 1344 (*CPRP I, 1342–1419*, p. 18).

977 *Rubric: Notarial instrument concerning the presentation of this bull to the archbishop of York: look in the Rillington and Bubwith bundle.*

[fol. 100r–v]
978 *Notarial instrument issued in the presence of the witnesses named below, in the porch of the parish church of Rillington, before the south door, by Brother John of Dishforth, monk of the monastery of Byland of the Cistercian order in the diocese of York, proctor of the abbot and convent, together with Brother John de Carleton his fellow monk and co-proctor, reciting their commission from the abbot and convent. Notification by the abbot and convent that they have appointed John de Carleton and John of Dishforth their fellow monks, and John of Rillington and William of Ingleby (?Greenhow), seculars, to act on their behalf in certain matters concerning their monastery and especially to take corporal possession of the moiety of the parish church of Rillington, vacant by the resignation of Ralph of Pockthorpe, last joint holder or rector, by reason of a bull of Pope Clement VI and according to the contents of a process of the archbishop of York. They are to take possession of the church and of all its profits in the name of the abbot and convent. Sealed with their seal.* The chapter house of Byland; 26 Nov. 1344.
Instruction to look among the privileges for the bull of Pope Clement VI.
Immediately afterwards John of Dishforth, proctor, exhibited certain letters patent of William, archbishop of York and legate of the apostolic see, sealed with his seal in red wax with silk threads of various colours, and written in the hand of John de Aldefeld, public notary and sealed by him. This declared the vacancy in the said moiety of the church. Letter of Ralph of Pockthorpe,

rector of Rillington, to the abbot and convent of Byland resigning his moiety
of the church which has, on papal authority, been appropriated to them.
When this had been agreed brother John de Carleton declared that he took
possession of the moiety of the church and entered and took corporal pos-
session with all its rights. The bells of the church were rung and after high
mass John de Carleton, proctor, in the name of his lords, received 14½ silver
pennies due to the moiety from the offerings at mass. Witnesses and notary's
attestation. Presentibus domino Iohanne rectore medietatis predicte
de Rill', Iohanne Hardyng, Willelmo . . . Thoma de Catton, Thoma
Spark presbiteris, Iohanne de Rillyngton' etc. Tues., St Andrew the
Apostle, 30 Nov. 1344.
Note: Ralph of Pockthorpe resigned as rector of a moiety of Rillington on 24 Nov.
1344 (BI Reg. 10 (Reg. Zouche), fols 180v–181r; *Fasti Parochiales*, V, 33).

[fol. 100v]
979 *Rubric: [Letter of] Proxy concerning the appropriation and the ordi-*
nation of the portion of the vicar.

980 *Rubric: Appeal* (provocatio) *by the abbot and convent for a moiety of*
the church. It is kept in the bundle named above.

[fols 100v–101v]
981 *Ordination of a new vicarage in the church of Rillington by William*
[de la Zouche], archbishop of York, primate of England and legate of the
apostolic see. Pope Clement VI, considering the needs of the abbot and
convent of Byland, has given permission for the appropriation of the parish
church of Rillington, which has been accustomed to be governed by two
rectors, reserving for the archbishop the ordination and decision about the
profits of the church for a perpetual vicar at the presentation of the abbot and
convent, that is 10 marks yearly, if that proves to be adequate. The incipit is:
Clemens episcopus servus servorum dei etc. *Look among the privileges.*
The archbishop, wishing to follow papal instructions and to provide for a
vicar in the church of Rillington, instructs that there shall be an inquisition
with the assent of the abbot and convent. First he ordains that there shall be a
perpetual vicar who shall be suitable and honest and prudent concerning the
cure of souls, and presented by the abbot and convent to the archbishop and
his successors, and during a vacancy to the dean and chapter. He is to be
admitted and instituted canonically in the same. The vicar is to have the cure
of souls of the parishioners of Rillington, and personally reside there. He is to
have the dwelling house of one of the rectors, that is, the part in which John of
Lutton lived, which contains 11 perches in length and in width 12 perches of

land. *The abbot and convent are to build a dwelling house for the vicar at their own expense for the first time. There are to be 2 bovates of glebe land, of annual value 20s. sterling. The vicar is to receive from the abbot and convent 12 marks sterling paid in equal amounts at two terms, Whitsuntide and St Martin in Winter (11 Nov.) and if this is not paid within 15 days of the agreed terms the vicar is to take all the fruits, profits and offerings until they reach that sum, and the abbot and convent are nonetheless to pay 40s. to the fabric of York if they do not pay. The vicar is to meet all ordinary expenses, and the abbot and convent all extraordinary expenses. The archbishop ordains that the house, land and money be limited to the suitable support of a perpetual vicar, as laid down. By John de Aldefeld, public notary by apostolic authority, scribe. Sealed with the archbishop's seal.* Ripon; 22 Nov. 1344.

Presentibus discretis viris magistro Thoma de Nevyll iuris civilis professore, dominis Willelmo de Feriby, canonico ecclesie Ebor' ac rectore ecclesie de Stokesleye, Thoma de Midelton' perpetuo vicario ecclesie de Silkeston', et Iohanne de Sutton' clerico Ebor' diocesis familiaribus nostris testibus ad premissa vocatis et rogatis.

Authentication and sign of John de Aldefeld, notary of the diocese of York, to the above.

Copy: BI Reg. 10 (Reg. Zouche), fol. 180r–v. This recites in full the bull of Pope Clement VI, dated 23 Jan. 1344 (see no. 976) It omits from the witness list the words 'perpetuo' and 'familiaribus nostris'.

[fols 101v–102v]

982 *Notification by William (de la Zouche), archbishop of York and legate of the apostolic see. It pertains to his office to end all disputes and scandals which might arise from lawsuits between his subjects. The abbot and convent of the monastery of Byland of the Cistercian order have brought to his notice that the parish church of Rillington, which was accustomed to be ruled by two rectors, has been appropriated to them by the pope. A moiety has become vacant through the resignation of Ralph of Pockthorpe. However John de Sancto Ivone, incumbent of the other moiety, strives to prevent the abbot and convent taking possession of the other moiety even though he has no right there. John has therefore been summoned before the archbishop and threatened with removal. The parties agreed to compromise. The abbot appeared through Nicholas of Ripon, clerk, proctor of the abbot and convent, and John appeared in person.*

Letters patent from the abbot and convent stating that a moiety of the church of Rillington which has been accustomed to be ruled by two rectors has been appropriated to them on apostolic authority, and that they are to take possession on the death or resignation of the rectors. Byland; St Clement pope and martyr [23 Nov.] 1344.

Acceptance, addressed to the abbot and convent of Byland, by John de Sancto Ivone, of arbitration, and his resignation. Recitation of letter of resignation. The archbishop accepts, and says that because John has no other income he is to get for life from the abbot and convent £20 yearly, that is 100s. at the feast of the Invention of the Holy Cross (3 May), 100s. at St Peter ad Vincula (1 Aug.), 100s. at St Martin in Winter (11 Nov.), and 100s. at the Purification of the B. V. M. (2 Feb.), two robes yearly, at Christmas and St John the Baptist, at York, through the abbot's proctor. They are obliged to pay, by sanctions. The fruits are to be sequestered until arrangements are made. Cawood; 7 Dec. 1345.

Notification by John de Aldefeld, public notary, scribe of the archbishop, of the above, done in his presence. Sealed with the archbishop's seal.

. . . una cum venerabilibus et discretis viris magistris Radulfo de Taravyll', canonico Lichefelden', Willelmo de Nassyngt' canonico Exonien', Willelmo de Langeton' curie Ebor' advocato, Roberto de Newenham et Eustachio Mundider notariis publicis et aliis testibus ad premissa vocatis et rogatis.

Copy: BI Reg. 10 (Reg. Zouche) fols 182v–183r.
Note: The cartulary rubric reads 'Resignation of John de St Ivo and the ordination of his portion'. See also below nos 983–4.

[fols 102v–103r]
983 *Notification by Brother John of Appleby, monk of Byland and proctor of the abbot and convent, reciting the instrument by which the abbot and convent notify that John of Carleton and John of Appleby, their fellow monks, and their brothers John of Rillington and William of Ingleby (?Greenhow), seculars, are appointed proctors to take possession of the moiety of the church of Rillington, vacant by letters of Clement VI, by process of the archbishop, and through the resignation of John de Sancto Ivone.* Sat. after St Nicholas [10 Dec.] 1345.

See the bull of Pope Clement among the privileges.

After reading the papal letters the proctor went to the door of the church and then quickly afterwards to the dwelling belonging to a portion of the church located in the vill of Rillington. He found the door of the church barred with an iron bar and the dwelling house with iron fixed in the door. He opened them and took possession of both of these, vacant by the resignation of John de Sancto Ivone. He rang the bells, mass was said at the high altar, with music, and offerings were received. Rillington; before the south door of the church; Sunday before St Lucy [11 Dec.] 1345.

Presentibus domino Willelmo de Burton', domino Roberto de Swaldale, Willelmo Scott de Rillyngton', Thoma de Cayton', Thoma

Spark capellano de Ryllyngton', etc., parochianis dicte ecclesie de Rillyngton' et aliis testibus ad premissa vocatis specialiter et rogatis. *Written and attested by John, clerk of Robert de Hakethorp in the diocese of Carlisle, public notary by apostolic authority, of all the above, in the presence of the above witnesses.*

[fol. 103r, old fol. 209]

984 *Rubric: Letter accepting arbitration of the archbishop of York for the ordination of a pension for Ralph of Pockthorpe and John de Sancto Ivone.* [Dec. 1345].

Note: These were the last rectors of the moieties of Rillington church. Ralph of Pockthorpe, resigned on 24 Nov. 1344 and was assigned a pension of £20 (BI Reg. 10 (Reg. Zouche), fols 180v–181); for the resignation of John de Sancto Ivone, who received the same pension, see above, no. 982. See *Fasti Parochiales*, V, 33–4.

985 *Rubric: Form of presentation of the vicar to the archbishop after the resignation or retirement of the rector.* [1345 x 1346].

Note: The abbot and convent presented the first vicar of the new vicarage, Adam de Barneby, on 12 May 1346. He was instituted and inducted on the same day: BI, Reg. 10 (Reg. Zouche), fol. 183v.

986 *Rubric: Surrender by Alexander (Neville), archbishop of York, copied* sub serico *both for Rillington and for a moiety of Bubwith. Look in the white or black chest* in evidentia premissorum. [Bishopthorpe; 8 Jan. 1376].

Text: BI Reg. 12 (Reg. Neville), fol. 56r. Notification by Alexander, archbishop of York, that it has recently come to his notice that the abbot and convent of Byland, against common law, possess and hold the parish church of Rillington and a moiety of the church of Bubwith, as appropriated and united to them, and take the rents and profits and convert them to their own use and dispose of them as they wish. He orders that the abbot and convent show the reason for the appropriation and appear at a certain place and time. The abbot and convent appeared through their proctor at the place and time appointed and displayed papal letters, instruments and muniments as well as certain evidences concerning the appropriation of Rillington. These were inspected and the archbishop concluded that the rights of the abbot and convent were demonstrated.

987 *Rubric: The proxy* (procuratorium) *to be shown in the visitation of churches: this is written in the white book in various forms.*

[fols 103v–104r]
RIEVAULX ABBEY (SE5785), Cistercian Abbey (NR). Rievaulx Abbey
was founded as a daughter house of St Bernard's abbey of Clairvaux
in 1132 by Walter Espec. It is situated in a deep valley on the banks of
the River Rye, just over 2 miles from Helmsley. In 1142 the monks
whom Roger de Mowbray had settled at Hood requested Roger's
mother, Gundreda de Gournay, to petition her son to provide them
with a new site; she suggested that she give them Byland on the
Moor, which was her dower. The move took place in 1142, the monks
taking possession of the vill and church of Old Byland and settling on
the banks of the Rye, just over a mile NW of Rievaulx. The *Historia
Fundationis* notes that the site was unsatisfactory because of its proximity to Rievaulx, that the monks remained there for five years before
relocating to their third site, Stocking, in 1147, and that the small cell
(*parva cellula*) constructed by the monks lay 'where their tile house is
now constructed' (*Mon. Ang.* V, 350–1). The site of the second settlement has been identified as Tylas Farm (SE566868), on the west bank
of the Rye. The *Historia* further notes that when the monks took possession of the vill they reduced it to a grange, granting part of the
land to the men who remained for a new vill. Old Byland and Byland
Grange lie approximately 1½ miles west of Tylas Farm. In addition to
being close neighbours from 1142 to 1147, the monks of Rievaulx and
Byland had benefactors in common. Roger de Mowbray and
Gundreda de Gournay were benefactors of Rievaulx, as were Roger's
tenants such as Hugh Malebisse (*Cart. Riev.*, nos 55–77, pp. 30–47; on
Rievaulx's estates generally see J. Burton, 'The estates and economy
of Rievaulx Abbey in Yorkshire', *Cîteaux: Commentarii Cistercienses*,
49 (1998), 29–94; *A History of Helmsley, Rievaulx and District*, ed.
J. McDonnell (York, 1963), pp. 102–21, and map at p. 111). This meant
that abbey lands bordered on each other, and this situation necessitated the agreements recorded in this section of the cartulary.

988 *Agreement of charity* (concordia caritatis) *between the house of
Rievaulx and the house of Byland, which, for fear of the future, Abbot Ailred
of Rievaulx and Abbot Roger of Byland ordained and confirmed with the
consent of both chapters, for the unity of spirit and the bond of peace.*
   *The monks of Byland will pray for a dead brother of Rievaulx as they do for
a brother of their own house, in masses and psalms and other prayers, and
the monks of Rievaulx will do the same for a brother of Byland.*
   *They shall stand together against any injury or persecution done to either
house by patrons, powerful men or neighbours, adhering to the advice and*

help of each other in all things.

If either is struck by misfortune, such as fire, the other will offer advice and assistance.

No-one is to trespass the boundaries which they have made between their pastures and lands, as written below, and if they do they are to be subject to the penalties contained in this agreement without dispensation.

The monks of Byland have granted to those of Rievaulx that they may have their bridge fitted with snares (laqueatus) to keep back the timbers (ligna) which are carried along the river Rye; the bridge shall be the same height as it was on the day on which this agreement was reached, but if the monks wish to heighten it they shall be allowed to do so. In the same way their mill weir shall be the same height as it was on the day of the agreement, and if they wish to heighten it they can raise it to the height of the bank. They have further granted them a road 18 feet wide from their bridge through the wood and field of Byland as far as their land stretches towards Hestelschet and they are to repair the road as often as is necessary and as often as the brethren of Rievaulx wish. They are free to repair their mill weir and bridges on Byland's bank, as the brothers of Byland are on Rievaulx's bank, but are to have no more on each other's side.

The land between Ashberry Hill and the river Rye as their ditch goes below Ashberry Hill shall remain with the monks of Rievaulx as laid down in the charter which they have of Byland, and the same applies to Oswaldehenges. The monks of Byland are to retain the houses that they have built at Deepdale with everything they have or might acquire in the vills of Gristhorpe, Lebberston, Cayton, Osgodby, Scarborough, Falsgrave, Seamer, Irton and Ayton (East or West), except for the meadows of Ayton. Here they will have nothing without the goodwill of the monks of Rievaulx. It has been agreed that henceforth neither the abbot nor anyone shall accept a place to build a house in Hutton (Buscel) or from Hutton to the vill of Brompton without first showing the place to the abbot and cellarer of the other house, in order that peace be maintained. The animals of Griff grange shall have pasture within the wood of Scawton from Bungdale towards Sproxton, but the remainder of Scawton will be retained by the monks of Byland.

The boundaries between Hesketh Grange and Byland Grange are these: from the spur and stone on Hesketh Dyke (Askeledic) by the boundaries agreed between them as far as the road from Boltby, and from that road in a straight line as far as the nearest head of the causeway across the brow of the hill and the boundaries which the monks of both houses have perambulated and agreed, as far as the boundaries between Byland and Cold Kirby and beyond, and as far as the land of Adam son of Odo stretches below the brow of the hill. The flocks of sheep and other animals of Hesketh shall not enter the pastures of Byland, nor the flocks of Byland the pastures of Hesketh from Hesketh Dyke as far as the boundaries which they have agreed. The king's highway is the boundary between them. From the boundary located near Hesketh as far as the ditch which divides Arden and Dale their boundaries extend as has been agreed, and from there towards the east the ditch is the boundary between them. From that place where the boundaries meet the said ditch, as a straight line might be drawn to the hill of Sowber Hill (Sotesberge), everything to the east shall be retained by the monks of Byland, and to the west by the monks of Rievaulx, with the exception that the monks of Rievaulx shall have all the plain of Arden near the said ditch. The boundary between the brethren in Laskill and Bilsdale and the brethren in Snilesworth shall be the road which runs from Helmsley to Cleveland as far as the land of Helmsley stretches.

The share between the forge which the monks of Rievaulx have in Shitlington and that which the monks of Byland have in Emley is this: the monks of Byland shall have ore and charcoal which they need for their forges from 6 vills, Emley, Bretton, Shitlington of Philip, Denby, Briestwistle and Thornhill, and those of Rievaulx shall have the same from 3 vills, the two Shitlingtons (of the fee of Adam son of Peter and Matthew son of Saxe), Flockton and Threpewda.

When this agreement had been in force for several years it was confirmed in many points and strengthened by adding certain items which were not included in the first agreement. All quarrels which had arisen between them were laid to rest from this day onwards. In particular the monks of Byland remitted all claim concerning 2 bovates in Welburn, Oswaldesenges, the ditch which they had made in the region of Scawton to conduct the river Rye, the smithy in Shitlington and Flockton, the bridge with snares, and concerning the road from the bridge through the middle of the wood towards Byland. The monks of Rievaulx remitted all claim concerning common pasture in Murton. The claims are all laid aside, and will not be invoked in any lawsuit. If the monks of Rievaulx or Byland shall construct mills or mill-ponds or bridges on the river Rye a pond is not to exceed custom but be just sufficient for a mill. Bridges must be sufficient to allow crossing. If the ponds or bridges exceed this, or if any other controversy arises, the disputes are to be settled by four monks, two monks of Rievaulx, chosen by the abbot of Byland, and two monks of Byland to be chosen by the abbot of Rievaulx. Both shall have use of Sproxton as before. If any brother trespasses within these boundaries through negligence and lack of care, he shall be scourged in chapter on the following Sunday and that day shall not eat with the others but on the ground. Judgement will decide if he did it unwittingly. If however he did this knowingly, he shall suffer the penalty on three Sundays. If he was *seen by another brother and ordered to leave and failed to obey he shall be removed from his grade* (ab ordine) *and shall be last of all until he has completed his penance, that is to drink only water on three Sundays. If this trespass is committed by boys of the house they are to be flogged until they bleed. If a hired worker commits trespass his master shall warn him twice, and if he does not correct his ways the master shall be punished as if he had committed the offence.*

The charter was read in both chapters in the presence of Abbots Silvanus of Rievaulx and Roger of Byland, and ratified by them and by the chapters. Byland and Rievaulx; 1170.

Marginal note: (at foot of fol. 103v) '1170 16 H 2'.

Pd: *Cart. Riev.*, pp. 176–80, no. 243, from BL MS Cotton Julius D II, fols 147v–151r, with minor variants.

Note: The rubric describes this as the first agreement between Byland and Rievaulx. Within a few years of the community moving from Hood to Old Byland arrangements began to be made concerning boundaries and access to abbey lands. Before 1145 Abbot Roger conceded to Abbot William (1132–45) and the brethren of Rievaulx the right to make a ditch across Byland's land at the foot of Ashberry Hill and to hold the land which they enclosed in peace (*Cart. Riev.*, pp. 180–81, no. 244). It was in the period after 1147, when Byland as a Savigniac house had become a member of the Cistercian order, and the move to Stocking had taken place, that the first agreement with Rievaulx, recorded here, was reached. This was ratified three years after the death of Abbot Ailred.

The agreement shows that there were a number of issues requiring clarification. The first was bridges and weirs on the River Rye. The second was the boundaries between lands to the west of the river. The bridge fitted with snares, which the monks of Rievaulx were to be allowed to have, seems to have been intended to catch wood drifting downstream; as Tylas House lies upstream from Rievaulx the force of this clause is not clear. However, it is clear that both houses were to be allowed onto each other's lands for the purposes of repair of bridges and weirs. The boundaries between Old Byland Grange, and Rievaulx's grange of Hesketh needed clarification (the distance between the latter and Tylas Farm is something over 4 miles) as did the pasture rights of Rievaulx's Griff Grange in Scawton wood, an area acquired by Byland. Hesketh Dyke, mentioned here as a boundary, is at SE5187. Adam son of Odo mentioned here is Adam of Boltby. With his consent his father, Odo, granted to Rievaulx part of his waste land below Hesketh next to Boltby, from the western side and south below the hill as 'Rutendesic' flows over the hill as the road leads from Murton (Byland property) to Boltby (held by Rievaulx) (*Cart. Riev.*, no. 76, pp. 45–6). For a discussion of the boundaries of Old Byland, based on Christopher Saxton's map of 1598 (PRO MPB 1(32), formerly part of E178/2779) see Maurice Beresford, *History on the Ground* (Lutterworth, 1957, rpt. Stroud, 1998), pp. 52–62). The common mining interests developed by both houses in the south of the county were addressed by laying down their access to ore and charcoal for the operation of their forges.

The agreement is of interest for the light it sheds on the interaction of these two houses in the moorland areas surrounding Rievaulx, the area west and east of the river Derwent on the southern fringes of the moors, and in the south of the county.

988A   *Rubric: Agreement between us and the monks of Rievaulx concerning certain injuries. In the first bundle of the abbots.*

[fol. 104r–v]
989   *Agreement reached in the time of William of Ellerbeck, abbot of Rievaulx, and Adam of Husthwaite, abbot of Byland. The agreements reached between their predecessors are not to be broken, in particular that between Abbots Ailred and Roger (no. 988), as well as other agreements known to have been reached. These have been renewed, and all claims and contentions have been set aside. The monks of Rievaulx have pardoned the monks of Byland a certain sum of money they thought due to them under a bond which they had in their possession. The monks of Byland have remitted and quitclaimed to the monks of Rievaulx an annual rent of 1 pound of incense which they demanded from Rievaulx's land in Thornaby; they are to be free from any further exaction and demand. Moreover they relaxed claim to 12d. annual rent in Fraisthorpe. The quarrel between them concerning the crossroads* (furcationem viarum) *from the leaden cross on Bloworth towards Cleveland between the boundaries of their pastures has been determined in this way: that the road which the two abbots rode around in the company of Thomas of Etton, layman, and Henry de Meinill, clerk, and certain monks from both houses on St Bartholomew the Apostle (24 Aug.) 1277, shall from henceforth be the boundary and division between the pastures of both houses. If the flocks of Rievaulx stray to the west of the road and those of Byland to the east because they are not guarded, they are to be returned to their enclosure in a friendly fashion. But if they stray when they are being carelessly guarded the shepherds, whether* conversi *or lay servants, shall suffer the penalties laid down by Abbots Ailred and Roger. There is strength in unity, therefore they pledge to defend each other in secular lawsuits. All action against William of Danby is to be dropped. This agreement is to be read each year in the chapter of both monasteries at St Stephen (26 Dec.) and the second day of Easter.* Laskill [Lachscales]; 31 Aug. 1277.

[fol. 104v]
990   *Rubric: Agreement with Rievaulx concerning pasture in Hawnby. 1181. Look in the abbots' bundle.*
Note: It is clear from the manuscript that the instruction applies to no. 990 and not to no. 991.

991   *Rubric: Chirograph agreement between Byland and Rievaulx made in the presence of the abbots of Furness and Combe, judges.* [? c. 1238].

Note: In 1225 a dispute between the abbots and convents of Rievaulx and Byland which had arisen in the time of Abbots R(oger) of Rievaulx and R(obert) of Byland concerning the boundaries of the granges of Byland and Hesketh was settled by the abbots of Waverley, Garendon and Combermere who had been appointed by the General Chapter to investigate the claims (NYCRO ZDV I 1 (Sandwith's *Exscripta*)). In 1238 the Cistercian General Chapter referred a dispute between Byland and Rievaulx to the abbots of Furness, Combermere and Beaulieu; in 1253 a further dispute was referred for investigation to the abbots of Furness, Fountains and Merevale (Canivez, *Statuta* II, 199–200 (no. 72) and 392–3 (no. 18)). This rubric probably refers to the 1238 investigation, with 'Combe' an error for 'Combermere'.

992 *Quitclaim, addressed to all the faithful of Christ who will see or hear this writing, by Abbot R(oger) and the convent of Rievaulx to the abbot and convent of Byland, of all right they had to saw wood in East Witton, so that they will not cut down in the wood nor will the monks of Byland lose wood there through the law of the land. Sealed with their seal, and with the seals of the witnesses. [c. 1236].*
Hiis testibus dominis M. de Kyrkestall, R. de Rupe, et M. de Melsa abbatibus, iudicibus super hoc datis a capitulo generali.
Dating: In 1236 the Cistercian Annual General Chapter committed the (unspecified) dispute of Rievaulx and Byland to the abbots of Kirkstall, Roche and Meaux: Canivez, *Statuta*, II, 163 (no. 48).
Note: The witnesses are Maurice of Kirkstall, Richard of Roche, and Michael de Bruno of Meaux.

993 *Rubric: Confirmation of the agreement between the abbots of Byland and Rievaulx by the abbots and Cîteaux and Clairvaux. Look as above.*
Note: This could refer to *Cart. Riev.*, p. 181, no. 245, a letter from G. abbot of Cîteaux and G., abbot of Rievaulx's mother house of Clairvaux. Fearing that geographical proximity might lead to the division of minds the two houses are urged to preserve mutual goodwill, and to refrain from accepting land or granges against the form of the order and the boundaries which have been laid down. This may refer to no. 988 above.

[fol. 105r, old fol. 211]
SUTTON UNDER WHITESTONECLIFFE (SE4882), in the parish of Felixkirk and the wapentake of Birdforth (NR), approximately one mile west of the first abbey site at Hood. The estate at Sutton was the result of grants by the Fossard family. The earliest acquisition appears to have been modest: Adam Fossard, who succeeded by 1183 and was dead by 1208, issued a charter relating to ½ carucate in 'Gildousdale' with woodland (no. 1017). This was the ½ carucate that was granted to the Vicars Choral of York (no. 1026) and that was the subject of a final concord of 1248 (no. 1022; see also no. 1027). However the main

benefactor was Adam's younger son, Thomas, who had succeeded his brother, Robert, by 1227. In 1225 Thomas confirmed common pasture throughout Sutton, and added to pasture granted by his brother, Robert (no. 1053). In 1237 Thomas granted a knight's fee in Sutton, and associated lands in Marderby, Laysthorpe, Hood and Felixkirk (nos 994, 997, confirmed by Thomas's son, Thomas, in nos 998, 1003), and he granted the homage and service of Geoffrey Fossard on 1 carucate (no. 1069). As heirs to the Stutevilles Hugh and Joan Wake acknowledged that the abbot and convent held one knight's fee of them (nos 1004, 1047–9). Others involved in minor grants, confirmations, and quitclaims were: Mary, wife of Peter de Richemund (nos 1007, 1008), and their daughters Petronilla (with her husband, Geoffrey of Thirsk, nos 1001, 1009, 1010, 1014), Christiana of Thirsk (nos 1012–13) and Constance (nos 1013, and possibly the Constance who occurs in no. 1036 with her husband, Robert of Myton); Geoffrey de Coigners (no. 1028) and his daughter, Helen, and Helen's husband, Bernard de Areyns (nos 1018, 1020–22) and son, Thomas (no. 1023); Elizabeth Conyers, possibly another daughter of Geoffrey, who was first married to William Ruthe and then to John of Danthorpe (nos 1027, 1030), and her son, Thomas (no. 1023), and Philip son of Philip of Sutton (nos 1015–16), a regular witness of Byland charters (nos 128–9, 584, 618, 646, 1027, 1042, 1044).

The lands in Sutton under Whitestonecliffe were used for sheep farming and pasture (see nos 999, 1000, 1053) and the monks enjoyed fishing rights in Gormire Lake (SE5083), to the north of Sutton Bank (no. 999). This section also demonstrates Byland's claim in Felixkirk church, the advowson of which was held by the Knights Hospitaller of nearby Mount St John (no. 1002), and agreements were reached with vicars of Sutton concerning tithes (nos 1054–5) and the provision of a chaplain (nos 1056–7, 1059).

Sutton became the centre of the Liberty of Byland, and the privileges claimed by the abbot are described in no. 544 above. Thomas Fossard granted the abbot suit of court in 1237 (no. 997), and the abbey court is mentioned in no. 1060. In 1271 Henry III ordered that pleas heard by royal justices were to be heard at the abbot's manor of Clifton rather than Sutton, probably because of the convenience of the location (no. 529).

994 *Rubric: Memorandum that Thomas Fossard son of Adam Fossard granted all the lordship which he had in Sutton and other vills.* Easter, 1237.
Marginal note: B(aculus) i. In later hand: 21 H 3.

Note: Thomas Fossard succeeded his brother Robert, son of Adam Fossard, between 1220 and 1227.

995 *Grant by Robert de Stuteville, addressed to all his men, French and English, to Geoffrey Fossard of 1 knight's fee in Sutton (under Whitestonecliffe), Marderby and Laysthorpe, with all appurtenances, to hold of him and his heirs as freely as Robert holds it of the king.* [before 1166].

Teste Helewisa uxore sua et Ricardo de Chedolm, Petro presbitero et Thoma clerico et Waltero de Peletoft, etc.

Pd: *EYC* IX, no. 15.

Dating: *EYC* points out that Geoffrey Fossard held the land of Robert de Stuteville in 1166.

Note: The rubric notes that the charter had been surrendered.

996 *Rubric: Charter of Thomas son of Adam Fossard concerning all his land in his lordship of Sutton (under Whitestonecliffe) and land which belonged to Joan, wife of Robert Fossard.* [*c.* 1237].

Marginal note: (in later hand) 'Juliana filia et heres Wm de Rillington in custodia Willi domini Latimer'.

Dating: This may have been issued at the same time as no. 997 (memorandum at no. 994).

997 *Notification to all present and future by Thomas Fossard son of Adam Fossard of Sutton (under Whitestonecliffe) of his grant in free alms to God and St Mary and the abbot and convent of Byland, of 1 knight's fee in Sutton, Marderby, Laysthorpe, Hood and Felixkirk, with all their appurtenances and rights, in demesne, arable and pasture, etc., marriage rights, wardships, reliefs and escheats, and suit of court. The grant is made for the salvation of his soul and of all his ancestors and heirs to do there whatever the monks wish. Pledge to warranty.* [Easter 1237].

Hiis testibus Rogero de Stapilt' tunc vic(ecomite) Ebor', Iordano Hayrun, Adam de Hiltona, Olyvero de Buscy, etc.

Pd: *EYC* IX, no. 88.

Dating: *EYC* dates this to between 1237 and 1238, because (i) the period of office of the first witness was 1236 until Michaelmas 1238, and (ii) the grant probably post-dated Thomas's grant of 1236 x 1237. Dated here by reference to no. 994.

998 *Confirmation, addressed to all the sons of holy mother church who will see or hear the present writing, by Thomas Fossard son of Thomas Fossard, to God and the monks of St Mary of Byland, of whatever right he had or could have by hereditary right in the region of Sutton (under Whitestonecliffe), Marderby, Felixkirk, Hood, Otterington and Laysthorpe, with all appurtenances and rights (as no. 997). To hold in free alms, quit of*

*all secular service except forinsec service due to the lord of the fee. Grant and
confirmation also of the lands and possessions which they have of the grant
of Thomas Fossard his father in Sutton, Marderby, Felixkirk, Hood,
Otterington and Laysthorpe, and quitclaim of all lands and possessions with
the wood of Sutton and all Gormire Lake and everything else which they
have of the grant of Baldwin de Paunton in Sutton and from others in the
said vills, to do there whatever they wish, according to the charters which
they have of Adam Fossard, grandfather of Thomas, Robert his uncle and
Thomas his father, as well as Baldwin de Paunton and all the other grantors.
Pledge to warranty as contained in their charters and in a chirograph made
in the king's court. Sealed with the donor's seal and those of the witnesses.*
[after 1237].

. . . cum sigillis testium subscriptorum . . . scilicet, domini abbatis de
Parco Lude, domini Ade de Hilton', domini Thome de Colevilla,
domini Alani de Lek, militum, etc.

Marginal note: In a later (post-Dissolution) hand is a genealogy showing the
descent from Adam Fossard, grandfather of Thomas, to Thomas son of Adam and
father of Thomas Fossard, to Thomas son of Thomas Fossard. Thomas had a
brother, Robert son of Thomas, who occurs in nos 816n, 1000, 1019, 1025, 1043.
Dating: probably on the grantor's succession to the tenancy.

[fol. 105v]

999   *Rubric: Chirograph made in the king's court between the monks and
Thomas Fossard concerning 18 bovates, 189 acres and others. It is in the
chest. It is annulled by the previous charter.* [Westminster; 27 Jan. 1237].
Text: MS Dodsworth 94, fols 19v–20v, no. 24; PRO CP 25/1/263/30,
no. 9. Final concord made at Westminster in the quindene of St Hilary
21 Henry III, in the presence of Robert of Lexington, Ralph of
Norwich, Adam Fitz William, William of Culworth, John de Kyrkeby,
and William de Sancto Edmundo, and other faithful men of the king
then present, between Abbot Henry, plaintiff, and Thomas Fossard,
defendant, concerning 18 bovates, 189 acres, 14 tofts and pasture for
260 sheep, 60 pigs, 20 cows, 1 bull, 20 oxen and 4 horses in Sutton and
Marderby, and the fishery of Gormire, which Thomas acknowledged
to be the right of the abbot and church of Byland as the grant of his
brother, Robert. Thomas moreover acknowledges that pasture for 60
sheep is the right of the abbot as his own grant. The abbot and
convent are to hold all the above, except for the 18 bovates, in free
alms, quit of all secular service. They are to hold the 18 bovates for
forinsec service to the chief lords of the fee. Pledge to warranty. In
return the abbot has received Thomas and his heirs into all the good
deeds and prayers of his church.

Pd: *Yorks. Fines 1232–1246*, p. 46 (from PRO copy).

1000 *Rubric: Chirograph made in the king's court between the monks and Robert Fossard concerning 2 bovates, 3 messuages in Sutton (under Whitestonecliffe) and 40 acres of woodland in* Gildusdale.   [York; 14 Jan. 1241].
Text: PRO CP 25/1/264/35, no. 4. Final concord made in the king's court at York on the morrow of St Hilary in the presence of Robert of Lexington, Ralph of Sudley, William of Culworth, Jollan de Neville, and Warner Engayne, justices, between Henry, abbot of Byland, plaintiff, and Robert Fossard, defendant, concerning 2 bovates and 3 messuages in Sutton and 40 acres of woodland in 'Gildusdale'. Robert acknowledged these, that is the woodland between the arable land of 'Gildusdale' and the pasture of Marderby, to be the right of the abbot and his church, of his own grant. Robert has also granted pasture in Sutton for 80 sheep, 6 cows, 6 mares, 6 sows and 60 she-goats with their issue up to three years, and 4 oxen. The abbot and convent are to hold the land in free alms. In return the abbot has received Robert and his heirs into all the good deeds of the church.
Pd: *Yorks. Fines 1232–1246*, pp. 94–5.

1001 *Rubric: Chirograph made in the king's court between Thomas Fossard and William, archdeacon of Durham. Surrendered.* [10 Sept. 1235].
Text: PRO CP 25/1/263/27, no. 18. Final concord made in the king's court at Beverley on the Mon. after the Nativity of the B. V. M. 19 Henry III, in the presence of Robert de Ros, William of York, Adam de Novo Mercato, and other faithful men of the lord king then present, between William, archdeacon of Durham, plaintiff, and Thomas Fossard, defendant, concerning 2 bovates and a mill in Sutton. Thomas acknowledged these to be the right of the archdeacon of his own grant, to hold of Thomas and his heirs for 1 pound of cumin yearly at St Felix (14 Jan.). For this the archdeacon gave 100s. sterling. The final concord was reached in the presence of Joan, formerly wife of Robert Fossard, who is to hold the mill as dower from the archdeacon for the term of her life, rendering yearly the 1 pound of cumin. After her death the mill is to revert to the archdeacon and his heirs.
Pd: *Yorks. Fines 1232–1246*, p. 41.

1002   Rubric: *Chirograph in the king's court between Robert Fossard and the Hospitallers concerning the advowson of the church of Felixkirk; surrendered.* [Lichfield; 1 Dec. 1210].
Text: PRO CP 25/1/261/12, no. 207. Final concord made in the king's court at Lichfield in the presence of the king, and of Simon of Pattishall, James of Poterne, Henry de Pont-Audemar, Robert de Aumar' and Roger de Huscart, justices, and other faithful men of the lord king then present, on the day after St Andrew, 12 John, between Brother Robert, prior of the Hospital of St John of Jerusalem in England through Brother Gilbert, and Robert Fossard concerning the advowson of the church of Felixkirk and 1 toft in the vill which was held by Christiana, formerly wife of Robert Hermit. Robert acknowledged the advowson and the toft to be the right of the prior and brethren of the Hospital, and they received him and his heirs into all the good deeds and prayers of their house.
Pd: *Yorks. Fines John*, p. 164.
Note: The document was noted in the cartulary because of the interest which Byland sought in the advowson of the church. In 1272 both Robert de Ver, prior of the Hospital of St John of Jerusalem in England, and the abbot and convent of Byland presented candidates to the living (*Reg. Giffard*, p. 46). In 1276 Archbishop Giffard declared that Conrad, whom both parties claimed to have presented, had been presented by the papal legate, Hugolinus (*ibid.*, p. 296). In 1279 Archbishop Giffard appropriated the church to the Knights Hospitaller and ordained a vicarage (*ibid.*, pp. 47–8). John de Craucumbe, Byland's nominee in 1272, was then rector, and Thomas of Cawood, vicar. See below, nos 1057, 1059.

1003   *Final concord made in the king's court in the presence of Robert of Lexington, Ralph of Sudley, William of Culworth, Jolland de Neville, Robert de Haya, Simon de Hales and Warner Engayne, itinerant justices, and other faithful men of the lord king then present, between Henry, abbot of Byland, plaintiff, and Thomas Fossard, defendant, concerning 1 knight's fee in Sutton (under Whitestonecliffe), Marderby, Hood, Laysthorpe and Felixkirk about which a plea of warranty was brought. Thomas acknowledges the knight's fee to be the right of the abbot and his church of the grant of Thomas himself, to hold of Thomas and his heirs in free alms for the service due to the chief lord of the fee. Pledge to warranty. The abbot has received Thomas and his heirs in all the good deeds and prayers offered in the church of Byland.*
York; one month from St John the Baptist 24 Henry III [22 July 1240].
Marginal note: (in later hand) '24 H 3'.
Copy: PRO CP 25/1/264/34, no. 174.
Pd (calendar): *Yorks. Fines 1232–1246*, p. 83 (from PRO copy).

1004 *Final concord levied in the king's court in the presence of Robert of Lexington, William of York, William of Culworth, Henry of Bath, justices, and other faithful men of the lord king then present, between Hugh Wake and Joan his wife, plaintiffs, through Joan's attorney, William de Mortuo Mari, and Henry, abbot of Byland, defendant through Brother Robert de Pavely, his monk and attorney concerning 1 knight's fee in Sutton (under Whitestonecliffe), Marderby, Hood, Laysthorpe and Felixkirk about which a plea had been brought. Hugh and Joan acknowledge the knight's fee as the right of the abbot and his church, to hold of them and Joan's heirs in free alms, rendering 60s., half at St Martin (11 Nov.) and half at Whitsuntide, and the service due from 1 knight's fee. Pledge by Hugh and Joan and Joan's heirs to make no further claim to suit of court nor to aid for making a son a knight nor for the marriage of a daughter, nor any other service except scutage. Licence to distrain on the chattels throughout their fee – but not the sheep of the abbot – should the abbot or his successors fail to pay the rent. If no chattels are found they may distrain on the sheep to the value of the rent. For this the abbot has given Hugh and Joan [40] silver marks.* St Bride's, London; quindene of Trinity 23 Henry III [5 June 1239].

Marginal note: (in later hand) '23 H 3'.

Copy: PRO CP 25/1/263/30, no. 31.

Pd (calendar): *Yorks. Fines 1232–1246*, p. 53 (from PRO copy). The amount of the payment, which is not readable in the manuscript, is supplied from this copy.

Note: Henry of Bath joined the King's Bench in 1238; he became chief justice at Westminster in 1245 and chief justice *coram rege* in 1249: Turner, *English Judiciary*, p. 193.

1005 *Rubric: Chirograph made in the king's court between the monks and Peter de Brus concerning ½ knight's fee in Otterington. Look there.*

Note: The text is entered in the cartulary at no. 841 above.

1006 *Rubric: Transcript of Mary wife of Peter de Richemund concerning half of 14 acres at* Roseheved.

1007 *Rubric: Charter of Mary of the charter [sic] of Adam de Brus which s/he made to Geoffrey Fossard of Otterington. Look under Otterington.*

Note: The sense of this rubric is unclear. Geoffrey Fossard, who was enfeoffed of lands in Sutton by Robert de Stuteville before 1166 (no. 995 above), also held land in South Otterington of Adam de Brus (no. 840 above).

1008 *Rubric: Quitclaim of the same [?Mary] of 2 acres in Sutton in the* cultura *of* Northanriddynges.

[fol. 106r, old fol. 212r]

1009 *Rubric: Charter of Geoffrey of Thirsk and Petronilla his wife concerning 4 acres in Sutton.* [*c.* 1250].

Dating: Geoffrey and Petronilla, and the monks of Byland, were parties to a final concord of 1252 (no. 1011 below).

1010 *Rubric: Quitclaim by Petronilla daughter of Peter de Rich<emund> of a third part of 2 bovates in Sutton.* [*c.* 1250].

Dating: as no. 1009.

1011 *Rubric: Chirograph in the king's court between the monks and the said G(eoffrey) and P(etronilla) concerning 7 acres and 1 acre of meadow in Sutton.* [York; 14 Jan. 1252].

Text: PRO CP 25/1/265/45, no. 123. Final concord made in the king's court at York on the morrow of St Hilary, 36 Henry III, in the presence of Silvester, bishop of Carlisle, Roger of Thirkleby, Hugh, abbot of Selby, Gilbert de Preston, and Adam de Hilton, justices, and other faithful men of the lord king then present, between Henry, abbot of Byland, and Geoffrey of Thirsk and Petronilla his wife, concerning 7 acres and 1 acre of meadow with its appurtenances in Sutton. Geoffrey and Petronilla acknowledge this to be the right of the abbot and church of their own grant, to hold of them and the heirs of Petronilla. The abbot has received them into the benefits of his house.

Pd: *Yorks. Fines 1246–1272*, p. 54.

1012 *Rubric: Charter of Christiana of Thirsk, daughter of Peter de Rich(emund) concerning 1 bovate in Sutton.*

1013 *Rubric: Charters of Constance and Christiana daughters of Peter de Rich(emund) concerning 2 acres in* Northmanriddyng *in the region of Sutton.*

1014 *Rubric: Confirmation of Petronilla of Thirsk of all the grants made by Mary her mother and Constance and Christiana her sisters, and G(eoffrey) her husband.*

1015 *Rubric: Charter of Philip son of Philip of Sutton of 2 bovates in the same. Copied.* [*c.* 1240].

Dating: by reference to the final concord of 1240 (no. 1016 below).

1016 *Rubric: Chirograph in the king's court between the monks and the said Philip [son of Philip] concerning the same.* York; quindene of St John the Baptist [8 July] 24 Henry III [1240].
Text: PRO CP 25/1/263/31, no. 12. Final concord, made in the king's court at York, in the presence of Robert of Lexington, Ralph of Sudley, William of Culworth, Jollan de Neville, Robert de Haye, Simon de Hales, and Warner Engayne, and other faithful men of the lord king then present, between Abbot Henry of Byland, plaintiff, and Philip son of Philip, defendant, concerning 2 bovates of land in Sutton. Philip acknowledged these to be of the right of the abbot by his own grant. The abbot has granted the whole to Philip to hold of him and his successors for 3s. yearly, at St Martin (11 Nov.) and Whitsuntide. The land is to revert to the abbot and convent on Philip's death.
Pd: *Yorks. Fines 1232–1246*, p. 68.

1017 *Rubric: Charter of Adam Fossard, surrendered, concerning ½ carucate in* Gildousdale *with woodland within specified bounds.* [before 1208].
Dating: Adam Fossard had been succeeded by his son, Robert, by 1208.

1018 *Rubric: Charter of Bernard de Areyns and Helen his wife, daughter of Geoffrey de Coigners, concerning ½ carucate in Sutton.* [1240].
Text: MS Dodsworth 91, fols 124v–125r, no. 86. Notification, addressed to all the faithful in Christ present and future, by Bernard de Arayns, with the consent of Helen his wife, of his demise to Abbot Henry of Byland and the convent, of ½ carucate in Sutton under Whitestonecliffe with all its appurtenances, liberties and easements inside and outside the vill, for 12 years from St Martin 1240, that is the ½ carucate to which Bernard and Helen established by assize title of Lady Elizabeth Conyers, formerly wife of William de Rue in the presence of itinerant justices at York. Pledge to warranty, and if they are unable to warranty the land they will give an exchange in Hayfield in Holderness until they can warranty the land in Sutton. At the end of 12 years the land is to revert completely to Bernard and Helen. For this the abbot and convent have given 16 silver marks. Hiis testibus domino Iordano Hairiam, Thoma de Colevyll, magistro Petro de Croft, Waltero Hairun filio Iordani Hayrun, magistro Waltero de Banebyrie, Roberto de Auford, Willelmo Arundell, Henrico Dyve, Gamello forestario de Baggeby at aliis.
Note: Geoffrey de Conyers was party to a court case in 1213: *EYC* V, 274.

1019 *Rubric: Charter of Robert Fossard concerning the same. Surrendered.*

Note: In the margin there is a genealogy, in a later hand, showing the descent from Adam Fossard to Thomas son of Adam, 21 H 3, to Robert son of Thomas and Thomas son of Thomas.

1020 *Rubric: Charter of Bernard Areyns concerning ½ carucate in* Gildusdale *with woodland and other appurtenances.* [mid 13th cent.].

Dating: For a charter of Bernard see no. 1018 above.

1021 *Rubric: Bond by the same [Bernard Areyns] to make a chirograph concerning the same.* [*c.* 1248].

Dating: This relates to no. 1022.

1022 *Rubric: Chirograph made in the king's court between the monks and the said Bernard [Areyns] concerning ½ carucate in* Gildusdale. *Reading; quindene of St John the Baptist [8 July] 32 Henry III [1248].*

Text: PRO CP 25/1/264/41, no. 21. Final concord made in the king's court at Reading on the quindene of St John the Baptist, in the presence of Roger of Thirkleby, Gilbert de Preston, master Simon de Wauton, John of Cobham, and other faithful men of the lord king then present, between Abbot Henry of Byland by Brother Adam his monk and attorney, plaintiff, and Bernard of Areynes, defendant, concerning ½ carucate in 'Gildusdale'. Bernard acknowledged this as the right of the abbot and his church, and has restored it to them, to hold of Bernard and his heirs in free alms quit of all secular service. In return the abbot has received Bernard and his heirs into all the good deeds of the house.

Pd: *Yorks. Fines 1246–1272*, p. 7.

Note: In the margin of the cartulary, opposite nos 1021–22, in a later hand, is a genealogy showing Elena as the daughter of Galfridus de Coigners and the wife of Bernhardus de Areyns.

1023 *Rubric: Quitclaim by Thomas son of Bernard of the same.*

1024 *Rubric: Charter, surrendered, of Thomas son of Adam Fossard concerning 2 messuages with crofts and 2 bovates and woodland in* Gildusdale. [before 1237].

1025 *Rubric: Charter of Robert son of Thomas Fossard of the same 2 messuages with crofts and 2 bovates and the woodland of* Gildusdale.

1026 *Rubric: Transcript of our charter of Byland which the vicars of York have concerning the said ½ carucate in free alms.* [1241 x 1243–4].

Text: This is to be identified as *Chs Vicars Choral*, II, no. 113 (where printed from the original charter, York Minster Library VC3/Vv89), a grant by Abbot Henry of Byland, at the request of William de Laneham, archdeacon of Durham (see no. 1001) to the vicars choral of York, of ½ carucate in 'Gildusdale' in Sutton, with all the liberties etc. contained in the charter of the archdeacon, which the vicars have.

I am grateful to Dr Nigel Tringham for this reference.

Dating: As *Chs Vicars Choral*.

1027 *Rubric: Charter of John of Danthorpe and Elizabeth Conyers his wife concerning 1 toft and ½ carucate in* Gildusdale. [1239 x 1241].

Text: MS Dodsworth 91, fol. 82r–v, no. 23. Notification addressed to all present and future by John of Danthorpe of his grant and confirmation, for the salvation of his soul and of all his ancestors and heirs, to God and St Mary and the abbot and convent of Byland, of ½ carucate in 'Gildusdale' which he has of the grant of Elizabeth Conyers his wife, formerly wife of William Ruthe, to hold of him and his heirs free of service, with all appurtenances, liberties and easements. Further grant of a toft in Sutton which he had of the same Elizabeth, which toft lies between the spring and the chapel of the vill, to hold with all the appurtenances, liberties and easements belonging to the toft, inside and outside the vill of Sutton. Pledge to warranty, and if he cannot warranty he will give an exchange. Sealed with his seal. Hiis testibus domino Willelmo de Midelton tunc vicecomite Ebor', Rogero de Stapelton', Ada de Hilton, Olivero de Buscy, Marmeduco Darel, Roberto persona de Kilvington tunc decano de Bulmer, Thoma de Siltona, Willelmo Arundel, Gamello forestario de Baggeby, Henrico de Karletona, Roberto de Buggedene, Philippo filio Philippi de Suttona, Thoma clerico de eadem villa, domino Honorio tunc priore et toto capitulo de Bellalanda, Andrea de Killebrune et aliis multis.

Dating: The tenure of William de Middleton as undersheriff to Nicholas de Molis, sheriff: *Lord Lieutenants*, p. 57.

Note: For a final concord between the monks and John of Danthorpe, see no. 1030 below. There is another version of no. 1027, with the witnesses in a different order, in MS Top. Yorks. e. 9, fol. 56r (old p. 85), continued on fol. 89v (old p. 152).

1028 *Rubric: Charter of Geoffrey Conyers concerning all his land in* Gildusdale *in woodland and meadow; surrendered.* [before 1208].

Dating: Adam Fossard, who issued a charter concerning the same land (no. 1029) was dead by 1208.

1029 *Rubric: Charter of Adam Fossard concerning the same; surrendered.* [before 1208].

1030 *Rubric: Chirograph made in the king's court between the monks and John of Danthorpe concerning ½ carucate in* Gildusdale. [c. 1241].
Dating: This refers to the final concord reached in the king's court in York on 20 Jan. 1241 between Abbot Henry, plaintiff, and John of Danthorpe and Elizabeth his wife, defendants, concerning ½ carucate in Gildusdale and a messuage in Sutton. It was recognized as the right of the abbot of the grant of John and Elizabeth, to hold of them in free alms. For this the abbot gave 40 silver marks. *Yorks. Fines 1232–1246*, p. 103, from PRO CP 25/1/264/36, no. 46. For a charter issued by John and Elizabeth see no. 1027 above.

1031 *Rubric: Quitclaim by William son of the said Elizabeth [Conyers] of the same ½ carucate of land in* Gildusdale.

1032 *Rubric: Charter of Thomas Fossard concerning a knight's fee in Otterington, with the advowson of the church. Look under Otterington.*
Note: There is no charter such as this copied into the Otterington section of the cartulary.

1033 *Rubric: Chirograph made in the county court of York between Adam Fossard and Philip son of Robert concerning a carucate in* Gildusdale. *Surrendered.*

1034 *Rubric: Charter of the master of* Lanum *concerning 4 bovates, 1 toft and croft and 11 acres in various places and concerning the mill of Sutton.*
Marginal note: B(aculus) ii.

1035 *Rubric: Charter of William son of Gamel concerning 2 bovates and various acres contained within them.*

1036 *Rubric: Charter of Robert of Myton and Constance his wife concerning 2 acres and ½ rood.*

1037 *Rubric: Charter of Reginald son of Adam of Islebeck concerning 1 acre.*

1038 *Grant, addressed to all the faithful in Christ who will see or hear this writing, by Abbot Henry and the convent of Byland to Roger son of Robert of*

Stretton that all his animals and those of his heirs and assigns except for pigs may have common pasturage in their park of Sutton. This park shall be fenced in from the beginning of April until the hay is brought in. If the animals and flocks of the abbot and convent enter the park before the hay is brought in <they shall allow> Roger and his heirs to have their animals there. Roger has quitclaimed for himself and his heirs all right he had in the said park. In the form of a chirograph, sealed with the seals of both parties. [mid 13th cent.].

Hiis testibus domino Waltero tunc priore de Bell', Henrico suppriore, Willelmo cellerario, Ada socio suo, etc.

Dating: The recipient witnessed a charter relating to 'Gildusdale' of date 1241 x 1243–4; see *Chs Vicars Choral*, II, no. 113 (no. 1026 above). By charter of the same date he received a carucate in 'Gildusdale' from the Vicars Choral of York (*ibid.*, no. 114). For the witnesses see also no. 155 above.

[fol. 106v]

1039 *Rubric: Quitclaim by Thomas <son> of the said Roger of Stretton of 2d. annual rent which John was accustomed to pay him.*

1040 *Rubric: Charter of Roger of Stretton in the form of a chirograph concerning common for his animals cultivating his land in Sutton and concerning a certain road.*

1041 *Rubric: Transcript of certain charters concerning lands which Roger of Stretton held of the abbot and convent in Sutton.*

1042 *Rubric: Charter of Hugh son of Robert of Sutton concerning 6 acres in the same.* [before 1227].

Text: MS Top. Yorks. e. 8, fol. 107r–v (old pp. 178–9). Grant in free alms, addressed to all the faithful in Christ present and future, by Hugh son of Robert of Sutton, for the salvation of his soul and of all his ancestors, to God and the monks of St Mary of Byland, of 6 acres in the region of Linton, as contained in the charter of Robert Fossard his lord (no. 1043), which he has given back to the monks with the present charter. Hiis testibus Ada de Bouteby, Roberto Fossard filio Gaufrido Fossard, Stephano de Meinill de Turkilby, Stephano de Blabi, Roberto de Auford, Roberto de Kereby, Simon de Marterby, Philippo filio Philippi de Sutton.

Dating: Robert son of Adam Fossard was dead by 1227. The second witness is probably Robert son of Geoffrey Fossard of South Otterington, who attests before 1223 and 1227 (see above, nos 606–8).

1043   *Rubric: Charter of Robert Fossard concerning the same; surrendered.*

1044   *Rubric: Charter in the form of a chirograph of Baldwin de Paunton concerning all the lands which he had in Sutton* super Southlitilclif *and other small portions in various places.* [1237 x 1238].
Text: MS Dodsworth 91, fols 109r–110r, no. 63. Notification to all present and future by Baldwin de Paunton of his quitclaim to the abbot and convent of Byland of all lands which he held of Thomas Fossard in Sutton on 'Suthlittelcliffe' and 'North Littel Cliffe' with woodland and meadow belonging to it, and its possessions, for homage and service, that is, all the land in Sutton with meadow called 'Megelingsty', the assart called 'Butterdalebanc' and ½ acre below 'Hertelaibes' and 1 rood at 'Blacscith' and the lake called Gormire, and of all the wood of Sutton with the land on the boundaries of Ravensthorpe to 'Butterdale' and from there to the foot of 'Aldegormiregate', and from there to the moor of 'Blakehow' towards the south and from 'Blakehow' moor to the arable land of Sutton. Quitclaim also of half the land which belonged to Thomas Fossard in 'Blakehow' moor towards the north; of 3½ bovates in Sutton which Joan, formerly wife of Robert Fossard, held as her dower, of which Philip son of Philip, William Pinchun and Adam son of Robert held 1 bovate each and Thomas the cleric ½ virgate; of 7½ tofts which Joan held in dower, held by William, Geoffrey, Elias of Kirkby, Gunna wife of . . ., Ivetta Lotrix, Reginald son of Emma, Matilda Lotrix and Alan son of Gunhild; of a ½ *cultura* called 'Wethelande' which Joan held in dower towards the west; of a ½ *cultura* called 'William Enges'; of ½ Stocking towards the west; of another ½ *cultura* which Joan held in dower; and of other parcels of land. The abbot and convent are to hold these for forinsec service, as laid out in the charter of Thomas Fossard, which he has surrendered to the monks. Testibus Rogero de Stapleton' tunc vicecomite Ebor', Ada de Hilton, Olivero de Buscy, Thoma de Colevill, Roberto persona de Kilvington, Stephano de [blank], Radulfo de [blank], Thoma de Sylton, Roberto de Auford, Henrico Dive, Eudone de Colevill, Willelmo Arundell, Willelmo de Carleton, Henrico de [blank], R. Buggedon et aliis. Sketch of seal.
Dating: after the death of Robert Fossard, and tenure of first witness as under sheriff of Yorkshire (1236–1238).

1045   *Rubric: Charter of Thomas Fossard concerning the same; surrendered.*

1046 *Rubric: Confirmation by Thomas Fossard of the grant of Baldwin de Paunton.* [early to mid 13th cent., probably 1237 x 1238].

Dating: probably as no. 1044.

Note: A final concord was made at York on 8 July 1240 between Abbot Henry, plaintiff, and William Arundel and Joan his wife, defendants, concerning 7 bovates and a messuage in Sutton held by Joan as dower of the freehold of her first husband, Robert Fossard. The abbot granted all this land to Joan, that is, 3½ bovates which the monks have of Baldwin de Paunton and 3½ of the grant of Thomas Fossard, to hold of the abbot and convent in the name of dower for 1 pound of cumin yearly. The land is to revert to the abbot and convent on Joan's death. See *Yorks. Fines 1232–1246*, p. 72, from PRO CP 25/1/264/34, no. 157.

1047 *Rubric: Confirmation and quitclaim by Hugh Wake and Joan his wife of all the grants of Thomas Fossard, rendering to them 60s. yearly.* [before 1241].

Text: MS Dodsworth 91, fols 100v–101r, no. 49. Confirmation, addressed to all the sons of holy mother church present and future, by Hugh Wake and Joan his wife, to God and St Mary of Byland and the monks serving God there, of all the grants which the monks have of the fee of Thomas Fossard in Sutton, with the capital messuage of the vill, and lands in Marderby, Laysthorpe, Felixkirk, and Hood, with all easements, liberties and appurtenances, to hold rendering 60s. yearly, 30s. at St Martin and 30s. at Whitsuntide, and scutage pertaining to 1 knight's fee. Hiis testibus Ricardo Duket, Walrano de Mortimer, Rogero de Stapeltona, Ada de Hiltona, Richardo de Saltfletby, Nicholao persona de Hettona, Hanneray de Brunne, Galfrido de Depehinges, magistro Iohanne de Sutteby, Nicholao de Dundeburc, Roberto de Stokisley, monachis de Bellalanda, et aliis. Sketch of two seals.

Pd: *Mon. Ang.* V, 347, no. IV.

Dating: death of Hugh Wake; see above, notes to no. 626.

Note: The seventh witness may be Alvered de Bruny of no. 1048.

1048 *Rubric: Chirograph between the monks and the same [Hugh and Joan Wake] concerning the same.* [before 1241].

Text: MS Dodsworth 94, fol. 19r, no. 22. Agreement between Hugh Wake and Joan de Stuteville his wife, and the abbot and convent by which Hugh and Joan quitclaim whatever right they had in Sutton, Marderby, Laysthorpe, Hood and Felixkirk saving to themselves scutage on 1 knight's fee. The abbot and convent are to pay 60s. annually, half at St Martin and half at Whitsuntide. Pledge to warranty. Sealed. Hiis testibus domino Nicholao tunc temporis abbate de Valle Dei, Ricardo Duket, Walranno de Mortemer, Rogero de Stapletone,

Ada de Hilton, Ricardo de Saufleteby, Nicholao et Roberto monachis de Bellaland', Nichola persona de Eton, Alveredo de Bruny, Galfrido de Depinge, magistro Iohanne de Sauteby, Willelmo de Karleton, Radulfo de Lech, Roberto de Auford, Henrico Dive, Willelmo Arundell.

Dating: at the same time as no. 1047. Nicholas, abbot of Vaudey, occurs on 16 Feb. 1227 though to 1238, and his successor, Godfrey, is first recorded in 1245 (*HRH* II, 319).

Note: The remainder of the rubric, *conliguntur*, probably means that 1047 and 1048 were bound together.

1049 *Quitclaim, addressed to all the faithful in Christ who will see or hear this writing, by Joan Wake in her widowhood and lawful power, to God and St Mary and the abbot and convent of Byland, of that annual rent of 60s. which the monks were accustomed to render for warranty of lands which they have of her fee in Sutton, Marderby, Hood, Laysthorpe, and Felixkirk under the terms of a chirograph made between them in the king's court (no. 1048). This grant is made for her and her heirs in free alms in order to support one monk whom she and her heirs will present in turn and who will celebrate for the soul of Hugh Wake her former husband and for the salvation of her own soul and of her father and mother and all her ancestors and heirs and for the souls of all the faithful dead notwithstanding the chirograph of the royal court between Hugh and Joan and Byland. Pledge to warranty. Sealed with the donor's seal. [after 1241].*

Hiis testibus domino Willelmo Ha . . . tunc seneschallo, domino Baldwino de Bruyncong', domino Willelmo de Sutton', domino Roberto capellano, Radulfo de Bruyncort, etc.

Dating: Death of Hugh Wake.

1050 *Rubric: Confirmation by Baldwin Wake of all the lands which the monks have of the lords Fossard. Look under the heading of the magnates.*

Note: This is copied into the cartulary at no. 674 above.

1051 *Rubric: Quitclaim by Thomas Fossard of all his demesne in Hood.*

1052 *Rubric: Charter of Robert Fossard concerning common below Whitestone Cliff; surrendered.*

1053 *Grant and confirmation, addressed to all the sons of holy mother church present and future, by Thomas Fossard son of Adam Fossard, to God and the monks of St Mary of Byland, of common pasture throughout the whole region of Sutton (under Whitestonecliffe) in order to increase the* *pasture which Robert Fossard his brother granted them for 260 sheep. They may have in that pasture 300 sheep by the long hundred. Grant and confirmation also of his sheepfold in the same pasture of Sutton, with adjacent meadow, with permission to use the pasture as they wish, according to the chirograph made in the king's court between his brother, Robert Fossard, and his heirs, on the one part and the knights of the Temple on the other. This grant is made for the salvation of his soul and of all his ancestors and heirs and for a certain sum of money which the monks have given him in his great need. Pledge to warranty.* Sutton under Whitestonecliffe; 1225.

Hiis testibus Olyvero de Buscy, Stephano del Meynill de Thurk', Hugone de Magneby, Henrico de Siltona, etc.

Note: There is a catchword, in the cartulary hand, at the foot of fol. 106v. Stephen de Meinill of Thirkleby, son of Gilbert, granted and quitclaimed lands in Osgoodby (nos 761–2, 787, 816, 827, 837).

[fol. 107r, old fol. 213]
1054   *Rubric: Agreement with the vicar of Felixkirk concerning the tithes of the mill of Sutton. Not to be paid into the hands of the monks.*

1055   *Peace agreement between Geoffrey, vicar of Felixkirk, on one part, and the men of the abbot and convent of Byland in Sutton and Marderby on the other, concerning the dispute between them heard in the presence of Master John de Langton, archdeacon of York, papal judge delegate, concerning the tithe of hens. The men have conceded for themselves and their heirs that they will give annually at Christmas 1 hen or 1 penny from any house which has a garden and from which smoke escapes, to the said Geoffrey and the vicars who succeed him in the church. For this Geoffrey has quitclaimed to the men, as far as his rights allow, all the tithes of eggs and chickens and produce of the hens and the produce of the garden, saving for himself and the vicars who succeed him the tithes of hemp and beans and corn. Sealed with the seal of the vicar and that of the abbot of Byland on behalf of the men and of the judge.* [1246 x 1262].

Dating: John de Langeton is first recorded as a canon of York in 1241; he held the prebend of Stillington. He occurs as archdeacon of Cleveland in 1246 x 49 and 1249, and appears to have held the office of archdeacon of York very briefly in 1262 (*Fasti York*, pp. 35, 39, 98). It is possible that the reference to him as archdeacon of York is to his tenure of an archdeaconry in the church of York, that is, the archdeaconry of Cleveland.

Note: On 26 Apr. 1225 the archbishop gave licence to Geoffrey, vicar of Felixkirk, to lease his vicarage for three years while he went to the Holy Land (*Reg. Gray*, p. 4). On 30 May 1233 the archbishop instituted Reginald de Suers, clerk, at the presentation of the prior and brethren of the hospital of St John of Jerusalem, to the church of Felixkirk, reserving for Geoffrey his vicarage, that is the whole church, from which he paid Reginald an annual pension of 30 marks (*ibid.*, p. 60). Geoffrey was still vicar in 1251 (see no. 1056). If this is the same Geoffrey then his tenure of the living was a long one. For the appropriation of Felixkirk to the Knights Hospitaller, and the ordination of a vicarage (1279), by Archbishop Giffard, see above, no. 1002n. The then rector, John de Craucumbe, who had been presented by the abbot and convent of Byland, received an annual sum of 40s. The vicar is named as Thomas of Cawood, but he is unlikely to be the same Thomas of Cawood, vicar in 1332 (no. 1059).

1056   *Memorandum that a controversy was brought before Dom. Walter, archbishop of York, between Abbot H(enry) of Byland and the convent on the one part, and Dom. Geoffrey of Husthwaite, chaplain, vicar of the church of Felixkirk, concerning a chantry chapel in Sutton. After many arguments between the two parties an agreement was reached. The abbot and convent granted Geoffrey for his lifetime 4 bovates in the region of Marderby with 4 tofts in the same vill, with meadow, which Robert the cleric, Robert the carter, and Adam Handson hold. Geoffrey is to find a chaplain – either himself or another – to celebrate mass in the said chapel for 3 days each week, on Monday, Tuesday and Friday, and on the Nativity of the B. V. M., the Purification, the Assumption, Christmas and Easter. In the form of a chirograph, sealed with the seals of both parties.* Bishopthorpe; the day after St Nicholas [7 Dec.], 1251.

Note: For occurrences of Geoffrey, vicar of Felixkirk, see no. 31 and no. 1055.

[fol. 107r–v]

1057   *Memorandum that there was brought in the presence of the official of the court of York the controversy which had arisen between the vicar of Felixkirk and the abbot and convent of Byland concerning certain matters relating to the chapel of Sutton, dependent on the church of Felixkirk. The parties, that is the vicar through Edmund his brother and attorney, and the abbot and prior through Robert de Baumburg, their attorney, submitted to judgement, that is, that four bovates of land, which time out of mind had been set aside to support a chaplain to celebrate for 3 days a week each year, and granted to the church of Felixkirk, should remain the property of the current vicar and his successors without contradiction, reserving for the official the right to compel the vicar to provide the said service.* York; 10 Jan. 1290 [1291].

1058   *Rubric: 2 writs of the king concerning the same 4 messuages, 4 bovates with their appurtenances in Marderby. Look in the Marderby bundle.*

Note: There are no writs copied into the Marderby section of the cartulary.

1059 *Indenture made at the termination of the dispute between John de Myton, abbot, and the convent of Byland on the one part, and Thomas of Cawood, perpetual vicar of Felixkirk, on the other, concerning 4 messuages, 4 bovates, and 1½ acres of meadow with their appurtenances in Marderby, about which a plea had been instituted in the king's court at Westminster in the presence of William de Herle and his fellow justices of the king's bench between the said abbot, plaintiff, and Thomas the vicar, defendant, by a writ of entry. The abbot and convent have granted and quitclaimed to Thomas of Cawood all right which they have or might have in the said messuages and lands. Thomas and his successors are to have and hold the land free from secular service for the provision of a chantry in the chapel of Sutton under Whitestonecliffe, as their predecessors did. Pledge to make no further claims in the land. Sealed with the seal of both parties. The part of the indenture remaining in Thomas's hands is sealed with the seal of the abbot and convent, and that remaining with Byland is sealed with Thomas's seal.* Byland; Tues. after St Matthew [22 Sept]. 1332.

Hiis testibus dominis Nicholao Cantilupe, [Willelmo Malbys], Iohanne de Colvill, militibus, Iohanne de Kylvyngton', Willelmo Wysebarne de Baxby, Marmeduco [Darell, Ricardo de] Estwra, Iohanne de Multona et aliis.

Pd: *Reg. Melton*, II, 157–8, no. 418, from BI Reg. 9 (Reg. Melton), fol. 257v, new fol. 310v. The lacunae in the witness list are supplied from this copy.

1060 *Rubric: Chirograph in the abbey court at Sutton by Hugh Fossard concerning 1 bovate in Sutton rendering 6s. yearly. Surrendered.*

1061 *Rubric: Quitclaim by Roger of Smeaton and Matilda his wife of the said 6s.*

1062 *Rubric: Chirograph made in the king's court between Robert Fossard and the Templars concerning all the pasture between the highway which stretches towards Cleveland and the brow of the cliff towards the boundaries of Kilburn, rendering 10s. to Robert Fossard. Surrendered.*

1063 *Rubric: Confirmation of Thomas Fossard concerning the same. Surrendered.*

1064 *Rubric: Charter of the canons of Newburgh, in the form of a chirograph, concerning raising a <millpond> as is necessary.*
Marginal note: B(aculus) iii.

1065   Rubric: Chirograph charter of the same [canons] concerning a certain park, and licence to strengthen 2 mill ponds. Look under the heading of Hood.

Note: The text is copied into the cartulary at no. 382 above.

[fols 107v–108r]

1066   Grant and confirmation, addressed to all the faithful in Christ who will see or hear the present <writing>, by Abbot Adam of Byland, to Robert of Foxholes of 2 bovates and 2 acres with their appurtenances which Peter Buterys held, near to the park of Hood, with a toft and its adjacent croft. To hold freely, with pasture, housebote and haybote, and sufficient wood to burn and build, and with all the appurtenances of the toft and croft, 2 bovates and 2 acres, rendering to the abbot and his successors 1 silver mark, ½ mark at Whitsuntide and ½ mark at St Martin in Winter (11 Nov.). Robert and his heirs are to make suit of court 3 times a year at Sutton at the next court after St Michael, and the next court after Christmas and at the next court after Easter. He shall also attend when itinerant justices are present at common pleas at Sutton. If he and his heirs fail to make suit of court at the appointed time, the abbot and convent may distrain on the toft and croft, 2 bovates and 2 acres and on their goods there. Pledge to warranty. Sealed with the seals of both parties. [before 1271].

Hiis testibus domino Ricardo de Malebys, Iohanne de Blaby, Thoma de Etton', Radulfo de Leke, Iohanne Maunsell, Thoma Maunsell in Hetona, etc.

Marginal note: The copyist has omitted the words 'our chirograph' between 'carta' and 'confirmavi', and written them in the margin, indicating their position in the text with a caret.

Dating: In 1271 Henry III ordered that his justices should hear pleas at the abbot's manor of Clifton rather than Sutton (above, no. 529).

Note: In 1284/5 Thomas Mansell held land in Hutton Sessay of John Mansell, who in turn held of Richard Malebisse (KI, p. 95). John and Thomas attest a charter of 1273: Chs Vicars Choral, II, no. 116.

[fol. 108r]

1067   Rubric: Chirograph between the monks and Robert of Foxholes concerning 2 tofts and 1 croft in Sutton, rendering yearly to the monks 3s. 8d.

1068   Friendly agreement reached on the Tues. before St Michael between the abbot and convent of Byland on the one part and Richard Malebisse on the other concerning all the disputes which had arisen between them, at York in the presence of John de Vaux and his fellow justices and before the official of York. *The abbot and convent have granted to Richard 4 acres of meadow in the region of Sutton under Whitestonecliffe in a certain meadow called the new park on the eastern side, lying towards the wood of Balk, to hold in peace and to enclose as Richard wishes from the time when other meadows there are enclosed until the hay is brought in. Grant also of a watercourse flowing towards Richard's mill in Scawton through the middle of the abbot and convent's meadow in Old Byland below Reins. The watercourse shall flow unimpeded by the abbot and convent and shall be 4 feet in width. Richard and his heirs may strengthen the water course on his own land in the open season as often as is necessary. For this Richard has granted licence to repair the millpond in Sutton and to enclose meadow in* Walkerheng *in Sutton with a hedge and ditch as they wish, saving to Richard and his heirs common pasture in the open season. Sealed with the seal of both parties.* York; Tues. before St Michael [24 Sept.] 1280.

Note: A rubric is given at no. 385 above. Reins Farm and Reins Wood lie just to the south of Old Byland.

[fol. 108v]

1069 *Notification to all present and future by Thomas Fossard son of Adam Fossard of his grant in free alms to God and the abbot and convent of Byland, of the homage and service of Geoffrey Fossard son of Robert Fossard on 1 carucate in Sutton (under Whitestonecliffe) and of 1 knight's fee in Otterington with the advowson of the church. The grant is made for the salvation of the donor's soul and of all his ancestors and heirs. Pledge to warranty.* [before 1237].

Hiis testibus domino Iordano Hayrum', Ada de Hiltona, Olyvero de Buscy, Thoma de Colevill, etc.

Dating: death of the grantor.
Note: A younger branch of the Fossard family held an undertenancy in South Otterington of the Fossards of Sutton. See *EYC* IX, 153.

1070 *Rubric: Chirograph charter of William son of Gamel concerning 2 bovates with toft and croft and 3 acres and 6 roods, rendering 4s. 2½d.*

1071 *Rubric: Chirograph charter of Stephen of Carlton concerning 1 toft in Sutton (under Whitestonecliffe) and 2 bovates, rendering 25s. yearly.*

1072 *Rubric: Quitclaim by the same Stephen [of Carlton] of the same.*

1073 *Rubric: Agreement between the monks and Richard Malebisse concerning the raising of the millpond in Sutton and concerning the boundaries between Cam and Sutton.*

1074 *Rubric: Quitclaim by the Templars of a close in* Whitstancote. *See above, Cold Kirby.*

1075 *Rubric: Enrolment of a plea concerning a new enclosure at* Whitstancote.

[fol. 109r, old fol. 215r]

SNILESWORTH (SE5296), in the parish of Hawnby and the wapentake of Birdforth (NR). Snilesworth Moor lies to the east of the River Rye, between Bilsdale Moor to the east, Whorlton Moor to the north, and Arden Great Moor to the south. In 1166 Hugh Malebisse held one knight's fee of Roger de Mowbray, which included lands in Dale Town, Murton and Snilesworth. His family's grants to Byland in Murton are included in the cartulary at nos 578–92; nos 1076–78 indicate that they were also responsible for the earliest grants in Snilesworth. The abbey lands on Snilesworth Moor bordered on Whorlton Moor, held by the family of Meinill of Whorlton. Robert de Meinill III, son of Robert II and Joan de Ros, died in 1207, leaving a young son, Stephen III, who was in the custody of Robert de Turnham, and who came of age between 1224 and 1226. A perambulation of the boundaries between Whorlton and Snilesworth took place in 1207, after the death of Robert III (no. 1080). The boundaries were still an issue after the coming of age of Stephen III (nos 1079, 1081, 1084) and in 1230 Stephen quitclaimed land within specified bounds (no. 1087). Stephen III died before 16 July 1269, and was succeeded by his second son, Nicholas, who became Lord Meinill shortly before his death in May 1299. His son, Nicholas II Lord Meinill, died in 1322 and was succeeded by his brother, John (d. before Oct. 1337); John's grandson died as a minor in 1349. In 1341 Whorlton passed to Nicholas, illegitimate son of Nicholas II and Lucy, daughter of Robert de Thweng. Nicholas confirmed the grants of his great-grandfather, Stephen III (no. 1088). He died before October 1341.

1076 *Grant in free alms, addressed to the archbishop of York and all the sons of holy mother church, by Hugh Malebisse, to God and the monks of St Mary of Byland, of Snilesworth, and all the land, woodland and pasture to the north and west of Blow Gill (Hawnby) as far as the land of Hawnby stretches towards Cleveland, to do with whatever they wish. The land is to be held free from service. Pledge to warranty.* [1150 x c. 1185].
Hiis testibus Iohanne [abbate] Iorevalle, Roberto de Dayvilla, Radulfo de Belver, etc.

Marginal note: B(aculus) i.
Pd: *EYC* III, no. 1846.
Copy: MS Dodsworth 63, fol. 75r, from cartulary fol. 215. This corrects the first
witness to 'Iohanne abbate Iorevall'.
Dating: John de Kynstan became abbot of Jervaulx in 1150, and had been
succeeded by *c.* 1185. The *Historia Fundationis* assigns the grant of Snilesworth to
Hugh Malebisse I (*Mon. Ang.* V, 351) and indeed land in Snilesworth was
confirmed by Roger de Mowbray in 1147 (*Mowbray Charters*, no. 44), indicating
that Byland's interest originated with Hugh Malebisse I, Roger's steward.
However the grant in no. 1076 was that of Hugh II is suggested by the confirmation by Hugh's son William (no. 1077) and his nephew Richard (no. 1078).
Hugh II occurs from *c.* 1166 as a witness to charters (see *EYC* III, 456), but as he
bore the same name as his father the two are difficult to distinguish.
Note: Blow Gill joins the River Rye about 2½ miles north of Hawnby.

1077   *Confirmation in free alms, addressed to all men present and future,*
by William Malebisse, for the salvation of his soul and of all his ancestors
and heirs, to God and the monks of Byland and their successors, of all the
land and pasture of Snilesworth by the boundaries contained in the charter
of his father (no. 1076). Confirmation also of 2 bovates in Thornaby and all
the land which they have in Tollesby which was granted by his father, and the
land and mill with its suit, and the meadow which the monks have in Silton
and its region of the grant of Simon Blund of Leake (no. 844). To hold freely
of the donor and his heirs. Pledge to warranty. [before 1206].
Hiis testibus Galfrido filio Arthuri, Willelmo de Baxeby, Roberto filio
Acke, Gilberto de Thurkilby, etc.
Copy: MS Dodsworth 63, fol. 75r, from cartulary fol. 215.
Dating: The grantor can be identified as William, son of Hugh Malebisse II; he was
still living in 1206. On the first witness see above, no. 739. Silton was part of the
knight's fee held by Malebisse of Mowbray.

1078   *Rubric: Quitclaim by Richard Malebisse of (Old) Byland and the*
church of the vill, and confirmation by the same charter of all the grant of
Hugh Malebisse his uncle in Murton and Snilesworth. Look under the
heading Old Byland. [1186 x 1187].
Text: MS Dodsworth 91, fols 74v–75r, no. 8. Quitclaim, addressed to
all the sons of holy church present and future, by Richard Malebisse,
to God and the monks of St Mary of Byland, of whatever right he or
his ancestors had in Byland on the Moor. By this charter he grants and
confirms it free from all service for the salvation of his soul and of his
wife and father and mother and all his ancestors and heirs. Pledge to
warranty. Confirmation also of the grant of his father (*sic*), Hugh
Malebisse, of Murton and Snilesworth, as contained in his charters.
Hiis testibus Ranulfo de Glanvill, Huberto decano Ebor', Ricardo

regis thesaurario, Hugone de Morewic, Rogero filio Reinfredi, Michaele Belet, Willelmo Mauduit camerario, Roberto de Wythefeld, Reinero vicecomite Ebor', Rogero de Bavent, Roberto de la Mara, Adam (*sic*) de Reinvilla, Adam (*sic*) filio Petri de Prestun', Radulfo de Bestona. This copy has the reading 'patris' in error for 'patrui', that is, 'of his father' rather than 'of his paternal uncle'.

Dating: The first witness was chief justiciar from *c.* 1180 to 1189. Hubert Walter was dean of York from 1186 to 1189, and also a royal justice and baron of the Exchequer (*Fasti York*, p. 8). The third witness was Richard fitz Neal, treasurer until 1196. That these three appear together suggests Westminster as a place of issue. Reiner de Waxham was under sheriff from 1184 to 1187. This suggests a date of 1186 x 1187, possibly after the death of Hugh Malebisse, Richard's paternal uncle, whose grants are here confirmed.

Note: The grantor is Richard Malebisse, son of Hugh's brother, William Malebisse of Acaster Malbis. Richard died in 1210 (*EYC* III, 456).

1079 *Rubric: Chirograph agreement between the monks and Stephen de Meinill concerning obtaining the king's writ that the boundaries between their pastures be perambulated by 12 knights.* [*c.* 1229].

Dating: This is related to no. 1084 below.

1080 *Notification to all who will see or hear these letters by William of Cornborough, William Engelram, William de Tanton, Drogo of Harome, Gikel of Smeaton, John of Romanby, Geoffrey Fossard, John de Coleville, Alan son of Brian, William de Hesding, William Hay, Henry of Silton, Robert of Kirby, that they, at the petition of Robert de Turneham and in the presence of his bailiffs Samson de Pomerario and Walter of Sowerby, had met on Byland Moor to perambulate the boundaries between Whorlton and the pasture of the abbot and monks. These are the boundaries between Whorlton and Snilesworth: from* Neleshou *as the water falls on either side as far as* Northou *and as the water divides at* Pruddalehou *and falls on both sides as far as the red road. They affirm that Robert de Meinill was not justly seised within these bounds towards Snilesworth on the day on which he went overseas with the lord king to Poitou. Sealed with their seals so that the monks may have the land and pasture freely.* 1207.

Marginal note: (in later hand) 'vj Jo. 1207'.

Copies: MS Dodsworth 63, fol. 75r; MS Dodsworth 94, fols 47v–48r.

Dating: Text.

Note: Robert de Meinill died before Jan. 1207, and was succeeded by his son, Stephen III, who was a minor and a ward of Robert de Turnham (*EYC* II, 137, *CP* VIII, 622–3). As the perambulation took place at Robert de Turnham's request and is concerned with the lands with which Robert de Meinill was seised, the date may be shortly after Robert's death. It is certainly before no. 1079, which may refer to a subsequent perambulation. As William of Cornborough, Drogo of Harome and

Gikel of Smeaton all occur in the late 12th century a date of 1229 for no. 1080 would seem too late. William Engelram was still living in 1206, and a date of *c.* 1207 is therefore possible. Robert de Meinill III was married to Emma, daughter of Richard Malebisse (no. 1078). Their son, Stephen (nos 1079, 1081), was still a minor in 1219 and came of age in 1224–5. There is a note in MS Dodsworth 94, fol. 48r: Finis instrumenti de bundis inter Wherlton et Snyleswath intus et in dorso.

1081   *Rubric: Chirograph agreement of the king between the monks and Stephen de Meinill concerning the boundaries of the moor, that is, from* <Neleshou *to* W>etherbrigg *and from* Wetherbrig' *as far as* Redegate. *In this chirograph half the moor is conceded to the monks [nearer to] the grange of Snilesworth.* Westminster; 3 weeks from St Hilary [3 Feb.] 14 Henry III [1230].

Text: PRO CP 25/1/262/22, no. 23. Final concord made in the king's court at Westminster in the presence of Thomas de Muleton, Stephen of Segrave, William of Raleigh, Robert of Lexington, William de L'Isle, William of London, master Robert de Scherdelawe, Richard Reynger and other faithful men of the lord king then present, between Abbot Robert of Byland and Stephen de Meinill concerning the moor between 'Neleshou' and 'Wetherbrig' and 'Wetherbrig' and 'Redegate'. The abbot conceded that the moor was Stephen's right, and for this recognition Stephen conceded a moiety of the moor, that is the moiety lying nearer to the grange of Snilesworth, to hold of Stephen in free alms. Stephen and his heirs were to have no part in the common of the abbot and his successors, nor the abbot in Stephen's part.

Pd: *Yorks. Fines 1218–1231*, p. 125.

Note: There is a note stating that the charter is in the chest bound with a certain roll of a legal process of the plea between them.

1082   *Rubric: Attestation of William of Cornborough concerning the same perambulation.*

[fol. 109r–v, old fol. 215]

1083   *Confirmation and quitclaim, addressed to all the faithful present and future, by William Malebisse, to God and the monks of St Mary of Byland, of all right and claim which he had or might have in land, woodland and pasture beyond Blow (Gill), that is, as far as the land of Hawnby extends towards Cleveland in length and width, to hold free from all secular exaction in free alms, for the salvation of the soul of the donor and of his father and mother and of all his heirs and ancestors. Pledge to warranty.* [mid 13th cent.].

Hiis testibus Thoma de Colvill', Willelmo de Harum, Ada de Hilton', Willelmo de Midelton', Ada de Nereford', Roberto de Renegile, etc.

Marginal note: There is a catchword, in the cartulary hand, at the foot of fol. 109r.
Dating: The grantor appears to be William Malebisse, son of John and Matilda, and grandson of Richard Malebisse (d. 1210). William occurs in 1233 and 1258 (*EYC* III, 456) and in 1247 (no. 1090 below).

[fol. 109v]

1084 *Rubric: Writ of the king which has force* (breve regis que habet vim). *A chirograph is bound with the aforesaid charter concerning the matters mentioned before* (de premissis). [Westminster; 24 Oct. 13 Henry III [1229]].

Text: MS Dodsworth 94, fol. 45r–v: Notification by the king to his sheriff of Yorkshire that in his court at Westminster, in the presence of justices, an agreement was reached between the abbot of Byland, plaintiff, and Stephen de Meinill, defendant, concerning the moor between 'Neleshow' and 'Wetherbrigg' and from there to 'Redgate'. A plea had been brought concerning making reasonable boundaries. The abbot acknowledged the moor to be Stephen's right, and for this recognition and final concord Stephen granted him half of the moor, that is, the half nearest to the grange of Snilesworth. T(este) W. de Raleng. This is followed in MS Dodsworth 94, fol. 45v by a copy of a writ addressed to the sheriff of Yorkshire, to cause Stephen de Meinill to receive at Westminster a chirograph between him and the abbot of Byland concerning the moor from 'Nelleshow' and 'Wetherbrig' to 'Redegate'. T(este) W. de Raleng. The text is followed by a note that Stephen came on the appointed day and received his chirograph. Through him and his friends none of the boundaries or bounds were put into the chirograph because they did not please them, and so they obtained another chirograph.

Note: On 6 May 1229 at Westminster a day was given to the abbot and Stephen de Meinill as to the moor, and for the taking of their chirograph on 20 Oct. They appointed as attorneys Brother Roger, monk of London, for the abbot, and William of Morton or Joseph le Mesager for Stephen. See *Yorks. Fines 1218–1231*, p. 125, note, and *Curia Regis Rolls*, XIII, 376, 383, 396.
Note: see no. 1079.

1085 *Rubric: Quitclaim by Robert son of Robert Breth of Carlton relating to not having common pasture in the monks' moor.*
Original: *Quitclaim by Robert son of Robert Breth of Carlton in Cleveland of all right to common pasture for his livestock in the moiety of the moor between Whorlton and Snilesworth according to the boundaries made in 1207 and perambulated by 12 men (no. 1080). [1294 x 1311].*

[Testibus] dom' Nicholao de Meynil, Engera de Bonyngtona, Willelmo de Coleville, Michael de . . . sale, Ricardo Malebisse militibus, Roberto Breth, Waltero de Steynisby, Roberto de Thormodeby . . .

Sealed.

Pd: *HMC Rutland*, IV, 76, from the original in the possession of His Grace the Duke of Rutland, Belvoir Castle.

Dating: The reference to the perambulation in 1207 suggests a date in the early 13th cent., and the fifth witness may be the Richard Malebisse who died in 1210. However, the first witness suggests a later date. The name Nicholas does not occur in the main line of Meinill of Whorlton before Nicholas, son of Stephen III (who died before 16 July 1269). Nicholas, his second son and heir, became Lord Meinill shortly before his death in May 1299; his son, Nicholas, died in 1322. If the fourth witness is Michael of Upsall, then this would place the quitclaim between his succession in 1294 and 1311, when his son had succeeded him.

1086 *Rubric: Note of a plea between the monks and Stephen de Meinill.* [? *c.* 1224].

Dating: This may refer to the assize of novel disseisin which Robert de Percy, John de Daiville, Henry of Ferlington and Gilbert of Ayton were ordered to hold in 1224, and which the abbot brought against Stephen de Meinill concerning a tenement in Snilesworth: *Cal. Pat. R. 1216–1225*, p. 489.

1087 Original: *Grant in free alms, confirmation and quitclaim, addressed to all the sons of holy mother church present and future who will see or hear the present writing, by Stephen de Meinill son and heir of Robert de Meinill, lord of Whorlton, to God and St Mary and the abbot and convent of Byland, of all the land and pasture, woodland and moor, with all appurtenances and easements both under and above ground, that is from* Nelishou *as the water falls from either side as far as* Northow *and from there as the water divides as far as* Pruddalehow *and from there as the water falls on either side as far as the red road. The confirmation and quitclaim is made for himself, his heirs and assigns, and for the salvation of his soul and of his father and mother and all his ancestors and heirs, to hold free of all secular service. As often as the animals, of whatever kind, belonging to the monks, transgress the boundaries towards Stephen's pasture of Whorlton and are found there, they shall be driven back into their own pasture without impounding or fine or impediment, unless they pasture through the forest watch* (per wardum factum). *Further confirmation of all boundaries perambulated and sworn by 12 knights (no. 1081). Pledge to warranty. Sealed with the donor's seal. On the day of sealing the monks have received Stephen into confraternity to participate in all spiritual good deeds in life and in death.* Byland; St Margaret Virgin [20 July] 1230.

Hiis testibus Roberto de Cokkefelde tunc vicecomite Ebor', Willelmo de Barton' tunc subvicecomite, Gaufrido de Thoreny, <R>adulpho de Tampton', Willelmo de Britton', Willelmo de Feugers, Gaufrido de Bakkeby, et aliis.

Location: NYCRO: Z1Q (MIC 3170/45–47); written under seal fold: et sciendum est quod ista tria verba negligenter erant oblita per . . . videlicet generis, suos, et monachi, sed fuerunt scripta et approbata ante consignationem.
Marginal note: (in later hand) '1230 14 H. 3'.
Copies: MS Dodsworth 63, fols 75v–76r; MS Dodsworth 94, fols 46r–47r.
Pd: (very brief calendar with the first witness only) *HMC Rutland*, IV, 76.
Dating: The original and cartulary copy have 1230. Robert de Cokefeld was sheriff of Yorkshire between 1226 and 1229, being succeeded in the latter year by William de Stuteville: *Lord Lieutenants*, p. 55.
Note: The cartulary copy has the first four witnesses only.

1088 Original: *Notification, addressed to all the faithful in Christ present and future, by Nicholas de Meinill, Lord of Whorlton, son and heir of Nicholas de Meinill, that he had inspected the charter of Stephen de Meinill his ancestor (no. 1087, recited), and confirmation of same. Sealed with his seal.* Byland; day after the Annunciation 14 Edw. III [26 Mar. 1341].
Hiis testibus dominis Petro de Malolacu, Iohanne Faucunbergh, Radulfo de Bulmer, militibus, Thoma de Moubray, Iohanne Gower de Sexhou, Thoma Sturmy de Kirkeby, Iohanne de Hamby, Thoma Longespyu, Roberto de Foxton.

Location: NYCRO: Z1Q (MIC 3170/39).
Marginal note in cartulary: (in later hand) '14 E. 3'.
Copies: MS Dodsworth 63, fol. 76r; MS Dodsworth 94, fol. 47r–v, from the original ('adhuc in dorso Ratificatio Nicholai de Menyll de carta Stephani de Menyll atavi sui de premissis').
Note: The cartulary copy has the first 3 witnesses only. The grantor was the illegitimate son of Nicholas II Lord Whorlton and Lucy de Thweng.

[fol. 110r, old fol. 216r]
SCAWTON (SE5483), parish in the wapentake of Ryedale (NR), 3 miles west of Helmsley. Scawton was part of the fief granted by Roger de Mowbray to Hugh Malebisse for one knight's fee (*Mowbray Charters*, no. 371 and p. 264), and Hugh granted to the monks of Rievaulx the meadow called 'Oswaldenges' in Scawton (*Cart. Riev.*, no. 74, pp. 43–4; see above, no. 988). The subject of the Scawton section of the Byland cartulary is a pension of 20s. due to the monks from Scawton chapel. According to the *Historia Fundationis* it was while the monks were at Old Byland (1142–7) that Abbot Roger, worried about the dangers facing the parishioners living in the vill of Scawton as they travelled to the mother church of Old Byland, persuaded Archbishop

Henry Murdac (1147–53) to allow him to build a dependent chapel at Scawton. He appointed a clerk named Richard, who served the chapel for 54 years (*Mon. Ang.* V, 351). Between 1177 and 1181 Archbishop Roger de Pont L'Evêque granted permission for the monks to appropriate Old Byland church (*EEA* XX, no. 8). To support a claim made in 1309 to pensions from the church of Rillington and 20s. from Scawton, the monks produced a sealed letter of Archbishops R. (probably Roger) and G (probably Geoffrey Plantagenet) (*ibid.*, no. 10).

1089 *Final concord levied in the king's court at York on Tues. before the Ascension, 4 John in the presence of G(eoffrey) fitz P(eter), earl of Essex and Hugh Bardolf, justices, and other faithful men of the king then present, between Richard Malebisse, plaintiff, and the abbot of Byland, defendant, concerning an assize of darrein presentment of the parson of Scawton chapel and the advowson of the same, about which a plea was made in the same court. The abbot has restored and quitclaimed the right of presentation and advowson to Richard and his heirs in perpetuity. The parsons who hold the chapel on the presentation of Richard and his heirs are to pay 20s. yearly from the chapel to the abbot and his successors, 10s. at Whitsuntide and 10s. at St Martin (11 Nov.). Richard and his heirs are not able to transfer the chapel to any house of religion other than Byland without the assent of the abbot and his successors.* York; 13 May 1203.

Copy: MS Dodsworth 63, fol. 76v.

Note: The grantor was Richard Malebisse, son of William Malebisse of Acaster Malbis; he died in 1210 (see also no. 1078). This action of darrein presentment evidently followed the death of Richard, chaplain of Scawton, who served the church for 54 years, and whose death would have therefore occurred in 1201 or 1202.

1090 *Notification by Henry III that the abbot had, in the king's court in the presence of his justices at Warwick, recovered seisin against William Malebisse of 20s. yearly rent to be received from each parson of the chapel of Scawton presented by William and his heirs for admission and institution. Order to his justices to restore seisin without delay, and to see that William pays arrears of £12.* Warwick; 18 Apr. 31 Henry III [1247].

Teste Rogero de Thurkilby apud Warwic xviii die Aprilis anno regni nostri xxx primo.

Copy: MS Dodsworth 63, fol. 76v.

Note: William was the son of John Malebisse and grandson of Richard Malebisse; he was the grantor of no. 1083. For confirmation of an annual rent from Scawton chapel see above, no. 968.

1091 *Rubric: Bond of John Malebisse and his heirs to compel payment of the said 20s.* [1211 x 1215].

Text: MS Dodsworth 94, fol. 16v, no. 17. Bond by John Malebisse for himself and his heirs that if it should happen that the parson of Scawton at the time should fail to render the 20s. due annually to the monks of Byland under the terms of a chirograph made in the king's court between the abbot and Richard Malebisse (no. 1089) then the monks may compel John to pay the 20s. Sealed. Hiis testibus domino Helya abbate Rievallensi, Gikello celerario Bellelande, Ingelramo socio eius, Ada magistro conversorum, Waltero cellerario Rievall', fratre Thoma bercario Bellelande, fratre Moyse, Willelmo de Herlesaie, Thoma clerico de Acaster, Thoma de Arneclive.

Dating: first witness. The bond may have been issued shortly after John succeeded his father, Richard, who died in 1210.

1092 *Notification to all the sons of holy mother church to whom the present letters shall come, by the official of the court of York, that an agreement was recently reached between the abbot and convent of Byland of the Cistercian order and Dom. Nicholas, rector of the church or chapel of Scawton, concerning an annual pension of 20s. which was held to be due to the abbot and convent from the chapel, and which it is claimed had been withheld. The abbot and convent through Bartholomew, their co-monk and proctor, and the rector in person appeared before the official, and the rector agreed that the pension had been paid from ancient times and that he was obliged to pay it in equal portions at St Martin in Winter (11 Nov.) and Whitsuntide. The official orders that the pension be restored under pain of ecclesiastical censure. Sealed with the seal of the officiality of the court of York.* York; Tues. before St Michael [28 Sept.] 1279.

Copy: MS Dodsworth 91, fols 113v–114r.

1093 *Rubric: Attestation of Master Andrew, notary public of the apostolic see, concerning the same sentence. Look under Byland in the first bundle.*

1094 *Rubric: Confirmation by Archbishop Geoffrey of York of an annual pension from the chapel of Scawton. Look under the heading of Rillington.*

Note: The text is entered in the cartulary at no. 968 above.

[fol. 110r–v]
1095 *Notification to all the sons of holy mother church to whom the present letters shall come, by the official of the court of York that on 1 Oct. 1333, in the consistory court of York, a diffinitive final sentence was handed*

down to the parties cited below, in this form. He has heard and understood
the merits of the possessory action concerning the spoliation of a pension of
20s. alleged to be due at three terms and not to have been paid, and the case
concerning the altering of the annual pension of 20s. brought in the presence
of the official between the abbot and convent, plaintiff, through William de
Twiford their proctor, and Dom. Henry, rector of Scawton chapel, by
William of Kendal, his proctor.
Recitation of the plea by the proctor of the abbot and convent, seeking from
Henry, rector of the chapel of Scawton, 30s., that is the annual pension of
20s. which has not been paid for 3 terms. The religious have asked for it, but
he has refused. The case has been heard, witnesses examined, and he has
made an order for the payment of 30s. Judgement for the abbot and convent,
and order for the restitution of the pension. Sealed with the seal of the
officiality of York. York, St Peter's ('the greater church'); 2 Oct. 1333.
Marginal note: (in later hand) '7 Ed. 3'.

1096 *Rubric: Attestation by William of Carlton concerning the sentence of*
the said 20s. [*c.* 1333].

1097   *Rubric: Attestation by the official of the archdeacon of Cleveland*
concerning the same. Look in Byland in the first bundle.

[fol. 111r, old fol. 217]
SPROXTON (SE6181), in the parish of Helmsley and wapentake of
Ryedale (NR), lying 1½ miles south of the town of Helmsley. No. 1098
is of interest for the field names it preserves.

1098   *Grant in free alms, addressed to all the sons of holy mother church*
present and future, by Simon son of William of Sproxton, to God and the
monks of St Mary of Byland, of 3 acres in the region of Sproxton, that is, 1
acre in Grantcornethwaith *near the* cultura *of the lord of Sproxton nearest*
to the west, ½ acre in Grenegatefeld *between the* cultura *of the lord of*
Sproxton and the land of Henry Wulf, ½ acre at Mapel *next to the nearest*
cultura *of the lord towards the west, and 1 acre at* Stodefald *next to the acre*
of Bernard son of Robert towards the east. Further grant of an annual rent of
6d. to be rendered by Simon and his heirs, 3d. at St Martin (11 Nov.) and 3d.
at Whitsuntide. These grants are made and confirmed by charter with the
donor's body. The grant is made free from all service for the salvation of the
soul of the donor and of all his ancestors and heirs. Pledge to warranty. [1210
x *c.* 1220].

Hiis testibus Iohanne Malbys, Symone de Stayngriva, Willelmo de Harum, Galfrido de Ampilford, etc.

Marginal note: A genealogy, in a later hand, shows the descent from William of Sproxton, to his son Simon (no. 1098), to William son of Simon (nos 1099, 1101), and to Simon son of William.

Copy: MS Dodsworth 63, fol. 77r, from cartulary fol. 217.

Pd: *EYC* X, no. 111.

Dating: The first witness is the son of Richard Malebisse (d. 1210) who occurs in 1227. As Clay noted, Simon of Stonegrave is unlikely to have lived beyond *c.* 1220.

Note: Clay notes that Richard of Sproxton transferred his land there to Robert de Ros II before John Malebisse, the first witness, succeeded his father, Richard (1210), and that it thereafter was part of the Ros fee. It is not easy to see how the donor fits into the main line of the family of Sproxton. Robert of Sproxton occurs in the time of Henry I. He was succeeded by his son Robert, who with his son, Simon, was a benefactor of Rievaulx Abbey, granting lands in Sproxton; this was confirmed by Simon's brother, Richard. Robert of Sproxton was a benefactor of Byland (no. 1102 below). Simon, who was alive in 1186, was succeeded by his brother, Richard, who was holding Sproxton in 1219 and 1226–7. Thereafter the names Robert and William occur in alternate generations (*VCH NR* I, 494, and *EYC* I, 326–8). The Byland benefactors appear to belong to another family in Sproxton.

1099 Rubric: *Confirmation by William son of Simon of the same 3 acres and rent of 6d. (no. 1098).* [early to mid 13th cent.].

1100 Rubric: *Charter of the said Simon concerning the whole tenement that William Drury formerly held of him for the service of 6d. Above under Laysthorpe; look in the third bundle there.* [early 13th cent.].

1101 Quitclaim, addressed to all the sons of holy mother church present and future, by William son of Simon of Sproxton for himself and his heirs, to God and St Mary and the abbot and convent of Byland, of all right and claim which he and his ancestors or heirs had or might have in the land and toft which William Drury and William his son held of his father Simon and afterwards of William, with all appurtenances and easements. To hold of the donor free from all service, with all appurtenances, liberties and easements belonging to the land inside and outside the vill. Quitclaim also of the rent which his father and he after him used to receive from the abbot and convent. The quitclaim is made for the salvation of his soul and of his wife and his father and mother and all his ancestors and heirs, in free alms. Pledge to warranty in the hand of the sheriff of York, and that he will give 10s. penalty and may be distrained. Sealed with the donor's seal. [early to mid 13th cent.].

Hiis testibus [Willelmo de Stokesley tunc] cellerario, W[illelmo] de

Wlsynden socio eius, Iohanne [de Ripona magistro] conversorum, etc.

Copies: MS Dodsworth 63, fol. 77r, from cartulary fol. 217; MS Dodsworth 91, fols 106v–107v, no. 60 (from the original in St Mary's Tower). Readings in square brackets are supplied from MS Dodsworth 91, where the witness list continues: Willelmo de Carleton, Willelmo Arundell, Henrico de Carleton', Roberto de Buggeden, Willelmo de Foxhol, Roberto Fossard et multis aliis.

1102   *Notification to all present and future by [Robert] of Sproxton of his confirmation [for the salvation of his soul and that of Albreda his wife], of the tenement which William Drury held and of all the land and rent which they have in the vill and region of Sproxton of the grant of Simon son of William. Confirmation also of the confirmation and quitclaim by Simon's son, William. Grant of free entry and exit across the land and moor of Sproxton. Pledge to warranty. Sealed with the donor's seal.* [late 12th or early 13th cent.].

Hiis testibus Symone de Stayngrive, Symone et Willelmo filiis eius, Willelmo Drury.

Copies: MS Dodsworth 63, fol. 77r, from cartulary fol. 217; MS Dodsworth 91, fols 71v–72r, no. 4 (from the original in St Mary's Tower). The latter reads 'filiis meis' for 'filiis eius' and the witness list continues: Roberto filio Line, Gaufrido capellano meo.

Note: At the foot of the folio in a ? fifteenth-century hand, is a note relating to annual rent from Sproxton. The donor granted pasture rights in Sproxton to Rievaulx Abbey, with the assent of his wife, Albreda (*Cart. Riev.*, no. 127, p. 79).

1103   *Rubric: Quitclaim by William Drury of 1 tenement in Sproxton surrendered to Simon son of William and William his son for 7 marks.* [early to mid 13th cent.].

[fol. 111v]

SCACKLETON (SE6472), in the parish of Hovingham and the wapentake of Ryedale (NR). Scackleton lies 2 miles SW of the town of Hovingham and midway between there and the abbey property of Skewsby. Gundreda de Gournay and Roger de Mowbray granted land in Scackleton by 1140 (nos 1104–5), and it appears to have been closely associated with lands in Airyholme (nos 1106–7). There was a grange at Scackleton (nos 1111, 1119, 1143). This lies at SE638725, just over ½ mile west of the vill.

1104   *Grant in free alms, addressed to the archbishop of York and the whole chapter of St Peter (York) and all the sons of holy church, by Roger de Mowbray, to God and the monks of St Mary of Byland and their successors,* *of his land in Scackleton, that is 3 carucates with their appurtenances and easements which he and his mother had, and common pasture in the region and forest of Hovingham wherever his and his men's animals pasture. Grant also of all Airyholme, in woodland, land and meadow, to do with as the monks please. Pledge to warranty.* [1140].

Hiis testibus Willelmo de Meynill, Mathia de Ramporn', Olyvero de Busceyo, Willelmo de Widevill, etc.

Marginal note: B(aculus) i.
Copy: MS Dodsworth 63, fol. 13v, which reads 'Morvill' for 'Meynill'.
Pd: *Mowbray Charters*, no. 35.
Dating: The Byland *Historia Fundationis* (*Mon. Ang.* V, 350).
Note: Since the monks were at Hood between 1138 and 1142 the address in this charter must be an interpolation or modernization. The rubric states that the charter is duplicated.

1105 *Rubric: Charter of Gundreda de Mowbray concerning 3 carucates in Scackleton.* [1138 x *c*. 1140].

Text: MS Dodsworth 91, fol. 93v, no. 38. Grant, addressed to all his men and all the faithful of holy church, by Roger de Mowbray and Gundreda his mother, to God and St Mary and the monks of Byland, of the land in Scackleton, that is, 3 carucates, free from all service, with appurtenances in woodland, plains, waters, and in all things. The grant is made for the salvation of their souls and for the souls of all their ancestors. Hiis testibus Willelmo de Menuham, Matthia de Romppei, Olivero de Bosceio, Waltero de Riva', Willelmo de Stutevilla, Olivero de Olgrs.

Pd: *Mowbray Charters*, no. 33.
Dating: As pointed out in *Mowbray Charters*, this charter, issued jointly by Roger and his mother, is likely to date from early in his majority, and to be associated with no. 1104. The first witness may be William de Meinill.

1106 *Rubric: Charter of Roger de Mowbray concerning Airyholme by boundaries, by which charter he also granted* Yneshous.

Note: This is probably a cross reference to no. 296, by which Roger granted his land in Airyholme and a *cultura* called 'Deneshous'

1107 *Confirmation, addressed to the archbishop of York and the whole chapter of St Peter (York) and all the sons of holy mother church, by Nigel de Mowbray, to God and the monks of Byland, of 3 carucates in Scackleton which his father, Roger, and Roger's mother, Gundreda, granted (nos 1104–5), with woodland and common pasture throughout the forest of Hovingham wherever the animals of the men of the vill pasture. Confirmation also of the meadow of Hovingham which the monks have of the grant of* *his grandmother Gundreda by the boundaries laid down in her charter, and of the grant of Hamo Beler, namely 10 acres of meadow in Hovingham and 5 acres called* Speules *in the region of the said vill, and ½ mark annually from his mill of Hovingham, as is contained in his charter. Confirmation also of the land of Airyholme which <lies> next to Howthorpe by the boundaries contained in the charter of his father. All this is granted in free alms for the salvation of his soul and of his father and mother and all his ancestors and heirs. Pledge to warranty.* [1186 x Dec. 1189].

Hiis testibus Roberto fratre meo, Willelmo filio meo et herede, Galfrido Hagat, Ricardo de Widevilla, etc.

Pd: *Mowbray Charters*, no. 74.

Dating: the respective departures of Roger and Nigel for the Holy Land. This charter confirms the part played by Gundreda in the grant of Scackleton.

1108 *Rubric: Agreement between the monks and the canons of Newburgh concerning the tithes of Scackleton. Look under the heading Newburgh.*

Note: The text is entered into the cartulary at no. 730 above.

1109 *Grant and quitclaim, addressed to the archbishop of York and the whole chapter of St Peter (York) and all the sons of holy mother church, by Serlo son of William son of Ingeler of Thirsk, to God and the monks of St Mary of Byland, of all right which he had or might have in the land of Scackleton which is of the fee of Roger de Mowbray. This quitclaim is made for the salvation of his soul and of all his own. Pledge to warranty.* [before 1186].

Hiis testibus . . . Gilberto del Meinil, Stephano . . .

Dating: the reference to Roger de Mowbray.

Note: Before 1190 Nigel de Mowbray confirmed the agreements made between the monks and William, nephew and heir of Ingelram of Thirsk, concerning 1 bovate in Bagby and 3 in Thirsk which Ingelram had granted (no. 662). Greenway suggested that Ingelram is the same as Ingelram de Torp, who made a grant to Byland of 3 bovates and a messuage in Thirsk which Roger de Mowbray had granted him (*Mowbray Charters*, no. 391, from a lost portion of the cartulary). This she dates to before the destruction of Thirsk castle in 1176. William is here called the son of Ingelram rather than his nephew. Gilbert de Meinill may be Gilbert of Thirkleby, who occurs in the 1180s; the second witness may be his son, Stephen.

1110 *Rubric: Charter of William Dreng remitting all his right in land <in Scackleton>.*

[fols 111v–112r]

1111 *Grant and confirmation, addressed to all the sons of holy church who will see or hear this charter, by Thomas de Richeburne, with his body, [to*

*God and the monks of St Mary of Byland], of all his right in Scackleton
within these boundaries: from the place [where the river runs from the
monks' garden] at Scackleton and flows northwards as far as the lowest head
of the pond of the old [mill, and from there] from the west as far as the road
which lies between Coulton and Scackleton grange, and from there by the
same road [as far as the hedge which] the monks made of old, curving around
until it comes to the head of the old ditch, and from there by the same ditch to
the corner of the court of [the monks' vaccary at] the said grange. The monks
are to do there whatever they wish, for the salvation of the soul of the donor
and of all his ancestors and heirs. Pledge to warranty.* [early 13th cent.].
Hiis testibus Galfrido de Hettona, Willelmo Burden de Grymston,
Bartholomeo de Torny, etc.

Copy: MS Dodsworth 7, fol. 173r–v, which omits 'etc' from the witness list and
continues: Galfrido de Ampleforda, Willelmo de Lundoniis. Readings in square
brackets are supplied from this copy.

Dating: Geoffrey de Etton of Gilling occurs in 1202–?1210 and 1218–19; in the early
13th century he granted the lay fee of William Burdon in Grimston to the dean and
chapter of York: *YMF* II, no 77 (p. 119); *VCH NR* I, 480, 482.

[fol. 112r, old fol. 218]

1112   *Rubric: Charter of Bernard of Scackleton concerning 1 toft and 3
acres and remission of all his right in Scackleton.*

1113   *Rubric: Confirmation of William [Bernard's] son concerning the
same.*
The rubric further states that these (nos 1113–14) are bound together.

1114   *Rubric: Charter of Henry le Noreys concerning 2 bovates in
Scackleton . . . in the king's court of York. Copied.*
Marginal note: B(aculus) ii.

1115   *Rubric: Charter of Pain concerning the quitclaim by Bernard son of
Walter . . .*

1116   *Rubric: Chirograph of the king between the monks and Henry and
Walter Cod' concerning 3 carucates in Scackleton for which the monks
granted 2 bovates. It is in the chest.*

1117   *Rubric: Charter of Gilbert de Thorny concerning free entry and exit
for the monks' flocks and carts by the road which lies on his land of* Parva
Bodehow *as far as* Aykscawe *rendering 1 axe annually.*

1118   *Rubric: Charter of Roger of Sessay (de Ceszay) and Matilda his . . .
concerning ½ acre in Scackleton in the* cultura *of . . . hill.*

1119   *Quitclaim, addressed to all the sons of holy church who will see or hear this charter, by Hugh of Howthorpe (pa. Hovingham), to God and the monks of St Mary of Byland, of all his right within these boundaries: from that place where the river leaves the monks' garden at Scackleton and flows towards the north, to the lower head of the pond of the old mill, and from there from the west as far as the road which runs between Coulton and Scackleton grange, and along that road to the hedge which the monks made, curving around until it comes to the head of the ditch below the monks' vaccary in the said grange. This grant is made in free alms for the salvation of the soul of the donor and of all his ancestors and heirs. Pledge to warranty.* [late 12th or early 13th cent.].

Hiis testibus Galfrido de Etton, W. de Richeburne fratre meo.

Dating: Hugh of Howthorpe occurs in 1165–6 and in the early 13th century (*VCH NR* I, 508), and below, no. 1138. The first witness is likely to be Geoffrey son of Thomas de Etton the elder; he occurs in 1218–19: *VCH NR* I, 480.

Note: The manuscript is badly damaged at this point. The second witness is William de Richeburne, who occurs in nos 1120, 1125, 1126, 1133 and 1134.

[fol. 112r–v]

1120   *Confirmation in free alms and quitclaim, addressed to all the faithful in Christ who will see or hear this writing, by John of Howthorpe, son of Hugh of Howthorpe, for himself and his heirs, to God and St Mary and the abbot and convent of Byland, of 4 bovates and 3 tofts in Scackleton which they have of the grant of William de Richeburna and which Roger Rawth formerly held of William, and of the homage and service of Peter of Coulton on 1 bovate in the same vill, and the homage and service of [Hugh] the brother of William on 1 toft and 1 bovate there with 2 crofts and appurtenances, and the whole woodland to the east side of Scackleton, as much as pertains to the grantor and his heirs. The monks are to do with these lands as they wish, to assart or to plough. Quitclaim also of an annual rent which Isabella de Bulmer granted in free alms for the salvation of her soul, and which the abbot and convent were accustomed to render to her for the said 4 bovates which they have of the grant of William de Richburne, and of 18d. which they rendered to the grantor. All these grants are to be held free from secular service, without suit of county or wapentake, for the salvation of the soul of the donor and of his father and mother and all his ancestors and heirs and for the benefits which the monks have conferred on him. Pledge to warranty. Sealed with the donor's seal.* [before 1242/3].

Hiis testibus domino Ada de Hilton', domino Iohanne de Dayvill, domino Willelmo Ma . . . Thoma de Colvill', etc.

Dating: The death of the second witness.

Note: Isabella de Bulmer may be the daughter of Emma, daughter of Bertram de

Bulmer; Emma was heiress of her brother, William. Emma married twice, and died in 1208. Her son, Henry de Neville by her marriage to Geoffrey de Neville, died without issue in 1227, and was succeeded by his sister, Isabella, who married Robert Fitz Meldred, lord of Raby (d. 1253). Their son was Geoffrey de Neville. See *EYC* II, 128. However, the Isabella who occurs in no. 1120 had a son named William, who is mentioned in nos 1130–1 below.

[fol. 112v]

1121   *Rubric: Charter of Hugh son of John concerning warranty.*

1122   *Rubric: Charter of John son of Hugh concerning 2 tofts and crofts in <Scackleton>.*

1123   *Rubric: Charter of Roger of Howthorpe concerning 1 toft in Scackleton. They demised this to Roger in perpetuity for 3s., by chirograph.*
Note: A Roger of Howthorpe occurs in 1244, along with William de Richeburne and Albreda his mother, Willia ıı de Tornye, Robert the cowherd, Robert son of John and Walter son of John ı,ı an enquiry as to whether they unjustly disseised the abbot of a free tenement in Scackleton. The abbot recovered seisin: *Curia Regis Rolls*, XVIII, 399.

1124   *Rubric: Confirmation by Walter de Percehay of all lands in his fee. Look under the heading of the Magnates.*
Note: The text is entered into the cartulary at no. 685 above. Walter de Percehay is a common name. One occurs in 1218–19; in 1284–85 Walter de Percehay held 3 carucates in Ryton of the Luterel fee; and a Walter occurs in 1316 (*EYC* VI, 143–4, 248–9).

1125   *Notification, addressed to all present and future by William de Richeburne of his confirmation to God and St Mary and the abbot and convent of Byland, for 4 pittances to be made for his soul, of 4 bovates and 3 tofts in Scackleton which Roger Raude held of him, as in no. 1120. Pledge to warranty. Sealed with the donor's seal.* [mid 13th cent.].
Hiis testibus Waltero tunc priore de B., Henrico suppriore, B . . . Ada socio eius, Thoma de Colvyll.
Dating: See no. 1038, where the same witnesses attest.

1126   *Rubric: Charter of the same William [de Richeburne] concerning woodland in the west of Scackleton and 3 villeins.*

1127   *Rubric: Returned charters of William de Rawth; there are 10 and they are bound together.*

1128 *Rubric: Charter of Roger Rawth concerning 1 bovate in Scackleton.*
. . .

1129 *Rubric: Charter of Isabella de Bulmer concerning the remission of 8[s.].*
Note: see no. 1120 and no. 1134.

1130 *Rubric: Charter of the same Isabella [de Bulmer] which she made to William her son . . .*

1131 *Rubric: Quitclaim by the same William called . . . Copied.*

1132 *Rubric: Chirograph of the king concerning the same 8s. In the chest.*
. . .

1133 *Rubric: Charter of Alice, widow of William de Richeburne concerning . . . of her dowry of a third part of 4 bovates and also a third part of 1 bovate. . . .*

1134 *Rubric: Chirograph in the king's court between the monks and William de Richeburne concerning 4 bovates and the service of Peter of Coulton etc. and Hugh his brother for 8s. annually. He remitted this to the monks by the charter of Isabella de Bulmer, as above (no. 1129). York; quindene of St Hilary [27 Jan.] 36 Henry III [1252].*
Text: PRO CP 25/1/265/46, no. 194. Final concord made in the king's court of York in the presence of Silvester, bishop of Carlisle, Roger of Thirkleby, Hugh, abbot of Selby, Gilbert de Preston, and Adam de Hilton, between Abbot Henry, plaintiff, and William de Richeburne, defendant, as to 4 bovates and 3 tofts in Scackleton. William recognized these as the right of the abbot and convent, of William's grant. William further granted to the abbot the homage and service of Peter of Coulton and his brother, Hugh, for the tenement they held of William, to hold of the abbot for 9s. 6d. yearly at Whitsuntide and St Martin (11 Nov.). William quitclaimed right of estover and common of herbage or mast in the abbot's wood in Scackleton, so that the abbot had right to assart and enclose as he wished. All articles contained in a former chirograph were annulled.
Pd: *Yorks. Fines 1246–1272*, pp. 70–1.
Note: The reference to an earlier chirograph may be to the final concord reached between William de Richeburne, plaintiff, and Abbot Henry, defendant, concerning estover in the abbot's wood of Scackleton (2 Aug. 1240). The abbot granted William and his heirs herbage and mast for their cattle and those of their

men of Scackleton, and reasonable estover in the wood to the west side of Scackleton grange between the grange and the wood which the abbot had of the grant of Elias de Flamville, and in the wood on the east side of Scackleton between the vill and the wood of Airyholme. The abbot undertook not to assart in the wood west of the grange (*Yorks. Fines 1232–1246*, p. 91, from PRO CP 25/1/263/33, no. 137). There was a further disagreement in 1244 when an assize of novel disseisin was summoned to investigate whether the abbot had unjustly disseised William of common pasture belonging to his free tenement in Scackleton. William was amerced for false claim. Moreover, an assize found that William, Albreda his mother, William de Tornye, Robert Vaccarius, Robert son of John, Roger of Howthorpe, and Walter son of John had disseised the abbot of a rood of land, and were amerced: *Curia Regis Rolls*, XVIII, 399.

1135 *Rubric: Charter of Thomas Fossard concerning ½ carucate with . . . in Scackleton.*

[fol. 113r, old fol. 219]
1136 *Rubric: Charter of Robert Fossard concerning 2 bovates which he had granted to Thomas his brother. Surrendered.*

1137 *Rubric: Charter of William de Wyville concerning licence to divert water to the mill.*
Note: This may be William de Wyville, son of Eustacia de Wyville and Nicholas de Yeland, who was restored in 1253 and who occurs in 1284/5, or William, son of John de Wyville (d. 1306).

1138 **Original:** *Grant in free alms, addressed to all the faithful in Christ who will see or hear this writing, by Richard de Riparia, for the salvation of his soul and of all his ancestors and heirs, to God and St Mary and the abbot and monks of St Mary of Byland, of free transit for their animals, their carts and draught animals and wagons through his wood of Brandsby towards Scackleton. The grant is made free from secular service. Pledge to warranty.* [before *c.* 1215].
Hiis testibus Ricardo de Wyvill, Thoma de Colevyll', Thoma de Richeburn', Hugone de Holthorp', Hugone de Upsale, Willelmo de Barton', Galfrido de Ampilford', Willelmo de Winton.
Location: NYCRO, ZDV I 47 (MIC 2889/3424); endorsed: Ric. de la River de via; Scakilden b. ii in fine, 'Scackleton, second bundle, at the end'; seal: black wax.
Dating: Richard de Wyville attests in late Henry II and the early 13th century and was dead by 1215 (*EYC* IX, no. 77, 107). Hugh of Howthorpe occurs before *c.* 1169 and in the early 13th century (*ibid.*, no. 157 and p. 250). Hugh of Upsall occurs in 1224 x 1233, and before 1227 (*ibid.*, nos 60, 87), and William de Barton and Geoffrey of Ampleforth in the early 13th century (*ibid.*, nos 79, 122). The cartulary copy has only the first four witnesses.

1139 *Rubric: Charter of Juliana Noreys concerning 2 bovates and 2 tofts and 2 crofts in Scackleton.*
Marginal note: B(aculus) iii.

1140 *Quitclaim, addressed to all the faithful in Christ present and future, by John of Stonegrave, to God and St Mary and the abbot and convent of Byland, of 8d. annual rent which he and his ancestors were accustomed to take, for one pittance annually. He makes this quitclaim for the salvation of his soul, of Ida his wife, his father and mother, and of Peter of Stonegrave his dead brother, and all his ancestors and heirs. Pledge to warranty. In the form of a chirograph, sealed with both seals.* [1278 x 1280].
Hiis testibus dominis Ranulfo de Daker' tunc vicecomite Ebor', Ada de Barton', Willelmo de Holtby, militibus, Ricardo Malbys, Rogero Rawt', etc.
Marginal note: (in later hand) '7 E I'.
Dating: the period of office of the first witness, sheriff of Yorkshire from 1278 to 1280: *Lord Lieutenants*, p. 60.
Note: John (d. 1295) was the last male heir of the family of Stonegrave. His wife was Ida, one of the three daughters of Baldwin Wake and his wife Ela. John's and Ida's daughter, Isabel, married the king's justice Simon of Pattishall. See *EYF*, pp. 84–5.

1141 *Bond, addressed to all the faithful in Christ to whom the present letters shall come, by Hugh of Howthorpe, son and heir of John of Howthorpe for himself and his heirs, to render service to Walter de Percehay on lands and tenements in Scackleton which the abbot and convent held of Hugh's father and hold of him. Pledge to warranty. Sealed with the donor's seal.* Byland; St Peter and St Paul, Apostles, 28 Edward I [29 June 1300].
Copy: MS Dodsworth 63, fol. 60r–v, from cartulary fol. 219.
Marginal note: (in later hand) '1299 27 Ed 1'.
Note: This bond follows claims in 1297 and 1298 by the abbot against Hugh that Hugh should acquit him of the service which Walter de Percehay demanded for a free tenement which the abbot held in Scackleton of Hugh: Baildon, *Monastic Notes*, I, 31.

[fol. 113r–v]
1142 *Quitclaim by John de Wyville, son and heir of William de Wyville, for himself and his heirs, of whatever right he had or could have in the manor of Airyholme. This is made for the love of God and for 100s. and one good colt which the abbot and convent have given him. Sealed with the donor's seal.* Byland; eve of St John the Baptist [23 June or 28 Aug.], 1300.
Hiis testibus Thoma de Colevyle, Iohanne de Barton' de Friton',

Iohanne de Iarpenvyle, militibus, Waltero le Graunt', Iohanne Maunsell, Roberto de Foxhole, etc.

Marginal note: (in later hand) '28 Ed. 1'.

Copy: MS Dodsworth 63, fol. 60v, from cartulary fol. 219, from which readings for the damaged portions of the charter have been supplied.

[fol. 113v]

1143 *Grant and confirmation, addressed to all the sons of holy mother church present and future who will see or hear this chirograph, by the abbot of Byland and the convent of that place to Simon of Lilling, son of Paulinus of Lilling, of common of woodland, that is for haybote and other necessities, and for all types of estovers, from the path which runs between Scackleton and Coulton from the eastern side through all the wood called* Coltonbusk. *Grant also of a perch of meadow lying below* Coltonbusk *saving to the abbot and convent common use of the meadow for their animals in the open season. The abbot and convent have also granted to Simon and his heirs pasture for 8 oxen only in Mugden at any time, saving meadow from the path leading between Coulton and Scackleton westwards as far as their grange of Scackleton. For this Simon has relaxed and quitclaimed all right which he had or could have in the wood called* Westwod *from the grange of Scackleton westwards. In the form of a chirograph sealed with the seals of both parties.* [late 13th cent.].

Hiis testibus Paulino de Lilyng prenominato, Iohanne de Iarpenvyle, Yvone de Etton', [Ricardo de] Malbys, militibus, Hugone de Bagg, Waltero de Coltona, Willelmo de Thorner de Wygynthorpe, etc.

Copy: MS Top. Yorks. d. 11, fol. 276r (old p. 517), from cartulary fol. 219, from which readings for the damaged portions of the charter have been supplied.

Dating: The third and fourth witnesses attest together in no. 906.

[fol. 114r, old fol. 220]

SKEWSBY (SE6271), in the parish of Dalby and wapentake of Bulmer (NR). Skewsby lies just over a mile SW of Scackleton Grange, on the southern edge of the Howardian Hills. Alan de Flamville, who entered Byland as a monk (no. 1144), was of a branch of the family of Roger de Flamville, second husband of Juetta de Arches (*EYF*, pp. 29–32). Alan's son, Elias, made a grant on the occasion of his father's entry, and this was confirmed and augmented by his son, Alan II (nos 1144–6). Alan II's son, Elias, intended to be buried at Byland (nos 1146–7, 1150). The lands obtained in Skewsby adjoined those of Scackleton, and comprised pasture (no. 1146).

1144   *Grant in free alms, addressed to all the sons of holy mother church present and future, by Elias son of Alan de Flamville, to God and the monks of St Mary of Byland, of all his part of his wood of Skewsby with his father Alan when Alan was received as a monk, by these boundaries: as* Stayngrifgata *comes from* Mugdala *and descends across the ditch which is the boundary between Scackleton and Skewsby, and from there as the ditch runs southwards from the east of* Braidethwhayt, *and from there by the boundaries which they have made, as far as the head of the ditch to the west of* Braidethwhayt, *and as the ditch crosses [the valley which] is to the west of Holgate and the bottom of the valley as far as* Mugdale *and from the ditch of* Mugdale *to* Stayngrifgata. *Grant of free entry and exit for themselves and their men and animals through his land and woodland to Scackleton. The grant is made free from all secular service for the salvation of the donor's soul and of his father and mother and of all his ancestors and heirs. Pledge to warranty. [c. 1172 x 1214].*

Hiis testibus Thoma de Colvill, Willelmo de Corneburgh, Petro Basset, Henrico de Queneby, etc.

Copy (abbreviated): MS Dodsworth 63, fol. 60r, from cartulary fol. 220.
Dating: Alan de Flamville witnessed charters of Roger de Mowbray between 1142 and 1157 (*Mowbray Charters*, nos 236–7, 240, 253) and occurs in 1169 and 1172. His son, Elias, grantor of this charter, reached an agreement with Hugh de Flamville, son of Roger, and in 1214 Elias's son, Alan (see no. 1145) paid 1 mark for a writ concerning the agreement (*EYF*, p. 31).
Note: Readings in square brackets are supplied from no. 1145.

1145   *Confirmation, addressed to all the sons of holy mother church present and future, by Alan son of Elias de Flamville, to God and the monks of St Mary of Byland, of all his part of the wood of Skewsby which they have of the grant of his father, Elias, by the boundaries specified in no. 1144. The grant and confirmation are made in free alms quit of all secular service for the salvation of the soul of the donor and of his father and mother and of all his ancestors and heirs. Pledge to warranty. [c. 1214 x 1232].*

Hiis testibus Henrico de Ferlyngton', Ricardo de Ryparia, Engelramo de Corneburgh, Willelmo Haghet, etc.

Marginal note: A later hand has added a genealogy showing the descent from Alan de Flamavile to his son Elias son of Alan, and his son Alan son of Elias.
Copy (abbreviated): MS Dodsworth 63, fol. 60r, from cartulary fol. 220.
Dating: In 1214 Alan, son and heir of Elias de Flamville, gave 1 mark for a writ in respect of a final concord between his father and Hugh, son of Roger de Flamville; Alan also occurs in 1226 and 1231; he died before July 1232 when his son was a minor (*EYF*, pp. 31–2).

[fol. 114r–v]

1146 *Grant in free alms, addressed to all the faithful in Christ who will see or hear the present writing, by Elias de Flamville, to God [and St Mary] and the abbot and convent of Byland, of common pasture in the pasture and wood of Skewsby [for 300 sheep with their lambs until separation and 40 animals] by the following boundaries, from the ford of the watercourse [of Dalby] west as far as the watercourse [which is between Skewsby and the grange of Scackleton]. Grant of free entry and exit for their carts and wagons, flocks and men throughout the whole pasture. The grant is made free from all secular service with the body of the donor and with the body of Beatrice his wife. Pledge to warranty. Sealed with the donor's seal. [c. 1240].*

Hiis testibus dominis Ada de Hiltona, Willelmo Malebys, Thoma de Colvyll, Alano de [Lek], etc.

Copy (abbreviated): MS Dodsworth 63, fol. 60r, from cartulary fol. 220.

Dating: The grantor was the son of Alan de Flamville, grantor of no. 1145. Elias, although not named, was the under-age heir who occurs in July 1232, and in 1242–43 he held 8 carucates in Skewsby (Dalby) of Peter de Brus. He granted woodland in Scackleton to Byland before August 1240 when it was the subject of a final concord (*Yorks. Fines 1232–1246*, p. 91, from PRO CP 25/1/263/33, no. 137, cited above, no. 1134n).

[fol. 114v]

1147 *Grant and confirmation in free alms, addressed to all the sons of holy mother church present and future who will see or hear this charter, by Elias de Flamville, knight, with his body, to God and St Mary and the abbot and convent of Byland, of 1 toft and 1 croft and 2 bovates in the vill and region of Skewsby which Richard son of Siward formerly held of Elias. Grant also of his villein, Richard son of Siward, with his household. The grant is made free from all secular service. Further grant of licence to mill at his mill of Skewsby without multure, suit of court or any other service. Pledge to warranty. [c. 1254 x 1260].*

[Hiis testibus domino Willelmo] le Latimer tunc vicec(omite) Ebor', Nicholao de Boltby, Galfrido de Upsall, etc.

Copies: MS Dodsworth 63, fol. 60r, from which the readings in square brackets are supplied; (abbreviated): MS Dodsworth 94, fol. 39v.

Dating: first witness. Geoffrey of Upsall occurs in 1244 and had been succeeded in the manor of Upsall by his son, Hugh, by 1284–5.

Note: The date of Elias's death is not known; he intended to be buried at Byland: see nos 1146, 1150.

1148 *Bond, addressed to all the faithful in Christ, by John de [Thornton, lord of Skewsby] concerning suit of court, county court, wapentake . . . Sealed with the donor's seal.* Byland; St Gregory [12 Mar.], 1305 [1306].

Hiis testibus dominis Yvone de Etton', Thoma de Colvyle milit(ibus),
Thoma de Riparia, etc.

Copy: (abbreviated) MS Dodsworth 63, fol. 60r, from which the readings in square
brackets are supplied.

1149 *Rubric: Quitclaim by Elias de Flamville of Hugh son of Roger of
Dalby. . . . [c.* 1240 x 1280].

1150 *Rubric: Charter of the same Elias [de Flamville] that he will not be
buried elsewhere. [c.* 1240 x 1280].

Marginal note indicating nos 1150–52: Scakilton B(aculus) iii.

1151 *Rubric: Chirograph of Adam de Eyndby concerning 1 toft and 2
bovates in the region of Skewsby and 7 acres in the region of Bagby. He
regranted them for 1 pittance to be made annually at the convent.* [1231 x
1242].

Text: MS Dodsworth 7, fol. 175v. Grant and confirmation in the form
of a chirograph, addressed to all the sons of holy mother church who
will see or hear this writing, by Abbot Henry of Byland and the
convent of the place, to Adam Aynderby of Thirsk of 1 toft and 2
bovates in the region of Skewsby which the abbot and convent have
of the grant of Elias de Flamville, and 7 acres in Bagby which they
have of the grant of Stephen de Blaby. To hold in fee and hereditary
right. Pledge to warranty. Sealed with the seals of both parties. Hiis
testibus dominis Iohanne de Eyvill, Willelmo Malebysse, Willelmo de
Buscy, Gaufrido de Uppes', Thoma de Colevyll, Willelmo de Barton,
militibus, Thoma de Etton, Iohanne de Holthorp, Waltero de Colton,
Nicholao Talvace de Tresk, Willelmo filio Ade de Aynderby de Tresk,
Waltero de Tresk, coco, et aliis.

Dating: Abbot Henry of Battersby. The first witness is John de Daiville who died in
1242/3 rather than his grandson, who died in 1291.

1152 *Rubric: Chirograph of the same [Adam de Eyndby] concerning the
collect 'Quare domine pro tua pietate' to be said at mass in the chapel in the
cemetery.*

Note: This relates to the annual pittance mentioned in no. 1151.

[fol. 115r, old fol. 221]

SCAMPSTON (SE8675), in the parish of Rillington and the wapentake
of Buckrose (ER). Scampston lies 1½ miles east of Rillington, the
church of which was appropriated to Byland.

1153 *Note: In Scampston the monks had 2 tofts and 2 bovates belonging to the glebe of the church of Rillington.*

[fol. 115r, old fol. 221]
SKIRPENBECK (SE7457), township and parish in the wapentake of Buckrose (ER), 2½ miles east of Stamford Bridge. This section of the cartulary contains three full texts and 17 documents represented by rubrics only. As discussed in the Introduction (pp. xliii–xliv) the reason for this selection was that Byland's property was conveyed to Easby Abbey. The main benefactors were members of the Chauncy family. Amfrey de Chauncy II, lord of Skirpenbeck, granted small portions of land and pasture for 400 sheep, by which time the monks had constructed sheepfolds (no. 1156). Possibly because of Byland's land acquisitions in the area St Leonard's Hospital demised to the monks 1 carucate that Amfrey had granted them, to hold of the Hospital for a small rent (no. 1154). By a final concord of 1207 Amfrey's son, Walter II, recognized the monks' lands (no. 1157), as did his brother, Roger, in 1231 (no. 1160). In 1249 the manor of 'Steynhow' in Skirpenbeck was granted by Byland to John le Romeyn, archdeacon of Richmond (no. 1171) and by him to the canons of Easby.

1154 *Rubric: Chirograph of the brethren of the Hospital of St Peter, York, concerning 1 carucate in Skirpenbeck which they have of the grant of Amfrey de Chauncy, rendering 2 marks yearly.* [1199 x 1201].
Text: BL MS Egerton 2827 (Easby cartulary) fols 254v–255r. Agreement between the monks of St Mary of Byland and the convent of the brethren of the hospital of St Peter in the time of Abbot Hamo of Byland and Master Paulinus, master of the Hospital. Paulinus and his brethren, by common assent, demised and confirmed to the abbot of Byland and the convent of the place that carucate of land that they have in the region of Skirpenbeck of the grant of Amfrey de Chauncy and by confirmation of King John. To hold free from all service except royal demands and for 2 marks paid yearly to the Hospital, 1 mark at St Martin (11 Nov.) and 1 mark at Whitsuntide. Pledge to warranty. In the form of a chirograph, sealed with the seals of both chapters. Hiis testibus etc.

Marginal note: B(aculus) i. A later hand has added a genealogy showing the descent from Amfrey de Chauncy, lord of Skirpenbeck, to Walter his son and heir (9 R. Jo.) to Roger de Chauncy (15 H 3).

Dating: Reference to King John and to Paulinus of Leeds, who was appointed master of St Leonard's Hospital in 1186 and died in 1200 or 1201 (*Fasti York*, p. 126).

Note: The family of Chauncy was a benefactor of Whitby Abbey in Skirpenbeck;

Amfrey's father, Walter, granted land and the church there, which Amfrey confirmed to the monks of Whitby (*EYC* II, no. 831, *EYF*, p. 16). Amfrey de Chauncy II granted property in Skirpenbeck to St Peter's Hospital, York (*EYC* II, no. 839, from the copy which precedes our no. 1154 in the Easby cartulary), and to Byland (*ibid.*, no. 838, no. 1156 below). He died before 1190; his son and heir, Walter, was then a minor (*EYF*, p. 16).

1155 *Rubric: Letter of the same [brethren of the Hospital of St Peter] concerning £20 to be paid to the monks if the land cannot be guaranteed to them.*

1156 *Rubric: Charter of Amfrey de Chauncy concerning land in Skirpenbeck in various places and pasture for 400 sheep.*
Original: *Grant and confirmation, addressed to the archbishop of York and the whole chapter of St Peter (York), by Amfrey de Chauncy of 11 acres in the region of Skirpenbeck next to* Haibrec; *32 acres in* Waitecroft; *13 acres and 1 perch in* Stainhou; *11 acres in* Rucroft *next to the mill; 5 acres to the south of his part of* Flagdthewat; *2 acres of meadow next to the meadow of Bugthorpe; and common pasture for their animals which cultivate the land, wherever his own flocks pasture. Further grant of pasture for 400 sheep wherever his flocks and those of his men graze, except for his enclosure of* La Bruce *as enclosed by a ditch. They shall pasture the 400 sheep throughout his demesne as the boundary runs between the land of his men in Thoralby and the said pasture. They shall have exits for the sheep,* 1 *two perches in width from their sheepfold to* Bildebrec *and from there to the highway running from Scarborough, and the other from their sheepfold above* Haibrec *to the spring of the vill and beyond the spring next to his garden throughout his meadow. They shall have a third exit from their sheepfold between the cultivated land and the spring of the vill as far as their pasture. All this is granted in free alms, free from service, to do as the monks wish, for the salvation of the soul of the grantor and of all his ancestors and heirs. Pledge to warranty. Grant also that neither he nor his heirs will receive the flocks of others within the region of Skirpenbeck, to the injury of the monks.* [1158 x 1186, probably *c.* 1166 x 1172].
Hiis testibus Roberto decano Ebor', Alano et Stephano canonicis, Roberto filio Petri, Willelmo de Buthum', Rogero de Bavent, Willelmo de Corneburgh, Normanno, Thoma, Paulino presbiteris, Ansardo, Willelmo filio Ingelberti, [Petro filio Gilberti *erased*], Willelmo le Norrais, Reinaldo de Cattona, Gaufrido de Ponte, Hugone de Cattona.
Location: BL Add. charter 20588; endorsed: iii Staynhou; Carta Amfredi de Chanc'

de terra in Scerpinbec; seal: round, red-brown wax; SIGILLVM ANFRID DE CANCI.

Pd (from original): *EYC* II, no. 838, where dated 1175 x 1186.

Dating: first witness, but this was probably the grant confirmed by Henry II between *c.* 1166 and 1172 (BL MS Egerton 2827 (Easby cartulary) fols 256v–257r; *EYC* II, no. 837; above, no. 524). Stephen, canon, is Stephen the Roman, canon of York, who occurs in 1164 x 1174, before 1173, and 1158 x 1181 (*Fasti York*, p. 129). He attests nos 225, 395, 491, 594 above.

1156A   *Rubric: Charter of Walter de Chauncy concerning 14 acres of meadow in the region of Skirpenbeck, 3 tofts in the same vill, and confirmation of the grant of his father.* [before 1228].

Dating: the death of Walter de Chauncy: *EYF*, p. 16. He died without issue and was succeeded by his brother, Roger, who died in 1238 and was succeeded by his son, Robert.

[fol. 115r–v]

1157   **Original:** *Agreement between the monks and Walter de Chauncy, by which the monks remitted all claims and quarrels against Walter. Walter has granted 14 acres of meadow in the region of Skirpenbeck next to the 2 acres of meadow which the monks have near the meadow of Bugthorpe, that is 11 acres in exchange for 11 acres of land and meadow which they had near* Haybrec *and 2 acres of meadow for the remission of pasture in* Haybrec *which they claimed against him in a case of novel disseisin at York in the presence of Simon of Pattishall and his fellow itinerant justices, and 1 acre for the remission of pasture for 100 sheep of the 400 which they ought to have in the common pasture of Skirpenbeck, by the charter of his father, Amfrey. Also 3 tofts in the same vill lying together between the toft which belonged to Thomas son of Elvive and the toft which belonged to Adam Bruisel, with all the headland in the open fields* (foraria) *nearest towards the south from the toft of Adam Bruisel to the public road which runs towards Sutton. The monks are to enclose and build at their will, and do there as they wish. Confirmation of all they have in the region of Skirpenbeck of the grant of his father, Amfrey, that is 32 acres in* Waitecroft, *13 acres and 1 perch in* Stainhou, *11 acres in* Rucroft *next to the mill, 5 acres near* Flagdewat *on the southern side of the road and 2 acres of meadow next to the meadow of Bugthorpe and common pasture for their animals which cultivate the land. Further grant of pasture for 300 sheep of the 400 sheep wherever his animals or those of his successors or men of Skirpenbeck pasture, except the whole of* Haibrec *towards the south, from that exit which the monks have from the spring of the vill, next to the garden as far as the land of the canons of St Andrews, and except for his enclosure of* La Bruce *which is enclosed by a* *ditch. Undertaking not to let in any animals of any other religious into the vill, to the detriment of the monks. If the monks wish to give as much as other monks, they may use common exits from the vill for their animals, one near the spring to the north by the road which runs westwards and eastwards, and through the green valley which divides the* culture *of* Haybrec *and the other towards* La Bruce *as far as the canons' land. The monks are to do there and improve these 16 acres as they wish, but are not to enclose them on Walter's side of the meadow nor build on them nor cultivate them. The monks are to have free entry and exit to their meadow from the highway near the cemetery between the profitable land and the great meadow. Pledge to warranty. Sealed with the seal of the abbot of Byland and those of Walter de Chauncy and Robert Murdac. 1207.*

Hiis testibus Simone decano, Hamone thesaurario Ebor', Radulfo magistro hospitalis Sancti Petri, Roberto Walensi tunc vic(ecomite) Ebor', Willelmo de Perci, Willelmo de Cornebergh, Gikello de Smedt', Gaufrido Fossard, Rogero Malleverer, Thoma de Lasceles, Gilberto de Torni, Drogone de Harum, Waltero de Angotebi, Gilberto de Thurkilby, Stephano filio eius, Gaufrido de Ampelford, Waltero filio Gille.

Location: BL Add. charter 20589; cut as chirograph; no endorsements; seal: round, red-brown wax; SIGIL.. WALTERI DE CANCI.

Marginal note in cartulary: (in later hand) '1207 9 Jo'.

Copies: BL MS Egerton 2827 (Easby cartulary), fol. 255r–v (witnesses omitted); MS Dodsworth 91, fols 144v–146r, no. 121; (brief mention) MS Dodsworth 63, fol. 59v.

Dating: given in text.

Note: The cartulary copy has the first four witnesses only. After the death of his father (by 1190) Walter de Chauncy, as a minor, was in the custody of Hugh Murdac, and he married Maud Murdac. Robert Murdac was presumably a relation. At the time of issue of the charter of Walter's father, Amfrey, the monks had a sheepfold at 'Hailbrec'. For the property in Skirpenbeck and Bugthorpe owned by the canons of the Gilbertine priory of St Andrew, Fishergate, York, see J. E. Burton, 'Historical Evidence', in *The Church and Gilbertine Priory of St Andrew, Fishergate*, ed. Richard L. Kemp and C. Pamela Graves, *The Archaeology of York*, 11, *The Medieval Defences and Suburbs*, fasc. 2 (Council for British Archaeology for the York Archaeological Trust, 1996), p. 59. On Simon of Pattishall see above, no. 1140, note.

[fol. 115v]

1158   *Rubric: Chirograph of the same Walter [de Chauncy] concerning an exchange of 1 toft in Skirpenbeck.* [1209 x 1212].

Text: MS Dodsworth 91, fol. 77r, no. 14. Notification to all present and future of the exchange made between the monks of St Mary of Byland and Walter de Chauncy by which Walter granted, to hold of him and his heirs, all the hill and cliff between 'Waitecroft' and the Derwent, from the land of Thomas son of Elvive below the hill towards the south to his land towards the north on the river bank. The monks have granted to Walter and his heirs the toft in Skirpenbeck which Nicholas the miller held between the land of Roger de Chauncy and the toft of Roger the carter. Pledge to warranty. Hiis testibus Henrico de Redeman tunc vicecomite Ebor', Rogero Malleverer, Nicholao Basset, Gilberto de Torny, Willelmo Haget, Willelmo Franceis, Roberto Borard, Willelmo filio Hugonis, Petro Britone.

Dating: first witness.

1159   *Rubric: Charter of Geoffrey de Breitona concerning 3 acres in the same vill.*
Text: BL MS Egerton 2827 (Easby cartulary), fol. 256r. Grant in free alms, addressed to the archbishop of York and the chapter of St Peter, York, and all the sons of holy church, by Geoffrey Breton, to God and the monastery of St Mary of Byland, of 3 acres next to 'Haybrech' on the southern side of the spring. The grant is made for the salvation of his soul and of his father and mother and all his ancestors and heirs. Pledge to warranty. Witnesses omitted.

1160   *Final concord in the king's court in the presence of Thomas of Moulton, William of Raleigh, Robert of Lexington, William de Insula, William of London, Master Robert of Schardlow, Ralph of Norwich, William of York and Richard Reyner, justices, and other faithful men of the lord king then present, between Roger de Chauncy, plaintiff, through Richard de Burgh his attorney, and Henry, abbot of Byland, defendant, through Brother Adam his monk and attorney, concerning 1½ carucates in Skirpenbeck, that is, all the land which the abbot held in the vill on the day the agreement was reached. Roger acknowledges that all this land is in the right of the abbot and his church, and has quitclaimed and remitted it. For this acknowledgement the abbot has given Roger 15 silver marks.* [Westminster; quindene of Easter 15 Henry III [6 Apr. 1231].
Copies: PRO CP 25/1/262/25, no. 125; MS Dodsworth 63, fol. 59v, from cartulary fol. 221.
Pd: (brief calendar): *Yorks. Fines 1218–1231*, p. 132 (from PRO copy).
Note: Roger de Chauncy succeeded his brother, Walter II, in 1228 and died in 1238 (*EYF*, p. 16).

1161   *Rubric: Confirmation by Jordan son of Geoffrey of 3 acres in Skirpenbeck.* [before 1190].
Text: MS Top. Yorks. e. 7, fol. 141r (old p. 229). Grant and confirmation in free alms, addressed to the archbishop of York and the whole

chapter of St Peter (York) and all the sons of holy church, by Jordan son of Geoffrey de Britonl, to God and the monks of St Mary of Byland, of the grant of his father, that is, 3 acres next to their grange of Skirpenbeck which is located on 'Haibrec' to the south of the spring. The confirmation is made for the salvation of his soul and of his father and mother and all his ancestors and heirs. Pledge to warranty. Hiis testibus Anfrido de Canci, Stephano de Killum, Roberto de Hothum, Iohanne de Rillingtun, Petro filio Grent, Radulfo presbytero de Skerpinbec, Pagano de Cattuna, Ada de Killum, Willelmo Norrais, Rannulfo fabro.

Dating: The death of Amfrey de Chauncy.

1162 *Rubric: Charter of Nicholas de Stuteville concerning water meadow* (holme) *and pasture in exchange for 2 bovates in Scrayingham.* [before 1233].

Text: BL MS Egerton 2827 (Easby cartulary), fols 255v–256r. Confirmation by Nicholas de Stuteville for the salvation of his soul and of all his ancestors and heirs, to God and the monastery of St Mary of Byland, of all his arable land with meadow, which they have in the water meadow called 'Harholvemilne' belonging to Skirpenbeck mill, as the water descends on either side of the holme from the meadow of William Thurkil as far as Stamford Bridge. This he grants in exchange for 2 bovates in Scrayingham which Geoffrey of St Peter granted to the monastery in free alms with his body. The monks are to to do there as they wish, and are to hold the land of Nicholas and his heirs in fee farm for 10s. yearly, 5s. at Whitsuntide and 5s. at St Martin (10 Nov.) for all service. Nicholas and his heirs are to take from the land water as necessary, in width 2 perches and the length of the mill-pond as far as the pond extends, and to repair the pond as necessary and with as little damage as possible to the said meadow beyond the profitable land. Pledge to warranty. Witnesses omitted.

Dating: death of the grantor.

1163 *Rubric: Charter of Nicholas [de Stuteville] concerning 1 pound of pepper paid yearly to Geoffrey of St Peter.* [before 1233].

Dating: death of the grantor.

1164 *Rubric: Charter of Ralph de Burdon concerning 1 acre in Skirpenbeck.* [before 1228].

Text: BL MS Egerton 2827 (Easby cartulary), fol. 256v. Grant in pure alms, addressed to all [seeing or hearing these letters], by Ralph

Burdun of Skirpenbeck, to God and the monastery of St Mary of Byland, of 1 acre with its appurtenances in the region of Skirpenbeck lying next to the monks' land in 'Flathewath' towards the south, free from all service for the salvation of his soul and of his wife and of all his ancestors and heirs. Pledge to warranty. Witnesses omitted.

Copy: MS Dodsworth 91, fol. 76v, no. 13, which adds: Hiis testibus Waltero de Caunci, Rogero de Caunci fratre eius, Michaele le Norrais, Petro Brett', Berteramo Burdun, Ada de Caunci et aliis.

Date: Death of the first witness.

1165 *Rubric: Quitclaim by the same [Ralph de Burdon] of his right in the ditch which the monks raised around* Staynhow *in the region of Skirpenbeck.* [early 13th cent.].

Text: BL MS Egerton 2827 (Easby cartulary), fol. 256v. Quitclaim by Ralph Burdun to the monastery of St Mary of Byland, of all right which he had against them in a ditch which they constructed at 'Staynhou' in the region of Skirpenbeck. The monks may freely enclose their land with a wall and a ditch as they wish. Pledge to warranty. Witnesses omitted.

Dating: By reference to no. 1164.

1166 *Rubric: Chirograph making a claim against the prior of St Andrew, York, concerning 10s. which the monks were accustomed to render to Nicholas de Stuteville.*

1167 *Rubric: Quitclaim by William son of Hugh of 1 toft.*

Text: BL MS Egerton 2827 (Easby cartulary), fol. 256r–v. Grant and quitclaim in free alms by William son of Hugh and William his son, to God and the monastery of St Mary of Byland, of all that open ground (*placea*) which they held of Walter de Chauncy in the vill of Skirpenbeck belonging to the toft which the monks hold of the Hospital of St Leonard's, York, from the moor which is the boundary between the grantors' land and that of the monks in a straight line beyond the road as far as the water. Pledge to warranty. Witnesses omitted.

1168 *Rubric: Quitclaim by the same [William son of Hugh] of his right in a messuage in* Staynhow.

Text: BL MS Egerton 2827 (Easby cartulary), fol. 256v. Quitclaim by William son of Hugh of all right which he or his heirs have or might have against the monastery of Byland in the wall and ditch which the monks have made around their houses in 'Staynhow' and in the buildings within the enclosure of the wall which have been constructed or will be constructed in the future. Pledge to bring no further claim. Witnessed omitted.

1169 *Rubric: Charter of William son of Hugh concerning 1 acre in Skirpenbeck.*
Text: BL MS Egerton 2827 (Easby cartulary), fol. 256r. Grant in free alms by William son of Hugh and William his son to God and the monastery of St Mary of Byland, of 1 acre in Skirpenbeck lying at the bridge of Buttercrambe near to the monastery's land on the southern side, to do with as they wish. The grant is made free from secular service. Pledge to warranty. Witnesses omitted.

1170 *Rubric: Letter patent from Nicholas de Stuteville concerning an annual rent of 10s.* [before 1233].
Dating: death of the grantor.

1171 *Notification, addressed to all to whom the present writing shall come, by Brother Henry, abbot of Byland, and the convent of that place, that they have granted to Master John le Romeyn, archdeacon of Richmond, the manor of* Steynhow *with all its appurtenances and pasture for 300 sheep. John is to hold the manor and pasture in ecclesiastical and secular right even though the abbot and convent may incur damage because of this. Quitclaim of all right except for 1 pound of cumin, and 16 acres of meadow in the great meadow of Skirpenbeck and 1 toft and croft in Skirpenbeck, that is, the toft which lies nearest to the exit to Full Sutton. John and his successors are to keep faithfully and indemnify the abbot and convent for their payment of 2 marks which they were accustomed to pay to St Leonard's Hospital (St Peter's), York, for 1 carucate in Skirpenbeck and 10s. which they were accustomed to pay to Nicholas de Stuteville for land and pasture and meadow in the water meadow in the region of Skirpenbeck. Pledge to warranty. In the form of a chirograph, both sides being sealed by both parties.* The eve of St Fabian and St Sebastian [19 Jan.] 1248 [1249].
Marginal note: (in later hand) '22 Ed. 3'.
Copies: BL MS Egerton 2827 (Easby cartulary), fol. 257r; (abbreviated) MS Dodsworth 63, fol. 59v, from cartulary fol. 221.
Note: Egerton 2827, fols 257v–258r, and MS Dodsworth 91, fol. 76r–v, no. 12, have copies of a similar but earlier grant made when John le Romeyn the elder was subdean of York, a post in which he first occurs in 1228 and which he held until he became archdeacon in 1241. This specifies an annual rent of 36s. 8d. in addition to 1 pound of cumin, payable at Whitsuntide and St Martin in Winter at the monks' house in Clifton, and omits the indemnity clause. No. 1171 was confirmed by

Hugh, rector, and the brethren of the Hospital of St Peter, York (MS Egerton 2827, fol. 257r–v). Joan de Stuteville, widow of Hugh Wake, granted to John le Romeyn, archdeacon of Richmond, an annual rent of 10s. which the abbot and convent of Byland were bound to render to her for meadow in Skirpenbeck next to the mill, and the mill itself, for 1 pound of cumin annually: *ibid.*, fol. 258r.

1172   *Rubric: Chirograph of Walter son of Ivetta concerning 1 toft in Skirpenbeck for his homage and service, rendering 3s. to the monks.*

[fol. 116r, old fol. 222r]
SLEDMERE (SE9364), township and parish in the wapentake of Buckrose (ER). This was isolated from most of Byland's estates.

1173   *Grant in free alms, addressed to the archbishop of York and the whole chapter of St Peter (York) and all the sons of holy church, by Thomas son of Roger of Dalton, to God and the monks of St Mary of Byland, of 6 acres in the region of Sledmere, and ½ acre in these places, that is, in the tofts and in* Langannelandes, *and pasture for 200 sheep throughout Sledmere. The grant is made free from secular service for the salvation of the soul of the donor and of his father and mother and of all his ancestors and heirs. Pledge to warranty.* [early 13th cent.].
Hiis testibus Rogero de Daivill', Radulpho clerico, Willelmo del Meynil', Rogero filio Roberti, Hugone de Cultona, etc.
Dating: Roger of Dalton attests in the reign of King John (*EYC* X, no. 97). The last witness is Hugh of Cowlam. It is not clear to what branch of the Meinill family William belonged.

1174   *Rubric: <Charter> of the same [Thomas son of Roger of Dalton] concerning ½ acre in the same vill.*

1175   *Rubric: Charter of Thomas of Dalton concerning ½ acre in Sledmere, that is, in* Scortenlandis.

1176   *Rubric: Charter of William Silvanus concerning 1 toft at the entry to the vill of Sledmere towards the west.*

1177   *Grant in free alms, addressed to the archbishop of York and the whole chapter of St Peter (York) and all the sons of holy church, by Richard de Wyville, for the love of God and salvation of his soul and of his relatives and heirs, to God and the monks of St Mary of Byland and their successors, of pasture for 120 sheep throughout the region and pasture of Sledmere. Confirmation of all that the monks have been granted by his men, both land and*

pasture, and of all they may acquire in the future. Pledge to warranty.
[? early 13th cent.].

Testes sunt Gilbertus . . . Nicholas Basset, Ricardus de la Ryver, etc.

Dating: Several of the Wyville family held the name of Richard. Nicholas Basset occurs in the early 13th century (see nos 1, 1158). Richard de Riparia made a grant to Byland in the early 13th century, which was attested by Richard de Wyville (no. 1138). This suggests that the donor is Richard, son of William de Wyville, who was dead by *c.* 1215.

1178   *Rubric: Charter of Henry de Thorpe concerning 2½ acres.*

1179   *Rubric: Charter of Walter son of Azce concerning 2 acres in free alms.*

1180   *Rubric: Charter of the same [Walter son of Azce] concerning 1 toft rendering 12d. from the heirs of Richard de Wyville.*

Note: The rubric states that these (nos 1179–80) are bound together.

1181   *Rubric: Charter of Walter son of Azce concerning 7 acres in free alms.*

1182   *Rubric: Confirmation by Ralph de la Mare of the grant which Walter son of Azce made, as his charters show.*

1183   *Rubric: Confirmation by Ralph son of Ralph of Sledmere concerning 6½ acres in Sledmere.*

Note: This is followed by a note: 'bound together'.

1184   *Rubric: Confirmation by Ralph de la Mare of 4 acres in the same.*

1185   *Grant in free alms, addressed to all the sons of holy church present and future, by Peter son of Gunewar of Sledmere, to God and the monks of St Mary of Byland, of that portion of profitable land which he had at* Thrillekeld *in the region of Sledmere, next to the* cultura *of Gerard Silvanus towards the south. The head of the land touches on* Severdaleclif *and the other head on the York Road* (Yorke Stret) *and is 1 perch wide, and at* Unerdail *he has granted 1 acre and 1 rood of 2 perches in width of which 1 touches on the highway between Sledmere and Cowlam . . . next to the* cultura *of Gerard Silvanus to the south in the fee of Nicholas de Yeland. Grant also of land 2 perches in width lying next to the boundary of Gerard. <Grant of> pasture for 2 horses and 4 pigs throughout his land with all liberties and easements belonging to the land. The grant is made free from* *secular service for the salvation of the soul of the donor and of all his ancestors and heirs. Pledge to warranty.* [before 1243].

Hiis testibus Iacobo de Cullun, Petro Silvani, Willelmo de Lutton', Roberto Putrell, etc.

Dating: Eustacia, daughter of Richard de Wyville married Nicholas de Yeland. Before 1243 she had married a second time, to William de la Launde. See *EYF*, p. 104.

Note: 'Yorkestret', here translated as in *EPNS ER*, p. 127, as the York Road, refers to the Roman road from York.

1186 *Rubric: Confirmation by Robert son of William de Palmer and Sibyl his wife of 2½ acres which Elias de Thorpe granted and 1½ acres of the grant of the same Robert and Sibyl.*

[fol. 116v]

1187 *Rubric: Charter of William son of William of Dalton concerning 2 acres which Walter son of Azce granted, whose charter is above. Surrendered.*

1188 *Rubric: Chirograph relating to the case of the canons of Kirkham concerning the tithes of 7 acres in Sledmere, which has been decided.*

Note: The canons of Kirkham held land in Sledmere and established a grange there: *EYC* X, no. 110.

1189 *Rubric: Two charters of Ralph de la Mare of Sledmere which have been surrendered.*

1190 *Grant in free alms, addressed to all the faithful in Christ present and future, by William son of William of Dalton, to God and the monks of St Mary of Byland, of 1 acre in the region of Sledmere, that is 3 roods and more lying between the field of Towthorpe and the king's highway which leads to York, and whatever might be lacking from a full acre within these boundaries he will make up in* Mykelgravelith *above* Hersewellegat, *so that they shall have the full acre. Grant also of pasture for 60 sheep throughout Sledmere, for the salvation of his soul and of all his ancestors and heirs. Pledge to warranty. Sealed with the donor's seal.* [before 1243].

Hiis testibus domino Iacobo de Collun, Roberto filio Nigelli, Petro Silvani, Roberto Putrell', Willelmo de Lutton', etc.

Dating: The same witnesses, except for Robert son of Nigel, attest no. 1185.

1191 *Rubric: Charter of Ralph son of Ralph of Sledmere concerning 4½ acres in the same vill.*

1192 *Rubric: Chirograph of Peter of Sledmere concerning 1 bovate in Sledmere, rendering 10s. yearly.*

1193 **Original:** *Notification addressed to all the sons of holy mother church present and future who will see or hear this writing, of the agreement between Dom. Henry, abbot, and the convent of Byland and Walter of Coulton (in Scackleton), son of Robert of Coulton, by which the abbot and convent have granted to Walter and his heirs in exchange for 2 bovates in Sledmere, their mill of Scackleton with meadow and ground lying between the ditch which brings water to the mill and the water course of Coulton. They have also granted the suit of their men holding 9 bovates of them in Scackleton and millsoke of all their men throughout Scackleton at the said mill, so that all grain, malt and flour shall be milled there to the twentieth measure. If the mill of Walter or his heirs shall be destroyed or moved, the men will be allowed to mill elsewhere without a claim being made by Walter or his heirs until Coulton mill is repaired. If they grind elsewhere or in any other way the grain which grows on their land in Scackleton or which they buy, the abbot and convent will compel them to pay multure to Walter and his heirs. The abbot and convent make this grant in exchange for 2 bovates in Sledmere without the tofts, of which one was held by Hugh the shepherd and the other by William Seger. The abbot and convent undertake to have no mill in the region of Scackleton to the prejudice of Walter's mill. Pledge to warranty. In the form of a chirograph. Sealed with the seals of both parties.* [1231 x 1268].

Hiis testibus domino Willelmo Haget', Roberto de Bulford, Willelmo de Thorny, Willelmo de Barthun de Hoton', Rogero Rawth, Roberto le Barn' de Gilling', Willelmo de Stodelay, Willelmo Nobel, Thoma de Ettun', Roberto de Croum, Galfrido filio Petri, Willelmo de Dalton', Petro de Briddal', et aliis.

Location: NYCRO, ZQG (F) (MIC 2894/1283).

Dating: The attestation of William Haget (see nos 1145, 1158), William de Thorny (nos 718, 1134), Roger Rawthe (nos 672, 1120, 1125, 1140) and Robert le Barn of Gilling (no. 507) suggest that this belongs to the abbacy of Henry of Battersby.

Note: The cartulary copy lacks the last 7 witnesses, and 'le Barn de Gilling'. The stream runs mid way between Coulton and Scackleton Grange and Mill Wood lies on its south bank.

1194 *Rubric: Confirmation of Richard son of William de Wyville of all the lands in Sledmere; look among the confirmations of the magnates.*

Note: The Magnates section of the cartulary contains no confirmation of Richard son of William de Wyville, only one of John son of William de Wyville (no. 686 above, also at no. 1197 below).

1195 *Rubric: Two enrolments, 1 of J(ohn de) Wyville and the other of Robert of Coulton. These are in the first bundle at the end.*

[fols 116v–117r]
1196 *Quitclaim, addressed to all who will see or hear this writing, by William of Sledmere, chaplain, son and heir of Jolland of Sledmere, for the salvation of his soul and of all his heirs and ancestors, to God and St Mary and the abbot and convent of Byland, of 10s. annual rent which the monks were accustomed to render from a certain bovate granted by Peter of Sledmere his grandfather, as appears in a chirograph between Peter and the abbot and convent. The grant is made for himself and his heirs and assigns. Undertaking to make no further claim to the rent. Pledge to warranty. Sealed with the donor's seal.* [7 Apr. 1312 x 1 Jan. 1333].
Hiis testibus magistro Roberto de Pykeryng decano ecclesie Beati Petri Ebor', dominis Willelmo de Wyvilla et Waltero de Percehay militibus, etc.

Dating: first witness.

[fol. 117r, old fol. 223]
1197 *Confirmation and quitclaim, addressed to all the faithful in Christ present and future, by John de Wyville, son and heir of William de Wyville, for the salvation of his soul and of all his ancestors and heirs, to God and the abbot and convent of Byland and their successors, of all lands which the monks have of his fee. Undertaking to make no claim. Pledge to warranty. Sealed with the donor's seal.* Byland; day after St Andrew, 28 Edward I [1 Dec. 1299].
Hiis testibus dominis Waltero de Tay', M[ilone de Stapi]lton, Ivone de Ettona, Waltero Percehay, militibus, Hugone de Calveton', Iohanne de Butterwyke, Willelmo del Bek, Hugone de Carleton', et aliis.

Marginal note: (in later hand) '1299 28 E 1'. There is also a genealogy showing 'Dominus Willelmus Wyvill' and his son and heir John de Wyvill, 28 E 1.
Copy: MS Dodsworth 63, fol. 59v, from which the readings in square brackets are supplied.
Note: There is a copy of this at no. 686 above.

[fol. 117v]
SCARBOROUGH (TA0388), township and parish in the wapentake of Pickering Lythe (NR). Scarborough castle was first constructed by William le Gros, count of Aumale, but it was under the patronage of King Henry II that the town grew to prominence, with the rebuilding of the castle as a royal castle, and the grant to the burgesses of the customs and liberties enjoyed by those of York. By the later middle

ages Scarborough was among the four wealthiest of Yorkshire towns, its wealth coming from fishing and from inland and international trade. See David Crouch and Trevor Pearson, ed., *Medieval Scarborough: studies in trade and civic life*, Yorkshire Archaeological Society Occasional Paper no. 1 (Otley, 2001). The Scarborough section is the last surviving section of the cartulary and is much damaged.

1198   *Rubric: Charter of Emma Wodecok, copied, concerning 3 messuages in Scarborough, that is 1 in the street called Newborough, another in the Oldborough and the third which Matilda of Kilham held, and concerning 3 acres in the* cultura *called Gildhousecliff and all the land which the monks have in the* cultura *called Store.* [mid 13th cent.].

Marginal note: Baculus i.

Dating: see no. 1201.

Note: An inquisition of 1240 stated that Scarborough castle was built by the count of Aumale, and that Henry II built a stronger castle on the site and established the old borough, and extended the borough with a further grant of land known as the new borough which lay outside the walls. See Paul Dalton, 'The foundation and development of Scarborough in the twelfth century', in Crouch and Pearson, *Medieval Scarborough*, pp. 1–6, and, in the same collection, Trevor Pearson, 'The topography of the medieval borough', pp. 85–91, especially pp. 87–91. Gildhousecliff, now Spring Bank, lay in Falsgrave, a mile to the west of Scarborough and the most important settlement in the area at the time of Domesday Book. In the 13th century a conduit was built at Gildhousecliff to supply water to Scarborough: Trevor Pearson, 'Falsgrave soke and settlement', *ibid.*, pp. 79–84 (pp. 82–3).

1199   *Grant, addressed to all the faithful present and future, by Abbot Henry and the convent of Byland to Richard of Falsgrave for his homage and service of 3 acres which lie in the* cultura *called Gildhousecliff between the land of Adam of Ruston and that of Adam Gamel, and the whole land which they have in the* cultura *called Store, with the meadow, to hold rendering yearly 10s. sterling, half at Whitsuntide and half at St Martin in Winter (11 Nov.). At Richard's death a third part of his chattels shall go to the abbey for the salvation of his soul and of all who are his. In the form of a chirograph, sealed with the seals of both parties.* [c. 1300].

Hiis testibus Roberto Wared, Roberto Farman, Iohanne Haldan, Ricardo de Osgotby, Thoma de Anelaby, etc.

Dating: The occurrence of Adam of Ruston (Roston, Royston, see no. 1217) suggests that this is the Abbot Henry who professed obedience in 1300. He had been succeeded by Abbot William by 1302 (*HRH* II, 270).

Note: The rubric is followed by a note that this charter is in the third Deepdale bundle.

1200   *Rubric: Charter of Emma Wodecok concerning 1 curtilege in the Newborough between the house of Richard son of Gerard and that of Ralph of Holderness.* [mid 13th cent.].
Dating: This may be related to the final concord of 1252 (no. 1201).

1201   *Final concord in the presence of Silvester, bishop of Carlisle, Roger of Thirkleby, Abbot Hugh of Selby, Gilbert de Preston, and Adam de Hilton, itinerant justices, and other faithful men of the lord king then present, between Abbot Henry, plaintiff, and Jordan Wodecok and Emma his wife, defendant, concerning 3 messuages, 4 acres and 3 roods of meadow in Scarborough about which a plea of warranty had been brought. Jordan and Emma acknowledge these to be of the right of the abbot and convent of their own grant, to hold of them in free alms quit of all secular service. They pledge to warranty the land. In return the abbot and convent have received them into all the good deeds and prayers offered in their church.* York; day after St Hilary, 36 Henry III [14 Jan. 1252].
Marginal note: (in later hand) '36 H 3'.
Copy: PRO CP 25/1/265/45, no. 127.
Pd (calendar): *Yorks. Fines 1246–1272*, p. 54 (from PRO copy).

1202   *Rubric: Charter of Jordan and Emma Wodecok concerning all their land in Scarborough.* [*c*. 1252].

1203   *Rubric: Quitclaim by Simon the cowherd and Hawise his wife of 1 toft in the Newborough . . . Emma Wodecok.*

1204   *Final concord in the king's court at York at Easter 41 Henry III in the presence of John, abbot of Peterborough, <Roger> of Thirkleby, Peter de . . . itinerant justices and other faithful men of the lord king then present, between Abbot Henry, plaintiff, and Emma Wodcok concerning 1 messuage with its appurtenances in Scarborough about which a plea of warranty had been brought. The messuage lies in the Newborough in the vill of Scarborough . . . and the house of Ralph of Holderness and was recovered by Emma Wodecok. Emma acknowledges that this is of the right of the abbot and his church and that they have it by the grant of the said Emma. Emma pledges to warranty, and in return the abbot has received her and her heirs into all the good deeds and prayers offered in their church.* York; Easter 41 Henry III [1257].

[fol. 118r, old fol. 224]
1205   *Rubric: Charter of Adam Ad portam concerning 2 tofts in Scarborough outside Sandgate* (Portum Sabulonis) *which he held of Simon*

son of Gamel and Beatrice de Thorny, rendering yearly to Simon 6s. 3d. and to Gilbert Thorny 5s.

Note: The Sandgate lay on the south side of the Oldborough, and a wall is mentioned in 14th-century documents. There were two entrances though the south wall, the West Sandgate and East Sandgate: Pearson, 'The topography of the medieval borough', in Crouch and Pearson, *Medieval Scarborough*, p. 87.

1206   *Rubric: Charter of Reyner of Deepdale and Matilda concerning the same tofts.*
Sub eadem forma.

1207   *Rubric: Charter of the same Reyner and Matilda his wife concerning 1 toft in Scarborough which lies between the barn of Robert Ughtred and <that> of John son of Gervase, rendering to the lord king 4d. for husgable.*

Note: The family of Uthred was prominent in Scarborough; see David Crouch, 'Urban government and oligarchy in medieval Scarborough', in Crouch and Pearson, *Medieval Scarborough*, pp. 41–7 (pp. 43–5).

1208   *Rubric: Charter of Beatrice concerning all the land in Scarborough towards the sea which Gerard* publicanus *sold to her and her husband Roger for husgable.*

1209   *Rubric: Charter of Ernisius de Havyrford concerning a moiety of his land below the castle of Scarborough, lying between the land of Andrew Barth' and the land of Richard son of Eche. To hold of the lord king, saving forinsec service.*

1210   *Rubric: Quitclaim by John Gernecyne of all the land which the monks have of the grant of Ernisius.*

1211   *Rubric: Charter of Lucy wife of Ernisius of the other moiety of that land which came to her after her husband, and confirmation of the grant by her husband.*

1212   *Rubric: Charter of Waleran Couper concerning 12d. rent to be taken from his house on the seashore in which Lawrence Manyfalde lived.*

1213   *Rubric: Quitclaim by Robert Carvisic of Beverley of all his right in the land with buildings which he held in fee of John of Ayton in the Oldborough of Scarborough between the land of Walter . . . and 'le goter' called The Dumple* (le Dympill) *rendering . . . s. for stabling to him or to the lord of the fee.*

Note: The Dumple was the marshy area in the Oldborough between High West-gate, St Sepulchregate, Cartgate and Cook Row. It lay within the precinct of the Franciscan friary. The name survived until the 1930s. See Crouch and Pearson, *Medieval Scarborough*, p. 111.

1214   *Rubric: Charter of John of Ayton; surrendered.*

1215   *Writ ad quod damnum from King Edward [II] to Gerald Salvayn, escheator. Since lawful men of the bailliwick have sworn on oath to enquire into the truth of the matter, he has granted to Master Adam of Ruston licence to alienate 2 shillings worth of land to his beloved in Christ the abbot and convent of Byland.*
Note: For a grant by Adam of Ruston, see no. 1217 below. The text of no. 1215 is much damaged.

1216   *Rubric: Reply of the escheator.*

[fol. 118r–v]
1217   *Grant by Adam of Ruston of rent of 2s. from his tenement which Thomas le Flauner held, lying in St Sepulchregate in Scarborough. Boundaries. The abbot and convent are to take half the annual rent at Whitsuntide and half at St Martin in Winter (10 Nov.), without impediment by Adam and his heirs. Pledge to warranty. Sealed with his seal, and handed to the abbot and convent in the presence of Guy de Bellocampo, constable of Scarborough castle, Robert Wawayne, bailiff of the same, John of Settrington etc.* Scarborough, 12 May 1319.
Marginal note: (in later hand) '1319'.
Note: The text is much damaged.

1218   *Rubric: Grant of the king concerning the same rent of 2s. Look among the royal charters.*
Note: This is preceded by 'Charter of Simon', deleted. There is a rubric for Edward II's confirmation (5 June 1309) of no. 1217 at no. 531 above (*Cal. Pat. R. 1307–1313*, p. 161).

1219   *Rubric: Charter of Simon of Ruston concerning land which the monks have in the Newborough in Scarborough, rendering gavel rent* (gabulagium).
Marginal note: B(aculus) ii.

1220   Rubric: *Chirograph of Norman the merchant concerning all the land lying between the road below the town outside the Sand Gate, and the land which William Brun held . . ., rendering the service due.*

1221   Rubric: *Chirograph of Adam son of Elewyn concerning all the land of the grant of . . . rendering gavel rent to the monks.*

1222   Rubric: *Chirograph of Simon of Folkton . . . Henry of Beverley, Adam son of Aldan (Haldain) and Robert Farman, rendering 2s. to the monks.*
Note: The Haldain family held lands in the fields outside the Newborough. Haldain of Scarborough lived around the end of the twelfth century, and his son, Adam, was an early bailiff. See Crouch, 'Urban government and oligarchy', in Crouch and Pearson, *Medieval Scarborough*, p. 45.

1223   Rubric: *Chirograph charter of Adam son of Aldain (Haldain) concerning all the land which . . . aldus . . . rendering to us 2s. etc.*
Note: On the family of Haldain see note to no. 1222.

1224   Rubric: *Charter of Henry the carter concerning the house in which . . . which Robert Freman built. It is worth more and he says that he . . .*

1225   Memorandum that on Mon. . . . . 11 Edward I William of Danby, monk and attorney of the abbot and convent came and <claimed> to have liberties under royal charters, bringing with him a writ of King Edward addressed to the bailiffs of Scarborough.
The remainder of the folio is faded.

[*Old folios 225–243 lost*] The evidence of MS Top. Yorks. d. 11, fols 276v–278v indicates that these folios contained documents relating to the following places:

STAINSBY (NZ4615), in the parish of Stainton and wapentake of Langbargh West (NR).

SAVIGNY, the mother house of Byland; charters in this section related to Byland's daughter house of Jervaulx.

THIRSK (SE4282), township and parish in the wapentake of Birdforth.

THIRKLEBY (SE4777), parish in the wapentake of Birdforth (see also MS Dodsworth 63, fol. 71r–v).

THORNTON-LE-MOOR (SE3988), in the parish of North Otterington and wapentake of Allerton (NR).

THOLTHORPE (SE4766), in the parish of Alne and wapentake of Bulmer (NR).

THORNABY IN CLEVELAND (NZ4516), in the parish of Stainton, and **LINTHORPE** (NZ4818), in the parish of Middlesbrough, both in the wapentake of Langbargh West.

MIDDLETHORPE (SE5948), detached portion of the parish of St Mary Bishophill Senior, now in the City of York.

WILDON (Wildon Grange, SE5178), in the parish of Coxwold and wapentake of Birdforth (NR).

WOMBLETON (SE6783), in the parish of Kirkdale and wapentake of Ryedale (NR).

OULSTON (SE5474), in the parish of Coxwold and the wapentake of Birdforth (NR).

WILSDEN (SE0936), in the parish of Bradford and wapentake of Morley (WR).

WHITLEY (Upper, SE1904), in the parish of Kirkheaton and wapentake of Agbrigg (WR).

WIND HILL (Gate and Wood, SE3113), **WOOLLEY** (SE3133) and 'MERSCHAW', in the parish of Royston and wapentake of Staincross (WR).

Charters of Byland Abbey

The intention was to compile a list of original charters; however, in some cases it has been deemed appropriate to include later transcripts. Where an original appears in the cartulary the number in the present volume is given in bold font. Where charters are not in the cartulary either a brief description or reference to a printing is given.

BELVOIR CASTLE, LEICESTERSHIRE
Manuscripts of His Grace the Duke of Rutland
301, 302, 1085

BRADFORD, WEST YORKSHIRE ARCHIVE SERVICE
9 D 74 (grant by Jordan de Dunlet, 13th cent. I am grateful to Dr Nigel Ramsay for this reference).

BRETTON HALL CAMPUS, UNIVERSITY OF LEEDS
Bretton Estate Archive (Allendale Muniments)
The Bretton Estate Collection comprises charters relating to the abbey estates in Bretton, Bentley/Emley, Flockton, and Shitlington. These are listed below. Many charters in this collection do not appear in the cartulary.
West Bretton: BEA C3/B7.1 **(42)**, C3/B7.2 **(44)**, C3/B7.3 **(43)**, C3/B7.4 **(46)**, C3/B7.5, C3/B7.6, C3/B7.7, C3/B7.8 **(45)**, C3/B7.13 **(41)**, C3/B7.14 **(40)**, C3/B9.10, C3/B9.11, C3/B.9.12, C3/B9.13
Bentley and Emley: BEA C3/B9.171, C3/B9.172, C3/B9.173, C3/B9.174, C3/B9.175, C3/B9.176
Flockton: BEA C3/10.60
Shitlington: BEA C3/B11.97 **(39)**, C3/B11.98, C3/B11.99
BEA C3/B7.1 **(42)**, C3/B7.2 **(44)**, C3/B7.3 **(43)**, C3/B7.4 **(46)**, C3/B7.8 **(45)**, C3/B7.13 **(41)**, C3/B7.14 **(40)**, C3/B11.97 **(39)**

CARLISLE, CUMBRIA RECORD OFFICE
D/Mus/Deeds Box 48 (Musgrave of Edenhall Archive)
69, 85, 88, 89
Not in cartulary: (i) Confirmation by Robert de Vipont, lord of
Westmorland, of all lands and rents which they have in Westmorland,
free from all service except for an annual farm which the monks owe
in Asby and Bretherdale, with right to suit of court. (ii) Confirmation
by J., prior of Carlisle, S., prior of Lanercost, and W., dean of Carlisle
of the termination of the dispute between the monks of Byland and
Hugh of Kaber concerning land in Warcop and a mill which the
monks had of Hugh's father, Robert.

DURHAM CATHEDRAL MUNIMENTS
5 The College, Durham
4. 1. Sacr. 18: **264**

HALTON PLACE, HELLIFIELD, YORKSHIRE
Deeds in the possession of Major J. E. E. Yorke
56 **(690)**, 58 **(688)**, 59 **(689)**
Not in cartulary: Yorke deeds nos 8, 55 (*Mowbray Charters*, no. 60), 57
(*ibid.*, no. 53), 60–67; also transcripts in no. 68 (*ibid.*, nos 52, 54)

KENDAL, CUMBRIA RECORD OFFICE
Deeds from the deposited collection of Fell, Kilvington and Co. solici-
tors of Kirkby Stephen
WD/Kilv/1/1/1 **(22)**, 1/1/3 **(25)**
Not in cartulary: 1/1/2, 1/1/4, 1/1/5, 1/1/6

LEEDS, WEST YORKSHIRE ARCHIVE SERVICE
Lane Fox Collection
LF135/47 **(521 or 522)**

LEEDS, YORKSHIRE ARCHAEOLOGICAL SOCIETY
DD/146/18/6 **(451, 684)**
DD/94/10 **(411, 415, 417, 421, 422, 424, 425, copy of 429)**
Not in cartulary: grant by Gilbert de Meinill of Thirkleby of land in
Thirkleby (DD146/47)
MD/70: Confirmation by William, son of William, lord of Emley, 1383
(I am grateful to Dr Nigel Ramsay for this reference).

LEVENS HALL, KENDAL, CUMBRIA
Bagot MSS, Levens Hall box A
nos. 26 (**310**), no. 23 (**314**), no. 24 (**315**)
Not in cartulary: (i) Grant by Gerald de Lasceles of land in Asby; (ii) Agreement between Byland and Richard de Cottesford; (iii) Confirmation by Richard de Redeman of the grants of Henry and Matthew de Redeman; Release by William of Threlkeld; (iv) Bull of Innocent III exempting from the payment of tithes; (v) Demise by Abbot Adam to Gilbert de Capella, rector of Lowther, of the manor of Fawcett.

LONDON, BRITISH LIBRARY
Additional Charters
Add. charters 7409–7482 relate to the abbey property in Denby, and were acquired by the British Museum in 1850.
7409, 7410 (**206**), 7411, 7412, 7413 (**213**), 7414 (**205**), 7415 (**205**), 7416 (**211**), 7417 (**236**), 7418 (**219**), 7419 (**254**), 7420, 7421 (**677**), 7422 (**239**), 7423 (**217**), 7424 (**247**), 7425 (**246**), 7426, 7427 (**225**), 7428 (**235**), 7429 (**229**), 7430, 7431 (**207**), 7432 (**224**), 7433 (**250**), 7434 (**228**), 7435 (**216**), 7436 (**208**), 7437 (**218**), 7438 (**?665**), 7439 (**240**), 7440, 7441 (**237**), 7442 (**244**), 7443, 7444 (**242**), 7445, 7446 (**253**), 7447 (**copy of 217**), 7448, 7449 (**209**), 7450, 7451 (**233**), 7452, 7453 (**243**), 7454 (**231**), 7455 (**226**), 7456 (**241**), 7457, 7458, 7459, 7460, 7461, 7462, 7463 (**221**), 7464 (**212**), 7465 (**?665**), 7466, 7467, 7468 (**copy of 254**), 7469, 7470 (**212**), 7471, 7472, 7473, 7474 (**212**), 7475, 7476, 7477, 7478, 7479, 7480 (**222**), 7481, 7482

8070, 8093, 8094, 8165, 8270, 8288, 8307, 8660

20546 (**309**), 20563, 20569, 20588 (**1156**), 20589 (**1157**), 20691, 20692

66799 (**214**), 66951A–C

70691, 70692, 70693 (**593**), 70694, 70695, 71764 (copy of 7421)

74770, 74771, 74772 (probably sold as part of the wrong lot in 1850 and acquired in 1933)

Egerton Charters
585 (**728**); 2139–2167: 2160 (**128**), 2161 (**414**), 2162 (**420**)
See *Yorks. Deeds II, passim.*

Stowe Charters
436 (**664**), 437 (**129**), 438, 439 (**733**), 440, 443 (**624**), 483, 496, 497, 499, 503

NORTHALLERTON, NORTH YORKSHIRE COUNTY RECORD OFFICE (NYCRO)

Further details are available in the unpublished guide to monastic records at NYCRO, compiled by Mr M. Ashcroft, former County Archivist, to whom I am most grateful for assistance. The references are to collection, number where applicable, and to microfilm and frame.

ZAZ Hutton of Marske

ZAZ 1/9 MIC 1315/290: Demise by Abbot Henry and the convent to Richard de Wasand and his wife Helewise, of 1 bovate in Thornton le Moor.

ZDV Newburgh (Belasyse/Fauconberg/Wombwell)

ZDV I 5 (Newburgh area)

MIC 1352/390–95: **330**

MIC 1352/396–7: **728**

MIC 1352/398–400: Quitclaim by William Mainilhermer of land in Thorpe le Willows; endorsed Gat Thorp vi ir xvii

MIC 1352/401–3: **323**

MIC 1352/404–7: **copy of 323**

MIC 1352/408–11: **copy of 323**

MIC 1352/412–5: **325**

MIC 1352/416–9: Confirmation by Sir Thomas de Coleville of previous grants; Byland, 8 Apr. 1344. *HMC Various Collections*, II, 7 (no. 13).

MIC 1352/420–3: Confirmation by Thomas de Coleville, lord of Yearsley, of previous grants; Yearsley, 3 Apr. 1359. *HMC Various Collections*, II, 8 (no. 14).

ZDV I 25 (Byland area)

MIC 2894/2377: **256**

MIC 2894/2379; grant by Ralph del Turp of land in Dale which he had given as her marriage portion to his daughter, Ymaine, which she had surrendered in exchange for land in Marton in Cleveland (much damaged); see *HMC Various Collections*, II, 5 (no. 5), and **255** note.

MIC 2894/2381: **258**

MIC 2894/2382: **257**

MIC 2894/2384: **259**

MIC 2894/2386: **260**

MIC 2894/2388: Confirmation by William de Coleville, son of

Robert de Coleville, of the charter of Ralph del Turp; Byland, 14 Aug. 1365. *HMC Various Collections*, II, 8 (no. 15).

MIC 2894/2390: Confirmation by William de Coleville, son of Robert de Coleville, of the charter of William Engelram; Byland, 8 Sept. 1365. *HMC Various Collections*, II, 8 (no. 16).

MIC 2894/2392: Confirmation by John de Coleville, lord of Dale, son and heir of William de Coleville, son and heir of Robert de Coleville; Byland, 20 May 1380. *HMC Various Collections*, II, 8 (no. 17).

ZDV I 47 (Brandsby area)
   MIC 2889/3424: **1138**
ZDV V 35 (Murton and Daletown)
   MIC 1440/406
   MIC 1440/410
   MIC 1440/412
   MIC 1440/415
   MIC 1440/416
   MIC 1440/417
   MIC 1440/418
   MIC 1440/421: Final concord between Abbot Henry and Nicholas of Boltby concerning common rights in Old Byland; 1246. *Yorks. Fines, 1232–1246*, p. 157.
   MIC 1440/423
   MIC 1440/424
   MIC 1440/442–3
   MIC 1440/447
   MIC 1440/545
   MIC 1440/458
[ZDV(L) MIC 1136: The 'Fauconberg Book', early 17th-century transcripts of Byland deeds and charters].
ZFL Mauleverer of Ingelby Arncliffe
   3 (MIC 1289/40)
Z1Q Meynell of Kilvington and Yarm
   MIC 3170/45: **1087**
   MIC 3170/39: **1088**
ZQG(F) Fairfax of Gilling (Fairfax-Cholmeley)
   I 7 MIC 2814/1283: ?**1193**
OUTFAC 85 This is a copy of an original confirmation by William son of William, lord of Emley, of the grants of his predecessor, William son of William, of lands in Emley, Bentley and Denby. It was sold at

Sotherby's in 1976, and a facsimile deposited in the British Library; this was subsequently deposited in NYCRO.

OXFORD, BODLEIAN LIBRARY
Douce charter 25 (Confirmation charter of Henry III, Winchester, 20 Feb. 1247).

APPENDIX II

Manuscripts containing post-medieval transcripts of Byland charters contained in the cartulary as text or rubric

Northallerton, NYCRO
ZDV I 1 (Henry Sandwith's *Exscripta*)
578, 584, 594, 878

Oxford Bodleian Library, Dodsworth Manuscripts
7: 186, 299, 365, 379, 638, 660, 669, 679, 840, 849, 885, 886, 888, 1111, 1151
8: 211, 220, 254
45: 683
63: 9, 13, 22, 23, 24, 25, 296, 366, 367, 395, 397, 403, 405, 406, 444, 445, 487, 520, 595, 622, 623, 624, 647, 685, 799, 810, 811, 812, 813, 816, 817, 831, 834, 836, 838, 870, 909, 927, 927A, 929, 1076, 1077, 1080, 1087, 1088, 1089, 1090, 1098, 1101, 1102, 1104, 1141, 1142, 1144, 1145, 1146, 1147, 1148, 1157, 1160, 1171, 1197
70: 71, 75, 82
71: 35
91: 9, 13, 121, 153, 156, 172, 300, 309, 312, 358, 452, 453, 490, 493, 494, 495, 498, 505, 507, 515, 628, 638, 675, 686, 716, 718, 720, 722, 842, 927A, 949, 968, 1018, 1027, 1044, 1047, 1078, 1092, 1101, 1102, 1105, 1157, 1158, 1164
94: 35, 39, 80, 316, 336A, 366, 486, 490, 578, 584, 585, 624, 671, 681, 683, 715, 965, 999, 1048, 1079, 1080, 1084, 1087, 1088, 1091, 1147
118: 623, 624
133: 227
157: 933, 935, 937, 959, 960

Oxford, Bodleian Library MS Top. Yorks.
d. 11: 26, 29, 30, 31, 32, 528, 529, 1143
e. 7: 106, 122, 452, 469, 492, 598, 602, 606, 611, 626, 637, 949, 954, 1161

e. 8: 39, 98, 351, 452, 460, 464, 506, 534, 578, 608, 628, 695, 926, 960, 1042
e. 9: 87, 106, 361, 453, 496, 498, 578, 624, 629, 851, 852, 930, 1027
e. 11: 956

BIBLIOGRAPHY

Unpublished primary sources

(Details of original charters of Byland Abbey are given in Appendix I, and are therefore omitted here.)

London, British Library
 Egerton MS 2823 (Byland cartulary)
 Egerton MS 2827 (Easby cartulary)

London, National Archives (PRO)
 CP 25/1/249, 261–266 (Feet of Fines 4 John–53 Henry III)
 E 368/166 (Memoranda roll of the Lord Treasurer's Remembrancer, 17 Richard II)

Oxford, Bodleian Library
 MSS Dodsworth 7, 8, 45, 63, 67, 70, 71, 76, 91, 94, 95, 118, 133, 157
 MSS Top. Yorks. d. 11, e. 7–e. 12

York, Borthwick Institute of Historical Research
 Reg. 9 (Register of Archbishop Melton)
 Reg. 10 (Register of Archbishop Zouche)
 Reg. 11 (Register of Archbishop Thoresby)
 Reg. 12 (Register of Archbishop Neville)

Published primary sources

Abstracts of the Charters and Other Documents contained in the Chartulary of the Cistercian Abbey of Fountains, ed. W. T. Lancaster, 2 vols (Leeds: privately printed, 1915)

Abstracts of the Charters and Other Documents contained in the Chartulary of the Priory of Bridlington, ed. W. T. Lancaster (Leeds: privately printed, 1912)

Abstracts of the Chartularies of the Priory of Monk Bretton, ed. J. M. Walker, YASRS, 66 (1924)

The Acta of Hugh of Wells, Bishop of Lincoln, 1209–1235, ed. D. M. Smith, Lincoln Record Society, 88 (2000)

Baildon, W. P., *Notes on the Religious and Secular Houses of Yorkshire*, 2 vols, YASRS, 17, 81 (1895, 1931)

The Bolton Priory Compotus 1286–1325, together with a Priory Account Roll for 1377–1378, ed. Ian Kershaw and David M. Smith, YASRS, 154 (2000)

Calendar of the Charter Rolls Preserved in the Public Record Office, 6 vols (London: HMSO, 1903–27)

Calendar of the Close Rolls Preserved in the Public Record Office: Henry III to Henry IV (London: HMSO, 1892–1938)

Calendar of Entries in the Papal Registers Relating to Great Britain and Ireland: papal letters, ed. W. H. Bliss, C. Johnson, J. A. Twemlow, M. J. Haren (London: HMSO, 1893–in progress)

Calendar of Entries in the Papal Registers Relating to Great Britain and Ireland: petitions to the pope, AD 1342–1419, ed. W. H. Bliss (London: HMSO, 1896)

Calendar of the Fine Rolls Preserved in the Public Record Office: Edward I to Henry VI (London: HMSO, 1911–49)

Calendar of Inquisitions Miscellaneous (Chancery) Preserved in the Public Record Office: Henry III to Edward III (London: HMSO, 1916–37)

Calendar of the Patent Rolls Preserved in the Public Record Office: Henry III to Henry IV (London: HMSO, 1891–1916)

Cartularium Abbathiae de Rievalle, ed. J. C. Atkinson, SS, 83 (1889)

Cartularium Abbathiae de Whiteby, ed. J. C. Atkinson, 2 vols, SS, 69, 72 (1879–81)

Cartularium Prioratus de Gyseburne, ed. W. Brown, 2 vols, SS, 86, 89 (1889–94)

The Cartulary of the Knights of St John of Jerusalem in England, Secunda Camera, Essex, ed. M. Gervers, British Academy Records of Social and Economic History, ns 6 (1982)

The Charters of the Anglo-Norman Earls of Chester c. 1071–1237, ed. G. Barraclough, Record Society of Lancashire and Cheshire, 126 (1988)

'Charters of Byland Abbey relating to the grange of Bleatarn, Westmorland' ed. J. E. Burton, *TCWAAS*, 79 (1979), 29–50

Charters of the Honour of Mowbray 1107–1191, ed. D. E. Greenway, British Academy Records of Social and Economic History, ns 1 (London: Oxford University Press, 1972)

'Charters to St Peter's, York and to Byland Abbey', ed. F. W. Ragg, *TCWAAS*, ns 9 (1909), 236–70

Charters of the Vicars Choral of York Minster I: City of York and its Suburbs to 1546, ed. N. J. Tringham, YASRS, 148 (1993 for 1988 and 1989); *II: County of Yorkshire and appropriated churches to 1538*, ed. N. J. Tringham, YASRS, 156 (2002)

Curia Regis Rolls . . . Preserved in the Public Record Office (London: HMSO, 1922–in progress)

Dugdale, William, *Monasticon Anglicanum*, ed. J. Caley, H. Ellis and B. Bandinel, 6 vols in 8 (London, 1817–30)

Early Yorkshire Charters, vols I–III, ed. W. Farrer (Edinburgh, 1914–16); vols IV–XII and index to I–III, ed. C. T. Clay, YASRS, extra series (1935–65)

English Episcopal Acta, V: York 1070–1154, ed. J. E. Burton (1988); *XX: York*

1154–1181, ed. Marie Lovatt (2000); *XXIV: Durham 1153–1195*, ed. M. G. Snape (2002); all Oxford: Oxford University Press for the British Academy

English Lawsuits from William I to Richard I, ed. R. C. Van Caenegem, 2 vols, Selden Society, 106–7 (1990–91)

The Fabric Rolls of York Minster, ed. J. Raine, SS, 35 (1859 for 1858)

Farrer, W., *Records Relating to the Barony of Kendal*, I, ed. J. Curwen, CWAAS, Record or Chartulary Series, 4 (1923)

Feet of Fines for the County of York, from 1218 to 1231, ed. J. Parker, YASRS, 62 (1921)

Feet of Fines for the County of York, from 1232 to 1246, ed. J. Parker, YASRS, 67 (1925)

Feet of Fines for the County of York, from 1246 to 1272, ed. J. Parker, YASRS, 82 (1932)

Feet of Fines for the County of York, from 1327 to 1347, ed. W. Paley Baildon, YASRS, 42 (1910)

Foedera, conventiones, literae . . ., ed. T. Rymer, 2nd edn (London: J Tonson, 1726–35)

Innocent III, Letters of, concerning England and Wales (1198–1216), ed., C. R. and Mary Cheney (Oxford: Clarendon Press, 1967)

Kirkby's Inquest: The Survey of the County of York taken by John de Kirkeby, commonly called Kirkby's Inquest, and Inquisitions of Knights' Fees, the Nomina Villarum and an Appendix of Illustrative Documents, ed. R. H. Skaife, SS, 49 (1867 for 1866)

Letters and Papers, Foreign and Domestic, of the Reign of Henry VIII, Preserved in the Public Record Office, the British Museum, and elsewhere in England, 23 vols in 38 (London: HMSO, 1862–1932)

Papsturkunden in England, ed. W. Holtzmann, 3 vols (Abhandlungen des Gesellschaft der Wissenschaften zu Göttingen, phil.-hist. Klasse, neue Folge, 25, 1930–31; 3 Folge, 14–15, 1935–6; 33, 1952)

Pedes finium Ebor. regnante Johanne, A.D. MCXCIX–A.D. MCCXIV, ed. W. Brown, SS, 94 (1897)

Placita de Quo Warranto temporibus Edw. I, II, & III in curia receptae scaccarij West. asservata (London: Record Commission, 1818)

Regesta Regum Anglo-Normannorum: the acta of William I, 1066–1087, ed. David Bates (Oxford: Clarendon Press, 1998)

The Register of Walter Giffard, Lord Archbishop of York, 1266–1279, ed. W. Brown, SS, 109 (1904)

The Register or Rolls of Walter de Gray, Lord Archbishop of York, ed. J. Raine, SS, 56 (1872)

The Register of William Greenfield, Lord Archbishop of York, 1306–1315, ed. W. Brown and A. Hamilton Thompson, 5 vols, SS, 145, 149, 151–3 (1931–40)

The Register of William Melton, Archbishop of York, 1317–1340, ed. R. M. T.

Hill, D. Robinson, R. Brocklesby and T. C. B. Timmins, 5 vols, Canterbury and York Society, 70–1, 76, 85, 93 (1977–2002)

Select Cases concerning the Law Merchant AD 1270–1638, I: Local Courts, AD 1270–1638, ed. C. Gross, Selden Society, 23 (1908)

Statuta Capitulorum Generalium Ordinis Cisterciensis ab anno 1116 usque ad annum 1786, ed. J. M. Canivez, 8 vols (Louvain: Revue d'Histoire Ecclésiastique, 1933–41)

Stenton, F. M. ed., *Documents Illustrative of the Social and Economic History of the Danelaw from Various Collections* (London: British Academy and Oxford University Press, 1920)

Taxatio Ecclesiastica Angliae et Walliae auctoritate Papae Nicholai IV, ed. T. Astle, S. Ayscough, and J. Caley (London: Record Commission, 1802)

The Thurgarton Cartulary, ed. Trevor Foulds (Stamford: Paul Watkins, 1994)

Valor Ecclesiasticus, ed. J. Caley and J. Hunter, 6 vols (London: Record Commission, 1802)

Walter Map, *De Nugis Curialium: Courtiers' Trifles*, ed. M. R. James, rev. edn C. N. L. Brooke and R. A. B. Mynors, Oxford Medieval Texts (Oxford, 1983)

William of Newburgh, *Historia Rerum Anglicarum*, in *Chronicles of the reigns of Stephen, Henry II, and Richard I*, ed. R. Howlett, 4 vols, Rolls Series (1884–89)

William of Newburgh, *The History of English Affairs, Book I*, trans. P. G. Walsh and M. J. Kennedy (Warminster: Aris and Phillips, 1988)

Year Books of Edward II, vol. XX, *10 Edward II, A. D. 1316–1317*, ed. M. D. Legge and W. Holdsworth, Selden Society, 5 (1934)

Yorkshire Deeds, ed. W. Brown (I–III), C. T. Clay (IV–VIII), M. J. Hebditch (IX), M. J. Stanley Price (X), YASRS, 39, 50, 63, 65, 69, 76, 83, 102, 111, 120 (1909–55)

Yorkshire Hundred and Quo Warranto Rolls 1274–1294, ed. Barbara English, YASRS, 151 (1996 for 1993 and 1994)

Catalogues

Catalogue of Additions to the Manuscripts in the British Museum in the Years 1848–1853 (London: British Museum, 1868)

Catalogue of Additions to the Manuscripts in the British Museum in the Years 1894–1899 (London: British Museum, 1901)

Catalogue of Additions to the Manuscripts in the British Museum in the Years 1946–1950, Part I, Description (London: The British Library, 1979)

Historical Manuscripts Commission Twelfth Report, Appendix, Parts IV and V, and Fourteenth Report, Appendix I, The Manuscripts of His Grace the Duke of Rutland Preserved at Belvoir Castle, 4 vols (London: HMSO, 1888–1905)

Historical Manuscripts Commission, Report on Manuscripts in Various Collections, 8 vols (London: HMSO, 1901–1914)

A Summary Catalogue of Western Manuscripts in the Bodleian Library at Oxford, ed. F. Madan, H. H. E. Craster and N. Denholm-Young, 7 vols (Oxford: Clarendon Press, 1895–1953)

Tenth Report of the Royal Commission on Historical Manuscripts, Appendix IV, The Manuscripts of the Earl of Westmorland, Captain Stewart, Lord Stafford, Lord Muncaster, and others (London: HMSO, 1885, reissued 1906)

Reference works

Beverley Minster Fasti, ed. Richard T. W. McDermid, YASRS, 149 (1993 for 1990)

The Complete Peerage, or a History of the House of Lords and all its members from the earliest times, ed. G. E. Cockayne and others, 13 vols in 14 (London: St Catherine's Press, 1910–40)

Davis, G. R. C., *Medieval Cartularies of Great Britain* (London: Longman, 1958)

Early Yorkshire Families, ed. C. T. Clay and D. E. Greenway, YASRS, 135 (1973)

Fasti Parochiales, 5 vols, ed. A. Hamilton Thompson and C. T. Clay (I–II), N. A. H. Lawrance (III), N. K. M. Gurney and C. T. Clay (IV), N. A. H. Lawrance (V), YASRS, 85, 107, 129, 133, 143 (1933–82)

Handbook of British Chronology, ed. F. M. Powicke and E. B. Fryde, Royal Historical Society Guides and Handbooks, no. 2, 2nd edn (London, 1961)

The Heads of Religious Houses: England and Wales, I, 940–1216, ed. D. Knowles, C. N. L. Brooke and V. C. M. London, 2nd edn (Cambridge: Cambridge University Press, 2001); *II, 1216–1377*, ed. D. M. Smith and V. C. M. London (Cambridge: Cambridge University Press, 2001)

John le Neve: Fasti Ecclesiae Anglicanae 1066–1300: II Monastic Cathedrals, ed. D. E. Greenway (London: University of London and Athone Press, 1971)

John le Neve: Fasti Ecclesiae Anglicanae 1066–1300: VI York, ed. D. E. Greenway (London: University of London School of Advanced Study, Institute of Historical Research, 1999)

The Lord Lieutenants and High Sheriffs of Yorkshire, 1066–2000, ed. W. M. Ormrod (Barnsley: Wharncliffe Books, 2000)

Medieval Religious Houses: England and Wales, ed. D. Knowles and R. N. Hadcock, 2nd edn (London: Longman, 1971)

Middle English Dictionary, ed. Hans Kurath and others (Ann Arbor: University of Michigan Press, 1952–)

Ordnance Survey Gazetteer of Great Britain, 4th edn (London: Macmillan, 1999)

Publications of the English Place Name Society: vol. V, *The Place-Names of the North Riding of Yorkshire* (Cambridge, 1928); vol. XIV, *The Place-Names of the East Riding of Yorkshire and York* (Cambridge, 1937); vols XXX–XXXVII, *The Place-Names of the West Riding of Yorkshire* (Cambridge, 1961–3); vols XLII–XLIII, *The Place Names of Westmorland* (Cambridge, 1967)

Revised Medieval Latin Word-List from British and Irish Sources, prepared by R. E. Latham (London: Oxford University Press for the British Academy, 1965, rpt. 1973)

York Minster Fasti, ed. C. T. Clay, 2 vols, YASRS, 123–4 (1958–9)

Secondary sources

Alfonso, Isabel, 'The Cistercians and feudalism', *Past and Present*, 133 (1991), 3–30

Beresford, Maurice, *History on the Ground* (Lutterworth, 1957, rpt. Stroud: Sutton, 1998)

Berman, Constance Hoffman, 'Cistercian development and the order's acquisition of churches and tithes in south-western France', *Revue Bénédictine*, 91 (1981), 193–203

———, *Medieval Agriculture, the South French Countryside, and the Early Cistercians*, Transactions of the American Philosophical Society, 76, no. 5 (Philadelphia, 1986)

———, *The Cistercian Evolution: the invention of a religious order in twelfth-century Europe* (Philadelphia: University of Pennsylvania Press, 2000)

Bishop, T. A. M., 'Monastic granges in Yorkshire', *English Historical Review*, 51 (1936), 193–214, 758

Bouchard, Constance Brittain, 'Cistercian ideals versus reality: 1134 reconsidered', *Cîteaux*, 39 (1988), 217–31

———, *Holy Entrepreneurs: Cistercians, Knights, and Economic Exchange in Twelfth Century Burgundy* (Ithaca and London: Cornell University Press, 1991)

Burton, Janet E., 'The Settlement of disputes between Byland Abbey and Newburgh Priory', *Yorkshire Archaeological Journal*, 55 (1983), 67–71

———, 'The abbeys of Byland and Jervaulx and the problems of the English Savigniacs', *Monastic Studies*, II, ed. J. Loades (Bangor: Headstart History, 1991) 119–31

———, *Monastic and Religious Orders in Britain, 1000–1300* (Cambridge: Cambridge University Press, 1994)

———, 'Historical Evidence', in *The Church and Gilbertine Priory of St Andrew, Fishergate*, ed. Richard L. Kemp and C. Pamela Graves, *The Archaeology of York*, 11, *The Medieval Defences and Suburbs*, fasc. 2 (Council for British Archaeology for the York Archaeological Trust, 1996)

———, 'The estates and economy of Rievaulx Abbey in Yorkshire', *Cîteaux: Commentarii Cistercienses*, 49 (1998), 29–94

———, *The Monastic Order in Yorkshire, 1069–1215*, Cambridge Studies in Medieval Life and Thought, fourth series, 40 (Cambridge University Press, 1999)

Butlin, Robin A., ed., *Historical Atlas of North Yorkshire* (Otley: Westbury Publishing, 2003)

Cheney, C. R., *Notaries Public in England in the Thirteenth and Fourteenth Centuries* (Oxford: Clarendon Press, 1972)

———, *Pope Innocent III and England* (Stuttgart: Hiersemann, 1976)

Chibnall, Marjorie, 'Dating the charters of the smaller religious houses of Suffolk in the twelfth and thirteenth centuries', in Michael Gervers, ed., *Dating Undated Medieval Charters* (Woodbridge: Boydell Press, 2000), pp. 51–9

Clanchy, M. T., *From Memory to Written Record England 1066–1307*, 2nd edn (Oxford: Blackwell, 1993)

Colvin, H. M., *The White Canons in England* (Oxford: Clarendon Press, 1951)

Cross, Claire, and Noreen Vickers, eds, *Monks, Friars and Nuns in Sixteenth-Century Yorkshire*, YASRS, 150 (1995 for 1991 and 1992)

Crouch, David, and Trevor Pearson, *Medieval Scarborough: studies in trade and civic life*, Yorkshire Archaeological Society Occasional Paper no. 1 (Otley: Smith Settle, 2001)

Dalton, Paul, 'Aiming at the impossible: Ranulf II, earl of Chester and Lincolnshire in the reign of King Stephen', in Thacker, ed., *The Earldom of Chester*, pp. 109–32

———, *Conquest, Anarchy and Lordship: Yorkshire 1066–1154*, Cambridge Studies in Medieval Life and Thought, fourth series, 27 (Cambridge: Cambridge University Press, 1994)

Declercq, Georges, 'Originals and cartularies: the organization of archival memory (ninth–eleventh centuries)', in *Charters and the Use of the Written Word in Medieval Society*, ed. Karl Heidecker, Utrecht Studies in Medieval Literacy, 5 (Turnhout: Brepols, 2000), pp. 147–70

Desmond, Lawrence A., 'The appropriation of churches by the Cistercians in England to 1400', *Analecta Cisterciensia*, 31 (1976 for 1975), 246–66

Donkin, R. A., *The Cistercians: Studies in the Geography of Medieval England and Wales*, Pontifical Institute of Mediaeval Studies, Studies and Texts, 38 (Toronto, 1978)

Donnelly, James S., 'Changes in the grange economy of English and Welsh Cistercian Abbeys, 1300–1540', *Traditio*, 10 (1954), 399–458

Drake, F., *Eboracum* (London: W. Bowyer, for the author, 1736)

Dumville, David, 'What is a Chronicle?', *The Medieval Chronicle* II, ed. Erik Kooper (Amsterdam and New York: Rodopi, 2002), pp. 1–27

English, B. A., and C. B. L. Barr, 'The Records formerly in St. Mary's Tower, York', *YAJ*, 42 (1967–70), 198–235, 358–86, 465–518

English, B. A., and R. Hoyle, 'What was in St Mary's Tower: an inventory of 1610', *YAJ*, 65 (1993), 91–4

Faull, Margaret L., and Stephen A. Moorhouse, *West Yorkshire: an archaeological survey to AD 1500*, 4 vols (Wakefield West Yorkshire Metropolitan County Council, 1981)

Fergusson, Peter, *Architecture of Solitude: Cistercian Abbeys in Twelfth-Century England* (Princeton: Princeton University Press, 1984)

Foulds, Trevor, 'Medieval cartularies', *Archives*, 18, no. 77 (April 1987), 3–35

Geary, Patrick, *Phantoms of Remembrance: memory and oblivion at the end of the first millennium* (Princeton: University Press, 1994)

Genet, Jean-Philippe, 'Cartulaires, registres et histoire: l'exemple anglais', in *Le metier d'historien au moyen âge: Etudes sur l'historiographie médiévale*, ed. Bernard Guenée, Publications de la Sorbonne, serie 'Etudes', 13 (Paris, 1977), pp. 95–138

Gilyard-Beer, R., 'Byland Abbey and the grave of Roger de Mowbray', *YAJ*, 55 (1983), 61–6

Golding, Brian, 'Burials and benefactions: an aspect of monastic patronage in thirteenth-century England', *England in the Thirteenth Century, Proceedings of the 1984 Harlaxton Symposium*, ed. W. Ormrod (Harlaxton, 1985), pp. 64–75

——, *St Gilbert of Sempringham and the Gilbertines c. 1130–1300* (Oxford: Clarendon Press, 1995)

Graves, C. V., 'The economic activities of the Cistercians in medieval England (1128–1307)', *Analecta Sacri Ordinis Cisterciensis*, 13 (1957), 3–60

Hector, L. C., *The Handwriting of English Documents* (Ilkley: Scolar Press, 1958, 2nd edn, 1966)

Hudson, John, 'Diplomatic and legal aspects of the charters', in Thacker, ed., *The Earldom of Chester*, pp. 153–78

——, *Land, Law, and Lordship in Anglo-Norman England* (Oxford: Clarendon Press, 1994)

——, *The Formation of the English Common Law: law and society in England from the Norman Conquest to Magna Carta* (London: Longman, 1996)

Hyams, P., 'Warranty and good lordship in twelfth century England', *Law and History Review*, 5 (1987), 437–503

Joynes, Andrew, ed., *Medieval Ghost Stories* (Woodbridge: Boydell, 2001)

Kaner, J., 'Clifton and medieval woolhouses', *York Historian*, 8 (1988), 2–10

Kimball, E. G., 'Tenure in frankalmoign and secular services', *English Historical Review*, 43 (1928), 341–53

McDonnell, J., ed., *A History of Helmsley, Rievaulx and District* (York: Stonegate Press, 1963)

Neilson, N., *Types of Manorial Structure in the Northern Danelaw, Customary Rents*, Oxford Studies in Social and Legal History, ed. P. Vinogradoff, vol. II, (Oxford, 1910)

Nicholl, D., *Thurstan, Archbishop of York 1114–1140* (York: Stonegate Press, 1963)

Nicolson, J., and Burn, R., *The History and Antiquities of the Counties of Westmorland and Cumberland*, 2 vols (London: W. Strachen and T. Cadell, 1777)

Palmer, Robert C., *The County Courts of Medieval England 1150–1350* (Princeton: Princeton University Press, 1982)

Platt, Colin, *The Monastic Grange in Medieval England* (London: Macmillan, 1969)

Postles, David, 'Securing the gift in Oxfordshire charters in the twelfth and thirteenth centuries', *Archives*, 19 (1990), 183–91

———, 'Gifts in frankalmoign, warranty of land, and feudal society', *The Cambridge Law Journal*, 50 (1991), 330–46

Raban, Sandra, *Mortmain Legislation and the English Church* (Cambridge: Cambridge University Press, 1982)

Raistrick, Arthur, *Lead Mining in the Mid-Pennines: the mines of Nidderdale, Wharfedale, Airedale, Ribblesdale and Bowland*, Monographs on Metalliferous Mining History, vol. 4 (Truro: D. Bradford Barton Ltd, 1973)

Robinson, D., ed., *The Cistercian Abbeys of Britain* (London: B. T. Batsford, 1998)

St John Hope, W. H., and Harold Brakspear, 'Jervaulx Abbey', *YAJ*, XXI (1910–11), 301–44

Sanders, I. F., *English Baronies: a study of their origins and descent 1086–1327* (Oxford: Clarendon Press, 1960)

Satchell, J. E., 'The Bretherdale wool weight', *TCWAAS*, 89 (1989), 131–40

Sayers, J. E., *Papal Government in England during the Pontificate of Honorius III* (Cambridge: Cambridge University Press, 1984)

Scammell, G. V., *Hugh du Puiset, Bishop of Durham* (Cambridge: Cambridge University Press, 1956)

Summerson, Henry, *Medieval Carlisle: the city and the borders from the late eleventh to the mid sixteenth century*, 2 vols, CWAAS extra series, XXV (1993)

Sutherland, D. W., *Quo Warranto Proceedings in the Reign of Edward I 1278–1294* (Oxford: Clarendon Press, 1963)

Tanner, Thomas, *Notitia Monastica, or a Short History of the Religious Houses of England and Wales* (Oxford: printed at the Theatre, and to be sold at the sign of the Black Swan at Pater-Noster-Row, London, 1695)

Thacker, A. T., ed., *The Earldom of Chester and its Charters*, *Journal of the Chester Archaeological Society*, 71 (1991)

Thompson, B., 'Free alms tenure in the twelfth century', in *Anglo-Norman*

Studies XVI, Proceedings of the Battle Conference 1993, ed. M. Chibnall (Woodbridge, 1994), pp. 221–43

Turner, Ralph V., *The English Judiciary in the Age of Glanvill and Bracton, c. 1176–1239* (Cambridge: Cambridge University Press, 1985)

The Victoria History of the Counties of England: A History of Lancaster, ed. W. Farrer and J. Brownbill, 8 vols (London: Constable and Co., 1906–14)

The Victoria History of the Counties of England: A History of Yorkshire, North Riding, ed. W. Page, vol. I (London: Constable and Co., 1914), vol. II and index (London: The St Catherine's Press, 1923–5)

The Victoria History of the Counties of England: A History of Yorkshire, The City of York, ed. P. M. Tillott (Oxford: Oxford University Press, 1961, repr. Folkestone: Dawson for the Institute of Historical Research, 1982)

The Victoria History of the Counties of England: A History of Yorkshire, III, ed. William Page (London: Eyre and Spottiswoode, 1913, rpt. London and Folkestone: Dawson for the University of London Institute of Historical Research, 1974)

Waites, Bryan, 'The monastic settlement of north-east Yorkshire', *YAJ*, 40 (1961), 478–95

————, *Monasteries and Landscape in North East England: the medieval colonization of the North York Moors* (Oakham (Rutland): Multum in Parvo Press, 1997)

Wardrop, Joan, *Fountains Abbey and its Benefactors 1132–1300*, Cistercian Publications, 91 (Kalamazoo, MI, 1987)

Washington, G. S. H. L., *Early Westmorland MPs, 1258–1327*, CWAAS Tract Series, 15 (1959)

'Yorkshire monastic archives', *The Bodleian Library Quarterly Record*, 8 (1935), 95–100 (author not given)

INDEX OF PERSONS AND PLACES

The roman numerals refer to page numbers; the arabic numerals refer to document numbers in the calendar.

Emley (Emelei, Emmelaie), WR   lxxii, lxxiii, lxxxi, 38, 42, 45, 228n, 666, 988
clerk of see Adam
granger of   lxxviii, 207
Bartholomew of   38
Henry son of Roger of   39
Simon of   222, 225
Thomas son of William of   lxiv, 38, 44, 214, 242, 254
Uviet of   222
William son of Arkil of   225
William son of Thomas of   253, 254
William son of William of   227
Emma, daughter of Richard Malebisse and wife of Robert de Meinill III 1080n
Emma, wife of Roger Cosin and daughter of Maleth   lxiv, lxxii, 343, 345, 347, 366
Emma, wife of Samson of Laysthorpe lxi, 497, 505, 506, 508, 515, 548n
Emmyng Croft (Hemmingcrokst, in Islebeck), NR   411, 420, 430
Engayne (Rugayne), Warner (Warin), royal justice   258, 722, 927, 927A, 1000, 1003, 1016, 1030
Engelram (Engeram)
Robert, son of William son of Walter   258, 259, 260, 840
Walter   256
mother of see Maud; wife of see Holdeard; brother of see Turp, Ralph del
William   256n, 1080
William son of Walter   255n, 256n, 257, 258, 259, 260, 591n, 840
Engleis see Anglicus
Engleys, brother William, Knight Templar   451
Engmar (Cayton), NR   141, 143
Epedecros (Nidderdale), WR   457
Epworth, Lincs.
document issued at   lvi, 106, 484
Erghum see Airyholme
Eringwatdala (Heringwath, Heringwar, Crinigleat, in Islebeck), NR   415, 421, 430
Ernald, steward   460
Esebrigge (Coxwold), NR   123n
Essex, earl of see Geoffrey fitz Peter
Esshur (Eschew, Essheur)
Richard de, the elder   9, 10
Richard de, the younger   9, 10
Estfeld (Clayton), NR   147
Esthfald (Nidderdale), WR   695n

Estington, William de   851
Estittesley, Michael de   851
Eston, John of   202, 703, 960
Robert of, brother of John   703, 704
Stephen of, abbot of Sallay (1225–c. 1233/4)   707n
Estre, Robert de   140
Esturmi
John   336A
Robert de   840
Estwra, Richard de   1059
Etton
Geoffrey de, of Gilling   1111, 1119
Ivo de (these may not all refer to the same man) 412, 452, 558, 685, 686, 703, 906, 1143, 1148, 1197
Thomas de (late 12th to early 13th cent.)   598, 611, 867, 1119
Thomas de (mid–late 13th cent.) 253, 254, 494, 496, 505, 507, 508, 509, 628, 718, 869, 909, 956, 1151, 1193
wife of see Felicia
Thomas de (late 13th cent.)   452, 490, 492n, 496, 497, 498, 558, 628, 671, 675, 869, 909, 949, 960, 989, 1066
Thomas de (14th cent.)   4, 18, 32, 123n, 366, 679
William de   718, 956
Etton (Hettona, Eton), ER, parson of see Nicholas
Eure (Ever')
Helen de   9n, 13
Hugh de   9n
Robert de   3, 8 (as Robert of Ampleforth), 9 (as son of Hugh), 10, 13
Isabel, Isabella, wife of   8, 10n
Eustace, abbot of Jervaulx (elected 1221, occ. to 1254)   125, 707
Eustace Fitz John   liii, 106n, 645, 738n
Eustacia, daughter of Richard de Wyville and wife of Nicholas de Yeland   297n, 1137n, 1185n
Eva, daughter of Gospatrick son of Waldef 48n
Eva of Warcop, daughter of Malreward of Appleby   65
Everley, Alan de   870
Evesham, Adam of, clerk, rector of Rillington   935, 945, 946, 964n
Eye, honour of   580n, 842

Magna Stene(s) (?How Stean Beck) 688, 698n, 700

Magneby, Magnebi *see* Maunby

Mainard, canon of York 224, 395, 491, 914

Mainild (Maynild), Richard 128, 129

Malebisse of Scawton

Hugh I (steward of Roger de Mowbray 1147 x 1154) lviii, lxx, 323, 326, 486, 578n, 690, 829n, 1076n

Hugh II, son of Hugh I (d. by 1187/8) xlix, lxvii, lxx, 486, 578, 579, 623, 632, 633, 648, 687, 829n, 1076, 1077, 1078

daughter of *see* Amice

wife of *see* Matilda

Hugh I or Hugh II 256, 688, 689, 725, 728, 888

Hugh III, son of Hugh II (d. 1206) lviii, 578, 579, 591, 634n, 1078

wife of *see* Constance

William son of Hugh II (still living in 1206) 257n, 634, 743, 845, 846, 1076n, 1077

Malebisse of Acaster Malbis

Hugh (possibly Hugh. occ. 1192, son of William Malebisse d. 1176) 585

John son of Richard Malebisse (d. 1210) 206, 580n, 583, 584, 585, 586, 591, 651, 655, 695, 701, 776, 836, 1083n, 1090n, 1091, 1098

wife of *see* Matilda

John (d. 1316) son of Richard Malebisse 684, 842

Richard (d. 1210), son of William, nephew of Hugh II lxx, 206, 260n, 580, 585, 591, 634n, 651, 655, 695, 701, 776, 836, 1076n, 1078, 1080n, 1083n, 1085, 1089, 1090n, 1091n, 1099n

Richard son of William Malebisse son of John Malebisse 13, 32, 385, 412, 490, 582, 588, 592, 658, 671, 700, 703, 906, 909, 959, 1066, 1068, 1073, 1140, 1143

Richard son of John Malebisse (d. 1316) 13, ?584, 1095

William (d. 1176) son of Hugh Malebisse I and brother of Hugh Malebisse II 634n, 845, 846, 1078n

William (still living in *c.* 1270) son of John Malebisse 505, 580, 583,

584, 587, 588n, 589, 590, 852, 1083, 1090, 1146, 1151

William (d. 1365) son of John Malebisse (d. 1316) lxix, 429, 430, 620, 842, 1059

Malebisse (branch uncertain)

Ralph 585

Richard (late 14th cent.) 32

Malecak, William 627, 879, 960

Malet (Maleth) 343

Malkael(l), Humphrey 50, 52

Malleverer, Roger 1157, 1158

Malocatulus, Humphrey 24, 60n

Malolacu, Peter de 1088

Maltby (Mauteby, Malthebi, Maltebi, Malteby), NR

Gilbert of 361

Robert of 337, 346, 840

William of 358, 361, 365, 720

William son of Fulk of 336A

Malton, NR 965

Robert of 322

William of 8

clerk of *see* Martin

Gilbertine priory 463n, 606n, 861n, 958n

prior of 958

Mancoys, William 664

Mandeville (Maundevyl, Maundeville, Maundevil)

Humphrey de 662

William de 128, 129, 306A, 411, 417, 464, 584

Manfield, NR, clerk of *see* Robert

Mansell (Maunsell)

John, chancellor of St Paul's London 528n

John, of Birdforth 558, 906, 1066, 1142

Richard (le) 122, 585, 937n

Thomas de 122

Thomas de, of Heton 588, 681, 1066

Manyfalde, Lawrence 1212

Mapel (Sproxton), NR 1098

Mara, John de la 712

Robert de la 1078

Marderby (Martherby), NR lx, lxviii, lxix, lxxi, lxxvii, 566, 598–625, 674, 995, 997, 998, 999, 1000n, 1003, 1004, 1047, 1048, 1049, 1055, 1058, 1059

grange lxxix

lordship of 618

manor of 618n, 624

Simon of 420, 424, 425, 602, 618, 1042

daughter of *see* Eleanor
and see Crossebergh; Heskeld;
Hestkeldeflat; Iokenewath;
Keldekeldsic; Le Plouland;
Northaskeholme; Northstow;
Ravenyldriddyng; Witheker
Mare *see* Sledmere
Marescale (Marshall), Richard de   558
Margaret (Margery, Mariota), wife of
John son of Richard of Batley   235
Margery, daughter of Hugh de Say
710n
Margery (Marioria), widow of John
son of Harding   237
Margery, widow of Middlesbrough
360, 361
son of *see* Ralph
Margery, wife of William of Acklam
335
Mariot rode (Denby), WR   249
Mariota, aunt of William son of
Michael of Briestwistle   238
Marketgate (Marton in Cleveland),
NR   632
Marmaduke   189, 667
Marrick, NR, nunnery
prioress of *see* Agnes
Martin, brother of Richard parson of
Seamer   930
Martin, clerk of Malton   717
Marton, NR, Augustinian priory
prior *see* Simon
Marton, Nicholas of   869
Marton, parson of *see* Robert
Marton in Cleveland, NR   lviii, 255n,
356, 527, 632, 633, 634, 635, 636
and see Crossebidaila;
Hovydlandflat; Marketgate;
Munkeflat; Wutskereflat
Mary, widow of Jordan of Denby
212n
Mary, wife of Peter de Richemund
1006, 1007, 1008
Mashamshire, NR   700
Mast, Emma   284n, 285, 369, 370
Helewise   284n
William the elder   284, 368, 370
William the younger   284n
Masyngile (Asby), Westm.   24
Matilda, daughter of Odo   480, 482,
483
Matilda, daughter of Roger Armiger
961
Matilda, daughter of Torphin son of
Robert   73, 81, 82, 575n

husbands of *see* Auno, John de;
Bueles, Nicholas de; Hugh son of
Jernegan
Matilda, Empress, daughter of Henry I
622
Matilda, wife of Adam son of Simon
298n
Matilda, wife of Hugh Malebisse II
632
Matilda, wife of John de Daiville
(daughter of Jocelin of Louvain and
Agnes de Percy)   305n
Matilda, wife of John
Malebisse   1083n
Matilda, wife of Reyner of Deepdale
1206, 1207
Matilda, wife of Roger of Smeaton
1061
Matthew, abbot of Newbo (occ. 1243)
580n
Matthew, *magister*   224
Matthew, parson of Kirkebi   598,
611n
Maud, mother of Walter Engelram
256n
Mauduit, John   523
William, chamberlain   1078
William   2
Maunby (Magneby, Magnebi), NR
Andrew of   844, 849
Hugh of   35, 220, 259, 260, 420, 424,
425, 1053
Robert of, prior of the Hospital of St
John of Jerusalem in England
157
Mauncuvenant
Geoffrey de   183
Laurence de   182n
Robert de   182n
William de   182
Maunsell *see* Mansell
Maurebergh (Warcop), Westm.   89
Maurice, abbot of Kirkstall (occ. from
1234, d. 1249)   992
Mauteby *see* Maltby
Mauvaisur, Henry   35
Meaux (Melsa), ER
John de   598, 611, 671
Robert de   647
Stephen de   221
Cistercian abbey
abbot of   884 *and see* Michael
Meburne *see* Milburn
Megelingsty (Sutton under
Whitestonecliffe), NR   1044

Meinill (Maynyll, Meinil, Menil) of
Osgoodby   lx
Alice de, daughter of Walter   755
Gilbert de, son of Gilbert   743n
Gilbert de, son of Thomas   743n,
807, 808n
Gilbert de, son of Walter   xlix, lxx,
257, 739, 743, 744, 747, 752, 776,
780, 782, 784, 793, 815, 822, 823,
834 (or Gilbert de, of Thirkleby
379, 623)
Thomas de, son of Gilbert   743n,
763, 764, 767, 773, 774, 775, 801,
803, 804, 805, 806, 807, 816, 817,
827n, 834
Walter de, son of Gilbert   257, 411,
415, 634, 743, 746, 748, 749, 750,
751, 752, 753, 754, 755, 756, 757,
759, 772, 776, 777, 778, 779,
782n, 783, 784, 793, 794, 815,
823, 834
Meinill of Thirkleby   lx
Alice de, daughter of Gilbert   785,
798, 799, 800, 816, 817
husband of *see* Holey (Holeghe),
Henry
Gilbert de   257, 264, 606, 634, 761,
762, 767n, 771, 786, 787n, 806, 816,
817, 830, 1109, 1157 (or Gilbert de,
of Osgoodby   379, 623)
Gilbert de, son of Gilbert   lxiii, 606,
(Cuthbert, recte Gilbert) 683,
743n, 767n, 796, 797, 816, 817n,
826
Gilbert de, son of Stephen   827
Nicholas de, son of Gilbert the elder
and brother of Stephen and
Gilbert the younger   606, 683,
767, 768, 817
Stephen de, son of Gilbert   257,
259, 260, 264, 305, 420, 421, 422,
424, 425, 445, 606, 608, 624, 634,
683, 743n, 761, 762, 787, 816, 827,
830, 837, 1042, 1053, 1109, 1157
William son of Alice daughter of
Gilbert   799
Meinill of Whorlton lx
Gilbert son of Robert (occ. before
1112)   lx
Nicholas I de (d. 1299), son of
Stephen III (d. before 1269)   452,
453
Nicholas II, son of Nicholas I, Lord
Meinill (d. 1299)   ?1085 and
note, 1088n

Nicholas III de, son of Nicholas II
and Lucy de Thweng (1322)
?1085, 1088
Robert III de (d. by 1207), son of
Stephen II (d. by 1188)   1080,
1087
wife of *see* Emma, daughter of
Richard Malebisse
Stephen son of Robert (occ. 1120 x
1143)   lx
Stephen III (d. before 1269), son of
Robert III (d. by 1207)   lx, 1079,
1080n, 1081, 1084, 1086, 1087, 1088
Meinill, Henry de, clerk   989
William de (occ. *c.* 1140) 1104, 1105
William de (early 13th cent.)   1173
Meldred, lord of Baxby   26
son of *see* Ralph
Meleclive (Melclyve) *see* Scencliffe
Melsambi, master R.   221
Melton, William, archbishop of York
(1317–40)   308
Menhou (Brimhou)   700
Merden, brother William de, preceptor
of the Knights Templars in
York(shire)   451
Merevale, Warw., Cistercian abbey
abbot of   991n
Merschagh (Mereschaw)   527, 665n
Merton, Andrew de   405
Mesager, Joseph le   1084
Methey (Meteleia, Metdeleia), WR
Peter of   218
Richard of   236
Mettingham, John of   547, 574
Meyingham, Thomas de   156
Michael (de Bruno), abbot of Meaux
(1235–49)   992
Michael son of Brian   379
Mickley, WR   xxxiii, 640
Middleberga (Midelesbergh, in
Coxwold), NR   116, 117, 486, 734
Middleburgh, North and South   748
Middlemoor, NR   622, 623, 625
document issued at   lvi, 623
Middlesbrough (Middleburge,
Midelesburg), NR   339n
deacon of *see* Jordan
Ralph of   720, 851
Roger of   362
Roger son of William of   357
Middlesbrough
cell of Whitby Abbey   339n
Nicholas monk of   339
William monk of   339

chaplain of see Walter
Mykelgravelith (Sledmere), ER   1190
Mylneholm (Milneholm, in
    Laysthorpe), NR   505, 508
Mynyoth see Miniott
Myrefeld see Mirfield
Myses, Geoffrey   462
Myton, John of, abbot of Byland
    (1322–34)   3, 322, 1059
    Robert of   1036
        wife of see Constance

Nassington (Nassyngton)
    John of   924n
    Philip of, master   734
    William of, canon of Exeter   982
Naturel, Ralph   323
Neill, Stephen de   602
Neleshow (Neleshou, Nelishou, in
    Snilesworth), NR   1080, 1081, 1084,
    1087
Nereford, Adam de   584, 1083
Ness (Nesse), East and West, NR   lix,
    708, 710, 712, 715, 716, 717
Nether Silton see Silton, Little (Nether)
Nettle Dale (Murton), NR   260
Neuby, John de   558
    William de   417
Neudik (Ormesby), NR   851
Neut', Thomas Scott of   241
Neuton, John de   718
Nevill (Neville, Novavilla)
    Alexander, archbishop of York
        (1373–88)   986
    Alexander   13, 670; son of Ralph
        and brother of Ralph   620
    Geoffrey de   262n, 1120n
    Geoffrey de, son of Robert fitz
        Meldred   1120n
    Henry de   272, 1120n
    Hugh de   212, 677
    Jolland de, royal justice   258, 488,
        722, 841, 927, 927A, 1000, 1003,
        1016, 1030
    Ralph de   211, 840
    Ralph de, father of Alexander and
        Ralph   620n
    Ralph, Lord   620
    Richard   479
    Robert de   629
    Thomas de   981
    Walter de   885
New House (Nidderdale), WR   695n
Newbo, Lincs., Premonstratensian
    abbey   lxx, 580, 584, 585

abbot of   578n, 589, and see Luke;
    Matthew; William
Newborough see Scarborough
Newburgh, NR
    Augustinian priory   xxiv, xxxiv,
        xxxvi, liv, lxii, lxvii, lxx, 332, 334,
        377n, 378n, 379, 380, 381, 382, 384,
        725, 727, 728, 729, 730, 731, 732,
        733, 734, 735, 736, 737, 738, 754, 781
    canons of   121, 122, 332, 334, 380,
        381, 442n, 725, 727, 728, 729, 730,
        731, 734, 736, 737, 738, 802, 901,
        904, 1064, 1065, 1108; and see
        William
    prior of   xliv, xlv, liv, 121; and see
        Augustine; Bernard; Foxholes,
        John of; Hovingham, Robert of; J;
        Philip; Richard; Roger; Simon;
        Skipton, John of; Walter
    prior and
        canons/convent/chapter   27n,
        123, 301, 327, 382, 732, 733, 735,
        754, 780, 781, 802, 816, 937
    chapter of   327, 688, 689
    document issued at   534, 563, 734
Newcastle upon Tyne, Northumb.
    document issued at   567
Newenham, Robert de, notary public
    982
Newerk, Malger de   844
Newsom, Odo de   737
Newstead, NR   735
    grange   lxxix
Newton (Neuton), John de   lxi, 496,
    508
    Robert de   366
    Thomas de   77, 78, 79
    Thomas son of Richard de   70
    Thomas son of Thomas de   79
    clerk of see John
Newton (Stonegrave), NR   6
    Peter of   6
        daughter of see Cecily
Nicholas, abbot of Vaudey (occ. 1227 x
    1238)   1048
Nicholas II, bishop of the Isles
    (1219–1224/6)   707
Nicholas the miller (of Skirpenbeck)
    1158
Nicholas, parson of Etton   1047, 1048
Nicholas, rector of Scawton   1092
Nicholas son of Ranulf   372
Nicholas son of Robert   912, 913
Nicholas son of Robert son of Simon
    291

Oulston (Vestona), NR   lix, 47n, 606, 607, 611

Ouse, river   lxxv, 124, 127, 261, 287, 288, 533

Ousefleet (Huseflete), WR, clerk of see Richard

Ousey Carr, NR   486, 488, 489

Over Silton see Silton, Over

Oxendale (NR)   323, 326, 327, 332, 725, 728

Oxford, John of, bishop of Norwich (1175–1200)   300, 517

Pallyng, Ralph de   163

Palmer, Robert son of William de 1186
   wife of see Sibyl
   William   899

Parva Bodehow (Scackleton), NR   1117

Patrick son of Thomas son of Gospatrick   lxxv, 397, 399n, 400

Pattishall (Patteshull), Northants.,
   Martin of, royal justice   487
   Simon of, royal justice   443, 619, 1002, 1140n, 1157

Paulinus, goldsmith   291

Paulinus, priest   1156

Paulinus son of William son of Gilbert   264n

Paumes, William   585

Paunton, Baldwin de   998, 1044, 1046

Paveley (Pavely), Robert de, monk of Byland   841n, 1004

Paynel family of Broughton
   Adam   75
   Adam son of Adam   73n, 75n, 80
      wife of see Agnes daughter of Torphin
   Fulk I or II   849
   Hugh I   849n
   Hugh II   849n
   William I (d. 1145 x 1147)   849n
   William II (d. 1184)   849n

Paynisdale (Osgodby), ER   859

Peche, Bartholomew   527

Peitevin (Peitevyn)
   Robert   613n, 615, 616
   William   669

Peletoft, Walter de   995

Peningtona (Peningtun), Alan de   69, 71

Peraut, Imbert de, master of the Knights Templar in England   451

Percehay (Percehai)
   Alan de   886

Hugeline (of Laysthorpe)   lxi, 500, 501, 503, 505, 506, 508, 513, 515
Walter de (mid 13th cent.)   514, 926, 927A, 928
Walter de (late 13th cent.)   685, 686, 1124, 1141, 1196, 1197
Walter de (mid to late 14th cent.)   927A, 928, 929
   wife of see Agnes
William de, son of Walter and Agnes   927A, 970

Percy
   Agnes de, daughter and co-heiress of William de Percy II   lx, 145n, 305n, 637, 638, 668n, 669
   Cecilia de, wife of Guy of Helbeck 36, 37
   Geoffrey de   638, 669
   Henry de (d. by 1198), son of Agnes lx, lxiv, 145n, 638, 639, 669
   Henry de, earl of Northumberland (b. 1341, cr. 1377, attainted 1406) 542n
   Richard de (d. by Aug. 1244), son of Agnes   145, 163n, 197, 668, 669
   Thomas de, steward of the royal hospitium   543
   William II de (d. 1175)   138, 145n, 158n, 189, 190, 194n, 637n, 667, 668n, 669n
   William III de, son of Henry son of Agnes   145n, 206, 669n, 1157

Percy family of Kildale   852n
   Walter de   852n
   William de, the elder, son of Walter ?35n, 624, 852
   William de, the younger, son of William   852n

Percy family of Bolton Percy
   Peter de, sheriff of Yorkshire (1261–63)   505; as royal justice 905
   Robert de   683, 1086

Perio, Richard   637

Peslandes   360

Peter of the chapel of the archbishop   224

Peter, clerk   688, 689

Peter, clerk of Wymund of Mirfield 212

Peter, constable   264

Peter, priest   339, 995

Peter, priest of Richmond   264

Peter son of Gilbert   1156

Peter son of Grent   1161

SUBJECT INDEX

The roman numerals refer to the page numbers; the arabic numerals refer to document numbers in the calendar.